Library of
Davidson College

ESSAYS PRESENTED TO
SIR LEWIS NAMIER

Walter Stoneman

SIR LEWIS NAMIER

ESSAYS
presented to
SIR LEWIS NAMIER

edited by
RICHARD PARES
and
ALAN J. P. TAYLOR

Essay Index Reprint Series

BOOKS FOR LIBRARIES PRESS
FREEPORT, NEW YORK

Copyright © 1956 by St. Martin's Press, Inc.

Reprinted 1971 by arrangement

320.9
P228e

INTERNATIONAL STANDARD BOOK NUMBER:
0-8369-2010-4

LIBRARY OF CONGRESS CATALOG CARD NUMBER:
70-134124

77-8705

PRINTED IN THE UNITED STATES OF AMERICA

PREFACE

THE essays in this volume have been written to express the admiration which historians feel for the work of Sir Lewis Namier. Their range, from the parliaments of Oliver Cromwell to the European diplomacy of the twentieth century, is evidence of the wide fields which Sir Lewis has covered. Some of the writers are his contemporaries; some have been his colleagues at Manchester or in journalism. All wish to acknowledge the debt that they owe to his help, his example and his ideas.

The Structure of Politics at the Accession of George III, his first great work, marked an epoch. It gave a new look to a century of British history, and established a method of studying past politics which has been applied fruitfully for other periods. Sir Lewis turned from what politicians said to what they did and who they were. He composed his picture from the biographical details of countless forgotten figures. The political history of England has been permanently reshaped; and its study will continue to bear the stamp of Sir Lewis Namier's inspiration.

This work would have occupied the life of a lesser man; but Sir Lewis has had an equally powerful influence in other fields. Equipped with a personal knowledge of east-central Europe and with a rare command of languages, he has given a new perspective to the liberal and national movements of modern Europe, especially during the revolutions of 1848. Nor has he arrested his attention at the nineteenth century. He has shown that a historian can write with the same accuracy and detachment about events that are strictly contemporary; and his study of the diplomatic origins of the Second World War set a standard that will not easily be surpassed. In every field, he has combined rigid attention to detail with a sweep of vision that can carry him across the centuries. He uses the microscope at one moment and the telescope at the next — both with equal effect.

He has judged himself and others rigorously, accepting correction as readily as he bestows it on others. The salutary stringency of his reviews has made him the *malleus maleficorum* of historians who misread their documents or perpetuate legends. No mistake has been too trivial to escape his notice; and many a historian must have verified his references more closely in the knowledge that he might have to appear before such a judge. Sir Lewis has brought to history a distinction of style which places him among the masters of English prose. He has been an artist as well as a scholar. Every sentence is pungent, weighty, decisive. He has shown, too, intuition both into individual character and into social classes. How else could the son of a Galician land-owner have come to know, perhaps even better than the English, what their ancestors were like two hundred years ago? His courage and confidence have stood out most of all. He never held a permanent university post until he was over forty, and at one time he went into business in order to save enough money to support himself for a few years in historical research. Few historians who have advanced smoothly up the ladder of academic promotion can be sure that they would have shown the same resolution.

Retirement from his chair has not brought leisure or abdication. He is now helping to direct the *History of Parliament*, perhaps the most important co-operative work of historical research since the *Dictionary of National Biography*. It is unlikely that he needs our encouragement; he cannot refuse our affection and esteem. The editors and writers of the present volume offer it to Sir Lewis Namier on behalf of all those who have admired his works and benefited from his example.

CONTENTS

	PAGE
PREFACE	v
OLIVER CROMWELL AND HIS PARLIAMENTS By H. R. Trevor-Roper	1
THE CITY OF LONDON IN EIGHTEENTH-CENTURY POLITICS By Lucy Sutherland	49
A LONDON WEST-INDIA MERCHANT HOUSE, 1740–1769 By Richard Pares	75
LETTERS FROM WILLIAM PITT TO LORD BUTE, 1755–1758 By Romney Sedgwick	108
A WINE-MERCHANT'S LETTER-BOOK By Sir James Fergusson of Kilkerran	167
HORACE WALPOLE, ANTIQUARY By Wilmarth S. Lewis	178
THE STEWARDSHIP OF THE CHILTERN HUNDREDS By Betty Kemp	204
THE REPORTING AND PUBLISHING OF THE HOUSE OF COMMONS' DEBATES, 1771–1834 By A. Aspinall	227
ENGLISH REFORM AND FRENCH REVOLUTION IN THE GENERAL ELECTION OF 1830 By Norman Gash	258
THE CHANGES IN PARLIAMENTARY PROCEDURE, 1880–1882 By Edward Hughes	289
ASPECTS OF RUSSIAN FOREIGN POLICY, 1815–1914 By G. H. Bolsover	320

Essays Presented to Sir Lewis Namier

	PAGE
'RUSSIA AND EUROPE' AS A THEME OF RUSSIAN HISTORY By E. H. Carr	357
THE INTELLECTUALS AND REVOLUTION: SOCIAL FORCES IN EASTERN EUROPE SINCE 1848 By Hugh Seton-Watson	394
PERSONALITY AND DIPLOMACY IN ANGLO-AMERICAN RELATIONS, 1917 By Stanley Morison	431
THE WAR AIMS OF THE ALLIES IN THE FIRST WORLD WAR By A. J. P. Taylor	475
MEN OF TRAGIC DESTINY: LUDENDORFF AND GROENER By J. W. Wheeler-Bennett	506
SIR LEWIS NAMIER From the photograph by Walter Stoneman	*Frontispiece*

H. R. TREVOR-ROPER

OLIVER CROMWELL AND HIS PARLIAMENTS

OLIVER CROMWELL and his parliaments — the theme is almost a tragi-comedy. Cromwell was himself a member of parliament; he was the appointed general of the armies of parliament; and the Victorians, in the greatest days of parliamentary government, set up his statue outside the rebuilt Houses of Parliament. But what were Cromwell's relations with parliament? The Long Parliament, which appointed him, he first purged by force and then violently expelled from authority. His own parliament, the Parliament of Saints, which to a large extent was nominated by his government, was carried away by hysteria, rent by intrigue, and dissolved, after six months, by an undignified act of suicide. Of the parliaments of the Protectorate, elected on a new franchise and within new limits determined by the government, the first was purged by force within a week and dissolved, by a trick hardly distinguishable from fraud, before its legal term; the second was purged by fraud at the beginning and, when that fraud was reversed, became at once unmanageable and was dissolved within a fortnight. On a superficial view, Cromwell was as great an enemy of parliament as ever Charles I or Archbishop Laud had been, the only difference being that, as an enemy, he was more successful: he scattered all his parliaments and died in his bed, while theirs deprived them of their power and brought them both ultimately to the block.

Nevertheless, between Cromwell and the Stuarts, in this matter, there was a more fundamental difference than this; for even if he could never control his parliaments in fact,

Cromwell at least never rejected them in theory. This is not because he was deliberately consistent with his own parliamentary past. Cromwell was deliberately consistent in nothing. No political career is so full of undefended inconsistencies as his. But he was fundamentally and instinctively conservative, and he saw in parliament part of the natural order of things. He did not regard it, as Archbishop Laud had regarded it, as 'that hydra' or 'that noise': he regarded it as the necessary legislature of England; and it was merely, in his eyes, an unfortunate and incomprehensible accident that his own particular parliaments consistently fell below the traditional standard of usefulness. Therefore again and again he summoned and faced them; again and again he wrestled with the hydra, sought to shout down the noise; and again and again, in the end, like the good man in a tragedy, caught in the trap of his own weakness, he resorted to force and fraud, to purges, expulsions and recriminations. He descended like Moses from Sinai upon the naughty children of Israel, smashing in turn the divine constitutions he had obtained for them; and the surprised and indignant members, scattered before their time, went out from his presence overwhelmed with turbid oratory, protestations of his own virtue and their waywardness, romantic reminiscences, proprietary appeals to the Lord, and great broken gobbets from the Pentateuch and the Psalms.

Why was Oliver Cromwell so uniformly unsuccessful with his parliaments? To answer this question we must first look a little more closely at the aims and character both of Oliver Cromwell and of that opposition to the court of Charles I of which he was first an obscure and ultimately the most powerful representative: an opposition not of practised politicians (the practised politicians of 1640 were dead, or had lost control, by 1644) nor of City merchants (the great London merchants were largely royalist in 1640),[1] but

---

[1] Mrs. Valerie Pearl, in her valuable MS. thesis, 'The City of London, 1640–43' (D. Phil., Oxon., 1954), has shown the strength of royalism in the effective City government until the internal revolution of Dec. 1641: a revolution described

Oliver Cromwell and his Parliaments

of gentry: the backwoods gentry who, in 1640, sat on the back benches of parliament, but who, as war and revolution progressed, gradually broke through the crumbling leadership which had at first contained them: the 'Independents'.

Now these 'Independent' gentry, it is important to emphasize, were not, as a class, revolutionary: that is, they did not hold revolutionary ideas. There were revolutionaries among the Independents, of course. There were revolutionaries in parliament, men like 'Harry Marten and his gang'— Henry Neville, Thomas Chaloner and others: intellectual republicans who had travelled in Italy, read Machiavelli and Botero, and cultivated the doctrine of *raison d'état*; just as there were also revolutionaries outside parliament: the Levellers and the Fifth Monarchy Men. But if these men were the successive sparks which kindled the various stages of revolution, they were not the essential tinder of it. The majority of the members of parliament, who at first accidentally launched the revolutionary movement and were afterwards borne along or consumed by it, were not clear-headed men like these. They were not thinkers or even dreamers, but plain, conservative, untravelled country-gentlemen whose passion came not from radical thought or systematic doctrine but from indignation: indignation which the electioneering ability of a few great lords and the parliamentary genius of John Pym had contrived to turn into a political force, and which no later leaders were able wholly either to harness or to contain. These were the men who formed the solid stuff of parliamentary opposition to Charles I: men whose social views were conservative enough, but whose political passions were radical, and became more radical as they discovered depth below depth of royal duplicity. These were the men who became, in time, the 'Independents'; and Cromwell, though he transcended them in personality and military genius, was their typical, if also their greatest, representative.

by Clarendon, *History of the Rebellion* (1843), pp. 149-50, and in the anonymous *Letter from Mercurius Civicus to Mercurius Rusticus* (1643), printed in *Somers Tracts* (1811), iv. 580.

Essays Presented to Sir Lewis Namier

Why were these men, in 1640, so indignant? They were indignant, above all, against the court. Curiously it was the court of James I rather than the court of Charles I which aroused their strongest moral feelings; but then most of them were now middle-aged and those of them who had previous parliamentary experience had necessarily acquired it before 1628 — the younger men, brought up under Charles I, tended to be royalist.[1] It was the corrupt, extravagant court of James I and the duke of Buckingham whose lavish expenses, 'so vast and unlimited by the old good rules of economy',[2] first insulted their own necessarily careful estate-management, and whose open, vulgar immorality further scandalized their severe puritan spirits.[3] But James I, by combining with his faults a certain political canniness, had postponed the impact of this indignation, and the very extravagance of his court, with its sinecures and monopolies and pensions, had often bribed the potential leaders of opposition into silence. His son had corrected the moral abuses,[4] but by his political faults had nourished and increased and armed that indignation which those abuses had first engendered. Indeed, by his very parsimony Charles I hastened his own failure: for by cutting down the extravagance of the court he had cut down the alleviating perquisites which had previously divided the Opposition, and by raising the revenue from wardships he had rendered 'all the rich families of England . . . exceedingly incensed and even indevoted to the Crown'.[5] By 1640 political and moral indignation were combined against the House of Stuart and

[1] This point — that the royalist members were, on an average, ten years younger than the Parliamentarians in 1640 — is clearly illustrated by D. Brunton and D. H. Pennington, *Members of the Long Parliament* (1954), pp. 14-20.
[2] Clarendon, *History of the Rebellion* (1843), p. 5.
[3] For the indignation which even courtiers, brought up at the orderly court, of Queen Elizabeth, felt at the vulgarity and immodesty of the court of James I see the letters of Lord Thomas Howard and Sir John Harington printed in McClure, *Letters and Epigrams of Sir John Harington* (Philadelphia, 1930), pp. 32-4, 118-21.
[4] As even the puritan Mrs. Hutchinson vividly admits. See her *Memoirs of Colonel Hutchinson* (Everyman edition), p. 67.
[5] Clarendon, *op. cit.*, p. 61.

were together a powerful force in the hands of those practical politicians who perhaps shared it, who could certainly exploit it, and who thought (but wrongly) that they could also control it.

And what were the positive ideals of these outraged but largely unpolitical conservative gentry? Naturally, in the circumstances, they were not very constructive. These men looked back, not forward: back from the House of Stuart which had so insulted them to the House of Tudor of which their fathers had spoken, and in the reign of Elizabeth they discovered, or invented, a golden age: an age when the court had been, as it seemed, in harmony with the country and the Crown with its parliaments; an age when a Protestant queen, governing parsimoniously at home and laying only tolerable burdens on 'her faithful Commons', had nevertheless made England glorious abroad — head of 'the Protestant Interest' throughout the world, victor over Spain in the Indies, protector of the Netherlands in Europe. Since 1603 that glorious position had been lost. King James had alienated the gentry, abandoned Protestantism for Arminian policy at home and popish alliances abroad, made peace with Spain, and surrendered, with the 'cautionary towns', the protectorate over the Netherlands. When the religious struggle had broken out anew in Europe, it was not the king of England who had inherited the mantle of Queen Elizabeth as defender of the Protestant faith: it was a new champion from the North, the king of Sweden. In the 1630s, when Gustavus Adolphus swept triumphantly through Germany, he became the hero of the frustrated, mutinous English gentry; and when he fell at Lützen, scarcely an English squire but wrote, in his manor-house, a doggerel epitaph on the new pole-star of his loyalty, 'the Lion of the North'.

Such were the basic political views, or prejudices, of the English back-benchers who poured into parliament in 1640. But they had social views also, and these too led them back to the same golden age of the Protestant queen. First there was the desire for decentralization — the revolt of the provinces and of the provincial gentry not only against the growing, parasitic Stuart court but also against the growing, 'dropsical' City of London, against the centralized Church, whether Anglican or presbyterian, and against the expensive monopoly of higher education by the two great universities. All this was implied in the Independent programme.[1] And also, what we must never forget, for it was a great element in the Protestant tradition, there was the demand for an organic society responsible for the welfare of its members. Ever since, among the first Reformers, 'the Commonwealth Men' had protested against the irresponsibility, the practical inhumanity, the privileged uselessness of the pre-Reformation Church, the English Protestants had laid emphasis upon the collective nature of society and the mutual obligations of the classes which make it up.[2] Under Elizabeth, and especially in the long reign of Lord Burghley, something more than lip-service had been paid to this ideal; but under the Stuarts, and particularly in the reign of James I (that formative era of English puritanism), the ideal had again been eclipsed as court and Church became once again openly parasitic upon society. Those were the years in which the cry for social justice had become insistent and the Common Law, so extolled by its most successful practitioner, Sir Edward Coke, became, in other eyes, one of the most oppressive of social burdens. When the Anglican Archbishop Laud had failed in his desperate, purblind but in some respects heroic efforts to reform society centrally and from above, the puritan Opposition inherited much of his programme and sought to realize it in another form, as a decentralized, 'Independent' commonwealth. The radicals would have achieved such reformation violently and devised new paper constitutions to achieve and preserve it. The conservative puritans, who

[1] I have touched upon this aspect of the Independent programme in my essay, *The Gentry 1540–1640* (Econ. Hist. Soc. 1954), p. 43.

[2] I do not mean to imply that such views were not held in the Catholic Church *after* the Reformation. The revolt was European, and both Protestant and Catholic Churches inherited it, and competed with each other in formulating it. Similar 'collectivist' doctrines were formulated by the Jesuits in Spain; but in England, being Protestant, it was part of the Protestant tradition.

were radical only in temper, not in their social or political doctrines, shied away from such novel remedies. Believing just as sincerely in a better, more decentralized, more responsible society, they looked for its achievement not to Utopia or Oceana but, once again, to a revived Elizabethan age.[1]

Such was the common denominator of positive philosophy shared by many of the back-bench members of parliament in 1640, as it emerges, by way of protest, from their pamphlets, their diaries, their letters to their patrons, their parliamentary ejaculations both before and after that crucial date. It is astonishing how faithfully it is reflected in the letters and speeches, as afterwards in the groping policy, of Oliver Cromwell. 'Reformation of law and clergy', social justice for the 'poor people of God' secured not by radical revolution but by patriarchal benevolence, a revival of the glories of 'Queen Elizabeth of famous memory'—a protectorate over the Netherlands, a privateering war in the West Indies, and the leadership of 'the Protestant interest' in Europe — all these recur in his later policy. Even the uncritical worship of Gustavus Adolphus is there. Perhaps nothing is more tragi-comic in Cromwell's romantic foreign policy than his cultivation of the robber-empire in the Baltic to which he would have sacrificed English commercial interests, and, in particular, of Queen Christina whom he fondly courted with a pompous embassy, rich gifts and his own portrait. For was she not both a Protestant heroine and a virgin queen — her father, the great Gustavus, and 'Queen Elizabeth of famous memory' rolled into one? In fact she

---

[1] Most recent writers — and not only Marxists and Fabians, for the same bias is to be found in the Roman Catholic W. Schenk's book, *The Concern for Social Justice in the Puritan Revolution* (1948) — have tended to find the evidence of such an interest in social reform only among the radical sects, who certainly made most noise about it. But I believe that just as much interest, in a more practical, less doctrinaire way, was shown by the 'conservative' Independents. It can be discovered in their projects for law-reform and church matters, in their educational work (on which see especially Mr. W. A. L. Vincent's excellent study, *The State and School Education 1640–1660* (1950)), in the ordinances of the Protector and Council between Dec. 1653 and Sept. 1654, and in the social policy carried out in the period of administration by major-generals.

was not. Even as he wooed her, that flighty Nordic blue-stocking was secretly being converted to Popery by Jesuit missionaries, and Cromwell had to transfer his uncritical devotion to her successor.

But this was in the future. In 1640 Oliver Cromwell was still, like the other country gentry who had followed their patrons to Westminster, a mere back-bencher, a lesser ally of his relatives the Barringtons, John Hampden and Oliver St. John, a client of the earl of Warwick. He never dreamed that his views would one day have more power behind them than theirs, or that the views which they all shared would be expressed otherwise than by the remonstrances of a faithful if indignant parliament to a wayward but, they hoped (once his 'evil counsellors' were removed), ultimately amenable king. None of them dreamed, in 1640, of revolution, either in Church or in State. They were neither separatists nor republicans. What they wanted was a king who, unlike Charles I, but like the Queen Elizabeth of their imagination, would work the existing institutions in the good old sense; bishops who, unlike the Laudian bishops, but like Bishop Hall or Archbishop Ussher, would supervise their flocks in the good old sense of 'the sweet and noble' Anglican, Richard Hooker.[1] At first they hoped that King Charles would adjust himself, would jettison a few Stuart innovations, give a few guaran-

[1] The conservatism of the Opposition in secular matters is generally admitted. In Aug. 1643 Henry Marten was sent to the Tower, without a division, for expressing republican sentiments. In Church matters the presbyterian clergy and the extreme sectaries naturally expressed clear anti-Anglican sentiments; but the laity (as the history of the Westminster Assembly showed) had no intention of submitting to such clerical extremists. In fact, the spiritual advisers of the Independents, William Ames, Thomas Hooker, Hugh Peter, etc., were 'non-separating congregationalists', who never disowned the Anglican Church (see Perry Miller, *Orthodoxy in Massachusetts* (Cambridge, Mass., 1933), pp. 177 foll.; R. P. Stearns, *Hugh Peter* (Urbana, 1954), p. 12, etc.). It was Henry Parker, a formidable Independent thinker, whose praise of Hooker I have quoted. Parker also described Bishop Hall as 'one of the greatest assertors, and in that the noblest, of episcopacy'. (W. K. Jordan, *Men of Substance* (Chicago, 1942), pp. 70-1). When in power, Cromwell granted far greater liberty to Anglicans than the revengeful Anglicans of the Restoration were disposed to admit (see R. Bosher, *The Making of the Restoration Settlement* (1951), pp. 9-14), and appointed for Archbishop Ussher a State funeral in Westminster Abbey, with an Anglican service.

tees, and become such a king of the State, such a supreme governor of the Church. It was only when King Charles had shown himself quite unadjustable that revolution, though unwanted, took place, generating its own momentum and driving basically conservative men to radical acts such as they would never have imagined before and would shudder to recollect afterwards, and facing them with fundamental problems of which they had never previously thought. It was only by an extraordinary and quite unpredictable turn of events that one of these back-benchers, Oliver Cromwell, having ruined all existing institutions, found himself, in 1649, faced with the responsibility of achieving, or restoring, the lost balance of society. It was a formidable responsibility for one so arbitrarily brought to eminence, but Cromwell took it seriously, for he was essentially a serious and a modest man; the question was, how could it be carried out?

The radicals, of course, had their plans: they were the intellectuals, or the doctrinaires, the new men and the young men of the revolution. They intended to continue the revolution, to create new engines of force, and to impose thereby new and untried, but, in their eyes, hopeful, constitutions. But Cromwell was not a radical or an intellectual or a young man. He did not want to continue the revolution, which had already, in his eyes and in the eyes of his fellow-gentry, got out of control. He wanted to stop it, to bring it under control, to bring 'settlement' after an unfortunate but, as it had turned out, unavoidable period of 'blood and confusion'. Nor did he believe in new constitutions, or indeed in any constitutions at all. He did not believe, as some of his more wooden colleagues believed, in the divine right of republics any more than in the divine right of kings. Forms of government were to him 'but a mortal thing', 'dross and dung compared with Christ', and therefore in themselves quite indifferent. He was not, he once said, 'wedded or glued to forms of government': had not the ancient Hebrews, God's own people, fared equally well, according to circumstances, under patriarchs, judges and kings?[1] Acceptability, or as he called it, 'acceptance', was to him the only test of right government. In his indignation against Charles I he might denounce monarchy, but in cooler moments he would admit that a government 'with something monarchical in it' was probably the most acceptable, and therefore the best. In his indignation against the earl of Manchester he might express his hope of living 'to see never a nobleman in England'; but in cooler moments he could insist that 'a nobleman, a gentleman, a yeoman' were 'the ranks and orders of men whereby England hath been known for hundreds of years', and that 'nobility and gentry' must be kept up.[2] Fundamentally, in his eyes, it was the fault of persons, not of institutions, which had been fatal to the *ancien régime*: 'the King's head was not taken off because he was King, nor the Lords laid aside because Lords, neither was the Parliament dissolved because they were a Parliament, but because they did not perform their trust.'[3] In politics Oliver Cromwell was not a theorist or a doctrinaire, but an opportunist.

Opportunists who do not believe in the necessity of particular constitutions take what lies nearest to hand, and what lay nearest to Cromwell's hand when he found himself called upon to restore his ideal Elizabethan society was naturally the surviving débris of the Elizabethan constitution. Parliament had been savaged — and by none more than himself — but its rump was there; the king had been destroyed, but he himself stood, if somewhat incongruously, in his place. Naturally he saw himself as a new Queen Elizabeth — or

[1] *Clarke Papers*, vol. i (Camden Soc., 1891), p. 369. This indifference to forms of government, which implied a rejection of Charles I's rule without any particular constitutional alternative, was a commonplace among the Cromwellian Independents. Sir Henry Vane similarly held that 'it is not so much the form of the administration as the thing administered wherein the good or evil of government doth consist' (*The People's Case Stated* in *The Trial of Sir Henry Vane Kt.* (1662), p. 106), and cf. the similar views of other Independents quoted in Ludlow, *Memoirs* (ed. C. H. Firth, 1894), i. 184-5, and Burton, *Parliamentary Diary*, iii. 260, 266.

[2] Whitelocke, *Memorials* (1853), iii. 374; *Camden Miscellany* (1883), viii. 2; W. C. Abbott, *Writings and Speeches of Oliver Cromwell* (Harvard, 1937-47), iii. 435; iv. 273.

[3] MS. Tanner, iii. 13, quoted in *Clarke Papers*, iii, p. viii, note 1.

rather, being a humble man, as a regent for a new Queen Elizabeth; and he prepared, like her, to summon a series of deferential parliaments. Surely, since he was one of them, and since they all earnestly pursued the same honest ideal, the members would agree with him, just as they had agreed with 'that Lady, that great Queen'? Surely he had only to address them in the Painted Chamber, to commend them in a few eloquent phrases, to leave them to their harmonious deliberations, and then, having received from them a few 'good laws', to dismiss them, in due time, amid applause, complimentingly, with a 'Golden Speech'?

Alas, as we know, it did not happen thus. It was not with golden speeches that Cromwell found himself dismissing his parliaments, but with appeals to Heaven, torrents of abuse, — and force. This was not merely because the basis of legitimacy and consent were lacking: Queen Elizabeth, like Cromwell, was disputed in her title, and Cromwell, like Queen Elizabeth, was personally indispensable even to those extremists who chafed at his conservatism. The fatal flaw was elsewhere. Under Oliver Cromwell something was missing in the mechanics of parliamentary government. It was not merely that useful drop of oil with which Queen Elizabeth had now and then so gracefully lubricated the machine. It was something far more essential. To see what that omission was, we must turn from the character to the composition and working of those uniformly unfortunate assemblies.

The methods by which Queen Elizabeth so effectively controlled her parliaments of — for the most part — unpolitical gentry are now, thanks to the great work of Sir John Neale and Professor Notestein, well known.[1] They consisted, first, in electoral and other patronage and, secondly, in certain procedural devices among which the essential were two: the presence in parliament of a firm nucleus of experi-

[1] Wallace Notestein, *The Winning of the Initiative by the House of Commons* (British Academy Lecture, 1924); J. E. Neale, *The Elizabethan House of Commons* (1949); *Elizabeth I and her Parliaments* (1953).

enced privy councillors, and royal control over the Speaker. Now these methods of control are of the greatest importance in the history of parliament, and if we are to consider Oliver Cromwell as a parliamentarian it is necessary to consider his use both of this patronage and of these procedural devices. This, I think, has not before been attempted. My purpose in this essay is to attempt it. I believe it can be shown that it was precisely in this field that Cromwell's catastrophic failure as a parliamentarian lay. In order to show this it will be necessary to take Cromwell's parliaments in turn and to see, in each case, how far the patronage of the government and its supporters was used, and who formed that essential nucleus of effective parliamentary managers, that compact 'front-bench' which, under the Tudors, had been occupied by the royal privy council.

Of course, Cromwell did not inherit the system direct from Queen Elizabeth. In the intervening half-century there had been many changes — changes which had begun even before her death. For in the last years of Elizabeth both methods of royal control had been challenged: the puritans had developed a formidable parliamentary 'machine' independent of the privy council, and the earl of Essex had sought to use aristocratic patronage to pack the House of Commons against the queen's ministers. But in the event, thanks to the parliamentary ability of the two Cecils, neither of these challenges had been successful. It was only after the death of the queen, and particularly after the rejection of Robert Cecil by James I, that the indifference of the Stuart kings and the incompetence of their ministers had enabled a parliamentary Opposition to develop and to organize both patronage and procedure against the Crown. By 1640, when the Long Parliament met, the tables had been completely turned. In that year the Opposition magnates — the earls of Bedford, Warwick and Pembroke — showed themselves better boroughmongers than the royal ministers, and the failure of Charles I to secure the election to parliament, for any constituency, of his intended Speaker could be described

Oliver Cromwell and his Parliaments

by Clarendon as 'an untoward and indeed an unheard of accident, which brake many of the king's measures and infinitely disordered his service beyond a capacity of reparation'.[1] Thus in 1640 both patronage and procedure were firmly in the hands of the Opposition. But this turning of the tables did not entail any change in the system by which Parliament was operated. It merely meant that the same system which had formerly been operated by the Crown was now operated against it. John Pym, the ablest parliamentary manager since the Cecils, resumed their work. He controlled the patronage, the Speaker, and the front bench. From 1640 until 1643 parliament, in his hands, was once again an effective and disciplined body such as it had never been since 1603.

With the death of Pym in 1643, his indisputable empire over parliament dissolved and lesser men competed for its fragments. Vane and St. John among the radicals, Holles among the conservatives, emerged as party leaders; but they cannot be described as successful party leaders: the machine creaked and groaned, and it was only by disastrously calling

[1] R. N. Kershaw, 'The Elections for the Long Parliament', *English Historical Review*, 1923; Clarendon, *op. cit.*, p. 68. The extent to which the party of opposition in 1640 was an aristocratic party, controlled by certain great borough-mongering lords, has, I think, been insufficiently emphasized by historians, although Clarendon, as a contemporary, takes it for granted. Pym was a client of the earl of Bedford ('wholly devoted to the earl of Bedford', Clarendon, *op. cit.*, p. 74); those who afterwards became Independents were largely (like the Independent preachers) clients of the earl of Warwick, to whom Cromwell himself remained a constant ally, even when their rôles were reversed (*ibid.* p. 874). For the earl of Warwick as head of a political party, see A. P. Newton, *The Colonising Activities of the Early Puritans* (New Haven, 1914), *passim*. For some of his electioneering activities, see J. H. Hexter, *The Reign of King Pym* (Cambridge, Mass., 1941), pp. 44-5. For the electioneering activities of the earls of Pembroke, see Violet A. Rowe, 'The Influence of the Earls of Pembroke on Parliamentary Elections 1625-1641', *English Historical Review*, 1935, p. 242. On the other hand, the electioneering feebleness of the government is shown by Archbishop Laud's refusal to avail himself of the borough-patronage at his disposal at Reading, or, apparently, at Oxford (see Laud, *Works*, vi. 587; M. B. Rex, *University Representation in England 1604-1690* (1954), p. 145). And yet, if Laud had chosen to recommend Sir Thomas Gardiner for Reading, there would have been a sound royalist Speaker instead of Lenthall, and the disaster so emphasized by Clarendon would never have occurred. It is difficult to over-estimate the consequences which might have flowed from so slight an exertion.

in external force — the army — that Vane and St. John were able, in the end, to secure their control. On the other hand, once parliament had been purged and the king executed, a certain unity of counsel and policy returned. The Rump Parliament, which governed England from 1649 to 1653, may have been justly hated as a corrupt oligarchy, but it governed effectively, preserved the revolution, made and financed victorious war, and carried out a consistent policy of aggressive mercantile imperialism. Its rule was indeed the most systematic government of the Interregnum; and since this rule was the rule not of one known minister but of a number of overlapping assemblies operating now as parliament, now as committees of parliament, now as council of state, while some of the administrative departments were notoriously confused and confusing, it is reasonable to ask who were the effective managers who made this complex and anonymous junta work so forcefully and so smoothly. This is a question which, in my opinion, can be answered with some confidence.

We have, unfortunately, no private diaries of the Rump Parliament which can show who managed its business or debates, but we have later diaries which show at least who claimed to have managed them, and from this and other evidence I believe we can say that, at least after 1651, the policy of the Rump was controlled by a small group of determined and single-minded men. Up to the summer of 1651 the ascendancy of these men is not so apparent, but with the policy which prevailed after that date it can, I think, be clearly seen. For in 1651, with the passing of the Navigation Act and the declaration of war against the Netherlands, the old Elizabethan ideal of a protectorate over the Netherlands was jettisoned in favour of a new and opposite policy, a policy of mercantile aggression against a neighbouring Protestant power. Furthermore, this policy, we are repeatedly told, was the policy not of the whole parliament but of 'a very small number', with allies in the City of London, 'some few men' acting 'for their own interest', 'some few persons deeply interested in the East India trade and the new Plantations.'[1]

Now the identity of these few men, or at least of their parliamentary managers, can hardly be doubted, for they never tired of naming themselves. They were Sir Arthur Hesilrige and Thomas Scot. In the later parliaments of the Interregnum, whose proceedings are fortunately known to us, Hesilrige and Scot appear as an inseparable and effective parliamentary combine. Together they head the list of those republicans whom Cromwell twice excluded from his parliaments. Together they are named by Ludlow as the principal champions of sound republican doctrine. Together they appear, in the *Commons' Journals*, as tellers for strictly republican motions. Moreover, not only did they repeatedly claim for themselves all the republican virtue of the Rump Parliament in general, but, in particular, the policy for which they most extolled the Rump was always precisely that policy of mercantile aggression which had been launched in 1651 with the triumphant but, in the eyes of serious-minded Protestants, fratricidal war against the Netherlands.

For Hesilrige and Scot were not only republicans. They were also, to use a later term, 'whigs'. If republics were to them the best of all forms of government, that was not merely because of classical or biblical precedents, nor because of the iniquity of particular kings: it was because republics alone, in their eyes, were the political systems capable of commercial empire. Like the later whigs, who were also accused of a preference for 'oligarchy', they found their great example in the mercantile republic of Venice. 'Is there anything but a Commonwealth that flourishes?' asked Scot: 'Venice against the pride of the Ottoman Empire';[2]

[1] These statements concerning the fewness of the makers of Rump policy, made by Pauluzzi the Venetian resident, Daniel O'Neil the royalist agent, and the later Dutch ambassadors, are quoted by S. R. Gardiner, *History of the Commonwealth and Protectorate* (1894), ii. 120, note.

[2] The fashionable cult of Venice reached its height under the Commonwealth. The republicans Harrington and Neville made it their ideal; the anonymous tract, *A Persuasive to a Mutual Compliance* (1652), prophesies for the Rump a future comparable with that of Venice (*Somers Tracts*, vi. 158); James Howell's laudatory *Survey of the Signorie of Venice, of her admired policy and method of government*, was published in 1651; etc., etc.

and he never ceased to urge a reversion to the aggressive commercial policy of 1651–3. 'We never bid fairer for being masters of the whole world.' 'We are rivals for the fairest mistress in the world — Trade.' 'It is known abroad — the Dutch know — that a Parliament of England can fight and conquer too.' 'You never had such a fleet as in the Long Parliament', echoed Hesilrige; 'all the powers in the world made addresses to him that sat in your chair'; 'trade flourished, the City of London grew rich, we were most potent by sea that ever was known in England'. When Cromwell expelled the Rump, he afterwards declared, 'there was not so much as the barking of a dog or any general or visible repining at it'; and his gentry-supporters agreed with him: 'there was neither coroner nor inquest upon it'. But some squeaks there were, and it is interesting to see whence they came. At the crucial moment, when an agreed solution was almost in sight, it was Hesilrige who swept down from seventy miles away and by his presence and oratory prevented the other members from surrendering to less than force; and when they had been expelled by force, it was from the City of London that the only plea for their restoration came: a petition whose paternity is easy to recognize — for six years later it was implicitly claimed by Thomas Scot.[1]

Now it is interesting to note that this policy, the 'whig' policy of mercantile aggression which I have ascribed to Hesilrige and Scot and their allies in the City, though it was carried out by an 'Independent' parliament carefully purged of unsympathetic elements, was flatly contradictory to the declared views and prejudices of those ordinary Independent gentry whom Cromwell represented and who, in their general attitude, foreshadowed rather the tory squires than the mercantile whig pressure-group of the next generation.[2] Cromwell himself always favoured the Elizabethan policy of

[1] Abbott, *Writings and Speeches of Oliver Cromwell*, iii. 453; Burton, *Parliamentary Diary*, iii. 97, 111–12, etc.

[2] This distinction between the 'whig' policy of the Rump and the 'tory' policy of the Cromwellian Independents is well illustrated in the person of a prominent champion of the former and the enemy of the latter, Slingsby Bethel. In his pamphlet *The World's Mistake in Oliver Cromwell* (1668) he attacked

an alliance with and a protectorate over the Netherlands, and it was this policy which Oliver St. John had, until 1651, pressed upon the Dutch government at the Hague; the defection of St. John in 1651 had enabled the 'whig' party to carry their war-policy, but in 1653, when Cromwell had expelled the Rump, he lost no time in ending the war they had begun. Further, Cromwell and his colleagues had revolted, in part, against the centralization of trade in the City of London, which had caused the decay of local boroughs and local industry: they had no wish to fight (and pay for) mercantile wars in the interest of the City, and afterwards, when they denounced the Rump, they 'cast much dirt and unsavoury speech' on it as 'a trading Parliament'.[1] Decentralization, the provinces against the City, and the Protestant Interest — these were their political slogans, the slogans which they had uttered in the 1630s and 1640s and would utter again after 1653, but which went altogether unheeded by those 'Rumpers' who had temporarily seized control of the revolution. Finally, the Rump Parliament — and this was one of Cromwell's greatest grievances against it — showed itself utterly indifferent to that Protestant 'concern for social justice' which loomed so large in the Independent programme. War on Protestants abroad in the interest of City merchants was accompanied at home, in those years, by a privileged scramble for public property which seemed a mockery of puritan ideals. The republic of Hesilrige and Scot might call itself a 'Commonwealth', but in fact, said a real republican, 'it was an oligarchy, detested by all men that love a Commonwealth';[2] or, if it were a commonwealth, it was only, according to the sour definition of Sir Thomas

Cromwell precisely because he had reversed the mercantilist policy of the Rump; in his *Interest of Princes and States* (1680) he attacks the gentry as the chief obstacle everywhere to rational mercantile policy; and in the days when whigs and tories existed in fact, not merely in embryo, he was whig sheriff of London in the year of the Popish Plot.

[1] Burton, *Parliamentary Diary*, i. pp. xxv, xxviii. For Independent complaints against the growth of the City of London and its monopoly of trade, see *ibid.* i. pp. cx, 177, 343-4. For the same complaint resumed by a tory backbencher a generation later, see *The Memoirs of Sir John Reresby* (1875), p. 333.

[2] Burton, *op. cit.*, iii. 134.

More: 'a certain conspiracy of rich men procuring their own commodities under the name and title of a Commonwealth'.

Thus the policy of the Rump in the years 1651–3 — the years, that is, when the army's resentment was mounting against it — was not only the policy of a small managing group which had obtained control of the assembly: it was also a policy essentially opposed to the aims of those Independents who had made the revolution. For all their insistence upon decentralization, social justice and Protestant alliances, those Independents had proved quite incapable of making such a policy even in their own parliament which their own leader had purged in their interest. Unable, or unfitted, to exercise political power, they seemed doomed to surrender it to any organized group, however small, which was capable of wielding it — even if that group only used it to pursue policies quite different from their own. Though the 'tory' Independents had made the revolution and, through the army, held power in the state, the 'whigs' had contrived to secure power in parliament. To correct this and create a government of their own, the Independents had the choice between two policies. Either they could preserve the republican constitution and beat the 'whigs' at their own game — or, if that was too difficult for natural back-benchers, they could remove their rivals by force and place over parliament a 'single person', like-minded with themselves, to summon, dismiss and, above all, guide and regulate their assemblies. This latter course was entirely consistent with their general political philosophy; it was also the easier course; and consequently they took it. The crucial question was, did the new 'single person' understand the technique of his task? He had in his hands all the power of the state; but had he in his head the necessary knowledge of parliamentary management? That is, patronage and procedure to prevent another usurpation of the vacant front benches? Would he now fill them with his privy councillors and thus cement, as Queen Elizabeth had done, the natural harmony between the faithful, if somewhat inarticulate, Commons and the Throne?

Oliver Cromwell and his Parliaments

If this was what Cromwell hoped to do, his first opportunity after the expulsion of the Rump was perhaps his best, for the 'Parliament of Saints', the 'Barebones Parliament' of 1653, was, after all, largely a nominated, not an elected, assembly. And yet, as it turned out, this experiment proved to be Cromwell's most humiliating failure. The Barebones Parliament is a classic example of an unpolitical assembly colonized from within by a well organized minority. It was so colonized not merely because the majority of its members were unpolitical — that is true of most assemblies — but because Cromwell himself, in summoning it, was quite unaware of the real inspiration behind it, and made no attempt to convert it, by preparation or organization, into a useful or even workable assembly. As he afterwards admitted, it was a tale not only of the members' weakness but of his own: 'the issue was not answerable to the simplicity and honesty of the design'.[1]

The evidence for this is sadly plain. For what was in the minds of Cromwell and his conservative allies when they decided, or agreed, to summon the Barebones Parliament? We look, and all we find is a well-meaning, devout, bewildered obscurity. The Independents had no political theories: believing that forms of government were indifferent, they counted simply on working with the existing institutions, and now that the existing institutions — first monarchy, then republic — had been destroyed, they were at a loss. 'It was necessary to pull down this government,' one of them had declared on the eve of the expulsion, 'and it would be time enough then to consider what should be placed in the room of it'; and afterwards it was officially stated that 'until the Parliament was actually dissolved, no resolutions were taken in what model to case the government, but it was after that dissolution debated and discussed as *res integra*'.[2] In other words, having expelled the Rump Parliament which had be-

---
[1] Abbott, *Writings and Speeches of Oliver Cromwell*, iv. 489.
[2] Ludlow, *Memoirs*, i. 351; [anon.] *A True State of the Case of the Commonwealth*, 1654 (quoted by Firth in Ludlow, *op. cit.*, i. 358, note).

trayed the Independent cause, the Independent officers found themselves in a quandary. They had acted, as Cromwell so often acted, not rationally nor with that machiavellian duplicity with which his victims generally credited him, but on an impulse; and when the impulsive gesture had been made and the next and more deliberate step must be taken, they were quite unprepared.

Over the unprepared the prepared always have an advantage. In this case the prepared were the new radical party which had replaced the broken Levellers: the extreme totalitarian radicals, the Anabaptists and their fighting zealots the Fifth Monarchy Men. These men had already established themselves in the army through their disciplined tribunes, the chaplains; they already controlled many of the London pulpits; and for the capture of direct power they had two further assets: an organization, in the form of the Committee for the Propagation of the Gospel in Wales, which was now totally controlled by their energetic Welsh leader, Vavasour Powell, and his itinerant missionaries; and a patron at the highest level in Major-General Harrison, the commissioner in charge of the Welsh Propagators and — what was now more important — the *alter ego* of the unsuspecting Cromwell. In the Rump Parliament, which after all had been the residue of a parliament of gentry, lawyers and merchants, these radical zealots had had little influence. Indeed, they had been its most violent enemies, for the Rump, unlike Cromwell, had been well aware of their subversive activities and had for some time been preparing, in spite of constant obstruction, to discontinue the Welsh Propagators who formed their essential committee. It was largely to forestall, or avenge, so crucial a blow that Harrison had urged Cromwell to expel the parliament.[1] When he had expelled it, Cromwell had played into the hands of the radicals. They had used him to destroy their enemy for them; and they now looked

---

[1] The history of the struggle over the Welsh Propagators can be followed in T. Richards, *The Puritan Movement in Wales* (1920). See also Alan Griffith, *A True and Perfect Relation of the whole Transaction concerning the Petition of the Six Counties*, etc. (1654).

forward to using him still further, as a means of achieving direct political power.

As so often in the history of Oliver Cromwell, there is something at once tragic and comic in the manner of his deception by the Fifth Monarchy Men. To him they were merely good religious men, and when he found that his own exalted mood of indignation against the Rump was shared by them, he followed their advice, little suspecting what deep-laid political schemes lurked behind their mystical language. 'Reformation of law and clergy': was not that precisely his programme? A milder, cheaper, quicker law, a decentralized, godly, puritan clergy; were not these his ambitions? How was he to know that by the same phrase the 'Anabaptists' meant something quite different and far more radical: wholesale changes in the law of property, abolition of tithe, the extension over England of the closely organized, indoctrinated religious tribunes who had already carried their gospel over Wales 'like fire in the thatch'? Oliver Cromwell suspected no such thing. When Harrison urged him to expel the Rump as the persecutors of the 'poor saints in Wales', he innocently acquiesced; and when the refusal of the Rump to renew their authority had still left the Welsh Propagators without a legal basis, he as innocently supplied them with a substitute, writing to them to ignore strict legality and 'to go on cheerfully in the work as formerly, to promote these good things'. Months afterwards the greatest crime of the Rump would still seem to him to be its attempt to disband those Welsh Propagators, 'the poor people of God there, who had men watching over them like so many wolves, ready to catch the lamb as soon as it was brought out into the world'.[1] This romantic view of a knot of Tammany demagogues, who concealed their sharp practices behind lachrymose Celtic oratory, was soon to be sadly dispelled.

As soon as they had secured the expulsion of the Rump, the Fifth Monarchy Men were ready for the next step. What they required was a legislature nominated by the supposedly

[1] Abbott, *Writings and Speeches of Oliver Cromwell*, iii. 13, 57.

'independent' churches, some of which had been completely penetrated and were now safely controlled by them. Only in this way could so unrepresentative a party achieve power. Therefore when Cromwell remained poised in doubt, he soon found himself besieged by willing and unanimous advisers. 'We humbly advise', the saints of North Wales wrote to him from Denbigh (the letter was composed by the local Fifth Monarchy panjandrum Morgan Llwyd), 'that forasmuch as the policy and greatness of men hath ever failed, ye would now at length, in the next election, suffer and encourage the saints of God in his spirit to recommend unto you such as God shall choose for that work'.[1] Another Fifth Monarchy preacher, John Rogers, was even more precise. He urged that an interim junto of twelve, 'like to Israel's twelve Judges', be first set up; that a Sanhedrim of seventy men 'or else one of a county' be then nominated, in which 'the righteous of the worthies of the late Parliament' might also be included; and that in all cases of doubt the General should 'consult with the Saints (Deuteronomy i. 13) and send to all discerning spirited men for their proposals'.[2] Through Harrison, these proposals were urged in the council of officers;[3] under this double pressure, direct and indirect, Cromwell easily yielded; and the Barebones Parliament, when it was summoned, was, in fact, a body constituted almost exactly as required in the Fifth Monarchy programme. The twelve councillors were appointed, and the members of the new parliament were to be nominated by the local churches which the radicals had often penetrated. Some few members were to be nominated directly by the council.

Whom would the churches elect? Cromwell's own demands were moderate and sensible. He called for 'known men of good repute'— that is, respectable puritan, even if

[1] *Milton State Papers*, p. 120; cf. J. H. Davies, *Gweithiau Morgan Llwyd* (Bangor, 1899 and 1908), ii. 264.
[2] John Rogers, *A Few Proposals*, quoted in Edward Rogers, *Life and Opinions of a Fifth Monarchy Man* (1867), p. 50.
[3] See Harrison's letters on this subject in Jones Correspondence (p. 23, note 2); also Ludlow, *op. cit.*, i. 358: *Clarke Papers*, iii. 4.

unpolitical, gentry; and such were the men he himself seems to have nominated, Lord Lisle, his own relatives, his own medical man Dr. Goddard,[1] etc. But the radicals had more definite, more positive, views: they were determined to send to parliament only reliable radical party-members. The chance survival of the correspondence of one of their Welsh sympathizers, Colonel John Jones of Merionethshire, clearly shows their electioneering tactics:[2] for in Wales at least there were now no 'independent' churches, only Vavasour Powell's dragooned itinerant missionaries. Consequently even the formality of election was there unnecessary. 'I presume', Harrison wrote to Colonel Jones, 'brother Powell acquainted you our thoughts as to the persons most in them to serve on behalf the Saints of North Wales: Hugh Courtney, John Browne, Richard Price out of your parts.' In other words, the three members for North Wales were simply nominated in London by Harrison and Powell and their names communicated, as a courtesy, to a prominent supporter in the district. It need hardly be added that all three were prominent Fifth Monarchy Men, and all were duly 'elected'. No doubt the three members for South Wales — Vavasour Powell's own district — were similarly chosen. Two of them also appear to have been Fifth Monarchists.[3] Similarly in England, wherever radical preachers controlled the churches, radical politicians were recommended to the council as mem-

[1] Lord Lisle was evidently nominated by the council, since he sat for Kent but had not been nominated by the churches of Kent, whose list of nominees survives (*Milton State Papers*, p. 95).
[2] Some of these letters were published in the *Transactions of the Lancashire and Cheshire Hist. Soc.* 1861, pp. 171 foll. (The originals are now MS. 11440 in the National Library of Wales.) Colonel Jones afterwards separated himself from the Fifth Monarchy Men, married Cromwell's sister, and supported the Protectorate; but at this time, as his letters show, he was a complete 'fellow-traveller' with Harrison and Vavasour Powell.
[3] The three members for South Wales were James Phillips, John Williams and Bussy Mansell. According to J. H. Davies, *Gweithiau Morgan Llwyd*, ii. p. lxiii, two of them were Fifth Monarchists. Louise Fargo Brown, *Baptists and Fifth Monarchy Men* (Washington D.C., 1912), p. 33, only identifies one of them, viz. John Williams, as a Baptist or Fifth Monarchy Man; but whether formally enrolled in the party or not, Bussey Mansell certainly voted with the radicals and was one of the last-ditchers on the radical side who were ultimately turned out by force (see his letter in *Thurloe State Papers*, i. 637).

bers of parliament, and Harrison, on the council, saw to it that they were approved.¹ So the Fifth Monarchists and their fellow-travellers, a compact minority, moved *en bloc* to Westminster. It was machine-politics, and it worked like magic. Complacently Harrison could write to a friend that 'the Lord had now at last made the General instrumental to put the power into the hands of His people'; but that, he added, 'was the Lord's work, and no thanks to His Excellency'.² The innocent Cromwell was still quite unaware of the revolutionary movement which he was sponsoring.

Thus the Barebones Parliament was 'elected', and when it met, on 4 July 1653, Cromwell addressed it in his most exalted style. Now at last, he thought, he had a parliament after his heart, a parliament of godly men, gentry of his own kind, back-benchers, not scheming politicians — with a sprinkling, of course, of Saints. He had a sound Speaker too, Francis Rous, a gentleman, a religious man and a typical Cromwellian: elderly, unpolitical, 'Elizabethan', a stepbrother of Pym and a friend of Drake. Surely so pure a body could be trusted to make good laws. Having urged them to do so, he withdrew altogether from the scene and waited for the good laws to emerge. He did not seek to control parliament; though elected to its committees he did not sit on them; in an honest attempt 'to divest the sword of all power in the civil administration' he drew aside, as Queen Elizabeth and her privy council had never done, from the business of managing parliament, and waited for results.

The results were as might have been expected. The Cromwellian back-benchers were as clumsy old bluebottles caught in the delicate web spun by nimble radical spiders. The radicals were few — there were only eighteen definitely

¹ Apart from the Welsh seats, I deduce that other constituencies were thus 'colonized' from the few surviving lists sent in by the churches. Thus, although the churches of Norfolk and Gloucester proposed miscellaneous names, many of which were not accepted by the council, the churches of Suffolk and Kent proposed solid lists of radical voters (*Milton State Papers*, pp. 92-5, 124-5).
² S. R. Gardiner, *op. cit.*, ii. 222.

identifiable Baptists or Fifth Monarchy Men,[1] of whom five were from Wales; but it was enough. They made a dash for the crucial committees;[2] Harrison, unlike Cromwell, sat regularly both in the House and on its committees; and outside the clerical organizers of the party had the London pulpits tuned. The oratory of Blackfriars created for the radicals that outside pressure which in the past had enabled Pym to intimidate the royalists and Vane to intimidate the presbyterians. Within six months the radicals had such control over the whole assembly that the Cromwellian conservatives, panic-stricken at their revolutionary designs, came early and furtively to Whitehall and surrendered back to the Lord General the powers which, through lack of direction, they had proved incapable of wielding.

Who were the parliamentary managers of the Barebones

[1] L. F. Brown, *op. cit.*, p. 33. It is often stated that the extremists had a 'party' of about sixty (*e.g.* by H. A. Glass, *The Barebones Parliament* (1899); L. F. Brown, *Baptists and Fifth Monarchy Men*, p. 33, and *The First Earl of Shaftesbury* (New York, 1933), p. 55; Margaret James, 'The Tithes Controversy in the Puritan Revolution', in *History*, 1941); but I do not think that so definite a statement can properly be made. It rests on the numbers in divisions, as recorded in the *Commons' Journals* and on two (slightly different) voting-lists for the last crucial debate, one of which is quoted from Thomason E. 669 by Gardiner, *op. cit.*, iii. 259 (it is also in *Thurloe State Papers*, iii. 132), and the other, without reference, by Glass. But divisions were not always on a straight conservative-radical issue and it is not proper to label members permanently as 'Cromwellians' or 'radicals' on the basis of one imperfectly recorded division (Glass's list gives Squibb as a conservative, which is ridiculous, and the lists anyway do not distinguish, among those who did not vote on the conservative side, between radicals, abstainers and absentees). Further, many of those who voted as radicals in 1653 afterwards, when separated from the radical leaders, conscientiously served the Protectorate, having no doubt been — like Cromwell himself — innocent fellow-travellers with the extremists. From a critical study of the tellers in divisions, and from other sources, it is certainly possible to identify the leaders on both sides: Sir Anthony Ashley Cooper, Sir Charles Wolseley, Sir Gilbert Pickering, Alderman Tichborne, on the conservative side; Harrison, Samuel Moyer, Arthur Squibb, Col. Blount, John Ireton and Thomas St. Nicholas on the radical side. No doubt there were others — like the solid bloc of Baptists and Fifth Monarchists — whose position can be as clearly defined. But it is likely that the ordinary back-benchers belonged to no 'party' but voted according to the occasion, and that the success of the radicals consisted in managing floating voters as well as in having control over disciplined voters.

[2] The committees most heavily colonized by the radicals were, naturally, those concerned with the essential parts of their programme, *viz.* tithes and the law. The Committee for a New Model of the Law contained all the principal radicals, and out of its eighteen members no less than thirteen voted on the radical side in the crucial last debate.

Essays Presented to Sir Lewis Namier

Parliament who thus filled the vacuum left by Cromwell's inability or refusal to form a party? Once again, I think, they can be identified. Arthur Squibb, a Fifth Monarchy Man, was a London lawyer with Welsh connexions,[1] and Samuel Moyer, a Baptist, was a London financier and member of the East India Company who had recently been added — no doubt by Harrison — to the council of state. Both were sincere radicals in politics and religion, as they afterwards showed in their eclipse; both had done well out of the revolution; they had worked together on important financial committees, particularly on the permanent Committee of Compounding; they are named together among the earliest public spokesmen for the Barebones Parliament;[2] and in the end, when Cromwell had discovered how he had been abused, it was Squibb and Moyer who, with Harrison and the preachers, were singled out for his revenge.[3] In the committees of the Barebones Parliament, where the radicals concentrated their strength, Samuel Moyer, their link with the council of state, headed the list by sitting, as no other man did, on seven standing committees; and we know from Cromwell himself that Squibb's house in Fleet Street was the central office of the party, 'and there were all the resolutions taken that were acted in that House day by day; and this was true *de facto* — I know it to be true'.[4] Against this

[1] He had begun his career in the office of a Welsh lawyer, Sir Edward Powell, and was connected by marriage with the Welsh judge, John Glyn.

[2] After Cromwell's opening speech, the members adjourned till 8 A.M. next day for 'a day of humiliation for a blessing upon their meeting, not any minister speaking before them (as was proposed), only themselves. Amongst the rest was Mr. Squibb and Samuel Moyer' (*Clarke Papers*, iii. 9).

[3] After the institution of the Protectorate, Squibb was forced to give up his offices as keeper of the prison at Sandwich and teller of the exchequer (*Cal. S.P. Dom. 1654*, pp. 116, 272). He was involved in Venner's Fifth Monarchy rising of 1656 (*Thurloe State Papers*, vi. 185). At the Restoration he and his brothers sought in vain to recover the tellership of the exchequer (*Cal. S.P. Dom. 1661–2*, p. 369; *1663–4*, pp. 121, 582; *1666–7*, pp. 182-3, 535). He was imprisoned in the Tower in connexion with a Fifth Monarchy sermon in 1671 (*ibid. 1671*, p. 357). Moyer disappeared from the council of state and all official positions at the same time. He reappeared to present the republican and Fifth Monarchy petition in Feb. 1659 (*Commons' Journals*, 9–15 Feb. 1659; Burton, *op. cit.*, iii. 288) and again another petition on 12 May 1659 (*Commons' Journals*, s.d.).

[4] Abbott, *Writings and Speeches of Oliver Cromwell*, iv. 489.

highly organized party-machine — the Welsh electioneering machine of Vavasour Powell, the publicity-making machine of the London pulpits now controlled by the party, and the parliamentary caucus of Harrison, Squibb and Moyer — Cromwell, for immediate purposes, had nothing: nothing, that is, except the ultimate basis of his rule — force.

It was by force, in the end, that the little group of radicals who refused to accept the suicide of the majority were expelled. While Speaker Rous, that 'old bottle', as Anthony Wood called him, who was unable to contain the new wine, went off 'with his fellow old bottles to Whitehall' to surrender their authority, some thirty radical members remained in the House at Westminster. Too few to count as a quorum, they could not legally act as a parliament; but they called Samuel Moyer to the mace and began to register their protests. They were interrupted by two colonels who ordered them to leave and then, meeting with no compliance, 'went out and fetched two files of musketeers and did as good as force them out; amongst whom', says a saddened Welsh radical, 'I was an unworthy one'.[1] 'And why should they not depart', retorted a conservative pamphleteer, 'when their assembly was by resignation dissolved, since they were but one degree above a conventicle, and that place, famous for the entertainment of so many venerable assemblies, was not so fit for them as Mr. Squibb's house, where most of their machinations were formed and shaped.'[2]

Cromwell's reply to the collapse of the Barebones Parliament was not to devise — he never devised anything — but to accept a new constitution. Just as, after his impulsive dismissal of the Rump, he had accepted the ready-made plans of Major-General Harrison and his party of Saints for a parliament of their nominees, so now, after the sudden disintegration of that parliament, he accepted from Major-General Lambert and his party of conservative senior officers the newly pre-fabricated constitution of the Instrument of Gov-

[1] *Thurloe State Papers*, i. 637; cf. [? Samuel Highland] *An Exact Relation of the late Parliament* (1654) (*Somers Tracts*, vi. 266-84); *Clarke Papers*, iii. 9-10.
[2] *Confusion Confounded, or a Firm Way of Settlement Settled* (1654).

ernment. By this the new Protectorate was set up, and Cromwell, as Lord Protector, carefully limited by a council of senior officers, was required, after an interval of nine months, to summon a new parliament based on a new franchise. Since this new franchise was, basically, the realization of the plan already advanced by the conservative senior officers seven years earlier in Ireton's *Heads of Proposals*, it must be briefly analysed: for if ever the Independent gentry got the kind of parliament for which they had fought, it should have been in the two parliaments of the Protectorate elected on the franchise which they had thus consistently advocated. If social composition were sufficient to secure a harmonious and working parliament, that success should now be assured.

Now the most obvious feature of the new franchise is that while preserving the old property qualifications, and thus the same social level of representation, it notably altered the distribution of membership, drastically cutting down the borough representation and greatly increasing the county representation. Compared with these facts, the creation of four new boroughs or three new county seats are insignificant adjustments of detail. In fact, the new franchise, in spite of these four new boroughs, reduced the total number of parliamentary boroughs in England and Wales from 182 to 109 and the total number of borough members in parliament from 419 to 136. At the same time the county representation was increased from 90 out of 509 seats to 264 out of 400 seats. In other words, whereas in previous parliaments borough members had occupied 83 per cent and county members 17 per cent of the seats, in Cromwell's parliaments borough members were now to occupy 34 per cent and county members 66 per cent. The county representation was thus quadrupled, the borough representation more than halved.

What is the significance of this sweeping change? The Victorian writers who saw in Cromwell an early nonconformist Liberal supposed that he had in some way 'modernized' the franchise. Had he not disfranchised rotten boroughs and enfranchised new boroughs? But the over-all change, the gigantic switch from borough seats to county seats, seems to me more significant than such modifications of detail. Modern Marxist historians, believing that the Protectorate was a device of the rich, a forcing-house of capitalism, suppose that the new franchise was 'designed to bring the electoral system into something like correspondence with the property-distribution in the country'.[1] But where was the wealth of England? Much of the new wealth was wealth from trade, concentrated — as the Independent gentry indignantly complained — more and more in the City of London. Even if we consider landed wealth only, it can hardly be argued that its distribution was better represented under the new franchise than under the old. Landed wealth was distributed among noblemen, merchants and gentry. Cromwell's parliaments under the new franchise contained no English peers and very few merchants.[2] They were parliaments of gentry, and not necessarily of the richer gentry either. The chief difference between the new and the old members was that whereas the old had been predominantly borough gentry the new were predominantly county gentry. What does this difference between 'borough gentry' and 'county gentry', in fact, mean?

A glance at English parliamentary history at any time between 1559 and 1832 provides the answer. The borough gentry were client gentry; the county gentry were not — they were, or could be, independent of patronage. It was largely through the boroughs that patrons and parliamentary managers had, in the past, built up their forces in parliament. It was through them that Essex had built up a party against Cecil and Cecil against Essex, through them that Charles I might have resisted the Opposition magnates and the Opposition magnates were, in fact, able to resist him. Further, at all times, it was through the boroughs that able men — lawyers, officials, scholars — got into parliament as the clients

[1] C. Hill and E. Dell, *The Good Old Cause* (1949), p. 445.
[2] For merchant representation in Cromwell's parliaments, see M. P. Ashley, *Commercial and Financial Policy of the Protectorate* (1934), pp. 6-8.

of greater men and provided both the Administration and the Opposition with some of their most effective members. The 'rotten' boroughs, in fact, performed two functions: first, they made parliament less representative of the electors than it would otherwise have been; secondly, they made it less inefficient as an instrument of policy.

Now, if, as I have suggested, the 'Independent' gentry were, in fact, the rural 'back-bench' gentry, such as were afterwards represented in the tory party of Queen Anne and the first two Georges, it is clear that they, like the later tories, would be opposed to the borough system as being, by definition, a device of the front-bench politicians to evade the 'equal representation' of 'the people' — that is, of the country gentry — and to introduce 'courtiers' instead of honest country gentry into parliament. It is true, many of them had themselves been returned in this manner in 1640; but their own front-bench leaders, the 'presbyterian' magnates, had then deserted them, and by 1647 they were clamouring for decentralization in parliament as in government, law, Church and education. They demanded a parliament not of untrustworthy 'courtiers' or experts but of sound, honest, representative men like themselves: a 'more equal representative' of real Independents, uncontrolled by any professional caucus; and since, in their own language, 'it was well understood that mean and decayed boroughs might be much more easily corrupted than the numerous counties and considerable cities',[1] they sought it by a reduction of 'corrupt' borough seats and a multiplication of 'independent' county seats.

That had been in 1647, when the Independents had been in opposition. Now they were in power; but their philosophy had not changed. It was not merely that they were committed by their past: that would be too cynical an interpretation. Their philosophy was genuinely held: experience had not yet shown the inherent impossibility of a completely

[1] Ludlow, *op. cit.*, ii. 48. The same argument was a commonplace among the later tories.

back-bench parliament or the inherent difficulty of decentralization by a revolutionary central government; and Cromwell no doubt supposed that honest, Independent country gentlemen, freely elected from within the puritan fold, would naturally agree with the aims and methods of his rule. Further, from the point of view of Cromwell and his council, there were certain compensations. If, by disfranchising the boroughs, the government had deprived itself of a system of patronage, it had equally denied that system to opponents who might, like the opponents of Charles I, be more skilful in using it. Besides, to make doubly sure, the new government prudently added to the English parliament a new system of exclusively government patronage which had not been, and indeed could not have been, considered in 1647. The sixty new Scots and Irish seats created by the Instrument of Government were not, of course, designed for genuine representatives of the newly conquered Scots or Irishmen: they were safe pocket boroughs for government nominees.

A parliament of congenial, unorganized, Independent county gentry, like-minded with himself, reinforced by sixty direct nominees and saved, by the franchise, from the knavish tricks of rival electioneers,— surely this would give Cromwell the kind of parliament he wanted. Especially after the radical scare of 1653, on which he was now able to dwell, and which had made him appear, even to many of those 'presbyterians' who shuddered at his regicide past, a 'saviour of society'. Therefore, when the members had assembled in September 1654, and had listened to a sermon on the arrival of the Israelites, after their years in the Wilderness, at their Land of Rest, Cromwell felt able to apply the text to them and to congratulate them too on having at last, 'after so many changings and turnings', arrived at a period of 'healing and settling'. Furthermore, he assured them, they were now 'a *free* Parliament'; just as he had not sought to control the elections, so he would not in any way control or interfere with their deliberations. Instead, he urged them to discover among themselves 'a sweet, gracious and holy understanding of one another'; and having so urged them, he once again swept off to Whitehall to await, in Olympian detachment, the results of their deliberations.

He did not have to wait long. Able men can work any system, and even under the new franchise the experienced republicans had contrived to re-enter parliament. Once in, they moved with effortless rapidity into the vacuum created by the Protector's virtuous but misguided refusal to form a party. The speed with which they operated is astonishing: one is forced to conclude either that Hesilrige and Scot were really brilliant tacticians (a conclusion which the recorded evidence hardly warrants), or that Cromwell had no vestige of an organization to resist them. At the very beginning they nearly got their nominee — the notorious regicide Richard Bradshaw — in as Speaker. Having failed, they displaced the rival Speaker by the old dodge of calling for a Committee of the Whole House. At once Hesilrige and Scot were in control of the debates; the floating voters drifted helplessly into their wake; and the whole institution of the Protectorate came under heavy fire. Within a week Cromwell had repented of his words about 'a free Parliament', and all the republican members, with Hesilrige, Scot and Bradshaw at their head, had been turned out by force. Legislation was then handed back to the real back-benchers for whom the parliament had been intended.

Ironically, the result was no better. Again and again Cromwell, by his own refusal to organize and his purges of those who organized against him, created in parliament a vacuum of leadership; again and again this vacuum was filled. A pure parliament of back-benchers is an impossibility: someone will always come to the front; and since Cromwell never, like the Tudors, placed able ministers on the front benches, those benches were invariably occupied from behind. The first to scramble to the front were always the republicans: they were the real parliamentary tacticians of the Interregnum. But when they were removed, a second group advanced into their place. It was this second group who now, by their opposition, wrecked Cromwell's first Protectorate parliament.

Who were they? As we look at their programme, shown in their long series of successive amendments to the new constitution which had been imposed upon them, we see that, basically, it is the programme of the old 'country party' of 1640. The voice that emerges from those 'pedantic' amendments, as Carlyle so contemptuously called them, is the voice of the original opponents of Charles I, the voice even of Cromwell himself in his days of opposition. It protests, not, of course, against the decentralization which by his ordinances he had been carrying out, which was still his policy, and of which the new franchise itself was one expression, but against the machinery of centralization whereby this policy was declared: against the new court, the new arbitrariness, the new standing army, the new taxes of that Man of Blood, Oliver Cromwell. Cromwell was caught up in the necessities and contradictions of power and found himself faced by his own old colleagues in opposition. In his days of opposition he too, like them, had demanded a parliament of back-benchers. Now he had got it — when he was in power. By a new franchise and a new purge he had confined parliament to the old 'country party' just at the time when he had himself inherited the position, the difficulties and the necessities of the old court.

But who were the leaders who gave expression and direction to this new country party? A study of the tellers in divisions, which is almost all the evidence we possess, enables us to name the most active of them. There was John Bulkley, member for Hampshire, Sir Richard Onslow, member for Surrey, and, above all, Colonel Birch, member for Hereford; and the interesting fact about these men is that they were all old 'presbyterians'— men who had been arrested or secluded in Pride's Purge. Thus, when the republicans had been removed, it was not the Independents who had occupied the vacant front benches — that indeed would have been contrary to their nature: it was the 'presbyterians'. Heirs of the original front-bench Opposition of 1640, first expelled by the army, then disgusted by the act of regicide, they had now decided to stomach the usurper as the only immediate guarantee against the even greater evil of social revolution; but they were not going to accept him on his terms: they were going to fight for their own.

And did no one seek to serve the cause of Independency against these new, revived 'presbyterian' opponents? Yes, the new Government had its champions, but it is interesting to note that they too were not Independents. In the Barebones Parliament it was Sir Anthony Ashley Cooper, a former royalist, since excluded as a 'presbyterian' in Pride's Purge, who had returned to politics as a 'Cromwellian' and had sought in vain, and without support from Cromwell, to organize parliamentary resistance against the radical extremists. He had been by far the most active parliamentarian on the 'conservative' side, one of their elected representatives on the council of state, their regular teller in controversial divisions; and when his efforts had been in vain, it was another former royalist, Sir Charles Wolseley, who had proposed and carried out the act of resignation whereby the radicals had been cheated of their victory. Now, in the parliament of 1654, the same two ex-royalists emerged again as the opponents of the new 'country' party. Only this time their rôles were reversed. Leaving Sir Charles Wolseley to inherit his position as the champion of Cromwellian government, Cooper, a far abler man, now appeared less as a protagonist than a mediator: he sought not to preserve the Protectorate in the new authoritarian form in which it stood, but to make such compromises with the Opposition as would make it a tolerable form of government, a form of government such as the original Independents had always demanded. Consistently with that original programme, he even sought to civilize the institution by making Cromwell king. But once again Cromwell, aloof at Whitehall, never supported this voluntary ally who now foreshadowed the only practical solution of his problem and was afterwards to prove the most formidable parliamentary tactician of the next reign; and before the abrupt end of the session Cooper drew the consequences. Despairing of Cromwell, he crossed the floor and joined Colonel Birch in opposition. A fortnight later the Protector, now dependent entirely on the army officers, came suddenly down to Westminster prematurely to dissolve yet another parliament. 'I do not know what you have been doing,' he declared, 'I do not know whether you have been alive or dead!'— it is difficult to conceive of Queen Elizabeth or Lord Burghley making such an admission — and with the usual flood of turbid eloquence, hysterical abuse and appeals to God, he dissolved prematurely what was to have been his ideal parliament.

For the next year Cromwell surrendered entirely to his military advisers. He still hankered after his old ideals — it is a great mistake, I think, to suppose that he ever 'betrayed' the revolution, or at least the revolution for which he had taken up the sword. But he resigned himself to the view that those ideals could best be secured by administration, not legislation. After all, 'forms of government' were to him indifferent: one system was as good as another, provided it secured good results; and now it seemed to him that the ideals of the revolution — honest rule such as 'suits a Commonwealth', social justice, reform of the law, toleration — would be better secured through the summary but patriarchal rule of the major-generals than through the legal but wayward deliberations of even an Independent parliament. And, in fact, the major-generals did attempt such things: as Cromwell afterwards admitted, even while he attacked them, 'you, Major-Generals, did your parts well'.[1] Unfortunately, like Archbishop Laud before him, he was soon to discover that in politics, good intentions are not enough. The major-generals, like the Laudian bishops, might seek to supervise J.P.s, to reform manners, to manage preachers, to resist enclosures; but all this was expensive, and when the Spanish war, like Laud's Scottish war, proved a failure, the major-

[1] Burton, *op. cit.*, i. 384.

generals themselves begged Cromwell, for financial reasons, to do what even Laud had had to do: to face a parliament. If Cromwell, like Laud, had apprehensions, the major-generals comforted him. Confident, as military men so often are, of their own efficiency, they assured him that they, unlike the bishops, could control the elections and secure a parliament which would give no trouble. So, in the autumn of 1656, after the most vigorous electioneering campaign since 1640, a parliament was duly elected.

The result was not at all what the major-generals had expected. Ironically, one of the reasons for their failure was that very reduction of the borough seats which the Independents had themselves designed. In the interest of decentralization, Cromwell and his friends had cut down a system of patronage which now at last they had learnt how to use. In the period of direct rule by the major-generals, the Government had 're-modelled' the boroughs and converted them into safe supporters;[1] but alas, thanks to the new franchise, the boroughs were now too few to stem the tide, and from the uncontrollable county constituencies, which the new franchise had multiplied, the critics of the Government — genuine 'Independent' critics of a new centralization — were returned, irresistible, to Westminster. The major-generals had secured their own election, but little more: thanks to their own new franchise, their heroic electioneering efforts had proved vain; and Cromwell, when he saw what they had done, did not spare them. 'Impatient were you', he told them, 'till a Parliament was called. I gave my vote against it; but you were confident by your own strength and interest to get men chosen to your hearts' desire. How you have failed therein, and how much the country hath been disobliged, is well known.'[2] He might well rub it in, for one of the first acts of the parliament thus called was to vote out of existence the whole system of the major-generals.

[1] See B. L. K. Henderson, 'The Cromwellian Charters', in *Transactions of the Royal Historical Society*, 1912, pp. 129 foll.
[2] Burton, *op. cit.*, i. 384.

Oliver Cromwell and his Parliaments

Thus, in spite of vigorous efforts to pack it, Cromwell's second and last Protectorate parliament consisted largely of the same persons as its predecessor; and in many respects its history was similar. Once again the old republicans had been returned: once again, as not being 'persons of known integrity, fearing God and of good conversation', they were arbitrarily removed. Once again the old back-benchers, the civilians, the new country party, filled the vacuum. But there was one very significant difference. It was a difference of leadership and policy. For this time they were not led by the old presbyterians. A new leadership appeared with a new policy, and the Independents now found themselves mobilized not against but for the government of Oliver Cromwell. Instead of attacking him as a 'single person', they offered now to support him as king.

The *volte-face* seems complete, and naturally many were surprised by it; but, in fact, it is not altogether surprising. The new policy was simply the old policy of Sir Anthony Ashley Cooper, the policy of civilizing Cromwell's rule by reverting to known institutions and restoring, under a new dynasty, not, of course, the government of the Stuarts, but the old system from which the Stuarts had so disastrously deviated. For after all, the Independents had not originally revolted against monarchy: the 'whig' republicans, who now claimed to be the heirs of the revolution, had, in fact, been belated upstarts in its course, temporary usurpers of its aims. The genuine 'tory' Independents, who had now reasserted themselves over those usurpers, had merely wanted a less irresponsible king than Charles I. Nor had they wanted new constitutions. They had no new doctrines: they merely wanted an old-style monarch like Queen Elizabeth. Why should they not now, after so many bungled alternatives, return to those original limited aims? Why should not Cromwell, since he already exercised monarchical power, adjust himself more completely to a monarchical position? In many ways the policy of the 'Kingship party' in parliament — however denounced by the republicans as a betrayal of the revolution which they sought to corner — was, in fact, the nearest that the puritans ever got to realizing their original aims. Consequently it found wide support. The 'country party' and the new court at last came together.

Who was the architect of this parliamentary *coup*? There can be no doubt about his identity. Once again, it was a former royalist. Lord Broghill, a son of the first earl of Cork, was an Irish magnate who had become a personal friend and supporter of Cromwell. He was now member of parliament for County Cork, and his immediate supporters were the other members for Ireland, whom, no doubt, as Cromwell's Irish confidant, he had himself helped to nominate. There was Major-General Jephson, member for Cork City and Youghal, where Broghill's family reigned; there was Colonel Bridge, member for Sligo, Roscommon and Leitrim; there was Sir John Reynolds, member for Tipperary and Waterford; and there was Vincent Gookin, member for Kinsale and Bandon, surveyor-general of Ireland. In other words, Lord Broghill was a great parliamentary manager, like the earls of Warwick and Bedford in 1640. While the major-generals, as officials, had organized the attenuated boroughs of England in their support, Broghill, a private landlord, wedded to an entirely different programme, had organized another area of influence, in Ireland. If the presbyterians had been, in some respects, a Scottish party, and the Fifth Monarchy Men a Welsh party, the 'Kingship-men' were, in their first appearance, an Anglo-Irish party.[1]

Once again the remarkable thing is the ease with which the new leadership secured control over parliament. Just as the eleven 'presbyterian' leaders, whenever they were allowed to be present in 1647–8, had always been able to win control of the Long Parliament from Vane and St. John; just as, after 1649, the little group of republicans dominated every parliament to which they were admitted; just as a score of radical extremists dominated the Barebones Parlia-

---

[1] The Irish basis of the Kingship party was pointed out by Firth, 'Cromwell and the Crown', in *English Historical Review*, 1902, 1903.

ment of 1653, or a handful of old presbyterians the Purged Parliament of 1654, so the little group of 'Kingship-men' quickly took control, against the protesting major-generals, of the parliament of 1656. Their success illustrates the complete absence of any rival organization, any organization by the Government — and, incidentally, the ease with which Cromwell, if he had taken the trouble or understood the means, could have controlled such docile parliaments.

For there can be no doubt that Cromwell himself, though he stood ultimately to gain by it, was at first completely surprised by Broghill's movement. As he afterwards said, he 'had never been at any cabal about the same'.[1] Indeed, when Broghill's party first made itself felt in parliament, it was positively opposed to the declared policy of the Protector; for Cromwell was still committed to the system of government by major-generals, and his faithful shadow, Secretary Thurloe, had already drafted a speech urging the continuation of that system — a speech which the sudden, belated conversion of his master and himself to the Kingship party left undelivered in his files.[2] Furthermore, the previous advocate of Kingship, Sir Anthony Ashley Cooper, had been firmly excluded from the present parliament by order of Cromwell himself. We are obliged to conclude that Cromwell at first genuinely intended to support the major-generals, and that, in jettisoning them, he did not follow any deliberate course. He simply wearied of them, as he had wearied in turn of the king, of the presbyterians, of the Levellers, of the Rump, of the Saints; and having wearied, he surrendered once again to a new party, just as, in the past, he had surrendered in turn to Vane, to Ireton, to Harrison, to Lambert — successive mentors who had successively promised to lead him at last out of the 'blood and confusion' caused by their predeces-

[1] Burton, *op. cit.*, i. 382.
[2] The draft is in *Thurloe State Papers*, v. 786-8, where it is described as 'minute of a speech in Parliament by Secretary Thurloe'; but, in fact, I can find no evidence that it was ever delivered, and I presume that it is a draft. In any case, delivered or undelivered, it shows that Thurloe, and therefore Cromwell, had intended to continue the major-general system which, in fact, they jettisoned.

sors to that still elusive elixir, 'settlement'.

Having captured a majority in parliament, the Kingship party set methodically to work. The government of the major-generals was abolished; the kingship, and the whole political apparatus which went with it — House of Lords, privy council, State Church, and old parliamentary franchise — was proposed. Except for the army leaders, whom such a policy would have civilized out of existence, and the obstinate, doctrinaire republicans, all political groups were mobilized. The officials, the lawyers, the Protectoral family and clients, the government financiers — all who had an interest in the stability of government — were in favour. At last, it seemed, Cromwell had an organized party in parliament. He had not made it: it had made itself and presented itself to him ready-made. It only asked to be used. What use did Cromwell make of it?

The answer is clear. He ruined it. Unable to win over the army leaders, he wrestled with them, rated them, blustered at them. 'It was time', he protested, 'to come to a settlement and leave aside these arbitrary measures so unacceptable to the nation.'[1] And then, when he found them inexorable, he surrendered to them and afterwards justified his surrender in parliament by describing not the interested opposition of serried brass-hats but the alleged honest scruples of religious nonconformist sergeants. Of course, he may have been right to yield. Perhaps he judged the balance of power correctly. Perhaps he could not have maintained his new monarchy without army support. There was here a real dilemma. And yet the army could certainly have been 're-modelled'— purged of its politicians and yet kept strong enough to defend the new dynasty. As Monck afterwards wrote, and by his own actions proved, 'There is not an officer in the Army, upon any discontent, that has interest enough to draw two men after him, if he be out of place'.[2] Cromwell's own personal ascendancy over the army, apart from a

[1] Burton, *op. cit.*, i. 382.
[2] *Thurloe State Papers*, vii. 387.

few politically ambitious generals, was undisputed. Instead of pleading defensively with the 'army grandees' as an organized party, he could have cashiered a few of them silently, as examples to the rest, and all opposition to kingship would probably have evaporated; for it was nourished by his indecision. The total eclipse first of Harrison, then of Lambert, once they had been dismissed — though each in turn had been second man in the army and the State — sufficiently shows the truth of Monck's judgment.

Be that as it may, Cromwell never, in fact, tried to solve the problem of army opposition. After infinite delays and a series of long speeches, each obscurer than the last, he finally surrendered to it and accepted the new constitution only in a hopelessly truncated form: without kingship, without Lords, without effective privy council. Even so, in the view of Lord Broghill and his party, it might have been made to work. But again, Cromwell would not face the facts. Neither in his new Upper House nor in his new council would he give the Kingship-men the possibility of making a party. Spasmodic, erratic gestures now raised, now dashed their hopes, and led ultimately nowhere; the leaders of the party wrung their hands in despair at the perpetual indecision, the self-contradictory gestures of their intended king; and in the end, in January 1658, when the parliament reassembled for its second session, the old republicans, re-admitted under the new constitution, and compacted by their long exile, found the Kingship-men a divided, helpless, dispirited group, utterly at their mercy.

At once they seized their opportunity. The lead was given by their old leader, Sir Arthur Hesilrige. Why, he asked, had the preacher, in his opening address, said nothing in praise of 'that victorious Parliament', the Rump? 'I cannot sit still and hear such a question moved and bide any debate.' Whereupon that other oracle of the republicans, Thomas Scot, 'said he could not sit still but second such a motion, to hear one speak so like an Englishman to call it a victorious Parliament'. From that moment the incorrigible combine was at work again, each seconding the other, filibustering unchecked with long, irrelevant speeches on the horrors of the *ancien régime*, boastful personal reminiscences, the divine right of parliaments, the virtue of regicide, the glories of the Rump. Hesilrige, who once spoke for three hours on past history, beginning with the Heptarchy, prophesied a two-months debate and 'hoped no man should be debarred of speaking his mind freely, and as often as he pleased'. As for himself, 'I could speak till four o'clock'. Within ten days all constructive business had become impossible: the parliament, the French ambassador reported to his Government, 'était devenu le parlement de Hesilrige', and as such Cromwell angrily dissolved it, 'and God judge between you and me'.[1] Before he could summon another, he was dead.[2]

If Oliver Cromwell's parliaments were thus consistently hamstrung through lack of direction, the one parliament of his son Richard was, if anything, more chaotic — and that in spite of immense efforts to prepare it. For weeks before it met, Secretary Thurloe and the council, on their own admission, did 'little but prepare for the next Parliament';[3] the old franchise, and with it the old opportunities of borough patronage, was restored; and the council, as Ludlow sourly

---

[1] Burton, *op. cit.*, iii. 874, 117, 141 ; ii. 437 (and cf. iii. 140); Bordeaux to Mazarin, 18 Feb. 1658, cit. F. Guizot, *Histoire de la République d'Angleterre* (Paris, 1864), ii. 629.

[2] For the failure of the Kingship party in Cromwell's last year see the analysis of their tactics in R. C. H. Catterall, 'The Failure of the Humble Petition and Advice', in *American Historical Review*, Oct. 1903 (ix. 36-65). Catterall concludes that Cromwell was wiser than the Kingship-men and was working, more slowly, more prudently and more patiently than they, to the same result : 'Time was the essential requisite. . . . Time, however, was not granted.' What one thinks of Cromwell's plans and prospects of success must depend on one's estimate of his character as revealed by his previous career, and here I must dissent from Catterall. I cannot agree that patience was 'a quality always at Oliver's disposal and always exercised by him', nor find, in his career, evidence of a slow and prudent progress towards a clearly envisaged political aim. Rather he seems to me to have successively borrowed and then impatiently discarded a series of inconsistent second-hand political systems ; and I see no reason to suppose that he was any nearer to a final 'settlement' at the time of his death than at any previous time in his history of political failure.

[3] *Thurloe State Papers*, vii. 562.

remarks, 'used their utmost endeavours to procure such men to be chosen as were their creatures and had their dependencies on them'.[1] But the result was as unsatisfactory as ever. The Kingship party was now dead: they would have fought to make Oliver king, but who would fight to put the crown on Richard's head rather than on that of Charles II? Lord Broghill did not even sit in the new parliament. On the other hand, the republicans were full of confidence: the demoralization of the Cromwellians gave them hope; in organization they were supreme; and when the parliament met it was soon clear that Hesilrige and Scot were once again its masters.

Masters for what? Certainly not to lead it to constructive legislation. Republicanism in England, except in their fossilized minds, was dead: perhaps it had never been alive outside that limited terrain. Certainly it had not inspired the beginning of the rebellion, and certainly it was extinct at the end of it. From 1653 onwards, when the 'whig' policy which they had grafted on to the revolution had been repudiated by it, Hesilrige and Scot and their friends were simply obstructionists. They had a doctrine and a parliamentary organization. Thanks to that doctrine, and that organization, and the absence of any rival organization, they had achieved power for a time; but when their policy had been rejected, and they proved incapable of modifying it or making it acceptable, they could never recover power and they could use their clear, hard, narrow doctrine and their unrivalled parliamentary organization solely to destroy every rival party in parliament, until the enemy they hated most of all, the monarchy of the Stuarts, returned to crush them and their rivals alike. From 1653 onwards the republicans were simply the saboteurs of every parliament to which they could gain admittance. The weakness of the executive was their opportunity: an opportunity not to advance a cause, but simply to destroy their own rivals; and in no parliament was that weak-

[1] Ludlow, *op. cit.*, ii. 49, and references there cited, cf. *Calendar of State Papers* (*Venetian*), xxxi. 276-7, 282, 284, 285.

ness so tempting to them, or that destruction so easy, as in the parliament of Richard Cromwell, who was too feeble to adopt his father's methods and expel them.

Consequently the record of Richard's parliament makes pitiful reading — even more pitiful than that of Oliver's parliaments, which at least is enriched by the serious purpose and volcanic personality of the Protector. In vain Richard's Speaker, regularly rebuked for his inability to control the debate, protested at the irrelevancy of members: 'we are in a wood, a wilderness, a labyrinth. Some affirmative, some negative, which I cannot draw into one question. . . . The sun does not stand still, but I think you do not go forward.' Even a new and more forceful Speaker, who himself pitched into the debate, answering everyone and laying about him 'like a Busby among so many schoolboys', proved hardly more effective.[1] Most pitiful of all was the fate of Mr. Secretary Thurloe, the chief representative of the Protector in his parliament, the man who was accused of having packed the parliament with at least eighty of his nominees. If only he had done so, as it was his duty to have done, the Government might have fared better.[2] In fact, attempting to defend the indefensible, romantic, irrational foreign policy of the Government, Thurloe found himself hopelessly left behind as one speaker after another carried the debate off into irrelevant by-ways: before long, Thurloe, instead of defending his foreign policy, was defending himself against a charge of having sold English subjects into slavery in the West Indies; and in a debate on the constitution he even found himself in a minority of one.[3] The secretary of state in a minority of one! The mere thought of such a possibility would have made Mr. Secretary Cecil or Mr. Secretary Walsingham — if they could even have conceived such a thought — turn in their graves. And yet this is the man whom historians have

[1] Burton, *op. cit.*, iii. 192, 269-70, 281, 333 ; iv. 205, 213, 234, 243.
[2] In fact, Thurloe protested 'I know not of three members thus chosen into the House'. Burton, *op. cit.*, iv. 301.
[3] *Ibid.* iii. 399, 287 ; and cf. [Slingsby Bethel] 'A True and Impartial Narrative . . .' in *Somers Tracts* (1811), vi. 481.

supposed — merely on account of the number of letters which he either wrote or received or steamed open — was the genius of Cromwellian government![1] When such a thing could happen it was clear that the old Elizabethan system of which the Cromwellians had dreamed, and indeed any parliamentary system, had indeed broken down.

Thus Oliver Cromwell's successive efforts to govern with and through parliament failed, and failed abjectly. They failed through lack of that parliamentary management by the executive which, in the correct dosage, is the essential nourishment of any sound parliamentary life. As always with Cromwell, there is an element of tragic irony in his failure: his very virtues caused him to blunder into courses from which he could escape only by the most unvirtuous, inconsistent and indefensible expedients. And the ultimate reason of this tragic, ironical failure lies, I think, in the very character of Cromwell and of the Independency which he so perfectly represented. Cromwell himself, like his followers, was a natural back-bencher. He never understood the subtleties of politics, never rose above the simple political prejudices of those other backwoods squires whom he had joined in their blind revolt against the Stuart court. His first speech in parliament had been the protest of a provincial squire against popish antics in his own parish church; and at the end, as ruler of three kingdoms, he still compared himself only with a bewildered parish-constable seeking laboriously and earnestly to keep the peace in a somewhat disorderly and incomprehensible parish. His conception of government was the rough justice of a benevolent, serious-minded, rural magistrate: well-intentioned, unsophisticated, summary, patriarchal, conservative. Such was also the political philosophy of many other English squires who, in the seventeenth century,

[1] The political ability of Thurloe seems to me to have been greatly overrated by historians. His skill in counter-espionage is attested by his own state papers, and it excited such admiration at the time that it afterwards became legendary; but otherwise he seems to have been merely an industrious secretary who echoed his master's sentiments (and errors) with pathetic unoriginality. A good secretary is not necessarily a good secretary of state.

turned up in parliament and, sitting patiently on the back benches, either never understood or, at most, deeply suspected the secret mechanism whereby the back benches were controlled from the front. In ordinary times the natural fate of such men was to stay at the back, and to make a virtue of their 'honesty', their 'independency', their kinship rather with the good people who had elected them than with the sharp politicians and courtiers among whom they found themselves. But the 1640s and 1650s were not ordinary times. Then a revolutionary situation thrust these men forward, and in their indignation they hacked down, from behind, the sharp politicians and courtiers, the royalists and presbyterians, who had first mobilized them. Having no clear political ideas, they did not — except in the brief period when they surrendered to the republican usurpers — destroy institutions, but only persons. They destroyed parliamentarians and the king, but not parliament or the throne. These institutions, in their fury, they simply cleaned out and left momentarily vacant. But before long the vacancy was refilled. By careful tests and a new franchise, parliament was reopened — to 'Independents' (that is, back-benchers) only; under careful reservations and a new title, the throne was reoccupied — by an 'Independent' (that is, a back-bench) ruler. At last, it seemed, Crown and Commons were in natural harmony.

Alas, in political matters natural harmony is not enough. To complete the system, and to make it work, something else was necessary too: an Independent political caucus that would constitute an Independent front bench as a bridge between crown and parliament, like those Tudor privy councillors who gave consistency and direction to the parliaments of Henry VIII and Elizabeth. Unfortunately this was the one thing which Cromwell always refused to provide. To good Independents any political caucus was suspect: it smacked of sharp politicians and the court. An Independent front bench was a contradiction in terms. Even those who, in turn, and without his support, sought to create such a front bench for him — Sir Anthony Ashley Cooper, Sir Charles Wolseley, Lord Broghill — were not real Independents but, all of them, ex-royalists. Like his fellow-squires (and like those liberal historians who virtuously blame the Tudors for 'packing' their parliaments), Cromwell tended to regard all parliamentary management as a 'cabal', a wicked interference with the freedom of parliament. Therefore he supplied none, and when other more politically-minded men sought to fill the void, he intervened to crush such indecent organization. In this way he thought he was securing 'free parliaments'— free, that is, from caucus-control. Having thus secured a 'free parliament', he expected it automatically, as a result merely of good advice, good intentions and goodwill, to produce 'good laws', as in the reign of his heroine Queen Elizabeth. He did not realize that Queen Elizabeth's parliaments owed their effectiveness not to such 'freedom', nor to the personal worthiness of the parties, nor to the natural harmony between them, but to that ceaseless vigilance, intervention and management by the privy council which worthy puritan back-benchers regarded as a monstrous limitation of their freedom. No wonder Cromwell's parliaments were uniformly barren. His ideal was an Elizabethan parliament, but his methods were such as would lead to a Polish Diet. Consequently, each of his parliaments, deprived of leadership from him, fell in turn under other leadership and were then treated by him in a manner which made them feel far from free. Only in Cromwell's last year did a Cromwellian party-manager, without encouragement from him, emerge in the House of Commons and seek to save the real aims of the revolution; but even he, having been tardily accepted, was ultimately betrayed by his inconstant master. In that betrayal Cromwell lost what proved to be his last chance of achieving the 'settlement' which he so long and so faithfully but so unskilfully pursued.

Thus it is really misleading to speak of 'Cromwell and his parliaments' as we speak of 'Queen Elizabeth and her parliaments', for in that possessive sense Cromwell — to his misfortune — had no parliaments: he only faced, in a helpless, bewildered manner, a succession of parliaments which he failed either to pack, to control or to understand. There was the parliament of Hesilrige and Scot, the parliament of Squibb and Moyer, the parliament of Birch, the parliament of Broghill, and the parliament of Hesilrige once again; but there was never a parliament of Oliver Cromwell. Ironically, the one English sovereign who had actually been a member of parliament proved himself, as a parliamentarian, the most incompetent of them all. He did so because he had not studied the necessary rules of the game. Hoping to imitate Queen Elizabeth, who, by understanding those rules, had been able to play upon 'her faithful Commons' like a well-tuned instrument, he failed even more dismally than the Stuarts. The tragedy is that whereas they did not believe in the system, he did.

LUCY SUTHERLAND

THE CITY OF LONDON
IN EIGHTEENTH-CENTURY POLITICS

A STUDY of the part which the City of London played in the politics of the eighteenth century involves the examination of two distinct but interrelated topics. The first is limited and specific: the nature and influence of the City in what was then a comparatively new sense, that of its 'monied interest'. The second is wider and more nebulous: the nature of the political opinion and political influence of the City of London in its older sense of a civic entity.[1] Though the borderline between the two is necessarily often more than a little blurred, they involve two very different issues: — the study of the first is a matter of the mechanics of government; that of the second is, in general, a study of the organization and inspiration of opposition. Though the first will be touched on in this article, its chief purpose is to indicate, however tentatively, the main considerations affecting the second.

The 'City' in the modern use of the term, the 'monied interest', was composed throughout this period of a small but growing number of persons closely and habitually concerned with that machinery for creating and mobilizing credit which had been taking shape since the late seventeenth century. Its organization was developing throughout the eighteenth century, particularly in time of war. Its institutional centre was to an increasing extent the Bank of England, assisted to a lesser degree by the other members of what contemporaries called the 'three great monied companies', the

[1] The phrase 'the City' was used in both senses by contemporaries throughout the century, and the context alone can indicate which is meant.

East India Company (with its own issue of short-term securities) and the South Sea Company, since its recovery from the crash of 1720 almost wholly a financial as distinct from a commercial organization.[1] With these were associated to some extent the two insurance companies formed in 1720, the Royal Exchange Assurance Corporation and the London Assurance Corporation.[2] Around this institutional centre there clustered the individual operators working on embryonic markets in stocks and shares, in insurance and in dealings in certain raw materials, a nexus of activities already foreshadowing the organization of a future when London was to become the money market of the world,[3] and already the opportunities it opened up to enterprising individuals were so promising as to lead the most vigorous and successful of the London merchants away from purely commercial activities towards those which were primarily financial. The purposes for which capital and credit were mobilized were much more restricted then than now, and were more limited than they had been before the Bubble Act of 1720.[4] They were, at least till the last quarter of the century, almost entirely restricted to the needs of overseas trade and public finance, and the second, particularly in time of war, bulked very large. Indeed the fortunes of the richest of the monied men would seem at this time to have been largely made by satisfying the credit needs of the State; in subscriptions to Government loans, in Government remittances and in

[1] For this, see J. Clapham, *The Bank of England ; a History* (Cambridge, 1944), vol. i; L. S. Sutherland, *The East India Company in Eighteenth Century Politics* (Oxford, 1952), chap. ii; and 'Samson Gideon and the Reduction of Interest, 1749–50', *Econ. Hist. Review*, 1946, pp. 15-29.

[2] The two Assurance Corporations were included, though in a lesser degree, with the three greater companies in arrangements for subscriptions to Government loans. The most able financier of the first half of the century, Samson Gideon, addressing the Treasury on the means of raising the loan in 1757, speaks of the importance of 'securing the five Companies' (Chatsworth MSS. 512.3).

[3] The history of the origins of the Stock Exchange is still an uncharted field. On the growth of marine insurance, see C. Wright and C. E. Fayle, *A History of Lloyd's* (1928).

[4] 6 Geo. I, c. 18. See A. B. DuBois, *The English Business Company after the Bubble Act 1720–1800* (New York, 1938), pp. 1-41.

The City of London in Eighteenth-Century Politics

financing Government contracts. It was this fact that gave the monied interest its significance in politics.[1]

Though the rise of an embryonic money market was making it possible for the State to mobilize to its own use the resources of the monied individual, there was as yet none of the impersonality of the modern public subscription. The method of raising loans was still so undeveloped and the number of credit-worthy lenders so small that — although shares in Government loans passed freely from hand to hand and market prices were regularly quoted — the actual subscription to loans was normally undertaken as the result of personal negotiations between the more important of the monied men and the Directors of the monied companies on the one hand and the Treasury on the other. Thus each Treasury in turn took pains to forge its personal links with the monied interest in the City, and the relations between them became very close. Moreover, in the intricate game of eighteenth-century political management the Treasury would often make it clear not only that they would tend to confine financial advantages to their friends in the City, but that they would give preference to those friends who were also members of parliament and could thus provide a vote on the Government's side in the House of Commons. In consequence the chief monied men in the City, unless they were disqualified by religion[2] or nationality,[3] found it worth while to buy expensive borough seats (they might, of course, have done so in any case if they were seeking to use their wealth to move into the ranks of the landed gentry) to qualify for the reception of financial favours from the Government. And the men who made up the nucleus of the monied interest, both within and outside the House, remained throughout the century in close alliance with the Government of the day.

The influence of such men on the Governments with

---

[1] Sir Lewis Namier first analysed this situation in *The Structure of Politics at the Accession of George III* (1929), i. 56 seq.

[2] As was Samson Gideon, the great Jewish financier.

[3] As was Sir Joshua Vanneck, of Dutch birth. See L. B. Namier, *op. cit.*, i. 70.

which they were in alliance was considerable, both in purely financial matters [1] and on other issues related to them. The combined opposition of the monied interest prevented the reduction of the interest on the National Debt, though Walpole was known to favour it, in 1737,[2] and Pelham only succeeded in carrying out his conversion operation of 1749–50 after making liberal compensations to the main institutions involved.[3] Not only were the terms of Government loans bargained for in advance between the Treasury and their leaders,[4] but their advice on the finance of war was taken on occasion in connexion with peace negotiations,[5] and those of them who sat in the House were often employed as experts on a variety of commercial issues. Their importance as a political force can, however, easily be over-emphasized. Eighteenth-century politicians sometimes gave credence to a myth not unlike that of the 'bankers' ramp' of the twentieth century, and maintained that ministries could be overthrown or rendered impotent by the 'loss of the City' engineered by political opponents. But their only illustration of a ministry 'losing the City' to opponents (and this a confused and inconclusive one) dated back to 1710–11.[6] Though it was some-

[1] Namier, *op. cit.*, pp. 56 *seq.*, and L. S. Sutherland, 'Samson Gideon: Eighteenth Century Jewish Financier', *Transactions of the Jewish Historical Society of England*, xvii. 79 *seq.*

[2] The best contemporary evidence for this abortive attempt is the diary of the first earl of Egmont *Historical Manuscripts Commission, Diary of the first Earl of Egmont*, ii. 380 *seq.*, and correspondence in the *Carlisle MSS., Hist. MSS. Comm.*, pp. 182 *seq.*

[3] L. S. Sutherland, 'Samson Gideon and the Reduction of Interest', *loc. cit.*

[4] This is shown by L. B. Namier, *op. cit.*, i. 68 *seq.*, for 1759, and L. S. Sutherland for other occasions in the two articles quoted above.

[5] For instance, W. Coxe, *Memoirs of the Administration of the Rt. Hon. Henry Pelham* (1829), ii. 318, H. Pelham to Newcastle, 23 Sept.–4 Oct. 1748. 'I have made the best inquiry I can, amongst all the men of business in the city, and I can assure you, they are all of opinion, that peace is absolutely necessary.' On 1 Oct. 1762 the duke of Cumberland consulted Newcastle, recently out of office, on the financial prospects if the peace negotiations fell through. Newcastle consulted a City friend, Thomas Walpole, son-in-law and partner of Sir Joshua Vanneck, who replied that, given a Minister they trusted, 'he thought the money might be had, taking advantage of the present general dislike to the terms of Peace' (Brit. Mus., Add. MSS. 32944, f. 36).

[6] The part played by the monied interest led by the Bank in the fall of Godolphin in 1710 (see J. Clapham, *The Bank of England ; a History*, i. 73 *seq.*,

times claimed that the attempt to oust the Pelhams in 1746 was defeated by the determination of the monied interest to refuse supplies to an alternative administration,[1] this does not seem to be supported by facts; the difficulties which the Devonshire-Pitt administration found in raising supplies in 1757 [2] were not due to political causes; and the hopes of the duke of Newcastle, when dismissed from office in 1762, that his successors would be unable to obtain credit, were disappointed.[3] In fact, the City, in the sense of its monied interest, was throughout the period a broken reed for the purposes of party politics, for the good reasons that the prosperity of all its members depended on their being on terms with the Government of the day, and that, even if it might have paid them to hold out for a short time, they were much too competitive among themselves to do so. As early as 1711 Daniel Defoe had argued that it was not the maxim 'They that have the Money must have the Management' which was true, but 'They that have the Management will have the Money'.[4]

So much for the City in the modern sense of the word. In its older sense the City was a great urban centre, by far the greatest in the British Isles, with a population within its ancient boundaries of about 150,000, and a dependent popu-

and C. Buck and G. Davies, 'Letters on Godolphin's dismissal in 1710', *Huntington Library Quarterly*, 1940, pp. 225 seq.) and the financial difficulties in Harley's Ministry (see 'Memoirs of the Harley Family, especially of Robert Harley, first Earl of Oxford, by Edward Harley, Auditor of the Exchequer', *Hist. MSS. Comm., Report on Portland MSS.*, v. 650 seq.) remains an obscure incident. Eighteenth-century politicians bore it in mind. In 1762 Newcastle deplored the threat of the governor of the Bank of England to retire in disgust at the Bute Ministry. 'Besides his successor would probably not be so good a friend as he is, and the Bank might fall into bad hands as it did when Sir G. Heathcote was overpowered by Sir James Bateman and John Ward in my Lord Oxford's time' (Add. MSS. 32940, f. 373, Newcastle to Hardwicke, 16 July 1762).

[1] H. Fox to Ilchester, 13 Feb. 1746, quoted in Ilchester, *Henry Fox, First Lord Holland* (1920), i. 125. But see W. Coxe, *op. cit.*, i. 289.

[2] Add MSS. 32870, ff. 437 seq.

[3] *Ibid.* 32944, ff. 22 seq. (Substance of a conversation with the duke of Cumberland, Oct. 1762), and Add MSS. 32940, ff. 302b-3 (Newcastle to J. West, 9 July 1762).

[4] *Eleven opinions about Mr. H[arle]y; with Observations*, 1711, p. 43.

lation of about 700,000.¹ It had a proud and ancient corporation from which many of its residents were excluded but which nevertheless comprised some 12,000–15,000 freemen by birth, apprenticeship or redemption ² (some 8000 of whom were also liverymen of the City Companies) and a vigorous corporate spirit which expressed the attitude of its 'middling men', as contemporaries called them, the class of small merchants, tradesmen and master craftsmen. It was they who dominated its Common Council, elected its four members of parliament and, both in the Common Hall and Common Council, played a great part in the election of City officers, from the Mayor downwards.³ And if the richest men in the City, its 'monied interest', were supporters of the Governments of the day, the City in this wider sense was almost always in opposition to them. If the state of City opinion be examined for the sixty-two years between the rise of Walpole in 1720 and the fall of Lord North in 1782, in the records of the Common Council,⁴ in the utterances of the City members, in pamphlet and press and the comments of contemporaries, it becomes clear that the City abandoned its anti-ministerialism only on occasions when there was some special explanation of the fact, and that the occasions were comparatively few. Such exceptions were the years 1747–54, when Henry Pelham had set himself to placate the City, as he was placating all the opponents of his Broad-bottomed Administration;⁵ the years 1756–61, when William Pitt was carrying on his two war ministries on principles with which the City was deeply concerned; to them may perhaps be added the first months of the Chatham administration, when the name of the late Great Commoner still exercised its spell.⁶

¹ For the problem of the population of London, see M. D. George, *London Life in the Eighteenth Century* (1930), pp. 21-9.
² S. and B. Webb, *English Local Government* . . . *The Manor and the Borough* (1908), ii. 574 *seq.*   ³ *Ibid.*
⁴ The Journals preserved in the Guildhall Records Office. See also vol. 8 of the Common Hall Books. 1751–88.
⁵ Sutherland, 'Samson Gideon and the Reduction of Interest', *loc. cit.*
⁶ The first Rockingham Administration, despite its active support of certain trading interests (Sutherland, 'Edmund Burke and the First Rockingham Ministry', *English Historical Review*, xlvii. 40 *seq.*), never succeeded in winning

But these years are, at the most, no more than eleven out of a total of sixty-two. For the rest of the time there was suspicion and antagonism, flaring from time to time, in the excitements of political life, into violent hostility.

The question arises, what was the reason for this remarkable consistency in opposition, a consistency which survived changes of kings and administrations and bore so little relation to the ruling persons or forces of the day? There are several possible explanations. Two of them are at bottom based on economic considerations. The first possible explanation is that the attitude was the outcome of friction and conflict within the City itself. In eighteenth-century London there was, partly as a heritage of seventeenth-century strife and even earlier traditions, and partly as a result of contemporary tendencies, a good deal of that latent hostility between the richest citizens and the lesser men which is familiar (as the struggle between 'Magnati' and 'Popolani') to students of the independent communes of Europe. The antagonism was social, economic and political in its origin and showed itself in friction within the City constitution (for instance, in disputes between the Court of Aldermen and the Court of Common Council)[1] and a tendency to seek emancipation from oligarchic leadership and control (for instance, in the choice of the four City members of parliament and sometimes of the chief City officers).[2] The fact that many of these rich citizens were supporters of the Government was in itself likely to lead the lesser men to array themselves with the Opposition,[3] and there were two special reasons

a good press in the City, even the repeal of the Stamp Act being generally attributed to Pitt (*e.g. Public Advertiser*, 1765, *passim*).

[1] The internal friction in the City and its connexion with national politics has been carefully analysed by A. J. Henderson, *London and the National Government, 1721–42* (Duke University Press, 1945).

[2] Instances of the latter are the election of Deputy James Hodges, as Clerk of the City in 1757 (for the controversy surrounding this, see *The Test*, 23 April 1757, pp. 134 *seq.*, and *The Contest*, 28 May 1757, pp. 165 *seq.*).

[3] The aldermen, though popularly elected, were elected by wards, the characters of which varied considerably; they held office for life and it was widely held that a fortune of not less than £30,000 was a necessary qualification. In consequence, though there were always some 'popular' aldermen among

which strengthened this trend. Firstly, in 1725, in his London Election Act, Walpole had ranged the Government on the side of the oligarchic faction in the City by giving the sanction of law to the traditional power of 'Aldermanic Veto' over the Common Council, and though Pelham repealed the relevant clause of the Act twenty-one years later, much bitterness had been engendered in the meantime.[1] Secondly, those outside the 'monied interest' were bitterly jealous of the advantages made available to the monied men by the method of taking up subscriptions to Government loans already referred to, and they clamoured loudly for an 'open' subscription in which they could all join, a demand which the Treasury seldom thought it prudent to satisfy.[2] Thus it felt of most ministers, as was said of Walpole (however unjustly), that 'he is hated by the city of London, because he never did anything for the trading part of it, nor aimed at any interest of theirs, but a corrupt influence over the directors and governors of the great monied companies.'[3] But this internal friction, though no doubt an important contributory factor to the City's attitude in national politics, does not seem of itself sufficient to explain the vigour of its anti-ministerialism. Nor does it explain why this anti-ministerialism was abandoned in special circumstances.

A second economic explanation might lie in the interest of the City in maritime and colonial war. The commercial classes of the eighteenth century were exceedingly bellicose in their sentiments, provided that the wars they were fighting were sea-wars and the aim of them was the retention or gain of colonial territory, for in such wars they saw prospects of private commercial gain as well as hopes of national

them, the majority tended to express the views of the monied interest, though few of them at any one time played a prominent or active part in this interest. When feeling ran very strong in the City, as in the later years of Walpole, or during Wilkes's predominance in the City, they tended to bow to it in the long run, but only after a considerable time-lag and always with a strong minority holding out.

[1] Henderson, *op. cit.*, pp. 74 *seq.*
[2] Sutherland, 'Samson Gideon and the Reduction of Interest', *loc. cit.*
[3] *Some Materials towards Memoirs of the Reign of King George II by John Lord Hervey*, ed. R. Sedgwick (1931), i. 138.

glory.¹ Indeed there is some truth in Burke's bitter description of the merchants in 1775 as beginning 'to snuff the cadaverous *haut gout* of lucrative war'.² They were also, however, the first to be struck in their pockets as well as their pride when such wars went badly, so that the events of the period in time of war, or in the years leading up to war, or (in the reign of George III) the years of conflict with the American colonies, gave ample opportunity for friction between the Governments and the body of commercial and trading opinion finding expression in the City. But this explanation, too, though it may account for the timing of most of the biggest outbursts of anti-ministerialism, is insufficient in itself to explain the whole movement, and fails to make clear why it was maintained in years of peace. Nor do either of these economic explanations account for the forms in which this feeling found expression.

If these two explanations are dropped the conclusion remains that the key to this tendency in the City must be sought in causes less obvious but perhaps even deeper-seated. These causes are best elucidated by considering the relations of the City with the other Opposition interests in national politics, bearing in mind at the same time the stamp set on the activities of the City by its own traditions and experience. If the parliamentary Oppositions of the eighteenth century are examined the first thing that becomes clear is that (oddly enough, at first sight, in an age when ministries made majorities and not majorities ministries) they always sought to bolster themselves up and embarrass their enemies in power by attracting the support of bodies of opinion outside the House. As Burke, one of the most experienced Opposition leaders of the century, remarked, 'we know that all opposition is absolutely crippled if it can obtain no kind of support without doors'.³ They sought this

---

¹ R. Pares, *War and Trade in the West Indies, 1739–1763* (Oxford, 1936), pp. 56-64.
² FitzWilliam and R. Bourke, *The Correspondence of the Rt. Hon. Edmund Burke* (1844), ii. 50.
³ *Ibid.* ii. 51-2.

support in general from two classes, the country gentry, who influenced and were influenced by those independent country gentlemen in the House whose role Sir Lewis Namier has so brilliantly analysed in his Romanes Lecture,[1] and in the body of organized commercial and trading opinion in the City of London. And, when they were successful in gaining this support, they did so by calling to their aid political assumptions and prejudices which were accepted by gentry and merchants alike without question — and which were indeed accepted by everyone except the small ring of persons directly concerned with the day-to-day questions of political power — the seventeenth-century suspicion of the Executive and the desire to limit the scope of its activities. For some forty-five years after the Hanoverian Succession every Opposition, whatever its nature and its real end, pinned its faith on rallying the support of these two powerful extra-parliamentary forces by 'out-whigging the whigs'. They produced a programme which expressed an archaic, academic whiggism, by incorporating the demand for a Place or Pensions Bill, the return to triennial parliaments and the reduction of the standing army.[2] And even in the reign of George III when Opposition found new and sometimes more realistic war-cries, the old ones had not lost their charm.

Moreover, though everyone with inside knowledge of politics knew that no group or party intended to implement these doubtful political principles, the fact that they were so widely accepted made them embarrassing to Governments. These even went so far on occasion (particularly just before a general election) as to let measures incorporating them through the House of Commons, to be quashed in the safety of the Lords, knowing, as it was said in 1731, that to vote

---

[1] L. B. Namier, *Monarchy and the Party System* (Oxford, 1952). See also his 'Country Gentlemen in Parliament 1750–1785', *History Today*, Oct. 1954, pp. 676–688. Both are reprinted in *Personalities and Powers* (1955).

[2] Extremists sometimes demanded annual parliaments and the total abolition of the standing army, but in the first half of the century they were rare and somewhat eccentric.

The City of London in Eighteenth-Century Politics

against such measures 'would put a great many gentlemen under difficulties' so that they 'must have left them or have hurt their own interest very much in the places they serve for'[1]—an argument which also throws some light on the passing of Dunning's famous Resolution of 1780.[2]

The counties and the City filled somewhat different rôles in the system of Opposition parties. Opinion expressed in the counties was intended to impress the country gentlemen in the House, and was dispersed and loosely organized. That stirred up in the City was much easier to organize and mobilize. City leaders were expert, from long experience of organizing commercial agitation affecting both London and the 'outports', in the art of bringing pressure to bear on authority from without. Petitions, instructions from the Common Council to the City representatives, pamphlets and press campaigns were rapidly planned there, while whenever political excitement ran high the London crowd could be relied on to emerge and give the added support of their clamour to the Opposition cause.

Both these extra-parliamentary allies presented Opposition leaders with some problems, but they were different ones. The country gentry might get out of hand, as from the point of view of the Opposition parties they did at the time of the County Associations. The duke of Newcastle warned his colleagues in Opposition in 1767, 'I know the

[1] *Hist. MSS. Comm., Carlisle MSS.*, p. 82. Hon. C. Howard to [Lord Carlisle]. The Pensions Bills of 1730, 1731 and 1732 were handled in this way. The Place Bills of 1734 and 1739 were thrown out by the House of Commons only by small majorities, the first by 39 and the second by 16 votes. The ministers tried to avoid speaking on them.

[2] 'That the influence of the Crown has increased, is increasing and ought to be diminished.' 6 April 1780 (*Parliamentary Register*, xvii. 453). It was passed by a majority of 18 votes in a full House against the Ministry, despite the fact that the North Administration was normally strong in the House at this time; but it had no consequences. The general election which took place later in the year had not yet been decided on, but it was clear it could not be long delayed. Lord Shelburne told the Common Council of London in reply to a congratulatory letter on the Resolution: 'It is universally acknowledged that the approaching Election has a considerable influence on the members who now support the petitions of the people', and added that the county members 'are understood to have voted for the most part uniformly on the same side'. Guildhall Records Office. Journal of the Common Council, 68, f. 49.

nature and the pulse of our country gentlemen. They are now as well and as quiet as possible; set them in motion and nobody can tell what may arise.'[1] But this problem was only an extension of the general one of handling the independent gentry in the Commons. But the City, though it could be rallied to the Opposition cause, always had to be handled as a separate entity, following (as the country gentry never did) some specifically City leader who was thought of as one of themselves, and it was a force which approached politics in a manner from outside. It was, indeed, this sense of separatism, of standing outside the dominant social and political system of the time, that gave the City in Opposition its peculiar flavour, and it was this sentiment (which lay at the root of the attitude which the nineteenth century was to call Radicalism) which really explains the persistency of the City's tendency to political opposition. Socially the attitude expressed itself in some resentment against and suspicion of the aristocracy and landed classes, with their easy arrogance and assumption of superiority, and in a somewhat self-conscious and self-righteous pride in their bourgeois virtues and bourgeois traditions — this finds its echo in literature and in drama intended largely for their consumption.[2] Politically, there is evidence of a feeling that they and their interests lay outside the framework of a political system dominated by and organized for the interests of the aristocracy and landed classes, and an irritation because they, with their stake in the prosperity of the country and their contribution to it, were apt to be in the position of outsiders having to bring pressure to bear on the political machine.

[1] Add. MSS. 32980, f. 355, Newcastle to Richmond, 20 March 1767. The occasion was a suggestion by Richmond that the Grand Jury of Sussex should thank the county members for their vote on the reduction of the Land Tax in which the Government was defeated. He remarked, '. . . I am not for opening a correspondence between the Grand Jury and their members. Every man may start a disagreeable thing in a Grand Jury, who can do no hurt in the County. It may put it in the head of some lively geniuses to give instructions, or, at any time, to observe upon the votes and behaviour of their members, which would not be pleasant.' *Ibid.* f. 354.

[2] The writings of Daniel Defoe are early expressions of this attitude. The so-called 'bourgeois' drama of the period shows its influence very strongly.

The City of London in Eighteenth-Century Politics

It is true that arguments have been adduced which would seem to run counter to such an explanation. It is pointed out that there was an easy and constant transit from the merchant classes into those of the landed gentry, and that, not only were commercial questions one of the major concerns of eighteenth-century parliaments, but also that a very considerable number of merchants sat in the House of Commons.[1] But it is important to bear in mind the cleavage between the rich merchant and financial classes and the lesser men. Most of the latter lived lives entirely circumscribed by their urban traditions; a seat in parliament was quite outside their ambitions, and they neither considered that their richer fellow-citizens who obtained seats in the House represented them nor that they represented the commercial interests with which they were concerned. The author of *The Remembrancer*, for instance, in 1748 complains bitterly of the prominent citizens who are to be seen cringing at levées and seeking seats in the House of Commons 'and instead of assisting as they ought to preserve and enlarge the traffic of the kingdom, assisting to traffic it away for the sake of a lucrative share in some contract, some remittance or some other dirty consideration of a like nature'; and he urges that a line should be drawn 'between the m[inisteria]l posse of stock-jobbers, contractors, remitters . . . etc., and the fair and upright exporter' and that one should 'confine the reputable title of *merchant* to the latter and admit of his verdict only in commercial matters'.[2]

This combination of participation in the general political assumptions and activities of the nation and of peculiar local separatism and self-consciousness can be traced throughout the history of the City's political activities during the century. It is possible also to trace the way in which the City's self-consciousness became stronger and more articulate under the pressure of events and with the passing of time; and as it grew, so too did the scope and effectiveness of City influence

---

[1] For the merchants in the House, see Namier, *Structure of Politics*, i. 56 seq.
[2] *The Remembrancer*, 3-10 Sept. 1748, quoted in the *Gentleman's Magazine* (1748), pp. 411-12.

in and over the parliamentary Oppositions with which they were in alliance. A brief (and necessarily imperfect) analysis of those stages in the City Opposition, corresponding also to stages in the history of eighteenth-century parliamentary Opposition, will illustrate this development. The same three periods correspond roughly with those of the personal predominance of three of that curious succession of leaders on which the City's political influence so strikingly depended.

The first period runs roughly from 1720 to 1754, that in which united parliamentary Oppositions, composed of combinations of discontented whigs and broken tories (grouping themselves for some years round the prince of Wales), fought what was on the whole a losing battle against the great whig governing connexion built up by Robert Walpole and continued by Henry Pelham — a losing battle, though Walpole himself was overthrown during its course. At this time the City's leader was a stout, high-principled merchant and ship-insurer of no more than moderate wealth, Sir John Barnard,[1] who represented the City in parliament for nearly forty years. During his prime he was a constant and effective speaker, hardly ever missed a debate [2] and never compromised a principle. He was an inveterate enemy of the financial interests,[3] was responsible for the Act for preventing 'the infamous practice of stock-jobbing',[4] 'which, if it had been effective, would have prevented the rise of the Stock Exchange altogether, and though he never compromised his independence, he seems to have believed implicitly that the purpose of the Opposition which hounded Walpole from power was to carry out those whiggish measures to which it paid lip-service. Under this leader the commercial interests of the City were kept well to the fore, and one of the biggest of the

---

[1] 1685–1764, b. Reading, son of a wine-merchant, M.P. for London 1722–61, knighted 1732, sheriff 1735, Lord Mayor 1737: *Memoirs of the late Sir John Barnard, Knight* (1776); *Reasons offered to the Consideration of the worthy citizens of London for continuing the present Lord Mayor . . . for another year*, 1738.

[2] *Reasons offered to the Consideration of the worthy citizens of London for continuing the present Lord Mayor . . . for another year*, 1738.

[3] See Sutherland, 'Samson Gideon and the Reduction of Interest', *loc. cit.*

[4] 7 Geo. II, c. 8.

The City of London in Eighteenth-Century Politics

Opposition drives, that against the Excise Bill of 1733, arose on a question primarily of commercial importance, but the remoteness of the City from the day-to-day realities of politics and its political naïveté made it little more than an adjunct to any Opposition leader who chose to play on its academic 'whiggism' and its sense of grievance and isolation. The oratory of William Pulteney,[1] for instance, greatly attracted City support and, on the fall of Walpole in 1742, it was widely believed that sweeping constitutional changes would follow. A contemporary describes the ferment of excitement on this occasion, in which the City warmly joined.

> Among those who thought themselves most moderate, no two men agreed upon what was necessary; — some thinking that all security lay in a good place bill . . . some in a pension bill. Some in triennial parliaments . . . some [were] for annual parliaments . . . some for a reduction of the Civil List . . . some for the sale of all employments . . . some for taking the disposition of them out of the Crown . . . some for allowing them to subsist but to be given only to those who were not in Parliament, that is, among themselves . . . some for making the army independent; others for no regular troops at all.[2]

When it became apparent that, in fact, nothing was to be done, the disillusionment in the City knew no bounds. For years Pulteney appears in City oratory as the great betrayer, whose example must be a warning to those who put their trust in politicians.[3]

During this time, though their detachment from the day-to-day preoccupations of politics was marked, there was still little overt expression of their political and social sense of separateness. There is, however, a good deal of indirect evidence of social and political malaise quite apart from their response to the demands of Oppositions upon them. It is usually disguised, in contemporary references, under the

---

[1] William Pulteney, earl of Bath, 1684–1764.
[2] *Faction Detected by the Evidence of Facts* [Lord Perceval, later earl of Egmont] (1743), pp. 69-70.
[3] E.g. [Richard Glover] *Memoirs of a Celebrated Literary and Political Character* (1813), pp. 1-7.

title of City Jacobitism; but the more this alleged Jacobitism is examined, the more it appears to be nothing other than a vague and unorganized dislike of the authorities. Horace Walpole said of the 'popular' Alderman Blakiston that he had 'risen to be an alderman of London on the merit of that succedaneum to money, Jacobitism'.[1] But the sober Lord Waldegrave was nearer the mark when he told George II in 1758 'that as to Jacobitism, it was indeed at a low ebb; but there was a mutinous spirit in the lower class of people . . .'.[2]

The next period, however, brought some major changes. This second period may be taken to cover that strange interlude in English political history when, in the war years between 1756 and 1761, William Pitt, the Great Commoner, broke through the chains of government by connexion and forced himself, on equal terms, on the group who had been ruling the country for the last forty years. He maintained himself in this precarious position by the general recognition of his essentiality to win the war and by his popularity not only with the country gentry in parliament but with public opinion outside the House. It has sometimes been claimed for the Great Commoner that he was the first eighteenth-century politician to realize the value of the support of public opinion. This is not true, but he was the first to try to continue using in power the support of outside forces hitherto thought to be available only to Opposition.[3] In consequence in this period the City suddenly found itself in alliance with Government instead of opposing it, and though, after Pitt's coalition with Newcastle in 1757, the City leaders continued as suspicious of his allies as ever — at one time Newcastle accused Pitt of 'letting the mob loose' on them [4] — they adopted

[1] Horace Walpole, *Memoirs of the Last Ten Years of the Reign of George II* (1822), i. 31.
[2] James, Earl Waldegrave, *Memoirs from 1754 to 1758* (1821), p. 130.
[3] In December 1761 the *Gentleman's Magazine*, p. 579, giving extracts from *Charges against the Late Minister with remarks extracted from a variety of Letters*, including the statement 'An opposition to government will always please and gain the people of England, who are great levellers', adds the note that this has not been true for the last four years.
[4] Newcastle to Hardwicke, 27 March 1758, quoted in P. C. Yorke, *Life and Correspondence of Philip Yorke Earl of Hardwicke* (Cambridge 1913), iii. 44.

The City of London in Eighteenth-Century Politics

with enthusiasm the rôle of representatives of the nation supporting the actions of a great national leader. The means by which this support was applied to Administration were the same as those by which it had been given to leaders of the Opposition. It was, as before, under the guidance of a City leader, no longer Sir John Barnard, who was not only nearing the end of his career, but had lost some of his popularity by coming to terms with the Pelham Administration, but a new man, Alderman William Beckford,[1] a rich Jamaica sugar-planter. The new leader was very different from the old: Barnard was first and foremost a merchant and citizen; Beckford had some interests in and connexions with the City,[2] but also much in common with the landed classes, had sat for Shaftesbury before he became member for London, and he began to foster his interest in the City (taking up his freedom in 1752, and becoming an alderman in the same year) only two years before offering himself as a parliamentary candidate. Active for some time in Opposition politics,[3] he obviously saw the chance of strengthening his political position by having the support of the City behind him, and after he had become the devoted supporter of Pitt he made no secret of the fact that he meant to use his power in the City to further the cause of his patron in national politics.

The propaganda and leadership of Beckford and the personal magnetism of Pitt produced, paradoxically, two conflicting results in the City during these years. In the first place, the City gained greatly in its sense of importance and

[1] 1709-70, born in Jamaica, where his family had great estates and his father was governor; M.P. for Shaftesbury 1747-54, London 1754-70; Lord Mayor 1761 and 1769. A statue was erected to him in Guildhall for his speech when delivering a petition to the king in 1770.

[2] He was described as a West-India merchant, but his trading interests seem to have been restricted to handling the produce of his own estates. In *The Gazetteer and London Daily Advertiser*, 25 April 1754, 'A Liveryman' asks 'If one of your candidates is not Member of a Club of Planters, where merchants are judged unworthy of admittance?' Beckford claimed that his 'family were citizens, and some of them had borne the highest offices for a century past'. (Speech when elected Lord Mayor in 1762, *Public Advertiser*, 30 Sept. 1762.)

[3] See, e.g., *The Diary of the late George Bubb Dodington* (ed. H. P. Wyndham, 1784), p. 100, and pp. 235-6; Namier, 'Country Gentlemen in Parliament', *loc. cit.*, pp. 683 seq.

65

the articulateness of its traditions and outlook. A speech by Beckford in the House in 1761 expresses the attitude of those he was leading. Having referred to the 'sense of the people', he proceeded to define it.

> The sense of the people, Sir, is a great matter. I don't mean the mob ; neither the top nor the bottom, the scum is perhaps as mean as the dregs, and as to your nobility, about 1200 men of quality, what are they to the body of the nation ? Why, Sir, they are subalterns, I say, Sir, . . . they receive more from the public than they pay to it. If you were to cast up all their accounts and fairly state the ballance, they would turn out debtors to the public for more than a third of their income. When I talk of the sense of the people I mean the middling people of England, the manufacturer, the yeoman, the merchant, the country gentleman, they who bear all the heat of the day. . . . They have a right, Sir, to interfere in the condition and conduct of the nation which makes them easy or uneasy who feel most of it, and, Sir, the people of England, taken in this limitation are a good-natured, well-intentioned and very sensible people who know better perhaps than any other nation under the sun whether they are well governed or not.[1]

Odd though these words must have sounded in the mouth of a wealthy slave-owner, they reflect accurately the social and political outlook of his followers, views middle-class, commercial, anti-aristocratic and clearly likely to prove difficult for Opposition groups trying to use them for their own purposes in the game of politics.

But if the strengthening of this feeling was one result of the experience of these years, there was another that was rather different. As a result of the example set by Beckford and soon followed by others, the City was brought more closely into day-to-day politics, since the leaders it trusted were themselves, as John Barnard had never been, the agents of political groups.

Both these effects were to become increasingly apparent in the third period under consideration, which was not slow in coming, for Pitt's position was essentially temporary, the

[1] Add. MSS. 38334, ff. 29 *seq.* [13 Nov. 1761].

product of war and crisis, and with his resignation and the return of peace this curious interlude was over. But it left behind it a City opinion more self-conscious, more closely engaged in national politics, in a state of frustration at the loss of its recent importance; and this at a time when post-war dislocation, bad harvests, political instability and the impact of a variety of national problems were to exacerbate all social and political problems. It is not surprising that the City was so deeply affected by the excitements surrounding the case of John Wilkes and General Warrants, nor that in 1763 a popular pamphleteer claimed that the constitution represented interests once predominant but now so no longer and that the merchant classes should enjoy a greater share in representation.[1]

The period 1762 to 1782 is that of the climax both of the eighteenth-century development of City self-consciousness and of its influence on national politics. The years which saw the rise of the whig Opposition *par excellence*, the years in which the whig interpretation of history was born, were those in which extra-parliamentary pressure on politics became open and organized, first in the City and then later, and for a limited period but with great effect, in the counties. In these years the parliamentary Opposition groups were forced to trim their sails and adjust their courses to meet the demands made on them by supporters whom they had hitherto been able to control and had been apt to have to stimulate, but whom less than ever they could afford to lose.

After the first confused eight years of George III's reign, two main Opposition groups emerged, that which followed Chatham, and of which Lord Shelburne and, later, Pitt the younger were the outstanding figures, and that which was built up round the person of the marquess of Rockingham, of whom Burke and, later, Charles Fox were the most active members. They were at one in their violent opposition to the king and his ministers, but united in nothing else. They

[1] *Political Disquisitions, proper for Public Consideration in the Present State of Affairs in a Letter to a Noble Duke* (1763).

were in active competition with each other in their attempts to capture the support of the extra-parliamentary forces on which Opposition traditionally depended. During the later years of the American War, they competed for the support of the counties, where the gentry were driven to unparalleled independence and activity by the expense and misfortunes of the war. Between 1768 and 1772,[1] and more sporadically up to 1775,[2] competition for influence in the City played a considerable part in their plans.

This competition would in itself have been likely to increase the concern of the City with the day-to-day business of politics but to detract from its position as a semi-independent political force, for the aim was to employ the machinery of City government for the needs of one or other of the groups active in national politics. The Chatham-Shelburne group had the initial advantage of the support in the City of William Beckford, who still had the most crowded years of his City career before him (he died in 1770, having completed a highly popular second term of office as Lord Mayor). Later, they had the support of certain close followers of Lord Shelburne in the City, Alderman James Townsend [3] and Alderman Richard Oliver.[4] The Rockingham group,

---

[1] Evidence of this activity is to be found in the *Burke Correspondence*, i. 228 seq., and the Burke and Rockingham MSS., Sheffield; Portland MSS., Nottingham University; *The Correspondence of William Pitt, Earl of Chatham*, ed. W. S. Taylor and J. H. Pringle (1839); and the Lansdowne MSS. at Bowood. At the general election of 1768 Barlow Trecothick, a successful candidate, was called in a City squib (*City Races* [1768]) 'Lord Rockingham's wall-eyed horse Mercator'.

[2] *Burke Correspondence*, ii. 55. E. Burke to Rockingham, 23 Aug., 1775. 'Lord John [Cavendish] has given your lordship an account of the scheme we talked over, for reviving the importance of the City of London, by separating the sound from the rotten contract-hunting part of the mercantile interest, uniting it with the corporation, and joining both to your lordship.'

[3] 1737–87. Son of Chauncy Townsend, a prominent London merchant; M.P. West Looe 1767–74, Calne 1782–7. Took up freedom of City by patrimony in 1769, alderman 1769. Lord Mayor 1772. In close touch with Shelburne at least from 1760. (W. P. Courtney, 'James Townsend, M.P.', *Notes and Queries*, 11th Series, v. 2-4.)

[4] 1734 ?–84. Born Antigua, brought up in London by his uncle, a West-India merchant; M.P. for the City 1770–80, alderman from 1770; committed to Tower by the House of Commons 1771. (*Notes and Queries*, 8th Series, iv. 217.)

however, tried to build themselves up a rival force, using as their chief City supporter Alderman Barlow Trecothick, member for the City and in 1770 Lord Mayor (who had been their agent in organizing the commercial agitation for the repeal of the Stamp Act in 1766).[1] They also had some hopes of using in the same way William Baker, son of Sir William Baker who had in his time been a prominent City supporter of the duke of Newcastle.[2] These tactics of Opposition led, as was inevitable, to comparable activity by the Government, who were able to give indirect assistance in the traditional way to the declining oligarchic influences in the City. Hence in the election of members for the City in 1768 and in elections for City offices for the next few years there was an obscure triangular struggle in process between groups who hoped to use the City as a political weapon, or at least to prevent their opponents from doing so.

This struggle was, however, interrupted almost before it began and suddenly cut across, by a startling revival of City independence in the political field. There emerged in 1768 the strangest of all the City leaders of the century, John Wilkes.[3] With his meteoric rise to power the City appeared once more as a powerful but external force in politics, as independent as in Sir John Barnard's day, but much more formidable and incalculable.

The sudden appearance of this cynical and able demagogue, whose cause had been fostered by Opposition leaders in the past, but who had not occurred to them as a possible rival for the control of the City, struck contemporaries, as it does posterity, with astonishment. Benjamin Franklin, who was in London in 1768, thought it inexplicable.

'Tis a really extraordinary event to see an outlaw and exile of bad personal character, not worth a farthing, come over from France, set himself up for candidate for the capital of the Kingdom,

---
[1] For him, see Namier, *ibid.*, 270, and L. S. Sutherland, 'Edmund Burke and the First Rockingham Ministry', *loc. cit.*; W. P. Courtney, 'Barlow Trecothick', *Notes and Queries*, 11th Series, iii. 330-2.
[2] Namier, *England in the Age of the American Revolution* (1930), pp. 280-1.
[3] H. Bleackley, *Life of John Wilkes* (1917).

miss his election only by being too late in his application and immediately carrying it for the principal county. The mob, spirited up by numbers of different ballads sung or roared in every street, requiring gentlemen and ladies of all ranks as they passed in their carriages to shout for 'Wilkes and Liberty', marking the same words on all their coaches with chalk, and No. 45 on every door; which extends a vast way along the roads into the country. I went last week to Winchester, and observed that for fifteen miles out of town there was scarce a door or window-shutter next the road unmarked.[1]

Posterity has found it no easier to explain. It has sometimes been assumed that his power rested essentially on his influence over the London mob. He certainly had remarkable success in whipping them up at a time when there were various causes for unrest — a fact which in the end contributed considerably to the collapse of the movement with which his name was associated. But examination of the stages of his career in the City suggests that his real political strength lay elsewhere. It lay in just those classes of lesser merchants and tradesmen on whose support Oppositions always depended, and he was thus directly competitive with the City leaders who were working to obtain the support of this class for the rival parliamentary Opposition groups. He was indeed assisted in his rise by their jealousy of each other. Though Beckford at first opposed him secretly,[2] he soon decided it was wiser to appear to back him; but when, in 1771, after Beckford's death his successors Townsend and Oliver quarrelled with Wilkes, Rockingham and Burke thought on the whole they would rather see Wilkes victorious than their political rivals. Rockingham thought Wilkes might be 'perhaps not so dangerous as the others would be ... and *probably Wilkes single* would be easier to manage than a whole *pandae-*

---

[1] *Memoirs*, quoted in W. P. Treloar, *Wilkes and the City* (1917), p. 56.

[2] Camden to Beckford, 28 March 1768. 'I give you joy of your success in London and hope Middlesex will follow the example of your City and send Wilkes to Jewry (?) which they say is to be his next excursion' If he fails there, I presume he will retreat into that strong fortress the King's Bench Prison' (Hamilton MSS., National Library of Scotland. I am indebted to Miss H. Allen for a transcript of this letter).

monium'.[1] It was an inept judgment, for it soon became apparent that Wilkes, in the strength of his popularity, could break through the webs of connexion which they were weaving, and, though his personal popularity depended on his remaining in active opposition to Government,[2] he could deal on equal terms with the parliamentary Opposition groups.

There seems to be no explanation of the phenomenon of his rise and the hold he gained on this type of follower but the fact that he appealed powerfully to forces in the City which resented subordination to Opposition as well as to Government, that he voiced their hostility to the aristocracy as well as to the Crown and the Executive and (a strong point in view of the personal nature of his power) that he appealed to them in his own person as the victim of the forces which they resented. Perhaps the best example of the attitude of his main City supporters — men of some substance and education — is the rich but misfit and plebeian parson Horne Tooke,[3] who played so big a part in his rise and was so bitterly disillusioned by its results.

Wilkes, strong in this support and backed by the funds of the Bill of Rights Society which his City friends founded, was soon not only driving the rival Opposition groups out of the City [4] but putting them at a grave disadvantage in national politics by forcing on them constitutional programmes which they had no desire to embrace. These programmes were not revolutionary, for his supporters were not revolutionaries; they clung to the idea of shorter parliaments and of traditional

---

[1] Rockingham to Burke [Jan. or Feb. 1771], Fitzwilliam MSS., Sheffield.

[2] This remained true even after the days of his great popularity were over. As late as 1784 John Robinson said : 'Mr. Wilkes's support of any government is very uncertain, because the safety of his situation depends on his watching as he calls it all administrations and having no apparent connexion with any, but taking the side of all popular questions'. *Parliamentary Papers of John Robinson, 1774–1784*, ed. W. T. Laprade (1922), p. 68.

[3] A. Stephens, *Memoirs of John Horne Tooke* (1813).

[4] Burke, *Correspondence*, ii. 111. 'It was but a few months after Lord Shelburne had told me, gratis (for nothing led to it), that the people (always meaning the common people of London) were never in the wrong, that he and all his friends were driven with scorn out of that city.'

methods of controlling the power of the Crown, but they added two new demands: an attack on the rotten boroughs as the centre of aristocratic as well as of royal power, and the proposal to bind their representatives to carry out their wishes by enforcing pledges on them at the time of their election, a proposal very unwelcome to all parliamentary parties.[1] How successful they were is shown by the fact that they forced Chatham to subscribe to triennial parliaments after he had explicitly expressed his disapproval of them;[2] and that they drove Burke not only to try to distract attention from those parts of their programme he thought most dangerous by developing other parts which his friends found less unattractive, but also to lay down as a maxim for preserving the 'true country interest' that they should not support candidates nominated by 'a mere club of Tradesmen'.[3] And most Opposition members would probably have agreed with his indignation at the 'infinite mischief' done 'by the violence, rashness and often wickedness' of that 'rotten subdivision of a faction amongst ourselves . . . the Bill of Rights people'.[4]

These years mark the climax of the influence of London on the political life of the country during the century, and its traces are to be found in the programmes of parliamentary Opposition and in the attitude of the country gentry when, during the American War, they followed the City's example and set up their own short-lived but spectacular extra-parliamentary organizations.[5] But it must be admitted that the climax was a short-lived one and that in the City, as in the

[1] Burke dated the driving from the City of 'all the honest part of the opposition' to 'all this professing, promising and testing'. (Burke, *Correspondence*, ii. 110).

[2] On 1 June 1770 he had refused to agree to the Common Council's demand that he should support triennial parliaments (Chatham, *Correspondence*, iii. 464), but by 1 May 1771, with much uncertainty and disquiet, he announced in the Lords his conversion.

[3] E. Burke to Portland [28 April 1770], Portland MSS., Nottingham University.

[4] E. Burke to R. Shackleton, 15 Aug. 1770, Burke, *Correspondence*, i. 229.

[5] The best account of these Associations is G. S. Veitch, *Genesis of Parliamentary Reform* (1913). The primacy of the City movement is shown by H. Butterfield, *George III, Lord North and the People, 1779–80* (1949).

counties, both the organization and the zeal for exerting pressure on politics disappeared as rapidly as they arose, leaving little obvious trace behind them. In both cases the explanation seems to lie in the limited nature of the aspirations of those supporting the movement, the dependence of these aspirations on the circumstances of the moment, and the unwillingness or inability of most men to realize that the issues they were raising had far wider implications. When something of the nature of what Burke was to call 'the portentous comet of the Rights of Man' appeared to them, the merchant and tradesman of the City, like the country gentleman, stopped abashed.

The check in the City came earlier than in the country as a whole, though even there it did not long outlive the exasperation of the American War. The withering away of the turmoils of the years of Wilkes's City dominance was partly due, no doubt, to the fact that Wilkes himself (never, as he said, a Wilkite) made his peace after 1779 with vested interests and retired to sedate ease in the most lucrative position the City had to offer, that of its chamberlain. But even before he did so the support he could count on was beginning to decline: he lost his following in the Common Council and his supporters became progressively limited to what George III had called 'a small though desperate part of the Livery'.[1] And when, in 1780, the London mob burst its bounds in the Gordon Riots, and this without any stimulation from those who normally expected to exploit it, Joseph Brasbridge spoke for many when he said: 'from that moment, though previously contaminated with the mania infected by Wilkes, the political mountebank of the day, I shut my ears against the voice of popular clamour'.[2]

But, though the City's fervour was thus summarily checked, the forces underlying it were not changed. In the turmoils which surrounded the political activities of Sir

---

[1] *Correspondence of George III*, ii. 256. The king to North, 26 June 1771. The king ante-dated the development.
[2] Quoted by J. P. de Castro, *The Gordon Riots* (1926), p. 147.

Essays Presented to Sir Lewis Namier

Francis Burdett [1] at the turn of the century, their continued vitality can be traced. And, when the great Reform agitation of the eighteen-thirties came on, one can see, in the organization and activities of the radical London master-tailor Francis Place,[2] the unmistakable mark of eighteenth-century City experience and traditions, with its long history of co-operation with parliamentary Oppositions but also its characteristics of isolation and separatism.

[1] M. W. Patterson, *Sir Francis Burdett and his Times, 1770–1844* (1931).
[2] Graham Wallas, *Life of Francis Place, 1771–1854* (1918).

RICHARD PARES

A LONDON WEST-INDIA MERCHANT HOUSE
1740-1769

BEFORE the great German air-raid of 29 December 1940 there stood, in a little court off the south side of Great Tower Street, a brick house built late in the seventeenth century.[1] The front room on the first floor was laid out and furnished, apparently about the time that the house was built, as a counting-house, with a long counter and panelled compartments. There was an inner room, to the right of the counter, with a fireplace surrounded by beautiful wood-carving. These were the offices[2] of Messrs. Wilkinson and Gaviller, a West-India merchant House which could trace its existence back to the day, in March 1740, when Henry Lascelles and his son Daniel wrote the letter which was copied into the first page of the oldest surviving letter book.

More than twenty years ago the partners of the House kindly allowed me to spend a whole winter and spring working through their oldest archives. In this article I propose, with their permission, to describe the first thirty years of this House's history, which is all that I had studied before the Germans came and the beautiful office with the counter, the carved fireplace and, worst of all, the archives, went up in flames.[3]

[1] The house is briefly described in *Royal Commission on Historical Monuments (England)*; London, iv. (1929), 185.
[2] Not their first offices: George Maxwell describes himself in his will, as 'of Mark Lane, merchant'.
[3] I should consider it a piece of useless ostentation to give continual footnote references to documents which no longer exist, but when occasion offers con-

A few years ago, in the second half of *A West-India Fortune*, I gave an account of a very similar merchant House, that of the Pinneys of Bristol. I must refer to that book the reader who wishes to see the business of such a House fully described. This will enable me to pass over quite briefly those things in which the business of the Lascelles resembled that of the Pinneys. On the other hand, I shall dwell particularly upon the differences between the business of a London House, dealing mainly with Barbados in the middle eighteenth century, and that of a Bristol House dealing mainly with Nevis from 1783 to 1850. Much is to be learnt from the differences between the two ports, the two islands and, above all, the two periods. Many important changes in West Indian history are reflected in them.

The Lascelles family had been connected with Barbados nearly half a century before 1740. Edward Lascelles was on the island in 1698; he seems to have been a merchant, for he had a wharf and dealt largely in wine; he also had something to do with the money affairs of the warships on the station. In 1700 he was a member of the island's Assembly. He must have returned to London soon afterwards. In 1706 he is described as a London merchant trading to Barbados. He was also the absentee owner of an estate on the island. He continued for twenty years to write occasional letters about the politics of the island and the African trade.[1]

There was also a Philip Lascelles, who traded from London to Barbados in 1702.[2]

Henry Lascelles was living on the island before 1714, married a Barbadian lady and became collector of Customs. He was a friend of Governor Lowther, whose defence against criticisms he undertook on a visit to England in 1720. Naturally, in that age of faction, he got into trouble during the

veniently, I shall try to give the date of any letter which I quote *verbatim* from my transcripts, so that, when I shall have deposited these transcripts in some public place, the more important quotations may be verified.

[1] *Calendar of State Papers, America and West Indies, 1697–8*, nos. 144, 739; *1701*, nos. 343, 1159; *1706–8*, no. 540; *1708–9*, no. 321; *1719–20*, no. 30; *1726–7*, no. 83.

[2] *Ibid. 1702*, no. 814.

next régime, that of President Cox, who accused him of various irregularities in the administration of the Customs and of the 4½ per cent export duty. According to the president, he had connived at illegal trade with Frenchmen, had obstructed prosecutions for Customs offences and 'being one of the chiefest shippers of sugars to private persons as well as the King, ships the good sugars received for duty to his private correspondents at high prices, and buys French sugars at low rates and ships to the King for duty'.[1]

In 1730 he turned over the collectorship of Customs to his brother Edward, but continued, at any rate until 1734, to collect the 4½ per cent duty and to reside on the island as a merchant. There is no means of telling whether it was Henry or Edward whom Governor Lord Howe called in 1733 'as considerable a merchant as any'. In any case Henry was back in London before the end of 1739.

Henry Lascelles was not only a whig, but a personal adherent of Sir Robert Walpole. This brought him certain advantages: for example, in 1740, by speaking personally to the prime minister, he obtained the privilege of transhipping some prize Spanish tobacco contrary to the letter of Customs regulations. After Walpole's fall, however, he had to pay for his politics. Those members of the new Ministry who had been no friends to the old minister tried to injure and to punish his friends and dependants wherever they could. Robert Dinwiddie, the surveyor-general of Customs for the southern district of America, went to Barbados in order to rake up what charges he could against the Lascelles brothers and their friends. According to a letter from George Maxwell to Edward Lascelles, 4 July 1744,

This matter has been brewing ever since the fall of the Earl of Orford, and your Brother became obnoxious to the New Ministry, I believe from some publick Declarations in favour of the old to which he was oblig'd. Not only the Treasury was put into other hands, but some new Commissioners of the Customs were made,

---

[1] *Ibid. 1714–15*, no. 654, vi; *1717–18*, no. 742, xv; *1719–20*, nos. 459, 563, 575; *1720–21*, nos. 687, 713, 754.

whereof Capt. Mead was one. The Majority at the latter Board are people of no importance, and Mr. Hill had formerly great sway there, which Mr. Mead has now in full possession. Ld. Wilmington who was at the head of the former was old and disregarded, and therefore the latter Board exerted a greater Power than belong'd to them, especially in the instance of Mr. Dinwiddie, and although at the old man's death the Treasury underwent a second change and came again into the hands of those that had been of the old Ministry, yet these did not care to intermeddle or discourage an Inspection proposed and countenanced before their time for the great Clamour of the necessity of it and for the same reason I fear the present Lords of the Treasury will not now interpose in the matter.

Dinwiddie suspended Edward Lascelles and Arthur Upton, the collector and comptroller at Barbados, and surcharged Henry Lascelles's own account with some monies due, as he said, for former irregularities. Henry Lascelles could not get his revenge until the end of 1744, when matters began to take a better turn for him. Lord Carteret, who seems to have encouraged his prosecutors, was dropped from the Ministry which his friends, the Pelhams, now dominated. To make quite sure of success, Lascelles entered the House of Commons himself. On 23 April 1745 William Smelt, member for Northallerton, was appointed receiver-general of His Majesty's Casual Revenue at Barbados;[1] a new writ was ordered and Henry Lascelles was elected in his stead. Probably at the same time, he bought the borough of Northallerton outright; I do not know what he paid for it, but the price was less, perhaps much less, than £13,000. It is very probable that he bought his way into parliament expressly to get himself rehabilitated and his brother restored; at any rate, when the negotiations for the latter of these objects was hanging fire, his partner observed, 'we expected no sort of disappointment after being chosen member for Northallerton'. With these advantages Henry Lascelles gained his object in the long run: in November 1745 the Treasury ordered the Customs to stay process against him, though the matter dragged

[1] *Calendar of Treasury Books and Papers, 1742–1745*, p. 841.

on for many years, and in 1747 Edward was restored by the good offices of Henry Grenville, the new governor of Barbados, who had a brother in the Ministry and a friend, George Lyttelton, at the Treasury Board. Henry Lascelles stayed in parliament until 17 March 1752, when he resigned in order to get his son Daniel elected.[1]

Daniel Lascelles is a colourless figure compared with his father. He was not exactly a sleeping partner in the House, but he never wrote its letters and did not always see them before they were sent off. For this reason the letter books tell us hardly anything about his politics. He held the seat for Northallerton until 1780. His elder brother, Edwin, was also member for Northallerton in the parliament of 1754, but in 1761, as befitted the head of a rich family,[2] he sat for the county seat of Yorkshire. In 1780, at a political crisis, he was turned out; his brother Daniel immediately obliged him by retiring from Northallerton in order to let him in.[3]

George Maxwell was not Barbadian born. He went to the island in 1721 or 1722 — possibly a significant date, for the losers in the South Sea Bubble were fleeing in all directions at that time in order to recover their injured fortunes by means of salaried office in the colonies. He became searcher of the Customs at Bridgetown, the chief port of Barbados, and so served for many years under Henry Lascelles. He does not seem to have made a large fortune in Barbados. He rented a plantation; there is no evidence of his possessing one, and if he once described himself as having been the owner of one hundred slaves, he may only have meant that he controlled them as renter, not as owner. He borrowed £1000 from Henry Lascelles in 1741, and if he in turn

[1] *Ibid.* pp. 528, 695, 716, 731. This affair is treated at length by Mr. Louis K. Koontz in his life of Dinwiddie (Glendale, Calif., 1941), pp. 67-94. Mr. Koontz scarcely seems aware of the political aspects of this prosecution. According to Miss Betty Kemp, Lascelles was the first M.P. to accept the Chiltern Hundreds, or a similar office, for the purpose of getting out of parliament altogether, not for that of changing his constituency (see p. 208 of this volume).

[2] Probably he was not his father's eldest son but, to judge from the will of the former, the eldest brother, Henry, was either feeble-minded or in some other way unsatisfactory, for he was cut off with a mere £34,000.

[3] Beatson, *Chronological Register*, i. 250; 311, 326. ii.

made loans to his fellow-planters, we know that the money was not his own but that of Lascelles. It is obvious that it was as Lascelles's junior partner that he returned to London in the autumn of 1743. In his letters to his friends in Barbados, he wrote as if he were in a foreign land. Like other West Indians, he fortified himself against the approach of winter by 'a frequent use of the Cold Bath', apparently at an establishment somewhere in Newgate Street. He disliked the winter, above all the 'nasty smoaky Coal fires', and would have liked to purchase some Barbados sunshine at any price; the meat was 'at first over luscious' to his taste. Worst of all, like many another returned colonial, he knew hardly any face in the country except that of the king. In time he got used to England and ceased to think of 'dear Barbados' as his mother country. The close friendships which he had formed in Barbados remained with him for the rest of his life: no doubt they brought the House a large part of its business, but they were also responsible for some of its most serious financial scrapes, for he did not like to refuse a loan to an old friend. The money he lent almost certainly belonged to Henry and, later, to Daniel Lascelles. Although Maxwell was credited with a half of the House's capital in the form of debts and credits, from beginning to end of his partnership, it is unlikely that he brought any money with him into the firm and he may have had obligations to his partner which rendered their financial equality a merely nominal one. In his will he called Henry Lascelles his 'dear friend and benefactor'.

When Maxwell died in February 1763 Gedney Clarke junior and William Daling were taken into partnership with Daniel Lascelles. Clarke's father had been associated with the House in various forms of business; he seems to have been an expensive, enterprising man who left his money affairs in a precarious state. The son, who had married a daughter of Henry Lascelles's brother Edward, succeeded him as collector of Customs in February 1765, a post which he clearly owed to the political efforts of the Lascelles brothers, and therefore left the House in order to return to Barbados. Not long after, he got into great financial difficulties, probably inherited from his father, and went bankrupt, some said for the spectacular amount of £150,000.

William Daling had risen from the ranks; he had been a clerk in the employment of the House. We do not know how large a staff they employed. According to their own account, their business was not one of the greatest in the West-India trade and they had not work for many subordinates. What there was consisted of three things: writing accounts and copying letters in the counting-house; going round to the grocers once a week in order to collect money due for sugar sold; and the 'waterside business'. Every factor had to have an agent in the Custom House in order to cast up the taxes due on the sugars imported, claim deductions for prompt payment, and know when to petition the commissioners for concessions; this agent also had to watch the sugars as they came ashore, compare the invoice weights with the landing weights and have the cask examined by his own cooper where any great discrepancy occurred, in order to detect pilferage. None of this was very advanced or responsible business; none of it, therefore, qualified an underling for the higher branches of the sugar-factor's profession, namely the art of selling sugars at the right time and, above all, of making loans to the right planters. Perhaps it was for this reason that, according to the House, sugar-factors very seldom took apprentices, even when money was offered with them. William Daling, however, seems to have risen above these difficulties and became Daniel Lascelles's partner in 1763.

The chief business of a sugar-factor was to sell his correspondents' sugars, for which he received a commission. The organization of the London sugar market at this time strongly resembled that of the Bristol sugar market half a century later, which I have described in chapter ix of *A West-India Fortune*, and I shall not waste time by describing it over again here.

It has sometimes been said that the factors discouraged the planters from turning their efforts from the main crop to alternatives because they were only willing or able to sell one thing. There is very little evidence of this in the correspondence of the House. There are many references to sales of rum and of the minor staples. It is true that the House did not much care for selling Barbados rum. This was chiefly because it did not meet with a ready market. Rum as a whole was, unlike sugar, an article for which the demand was intermittent and capricious; moreover, if an Englishman bought rum, he preferred that of Jamaica which was stronger and went further in punch than Barbados rum, however well flavoured. Only once or twice in the correspondence of the Lascelles House is a general demand for rum mentioned: for example, in February 1768 they reported a rise of price 'occasioned by a great many Rums being bought up in hopes of a large consumption this year as it is the General Election year'. There was, in addition, a particular nuisance in the sale of rum: it was commonly sold on board ship in order that the purchaser might pay the duties and excise, and these importers too often delayed landing the rum, which therefore cluttered up the ship when it was ready to go into dock. The House also sold ginger and cotton, though without enthusiasm: ginger was chiefly wanted for re-export to the German market which was often obstructed in this period by war, and West-India cotton, even though well cleaned, was subject to competition from Turkish cotton. The House seems to have believed that the manufacturers could not work Turkish cotton without some admixture of West-India, but the proportions between the two seem to have been arbitrary, so that when Turkish cotton was cheap the consumption of the West-India article would be reduced.

Besides selling the planters' crops, the factors fulfilled their orders for every article which they wanted from the mother country. The only article which was constantly sent in bulk from London at this time was hoops for the sugar casks; but the House had, at one time or another, to buy luxuries and conveniences of every sort — it might be anything from a spinet to a copy of Gay's *Fables* or a rat-catching dog. The House had few dealings with provincial producers but contented itself with buying from the London tradesmen. (In this way the sugar- and tobacco-factors, like the East India Company, must have helped to sustain London industry against the competition of the provinces.)

You complain [they wrote on 21 February 1745/6 to Samuel McCall of Philadelphia] of the goods by breame being dear bought, and particularly the Cutlery of Rogers's make. We have lately heard that Rogers lives at Sheffield in Yorkshire, and as we have not had orders of any great consequence in the Course of our business for the Country made goods, we never Settled any Correspondence with Sheffield or Birmingham, but have always given them to the Tradesmen in town to furnish with town made goods. It's not to be doubted but they charge some profit in consideration for their knowledge and trouble in sending to the proper places and Makers in the Country, which we are unacquainted with, but as we deal for ready money we expect to be served at a moderate profit ; however, if we had any tolerable share of orders in the Country made goods, we would go to Sheffield and Birmingham on purpose, to make an acquaintance with the artificers themselves.

Evidently the London tradesmen sometimes acted as middlemen, and the House seems to have bought even London goods of the wholesalers : Maxwell described a visit to a London textile wholesaler which he and Henry Lascelles both made in order to buy the product of the Spitalfields weavers 'from some of whom we have found exactions, but', he added, 'as some of your orders were circumstanced in respect of lengths, we could not be so well supplied but by Browne & Co., who have a general accquaintance among all the weavers'. The partners usually bought from a restricted circle of tradesmen whom they could trust and, on the strength of this, they by no means always examined the goods, though they would usually do so if, in pursuance of their correspondents' orders, they had patronized a West End tradesman with whom they were not well acquainted.

For the goods they bought they paid cash and obtained a discount with which they credited their correspondents. From an arbitrarily chosen date (generally four months after the date of shipment, by which time they would, on an average, have received and paid the bills) they charged their correspondents with interest on these purchases. Some correspondents complained, evidently believing that the House had itself bought the goods on credit. It may be significant that most of these complaints came not from planters but from merchants, either in the West Indies or on the continent of North America. These merchants wrote as if they could obtain goods at nine or twelve months' credit from the manufacturers. It seems probable that there were, side by side, two different systems of exporting to the colonies — that, on the one hand, merchants in the colonies bought on credit from British manufacturers while, on the other hand, planters bought through factors in London who paid cash, passed on the discount and charged interest. On 1 February 1742 Henry Lascelles had to answer a complaint from Samuel McCall of Philadelphia.

I have attentively looked into your Invoice and am observing your directions as near as possible, in the orders to the Tradesmen, it will be best buying the whole with ready money which I believe will be for yr. Int^t, and for the time I may be in Advance for any part I can only Charge Int^t allowing the Discount for prompt payment where any is Customary. Richd King is the pewterer I employ, I spoke to him about the parcel you had ordered, that I was to give him the Marks and Numbers, I made no doubt of his providing it for you, seeing you had writt to him, but he pretends to decline meddling with it, and says his business is to take his orders from the Merch^t here, and not to send his Goods abroad as if he were a Factor, so that I am to include his Bill in your Invoice and pay him the Money here.

I doubt if a Birmingham manufacturer would have behaved in the same way, at any rate twenty years later.

In order to send all these goods to and fro, the factors found it necessary to hold an interest in shipping. Here the differences between London in the middle eighteenth century

A London West-India Merchant House, 1740–1769

and Bristol after 1800 are considerable. The partners held shares in many ships — indeed, in so many that they complained that their ships got in each other's light — but these shares were seldom large (five-sixteenths was exceptional) and only by accident, when the other prospective owners had let them down, did the House ever own a whole ship. One-sixteenth or one-eighth was a very usual share and the House once owned as small a part as one-thirty-second. The other owners were sometimes rival sugar-factors and, still more commonly, planters. A planter who had sugars to ship might like to take an interest in a number of vessels in order to be able to claim a preference in getting his sugars aboard them. One or two vessels seem to have been entirely owned by planters or by merchants in the colonies.

This fragmentation had several consequences. For one thing, since nearly every ship had some owners in the colony, it was virtually tied to the trade of that colony and could not easily be shifted to another destination even when the colony in question had a small crop and was likely to abound in shipping. As it happens, this did not make a great difference in the case of Barbados, since the island was to windward of all others: if there was a bad crop in Barbados and news of good crops elsewhere, the owners on the spot would know this and would consent to let their ship go down for a better freight. Secondly, since the House seldom had a very large interest in any one ship, it had only a weak inducement to give the preference to its own ships at the expense of others: hence, it often gave its good offices to the vessels owned by its friends in the colonies when they arrived in London even though it had vessels of its own in the same trade. The last and most serious consequence of this fragmentation was to strengthen the importance and the power of the captains. The captain was always a central figure in this trade, for it was his personal relations with the planters that got the vessel her freight home; but when the captain was faced, not with a single owner but a collection of owners on both sides of the Atlantic, his control must have been still stronger, especially if he was an owner himself. The captain-owner seems to have had a veto on all the proceedings of the ship. In 1755, when the Seven Years' War was obviously coming on, the House endured torments from Captain Holland of the *Judith*. He was too lazy to collect a crew or put up the ship for freight; he would not let the owners sell and they were reduced to blockading him by saying that she should lie by the walls until further notice. They offered that, if he would let them sell her, their share of the price should be invested in the funds for his benefit as long as he lived, but even this offer was declined. Finally they got him to consent to her sale on condition of giving him the command of a new ship (but without any share of the ownership this time). So bitterly did they remember this incident that ever afterwards they accused of 'treachery' or 'ingratitude' any owner of a ship in which they were concerned who sold his share to the captain.

They often claimed that they were only interested in shipping in order to serve their friends. If so, they did not always get value for their investment, for these headstrong captains often neglected their owners' friends when accepting goods for shipment. Sometimes this was excusable, if, for example, there was a hurry to catch a convoy. Only once or twice did a captain in the West-India trade refuse to accept goods for shipment unless they were consigned to the owners.[1] A planter, for his part, was only bound morally to favour a particular ship belonging to his factors. He might reserve his early sugars for their first ship, but he could not be expected to do so unless the ship appeared punctually, and the House never liked to make a stipulation of it.

These collateral benefits were probably the chief advantage which the House made from its investment in shipping. Its books do not give enough detail to show conclusively the profit or loss that it made on ship-owning. There are particular instances of small losses or small profits — £200

---

[1] I have stated on p. 210 of *A West-India Fortune* that this was quite common in the experience of this House. I find on closer examination that this is an exaggeration.

A London West-India Merchant House, 1740–1769

or £500 per voyage; only occasionally, and then in war-time, do we hear of so great a profit as £2000.

Ship-owners in the Barbados trade appear to have relied more than most others on freight outward from London to the West Indies. This seems to have been a peculiarity of the island, which had an unusually large white population and therefore consumed a lot of European goods. In consequence there were some occasions (especially in war-time when fewer ships frequented the island and none could make more than one voyage a year) when a ship could be filled up entirely with high-class freight so that bricks, hoops, coal and lime could not find room at all. More often, however, there was room for these heavy goods, unless an owner preferred seeking a profit from shipping them to the island on his own account, and refused to take those of anybody else. There are no instances in the Barbados trade of coal or lime carried out to the island freight-free. This was common later in the experience of the Pinneys, who dealt with the Leeward Islands, and even at this earlier period the Lascelles House arranged for one such shipment — but to St. Christopher's, not to Barbados, which points the lesson that the islands with smaller white populations were those in whose trade the outward freight was insignificant.

Even at Barbados, it was homeward freight that really counted. The House made many attempts to get as high a rate of freight as possible, but it could only persuade, not command: besides the regular ships which were tied to the trade of the island year by year, any ships from any other part of the world could go there in the hope of a great crop on a particular occasion, and lower the rate by its competition. Even the House itself might charter an additional ship, or a rival sugar-factor might do so. The House was particularly jealous of the standing competition of the North Americans, and of the slave traders who were only too glad to fill up with a cargo of sugar on the last lap of their voyage from the islands. The House often claimed, and evidently believed, that this alternative shipping was inferior and that the planters would be unwise if they trusted their produce to it. But it continued to compete with the superior London-built ships which the House put into the trade.

The rate of freight was necessarily settled in the West Indies — at any rate in Barbados. In the spring of 1746 (according to the House's letter to Thomas Applewhaite, 1 March 1745/6):

> The planters and owners of ships that are here [in London] having agreed, as by the original papers enclosed, that good ships can not be sent to bring home the Crops, during the continuance of the War at a less freight than nine shillings per cwt. for Sugar, on accot of the high charges of fitting, navigating and insuring, we hope for the Concurrence of the Gentlemen of Bdos. with us in the same opinion. We do not allow the Ships from North America, by any meanes, to be upon the same footing as they are never so well found nor navigated at the same expence and therefore they do not deserve so good a freight.

This attempt to impose upon the planters evidently failed, for next year (on 13 February 1746/7) the House wrote to Foster March:

> The freight must always be settled abroad and not at home. We attempted to settle it at home last year for Barbados and thought to have fixed it at Nine Shillings per cwt. but the Gentlemen there would not allow more than 7/6, and at that rate the Ships loaded, and indeed high or low freights must always depend upon the plenty or Scarcity of shipping.

At the beginning of the Seven Years' War the owners in London made another attempt to dictate the rate:

> The present immoderate Expense that now attends the fitting out ships [so ran the House's instructions to Captain Thomas Mapstone, 16 February 1757] Provisions of all kinds being extravagantly dear, and Sailors' Wages £4 per month — a Circumstance never known before — it will be impossible to support the Navigation without some considerable additions to the homeward bound freight. And therefore, upon a meeting of the Gentlemen concerned in Ships employed in the Barbados Trade, it was unanimously [sic] to give orders to all Captains under their respective directions not to take in Sugar at less than 7/6 per cwt.

A London West-India Merchant House, 1740–1769

Freight — the same that was paid during the last war, when the Charges did not run near so high. We flatter ourselves that the Gentlemen of the Island in general will think it very reasonable, and just, under the unhappy Circumstances of Publick affairs, and these orders you are punctually to regard.

I do not know whether they were successful in imposing their will, but if they did so, it was only in war-time. Their jeremiads about the high expense of ship-owning, especially the high wages, after the war are almost plaintive and do not seem to have produced any results. Only in the different out-ports of Jamaica, where there was no strong centre of local opinion, and the rate of freight at the capital, Kingston, was not known, bills of lading were filled up in such a manner as to leave the rate of freight to be settled in England.

Besides selling sugars, purchasing stores and ship-owning, the factor had to perform services of every kind for his correspondents. He invested their money for them if they had any; he dealt with government departments on their behalf; he got sugar machinery made in accordance with the models or drawings which they sent him; he interviewed suppliers of unsatisfactory goods; he prosecuted their law-suits (although the partners once said that this was not in their line, there is evidence that they feed lawyers and sometimes even attended the courts on behalf of their correspondents who sent home appeals from the colonies to England, especially in prize cases).[1] On one occasion the House even looked out for a seat in parliament for a friend who was an officer in command of the squadron on the Jamaica station.

Perhaps the best way of illustrating this diversity is to give an account of the miscellaneous commissions which the House executed in September and October 1743, just after George Maxwell had become a partner. For Mary Croasdaile of Jamaica they bought two tickets in a state lottery and received the interest on her East India Company bonds. For John Denny of Barbados they bought some more lottery

---

[1] See my book, *Colonial Blockade and Neutral Rights* (Oxford, 1938), p. 107.

tickets, also Gay's *Fables* in two volumes. For John Frere they got a gown dyed and a bell re-cast, and they interviewed a milliner on behalf of Miles James in order to complain of the inferior quality of the fur with which Mrs. James's nightgown had been trimmed. On behalf of Samuel Husbands they interviewed the secretary of the island of Barbados (whose deputy on the spot Husbands was) about the terms of the deputation. Henry Lascelles ordered a spinet for the granddaughter of William Gibbes. George Maxwell went to Thomas Alleyne's school to report on his progress; the House also put to school the stepson of the governor, Sir Thomas Robinson, and on this occasion their task was complicated by the fact that when the child arrived, the school he was to have attended no longer existed. They sent out some gold coin for H. P. King; they wrote to Nicholas Wilcox that they had ordered their correspondent at Cork to send him some beef, candles, tongues and claret, would order some Dutch clinkers from Holland when they could be sure of getting a ship to take them from England, and would speak to the coppersmiths about some work that he wanted done.

Amid this welter of miscellaneous services, there were certain things which they had to do repeatedly.

They insured homeward-bound sugars and the outward-bound stores of their correspondents. Usually they had express orders for this, but some planters preferred to leave them to judge whether to insure or not, and even without this latitude they sometimes took it upon themselves to do so in an emergency, such as the outbreak of war, which could not be known in time at the islands. As they said, nobody was likely to thank them for this; if they insured and the sugars arrived safe, the planter would think them officious, whereas if they did not insure and the sugars were taken, he would think them negligent. On occasion, they insured in peacetime the sugars of such correspondents as were deeply in debt to them; this precaution was one which, fifty years later, the Pinneys considered that every factor had a right to take, but this House only took it seldom and with apology.

A London West-India Merchant House, 1740–1769

For this business the House preferred to deal with the public insurance companies, especially the London Assurance, with whom they had an open account and settled once a year. They would only take out a policy with an unknown insurer for a risk which the companies would not underwrite, for example, upon a ship already overdue. Some of these outsiders proved to be bankrupts: when this happened the planter was apt to claim that the House ought to pay his loss, but they always replied that it was not the custom of merchants 'to insure the insurer'.

The House had a lot of trouble in obtaining skilled employees for their correspondents. Here they found repeatedly that the colonies must expect to put up with the second best. When they wanted a plumber they were told 'that he must be a Person in debt, that is a good Workman, to leave this Country where there is good Encouragement, to go to the West Indies'. When they wanted a private tutor, they found 'it would have been an easy matter to have obtained a Clergyman for the business, as he would have had the prospect of otherwise advancing himself in the Island. We have had many Laymen recommended to us, but some we thought too young, others we were told were mere Scholars and not men of breeding, and we think the last qualification as necessary as the former for the tuition of young Gentlemen.' The best they could suggest was to offer a lay tutor an additional encouragement by building a school-house for him and permitting him to take day scholars in order to supplement his salary. When they wanted a doctor, they found 'there is great plenty of such from Scotland and Ireland and these will not do'—I do not know why, since the great age of the Edinburgh medical school was just beginning. They even resorted to a crimp to get them a surgeon and, failing that, they took up with a Scot who brought 'very good Credentials from the professors at Edinburgh'—but he proved to be an idle worthless fellow.

They had just as great difficulty in procuring a boy of fourteen or fifteen without any professional qualification.

The West-India planters liked to obtain young boys for book-keepers and overseers from the Blue Coat Hospital. The authorities of the Hospital made difficulties; they would apprentice a boy to a planter but not to an agent on his behalf, for there were ugly stories of cruel and neglectful treatment in the West Indies. Pursuing the matter further, George Maxwell found that he had no hope of getting a boy unless he enlisted the interest of Mr. Smith the writing-master. There were two ways of doing this: either one might force his hand by making interest with one of the governors of the Hospital such as Sir Hans Sloane, or one might put money into his pocket by sending to him West-India lads to be instructed in writing and accounts (this seems to have been a common practice). Maxwell employed both these means but even then he came up against a further difficulty — he had to have the consent of the parents.

By G. M.'s going often to the Hospital, he became known to some hundreds of Boyes, and it required no difficulty to get the Consent of any of them, for he was encircled by a multitude all crying out, 'I'll go Sir!', and with their own goodwill, if that was all, he might have loaded a ship with them. He took a fancy to one James Lowman, a sprightly boy, whom the Master spoke well of, and got the Consent of his Mother, who keeps a School, after using all his eloquence in expatiating very justly in praise of the Delights and beauties of dear B^{dos}, in so much that the poor woman was possessed with an ardent desire to go with her son, but there was no need of her.

This embarrassing success was not repeated very often; for ten years on end, the House could not get a Blue Coat boy and had to fall back upon Scotland. Even in Glasgow there were rumours of ill-treatment in the West Indies. One agent wrote to know what the lads were to do? 'We answered to be Brought up Planters and See the business of your Plantations carefully and Properly done. It was dreaded by some, that they were to be put to the hard labour of Negroes.' Other boys were afraid of the climate — one actually ran away a few days before he was due to sail because he had heard of Scots boys who had lately died in the West Indies. Nevertheless,

A London West-India Merchant House, 1740–1769

the Scots boys did well and the House had to fulfil repeated orders for more.

The partners often had to obtain for their correspondents offices in the Customs and seats on the council of the island and to negotiate between the secretaries, provosts marshal, etc., of the colonies, who seldom left England, and the planters or merchants who wished to rent their offices from them, perform the duties and receive the profits.[1] In these last cases the House offered its own security for the due payment of the rent and, in return, charged 5 per cent commission upon the rent itself.

For all this business, some political influence was necessary. The House relied most on the powerful John Sharpe, who was agent for Barbados and for other islands, solicitor to the Treasury, and general factotum for the Pelhams and their friends.[2] The partners once said that most of their business was negotiated through Sharpe. They had some hold upon his goodwill for, besides everything else, he was a solicitor and they could direct to him all the lucrative law business arising out of the appeals which their correspondents sent home from the colonial courts. Besides this, it was usual to make him a present of £50 whenever one of their correspondents was elevated to the council by his means. The House did not, however, rely on Sharpe alone, especially after Henry Lascelles himself became a member of parliament. Writing to Thomas Applewhaite on 31 July 1745, they said that they had paid Sharpe the usual present, although it had been Henry Lascelles who had got the business done, as Sharpe was engaged in soliciting it before Lascelles became a member of parliament. The implication must be that an M.P. did not need to fee agents as he commanded enough interest of his own. But this was not always so. Although Henry Lascelles thought well of his family's political influence, he had to admit at least once that a dozen members of parliament

[1] See J. H. Parry, 'The Patent Offices in the British West Indies', *English Historical Review*, lxix. 212-14.
[2] For his career as agent, see Lilian M. Penson, *The Colonial Agents of the British West Indies* (London, 1924), *passim, especially* pp. 167-8.

could not have prevailed against Sharpe. The House also used, on occasion, the influence of the governors of the islands. Sir Thomas Robinson, governor of Barbados, was a fellow-Yorkshireman and dined at Henry Lascelles's house even before he accepted the office, probably in order to find out what additional salary he was likely to get from the legislature of the island. He continued to show goodwill but unfortunately he ceased to be a political asset, for he got involved in quarrels and had to be recalled. The House started on very good terms with Henry Grenville, his successor, an even more powerful character since he had at one time brothers at the Admiralty and the Board of Trade and a friend at the Treasury. The favour of both these governors was particularly necessary to the Lascelles family so long as Edward had not been restored to his collectorship of Customs. Soon after this happened, the House quarrelled with Grenville for reasons unknown, and found that they could hardly get anything done against his will.

The partners used such political influence as they had, for promoting not only the interests of particular correspondents, but that of the island as a whole. George Maxwell, in 1744, lobbied thirty M.P.s in a day against a proposed tax on sugar. Henry Lascelles soon afterwards got a relation who was surveyor-general of the Ordinance, to expedite the dispatch of small arms ordered by the colony and to ensure that their quality was good. Both partners waited upon Sharpe in 1744 in order to discuss with him the danger from the French at St. Lucia and the necessity of a cartel for dealing with the French and Spanish prisoners of war. The partners were tempted once or twice to use their interest against, rather than for, the wishes of the majority of the island: for example, they tried, apparently without success, to prevent the confirmation of a bill for reducing the rate of interest from 8 per cent to 6 per cent. As creditors to the planters, they naturally liked to keep the rate high.

From the internal politics of the island they tried to stand clear, for they were likely to lose business by taking one side

A London West-India Merchant House, 1740–1769

or the other. Even neutrality did not always satisfy their angry friends. Thus, when Governor Robinson removed Judge Harrison from office, they declined to sign a memorial on Harrison's behalf and he accused them quite unjustly of being 'retained' by his enemies. They had to answer a similar complaint from their friend Gedney Clarke who, as collector of Customs, got into a quarrel with the attorney-general of the island.

> Don't think [they wrote to him on 28 December 1750] that We are so anxious after the Commissions as you take upon you to represent us. The Gentleman to whom you have so great an invetteracy, offered Us his Business, and in course We accepted of it. We must tell you, that People in the West Indies have their passions greatly inflamed by the heat of the Climate, and are apt to take fire upon every occasion, which they cannot be sensible of themselves, nor will be so, unless they change the Climate and come to a Colder.

No doubt George Maxwell was here writing from his own experience.

Nothing gave the House more trouble than the duty of looking after the children of their correspondents in the islands. If it had been a mere matter of social duty, such as asking them to stay in the Christmas holidays, or taking a post-chaise to Honiton in order to rescue a stranded Creole maiden, it might have been tolerated. But the House had to take serious financial decisions, such as that of supplying a young man with money without order from his father, in order to rescue him from the money-lenders or from the sharks who offered to get his life insured, with no good purpose, we may be sure. Worst of all was the supervision of these children's education.

They arrived with a sallow complexion and a sing-song accent, and it was much if they could be got to look and speak like Englishmen. Their book-learning was grossly behindhand and the factors sometimes shrank from putting them to a school where they would have to sit below the smallest boy. It was too late for them to take Latin — French and arithmetic were the most that could be expected, and if they were put upon higher things they complained of being made to waste their time 'learning Greek derivations'. With all this ignorance and, often, ill-health they combined extravagant ideas of their fortune and expectations and a total aversion to discipline. Conrade Adams was always running away from school and had to be placed in an 'Academy' where the discipline was looser. Young Upton Law likewise ran away from the ironmonger to whom he was apprenticed and, when the House spoke of sending him back to Barbados, threatened to drown himself. James and William Dottin Maycock were made of sterner stuff. They were expelled from an Academy near London for knocking down the usher who got them a punishment from the headmaster for impudence; in addition they went about to plays and concerts without the headmaster's leave. The House took lodgings for them in London and provided them with proper masters, but the elder boy had high words with his landlady and struck her, then drew his sword upon her husband who took her part. These boys had to be shipped home to Barbados. So likewise did Peers and Tom Alleyne, who were grossly extravagant at Oxford. Peers was at The Queen's College — according to him the most expensive in the university, where the Tutor took no pupils, but farmed them out to a certain Dr. Brown, who charged an extra twenty guineas a year. The Doctor complained of Peers for 'being continually in Company with a Young Gentleman of the Leeward Islands whom he wrote a very bad Character of'. This undesirable companion left the university, and Peers was, for a time, charged with no more than going to bed and getting up too late. The House tried to persuade him to be 'a good Oeconomist', but in vain: he insisted on drawing a bill of exchange because he 'liked better to be allowed to draw for his allowance himself, as most of the Young Gentlemen do, than to receive it in a Guinea a time from his Tutor, and he alledged also that he could be a better Oeconomist by having the whole under his own management'. How often have undergraduates told that story! His brother Tom, at Magdalen, was just as expensive, and when the two of them were shipped home £2220 had to be paid in order to get them out of the country.

I could continue for a long time this catalogue of tiresome youths; but let the story of young Sam Husbands stand for the whole. Soon after he arrived at Westminster school he was nearly turned out because his Tutor refused to pay the Under Master a fee which he claimed of right. The boy's father then started complaining of his heavy expenses. The partners replied that they could not be expected to see to these in detail — they preferred that the schoolmasters should pay the necessary bills, subject to an examination of their accounts. In any case, if Sam had too much pocket money, that was the fault of a Mrs. Gordon, who was supposed to be looking after him and doled out his allowance through a milliner. Worse was to come. Sam could not go back to school after the Christmas holidays of 1755, because he had been 'unfortunately drawn into the embraces of a vile wicked Strumpet who gave him the foul disease'. He was reported to be 'a sincere penitent', and when he was cured and ready to return to school 'our G. M.' felt that he owed some explanation to the headmaster. The great Dr. Markham 'expressed a concern for what had happened but said, Sammy was a lad of parts and to be regarded, that he should not take the least notice of it to him nor seem to know of it, and he hoped he would keep the thing a secret from the other Boys at School. He further said, you know, many Lads have met with the same mischance, and afterwards proved and turned out good Men, and this Lad therefore is not to be neglected or lost.' For a time Sam prospered: he reported himself to be on good terms with the headmaster and to have 'executed themes, on two subjects set him, with great applause vizt., one on diligence and the other on prudence'. This good reputation was not to last. A few months later Dr. Markham found himself forced to expel the boy from school. His offence was that of setting a bad example by lying in bed until eight or nine in the morning: evidently headmasters' sense of proportion has changed since the eighteenth century. Sam proceeded to Cambridge where he continued to give trouble: he went on lying in bed and, on the pretext of living by a 'regimen', he would not dine in Hall — although he paid for his dinner whether he took it or not; he pestered the House to buy him a horse because a doctor had ordered him riding; 'to say truth, we were apprehensive this was only a Scheme, to have a horse of his own, and be like others of his rank, who keep horses'. In the end they became so tired of him that they washed their hands of him. Indeed they were heartily sick of all such business. When the father of Conrade Adams complained of their charging $2\frac{1}{2}$ per cent on his disbursements, they retorted that the money was dearly earned as this sort of business was so far more troublesome than 'a common cash article'. Before they had done with Sam Husbands they exclaimed, 'When young People will follow their own ways, it is an office more eligible to be a Hog Driver than to have any concern with them.' The worst of it was that they were not even casting their bread upon the waters: as they observed, very few of the young men of whom they had taken charge in this way became or even continued their correspondents after getting possession of their estates.

For all the services which I have been describing, the House needed a considerable capital. Even for paying the freight and duties of incoming sugars and accepting the bills of exchange which the planters had drawn on the strength of them, a sum of at least £20,000 was needed. But the matter did not stop there. Most planters expected a fair-sized advance upon account current and many of them wanted loans of a more specific nature.

In chapters xi and xii of *A West-India Fortune* I have described fully the system of West-India finance — the loans on account current; the contract debts fortified, perhaps by a bond to repay twice the sum borrowed, perhaps by a formal judgment in the colonial courts or at least a warrant of attorney to confess judgment; lastly, the mortgages. I refer the reader to that description, nearly all of which holds good for the history of the House I am now discussing. I shall now

A London West-India Merchant House, 1740–1769

concentrate on the differences between the history of the Lascelles and that of the Pinneys, many of which are significant.

The greatest of all these differences was this: the planters were much less deeply in debt in the earlier period than in the later, and the factors had far more confidence in the ability of the sugar industry to carry and repay these debts. There were many reasons for this. Barbados was an island with plantations of moderate size, whose owners generally resided on the spot. The initial capitalization had been made — that is, the slave population had been bought — at the low prices of the seventeenth century, even though current replacement had to be made at greater cost. In the decade before the House began business the sugar prices had been at their lowest, and it was not likely that the factors would have allowed the planters to get deeply into debt; and these lean years were succeeded by a generation of higher prices and optimism, which might well be called the silver age of the British West-India sugar industry. Lastly, the House itself was relatively new, and started with a clean sheet — not that that would have mattered after 1800, when a new House had to begin by raising capital to pay off the previous encumbrances of its would-be correspondents.

There are many symptoms of this relative buoyancy. In the first place, the House of Lascelles was content with much less security than the House of Pinney would have demanded. The partners allowed the debts on account current to run into thousands without asking for a bond or a mortgage: one of their correspondents, John Frere, owed them more than £14,000, and they still disclaimed any wish for better security. There was little talk of mortgages: it was generally believed that a planter's credit was blasted by a mortgage, and the House itself must have acknowledged this to be true, for it more than once refused to pay bills of exchange for a planter who was believed to be mortgaging his plantation. The Pinneys could not have taken these risks, and nearly every big debt on their books was a mortgage debt. Secondly, the Lascelles, unlike the Pinneys, never objected to their correspondents selling their sugars in the island instead of consigning them home. Indeed they often congratulated their correspondents on having done so. They could not have held this opinion if they had looked upon consignments of sugars as the only means of repaying debts otherwise desperate. They thought only of the commission, and did not even mind very much when their correspondents left them for new factors. This, again, would have been unpardonable in the later age. Lastly, it is clear that Henry Lascelles, at least, was looking for opportunities of investing money in Barbados: he welcomed opportunities of buying judgment debts from good debtors and was angry when others tried to buy good debts owed to himself. When a prospective bond or judgment debtor asked for a 'defeasance' —that is, an undertaking not to demand repayment within a given term of years — he stipulated that the defeasance should be mutual, in order that he might not have his money returned sooner than he wanted it. He sold out of the public funds in order to make these loans, and he wanted, in return, an investment equally permanent. He could not have behaved like this if he had doubted the security of his money.

The greater security and prosperity of sugar business showed itself in another way — in the greater financial independence of Barbados as a community. There were sterling debts and currency debts — that is, debts repayable in England and debts repayable on the island: interest on the former was limited by law to 5 per cent, on the latter to 6 or 8 per cent. Many of the debts which the Lascelles family handled were currency debts. They arose from judgments in the colonial courts. All these 'judgment debts' (often, as I have said, little more than a formal means of registering the debt) were the object of a lively traffic: people bought and sold them. It is clear that, at any rate in the preceding age, Barbadians had owed money not so much to Englishmen as to other Barbadians, and had had some prospect of repaying them; there must have been a class of prosperous planters who could afford to lend to newcomers and the weaker brethren. Probably this class had not altogether disappeared in Henry Lascelles's time.

There was some disadvantage in holding currency debts. Money repaid in the island could only be remitted to England by shipping sugar and standing the risk of the seas, or by purchasing a bill of exchange, at a rate which varied. Often this rate was disadvantageous to the remitter, that is, a lot of Barbados money was needed to buy a moderate quantity of sterling. Henry Lascelles disliked having his currency debts remitted to him at such a disadvantage: sometimes he insisted on leaving the money in the islands, at other times he would stipulate beforehand the rate of exchange at which remittance was to be made. All these difficulties were avoided by making the debt a sterling debt. This was not the only reason why sterling debts tended to supersede currency debts. The latter could only exist on a large scale either where there were still local capitalists or where the debtors readily repaid money on the island and the sum so repaid became available for new loans. Both these conditions were disappearing, and when the only source of fresh capital was England (even if it came from the West-India trade itself, that is, from the payment of interest in London by planters to factors), then every important debt would be a sterling debt. This condition had come into existence by the time the House of Pinney and Tobin began business in 1783.

Even in the later pages of the Lascelles letter-books there are symptoms of increasing debt. Mortgages were more frequent and excited less repugnance than they had done a generation earlier. Debts on account current were swelling, and the planters with favourable balances were fewer and fewer in comparison with the others. The Lascelles even began to find that when they got a debtor to sell his plantation the purchaser was no better able to pay for the debt, and, little as they liked it, they had once or twice to threaten that in the end they would take the debtors' plantations to themselves. In fact, they must have done so more than once. In

1836, when the slave-owners were compensated for the abolition of their property in the slaves, the heirs of Henry Lascelles were recorded as possessing four plantations in Barbados, with 933 slaves in all. At least two of these plantations, it seems, must have been taken over from their debtors.

In one important respect the Lascelles differed from the Pinneys very much: they dealt much more largely with merchants resident in the islands. This kind of business lacked many of the advantages which could be got from dealing with planters: a merchant might have no landed security to offer and, though his business brought in a larger commission on purchases, it yielded much less on returns, since these often took the form of bills of exchange, on which only $\frac{1}{2}$ per cent was paid, instead of sugars yielding a commission of $2\frac{1}{2}$ per cent or more. The merchant's debt would carry 5 per cent interest, but so would that of a planter with better security. Some of these disadvantages the Lascelles tried to overcome: in particular, when they dealt with a merchant they tried to get some other better established merchant, preferably one with some landed property, to go security for him. At any rate, a large part of their business was done with merchants, and this is not altogether surprising. Henry Lascelles himself had been a merchant in the island; his brother Edward still was one; his wife's nephew Samuel Carter and many of his closest associates, especially the Gedney Clarkes, father and son, and Thomas Stevenson, still were merchants.

Some of these men had a miscellaneous business in dry goods, and in prize sugars when opportunity offered in wartime. But, as a rule, big business was slave business, especially in Barbados. The reasons for this were largely geographical: Barbados was the first port of call in the West Indies and many a captain threatened with mortality, mutiny or scarcity of provisions, and ignorant of the state of the markets, would call at Barbados, if only to refresh the Negroes and ask for news of commercial conditions. Barbados, therefore, was an island of great slave merchants.

A London West-India Merchant House, 1740–1769

The method of selling the slaves in the islands was changing. In the old days the captain, with or without the assistance of a local merchant, would hold an auction in which the slaves were sold for sugars to be paid promptly and carried home in the ship. This way of doing business had its risks: above all, the captain could hardly know which planters were capable of paying for their purchases in a reasonable time. This difficulty increased when the payments began to be made largely in bills of exchange — a development which came about, perhaps, because, as the price of Negroes rose and the price of sugar fell, no slave ship could have carried the entire value of her slaves in sugar. In these new conditions the captain needed the help of a merchant, who seems at first to have acted simply as a factor, selling the slaves on commission. In time, however, the factor became something more. The owners of the slaves would expect him to contract, and even bind himself by a penal bond, to sell the slaves at or above a certain limit of price and to return the proceeds by the ship which had brought them. In these cases the factor insensibly became the real purchaser of the slaves: he paid the limit demanded by the owners, resold the slaves to the planters for payment in six, nine or twelve months, and compensated himself — indeed, made his fortune — out of the difference between the cash price and the credit price. But as he was to lie out of his money, he had to have either a large capital or a financial backer in London. Gradually his relations with this backer took a more precise form: the Liverpool and Bristol slave merchants would expect the London financier to give security on behalf of the local slave merchant in the colonies. Usually this was a 'specific security'— that is, the financier would bind himself in a penalty of, say, £10,000 that the local slave merchant would comply with the conditions imposed by the owners of the ship. The letter-books of the House do not show what return the financier got for this business. The House did not go into partnership with the merchants in the islands, for whom they gave these securities, and it is not certain that they got anything more than the usual 5 per cent interest on the money advanced.

Much of their business was of this kind. Moreover, besides this security business, which only involved a risk of actual outlay, they advanced money to slave merchants in the islands in large sums. Some of this money was used for outright purchase of slaves to be sent from Barbados to another island or to Carolina; the rest was used in miscellaneous ways, probably in part for buying plantations. At various times Samuel Carter and the Stevensons owed the House between £10,000 and £20,000 and Gedney Clarke, senior, an enterprising, showy man, with all sorts of irons in the fire, owed at his death nearly £50,000, to which his son added a further debt of £25,000, nearly all of which must have been lost when he went bankrupt in 1774.

The biggest business of all was done with the family of the Harvies, and I shall tell this story in more detail, partly because it explains why a family which specialized in the trade of Barbados ended by owning two plantations in Jamaica.

In 1740, one John Harvie was procured by the House to go over to Barbados as a private tutor. He seems to have married a daughter of Thomas Stevenson and in 1744 he was home in England asking for an advance which would enable him to start business as a dry goods merchant in the islands. Fortified by the security which Thomas Stevenson offered, the House agreed to advance £4000 to Harvie for the purchase of linens and calicoes. He remained in Barbados until 1753, by which time his debt had insensibly swelled to more than £10,000. He then decided to go down to Jamaica with his brother Alexander and enter the business of slave consignments. For the purpose, the House agreed to advance for him a sum which was never to exceed £20,000, and the partners sent their friends in Bristol and Liverpool a letter to this effect. For a year or two all went well, but the Harvies seem to have been plungers. The years just before the Seven Years' War were not a good time for selling slaves — the prospects of Jamaica and its industry seemed doubtful. The Harvies, however, rushed in where others feared to

A London West-India Merchant House, 1740–1769

tread, and by the end of 1754 their debt to the House approached £60,000. This was too much, and George Maxwell was driven nearly distracted by financial anxiety. But he could do little. The agreement with the Harvies did not expire until July 1757: the House could have denounced it on the grounds that the £20,000 limit had been exceeded, but, lured by promises of repayment from the Harvies and fearing to blast their credit by a violent move, the House did not take this step. Maxwell tried in vain to induce the Harvies to give up slave consignments, but they refused to do this. Their idea was to 'push the business' for a few years and then shut up shop completely and collect their debts. This was not altogether silly; for a merchant, whether dealing in slaves or in dry goods, was apt to find that planters would cease coming to his shop if he asked them to pay their old debts, so he could only dun them after he had wound up his business. But the Harvies trespassed too much on George Maxwell's good nature: even when they had given up the slave consignment business they started it again more than once; besides this, although they promised not to do so, they went into the dry goods business, shipped cargoes to the Spanish colonies and, worst of all, started buying plantations right and left. Their debt to the House, which had at one time reached £80,000, came down to £60,000 but could not be reduced further. Three Harvies died one after another; although they believed that they had (besides plantations worth £50,000) enough money owing them to pay off the House, most of these debts proved bad, and they were reduced in the end to asking Daniel Lascelles to take over their plantations. This he had no wish to do. He would rather have got them sold to a purchaser who could repay him his money. At this point the story, so far as I know it, stops; but it is easy to see what was going to happen. The Harvies' plantations, already mortgaged to the Lascelles family, were going to fall into their reluctant hands and to stay there. In 1836 the heirs of Henry Lascelles owned two plantations in Jamaica, with 344 slaves in all.

By the middle 1760s, the House was owed at least £120,000 by merchants (though most of these merchants had, in the course of their business, yielded to the craze for becoming planters as well). Probably — although there is no means of knowing this — the debt owed to the House by mere planters was smaller than this; indeed, the partners often complained that if they had not been forced to lend so much to merchants they could have had a much larger consignment business from planters. But it all came to the same thing in the long run. Whether the House lent money directly to planters or lent it to merchants who sold the planters slaves for which they could not pay, the money was, in fact, financing supplies of slaves to the plantations; and it was only just that in the end, directly or indirectly, the money-lender should become the owner of the plantations.

There are two last questions — where did all the money come from, and what did it all amount to?

Clearly the money did not come from George Maxwell. He always spoke as if it was his partners' money that he was lending, not his own, and they often scolded him for the terms on which he lent it. The mainstay of the House was Henry Lascelles. He may have inherited part of his fortune from a father or uncle who had himself made it in the West Indies. He certainly added to it by his career as a merchant in Barbados, and by the profits of the business I have been describing. When he ceased to be a partner in 1750, he handed over to his son Daniel and to George Maxwell the credits which the House had given to the planters up to that date. He continued to invest directly in Barbados by lending to the planters; probably he also advanced to the House much of the money which they lent — in 1752, for example, we learn that when he made a loan he sold securities, whereas when the House made a loan, it had to take up money, probably from him. After his death in 1753 the House was much weakened financially, for only one-third of his fortune descended to Daniel, and even that seems to have been held for him on trust. From this time the House frequently complained of the pressure on

A London West-India Merchant House, 1740–1769

its means. There had been squeezes even in Henry Lascelles's time — at the outbreak of war with France in 1744, the invasion scare of 1745, the high price of money in 1746–8 and again in 1750–1 — but these squeezes became much worse after 1753, and the House was working on an overdraft at the bank for much of the time. We do not know the size of this overdraft, but it frequently troubled the partners, especially at times of financial stringency (above all, war-time), when much money could be made by investing in the public funds and holding them for a rise. Evidently the big loans to the Harvies and the Clarkes, and such loans as were made to the planters, took the House and kept it very near the edge of its means or its credit. In the end the storm was weathered — we know that, but we do not know how.

Even if the House had collapsed something would have been added permanently to the national capital. When Henry Lascelles made his will in August 1753, he bequeathed, besides annuities, sums amounting to £284,000. (It does not follow that he possessed all this, but I do not think Henry Lascelles was likely to make a mistake.) Of this sum, £53,000 was invested in lands in Yorkshire; the rest seems to have been in the public funds, in Henry Lascelles's own plantation in Barbados and, above all, in loans to the planters. Only one-third of this money was bequeathed to Daniel, who continued to be engaged in the West-India trade. £166,666 went to Edwin, who never had anything to do with the business. Daniel's share might have been lost — I have no reason to believe that it was — but Edwin's share was enough by itself to found one of the noble families of England.

ROMNEY SEDGWICK

LETTERS FROM WILLIAM PITT TO LORD BUTE: 1755-1758

IN 1934 Sir Lewis Namier and I were given access by the late marquess of Bute to a portion of the Bute papers which had recently come to light and was temporarily deposited in London. Among these documents we found a series of unpublished letters from Pitt to the third earl of Bute, complementary to Bute's letters to Pitt in the Chatham papers, some of which have been published in the *Chatham Correspondence*. The more important of Pitt's letters to Bute are printed below.

The correspondence opens in June 1755, shortly after Pitt's acceptance of Bute's invitation to 'enter into the closest engagements with Leicester House'. It ends towards the close of 1758, when Pitt, like other politicians before him, found that in the long run it was impossible for him to become a minister without giving up his connexions with the heir-apparent. The last surviving document in the correspondence, as in Bute's correspondence with George III, is a hysterical letter from Bute, which is printed in Appendix I.

Most of Pitt's letters are dated only by the day of the week, but the precise dates can usually be fixed on internal evidence. The dates assigned to them are given at the head of each letter; the grounds for the dating are shown in the notes, which have generally been confined to this purpose. A brief account of the circumstances of the termination of the correspondence is contained in Appendix II.

Letters from William Pitt to Lord Bute: 1755–1758

(1) MONDAY, 2 JUNE 1755

Hayes. June 2nd.

Mr. Pitt's affectionate compliments attend Lord Bute. He proposes being in Town by one o'clock today, and if it will not be inconvenient to his Lordship to call at Privy-Garden, he will give great satisfaction to his very anxious and truely devoted friend.

(2) SATURDAY, 9 AUGUST 1755

See Hardwicke to Newcastle, 9 August 1755, giving an account of his conversation with Pitt (P. C. Yorke, *Life of Lord Chancellor Hardwicke*, ii, 230-3).

Saturday 9 o'clock.

MY DEAR LORD,

I have just received a letter from Sunning Hill, writ to Mr. Fury, a gentleman in my office. This letter to him desires, in the Duke of Newcastle's name and Lord Chancellour's, that I wou'd call at Powis House any time before Wednesday next, when his Lordship goes to Wimple. If I find Lord Chancellour at home, I wou'd beg leave to trouble your Lordship for a quarter of an hour before I set out for Sunning Hill; if this shou'd confine you inconveniently at home, a line from your Lordship shall prevent me. Believe me with the truest respect and affectionate esteem

Your Lordship's most faithful friend
and most humble servant
W. PITT.

I cannot get to Powis House before eleven.

(3) SATURDAY, 9 AUGUST 1755

From this and the next letter it looks as if Pitt had called and found Hardwicke out riding but caught him later on in the day.

Mr. Pitt, who is really ashamed to redouble his persecution of Ld Bute, now begs leave to let him know that he has miss'd my Lord Chancellour, and therefore thinks it but conscionable to defer troubling Ld Bute till he returns to London again. He has seen Sir George Lee, by his own appointment, and is highly satisfy'd with him. What shall he say he is at Ld Bute's infinite goodness to him?

(4) SUNDAY, 10 AUGUST 1755

Sunday morning.

Mr. Pitt will expect the honour and pleasure of seeing Lord Bute at the Pay Office. He fears he can hardly be at home much before one, as he means to try to find the Duke of Devonshire this morning. He has a relation to make to Ld Bute of a conversation at Powis House,[1] which took place the same day after the Ld Chancellour returned from riding.

(5) SUNDAY, 31 AUGUST 1755

Replying to a letter from Bute dated 'Sunday August 31st' in Chatham MSS. asking Pitt to meet him for 'two hours' early 'tomorrow'.

Sunning Hill. 2 o'clock.

MY DEAR LORD,

I wou'd set out this moment in order to meet the sooner the two hours your Lordship is so good to promise me, if I did not expect Mr. Legge this day in his return. I am surprised that you have not seen him. I will be with you by ten o'clock tomorrow. I had determin'd not to fix an interview with Ld Egmont, nor on any account to see the D[uke] of N[ewcastle] till I cou'd have an ample conversation with your Lordship, and learn from you that final will and pleasure which shall entirely dispose of me and all my actions. All my ambition is to devote myself truely and sincerely (that is, by and with my dear Lord Bute) to the same great and truely respectable objects. Non ego perfidum, dixi, sacramentum. When I return'd from Mr. Legge's, I found a keeper had

---

[1] Presumably that referred to in the previous letter.

Letters from William Pitt to Lord Bute: 1755–1758

been to acquaint me that the Duke [of Cumberland] had been pleased to order a warrant for a buck for me. This great honour surprises me not a little. I shall count every hour till I embrace you. The odd face, you say, things wear gives me a painfull impatience to receive your ideas concerning them. I am with the highest regard

       my dear Lord Bute's most faithfull
          and affectionate humble servant
                      W. PITT.

Lady Hester presents a thousand thanks to Ld. Bute.

(6) TUESDAY, 2 SEPTEMBER 1755

See Newcastle to Hardwicke, 3 Sept. 1755 (Yorke, *op. cit.*, ii. 237-244), and George Bubb Dodington, *Diary*, 363.

                      Tuesday. 3 o'clock.

I am to see the Duke of Newcastle at eight this evening, instead of seven, his Grace being to dine late. As I do not imagine the Conference will be very long, I hope to be with your Lordship in a reasonable time. I have seen Mr. Dodington who holds a very good language.
        Your Lordship's truely devoted
                             W. PITT.

(7) THURSDAY, 11 SEPTEMBER 1755

At the interview referred to in the preceding letter Pitt and Newcastle had agreed to meet again in Hardwicke's house on 12 Sept.

              Sunning Hill. Thursday morning.

As I am to have a Conference with great men, soi disant tels, tomorrow evening, will my dear Lord Bute give me an hour in the morning at his house? I will be in town by eleven. Legge has been in London, and Ld. Guilford has answer'd all our wishes. The Duke of Newcastle was gone to Wimple, so no Treasury, nor consequently any interview between his Grace and Mr. Chancellor of the Exchequer. Believe me ever Your Lordship's truely devoted

W. PITT.

(8) MONDAY, 3 NOVEMBER 1755

Monday. 12 at night.

I have this evening imparted to Mr. Legge what I was charged with to him. He will himself best express the sense he has of what has pass'd on his subject. He has a letter from the D. of Devonshire who will be in town Friday, and we have reason to hope with the same dispositions he carry'd into the country.¹ This news is so good and so very seasonable that I cou'd not defer communicating it. I learn Lord Chanc^r. has been this night upon an errand of overtures to Bedford House.² The D. of B[edford] and I have miss'd each other but I shall try to find him tomorrow upon a message he left at my house desiring to see me before he gos out of town Wednesday. I go without the least expectation of any effect.

(9) THURSDAY, 6 NOVEMBER 1755

Thursday Evening.

The D. of B[edford] was gone on horseback Tuesday morning when I was at his door. We have not met since, and he is gone out of town today. The result of the Chancellour's visit Monday night ³ has not reach'd me, but I believe it left the D. of B. as it found him; determin'd to accept no place while the D. of N. is of the Ministry. It is said he is for subsidies at the Duke's desire. This softness to measures and firmness against persons shews him more of one faction than I thought him. May attachments to the quarter of [illegible] to England be as warm and as firm as those are to

¹ To attack the Hessian Treaty in the House of Lords (Yorke, *op. cit.*, ii. 241).
² See *ibid.* 252, as to their interview.
³ See preceding letter.

Letters from William Pitt to Lord Bute: 1755–1758

the men who meditate the most dangerous designs! I am in inquietude to hear of that health without which all must sicken. You will probably have heard that H. Campbell is to be Chancellour of the Dutchy for life.[1]

(10) THURSDAY, 20 NOVEMBER 1755

Pay Office. Nov. 20th.

I am to acquaint my dear Lord that I have just receiv'd a letter from Lord Holdernesse signifying to me the Kings commands that His Majesty has no further occasion for my service as Paymaster General. To which I have answer'd that 'I receiv'd His Majesty's commands with the deepest sense of duty and most respectful submission to His Majesty's pleasure'. I trouble your Lordship with the words, because it is not impossible I may be misrepresented on this as I have been on so many other occasions. Good-night my dear Lord: I believe I shall sleep very quietly and wake as happy as any Minister now in England. Heaven defend and prosper the great cause we have the glory to serve.

(11) SUMMER OF 1756

This may refer to the loss of Minorca.

Wednesday noon.

MY DEAR LORD,

I long with the utmost impatience for tomorrow morning when Mr. J. Grenville informs me your Lordship is to be in town. I will be with you by nine o'clock. The Interval that has passed since I left London has been productive of such events as will have afforded abundant occasion for the trial of all those virtues and the exertion of those abilities which are made for the saving of a country exposed to variety of dangers; and for the true service of a Royal Family whose safety, independency and glory are involved in this great crisis. My ambition and my happiness is to devote myself with you

[1] Actually he had been made Lord Registrar of Scotland.

to this transcendent, animating object; wou'd I cou'd assist half as much as I admire and love so generous and honourable a work! Your Lordship's
> most faithfull and affectionate servant
>
> W. PITT.

(12) WEDNESDAY, 6 OCTOBER 1756
> Hayes. October 6th 1756.

The subject on which I now trouble my dear Lord Bute is a letter I received this morning from Potter. This letter has explain'd that with the Wooburn post-mark which was destroyed unread. Potter gives me to understand that he had waited on your Lordship in town but not finding you he took the liberty to ask a favour of you by letter, to which having received no answer he fears it has by some accident failed reaching you. His request was in favour of a Mr. de Marville, private tutor to his son, who having compiled a stout system of modern geography begs the permission to have the honour to dedicate his book to Prince William, and Potter had in his letter asked your Lordship's favour in obtaining of the Princess this honour, if there shall be nothing improper in the request. A line from your Lordship on this subject would, I know, give Potter great pleasure.

I long to hear a good account of your health, for which no one can be more truely interested. Lady Hester continues still up and well; she is most sensible of the honour of your Lordship's obliging attentions to her, and desires her best compliments in Audley Street. Mr. Pratt will wait on your Lordship Sunday morning. Believe me ever, Lord Bute's faithfull and affectionate
> W. PITT.

(13) THURSDAY, 7 OCTOBER 1756
> Hayes. October 7th 1756.

Mr. Pitt presents his truest felicitations to Ld Bute.[1] He rejoices at this triumph of merit over malice, and that worthi-

[1] On his appointment as Groom of the Stole to the prince of Wales.

ness and consideration are no longer strangers to each other. May he presume (silently in his breast) to wish the P[rince] and P[rinces]s joy of the publick avowal of their just predilection? Thank God their R[oyal] H[ighnes]s's are delivered from all sollicitudes about their immediate family. Would to heaven we cou'd say as much for their great family, the Nation!

Lady Hester still holds out well. We are both gratefully sensible of the honour of Ld. Bute's obliging good wishes for us. The flames have already obeyed your orders.

(14) SUNDAY, 10 OCTOBER 1756

Sunday morning 1 o'clock.

Lady Hester is safely deliver'd of a Boy;[1] who I think will live to be one day an Englishman, and to bless, together with millions yet unborn, the happy influence of the princely virtues Ld Bute cultivates so successfully. The good condition Lady Hester is in fills me with the greatest joy, and the goodness that interests itself for the cottage of Hayes will pardon this gossip's note.

(15) TUESDAY, 12 OCTOBER 1756

This replies to Bute's acknowledgment (in Chatham MSS.) of the preceding letter.

Tuesday night.

MY DEAR LORD,

Give me leave to return your Lordship a thousand thanks for the very obliging interest you are so good to take in the Domestick event at Hayes. Lady Hester will not disown me in expressing for her, beforehand, how sensibly she will feel your Lordship's and Lady Bute's kind remembrance of her. I left her last night in as good a way as can be and the child in perfect health. May I beg Lady Bute to accept my respectfull compliments and at the same time let me express my

[1] Afterwards the second earl of Chatham.

acknowledgements of the kind part your Lordship takes in what touches me so nearly. I am ever with the truest regard
My dear Lord Bute's most affectionate friend
and faithfull servant

W. PITT.

(16) WEDNESDAY, 1 DECEMBER 1756

Brook Street. past 4.

The Reception in the Closet was favourable, considering the long impressions against me; and longer than I expected, for it lasted several minutes. As to the rest, I am extremely hurt at an intention to insert in the address of the Lords thanks to his Majesty for bringing the H[anoverian] troops last year. I told the Duke of Devonshire that if it had been attempted in our House I would have warmly opposed it; that if Lord Temple cou'd go to the House of Lords, I was sure he would think his honour concerned to resist it highly there.[1] He did not need my advice, but I shou'd certainly desire his Lordship to do so, and wou'd understand it as a step taken by the enemies of the present system, to throw it into confusion, and I believ'd dissolution. His Grace says it is against his opinion and that of the Cabinet. What is this latent malignant influence? It is the Duke of Cumberland, I dont doubt. I waited on Lady Yarmouth but cou'd not get at any conversation with her beyond that of a visit. If your Lordship can call at seven, I shall be at home; having desired Mr. Legge to read the speech at the Cockpit. Ever, ever yours

W. PITT.

(17) SATURDAY, 4 DECEMBER 1756

Saturday morning.

I will just trouble dear Lord Bute with a word to let him know that the Duke of Devonshire came to me last night, had

[1] See Temple to Devonshire, 1 Dec. 1756 (*Grenville Papers*, ed. W. J. Smith, i. 182).

Letters from William Pitt to Lord Bute: 1755–1758

been long with the King after I left Court; and also had seen Lady Yarmouth in great inquietudes upon the incident which had happened.[1] I was given to understand that, if I wou'd take the Seals, the King wou'd not receive me as I apprehended (in which case I had declared I wou'd lay them at his Majesty's feet, as despairing of being able to do him any real service): that he, D. of Devonshire, still declared he believ'd the thought of being thank'd arose in the King. I said wherever it had arisen I was informed *that Mr. Fox* in *concert with Ld. Egmont* had wish'd to throw the House into confusion upon it. His Grace hoped and believ'd that intelligence was not founded; that the *D. of Bedford* had contributed also to stop the progress of the mischief in the House, as soon as the D. of Devonshire had told him the consequence, which they all agreed wou'd be fatal to the King's affairs. That all were desired to kiss hands today; that the King consented to Mr. Forbes, who was also desired to kiss hands. In short that I was to understand the Storms of the Closet wou'd subside. What they will end in, time must show. I propose to receive the Seals, if I find before hand that the Closet is subsided.
 Your Lordship's
  unalterably affcte
   W. Pitt.

(18) Saturday, 1 January 1757

Saturday 2 o'clock.

Mr. Pitt's affectionate compliments wait on Lord Bute, and he will expect the pleasure of seeing him tomorrow, if his Lordship can without inconvenience come by half an hour after twelve, it will be extremely good to an invalid, who ought to take air and motion, the rather as he is forced to lose it today.

The matter is, a change in a certain place. I am told by the D[uke] of D[evonshire] that they will not take the £300000 but have the Hessians paid by England according to treaty,

---
[1] See preceding letter.

and only £200,000 as a succour in money.[1] Quid non mortalia pectora cogis, Auri sacra fames? What can be done with such a spirit? I suppose some such noble object as £40,000 or £50,000 difference is the motive of this disarrangement of plan.

(19) MONDAY, 31 JANUARY 1757

This and the next letter relate to the number of troops to be sent to North America.

Jan. 31 : 1757. Monday night.

I have the satisfaction to acquaint Lord Bute that the Duke of Devonshire has just been with me to let me know H.R.H. consents to a Bataillon or draughts to the amount, whichever your humble servant shou'd chuse. I have desired it might be a Bataillon and the Duke of Devonshire wrote in my presence to the Secretary at War to that effect. I shall send the King's pleasure upon it to the Duke of Bedford tomorrow to be forwarded to Ireland by express. The regiment is Perry's. I hope the train will also be increased. This point carry'd will be no small pleasure to your Lordship and indeed it shou'd be so, for in truth it is all your own work, if things are traced to their true efficient causes. I was forced to put off Sir John Ligonier till tomorrow, for the Duke of Devonshire. Believe me ever with the warmest affection and highest esteem

Your Lordship's unalterable friend
and devoted servant.

W. PITT.

(20) FRIDAY, 4 FEBRUARY 1757

See preceding letter.

Friday morning

Our meeting passed very well. Instructions unanimously approved, additional train and stores, 6 engineers, and 2 more

---

[1] Pitt had proposed to save his face by arranging for the Hessian subsidy to be paid by George II, in his capacity of Elector, out of the grant for the Hanoverian forces, which was to be increased by the amount of the subsidy, *i.e.* from £200,000 to £300,000. The King refused to agree to this. (Newcastle to Hardwicke, 4 January 1757; Add. MSS. 32870, f. 21.)

companies of Artillery agreed to, and the sloop, I hope, to be dispatcht to America today or tomorrow. The D. of Marlbrough shew'd great facility and promises to be ready very soon with the additions, and that the first train and stores shall sail with the transports. The unexampled injury done Sir Richard Lyttelton if he is left out of the promotion, astonishes me. I have just writ to the D: of Devonshire upon it [1] and shou'd not think this oppression will be pushed. I expect no answer, and add entreaties that your Lordship will not exercise your hand. Believe me with every sentiment of a heart devoted to the best and noblest of friends ever yours

W. PITT.

(21) SATURDAY, 19 FEBRUARY 1757

This replies to a letter from Bute, dated 'Saturday', which is printed and misdated 2 March 1757, in *Chatham Correspondence*, i, 223, congratulating Pitt on the success of his speech asking for £200,000 for the Hanoverian forces — see No. 18.

Whitehall. Feb. 19th.

The undeserved success of yesterday cou'd have given but a satisfaction of a very inferior kind, if the most noble and generous friendship had not imparted to it a value most transcendent and most dear by kindly sharing it with all the warmth and sensibility of a superior and elevated spirit. The perseverance my noble friend applauds so partially as mine was, in effect, his own constancy of mind and clearness of view animating and confirming wishes of mine into resolution and execution. It is no compliment, but a litteral truth, that I feel the constitution and temper of my heart (I hope not void of some good) yet not of a nature insuppressive enough to struggle thro' this sad period, were it not link't and united by the warmest and most grateful sentiments to a virtue and a constancy of spirit that I will aspire to make the object of my imitation, as it most truely is of my whole esteem and love. The Reception today was gracious; but I will decline filling

[1] See W. M. Torrens, *History of Cabinets*, ii. 355.

this paper with anything but the concerns of the heart, and finish the chapter of St. James's. The whole devotion of that heart is offer'd at another place, where your friendship alone cou'd have made it appear an undespicable oblation. The most gracious acceptance of my ardent vows for their glory and happiness shall be my perpetual support under every difficulty. So protected and associated, and united with the abilities and firmness of the noblest of friends I will never disperare de republica.

Let me not omit to do a word of justice to Lord G. Sackville. His part was most friendly and handsome, and his weight decided the success of the day. I was large on his subject to Lady Y[armouth]. He deserves every return in our power. My paper is at an end; till life is so, I shall be warmly and devotedly yrs.

W. PITT.

(22) WEDNESDAY, 23 FEBRUARY 1757

Whitehall. Wednesday night.

If my noble and kind friend had not bid me, I shou'd blush to notify to him my intention of having the honour to be presented to H.R.H. the Prince of Wales tomorrow. My feet, thank God, hold out tolerably, and in default of feet, a heart truely penetrated with ardent gratitude and most dutifull affection will bear me to Saville House. By the appearance at Westminster today English humanity is no more. Fox's attack on the Admiralty came to utter disgrace.[1] Our friend Elliot did admirably, Hunter sensibly and like a man. I am, my dear Lord, ever affectionate and devoted

W. PITT.

(23) WEDNESDAY, 6 APRIL 1757

4 O'clock Wednesday.

Having just received a letter from Lord Holdernesse, appointing seven this evening for executing the same sort of

[1] Fox had accused the Admiralty of trying to throw the odium for Byng's execution on the king.

Letters from William Pitt to Lord Bute: 1755–1758

commission His Lordship was charged with to Lord Temple,[1] I will propose the hour of eight to my noblest and kindest friend for the pleasure of seeing him.

(24) SUNDAY, 17 APRIL 1757

Sunday April 17th.

Mr. Pitt is not a little anxious for the health of his noble friend. He hopes to hear that the air of the country and exercise has done good to him, on whom the good of all so much depends. He was most unlucky yesterday in not arriving till between 7 and 8 o'clock, much too late for Lord Bute's kind intentions. He has no hopes of the pleasure of embracing his Lordship till tomorrow, having a meeting at seven this evening to consider of the enquiry.[2]

(25) TUESDAY, 3 MAY 1757

Newcastle had asked the Primate of Ireland, Andrew Stone's brother, to arrange a meeting with Bute on 3 May (Newcastle to Hardwicke, 1 May 1757; Add. MSS. 32871, f. 1).

Tuesday night 9 o'clock.

A thousand thanks to my noble friend for his kind note. Legge is here and in the temper you describe him. The Duke of Devonshire has imparted nothing worthy of much notice. His Grace declares he is ignorant of further new arrangements. Four and twenty hours will bring forth the promised birth of the Primate's negotiation. I wait, with expectation of but little fruit from the poor soil his Grace has to work upon. Your ever affecte. and devoted

W. PITT.

(26) TUESDAY, 24 MAY 1757

See Hardwicke to Newcastle, 24 May 1757; Add. MSS. 32871, f. 128.

Tuesday 11 o'clock.

Lord Hardwicke desires, by a note, to see me this day, at the hour I shall name. I have proposed three o'clock. I

---

[1] *I.e.* notifying him of his dismissal.   [2] On the loss of Minorca.

conceive the Duke of Newcastle finds the distress urgent and is playing his last resources. The sooner the meeting we talked over last night is had, I think the better. Ever, ever your devoted friend

W. PITT.

(27) TUESDAY, 24 MAY 1757

Tuesday. past 3

Lord Granby has not proposed any meeting between us and the D[uke] of N[ewcastle]. He express'd much desire of Union; fear'd there was no light for agreement upon Chan^r. of Exchequer, but wou'd go and report to his Grace my reasonings upon that matter, which, he thought, had one side very strong; that those in favour of the Duke's wishes had also great weight. I collect his Grace is to return a final answer to the K[ing] Friday.

Ld. Temple just sends me intelligence from Nugent that one point unalterable with the K[ing] is Fox Paymaster. Lord Hardwicke being engaged at the House of Lords at three has, by an answer to my note,[1] desired to see me this evening. There is certainly l'alarme au Camp, and I think the enemy have taken strong post in the closet; so between Knaves and Fools, this miserable country is going to destruction. Providence guard the sole hope of England!

(28) TUESDAY, 24 MAY 1757

See two preceding letters.

at Dinner.

Lord Hardwicke is to be with me at half an hour after seven. I conclude an hour must finish our Conference. I shall hope to see dearest Lord Bute at nine, as I imagine a letter wou'd not so well give him the true idea of what may pass.

[1] See preceding letter.

Letters from William Pitt to Lord Bute : 1755–1758

(29) MONDAY, 6 JUNE 1757

                                    Past 11 o'clock.

Lord Hardwicke was just going to Newcastle House, when I stop't at his door. He wou'd not let me be refused. I found him grave and full of thoughts, but not admitting the thing was finally over. I left him after a quarter of an hour's conversation, he promising to let me know by a note tomorrow morning, if any meeting was to be fix't for the evening. The D. of N. he told me is to see the King tomorrow.[1] Ld. Temple's news, from the opera, is that Fox is to kiss hands as first Lord of the Treasury, tomorrow. This does not accord with the intended audience of his Grace.

(30) WEDNESDAY, 15 JUNE 1757

See letters printed in Yorke, *op. cit.*, ii, 400-6, which explain the points referred to in other letters.

                                    Wednesday 10 o'clock.

Lord Hardwicke came to me late last night, brought the paper produced by Ld. Granby, and told me he (Ld. H.) had orders from the King to attend him this morning. His language concerning Ld. George in the War Office much the same as Ld. Granby's. Admiralty still the King's points, as well as Fox. Lord Anson being totally drop't, a hardship; and a point of honour to Ld. Hardwicke to mention him to the King. I shall be impatient till I have the pleasure of seeing dear Lord Bute and will wait on him between eleven and twelve.

(31) JUNE 1757

                                    11 o'clock

The inclosed letter to me conveys the best information I can have. I beg your Lordship will be so good to burn it as soon as you have read it, as Lord Hardwicke would dislike to

---

[1] To convey his final decision not to form a Government without Pitt.

123

have it seen. I will not set out for Hayes till after one o'clock, in case you have any commands for me. Your ever devoted friend

W. PITT.

(32) WEDNESDAY, 22 JUNE 1757

See Pitt to Hardwicke of same date (Yorke, *op. cit.*, ii, 406-7).

Wednesday 4 o'clock.

Nothing having pass'd, as the D. of N. says, which alters the state of things for better or worse since yesterday, I have declin'd meeting tonight, leaving it with his Grace to ripen matters for immediate execution, if his Grace thinks proper. That I, having nothing more to say, wou'd go and sleep at Hayes this night. His Grace desires to meet tomorrow night at his house at nine o'clock, and wish'd to know if Lord Bute would do him that honour. Legge's agitations continue. He must accept.[1] I have again press'd it, and I understand that he will accept, but a more miserable being I have not seen. I pity him with all my heart, and I leave him and all his weaknesses to Lord Bute and all his generosity. Ever most affectionately, yrs

W. P.

I propose to be in town tomorrow between seven and eight.

(33) TUESDAY, 28 JUNE 1757

Tuesday 11 o'clock.

All is settl'd for kissing hands tomorrow, the whole number, except Sir Robt. Henley and Mr. Pratt, who are to do it on Thursday, the ending of the term not permitting it tomorrow.

I go to this bitter, but necessary cup with a more foreboding mind, even since last night. Can my noble and generous friend hear without being deeply shock'd that the D. of

[1] The post of Chancellor of the Exchequer.

Letters from William Pitt to Lord Bute: 1755–1758

Newcastle had the front to affirm that he proposed to me in our conferences Lord Halifax's being Secretary of State for America, and worst of all, Lord Hardwicke's memory was too ready to countenance this shameless assertion. I own, I was enraged beyond bearing and did repell such a misrepresentation in warm terms, and by a declaration that I cou'd not serve the King with honour and safety if no candour and fidelity of repetition were to prevail. I put their Lordships in mind that whatever was said concerning Lord Halifax arose from me, who declared, at the time, that I did it to forestall any idea coming again of what had been press'd upon me by Mr. Legge in October last; that this was the fact; that I had declared to Lord Halifax his Lordship was never mention'd to me for Secretary of State for America, or the least mention made of any engagement to him for it, and that I wou'd not suffer an averment upon my honour to be contradicted. His Grace admitted then that I did anticipate the matter by declaring so strongly against it, and that the proposal was not made. How hard is the lot of this vile age? This is the wretch who draws the great families at his heels, and for whose elevation and power the pretended friends of the publick have so loudly pass'd sentence on my inflexibility. But no more of these exanimating heart-breaking reflections — I will fix my thoughts on the honours, comforts and security of noble and true friendship, warm my heart and arm my mind to encounter every difficulty in that service to which I have the glory, in conjunction with your Lordship, to be unalterably and totally devoted. I am ever ever yrs

W. PITT.

(34) WEDNESDAY, 29 JUNE
                        Whitehall. Wednesday past 11 o'clock.

A thousand truely affectionate thanks to dear Lord Bute for the pleasure and consolation of his kind letter.[1] I am just

---

[1] In Chatham MSS. dated 'Kew, Tuesday night', and incorrectly endorsed by the editors of the *Chatham Correspondence* 'August 28th, 1757'.

returned from Hayes, and making ready in no small hurry to attend the King. I will, after your own example, suppress disgusts and face difficulties as well as I can, and say ne cede malis sed contra audentior ito

Quo fortuna vocat.

I long to see you, and wou'd propose as soon after ten as is convenient to your Lordship, my first return to Office filling my hours so as to press me in time. I will keep from ten to eleven vacant, in hopes of seeing that last and only support, a truly noble and generous friend.

Dear Lord Bute's ever affectionate

W. PITT.

(35) FRIDAY, 1 JULY 1757

Bute's reply, dated 'Friday 10', is printed and misdated 5 August 1757 in *Chatham Correspondence*, i, 240.

Past seven Friday morning.

MY DEAR LORD,

I am just waked to read a note from Lord Holdernesse containing the melancholy news that the King of Prussia has been entirely defeated by Marshal Daun between Milhowitz and Kaurzim, within six miles of Prague, and that his P[russia]n Maj$^{ty.}$ had raised the blocus of Prague, not without loss from a sortie of the garrison. The accounts are yet imperfect, as Ld. Holdernesse's note informs me.

The King of Prussia, with his whole army, is retir'd to Leutmanitz.

I will not stay to make any reflections on this sad revolution of war. The campaigne must be eventfull yet, and a general battle, I expect to hear of very soon, which will probably be finally decisive. I am ever, with the truest affection and attachment,

Dear Lord Bute's unalterably devoted
friend and servant

W. PITT.

Letters from William Pitt to Lord Bute : 1755–1758

(36) FRIDAY, 8 JULY 1757

Friday.

I am too happy to be able to send my noble friend a little good news in this dreadfull crisis. Admiral Watson has retaken Calcuta on the Ganges, without considerable loss. He had also taken Hughly, somewhat higher up the river. No booty but some cannon.

This cordial, such as it is, has not power enough to quiet my mind one moment till we hear Lord Loudoun is safe at Hallifax and the troops also with Holburne. On the 25th June the 6000 men from New York were on the sea, at about three days sail from Hallifax. On the 28th May 8 sail of French men of war were seen about 20 leagues off Hallifax. Lord Loudoun writes that Beaufremont's own ship cou'd destroy them, but he trusts that he shall find Holburne arrived, and on the coast for his protection. I have litterally hardly slept since this news. What a catastrophe may have fallen on this, perhaps devoted, country ! But I will suppress too black presages, and trust that providence means to awaken, not totally extinguish, a declining nation. I have had a conversation with the D. of N. on the subject your Lordship mention'd to him.[1] I am persuaded he means to go about it. I am just running to Kensington. Ever, ever dear Lord Bute's devoted friend and servant.

(37) WEDNESDAY, 3 AUGUST 1757

Wednesday. 10 o'clock.

I have just heard that the melancholy news is arrived at Kensington that the Duke [of Cumberland]'s army was beat by Ml. d'Etrée's on the 26th past. My noble friend, what a complication of dangers and various ills press this unhappy, degenerate country ! I tremble for the news from America, whenever it shall come ; but no more forebodings. Providence

---

[1] Certain changes in the prince of Wales's establishment referred to in Newcastle to Primate of Ireland, 20 Aug. 1757 ; Add. MSS. 32872, f. 181.

may yet deliver us. In extreme haste, give me leave to break off. Yours ever devoted

W. PITT.

(38) FRIDAY, 5 AUGUST 1757

See Pitt to Grenville, 11 August 1757 (*Grenville Papers*, i, 206). Bute's reply, dated 'Saturday morning', is printed and misdated 11 March 1758 in *Chatham Correspondence*, i, 301.

Friday evening.

I must at all times wish to see dear Lord Bute after so many days absence, and in a very particular manner do I wish for that satisfaction at present. Things are in a most dangerous state. British troops have been strongly press'd by the K[ing] of P[russia] to be sent to reinforce the D[uke of Cumberland]. The D. of N., Ld. H[ardwic]ke and Ld. H[oldernes]s have declared for the measure. Your humble servant's negative has prevail'd to wave it,[1] but the fatal situation of the present gloomy moment is that under the disappointments of this darling measure, a total insensibility to all other objects, and non-execution for want of the necessary *authority* is like to ensue. I am almost ready to succumb with fatigue and disgust; having set up, to little purpose, at a meeting last night, till past two o'clock. I have nothing to complain of my colleague; we differ but his proceeding is fair and manly. I am going to sleep at Hayes tonight, and am to dine at Claremont tomorrow. I will return to town that night and will do myself the honour and pleasure to wait on your Lordship Sunday morning about eleven, if I don't hear to the contrary from you before. If my mind had not the consolation of a friendship like that you have given me to repose on, it cou'd not find strength to carry me thro' the distress of the present conjuncture, and the risque of my particular situation. With that firm support and truest consolation, I am determin'd to meet all events in pursuit of that honest and animat-

[1] Bute's reply states that 'the idea of sending troops abroad is totally inconsistent with the being of this administration'.

Letters from William Pitt to Lord Bute: 1755–1758

ing cause in which it will be ever my happiness and pride to be united with the best and noblest of friends. I am with the truest affection

Your Lordship's unalterable and devoted etc.

W. PITT.

(39) SUNDAY, 7 AUGUST 1757

Sunday night. 10 o'clock.

After all the glooms of our conversation of this morning I have the joy to send my dear Lord Bute the happy news that Lord Loudoun is arrived safe, with all his people at Hallifax, and that Holburne was also arrived there with his whole convoy, one 60 gun ship, which separated, missing. He luckily took on his way 4 transports with 1000 men on board. I cannot leave my noblest friend in ignorance of this providential event till morning, tho' almost afraid of my note breaking a repose that I fear your indisposition makes quite necessary for you. I am infinitely happy to think the joy this news will give at Kew.

Ever most affly. yrs.

W. PITT.

(40) WEDNESDAY, 17 AUGUST 1757

I will with the greatest pleasure wait on dear Lord Bute Thursday at dinner. I am sorry to lose a conversation with you this evening, tho' nothing new has happened since I had the pleasure of seeing you, except that the transports [1] sail'd out of the Downs yesterday and that reports from Harbourgh, well vouched, make the Empress of Austria at the point of death. We meet tomorrow night on the idea of doing something to engage Spain, if possible.[2] There seems to be the only chance of salvation to us and all Europe, but I doubt much we are too late.

---

[1] The Rochefort expedition.
[2] See Chatham MSS. 92 for minutes of this meeting and *Chatham Correspondence*, i. 247-54, for Pitt's dispatch to Keene.

The ill state of the Duke [of Cumberland]'s legg was more evident yesterday, from the manner of speaking of it. I am with unalterable affection
My dear Lord Bute's truely devoted
W. PITT.

(41) TUESDAY, 30 AUGUST 1757
Tuesday night.

I was in no great haste to convey to my noble friend the particulars of news that dashes all our hopes from America for this year. Lord Loudoun has laid aside all thoughts of Louisburgh or Quebec; the latter was become impracticable, but that the former shou'd be judged so, I am somewhat disappointed. It were injurious to blame a conduct not sufficiently before us, nor must any but a military man decide upon military matters. His Lordship seems to reduce his ideas to a defensive for this campaigne. A poor issue for an army of 21 Battallions, besides independent companies and provincials. Holburne talks of offering the French fleet in Louisburgh battle, if they think fit to accept it and come out to him. I wish the 4 ships arrived before it happens. I confess I find it hard to keep up my mind under this unhopefull state of things; I had my heart in America and in our windbound expedition. Let me not however communicate the gloomy cast of my present thoughts to yours; may you ever support your own mind, and fortify against misfortune those whose virtues may be call'd (which Heaven avert) to that severe but noblest trial. I write before I go to bed, lest your Lordship shou'd go early to Kew. I am with truest affection
Dear Lord Bute's ever devoted
W. PITT.

(42) MONDAY, 19 SEPTEMBER 1757
Monday. 5 o'clock.

The present most calamitous and ignominious conjuncture[1] has something so astonishing which accompanies

[1] The Convention of Closterseven.

Letters from William Pitt to Lord Bute: 1755–1758

it [1] that I beg to see my noble friend Lord Bute tomorrow, if it be but for a few minutes. I wou'd have come to Kew from Kensington had [not] I left it till long after three o'clock, as well as being engaged at a meeting tonight. If your Lordship cou'd alight tomorrow morning at my house, when you arrive, and be with me by half an hour after nine, the foreign ministers will not be come and when once they begin their conferences, it is difficult to interrupt them. Some way or other I beg my dear Lord Bute will let me see him before he returns to Kew. The moment is dreadfull, and some circumstances most stupendous. I am ever with the truest affection
my dear Lord Bute's most devoted
W. PITT.

(43) MONDAY, 3 OCTOBER 1757

October 3rd. 1757.

I am happy to be able to send my dear Lord Bute one piece of good news, at least to felicitate, if I tell you what you perhaps already know. The 13th of September Marshall Apraxin retreated *a la sourdine* into his own country, leaving behind, in his very precipitate march, all his sick and wounded, to the number of between 15 and 16^m men and eighty pieces of cannon. He cover'd his design so well that Ml. de Leiwald had no notice till three days after it was put in execution and, tho' late, he then detach'd his cavalry to harrass him. It is reported in Holland that Ml. de Leiwald was marching to Pomerania. The King of Prussia was at Gotha the 14th, and marked a camp there. P. de Soubise retired to Eisenach. I am extremely concerned to see that Gotha [2] has been exposed to formidable alarms which most happily came to no effects.

My dear Lord, your generous heart will least suggest what wounding and humiliating regrets this happy revolution in the affairs of that truely great King, his Prussian majesty,

[1] George II's anger with the duke of Cumberland — see Newcastle to Hardwicke, 9 Sept. 1757 (Yorke, *op. cit.*, iii. 181-2).
[2] The princess of Wales came from Saxe-Gotha.

must infix in the inmost reflections of ——.[1] May we redeem the past by our expiatory acts of common manhood, nay of commonsense! It is not yet too late. Indignation is as high as ever.

The enclosed[2] is so pretty I could not help sending it. But it must not, if you please, come from me. Believe me ever unalterably yrs

W. PITT.

(44) WEDNESDAY, 5 OCTOBER 1757

See Pitt to Newcastle, 5 October 1757; Add. MSS. 32874, f. 452.

We have no letter from the Fleet, but I have the pleasure to let my noble friend know that authentick accounts from France inform us that we are in possession de l'Ile d'Aix and that on the 24th past the troops landed, without much resistance, at Chatel-Aillon, a place between Rochelle and Rochefort, 3 leagues distant from the latter. There are but 4000 men in all those parts. The Household, 6 Bataillons and some detachments of garde-corps and mousquetaires, march'd for Rochefort the 27th past and cannot arrive till the 14th inst. The consternation at Paris is great; the success in India and this alarm has shaken credit, so that their actions bear no price. Heaven prosper our arms! Germany is redeem'd si l'on veut. Richelieu has publickly declared at Brunswick that the intentions of the King his master was to disarm the troops of Hesse and Brunswick when they arrived in their respective countries. Both those Princes have ordered their troops to halt and have declared they will perish rather than submit to such indignity. If I hope, I must adopt your quotation, spero contra spem. Yet I found a better aspect of things today. I am as yet undined, half an hour past five and to meet at seven. So I recommend my noble friend and all his generous purposes to the care of that power, which saves degenerate states and raises them up again to virtue.

[1] George II.   [2] Not preserved.

Letters from William Pitt to Lord Bute: 1755–1758

The Princess of Hesse is to come to England. Is it important or not? I beg to know who the panegyrist of the expedition is, for my conjecture fails me.

(45) THURSDAY, 6 OCTOBER 1757

Hayes. Thursday 2 o'clock.

MY DEAR LORD,

I just receive the afflicting news that our Fleet and troops resolved the 30th past not to attempt Rochefort. The road was found spacious and safe riding for the whole fleet of England. The *Magnanime* silenced the batterys on L'lle d'Aix in 35 minutes incessant firing and the forts surrender'd. This is all the short extract of this sad dispatch, which alone has been sent me here, contains. My heart is too full to write more. I am ever with the truest affection unalterably yours

W. PITT.

(46) SUNDAY, 16 OCTOBER 1757

Hayes. Sunday 16th.

Nothing but an absolute want of air and some remedies wou'd have made me leave town Saturday. I hope to find my noble friend tomorrow, not return'd to Kew. If he can give me the early part of the evening, from six till eight, I will set aside every business of what nature soever. I know not well where we are; perhaps my dear Lord Bute can impart more lights than he has to receive. At all events, I most earnestly beg to meet, shou'd it be only to mingle afflictions and despair. I have been for some days in constant threatnings of gout, but I trust I shall not fall down, at least at present. I don't know if the mind be strong enough for such a sad complication of publick dangers and dishonours; I much fear the body is not. Your advice, however, '*Tu ne cede malis, etc*' shall not be forgot; in minds well resolved, fortitude ought to outlive hope. I am ever with the truest affection

My dear Lord Bute's unalterably devoted

W. PITT.

(47) MONDAY, 17 OCTOBER 1757

St. James's Square Monday—4 o'clock

Tomorrow being my day for seeing the foreign ministers, I will propose Wednesday morning for the comfort and joy of embracing my dear Lord Bute. The sooner after ten you shall not find it inconvenient to come, the better, as we shall have more time before us. The event of the Duke's retreat from all military and civil business opens a scene of vast consequence.[1] I have just learnt this great decision, which, I conclude, has reach'd Kew before now. I have told the D. of Newcastle my opinion and urged it with my whole force, that a moment shou'd not be lost in making Sir John Ligonier Marshall and giving him the first regiment of Guards, conceiving the last point to be essential on more accounts than one. Ld. George Sackville should be Lieutenant General of the Ordnance. I think his Grace is convinced of the importance of speedy decision, to show there is neither consternation or distress. I feel more and more I never shall get Rochefort off my heart. Nor do I believe England, (which is the misery) will cease to feel, perhaps for an age, the fatal consequences of this foul miscarriage. I am ever, my dear Lord Bute's truely devoted

W. PITT.

I need not desire your Lordship to burn this note; the matter being so delicate for [the king] means to be his own General and intends I guess the Guards for ―― .[2]

(48) FRIDAY, 25 NOVEMBER 1757

Friday 1 o'clock.

Jemmy [Grenville] has just told me that the reports of the Generals[3] had not reach'd my dear Lord Bute. The enclosed

---

[1] This took effect on 16 Oct. (Newcastle to Hardwicke, 23 Oct. 1757; Add. MSS. 32875, f. 225).

[2] Prince Edward. Pitt told Newcastle that 'Leicester House did not wish Prince Edward to have the regiment' (*ut supra*).

[3] A military commission had been appointed to enquire into the Rochefort expedition. It reported on 21 Nov.

Letters from William Pitt to Lord Bute: 1755–1758

is a copy that has been sent to me by Lord Barrington, which your Lordship will be so good not to let go out of your hands. No accounts yet arrived carry us farther than the night of the battle.[1] Major Grant is hourly expected.[2] He will satisfy our thirst to learn the detail and consequences of this stupendous providential victory.

Ever yr. devoted

W. PITT.

(49) FRIDAY, 25 NOVEMBER 1757

Friday 5 o'clock.

I am just setting out for Hayes, but cannot go without sending dear Lord Bute a line, to tell him things are ripen'd at Stade and the resolution taken. God be prais'd, Prince Ferdinand is to command.[3] I learn'd these happy circumstances just before I left St. James's. Grant's arrival will give lights into the plan of this long-wish'd for and necessary operation. The circumstance your Lordship mentions about promises of Embassy's to Madrid [4] surprises me not a little. I certainly am not acquainted with it, and will suppose your Lordship *suppose* an irony on your friend. For if I knew of such a thing, it wou'd not be a secret to Lord Bute. I am

my dear Lord's faithfull friend
and servant

W. PITT.

(50) SUNDAY, 27 NOVEMBER 1757

Hayes Sunday 11 o'clock.

By what I learn, since I am here, I think things will have a good issue in Germany. The K. of P. is march'd himself to Lusatia, and to raise the siege of Schwednitz, leaving Prince Henry and Marshal Keith with a part of the troops to co-

---

[1] Rossbach.
[2] A.D.C. to the king of Prussia; he arrived on 28 Nov., having been detained by contrary winds.
[3] Prince Ferdinand of Brunswick had arrived in Stade to take command of the Hanoverian army.
[4] Bute had heard that General Conway might be appointed Ambassador to Spain in succession to Sir B. Keene (Bute to Pitt, 'Friday, past 5'; Chatham MSS.).

operate with Prince Ferdinand of Brunswick. Providence seems to open to us the means of retrieving some of the great opportunities lost this fatal summer; others, I fear, will not return this war. I am still anxious till the army here is settled.[1] I put my whole force to it, on Friday last, and his Grace has sworn wonders for Monday. I have declared that I expected every thing alarming in Parliament and City, if a Corp of 3,000 men were to be left in the seat of Government at the orders of Lieut. Col. Durée. I have insisted for decision before the Parliament meets. I shou'd not omit, that the D. of Newcastle dropt, en passant, but wanted my opinion, as to *Ld: Bathurst* seconding Lord Northumberland on the Address. I answer'd off, saying I thought no seconder usual in the House of Lords, that I cou'd not see well how Ld. Bathurst was proper, or improper; this matter seems to me by no means *indifferent*. It is either right or wrong, to a considerable degree. Your Lordship may perhaps have heard something about it; at least, you surely must hear, if it goes any farther. Ld Hardwicke has prepared a draught of the speech, and I think a very proper one which I shall be able to send your Lordship tomorrow. I am full of gouty pains flying about me, but hope not to fall down. A little repose wou'd save me, but I am at present press'd with more business than I can well suffise to, not having had one hour's recess even here. However, as far as valeant humeri, I go on. I have engaged Ld. Royston to move our Address, which I dare say you will approve. Our seconder is not fixt.

  I am ever dear Lord Bute's
    most faithfull and affectionate
        W. PITT.

(51) MONDAY, 28 NOVEMBER 1757

Monday 5 o'clock.

  Schwednitz is taken and seven Battalions in it. The King of Prussia learn'd the news at Dresden and is gone to Silesia

---

[1] The promotions consequential on Ligonier's appointment to be Commander-in-chief — see Pitt to Newcastle, 27 Nov. 1757 (Add. MSS. 32875, f. 152).

with 18 Battalions and some horse. This is an ugly contretems. I am far from satisfy'd with the indecision at home about our British army. Something is not right; but I trust will be got over. Nothing yet resolved upon the expedition Generals. The Draught of speech and motion not yet passed in form, so reserve in showing them is necessary. Ld. North will second. The idea of Ld. Bathurst is at an end, as I understand. I write this in the midst of dinner, so without farther ceremony allow me to say, adieu.

(52) THURSDAY, 8 DECEMBER 1757

Holdernesse passed on this incorrect report to Bute on the above date (Bute MSS.).

Thursday 1 o'clock.

Thanks be to heaven, the Prince of Bevern, who was attack'd by the Austrians near Breslau on the 22nd past, at 7 o'clock in the morning, after an action of four hours, broke them and pursued them 4 German miles from the field of Battle. The King of Prussia was on the 24th but 3 marches from Lignitz, whither one Division of the Austrians had retreated.

The operations are begun on the Elbe and his Majesty's troops are before Harbourgh.

Yr. Lordship's most faithfully
W. PITT.

(53) FRIDAY, 9 DECEMBER 1757

10 o'clock.

I am quite sorry to have been abroad when my dear Lord Bute was so good to call, happy at all times to see him, and peculiarly when there is matter to rejoice with him from such favourable strokes of providence. I rejoice truely with my noble friend on the intelligence he sends me of a right treatment of the Prince of Wales.[1] (For tho' a little embarrassing

[1] No letter from Bute on this point has been preserved and the nature of the 'intelligence' is unknown.

as to a particular object) I understand it to be intended by the King as an agreeable thing to H.R.H.

I fear the hours of the morning are not convenient to your Lordship, and am ignorant which may be least so. If half an hour after eleven be not disagreeable, I shall be happy to receive your commands at that time. I understand your Lordship will send to Ld. G: Sackville. I am ever my dear Lord Bute's
faithfull and affectionate friend

W. P<small>ITT</small>.

I am not sure if in my hasty note[1] I mentioned the King's troops having taken possession of Harbourgh and preparing to attack the Fort where twelve hundred French had retired.

(54) S<small>ATURDAY</small>, 10 D<small>ECEMBER</small> 1757

Holdernesse also wrote to Bute about this in a letter dated, 'Saturday' (Bute MSS.).

Hayes, 8 o'clock.

I grieve to send my dear Lord Bute a sad contradiction to all the good news from Silesia.[1] Mitchel's letter to Yorke, written the 30th Novr. at Leipsick retracts his former account, adding it was from the greatest authority, and admits the issue of the action to be unfavourable to the Prussians. Letters decyphering will probably contain the particulars of this unhappy event. Prince Ferdinand was marched forwards towards *Isterbourgh* in order to oblige Marshal Richelieu who was assembled at *Soltow* to fight him, or retire. The Prince had left a small corps to carry on the siege of the Castle of Harbourgh.

I must not detain the messenger, who returns with the letters to add more than that I am ever with greatest truth
Lord Bute's affectionate friend

W. P<small>ITT</small>.

[1] See No. 52.

The Austrian account from Brussels says Breslau had surrendered in consequence of the battle, the most bloody of this war.

The French Fleet is got into Brest, but the distemper and mortality excessive.

(55) MONDAY, 12 DECEMBER 1757

Dated by the reference to the Army Estimates.

Monday past 4 o'clock

The Duke of Newcastle has mentioned Lord George Sackville for the Ordnance and the choice will do, I hope; the execution may be obtain'd before Wednesday, the day the army comes on. His Grace told me, without my asking, that he had not judged proper to mention the Prince's Bedchamber today.[1] I said nothing to urge him, as I understand a little time is the thing wished. I find the Austrian slaughter is such that their army is ruined; accounts from Vienna avow 20000 men, as large a number as the whole Prussian corps before the action. The King of Prussia was in that neighbourhood and a second action is highly probable. General Schulenbourgh at the head of two or three regiments of Hanoverian Dragoons has beat very handsomely from twelve to fifteen hundred French Horse. Harbourgh is still bombarding.

Ever dear Lord Bute's affectionate
W. PITT.

(56) MONDAY, 19 DECEMBER 1757

This replies to a letter from Bute dated 'Friday night' in Chatham MSS., enclosing a letter from Elliott dated 'Thursday, 15 December'.

MY DEAR LORD,

I am this moment going to a meeting at Ld. Holdernesse's and will mention Genl. Elliot's wish to him, the thing being

---

[1] The filling of two vacancies in the prince of Wales's Lords of the Bedchamber — see Nos. 61-5.

in his province. The General's name has been in question as a person that would be very able to serve the King in the room of Amherst, attending the army as Commissary. Sir John Mordaunt was in that capacity with the Hessians last year. I doubt if Elliot would like it, and I find his present illness forbids the idea. I have mentioned Moreton to the Duke of Newcastle, who seems to like it very well, and coupled de Grey with him. What difficulties may arise from real or pretended promises to others, I know not; but I hope not such as will be unsurmountable.

   I am
     Dear Lord Bute's most affectionate
                W. PITT.

(57) MONDAY, 19 DECEMBER 1757

                Past 4 o'clock.
MY DEAR LORD,

I am this moment come from St. James's. The news from Silesia is most happy. The account is that the King of Prussia on the 5th inst. beat the Austrians, near Neumarkt; has taken 4 regiments of infantry, canon, colours, etc.[1] The authenticity of this is good, namely, a letter of the *King of Prussia* to Mr. *Eichel,* and a transcript of that very account to *Michel* here.[2] I dare not however indulge my entire joy till news more direct and authentick still. A letter is just come from Hanover, writ by an Individual to his Friend, dated the *13th,* which says 'nous entendons ronfler le canon; nous distinguons même le feu de la mousqueterie, et nous savons que le Prince Ferdinand contait d'attaquer M. de Richelieu aujourdhui', so that an action is believ'd, and a messenger expected hourly with the event. Heaven send it be a prosperous one! 'tis decisive, if well push'd. Ld. Holdernesse promised, with much pleasure, to write to Col: Yorke on Genl Elliot.[3] The King refuses Amherst flat and peremptory.[4]

[1] The battle of Leuthen or Lissa.
[2] Copy in Add. MSS. 32876, f. 238, endorsed as received on 19 Dec.
[3] See preceding letter.
[4] For the command of the Louisbourg expedition.

Letters from William Pitt to Lord Bute: 1755–1758

I wish the Duke of Marlbrough. What a consideration, that such commands go a begging. We cannot be a country long.

    I am
        Dear Lord Bute's affectionate friend,
                              W. PITT.

There is some mystery about the Prince of Bevern being taken. The K. of P. has made a new field marshal in that army. Name I don't remember.

(58) FRIDAY, 23 DECEMBER 1757
                                    Past 4 o'clock.

Mr. Pitt presents his compliments to Lord Bute. The Convention[1] goes away tonight or tomorrow and is quite right. Orders will go to America about Monday. Amherst still hangs.[2] Abercrombie is to command;[3] Ld. Loudoun to return home immediately. Letters from Germany say that Prince Ferdinand was before Zell the 14th. The French had set fire to the suburbs, and were filing off by the road of Brunswick; Prince Ferdinand had sent a very proper, firm message to the Duke of Richelieu, that he wou'd retaliate threefold such *incendies a la Russienne*, if they continued, on the friends of France. The Prince was to pass the Aller the next morning the 15th. It was thought the D. of Richelieu might stand him between Brunswick and Wolfenbuttle. The news from abroad (tho' not direct from the K: of Prussia to Government here) leaves it hardly to be doubted that the victory of the 5th is a great and glorious one. If Prince Henry moves, as is hoped, on the side of Magdebourgh, it must extremely embarrass the French. Harbourgh still holds out, this is the news of today; upon the whole good, tho' not decisive.

I forgot to mention that Marshal Daun is said to be taken prisoner.

[1] With Prussia. It went on 23 Dec. 1757 (Add. MSS. 32876, ff. 373 and 393).   [2] See preceding letter.   [3] In America.

(59) WEDNESDAY, 28 DECEMBER 1757

Wednesday 4 o'clock.

MY DEAR LORD,

The melancholy event at St. James's [1] has hindered Ld. Ligonier from having an audience today, in consequence of which, we had reason to hope Amherst wou'd have been granted; our dispatches to America will also be retarded for a day or two. I hope to send the messenger away Friday evening.

The letters from Prince Ferdinand's quarters bring nothing but that the Headquarters were still at Altenhagen, the Aller unpass'd, and Harbourgh unsurrendered. These letters go no lower down than the 17th. I am not a little uneasy at these delays. On the other side, the King of Prussia's victory and its consequences surpass all expectation and almost belief. The State of Russia, by the last accounts leaves little to fear; that Empire and Court especially is plunged in corruption and turpitude; no army, no Government, no finances; in a word, annihilation.

I cannot hope to get away for Bath before next week, if at all. I am always

Dear Lord Bute's, most faithfull and
affectionate friend and humble servant

W. PITT.

May I beg to know if any enquiries are proper at Leicester House and Saville House and in what manner if at all?

(60) WEDNESDAY, 4 JANUARY 1758

Wednesday January 4th.

I am happy to send, as a New Year's gift, to dear Lord Bute, the joyful and glorious news that Breslau surrender'd the 30th past. 15 general officers and ten thousand men bearing arms are Prisoners of War.

[1] The death of Princess Caroline.

Letters from William Pitt to Lord Bute: 1755–1758

(61) SATURDAY, 14 JANUARY 1758

12 o'clock Saturday.

To my great surprize, I have just received a note from the Duke of Newcastle to tell me he thinks it best to go to Claremont today, lest going to the King[1], on an unusual day, might have a bad effect. I think with my noble friend that the business is to be done; but I incline to believe that the difficulties are real not pretended. I am still far from well. Believe me ever,

Dear Lord Bute's very affectionate

W. PITT.

(62) 1758

This and the next three letters, which it has been impossible to date more precisely, relate to the vacancies in the prince of Wales's Bedchamber — see Nos. 55 and 61. In October 1758 Newcastle learned that Bute had 'found some fault with me, particularly that the prince's Lords of the Bedchamber were not filled up', but 'that Mr. Pitt said, he knew the D. of N. had done all that it was possible for him to do in that respect' (Add. MSS. 32884, f. 308). A year later Leicester House cut the knot by appointing Lords Carnarvon and Pulteney without notifying the King (Namier, *Structure of Politics*, p. 320).

Thursday 6 o'clock.

I am very sorry I lost the pleasure of seeing dear Lord Bute this forenoon by being out to get a little exercise in a coach. I continue ailing, but hope I shall crawl on without being laid up. I receiv'd just before dinner a note from the Duke of Newcastle to let me know that, to his great disappointment, he had not met your Lordship at Leicester House today, where he proposed to give you an account of what pass'd on Tuesday, relating to the Prince's bedchamber; that he is to try again tomorrow, *below stairs*,[2] where he is sure nothing will be wanting, as nothing shall on his part. So

---

[1] About the vacancies in the prince's Bedchamber — see no. 55. A copy of Newcastle's note, endorsed 14 Jan. 1758, is in Add. MSS. 32877, f. 120.

[2] *I.e.* Lady Yarmouth.

much for his Grace's note. On Tuesday he told me at Court that things stood in the closet as he left them on Friday, nothing absolutely decided; that he wish'd I would assure your Lordship it was not his fault; that he had done, and wou'd do, all that was possible. As I do not well understand this delay, I told his Grace I thought it best that he should inform your Lordship how things stood. He reply'd, he would do so on Thursday. To which I added that I wou'd not advise him to let Thursday arrive without his being able to carry to Saville House a decision of the matter. I still continue to think, as we both did, when I had last the pleasure to see your Lordship, viz. that the thing cannot fail. Lady Yarmouth is certainly in earnest to promote everything that is right, but his Grace's foible of procrastination keeps all things longer in suspense than I believe prudence requires. I am ever, dear Lord Bute's
        most faithfull and affectionate friend
                                W. PITT.

(63) 1758

See preceding letter. Bute's reply is printed in *Chatham Correspondence*, i, 170, where it is misdated 20 July, 1756.

                                      Tuesday night

MY DEAR LORD,

I am sorry my message did not reach your Lordship early enough to give me the pleasure of seeing you this evening, as I shou'd be glad to be fully instructed by a conversation with you what sort of answer is to be made upon the intimation I received today. Tho' a note but ill conveys insinuations of the kind hinted to me, I may however in one word inform your Lordship that the Duke of Newcastle protests his zeal and his distress, and adds that if he might be trusted with the names, *indirectly* and *as a private secret*, not *a step of His R: Highness* and at liberty to impart it below stairs, that assurance wou'd be given that the persons shou'd not have a negative. I will not hazard any opinion, but leave what I am charged

Letters from William Pitt to Lord Bute: 1755–1758

with for your Lordship's consideration. If you can, without inconvenience, call from twelve till one tomorrow morning, I will be at your orders, or at six in the evening as you shall chuse. I am ever dear Lord Bute's
most faithfull and affectionate
friend and servant
W. Pitt.

(64) 1758
See preceding letter.

Friday 4 o'clock.

Mr. Pitt presents his compliments to Lord Bute. He was sorry not to have the pleasure of seeing his Lordship at Leicester House yesterday, and letting him know that he had read to the Duke of Newcastle the answer he was charged with, to his Grace. Mr. Pitt is extremely concerned that the affair in question is still as undecided as it was.

(65) 1758
See preceding letter.

Tuesday 4 o'clock.

Mr. Pitt presents his compliments to Lord Bute and thinks himself most unfortunate in being abroad when his Lordship has had the goodness to call. If Lord Bute can take him in his way, any time before eight o'clock this evening, Mr. Pitt wishes extremely to impart to him a particular circumstance relating to the Prince of Wales's Lords. That matter, to his great concern, not yet being where it should be.

(66) Tuesday, 28 February 1758
Tuesday 7 o'clock.

Mr. Pitt is extremely concern'd he lost the pleasure Lord Bute was so good to intend him. He learnt after his return from dining the happy openings in the Electorate. P. Ferdinand's operations were begun and all looks auspiciously. He [Pitt] dos not think the French will stand it. He is as yet uninformed of the decision of Prussia, if any be arrived. A crowd of office business presses extremely, so that Mr. Pitt has no hour to propose to Ld. Bute but twelve tomorrow noon, which will allow him to air at one. This day's news has, in great part, given him his hand.[1] The completion of the plan will set him upon his leggs. He hopes the hour of twelve will not be inconvenient to Lord Bute.

(67) MONDAY, 6 MARCH 1758

Monday March 6th 1758.

Mr. Pitt presents his compliments to Lord Bute and regrets extremely that he has lost the pleasure his Lordship has been so good to intend him. If Lord Bute will do him the honour to call any time today from twelve till one, he will make him very happy.

(68) MONDAY, 6 MARCH 1758

Monday the 6th.

By a courier arrived from Stade certain account is come that the French have evacuated, in the utmost consternation, not only Bremen, but Hanover, Brunswick, Wolfenbuttel and it is thought Hesse Cassel. Prince Ferdinand is pursuing them on all sides. I write this note to dear Lord Bute with that sincere joy which he will feel on so happy event.

---

[1] See Pitt's extremely characteristic letter to Newcastle on the same date: 'I make this first use of my Lame Hand (or rather I recover it on this happy event) to express the true Joy of my Heart at these favorable openings of a Plan worthy of His Majesty. So should and I doubt not so will Dignity and Firmness of Resolution be crown'd with Success, Glory and Safety. May the sword of Prince Ferdinand confound the insidious Friendship of the French Pensioner Bernstorf and the Collegiate Cunning of the Pedants of Stade' (Add. MSS. 32878, f. 48).

Letters from William Pitt to Lord Bute: 1755–1758

(69) END OF MARCH 1758

5 o'clock.

MY DEAR LORD,

As I find it is probable that the choice will fall on Ld. Bristol for the Court of Spain,[1] I mention'd to the Duke of Newcastle the exigency of a proper person for Turin, Sir Richard Lyttleton not caring for such a commission. His Grace immediately suggested a name very near to me, Mr. H. Grenville. I told the Duke that obliging as that suggestion was towards me, that I had not once had him in my thoughts for that commission, nor I believed had any of his family; that I should wish some young man of Quality, of Hopes for business, who might form in such a wise, able Court, where the good intentions of the Prince did not greatly need a surveillant, much versed in affairs, and such a young man I thought was Lord North. I mention him to your Lordship, as supposing Leicester House and Saville House wou'd approve such a nomination. I shou'd be happy to know your Lordship's sentiments, as soon as convenient, till which I shall take no steps towards Lord North. I write with difficulty what you will hardly read. I am

ever ever faithfully yrs

W. PITT.

(70) SUNDAY, 2 APRIL 1758

April 2^d 1758.

A thousand thanks to dear Lord Bute for the kind trouble he is so good to take on the subject of our conversation relating to Turin. General Elliot is an excellent subject for such a conversation if a title be not necessary. I will sound the dispositions towards him, and if the thing will drive, I shall think no arrangement can be better. I am ever dear Lord Bute's most affectionate

W. PITT.

---

[1] On 24 March Newcastle informed Pitt that the king had agreed to Lord Bristol's appointment as ambassador to Spain (*ibid.* f. 330).

(71) Thursday, 27 April 1758

past 11 at night.

Mr. Pitt has pleasure to acquaint Lord Bute that Schwednitz surrendered the 16th; a post having been carried by assault the 15th. Prisoners of war, 250 officers, soldiers 3500 and from 2 to 3000 men of the garrison perished during the siege.

(72) Monday, 29 May 1758

In reply to Bute's letter of 28 May suggesting his brother, Stuart Mackenzie, for the post of minister at Turin (Bute Register).

Monday past 8 o'clock.

My dear Lord,

I am happy to have learnt Mr. Mackenzie's thoughts and your Lordship's with regard to Turin, before I had taken any step in consequence of our last conversation concerning Lord Coventry. The matter is where it was left, some time ago, with the Duke of Newcastle, and I hope his Grace has taken no farther measures on the subject. Every circumstance meets in Mr. Mackenzie that can ensure the publick service, and I shall ever think my own particular security and satisfaction as well consulted in the appointment of such a friend and of the brother of Lord Bute, as if a brother of mine were my correspondent. I propose being in town tomorrow morning, and shall wait with great impatience your Lordship's farther thoughts with regard to the manner of giving the properest movement to a matter wherein no time should be lost. Both the invalids of Hayes join in a thousand thanks for the obliging remembrance of their health. Lady Hester is better and I still muffled up with a swell'd face, which abates. I am ever
      my dear Lord Bute's
         most faithfull and affectionate friend
                        W. Pitt.

Letters from William Pitt to Lord Bute: 1755–1758

(73) WEDNESDAY, 31 MAY 1758

Dated by enclosure

5 o'clock.

I am extremely sorry to have lost the pleasure which dear Lord Bute intended me, by not being return'd from Kensington. I stayd late there in order to learn, if I cou'd, any news of what I have so much at heart. I have the satisfaction to find the ground has been sounded, and I trust in manner so favourable to our wishes, that the Duke of Newcastle, who has promised to try tomorrow, will find things well prepared, and disposed for success.[1]

Wind yesterday at 3 o'clock south west at Portsmouth. Ld. Loudoun arrived there in ye *Hampshire*. Durel, with the troops, sail'd for Halifax the 3d of May. Hardy was cruising before Louisburgh. Boscawen not mentiond; notwithstanding which, he might be arrived, altho' his arrival unknown at New York. I write at dinner; pardon haste and believe me ever most affectionately yrs

W. PITT.

Enclosed with the preceding letter. Not in Pitt's hand

St. Hellens 31st May 1758.

The *Hampshire* is this moment arrived with Lord Loudoun. The Captain gives a very good account of the situation of our affairs in America; Hardy and Durell arrived there the beginning of March, the latter with the troops sailed for Halifax the 3rd of May, and the former was cruizing before Louisburgh.

(74) FRIDAY, 2 JUNE 1758

Mr. Pitt's compliments attend Lord Bute. He had order'd the extract of Lord Anson's letter to be sent his Lordship,

[1] This refers to Stuart Mackenzie's appointment to Turin; see No. 72 and Add. MSS. 32880, f. 301.

when his obliging note arrived. Last night he had the satisfaction to receive accounts from Gl. Abercrombie [1] that all the troops destined for Louisburgh were sail'd from New York, Boston and Pensylvania; the last division consisting of two battallions, with the train, sail'd from New York the 3d May, the other two the end of April. Amherst's regiment was arrived, and the empty transports. The Northern Colonies have voted 17000 men; the Southern 5000 m. Pardon extreme hurry, having the room full of ministers. I am sure dear Lord Bute's heart will truely feel this favorable prospect in America; ever most affectionately

yrs
W. PITT.

(75) WEDNESDAY, 7 JUNE 1758

This refers to Prince Ferdinand's crossing of the Rhine, news of which reached London on 7 June, and the expedition against St.-Malo — see succeeding letters.

Mr. Pitt presents his compliments to Ld Bute. He mixes his warm felicitations with those of his noble friend on the spirited opening of the campaign by Prince Ferdinand. Lord Bute's information is the only authentick one that has yet reached St. James's Square on this happy event. May the arms of England do their part!

(76) THURSDAY, 8 JUNE 1758

Bute's reply, dated 'Thursday night', is in Chatham MSS.

½ past 12 Thursday night.

MY DEAR LORD,

An officer is just arrived from Captain Howe. The troops, after being detain'd by contrary winds, several days on the coast of France, landed on the 5th in the evening and during the course of the next day, with a trifling opposition of small

---

[1] Abercromby to Pitt, 28 April 1758, received 1 June (*Correspondence of William Pitt with Colonial Governors*, ed. Gərtrude S. Kimball).

Letters from William Pitt to Lord Bute: 1755–1758

batteries, soon silenced by Captain Howe, some little appearance of militia or arm'd peasants which made no stand before the troops. The landing was made in Cancale Bay, about 7 miles from St. Maloes. Heaven send us a prosperous issue! I have directed that my noble friend shou'd not be wak'd, in case he should be retired to rest, not thinking this news may not stay till he wakes.

    Ever most affectionately
        My dear Lord Bute's most faithfull friend
                W. PITT.

(77) THURSDAY, 15 JUNE 1758

                past 12 at night.

St. Malos stands as it did: the attack of the place being found, from the strength of the fortification as well as from the impracticability of the roads to draw artillery, not adviseable, and intelligence being got from Prisoners of a body, *which might consist of 10000 men* being on their march, the troops were well order'd to re-embark and were all *safe* on board the 12th in the afternoon. On the 9th the light troops and some pickets push't into St. Servant and burn't near that place a man of war of 50 guns, another of 20, and privateers of 30 and 20 guns, the number of ships burnt making in all above 100. The Duke of Marlbrough's private letter speaks doubtfully of their next attempt. Being at some loss where to land next, his Grace thinks in Normandy.

My dear noble friend, I wish the *enterprise* may not prove a *sort of expedition*, but give it a fair trial and let us see if our heroes will mend their hand in some future operation.

(78) FRIDAY, 16 JUNE 1758

Bute's reply, dated 'Friday', is in Chatham MSS.

                ½ past 9.

MY DEAR LORD,

    I send inclosed the Duke of Marlbrough's letter for their R.Hs's. information. On reading the account again, I think

its a justice to acknowledge that I see little else was left for the troops to do, in such a state of things, but to re-embark in good order. I say this on a supposition that their intelligence of the body of troops marching to them was not lightly taken up. May the next attempt answer better, and the British arms share one sprig of laurel with the rest of Europe! I beg your Lordship will be so good to send back as soon as conveniently may be the Duke of Marlbrough's letter. I am ever
    Dear Lord Bute's
     affectionate friend and servant
          W. PITT.

(79) TUESDAY (?) 20 JUNE 1758

      St. James's Square, Tuesday 4 o'clock.
MY DEAR LORD,
 I will be at Kensington tomorrow where your Lordship gives me hopes of meeting you. There is no news yet arrived from Prince Ferdinand or King of Prussia. All this is anxious; the farther operations of the enterprise doubtfull, and Louisburgh far off, and the event consequently long before it arrives here. The interval must be filled up with the best hope one may, and the great issue be left to that providence which has saved this country in worse times. The present however are so bad that those worse times do not very readily occur; but some such are to be found. May my noble friend's honest labours in planting the seeds of moral virtue never be frustrated! and may the reviving country reap the happy fruits of a Prince train'd to love his people enough to wish generously to reform them! I am ever
    Dear Lord Bute's most affectionate
      friend and servant
         W. PITT.

(80) THURSDAY, 22 JUNE 1758

       Thursday night past 11.
 Mr. Pitt presents his compliments to Lord Bute and acquaint his Lordship that an officer is just arrived from the

Letters from William Pitt to Lord Bute: 1755–1758

Duke of Marlbrough, with an account of the fleet being detain'd by contrary wind in Cancale Bay. The letters are dated ye 19th. The Duke of Marlbrough will proceed (without naming any particular place) with the first fair wind.

(81) FRIDAY, 23 JUNE 1758

This important letter, reversing Pitt's previous veto on sending troops to Germany (see 38), is dated by Newcastle's letter to Rockingham, 24 June 1758 (Add. MSS. 32881, f. 37), stating that in addition to the cavalry mentioned in Pitt's letter, which were to go at once, it had been agreed, at Pitt's suggestion, to send 6000 infantry to join Prince Ferdinand's army when the combined operation against the French Coast was over. Bute's reply, approving the proposal on the understanding that Pitt had made it clear that 'a small body shall not lead to a great one', is in the Chatham MSS.

Friday ½ past 5.

MY DEAR LORD,

As nothing can be of greater consequence than that the War should continue, on our part, on the offensive, and that Prince Ferdinand shou'd be enabled to maintain and push his operations on this side of the Rhine, I have ventur'd to suggest the sending some squadrons of English cavalry to reinforce the King's army there. Such a succour, I believe, will effectually tend to prevent repassing the Rhine, which, *at some moment of low spirits*, I confess I apprehend. Lord Ligonier's ideas will decide of this measure. In the mean time transports will be taking up in order to be in some forwardness. As all our operations at present consist of infantry, we have evidently an over-proportion of cavalry here at home, part of which may be safely spared and apply'd, I conceive, to the greatest advantage, both for the common cause and for the good of the troops themselves, under such a General as Prince Ferdinand. As we have had more conversations than one on the subjects of *some troops* joining for an *offensive operation, on the Rhine*, I have the satisfaction to understand your Lordship's ideas favour mine on this important question.

The publick approbation I have no reason to doubt of, and the rectitude and efficacy of the measure enough demonstrate themselves. No news when I left Kensington. I am just going to Hayes, to return on Monday, by which time, I trust, some satisfactory accounts may arrive.

I am ever
Dear Lord Bute's
most truely affectionate friend and servant
W. PITT.

(82) MONDAY, 26 JUNE 1758

See No. 81. Bute's reply is printed in *Chatham Correspondence*, i, 320. For Leicester House's real views, see *Letters from George III to Lord Bute*, 1756–1766, ed. R. Sedgwick, No. 14.

Monday evening.

MY DEAR LORD,

I delay'd returning you my sincere thanks for a most friendly and kind letter, till I could, at the same time, send some account of the situation of things. The prosperity and lustre of the campaigne in Germany surpasses hitherto our most sanguine hopes. By the letters of yesterday the French seemd to be possess'd with a pannick, that wou'd not suffer them to make one stand. Those of this morning represent the position of the two armies, near Crevelt, so close to each other that it appears almost impossible for either to retrograde, without giving to the other an attack upon their rear-guard at least. Things in Moravia have a very promising aspect; the King of Prussia having receiv'd his grand convoy without losing a single waggon. The besiegers were about 400 paces from the covert-way and it was expected they wou'd be masters of the place in the course of this month. The Russians are, as yet, little felt, and the Swedes, reduced by mortality to 10,000 men fit for service. Our enterprise meets with very untoward delays. The Fleet was however off Cape La Hogue the 24th, and purposing, I would fain hope, to attempt something handsomely. Five regiments are

intended to reinforce Prince Ferdinand, which will make him nearer a match in cavalry. This succour will be about 2,000 men. A thousand real thanks for my noble friend's salutary caution. Be assured, I will not be drawn further than my own conviction, authorised and confirmed by your concurrence, shall suggest. It is proposed to bring some horse hither from Ireland. The King has named Blyghe to command. I am ever
    Dear Lord Bute's most affectionate friend
                W. PITT.

(83) WEDNESDAY, 5 JULY 1758

Nos. 83-88 relate to the proposal that the prince of Wales's younger brother should join the navy and serve as a volunteer in the combined expeditions against the French Coast.

        Wednesday past 6 o'clock.
MY DEAR LORD,

In consequence of the commands which your Lordship did me the honour to bring me this morning, I have, in concert with the Duke of Newcastle, open'd the matter with which I was very proud and happy to be charged, in the place where I had permission to mention it. I had not the least doubt of the manner in which every overture of the wishes and intentions your Lordship had done me the honour to signify would be embraced, and I have the satisfaction to acquaint your Lordship that I think the thing in a very good train, and have great reason to hope that the success will be favourable. I shall be happy in seeing an agreeable and speedy issue to an idea, of which I cannot enough applaud the wisdom and many good consequences. Nothing, humanly speaking, will be preventive of more inconvenience and productive of more good to the service of the whole, at this time, than this happy temperament. I am ever
    my dear Lord Bute's
      most affectionate friend and servant
              W. PITT.

(84) FRIDAY, 7 JULY 1758

This replies to Bute's letter, dated 'Thursday evening', printed and misdated 3 June 1756 in *Chatham Correspondence*, i, 156.

Friday July ye 7th past 5 o'clock.

Truely penetrat'd with the sense of their Royal Highnesses gracious acceptance of my entire devotion to their commands, let me entreat your Lordship to lay me at the feet of the Prince and Princess of Wales and to express for me the most respectfull and gratefull sentiments of my heart.

As to the doubts with regard to Prince Edward's acknowledgements to the King for his Majesty's gracious compliance with his desires, I have consulted where I thought I might obtain the best light, and I am to recommend to your Lordship that Prince Edward may safely defer taking any step on Sunday, and to apprise your Lordship that on Monday morning, at the Review, intimation will be convey'd, by the Duke of Newcastle, who will be there, with regard to what shall be then found most adviseable to be done. This day has been very little favorable, I know not why, for advancing any that is right and necessary; but cloudy skies clear up, and the public service finds its way, tho' most painfully to those at the oar. I am just getting into my chaise for Stowe, to return by dinner on Monday next. I am ever my dear Lord Bute's

most affectionate friend and humble servant

W. PITT.

(85) TUESDAY, 11 JULY 1758
See preceding letter.

Tuesday past 5 o'clock.

I have the satisfaction to acquaint my dear Lord Bute that the King has signified his pleasure to the Duke of Newcastle that Prince Edward may come to thank his Majesty whenever he will. At the same time, I understand that it is conceived

Letters from William Pitt to Lord Bute: 1755–1758

the time the most proper for doing this may be tomorrow, after that Prince Edward shall have been at the Levée.

Lord Panmure has wrote to Lord Ligonier a second letter, whereby he accepts the command of the expedition. I am more than ever impatient to get it away, finding by a letter from Lord Anson that his Lordship is laying in for a reason to come into port, before it is long. Whether this be all from his own movement, or by concert, to embarrass and render impracticable farther operations on the coasts of France, I will not venture to decide. But it is too evident that difficulties and obstructions swarm upon me. However, nil desperandum, under *happy auspices*, and *upon firm system*. I am ever
my dear Lord Bute's most affectionate
friend and servant
W. PITT.

I found the King, I think, much better.

(86) FRIDAY, 14 JULY 1758

See Newcastle to Hardwicke, 15 July 1758 (Add. MSS. 32881, f. 329).

Friday ½ past 4.

MY DEAR LORD,

I have the honour to be charged with the agreeable commission of acquainting your Lordship for the information of the Prince and Princess of Wales and of Prince Edward, that the King has been graciously pleased to approve of his Royal Highness's intention to serve as volunteer with the squadron under the command of Captain Howe, and the necessary orders are given for making preparations for receiving Prince Edward and his retinue on board the Commodore's own ship.

I am sorry to have nothing satisfactory to say to my dear Lord Bute concerning a commander in chief of the land forces on the expedition. Lord Panmure can not go. Lord John Murray will not be let to go, Durée remains eldest major general and will, I understand, go with the command. This seems His Majesty's pleasure. Letters from France inform us that Louisburgh was begun to be besieged the early days of June, this account seems worthy of credit. D'Estrée has refused the command, and France knows not on whom to cast an eye to replace M. de Clermont, fallen into great disrepute.

I must not omit to acquaint your Lordship, for Prince Edward's information, that it is likely the expedition will be to sail, by the middle of next week. At least, all will be ready, and nothing wanting but final orders. I am going to Hayes and hope to be recall'd by letters from America. I am ever my dear Lord Bute's
most affectionate friend and servant
W. PITT.

(87) MONDAY, 17 JULY 1758

This replies to Bute's letter, endorsed 'July 14th', which is printed and misdated June 27, 1758, in *Chatham Correspondence*, i, 319.

Monday past 11.

MY DEAR LORD,

I am this minute return'd from Hayes, where your Lordship's note of ye 14th reachd me but yesterday, in the afternoon, by some delay, I believe, of your servant. I have sent to the Admiralty to enquire if any commission was given to the Duke [of Cumberland]. I presume not, but precedents need not govern, in this case, if judged necessary. I do not conceive there can be the least room for doubt as to the destination of Prince Edward, His Royal Highness having desir'd the King's permission to *serve as volunteer on board the Squadron commanded by Captain Howe*, and His Majesty having been pleased to signify his approbation thereof. Nothing, my dear Lord, can have been more fully explained than the idea that Prince Edward prefer'd *entering into the Department of the Navy* and that this destination had the entire approbation of the Prince and Princess of Wales.

There has been some little misunderstanding with regard

to Howe's intended return to London. I did not apprehend any the least necessity for seeing the Commodore any more before he sails, and shou'd much fear that all preparations must suffer, in point of dispatch, by his absence. Any proper person sent to the Admiralty I shou'd not doubt would receive every sort of information, with regard to the preparations, your Lordship mentions. I will write again, when I return from Kensington. I know of nothing, but contrary winds, that need delay Howe's sailing by Thursday or Friday. I am ever dear Lord Bute's
most affectionate
W. PITT.

P.S. Saunders being arrived with two or three ships, I have got the *Revenge* of 64 guns, for Howe, in place of a 50, a very essential addition of weight of metal. I have obtained the promotion of three excellent Rear-Admirals, Stephens, Durell and Homes.

(88) TUESDAY, 18 JULY 1758

Tuesday past 4.

MY DEAR LORD,

Since I had the honour of seeing Prince Edward at the Levée I have receiv'd his Majesty's commands for ordering the troops destin'd for the expedition to embark and be ready to sail, in the *course of Saturday or Sunday next*. This is the soonest, I understand, that General Bligh can be ready with his horses and baggage. I beg your Lordship will acquaint his Royal Highness how far this matter now stands settled. Shou'd any alteration happen, which I cannot expect, I will not fail to send your Lordship the earliest notice for His Royal Highness's information. The King is very impatient for the departure of the expedition. I like our General extremely, and never saw a more soldier-like man. Lord Fitzmorris is appointed to act as Adjutant-General on the expedition, which gives me great satisfaction.

I hoped to have had the pleasure of dining at Kew Green today, but the adjourn'd examination of Hensey,[1] which kept us very late last night, is to be resumed again at seven this evening. The three regiments of cavalry sail'd from the Nore, with a fair wind, yesterday, and yesterday also a fourth regiment of Dragoons and one of foot fell down the river, and will, I conclude, have sail'd today. I am ever my dear Lord Bute's
     Most affectionate friend and servant
               W. PITT.

(89) FRIDAY, 21 JULY 1758
              Friday past 5 o'clock.
MY DEAR LORD,
 The news of this day is very unfavourable; however, all that is come to my knowledge is reducible to the single fact that the siege of Olmutz is raised. The various particulars spread and propagated are all from French and Austrian authorities, suspected consequently, full of contradictions, and deserve, as yet, but little attention. Yorke's letter gives us to hope that the King of Prussia has assembled his whole army at Littau, without loss. If this proves founded, an action is to be expected. On the whole, I see nothing yet but an échec which affects more the honour of the Prussian arms than that it decides at all of the sum of things for the campaigne. Prince Ferdinand has moved nearer Nuys, and the French look as if they intended another action, probably before our troops join. General Bligh will be at Portsmouth in the course of Sunday next, and, by a letter I received yesterday, from Commodore Howe, every thing would be ready to sail tomorrow. Lord Anson's orders to put to sea will reach him this night, and I am informed by Cleveland he will have taken in his water and be ready to put to sea by the time the orders will reach him. Your Lordship will imagine that the news from Moravia cannot but make con-

---

[1] For conveying military information to the French Government by the Spanish ambassador's courier (Add. MSS. 32998, ff. 171 *et seq.*).

siderable impressions; however, I have the satisfaction to acquaint you that I found those impressions rather less than I had apprehended they might be; an uninterrupted course of prosperity must not be expected in war, and I see nothing that may not be repaired, and perhaps by one decisive battle in Moravia, converted into greater and more important advantages. If the King of Prussia is still at the head of his army, not much impair'd, I trust, under Providence, that all will be well. I am ever my dear Lord Bute's most affcte

W. PITT.

(90) TUESDAY, 1 AUGUST 1758

Tuesday past 5 Augt. ye 1st 1758.
MY DEAR LORD,

Lest the inclosed printed relation of ye campaigne should happen not to have reach'd you, I send it to your Lordship. It contains a very happy event, which is, the safe arrival of the Prussian army at the post of Coninsgratz. The actions that have pass'd have had nothing farther decisive in them, than that the march has been happily executed. This is a great point, considering the situation things were in. As to the ulterior operations on that side, I find they are very precarious, and must depend on the practicability of subsisting.

Prince Ferdinand march'd ye 24th past to Roermond. What his object may be, exercises the conjectures of Kensington, as no letters are come from the army. For my part, I repose entirely on the great capacity and interior lights of the General, and wait the clearing up of this unexpected movement with more hope than inquietude. Prince d'Ysensbourgh's action near Cassel is an ugly contretems, it having been the intention of Prince Ferdinand that his operations on that side shou'd have been defensive, and a war of posts. The French, however, have bought their advantage very dear. On the whole, my noble friend will see the present moment big with mighty consequences, and the operations so manifold and corps of armies so spread in different parts that who can form, as yet, any sure conjectures concerning the final issue upon the total of this eventful campaigne? The accounts by way of France look well for us at Louisbourgh. Howe was obliged to anchor at the Northern bank of the Isle of Wight the wind being too fresh for the transports, and was waiting yesterday the first occasion to sail.

I am ever, my dear Lord Bute, most affectionate
W. PITT.

(91) FRIDAY, 11 AUGUST 1758

Friday Aug. 11th 1758.
MY DEAR LORD,

I can imagine what your Lordship's impatience must be till we hear again from the coast of France, by the sollicitude I feel in such a situation. General Bligh's letter is that of a soldier; he writes and will, I doubt not, act like one. The Lieutenant of the *Cutter* tells me that nothing could be better than the countenance and ardour of the troops at landing. He saw them, on ye 8th when he came away, in full march for Cherbourgh, and Mr. Howe under sail with a fair wind for the town and batteries. As the officer is to return this evening, I beg leave to apprize you, for their Royal Highnesses information, in case they have any commands. The messenger will attend and bring any letters for Prince Edward.[1] I am ever

My dear Lord Bute's most affectionate friend
W. PITT.

APPENDIX I

BUTE TO PITT: Monday, 25 September 1758

The register of Lord Bute's correspondence (Add. MSS. 36796) shows that between 11 August and 2 September Pitt wrote at least four times to Bute, reporting Prince Ferdinand's repassage

[1] This letter is endorsed by Bute: 'I keep the messenger till I know whether Y.R.H. intend to write'.

Letters from William Pitt to Lord Bute: 1755-1758

of the Rhine, the capture of Louisbourgh, Abercromby's defeat at Ticonderoga and the battle of Zorndorff. None of these letters has been found but Bute's replies to the last two are in the Chatham papers. After that there is nothing more till this letter.

Monday.

MY WORTHY FRIEND,

I intended to have call'd upon you this morning but Mr. Wood told me that Lord Howe was to be with you early. A thousand thanks for the trouble you have taken about my brother. He now has nothing to detain him but the necessary passports and instructions. The more I hear about Bligh's usage and reception the more it fills me with amazement and indignation. Is the only man that has been victorious in France, that has forc'd a diversion and eagerly executed his orders, is he to be singl'd out; to suffer harsher treatment than Conway, Mordaunt, Cornwallis? These all were allow'd to appear before their Sovereign; nay to exercise their functions about his person; pity and compassion whisper'd for them in every corner of the Court; while poor Bligh is told that Lord Falconbridge had directions from Legonier, in case he came to Court, to let him know his presence was not proper there.[1] What has he done; why after the most vigorous execution of his orders he thinks it safer to rely upon the unanimous opinion of his general officers; if he had not call'd upon them, where would this mighty crime have been? Only an error in judgement; he thought it more expedient to retreat than hazard a battle, *and that* however no one man in his army dare say he was affraid of; When I read over Turenne, Luxembourgh's, Conde's campaigns, how often do I observe these great men blaming themselves, owning they had lost this or that advantage, suffer'd this or that affront, by their own faults; but the conqueror of Cherbourgh must not err. Again is not the loss sustained nearly equal, by the confession of the enemy. If numbers wont damn him, the superior *excellency* of the Guards is vaunted, the *unheard of infamy* that

[1] In the end Bligh was presented at Court but met with an unsatisfactory reception — see *Letters from George III to Lord Bute*, No. 20.

has overtook the most quiet virtuous disciplin'd body is to run him down. Excuse this long letter, my dear friend, my heart is full, and feels for you as well as Bligh whom I never spoke to. This is in my firm opinion, the factious measure of men, who abhorr vigour and expeditions, and that this day breath revenge for a Habeas Corpus Act.[1] Our Commander in Chief is now theirs, and co-opperates in their revenge. Nothing has ever happen'd since we put the crown once more on that little Pelham's head that so thoroly opens my eyes. This is a trait a greater person than me never will forgive. Don't think this the sentiment of passion. I never was cooler, tho' never more determin'd in my life. Adieu, my dear friend, better days attend us, tho' in bad as well as good, I am ever most affectionately yours, &c.   BUTE.

Bligh declares that were he reduc'd to £50 a year the universe should not make him keep any office whatever.

APPENDIX II

Pitt's reply to Bute's letter of 25th September (printed in Appendix I) is entered in the Bute Register. The letter itself has not been found, but its tenor and consequences were disclosed to Newcastle by Viry,[2] the Sardinian Minister, in a series of remarkably well-informed communications,[3] which were assumed to have been inspired by Pitt.[4]

After giving an accurate summary of Bute's letter about Bligh, Viry told Newcastle that Pitt's reply, which he had seen, had taken the line that Newcastle knew no more than Pitt himself about the affair; that Ligonier had handled it clumsily; but that it would look strange if Bute and Pitt,

[1] A bill for extending the provisions of the Habeas Corpus Act; promoted in the previous session by Pitt and Pratt and passed by the House of Commons; but opposed by Newcastle, Hardwicke and Mansfield and thrown out by the House of Lords.
[2] For Viry, see L. B. Namier, *England in the Age of the American Revolution*, pp. 91-3.
[3] Add. MSS. 32884, ff. 268, 317 and 412, and 32886, f. 384.
[4] *Ibid.*, ff. 289 and 335, and 32885, f. 36.

Letters from William Pitt to Lord Bute: 1755-1758

'who had been so uneasy, at the reception of Sir John Mordaunt and General Conway, should now complain that too much severity had been shown to General Bligh'. This had led to an interview in which Bute had attacked Pitt's policy of sending British troops to Germany and accused him of always giving in to Newcastle; while Pitt had shown himself determined to continue his German measures and his co-operation with Newcastle. Bute had then written to Pitt 'insisting that he should ask, and even *force* the King' to make Clark, the officer believed to have been primarily responsible for the attack on St.-Malo, a colonel of Marines. To this Pitt had sent a 'short negative', adhering to his decision when Bute returned to the charge.

Viry also gave Newcastle two pieces of information bearing on Bute's concern about the treatment of Bligh and Clark and on his correspondence with Pitt. The first was that Bute had admitted that the unfortunate plan of attacking St.-Malo a second time, after it had already been alerted by the previous abortive attempt in June, had been concerted at Leicester House with the commanders of the expedition 'à l'inseu du duc de Newcastle et Mr. Pitt'. The second was that Pitt's colleague, Holdernesse, was making court to Bute by sending him minute accounts of all the foreign dispatches as soon as they came in; whereas 'the other Secretary [*i.e.* Pitt himself] is not so minute; and that does not please'. The last words of course refer to Pitt's letters to Bute, supplying Leicester House with the latest news from the various war-fronts.

After this Pitt discontinued his correspondence with Bute, except for an occasional routine communication. This led the Prince of Wales to write to Bute on the 8th December:

> I suppose you agree with me in thinking that as Mr. P. does not now chuse to communicate what is intended to be done, but defers it till executed, he might save himself the trouble of sending at all, as I should hear only a few days later, as well as other people, what measures have been taken.
>
> Indeed my Dearest Friend he treats both you and me with no

more regard than he would do a parcel of children, he seems to forget that the day will come, when he must expect to be treated according to his deserts.¹

On 19th December Viry told Newcastle of a further interview between Bute and Pitt, at which Bute, presumably as a result of the Prince of Wales's remarks, had

complained of Mr. P.'s reservedness in not having acquainted him with the occurrences as they had happened. Mr. P. said the reason was that most things that had passed were immaterial ; but that as to others, when he informed his Lordship of any material news, he had found that my Lord Bute had been informed of them before (viz. by my Lord Holdernesse).²

At the same interview Pitt told Bute that Newcastle would have to be included in the future government in the next reign, thus confirming the impression of Leicester House that, as the Prince of Wales put it, 'he has given himself either up to the K. or the D. of N. or else he could not act the infamous and ungrateful part he now does.' This marks the end of Pitt's 'fraternal union' with Bute and of the long personal correspondence that arose out of it, and the beginning of their total estrangement.

[1] *Letters from George III to Lord Bute*, No. 24.
[2] *Ibid.*, No. 25, and Namier, *op. cit.*, pp. 110 *et seq.*

SIR JAMES FERGUSSON OF KILKERRAN

A WINE-MERCHANT'S LETTER-BOOK

In 1950 there was deposited in Her Majesty's Register House the letter-book of a firm of wine-merchants which carried on business in the town of Ayr during the early years of George III. It was in a very tattered and fragile condition and had lost one or two of its opening pages and portions of others; but on being repaired and rebound it could be thoroughly examined, and turned out to be of unusual interest. It covers only four and a half years, from the autumn of 1766 to the early months of 1771; but even in that brief period the business of the firm, Alexander Oliphant and Company, ranged from Stirlingshire to Barcelona, touched many social levels, and dealt with several other commodities besides wine.

The firm was founded in 1766, and the names of the eight partners were recorded some years later in a bond registered in the Books of Council and Session.[1] Four of them, Alexander Oliphant himself, John Christian, George McCree and Robert Whiteside, were merchants in Ayr; the other four were small lairds — Gilbert McAdam of Merkland, Dr. John Campbell of Wellwood, William Logan of Castlemains and David McClure of Shawwood. McCree and Christian shortly became landed proprietors also; for McCree, in 1770, bought Pitcon, in the parish of Dalry, from the last of the Boyds of that name; and Christian, in 1772, bought the little estate of Cunningpark, near the mouth of the Doon, from Captain Hew Whitefoord Dalrymple.[2] By 1774 no less than five of the eight partners were on the roll

[1] Register of Deeds, vol. 238, part i (Durie), f. 497.
[2] Paterson's *History of Ayrshire* (1863), iii. 189; i. 142.

of parliamentary voters for Ayrshire, who at that time numbered only 128.

The group touches the circles of both Burns and Boswell. David McClure of Shawwood was the man who, as Burns admitted, 'sat for the picture' of the harsh factor in *The Twa Dogs*,[1] and Dr. Campbell was the brother-in-law of John Ranken or Rankine of Adamhill, to whom he wrote one of the most outspoken of his *Epistles*. Dr. Campbell also attended Mrs. Boswell in her last illness.[2] Boswell knew Gilbert McAdam and many of his near relations.[3] The firm's customers, moreover, included several of Boswell's acquaintance.

Although the beginning of the book has been destroyed by damp, it is clear that it began with the firm's inauguration. On 24 October 1766 a correspondent was told, 'We have not yet engaged a wine cooper, and as our cellars are not finish'd and consequently our stock not laid in, we will not have occasion for one for a while'. By early December, however, a cooper had been engaged, and the cellar was built — though actually above ground, and, says one letter, 'on a sand bank'. It was on sloping ground with an easy approach to its entrance from the harbour. It is still in use to-day, and still holds wine.

By the spring of 1767 business was already brisk. Alexander Oliphant and Company seem to have aimed at building up a connexion all over the south-west of Scotland. Before long they also had customers in the north of England, and through an agent in Greenock were exporting wine to the West Indies. But their main business evidently lay between Clyde and Solway. Besides their headquarters at Ayr, they had cellars of their own in Glasgow, Kilmarnock, Moffat and Stranraer. In 1770 they were negotiating for another in Lanark, and also writing detailed instructions to their agents in Greenock, Robert and Alexander Sinclair:

---

[1] *Letters of Robert Burns*, ed. Ferguson, i. 107.
[2] *Private Papers of James Boswell*, xv. 145-6 ; xvii. 44, 111, 117, 150-1, 159.
[3] Ibid., vii. 122, 132 ; i. 57-60.

We hope you have got a good cellar to keep the wine in, so that it will be cool in summer and pretty warm in winter. You shou'd have catacombs in the cellar and the wine shou'd be pack'd on the side of the bottles with sarvings of timber.

It was probably due to the social standing of some of the partners that the firm seems to have built up very quickly an extremely promising connexion with many well-known families. Some of their customers were wealthy, and must have entertained on a large scale. One of the first was the duke of Montrose. In October 1766 his chamberlain was ordering on his behalf two hogsheads of claret; and three years later he ordered three hogsheads. The second consignment was ordered after the firm had sent six bottles of claret 'for a tryal', with the message, 'The wine we propose sending is very old and don't doubt it will please his Grace's taste'. The six bottles were sent by Thomas Hunter, carrier, 'with directions to leave it with the Buchanan carrier at Mr. John Scott's in the new wynd in the Trongate, Glasgow'.

Lord Marchmont was another customer, who, in September 1767, was sent seventy-five dozen of claret and madeira; and William Mure of Caldwell, Baron of Exchequer, was another who liked to order his claret by the hogshead — 'which', wrote Alexander Oliphant, 'we shall be carefull in the choice of, and hope it will please your taste'. Another Baron of Exchequer, John Maule of Inverkeilor, formerly M.P. for Aberdeen burghs; Patrick Craufurd of Auchenames, a former member for Ayrshire; the earls of Cassillis and Dumfries and Sir Thomas Dunlop of Craigie were other customers who had large accounts with Alexander Oliphant and Company. Sir John Cathcart of Killochan appears once, with an order for a puncheon of rum.

Before the firm had been in existence for more than a few months, the partners decided to build a ship of their own in which to fetch their consignments of wine to Ayr. In April 1767 they placed an order with an Ayr shipbuilder named John Fraser. The ship, a sloop of fifty tons, was built in the course of that summer and launched in October. She cost

£600 and was named the *Buck*. It was fortunate that she was ready so soon, for in December the company had news that the *Nelly*, Captain Brackenridge, on which they had apparently been depending hitherto for their cargoes from abroad, had run ashore in the West Indies, during a voyage from Madeira to Ayr by way of New York. She had had fifteen pipes of madeira on board consigned to Alexander Oliphant and Company, and they lost over £700 worth of goods in her and only recovered some £200 through insurance.

The *Buck*, however, which made her maiden voyage to Cadiz and Madeira in the spring of 1768, served her owners well. The skipper, after the first voyage, was one Captain William McRae, and he seems to have been conscientious and skilful. The letter-book contains copies of his sailing orders and also of the orders he carried with him to the company's agents in Madeira, Cadiz, Lisbon, Oporto, Barcelona, Bordeaux and Guernsey, from which a very fair idea can be had of the *Buck's* cargoes, and occasional glimpses of what sort of passages she had. Sixteen days was reckoned a good passage from Lisbon to Ayr.

The one misfortune the firm suffered through the *Buck*, as far as the letter-book's evidence shows, was the fault of neither the company nor Captain McRae. It happened in the early summer of 1769. The company heard from their agents at Oporto that their ship had been seized by the Portuguese customs authorities, as 'some of the scoundrels of sailors' had been smuggling tobacco on board. The agents managed in a few days to get the ship cleared, but the sailors were detained in prison, and when the news got to Ayr the company seem to have been a good deal embarrassed by the clamour of their relations round the office doors. They wrote to the agents asking if it would be of any use to raise a fund in Ayr for the men's release; but this plan apparently hung fire. The following February a letter repeats, 'The sailors' wives are very uneasy about their husbands'. In March the agents found means at last to get the men out of jail, having apparently advanced the money for their fine — unless

A Wine-Merchant's Letter-Book

perhaps a bribe to the authorities worked equally well. It was not, however, until June that Alexander Oliphant and Company heard about it, and then they wrote,

We wish you could have let us know before the sailors were set at liberty what sum would have been expected as we doubt it will not now be so easily got, however we will try what can be done.

The names of several other ships besides the *Buck* appear in the correspondence, such as the *Peggy*, the *Hercules*, the *Greyhound*, the *Mally* and the *Flora*. The two most picturesque of these names are the *Seaflower* and the *Charming Molly*, a brig from Bristol. One skipper bore a name that might have inspired Stevenson — that of Captain Hannibal Lusk.

The *Flora*, a Greenock brig, came to a sad end in the bay of Ayr on the 8th of December 1770, and her fate is described in one of the longest letters in the book, written by Alexander Oliphant and Company to her owner, Mr. James Gammell.

We are extremely sorry to advise you of your brig Captain Francis's misfortune in being forc'd on shore here this morning in a hard gale of wind at north-west about 10 o'clock and about half-flood. The sea was so high that it was some time before any body could think of going off to her which a few sailors did at last at the risque of their lives in order to save the people on board. They got 3 seamen on shore but the captain, mate and boy refus'd quitting the vessel so that [they] continued from that time till about 4 o'clock in [a ver]y distress'd situation being almost constantly under water till the people on shore ventur'd again off with the boat and brought the captain and boy ashore but the mate was dead, occasion'd by fatigue and the severity of the weather. We are much afraid the brig will be loss'd as we hear she is bulg'd, but are hopeful a good part or all of the cargoe will be sav'd except what may be damag'd by salt water. We shall do what lyes in our power to preserve both ship and cargoe and have employ'd some good hands to get what they can out of her this night as soon as the tide leaves her. We apply'd to the captain for what letters or other papers he might have for you, but he says they are all on board in his chest and must be all wett. As soon as they can be got at he will get them dry'd.

The company proved themselves good friends to the *Flora*'s owner, arranging for a cooper to help in landing and securing the goods, 'also a sergeant's command to watch them and keep off all pilferers'. A fortnight later they offered advice against selling the wreck 'by publick auction', and recommended John Fraser, the builder of the *Buck*, if Mr. Gammell proposed building a new ship to replace the *Flora*, suggesting that in that case Fraser would probably give a price for what remained of her, which was apparently her dismasted hull.

To any historian of the Scottish wine trade Alexander Oliphant and Company's letter-book would certainly be of great value for its evidence of the kind of wines which were in favour in the age of Boswell. As might be expected, claret predominates; and it is interesting to read how such famous names of to-day as St. Julien, Cantenac and Margaux were equally esteemed then. Port and madeira were alike evidently popular. The company ordered thirty pipes of port of the '67 vintage in November 1768. White port, sherry, malaga, canary and various red Spanish and white Portuguese wines also figure among their orders, but burgundy very little, and champagne hardly at all. Nor does there seem to have been any demand for Rhine or Moselle wines, except for that favourite tipple of Boswell's, old hock. The company ordered some old hock in July 1768, through their agent in Guernsey, and two years later sent an order direct to an agent in Hamburg, as follows:

By the recommendation of our friend Mr. Charles Fergusson in London [1] we use the freedom to apply to you for some old hock. He mentions that his house in Madeira propos'd sending a vessell to your place this season and hope this may yet overtake her with you. If so you'l please ship on board of her for our account one hundred doz. of old hock. We beg you'l send it good and address it to the care of Messrs. Fergusson and Murdoch in Madeira. . . . Mr. Fergusson says they had some from you which was esteem'd very good.

[1] Younger brother of Sir Adam Fergusson of Kilkerran, later M.P. for Ayrshire.

A Wine-Merchant's Letter-Book

A letter of a month later mentioned that the company hoped to buy the old hock at two shillings a bottle, but were willing to go up to two and sixpence. This was quite a high price, for when the price of port went up to 18s. a dozen the company reckoned it an 'extraordinary rise'. Port, sherry and malaga were all in much the same class as regards price, along with the light Spanish and Portuguese wines, which included 'Packarete, a pleasant sweet wine', 'Methuen, a light red wine', and 'White Carcavella'. The expensive wines were madeira and claret; and the 'very old' claret sold to the duke of Montrose was charged at £30 a hogshead, 'with bottles, corks and all other charges except carriage', or £31 : 10s. inclusive. The company's stock clarets were retailed in bottles at prices ranging from 46s. down to 30s. a dozen. These were high prices, but of course the clarets for which they were charged were all vintage wines. The evidence of the letter-book need not be taken as disproving the well-known assertions of all the English travellers in eighteenth-century Scotland about the goodness and remarkable cheapness of claret in all the Scottish inns. Such wine was evidently of the non-vintage kind, as might be expected.

The company did not deal much in spirits. They wrote to their Bordeaux agent in January 1769, 'We find brandy will not do here'— the reason, presumably, being that smugglers could always undersell them. The Clyde coast from Fairlie to Girvan was notorious for the activity of smugglers. Once at least the company ordered some arrack through their Lisbon agent. In whisky they did not deal at all. At this date it was not drunk in the Lowlands.

But the *Buck* carried a good many other things in her hold besides wine. The company dabbled, at various times, in importing salt, fruit, grain, meat and silk. 'We do a great deal of business in the corn trade', they wrote in 1770. Occasionally they seem even to have chartered the *Buck* to other firms for short voyages: thus in November 1769 she was carrying a cargo of lead from Creetown to Dublin — it had probably come down on packhorses from the old mines at Wanlockhead. Once they sent the *Buck* out to Lisbon ballasted with coal, 'which', they told their agent, 'please sell and credit us the proceeds'. She seldom returned from abroad without various interesting goods stowed among the wine-barrels. One special order to the Bordeaux agent in December 1769 was for burgundy, champagne, 'the oldest and best claret that can be got', cork-wood, vinegar, olives, oil, silk gloves and mittens, anchovies and 'St. Catherine's prunes'. And in September 1770, when Captain McRae sailed for Cadiz, with orders to load wine, cork-wood — 'as much cork-wood as will stow the cargoe'— lemons, sweet and bitter oranges, and 'raisins of the sun' or sultanas, he carried also with him this curious request to the Cadiz agent:

> Please send as much strip'd lutestring as will make a gown for a lusty woman. We suppose Cadiz is a good place for buying silk.

The letter-book naturally contains many orders for the essentials of a wine-merchant's business: cork-wood, bottles, and wax for sealing the corks — red, green, black and yellow. Bottles gave the company a good deal of trouble. They got them first from Glasgow, but their cooper complained that the Glasgow manufacturer made the mouths so large that 'there is no getting corks large enough to stop them'. They next tried a firm in Bristol, from which they ordered 100 gross 'for a tryal', to be sent in the brig the *Charming Molly*; and then three Liverpool firms in turn. None of these manufacturers seems to have been dependable enough to supply bottles of the exact shapes and sizes asked; and Alexander Oliphant and Company had in particular great difficulty in getting their favourite size of bottles — 'long thirteens'. 'What we mean by 13's', they wrote to the Bristol firm, 'is 13 bottles to hold 3 gallons, but those you sent us are all quarts.'

They had other difficulties too. In 1770 there was an appearance in Galloway and Carrick of forged banknotes, the first of which reached the company in a remittance from their agent in Stranraer. Some customers, again, were very slow in paying their accounts. Sir Thomas Wallace of

Craigie at one time owed the company over £70,[1] and Lord Dumfries over £125.

Some other troubles were probably due to the partners' inexperience in the wine trade. Despite constantly telling their agents abroad, 'We must have the best. . . . We depend on your care in choosing the wine. . . . We beg you'l send good wine. You must know how material it is to have our wines of equal quality to our neighbours',' they seem to have been several times badly or dishonestly served. Lord Cassillis, Baron Mure, Baron Maule and Patrick Craufurd of Auchenames all complained about the quality of certain clarets supplied to them. Some at least of this wine must have come through the Belfast agent with whom the company had dealt in their early months, and to whom they complained in August 1768 that of the last two consignments from Belfast most of the bottles were 'prick'd', and the rest 'very ill tasted'. To some of their customers Alexander Oliphant and Company apologized, and took the bad wine back; but to Mr. Craufurd of Auchenames they protested,

We are convinc'd that if the wine had been used in time it would have pleas'd well but it is loss'd merely by being too long kept for wine of that body. It was in very good order for drinking when we sent it away. . . . It was exceeding well lik'd and much in demand.

A month later they took back two dozen of claret from Baron Maule, declaring at the same time, 'It is the only wine ever we took back but what was sold in bottles and seal'd with our own seal, and return'd so'.

But the main cause of the company's ultimate downfall seems to have been simply bad financial management. They had their fingers in too many pies, and from the very beginning seem to have been carrying a large load of debt, increased, perhaps, by the loss of the *Nelly* and the building of the *Buck*. Before the company was two years old it was risking its credit in other ventures. A letter of April 1768 says, 'We are now

[1] Register of Deeds, vol. 247 (Durie), f. 810.

considerably in advance for the cost of the grain got from Ireland and little money coming in'. A few months later the partners describe themselves as 'disappointed in some sums we thought to receive', and negotiating with Mr. John Bushby in Dumfries for a loan of £3000, 'on the joint security of our whole company'. Early in 1770 they were uneasy about the import duty they were having to pay on French wine, their principal stock-in-trade, and toying with a subterfuge for avoiding it. This is revealed in a letter to their agent in Barcelona:

> Pray is it practicable to import wine into your place from the south of France . . . and if so what duty or other charges on it with you and could that wine be ship'd again with you for Brittain as Spanish wine by this manner to save the extravagant high duty which those kind of French wines will not bear? If this could be done it must be unknown to the captain of the vessell who takes it. . . . Pray let this be between ourselves. . . .

They were nervous in November 1770 about the risk of sending the *Buck* to Portugal in view of the possibility of 'a rupture' with France, though hoping there would not be 'a warr for some time'. But the mortal wound was received three years later through the failure of Douglas, Heron and Company's bank, which closed its doors, after a spectacular career of less than four years, on 12 August 1773. The bank, like the wine company, was an Ayr venture which had spread its activities over a good deal of the south-west of Scotland; and its collapse involved in its ruin a large number of west country lairds and many small business firms. Alexander Oliphant and Company were only one of 'a variety of enterprising companies, engaged in different kinds of foreign and domestic trade . . . all of them closely connected or linked together' and 'all of them partners of Douglas, Heron and Company'.[1] When the bank failed, Alexander Oliphant and Company could not hope to carry on.

The partners suffered individually. John Christian had to raise money by a bond on his newly acquired estate of

[1] Paterson, *op. cit.*, i. 38-40.

A Wine-Merchant's Letter-Book

Cunningpark, which was sold a few years later at the instance of the bank's creditors. Dr. Campbell of Wellwood was 'stripped of nearly all he possessed' and was obliged to sell his family estate.[1] So was Gilbert McAdam, who on his death in 1788 left many debts and no assets but a gold watch.[2] McClure of Shawwood was in financial difficulties in 1783 when he was pressing Robert Burns's father for the arrears of the rent of Lochlie.[3] None the less, the firm seem to have carried on for a while. In 1774 they were borrowing the sum of £1100 from Archibald Craufurd of Ardmillan.[4] But that seems to have been their last effort, and their affairs were shortly in the hands of trustees for behoof of their creditors, Ardmillan being one of the trustees.[5] They must have given up business soon afterwards, but their stock and goodwill were evidently bought by another wine-merchant, for their premises, like their letter-book, ultimately came into the possession of the later, and still flourishing, firm of wine-merchants who presented this record of their predecessors' activities to the Scottish Record Office.

[1] *Ibid.* pp. 142, 612.
[2] Glasgow Testaments, vol. 70, ff. 803-4.
[3] Hans Hecht, *Robert Burns*, 1936, pp. 46-7.
[4] Register of Deeds, vol. 238, part i (Durie), f. 497.
[5] *Ibid.* vol. 242, part i (Dalrymple), f. 689.

WILMARTH S. LEWIS

HORACE WALPOLE, ANTIQUARY

THE subject of English antiquarianism in the eighteenth century is one that has had relatively little attention. That admirable compendium, *Johnson's England*, 1933, has no chapter devoted to it, nor is there any reference to English antiquarianism in the index. As early as 1811 Scott, in the introduction to his edition of *The Castle of Otranto*, said that Walpole's taste for English antiquities was then uncommon. How mistaken he was, became plain in the following year when the first volumes of Nichols's *Literary Anecdotes of the Eighteenth Century* were published. There were in all nine volumes of *Anecdotes*, and they were followed by eight volumes of *Illustrations of the Literary History of the Eighteenth Century*. Those seventeen volumes of some seven million words are given over exclusively to antiquaries, the parsons and country gentlemen who communicated their discoveries and speculations to one another with a fervour that might at any time burst into flames. In that set Horace Walpole was an eager and, on the whole, respected visitor.

What did the eighteenth century mean by 'antiquary'? Johnson is not very helpful. In his *Dictionary*, 1755, he said that an antiquary was 'a man studious of antiquity; a collector of ancient things'. And what was 'antiquity'? 'Old times,' said Johnson, 'time past, long ago.' The *Encyclopaedia Britannica*, 1771, adds little except to observe that antiquarian researches, 'unless they are conducted with judgment, are extremely liable to ridicule'. The Introduction to the first volume of *Archaeologia*, which was published by the Society of Antiquaries in 1770, is more instructive. The antiquary was one 'who will never be deemed an unserviceable member of the community, whilst curiosity or the love of truth subsists; and least of all, in an age wherein every part of science is advancing to perfection, and in a nation not afraid of penetrating into the remotest periods of their origin'.[1] This last is significant. 'Ancient things' might be Egyptian, Greek, Roman or Etruscan objects of art or utility, but as the century progressed 'antiquarianism' became more and more associated with the British past, in spite of the uncovering of Herculaneum and Pompeii, and the researches of Robert Wood, Stuart, Revett and others. Of the sixty-three contributions to the 1770 volume of *Archaeologia* fifty-two dealt with British antiquities; in the 1796 volume all the contributions did so. Among the subjects discussed in 1770 are the registers of the bishops of Lincoln, Leves Abbey, the crucified child at Lincoln and 'A Roman Inscription upon a Rock at Shawk'. The earliest subject in the volume is 'On the First Peopling of this Island'; the latest is the miraculous victory over the Irish in 1641. As the century wore on the range of antiquarianism became wider and wider. There were still those who concerned themselves with Romans and Druids, but there were more who wrote on architecture, sculpture, painting, poetry, music, heraldry and genealogy, dress, money, customs and other matters that reveal the life of former ages in Britain.

Horace Walpole did not find these articles of equal interest. 'A barbarous country, so remote from the seat of empire, and occupied by a few legions, that very rarely decided any great events, is not very interesting, though one's own country — nor do I care a straw for the stone that preserves the name of a standard bearer of a cohort or of a colonel's daughter. . . . I do not say that the Gothic antiquities that I like are of more importance; but at least they exist. . . . How often does it happen that the lumps of earth are so imperfect, that it is never clear, whether they are Roman, Druidic, Danish, or

[1] *Archaeologia*, 1770, i. 2. The author was Richard Gough (Nichols, *Literary Anecdotes*, vi. 4 n.).

Saxon fragments — the moment it is uncertain, it is plain they furnish no specific idea of art or history, and then I neither desire to see or read of them.' 'Ideas of art and history' were what Walpole sought in antiquities.

He pursued the study of them in four ways, by collecting, by visits to country houses and churches, by building and remodelling, and by his publications and correspondence. For him the attraction of this study lay in its biographical, aesthetic and romantic aspects; above all, antiquarianism was for him an exercise in the patriotic and entertaining demonstration of England's past (and present) greatness. His patriotic motive was not singular, as Dr. Johnson showed in the *Rambler*, in which he ridiculed antiquaries and collectors.[1]

I

As one turns the pages of Walpole's *Description of Strawberry Hill* and the *Catalogue of the Classic Contents of Strawberry Hill Collected by Horace Walpole*, 1842 (the sale catalogue), one gets an impression of indiscriminate clutter. The walls were crowded with pictures and drawings, the closets and cabinets were filled with china, glass, snuff-boxes and curiosities of every sort. Gradually one can sort out and put together certain accumulations of cognate pieces that may be described as collections.

Like most eighteenth-century collectors, Walpole's first serious collecting was of classical antiquities. 'I am far gone in medals, lamps, idols', he wrote to Conway from Rome in 1740, 'I would buy the Coliseum if I could', but with the purchase in 1743 of Conyers Middleton's extensive collection, his concentration on classical antiquities came to an end.

Walpole had already begun his second big collection, coins and medals; on the Grand Tour he bought 'a silver medal; on one side the head of Queen Mary of England, on the other, of Philip 2d', a trial-piece, and 'certainly the finest

[1] Number 177, 26 Nov. 1751.

modern medal known'.[1] In 1742 at Lord Oxford's sale of coins and medals he bought many of the best pieces in the English series, purchases that made him, at the age of twenty-four, one of the leading English virtuosi. He was elected F.R.S. in 1747 and F.S.A. in 1753. His sponsors at the latter Society were Lord Fitzwilliam, Charles Lyttelton, Henry Baker, George Vertue and Joseph Ames. Sir Hans Sloane appointed him one of the original trustees of the British Museum in 1751.

Among the English collections that he formed during the next fifty-odd years high place should be given to his miniatures and enamels. This collection he believed was 'the largest and finest in any country. His Majesty has some very fine, the Duke of Portland more; in no other is to be seen, in any good preservation, any number of the works of Isaac and Peter Oliver.'[2] Holbein, Nicholas Hilliard and Samuel Cooper were also well represented at Strawberry Hill.

Then there were the drawings and prints, many hundreds in all, together with the drawings and prints of portraits of English painters and engravers that Vertue had collected, and Vertue's notebooks. These materials, which Walpole bought from Vertue's widow in 1758, formed the basis of his *Anecdotes of Painting in England*. Before and after he acquired them Walpole collected engraved English heads, several thousand of them, which the Strawberry Hill sale catalogue called 'unquestionably the most complete collection that has ever been made', and which may have been so, if the cataloguer meant a collection confined to the efforts of one person. It took ten days to sell them in 1842 (included with them were books of prints). The prints were arranged by reigns, beginning with, no less, King Arthur. This was the most extensive and complete of Walpole's collections.

There were upwards of five hundred county histories and books of British topography at Strawberry Hill. As with all

---

[1] Walpole, 'Description of Strawberry Hill', Lord Orford's *Works*, 1798, ii. 450.   [2] *Ibid.* 396.

his books, Walpole bought them as a reader, not as a collector; he did not collect books as he collected coins and prints, mindful of first issues and states. His copies of Stowe's *Chronicles*, *Annals* and *Survey* were the third, second and fourth editions respectively. He had Kennett's *Parochial Antiquities*, 1695, but not Lambarde's *Perambulation of Kent*, 1576. His edition of Dugdale's *Warwickshire* was the second, his *St. Paul's* the first. Which edition he had of the earlier antiquarian books seems to have been a matter of indifference to him. He bought most of the topographical books that came out during his lifetime. 'I am sorry I have such predilection for the histories of particular counties and towns: there certainly does not exist a worse class of reading.' He read these books carefully and annotated them. In some, his marginalia are merely pencilled marks of approval or disapproval; in others, there are extensive notes, chiefly of a biographical nature; in still others his remarks overflow on to separate sheets, which he had bound into the book.

Walpole supplemented his county and family histories with a small miscellaneous collection of manuscripts. The most important of these were probably Sir Julius Caesar's papers, letters and accounts, Orders of Council, etc., of the time of James I and Charles I, but of greater interest to Walpole were his heraldic and genealogical manuscripts and visitations, particularly those relating to Norfolk and Suffolk. 'I am the first antiquary of my race — people don't know how entertaining a study it is. Who begot whom is a most amusing kind of hunting; one recovers a grandfather instead of breaking one's own neck — and then one grows so pious to the memory of a thousand persons one never heard of before.' Genealogic and heraldic manuscripts were his hunting field. On the fly-leaf of one of them now in my possession he noted, probably in 1777, that on three later pages 'are wills of three Bacons of Hesset in Suffolk, who were my ancestors; Callybot Walpole, who died 1646, married Elizabeth Bacon of Hesset. H. W.' In the last year of his life he added, 'I am descended from the Bacons

Horace Walpole, Antiquary

of Hesset. Hor. de Orford, 1796.' His first attempt to write this ended in a smudge, but he tried again and carefully and laboriously succeeded in transmitting his note to posterity.

II

As early as 1736, when Walpole was only eighteen years old, he recorded visits to Wrest, Cornbury, Althorp, Easton Neston and Blenheim. At Cornbury he found 'a prodigious quantity of Vandykes, but I had not time to take down any of their dresses'. He continued such visits and comment as long as he lived, in his letters and notebooks, or 'Books of Materials', as he called them. In the latter are notes on upwards of eighty country houses visited between 1758 and 1784.[1] He made no attempt to travel all over Britain; he was never in Scotland or Wales, or several counties in England. The accident of where his friends lived largely determined which houses he saw. The Straffords in Yorkshire, George Montagu in Northamptonshire, George Selwyn at Gloucester, account for his seeing the houses in their neighbourhoods. Had Lord Carlisle lived in Northumberland and Lord Edgcumbe in West Cornwall, Walpole doubtless would have seen Alnwick and Michael's Mount, but as it was, he never got north of Castle Howard or farther west than Mount Edgcumbe.

He was very keen about what he did see. All country houses had their surprises, whether or not they had 'the true rust of the Barons' Wars'. One entered them for the first time with an expectation that was seldom disappointed. The owners had played at least a local part in the ruling of England and had their place in the great panorama of English history. Their houses were filled with the tacit assumptions of earlier generations. The pursuit and discovery of these hidden clues were perhaps the chief pleasure of antiquarianism. Gardens, furniture, pictures, all contributed their answers. And one

---

[1] They were printed by Paget Toynbee in vol. xvi of *The Walpole Society* (Oxford, 1928), pp. 9-80, 'Horace Walpole's Journals of Visits to Country Seats'.

could never tell when one might unearth a Holbein or Vandyke or Mabeuse. Walpole made discoveries of notable pictures everywhere, even at Kensington Palace, when, in the absence of his sister, the housekeeper, he was in superintendence. England was a virtually unexplored paradise for the antiquarian collector.

Only occasionally did he uncover family papers, which is odd in view of his interest in family histories and his delight in the few discoveries — or 'recoveries', as he more properly called them — of such papers as he did make. Chief among them were the Conway papers at Ragley, where in the lumber room he found what was left after the depredations of damp, rats and an ignorant steward.

His interest in churches centred in their monuments, whose they were, whether they were plain, pretty, 'genteel', or 'fine', and whether they had any particular feature worth noting, a pulpit, perhaps, with friars around it, a wainscot roof with roses in stars. The importance of tombs could not be exaggerated, 'for you know the great delicacy and richness of Gothic ornaments was exhausted on small chapels, oratories and tombs'. Walpole made this discovery at the outset of his antiquarian career. 'Ornament' was what was illustrated in the remodelled Strawberry Hill.

III

The remodelling of Strawberry Hill was inspired by Walpole's antiquarian researches. The original cottage was built in 1698. When he rented it in 1747 Walpole described it as 'the prettiest bauble you ever saw', a character not sustained by his sketches of it. Two and a half years later he wrote Mann, 'I am going to build a little Gothic castle at Strawberry Hill. If you can pick me up any fragments of old painted glass, arms, or anything, I shall be exceedingly obliged to you.'

This last indicates the eclectic nature of the undertaking. Bits and fragments were to be picked up here and there and stuck into and upon the house, which was to be composed of details copied from Gothic models. To help him in this task Walpole formed 'The Committee on Taste', which included, besides himself, John Chute (1701–76) of the Vyne, Basingstoke, and Richard Bentley (1708–82), son of the Master of Trinity. Chute's recently discovered drawings for the improvements at Strawberry Hill make it clear that he played a major part in its design, but Bentley was the chief draughtsman of the earlier rooms, those built between 1750 and 1761. His and Chute's drawings, with Walpole's *Description of Strawberry Hill*, 1784, and certain of the books from his library, show us how the house was put together, room by room.

The *Description* tells us, 'You first enter a small gloomy hall . . . hung with Gothic paper, painted by one Tudor, from the screen of Prince Arthur's tomb in the Cathedral of Worcester'. When Walpole went to Worcester shortly after the paper was on the wall he was surprised to find that the tomb was on a smaller scale than the paper and was not of brass but stone. What the Committee on Taste had done was to study two books at Strawberry Hill, Sandford's *Genealogical History of the Kings of England*, 1677, the plate at page 447 (which bears their annotations), and the plate on page 38 in Thomas's *Survey of the Cathedral Church of Worcester*, 1737. In other rooms the sources of various features are stated in the *Description*: Chute's bookcases in the library were copied from the side doors of the choir of old St. Paul's as shown in Dugdale's *St. Paul's Cathedral*, 1658, page 168; the chimney-piece was from Dart's *Westminster*, 1742, page 106; its stone work was imitated from the tomb of Thomas, duke of Clarence, at Canterbury, as seen in Dart's *Canterbury*, 1725, page 67, and so on.[1]

Walpole and his two friends were not alone in their attempt to revive the Gothic style, but the Committee on Taste believed that the others who were attempting to build in it

[1] Further details may be found in my 'Genesis of Strawberry Hill', *Metropolitan Museum Studies*, vol. v, part i, June 1934, pp. 57-92.

were, for the most part, fumblers who did not understand the science. They did not go, as did the Committee, to the prints of authentic Gothic structures, and so they were not on solid ground. What the Committee created was a museum in which was displayed 'genuine' Gothic architecture. More than thirty years after the Committee was formed, Walpole wrote in his preface to the *Description* that that work was perhaps excusable because it exhibited 'specimens of Gothic architecture, as collected from standards in cathedrals and chapel-tombs' and showed 'how they may be applied to chimney-pieces, ceilings, windows, balustrades, loggias, &c. The general disuse of Gothic architecture, and the decay and alterations so frequently made in churches, give prints a chance of being the sole preservatives of that style.' Walpole believed that 'the designs of the inside and outside [of Strawberry] are strictly ancient', but he did not mean, he said, to make his house 'so Gothic as to exclude convenience and modern refinements in luxury'. A line had to be drawn somewhere. Strawberry Hill was a pasticcio in which students of taste might learn to appreciate and adapt the beautiful earlier English architecture to everyday living.

The success of these methods was acknowledged by all who saw them; the inappropriateness of converting a tomb to a chimney-piece does not seem to have been noted. Walpole's help was sought by his lay and clerical friends in redesigning their houses, adorning their gardens, and re-modelling their churches. In the collection of Bentley's drawings and designs that Walpole pasted into a folio notebook are sketches not only for Strawberry Hill, but for other houses: a design 'of a fictitious steeple for Nich. Hardinge Esq. at Kingston' (the Gothic steeple was tacked on to the roof of what appears to be a Georgian house); 'The Priory of St. Hubert, a farm belonging to the Countess of Suffolk at Marble Hill near Twickenham'; a 'Gateway designed for Dr. Trevor, Bishop of Durham'. The Committee on Taste also provided Gothic garden seats for their friends, the most striking one by Bentley being for 'Lord Strafford's Menagerie at Wentworth Castle, Yorkshire, 1756'. The idea for this, Walpole explained, he got from Chichester Cross. Chute was also busy at Hagley, at his own house and at Chaucer's Grove.

The clergy turned to Walpole for help. Bishop Mawson of Ely, having decided 'to rummage among the old tombs and antiquities', and having, with the Chapter, put up £2000 to ornament the cathedral, applied to Walpole for advice about the east window. Walpole gave such satisfaction that his name was later invoked in a quarrel that divided the Chapter on the subject of replacing the organ. When he was consulted by the bishop of Rochester and dean of Westminster about an altar-piece for the choir at Westminster he came up with 'an octagon canopy of open arches', another invocation of Chichester Cross. What had proved so successful as a menagerie in Lord Stafford's garden at Wentworth was 'to be elevated on a flight of steps, with the altar in the middle, and semi-circular arcades to join the stalls, so that the Confessor's chapel and tombs may be seen through in perspective'. It is perhaps as well for Walpole's posthumous reputation that his proposal was not executed.

One pious act of restoration was accomplished. On visiting York Minster in 1772 Walpole found the tomb and figure of Edward II's second son, William of Hatfield, 'thrown aside into a hole'. He persuaded William Mason to help restore it, and it may be seen to-day in the westernmost bay of the north aisle.[1]

IV

Walpole's most ambitious antiquarian books were *A Catalogue of the Royal and Noble Authors of England with Lists of Their Works*, 2 volumes, 1758; *Anecdotes of Painting in England*, and *A Catalogue of Engravers*, 5 volumes, 1762–71; and *Historic Doubts on the Life and Reign of Richard the Third*, 1768.

The epigraph on the title-page of the first volume of the

The Cathedral Church of York, ed. F. Harrison (1931), pp. 129-30.

Royal and Noble Authors is '*Dove, diavolo! Messer Ludovico, Avete pigliato tante coglionerie?*' a question that gave Walpole a chance in his Advertisement to explain and apologize:

> How many German, Dutch, and other heralds have marshalled authors in this manner ! Balthazar Bonifacius made a collection of such as had been in love with statues; Ravisius Textor, of such as have died laughing; Vossius, of chronologers: Bartholinus, of Physicians who have been poets. There are catalogues of modern Greek poets; of illustrious bastards; of translators; of Frenchmen who have studied Hebrew; of all the authors bred at Oxford, by Antony Wood; and of all British writers in general by Bale, Pitts, and Bishop Tanner.

Walpole had made up his book largely from the works of noble authors on his own shelves, the less than five months that he spent in writing it having left him little time for more extended researches. He printed 300 copies of the book at his press at Strawberry Hill. Within a year Dodsley brought out a second edition of 2000 copies. Walpole made a few corrections and additions that were suggested by Dalrymple and Zouch, but, as he was fond of pointing out, he was not one to revise. Five later editions were subsequently printed. For a century after its first appearance 'Walpole's Noble Authors' was to be found in every gentleman's library, and the epithets 'ingenious and elegant' became attached to his name.

His most important antiquarian work was his next one, *Anecdotes of Painting in England*. The key to it is the statement in the preface that the Walpole Society have placed in all their publications, 'This country, which does not always err in vaunting its own productions'. The remainder of the sentence reads, 'This country . . . has not a single volume to show on the works of its painters'. The *Anecdotes* was a pioneer work whose inspiration owed much to patriotism. Its full title is *Anecdotes of Painting in England; With some Account of the Principal Artists; and incidental Notes on other Arts; Collected by the late Mr. George Vertue; and now digested and published from his original MSS by Mr. Horace*

Walpole. Thirty-nine volumes of Vertue's manuscripts were in the collection that Walpole bought from his widow in 1758. They are a jumble of notes, invaluable and unreadable. Walpole spent, in all, about a year and a half turning them into five orderly volumes (including the *Catalogue of Engravers*), which he printed at his press, 1762-71. His achievement may now be gauged, since thirty-three of the notebooks (which are now in the British Museum) have been printed by the Walpole Society. Reviewing the first volume in a signed article in *The Times Literary Supplement*,[1] the late Mrs. Esdaile pointed out that 'though scholars have long treated the *Anecdotes of Painting*, that solid achievement based on the inchoate notebooks of George Vertue, as the ultimate authority on the subject of English art, its author is too often spoken of as a mere gentleman amateur. Yet few professed scholars have achieved so great a task in so brief a time.' Publication of Vertue's notebooks has borne out Lionel Cust's statement in 1914, that 'an examination of the actual manuscripts themselves will justify in full the extraordinary importance of the work achieved by Horace Walpole', which 'laid the foundations for an historical study of the Fine Arts in England'.[2]

The *Anecdotes* brought Walpole a still greater reputation as an antiquary, and many new correspondents. Of these, two are noteworthy.

The first was the Rev. William Cole, the Cambridge Anthony Wood, the dean of mid-eighteenth-century antiquaries, who bequeathed to the British Museum the 114 volumes of antiquarian manuscripts that he called 'my wife and children'. In the 'forties and 'fifties he and Walpole had probably exchanged a letter now and then (they were contemporaries at Eton and King's), but their correspondence did not begin in earnest until the *Anecdotes* were published. 'The extreme pleasure and entertainment', Cole wrote, that he had received from the *Anecdotes* called for his most grateful acknowledgements; the *Anecdotes* furnished 'a continual

---

[1] 19 March 1931.
[2] *The Third Annual Volume of the Walpole Society*, 1914, p. 122.

feast from one end to the other'. The key word here is 'entertainment'; no word that Cole could have used would have pleased Walpole as much. After this happy beginning Cole proceeded for page after page, throwing fresh light on Petruccio Ubaldini and Horatio Palavicini, Lady Danvers's tomb at Stow Nine Churches, Lord Grey rewarding the executioner of King Charles, Walker's portrait of Oliver at Horseth and many other matters. Walpole found this 'the most kind and obliging letter in the world', and thus began the correspondence that lasted until Cole's death twenty years later. Week after week and month after month letters went back and forth between Strawberry Hill or Arlington Street and Cambridgeshire, discussing the oaken head of Henry III at Oundle, the parliament held at Bury in the presence of the king on the Feast of St. Scholastica in 1446, and scores of similar subjects.

The *Anecdotes* also brought Thomas Chatterton into Walpole's life. Chatterton was only nine when the first volume appeared, but seven years later he came across a copy in an evil hour and with great discernment fastened upon the passage that would most readily convince Walpole of his competence as an antiquary and his worthiness as a correspondent, the long passage [1] where Walpole wonders if John Van Eyck learned the secret of oil painting in England. This question fascinated Walpole. He had raised it with the Society of Antiquaries in 1760 and had had no satisfactory answer to it.[2] 'Being versed a little in antiquitys,' Chatterton wrote him from Bristol, 'I have met with several Curious Manuscripts among which the following may be of Service to you in any future Edition of your truly entertaining Anecdotes of Painting.' This is the way Walpole's new antiquarian correspondences began; Chatterton might have been Hillier,

[1] *Anecdotes* (1762) i. 24-9.
[2] He printed his question in two versions at his press (Allen T. Hazen, *A Bibliography of the Strawberry Hill Press*, pp. 172-5). In 1781 Walpole paid for the publication of *A Critical Essay on Oil Painting; Proving that the Art of Painting in Oil was Known before the Pretended Discovery of John and Hubert Van Eyck*, by R. E. Raspe (better known as the author of *Baron Münchausen's Narrative of his Marvellous Travels and Campaigns in Russia*, 1786).

Henry, Gough or three dozen others. 'The following' that Chatterton enclosed was nothing less than a fifteenth-century manuscript, 'The Ryse of Peyncteynge yn Englãde, wroten bie T. Rowleie. 1469 for Mastre Canynge.' Rowleie, Chatterton said, was a 'Secular Priest whose Merit as a Biographer, Historiographer is great, as a Poet still greater'; Canynge was 'the Mecenas of his time: one who could happily blend The Poet, the Painter, the Priest and the Christian — perfect in each'. The manuscript that Chatterton sent began, 'Peyncteynge ynn Englande, haveth of ould tyme bin yn use; for saieth the Roman Wryters, The Brytonnes dyd depycte themselves, yn sondrie wyse, of the fourmes of the Soune and Moone, wythe the hearbe Woade'. It got better and better as it went on until Abbate John was reached, 'the fyrste Englyshe Paynctre yn Oyles', and, Chatterton explained in a note, 'the greatest Poet of the Age, in which he lived. . . . Take a Specimen of Poetry, On King Richard Ist.' The hook could not have been more attractively baited. Walpole replied by return post: 'I cannot but think myself singularly obliged by a gentleman with whom I have not the pleasure of being acquainted. . . . You do not point out exactly the time when [Abbot John] lived, which I wish to know, as I suppose it was long before John ab Eyck's discovery of oil painting. If so, it confirms what I had guessed, and have hinted in my *Anecdotes*, that oil painting was known here much earlier than that discovery or revival.' What followed need not be told here.[1] It will perhaps be enough to point out that one of the bright colours on the fly cast so adroitly before Walpole was patriotism.

From 1768 to 1793 *Historic Doubts on the Life and Reign of King Richard the Third* engaged Walpole intermittently in controversy with many of the most formidable critics and scholars of the day, Hume and Gibbon among them. The opening sentence of his preface was not propitiatory. 'So

---

[1] I have repeated it recently in the Introduction to volume 16 of the *Yale Walpole*, pp. xxvi-xxxi; it is given, step by step, in E. H. Meyerstein, *A Life of Thomas Chatterton* (1930).

incompetent has the generality of historians been for the province they have undertaken, that it is almost a question, whether, if the dead of past ages could revive, they would be able to reconnoitre the events of their own times, as transmitted to us by ignorance and misrepresentation.' The bias and incompetence of historians were particularly gross, Walpole observed, when dealing with the reigns of Edward IV, Richard III and Henry VII. 'The more I examined their history, the more I was confirmed in my opinion . . . that we have either no authentic memorials of Richard's crimes, or, at most, no account of them but from Lancastrian historians.' In other words, Richard had been traduced. Walpole was by nature happy in opposition. Throughout his life he was a supporter of the under-dog: Sir Robert Walpole when he fell from power, Maclean the highwayman, Theodore of Corsica, Admiral Byng, the French royal family in the Revolution, it made no difference who they were so long as they were on the losing side. His defence of Richard III was inspired by the same charitable impulse. Unfortunately, he laid himself open to attack by less emotional and more plodding students of the fifteenth century. As Mr. Ketton-Cremer has said, '*Historic Doubts* was an original and spirited piece of special pleading, but its theories were based on inadequate material, and were often supported by decidedly flimsy reasoning'.[1]

Historic Doubts was published by Dodsley, 1 February 1768, in an edition of 1200 copies; the following day the second edition of 1000 copies was begun and rushed through the press in eleven days. Cole and Walpole's other friends stood loyally by it; even Gray, who objected to certain 'inaccuracies of style', said 'as to your arguments, most are made out with a clearness and evidence that no one would expect when materials are so scarce'. Final victory, however, went to the opposition. Besides Gibbon and Hume, the book was successfully attacked by others. The Coronation Roll that the bishop of Carlisle and Thomas Astle produced for

[1] R. W. Ketton-Cremer, *Horace Walpole* (1940), p. 278.

Horace Walpole, Antiquary

Walpole as new evidence that Edward V walked at Richard's coronation, Walpole's most telling point, was shown by Dean Jeremiah Milles, president of the Society of Antiquaries, to have been not the Coronation Roll but merely a Wardrobe Account.[1] By comparison with Walpole's tone this refutation and another (which engaged the Society for two entire meetings) by the Rev. Robert Masters, rector of Landbeche in Cambridgeshire, were mild, but Walpole drew up sarcastic replies that appeared in his posthumous *Lord Orford's Works*, 1798. His answers fill sixty-six pages, almost as many as *Historic Doubts* itself. The Society of Antiquaries and *Archaeologia* became so offensive to him that he withdrew from the Society, not at once, but when Foote ridiculed it in 1772 in *The Nabob*, for sitting in council on Dick Whittington and his cat. We are not concerned here with Walpole as a person, but in the long and rather ridiculous episode of the *Historic Doubts* it may be said, I think, that he appears at his worst, both as a person and as an antiquary.

In addition to these three works Walpole published a catalogue of his father's pictures at Houghton, *Aedes Walpolianae*, 1747, and a *Description of Strawberry Hill*, 1774, 1784. The *Aedes* was by way of being a pioneer work in England. Walpole bagan work on it in his nineteenth year. He gave the history of the pictures and references to similar subjects elsewhere. For good measure he threw in allusions to Pliny, Livy and Tacitus, Amelot de La Houssaie and Mézeray, to Zosimus and other learned and obscure authors into whose works he had at least glanced in his wide and curious reading. A second edition of the *Aedes* was published in 1752 and a third in 1767.

'Catalogues of this sort are deservedly grown into esteem', Walpole wrote in 1757 in his Advertisement to Vertue's *Catalogue and Description of King Charles the First's Capital Collection*. 'It is to be wished, that the practice of composing catalogues of conspicuous collections was universal' in a

---

[1] In a paper read before the Society of Antiquaries, 8 March 1770, and published in *Archaeologia*, i. 361-83.

country where 'for some years has been assembling the arts and works of the politest nations and greatest masters.' He pointed out that the establishment of the British Museum invited the opening of a new era of *virtù*. Collections that were wont to straggle through auctions into obscurity should now be rescued by patriotic persons with redoubled spirit and placed in the Museum, which would thus become an academy of arts where British artists might study Greece and Rome, Praxiteles and Raphael, without stirring from their own metropolis. In his Advertisement Walpole also noted that the late prince of Wales had proposed to buy back as many as possible of Charles I's pictures that had been sold abroad; 'but painting has still been unfortunate in Britain!'— a compliment intended for the eyes of his son and Lord Bute and which was conveyed to them a few years later, as will presently be shown. In 1758 and 1759 Walpole wrote Advertisements to similar catalogues of the collections of James II and Queen Caroline and of the second duke of Buckingham and others.

Other antiquarian and historical works were issued from the Strawberry Hill Press. The first book printed there (Gray's *Odes* apart) was *A Journey into England, 1598*, a translation by Bentley of that portion of Hentzner's *Itinerarium* (Nuremberg, 1612) that dealt with England. Walpole dedicated it to Lord Willoughby of Parham, president of the Society of Antiquaries, signing himself 'F.S.A. and F.R.S.', the only time, I think, when he did so. In 1764 he printed the first edition of *The Life of Lord Herbert of Cherbury*, by himself. Public editions followed in 1770, 1778 and 1792, and it has been frequently reprinted since. Walpole suffered one small mortification in connexion with it. The pedigree of the Herbert family which he had engraved and tipped into the book, and of which he was particularly proud, proved to be so full of errors that he suppressed it in the copies remaining on his hands.

In 1772 Walpole issued *Copies of Seven Original Letters from King Edward VI to Barnaby Fitz-Patrick*. The originals were lent him by Fitzpatrick's descendant, the earl of Upper Ossory. This publication was especially attractive to Walpole: letters written by a sovereign to a favourite, in whose family they had lain unprinted for two hundred years. Their being letters gave them a special significance, for 'nothing gives so just an idea of an age as genuine letters; nay, history waits for its last seal from them'. The two principals were young men of exceptional charm, a king uncorrupted by 'the arrogant royalty of his condition', and his whipping-boy 'who made so great a figure by his merit, after he had missed making a more showy one by favour'.[1] Furthermore, the descendant and present owner of the letters was the husband of the friend to whom for thirty-six years he wrote the most carefully composed letters he was capable of writing. Half the printing of 200 copies Walpole sent to the Ossorys, the other half he kept and gave away to friends; the pedantic Milles and other querulous persons were excluded from enjoyment of this treat.

As soon as King Edward's letters were off the press Walpole began to print the first of his *Miscellaneous Antiquities; or a Collection of Curious Papers: Either republished from scarce tracts, or now first printed from Original MSS.* The 'Advertisement by the Editors' begins, 'The taste for anecdotes and historic papers, for ancient letters that record affairs of state, illustrate characters of remarkable persons, or preserve the memory of former manners and customs, was never more general than at present. To indulge this disposition in the public and in themselves, the Editors of the following pages, being possessed of several original MSS and being promised the use of others, propose to publish in numbers some of the most entertaining.' That is, Walpole was to have his own *Archaeologia*, edited and printed by himself, with the assistance of Gray and Cole and his many other antiquarian friends whose good sense and taste could be relied upon.

[1] *Copies of Seven Original Letters from King Edward VI to Barnaby Fitzpatrick*, pp. iii, viii.

The First Number was 'An Account of some Tournaments and other Martial Diversions extracted from a thin folio written by Sir William Segar, Norroy; and is called by the Author, Honour Military and Ciuill; printed at London in 1602'. The extracted pages related to 'some of the splendid and romantic ceremonies practised in the reign of our Heroine Elizabeth'. The Second Number (which was printed three months after the First) was 'Sir Thomas Wyatt's Defence after the Indictment and Evidence'. It had been copied by Gray from the Harleian Collection. Walpole added an extended account of the elder Wyatt. In his Introduction he made it clear that he was attracted to Wyatt because he thought that justice had never been done to his many merits. He printed 500 copies of both numbers on ordinary paper and twenty-five copies on writing paper for presents. Believing that 'the affectation of loving veteran anecdotes was so vigorous' he offered the copies on ordinary paper for sale, but only 130 of them were sold, and there was no Third Number.[1] *Miscellaneous Antiquities* concluded Walpole's direct contributions to the study of antiquities, if we except his *Postscript to the Royal and Noble Authors*, 1786, an account of John Montacute, earl of Salisbury, in the reign of Richard II, of which he printed only forty copies for presents.

A monumental work under royal patronage seemed at one time about to be placed under his charge. When George III came to the throne the *cognoscenti* had high hopes of his becoming an active patron of the arts. In 1762 Walpole sent Bute the three catalogues of royal collections that he had recently edited and that contained his flattering allusion to the late prince of Wales.

Having dabbled a good deal in this kind of things [he wrote] if there is any point in which I could be of use to your Lordship for his Majesty's satisfaction, I should be very ready and happy to

[1] Walpole noted on British Museum Add. MS. 12528, 'Sir Sackville Crowe's Book of Accounts . . . 1628', that it was 'collected for my *Miscellaneous Antiquities*'. In Pinkerton's *Walpoliana* (1799), i. 65-7, is a list of twenty-two other articles 'intended for other numbers of my *Miscellaneous Antiquities*, if that publication had been encouraged'.

employ my little knowledge or pains. . . . The mere love of the arts, and the joy of seeing on the throne a prince of taste, are my only inducements for offering my slender services. I know myself too well to think I can ever be of any use but as a virtuoso and antiquarian.

At the same time he wrote some flattering verses on the king, 'The Garland', which he sent to Lady Bute. A letter from Bute encouraged him. On looking over Walpole's catalogues, Bute observed that Walpole had mixed several curious remarks on the customs, etc., of the times he treats of ; 'a thing much wanted, and that has never yet been executed, except in parts by Peck, etc. Such a general work would be not only very agreeable but instructive — the French have attempted it; the Russians are about it ; and Lord Bute has been informed Mr. Walpole is well furnished with materials for such a noble work.' Walpole replied that a work like Montfaucon's *Monumens de la monarchie françoise* was what he had long wished to see executed, nor would it, in point of materials, be a very difficult one to carry out. The chief obstacle would be the expense, which would be too much for his private purse, 'but I own I think I could be of use in it, in collecting or pointing out materials, and I would take any trouble in aiding, supervising, or directing such a plan'. A week later when Dr. Ducarel wrote to him about the need for an English Montfaucon — the proposal was apparently stirring the antiquarian world — Walpole confessed that the suggestion 'accords perfectly with a design I have long had of attempting something of that kind, in which, too, I have been lately encouraged'. Alas, for these hopes ! So far as Bute and the king were concerned, the rest is silence. But not so far as Walpole went. He was ready to be the English Montfaucon as well as the English Vasari. He must have been pleased when Cole told him that he had done more in the way of Montfaucon than all the English world beside.

As the years went by an even larger work formed in his mind, a history of Gothic architecture in England to be undertaken by the most informed antiquaries. He wrote about it at some length to Cole: 'I would give a series of plates, even from the conclusion of Saxon architecture, beginning with the round Roman arch, and going on to show how they plastered and zigzagged it, and then how better ornaments crept in, till the beautiful Gothic was arrived at its perfection; then how it deceased in Henry the Eighth's reign, Archbishop Warham's tomb at Canterbury being I believe the last example of unbastardized Gothic. . . .' James Essex was to do the next part, which 'should consist of observations on the art, proportions and method of building, and the reasons observed by the Gothic architects for what they did. . . . The prices, and the wages of workmen, and the comparative value of money and provisions at the several periods, should be stated, as far as it is possible to get materials.' Cole was to determine the date of each building and tomb. As to Walpole himself, he would add

> detached samples of the various patterns of ornaments, which would not be a great many, as excepting pinnacles, there is scarce one which does not branch from the trefoil; quatrefoils, cinquefoils, etc., being but various modifications of it. I believe almost all the ramifications of windows are so: and of them there should be samples too. . . . Mr. Tyson's history of fashions and dresses, would make a valuable part of the work, as in elder times especially much must be depended on tombs for dresses.

Walpole's letter reached Cole when he was removing from Waterbeche to Milton two miles away, a very trying time indeed; months passed, and when the correspondence was resumed nothing further was said on either side about the great history of Gothic architecture. Not that Cole had destroyed or mislaid Walpole's letter. It turned up almost *verbatim* in the preface to Gough's *Sepulchral Monuments in Great Britain*, 1786. Since the epigraph on the title-page is from Montfaucon and Walpole is identified with him and his methods from the start, the letter to Cole was not without its effect, after all.

One other ambitious project never got beyond Walpole's Books of Materials. This was a book on the streets of London, like St.-Foix's *Rues de Paris*. His first notes for this unpublished work appear on page 3 of the notebook begun in 1759. As he read in the Harleian MSS., Wood's *Fasti*, Stowe's *Survey*, Morgan's *Sphere of Gentry*, or whatever, he entered any references he found to London streets. Cole sent him a report on the stews in Southwark in the reign of Edward III and followed it up from time to time with other notes 'in your way', but the project required something more constant than occasional notes. 'I found the labour would be too great', Walpole later confessed to Pinkerton.[1]

No account of Walpole's antiquarian writings would be complete without reference to his works of imagination. As early as 1736 he addressed himself in verse to King's College Chapel:

> When Henry bade this pompous temple rise,
> Nor with presumption emulate the skies,
> Art and Palladio had not reach'd the land,
> Nor methodiz'd the vandal builder's hand :
> Wonders, unknown to rule, these piles disclose ;
> The walls, as if by inspiration, rose.

King's Chapel had a special hold on him throughout his life. Years later he told Cole that 'the beauty of King's College Chapel, now it is restored, penetrated me with a visionary longing to be a monk in it'; and to Mason he paid it the supreme tribute: 'King's Chapel is more beautiful than Strawberry Hill'.

Two other works owed their inspiration to 'a head filled like mine with Gothic story', *The Castle of Otranto*, 1765, and *The Mysterious Mother*, 1768.

Walpole was the first to point out that *The Castle of Otranto* and Strawberry Hill were one and the same,[2] and it is a simple matter to pair off the rooms in each.[3] Walpole

---

[1] *Walpoliana* (1799), i. 57.
[2] In the concluding sentence of the preface to his *Description of Strawberry Hill*, 1784.
[3] See 'Genesis of Strawberry Hill', *loc. cit.*, pp. 88-90. The one feature that was not the same has since been shown by Dr. Warren H. Smith to be Neville's Court at Trinity (*Times Literary Supplement*, 23 May 1936).

concealed his authorship in the first edition, pretending that 'the following work was found in the library of an ancient Catholic family in the north of England. It was printed at Naples, in the black letter, in the year 1529', but 'if the story was written near the time when it is supposed to have happened, it must have been between 1095, the era of the First Crusade, and 1243, the date of the Last, or not long afterwards'. Three months later, when the second edition appeared, Walpole acknowledged his authorship in a preface and confessed that the story 'was an attempt to blend the two kinds of Romance, the ancient and the modern'. He also called attention to the 'deportment of the domestics', the simplicity of whose behaviour was consonant with the aims of one whose 'rule' in telling the story 'was nature'. How seriously he took *The Castle of Otranto* may be seen in the letter to Cole in which he described how he wrote it. 'You will laugh at my earnestness, but if I have amused you by retracing with any fidelity the manners of ancient days, I am content, and give you leave to think me as idle as you please.' In this confession he summarized his attitude to all his writing.

The setting of *The Mysterious Mother* is the Castle of Narbonne. The tragedy begins:

> *A Platform before the Castle*
> Florian. What awful silence ! How these antique towers
> And vacant courts chill the suspended soul,
> Till expectation wears the cast of fear.

Gothic touches are stuck in here and there, as they were at Strawberry Hill and in *The Castle of Otranto*; we have the same 'monumental stones', meddling monks and 'natural' peasants. The time is again, presumably, of the Crusades, although the footnotes Walpole supplied to elucidate and inform the reader bring in authors who lived after the period of the play — two, indeed, allude to Addison; but, as in *The Castle of Otranto* and Strawberry Hill itself, the modern was made to blend with the ancient.

Horace Walpole, Antiquary

V

In 1781 Walpole was elected an honorary member of the Society of the Antiquaries of Scotland. His letter of acceptance to Lord Buchan must have mystified that humourless man: 'In my best days, my Lord, I never could pretend to more than having flitted over some flowers of knowledge. Now worn out and near the end of my course, I can only be a broken monument to prove that the Society of the Antiquaries of Scotland are zealous to preserve even the least valuable remains of a former age, and to recompense all who have contributed their mite towards illustrating our common islands.' In spite of the indifference to this honour that he professed to his English friends, he got some balm from it, for the wounds inflicted by Dean Milles and Mr. Masters never quite healed.

His interest in British antiquities continued unabated as long as he lived. Anyone who wrote to him could draw upon the collections at Strawberry Hill and its master's vast stock of knowledge and anecdote. In spite of his protests, several of his correspondents dedicated their books to him. Of these the most important are Granger's *Biographical Dictionary of England*, 1769, Carter's *Specimens of Ancient Sculpture and Painting*, 1780, and Daniel Lysons's *Environs of London*, 1792. In their dedications some authors were doubtless moved by the thought of how much Walpole could do for their books if he would, but others were clearly sincere in their encomiums.

To his friends Walpole frequently expressed exasperation with the results of all this study. 'I love antiquities, but I scarce ever knew an antiquary who knew how to write about them. Their understandings seem as much in ruins as the things they describe.' When *Archaeologia* offended him a third time, he said, 'I was the first soul that ever endeavoured to introduce a little taste into English antiquities, and had persuaded the world not to laugh at our Hearnes and Holinsheds, and the graceless loggerheads fly in my face!' Futile and foolish were antiquarian labours when they were compared to others: he snubbed Buchan on the possibility of finding 'secret stores' in the Scots College at Paris, 'If there were, how puny, now diminutive, would all such discoveries, and others which we might call of far greater magnitude, be to those of Herschel, who puts up millions of coveys of worlds at a beat!' When it was clear that America was lost he did not wish to be the trumpeter of my country's calamities. Yet as they must float on the surface of the mind and blend their hue with all its emanations, they suggest this reflection, that there can be no time so proper for the institution of inquiries into past story as the moment of the fall of an empire — a nation becomes a theme for antiquaries, when it ceases to be one for an historian! — and while its ruins are fresh and in legible preservation.

Such depressed moods were succeeded by others. The long line of English antiquaries from Leland, Parker and Cotton to the present showed no sign of coming to an end. Quite the contrary. New antiquaries were appearing and new historians; new poets and painters, too; a very promising and agreeable generation who were aware of their indebtedness to the past. The younger Bertie Greatheed's drawings for *The Castle of Otranto* had 'indubitable indications of real genius'; William Roscoe was 'a pure writer of history' and a poet superior to Lorenzo; James Wyatt after executing the New Offices in 'Collegiate Gothic' at Strawberry Hill had gone on to build Lee Priory, 'a child of Strawberry, prettier than the parent'. Netley Abbey still stood. 'Visions' that alone give reality to the past would lead posterity back 'to the ages that do not disappoint', just as visions had led him and all others of like mind from time immemorial. In due course the eighteenth century would be such an age, and when that time came, whatever posterity might think of the *Anecdotes of Painting, Historic Doubts* and his other works, it would have his *Memoirs* and some thousands of his letters to aid it in understanding the English of his day. He had left something for the Tom Hearnes and Vertues of the future; he had left more for the Horace Walpoles.

Horace Walpole, Antiquary

In his last years he would be carried by two footmen into the library or the Blue Bedchamber at Strawberry Hill. The books and prints that he wanted would be brought to him. If the gout was not too active in his hands, he would add a note in the margins or in his Book of Materials. The final note in his last Book of Materials must have taken him some time to write. The book is tightly bound, and to keep it open he must have had to press his left hand, knobbed with chalk stones, upon the open pages while with his right he laboriously spelt out at the top of page 87:

In Murphy's *Travels in Portugal* in quarto, 1795, it is said, p. 44, but not positively, that the fine Gothic Church at Batalha was built after a design of Stephen Stephenson, an Englishman. Mr. Murphy gives a reason that makes it probable, though not very, he supposing that Philippa Queen of Portugal, daughter of John of Gaunt, might have introduced English architecture into Portugal; but I think she lived too long before the erection of Batalha.

In spite of the stupidity and tastelessness of some of its practitioners, 'antiquities' absorbed him until he died.

BETTY KEMP

THE STEWARDSHIP OF THE CHILTERN HUNDREDS

THE office of steward or bailiff of Her Majesty's Three Chiltern Hundreds of Desborough, Stoke and Burnham was first used for the purpose of vacating a seat in the House of Commons in 1750. But the constitutional problems of vacation, whether members may resign and, if so, on whose authority, are as old as the House itself. They were not solved but reopened in 1750. Before the sixteenth century these problems, like all those connected with the composition of parliament, were the concern of the king. They became of theoretical importance to the Commons in the sixteenth century, when the House successfully maintained that its right of exclusive jurisdiction over its members covered questions of resignation, as it did questions of absence [1] and replacement. But in the sixteenth and seventeenth centuries, when only a few parliaments were of long duration, the problems of vacation were of practical importance only intermittently. In the eighteenth century the House lost its control to the king: it neither provided the increased opportunities for vacation necessary in the period of regularly long parliaments which opened in 1716, nor objected when the king did so. In the nineteenth century the king seldom exercised his control, but the Commons never regained it: resignations came to depend, in practice, neither on king nor on Commons but, with few exceptions, only on the wish of the members concerned.

[1] An Act of 1515 (6 Henry VIII, c. 16) gave the Speaker and the House of Commons power to license the absence of members.

The Stewardship of the Chiltern Hundreds

Permission to be excused from serving the king in parliament was a privilege which the king was seldom willing to grant, and when the right to grant the privilege passed to the Commons it was not granted more easily.[1] During Elizabeth's long parliament (1572–83) the House successfully claimed that it alone could authorize both the resignation of members and the issue of writs for by-elections to replace them.[2] Its resolution of February 1575,[3] that members 'in service of Ambassage, or else in Execution, or visited with sickness, shall not in any wise be amoved from their place in the House' did not stop resignation: rather it emphasized that resignation was in no circumstances automatic. For example, in March 1581 the House appointed a committee to consider the claims of nine 'new returned Persons in lieu of others absent, being either sick, or employed in Her Majesty's Service, or otherwise, and not dead',[4] and, following its recommendations, allowed three of them to stay on the grounds that their predecessors were 'incurably sick and diseased', and removed the other six, including two whose predecessors were employed in the queen's service. In November 1606, at the beginning of the third session of James I's long parliament (1606–10), the House was asked by the lord chancellor to consider the case of seven members who since the last session had been appointed to Crown offices, and gave three of them permission to resign.[5]

---

[1] It was granted in 1377, when a member was allowed to retire from the House on the grounds that he was engaged on the king's affairs beyond the seas; in 1534, 1543 and 1552 on grounds of sickness; in 1542 on grounds of captivity in Scotland.

[2] *Commons Journals*, i. 136, and Simonds D'Ewes, *Journal of the Votes, Speeches and Debates both in the House of Lords and in the House of Commons throughout the whole Reign of Queen Elizabeth*, p. 307 (18 March 1581); p. 377 (9 Nov. 1586). The House also resolved, on 18 March 1581, that members absent for a whole session without the permission of the House should be fined and lose their wages.   [3] *Ibid.* p. 244.

[4] *Commons' Journals*, i. 135.

[5] Winch, chief baron of exchequer in Ireland; Ridgeway, treasurer at wars in Ireland; Oliver St. John, master of ordnance in Ireland. Three ambassadors were refused permission, on the grounds that their appointments were not 'for life' (*ibid.* 316, 323; *Diary of Robert Bowyer*, 1606–7 (ed. D. H. Willson), pp. 186, 188, 189. After much controversy the attorney-general was

The formulation of general rules of disqualification — for example, that judges of the common law courts, sheriffs and mayors could not sit in the House — further emphasized the distinction between disqualification and privilege. Resignation for reasons other than sickness and service was never allowed: in 1614 and in 1623[1] the House refused to allow members to decline their election merely because they were unwilling to serve, and in 1641 the Long Parliament, later much concerned with problems of absence and disqualification, refused a similar request.[2] Although the question of resignation did not recur during Charles II's long parliament (1661–79),[3] the question of the authority for the issue of writs for by-elections recurred at the beginning of the tenth session, when thirteen new members were discovered to have been returned as a result of writs issued by the lord chancellor. After debate, the Commons resolved that these elections were void, ordered the Speaker to issue warrants for new writs and declared that 'the Right and Power of issuing writs for electing Members to serve in this House . . . is in this House, who are the proper Judges also of Elections and Returns of their Members'.[4]

Before the question of resignation became of regular practical importance the theoretical constitutional position had been radically altered by the partial success of the Commons' attempts to extend disqualification to all Crown office-

---

allowed to take his seat (*Commons' Journals*, i. 323 ; *Diary of Robert Bowyer*, p. 189), but in 1614 the House resolved that in future the attorney-general should not sit in the Commons (*Commons' Journals*, i. 459). In the same parliament, 1606–10, the House allowed five members to resign on grounds of sickness.

[1] The Commons' decision in 1623 was followed by a resolution that 'a man, after he is duly chosen, cannot Relinquish' (*Commons' Journals*, i. 724 ; John Glanville, *Reports of Certain Cases Determined and Adjudged by the Commons in Parliament in the Twenty-first and Twenty-second Years of the Reign of King James I*, p. 101). This resolution must be taken to mean that members could not 'decline election' at will, not that the House would not consider applications for resignation.   [2] *Commons' Journals*, ii. 201.

[3] There were during this parliament 271 by-elections caused by death.

[4] *Ibid.*, ix. 245, 248 (4, 5 and 6 Feb. 1672-3) ; Anchitell Grey, *Debates of the House of Commons, 1667–94*, ii. 3-7 ; John Hatsell, *Precedents of Proceedings in the House of Commons* (1818 edition), ii. 80.

The Stewardship of the Chiltern Hundreds

holders: after 1707 [1] members who accepted any Crown office automatically forfeited their seats in the House; all offices created after 1705 and certain specified offices, including revenue offices, carried with them disqualification; members who accepted other offices were allowed to stand for re-election.[2] This meant that, without asking the permission of the House, members could use Crown offices either to withdraw from the House altogether or to withdraw in order to stand for another constituency. The task of finding suitable offices for the purpose was made easier because, under the 1707 Act and other Place Acts, not only active offices but sinecures and semi-sinecures were available, provided only that the king was willing to grant them.

It is possible that the king granted a few offices to members who wished to vacate their seats even in the period 1707–16, when parliaments were short: it is certain that he did so between 1716 and 1750, when the stewardship of the Chiltern Hundreds was given to John Pitt in order to enable him to resign his seat for Wareham and stand for election at Dorchester. It is not possible to give an accurate list of these forerunners of the Chiltern Hundreds, which were seldom used more than once or twice, nor to say definitely how many of the eighty or so members who lost seats in this period as a result of appointment to office used their offices for the purpose of quitting their seats. But it is likely that the offices known to have been used for this purpose are only a proportion of those actually used. The earliest example of an office certainly so used was that of outranger of Windsor Forest, used in 1715 and again in 1717 in order to transfer from a

[1] The date from which these provisions operated was not 'the accession of the Hanoverians'. The operative Acts of 1705 (4 and 5 Anne, c. 20) and 1707 (6 Anne, c. 41) were to take effect from the end of the parliament which passed them, that is, from April 1708. But a Commons' resolution of 10 Nov. 1707 applied them to the existing parliament (*Commons' Journals*, xv. 396). As a result, seven members lost their seats immediately and three later in the parliament: all but one were re-elected.

[2] This is the usual interpretation of sections 25 and 26 of the 1707 Act. But it is clear that some members who accepted post-1705 offices and other disqualifying offices were also re-elected both in the 1705–8 parliament and in later parliaments.

borough to a county constituency: among others probably used were those of receiver-general of House Duties for Yorkshire, Durham and Northumberland in 1717; auditor of accounts of Duties on Leather in 1722; head steward of the Honor of Otford in 1742; commissary-general of musters in 1745; master of the Jewel House in 1745; receiver of Crown and fee farm rents for the counties of Warwick and Leicester in 1747, and for the counties of York, Durham and Northumberland, the archdeaconry of Richmond, and the counties of Lancaster, Westmorland and Cumberland in 1748. In the parliament of 1747–54 two stewardships were used: the stewardship of the Chiltern Hundreds, in 1750 by John Pitt and in 1753 by Henry Vane, who used it to transfer from Downton to Durham county; and the chief stewardship of the Honor of Berkhampstead, in 1752 by Henry Lascelles, member for Northallerton, who was the first to use a stewardship in order to retire from the House altogether.

Although after 1754 other offices were still occasionally used for vacation of seats,[1] stewardships came to be regarded as particularly fitted for the purpose, and the number of applications for them increased from thirteen in the 1754–61 parliament to thirty-nine in the 1774–80 parliament.[2] The nature of the eighteenth-century stewardships made them suitable vacating offices.[3] Originally Crown stewards or

---

[1] For example, there were four instances in the parliaments of 1774 and 1780 of vacation by the acceptance of the agency to a regiment of militia. This was not an old office, but it was held to debar from later election. Cf. Hatsell, *op. cit.*, ii. 54, and *Rogers on Elections* (18th edition, C. W. Williams), ii. 53.

[2] There were 110 applications in the period 1747–80 : 68 for the stewardship of the Chiltern Hundreds, 29 for the stewardship of the manor of East Hendred, 10 for the stewardship of the manor of Old Shoreham, one each for the stewardships of the manors of Berkhampstead, Kennington and Shippon.

[3] Several Crown stewards sat in parliament in the first half of the eighteenth century, but the first re-election of a Crown steward seems to have been in 1740, when the House decided that the inheriting of the stewardship of the lordship and manors of Bromfield and Yale was tantamount to its acceptance (*Commons' Journals*, xxiii. 538). This has been cited as evidence that Crown stewardships were not always regarded as offices of profit under the Crown (*Parliamentary Papers*, 1894, xii (278), p. 56). It seems more likely that there was no case between 1707 and 1740 where an appointment to a stewardship was made after election to parliament. The Commons' decision in 1740 was based on other instances of reversionary grants of offices to members (Hatsell, *op. cit.*, ii. 51,

The Stewardship of the Chiltern Hundreds

bailiffs were officers deputed to supervise the judicial and financial administration of Crown estates, but as the jurisdiction of their courts had been restricted by law and their financial duties had been curtailed by the loss of the Crown's feudal rights, those which survived had few duties, small salaries and shrunken fees. By the seventeenth century the appointment of stewards, usually for life or during pleasure, was made through the lord treasurer and chancellor of the exchequer, and by the end of the eighteenth century about twenty stewardships had come to be regarded as wholly within the gift of the chancellor.[1] Of the stewardships used for vacation before 1780, that of the Chiltern Hundreds had no duties,[2] and the others, though active offices, were not onerous. But they were never threatened with the danger of abolition as a source of undue Crown influence, as were other offices suitable for vacation, and they survived even the suppression, in the nineteenth century, of the territorial units on which they were based.

By 1780 the practice of vacating seats in the House of Commons by accepting Crown stewardships seemed to have been 'so long acquiesced in, from its convenience to all parties' that it was impracticable to disturb it. Hatsell questioned its legality, for he doubted whether nominal or nearly nominal offices properly were 'offices of profit, granted by the Crown'.[3] But he did not raise objection to the practice on

---

gives instances in 1717, 1726, 1737) : the point at issue was not whether stewardships were offices of profit under the Crown but, clearly, the date at which reversionary grants were to be regarded as acceptances of office, vacating seats.

[1] 'A List of Offices in the Gift of the Chancellor of the Exchequer', dated 21 Jan. 1808, contains nineteen 'Stewards, Bailiffs etc.' (eleven without salary) — including the steward of the Chiltern Hundreds (with a note that the Hundred courts had been long discontinued, and that the office had no salary and was used only for vacating seats in parliament) and the steward of the manor of East Hendred (with a note that the duties were executed by deputy, that the salary was £1 and the office often used for vacating seats) — and eleven receivers of land revenues (*Parliamentary Papers*, 1894, xii. Appendix 5).

[2] This perhaps increased its suitability for the purpose of enabling members to vacate their seats, but it decreased its suitability to rank as an office of profit (cf. Henry Pelham to William Pitt, 20 Oct. 1750, *Chatham Correspondence*, i. 53, for John Pitt's anxiety lest his application be refused). This is perhaps one reason why the Chiltern Hundreds was not the only office used for vacation.

[3] Hatsell, *op. cit.*, ii. 55 (footnote).

constitutional grounds. It is more surprising that the House of Commons showed little concern either at the increasing number of vacations or at its own loss of control over them, for there are strong constitutional objections both to resignation in general and to this particular method of resignation. Service in parliament is a duty, originally a feudal obligation, required of members for the duration of the parliament to which they are elected. Dispensation from this duty is a privilege: resignation therefore can never be voluntary but must be subject to the permission of the king, or, when control over membership passed from king to Commons, of the House itself. It is not a matter in which any other body has competence: constituencies, for example, may protest either against the burden of representation, or, later, against being unrepresented by reason of their members' absence from the House, but they have no authority to accept or demand resignations. It was on these grounds that the House of Commons at the end of the sixteenth and in the early seventeenth century asserted its sole competence in matters of resignation, denied that members could in any circumstances resign voluntarily, and insisted that by-elections should take place only on the authority of the House. And in the middle of the nineteenth century, when the House had surrendered its control over the only class of by-elections which could be controlled — those caused by members' wish for retirement — and the Crown had ceased to exercise its right to refuse applications for the Chiltern Hundreds, Peel was moved, on similar grounds, to disquietude at the vacation of seats by the 'voluntary act' of their holders.[1] Indeed, cause for disquietude seemed greater in the middle of the nineteenth century, for the voluntariness of resignations was often an illusion: the removal of the control both of the Commons and of the king left members more vulnerable to 'unconstitutional' pressure from outside parliament, from patrons or from constituents.

Whatever may be thought of the general question of

[1] C. S. Parker, *Sir Robert Peel from his Private Correspondence*, iii. 337.

The Stewardship of the Chiltern Hundreds

resignation, there can be no doubt that the constitutional objections to the practice of using the stewardship of the Chiltern Hundreds and other Crown offices in order to enable members of parliament to resign their seats without asking the permission of the House were not merely theoretical. Appointments to Crown stewardships were part of Crown patronage. There were occasions in the second half of the eighteenth century when applications for them were granted and refused for party reasons, and there were occasions both in the eighteenth and in the nineteenth century when they were granted in circumstances detrimental to the House of Commons. For example, the Chiltern Hundreds was used twice during the 'tragi-comedy enacted... for the benefit of Mr. Wilkes, and at the expense of the constitution'.[1] After Wilkes's third election as member of parliament for Middlesex in March 1769, and his third expulsion by the House of Commons, the 'prudent conduct' of 'electing and declaring void' was abandoned, and the Government gave the Chiltern Hundreds to Henry Lawes Luttrell, member for Bossiney, in order to free him to stand against Wilkes. Wilkes's prophecy that 'if once the ministry shall be permitted to say whom the freeholders shall *not* choose, the next step will be to tell them whom they *shall* choose'[2] was now fulfilled: Luttrell received 296 votes, Wilkes 1043, but the House declared Luttrell elected and he took his seat.[3] Five years later, on the death of John Glynn, the other member for Middlesex, Lord North made a 'secret promise' of the Chiltern Hundreds to Colonel Tufnell, member for Beverley, in order that he might stand for Middlesex in the Government interest, and 'an open and avowed Refusal of the same privilege'[4] to George Byng, member for Wigan, who had been asked to stand by the 'patriotic party'.

---

[1] Burke in *Parliamentary History*, xvi. 546.
[2] T. H. B. Oldfield, *History of the Boroughs of Great Britain*, ii. 230.
[3] Wilkes was elected again at the general election of 1774 and allowed to sit.
[4] Petition of the Freeholders of the County of Middlesex, 10 December 1779 (*Commons' Journals*, xxxvii. 506). The promise to Tufnell was not implemented, and a third candidate, Thomas Wood, was elected.

Essays Presented to Sir Lewis Namier

In the 1780 parliament, with both Wilkes and Byng as members, attacks on the Government's attempts to 'obtrude a representative on the county'[1] ended, in May 1782, with the Commons' decision, by 115 votes to 47, that its resolution of 1769, declaring Wilkes incapable of being elected, was 'subversive of the Rights of the Whole Body of Electors of this Kingdom'.[2] In 1842, owing to the exertions of another Radical, John Arthur Roebuck, member for Bath, a select committee investigated six 'corrupt compromises', made shortly after the general election of 1841, between successful and defeated candidates at Harwich, Nottingham, Lewes, Penryn, Reading and Bridport. The purpose of the corrupt compromises, to terminate parliamentary enquiries into alleged bribery at the time of election, was achieved by the use of the Chiltern Hundreds. The general pattern of the corrupt compromises was the same. At Nottingham,[3] for example, where petitions had been presented on behalf of John Walter, one of the defeated candidates, against the return of both successful ones, Sir John Cam Hobhouse and Sir George Larpent, on the grounds of bribery and corruption, the appointment of a committee to investigate the charges was immediately followed by the making of a compromise between the agents of Walter, Hobhouse and Larpent: all petitions were to be abandoned, one seat was to be vacated within four days by application for the Chiltern Hundreds, Walter was to be returned at the ensuing by-election. This agreement was carried out — Larpent applied for the Chiltern Hundreds and was succeeded by Walter, the petitions were withdrawn and the committee's enquiry thereby brought to an end. Although an Act of 1842,[4] sponsored by Lord John Russell, included a clause empowering the House of Commons to investigate a charge of corruption even if the

---

[1] Oldfield, *op. cit.*, ii. 239. The moral of the Wilkes case — that a constituency may elect whom it pleases — was recalled during the debates on the new procedure rules of 1902 (see my article 'Resignation from the House of Commons' in *Parliamentary Affairs*, v. (2)).

[2] *Commons' Journals*, xxxviii. 977.

[3] *Parliamentary Papers*, 1842 (v), p. vi.   [4] 5 and 6 Vict., c. 102.

The Stewardship of the Chiltern Hundreds

petition alleging it was later withdrawn, it is certain that compromises of this kind continued to be made, and that they were facilitated by the ease with which the Chiltern Hundreds were given. In August 1859 Roebuck drew attention to a corrupt compromise at Bodmin, and proposed that the House should state its disapproval of the indiscriminate grant of the Chiltern Hundreds to its members. He put before the House a motion: 'That in the opinion of this House, any Minister would be guilty of a breach of the privileges of this House who should advise the Crown to confer the office of Steward of the Chiltern Hundreds (etc.) upon any person charged with corrupt practices at an election, and who for the purpose of evading the jurisdiction of this House, has entered into an agreement to vacate his seat, upon the withdrawal of the petition'.[1] He was supported by Disraeli, who urged the House not to allow itself to be made 'a party to a corrupt contract',[2] by James Whiteside, attorney-general for Ireland, who begged the House to 'strengthen the hands of the Chancellor of the Exchequer in the effort to baffle (corruption)'[3] and by Lord Stanley. Palmerston supported Roebuck 'in principle' but opposed the method of a general rule, and Bright opposed him on the grounds that every case of compromise was not necessarily a case of corruption. Gladstone, chancellor of the exchequer, agreed that the Chiltern Hundreds, 'a very delicate office', should not be granted if there were a *prima facie* case for corruption, and quoted the precedent of Goulburn's refusal of it in 1842 to Lord Chelsea, member for Reading, who had confessed himself a party to a corrupt compromise. But Gladstone did not consider that the mere existence of a petition was sufficient reason for refusal of the Chiltern Hundreds,[4] and maintained that the chancellor of the exchequer had no right to enquire into the reasons for application, since such an enquiry would infringe the 'exclusive jurisdiction' of the House. Finally, Gladstone

---

[1] *Hansard*, 3rd series, clv. 947.   [2] *Ibid.* 949.   [3] *Ibid.* 959.
[4] A few days later he granted the stewardship of the manor of Northstead to Michell, the member for Bodmin.

declared what is still the accepted doctrine: that the duty of a chancellor of the exchequer was to grant the Chiltern Hundreds without enquiry unless in any particular case the House of Commons was prepared to restrain him from 'exercising the power which is formally, and I may say Ministerially, lodged in his hands, of granting certain offices under the Crown to persons who wish to be enabled to resign their seats in Parliament'.[1] Roebuck's motion was defeated by 214 votes to 30.[2] It is clear that the defeat was due to the fact that Roebuck and his supporters were interested in corruption and not in the anomaly which made corruption possible — the accidental combination of the power of granting the Chiltern Hundreds, 'the only patronage that belongs to the Chancellor of the Exchequer',[3] with the problem of resignation from the House of Commons.

The first attempt to draw attention to the possible abuses of this combination, and to provide an alternative method of resignation from the House, was made in March 1775, when George Grenville, member for Buckinghamshire, asked leave to introduce a bill to enable members of parliament to resign their seats, 'under certain regulations', if the Speaker gave them permission to do so. Grenville did not object to resignation—on the contrary, he considered that there were many 'situations where it is expedient and proper for a member to wish to divest himself of his trust',[4] and he quoted a number of instances, taken from the period 1575–1609, when the House had authorized the issue of new writs where members were sick or employed in the king's service — but he objected to resignation by means of the Chiltern Hundreds.[5]

The Place Bill[6] (he said) was originally meant as the great security to independence in this House, by giving the electors the power

---

[1] *Hansard*, 3rd series, clv. 1343.   [2] *Ibid.* 1042.   [3] *Ibid.* 952.
[4] *Parl. Hist.*, xviii. 412.
[5] In May 1774 Grenville had refused to enter parliament as member for Buckingham in place of his uncle, Henry Grenville, who had been asked by Earl Temple, the patron of the borough, to apply for the Chiltern Hundreds. And his father, George Grenville, had opposed the use of the Chiltern Hundreds against Wilkes.   [6] The 1707 Act.

The Stewardship of the Chiltern Hundreds

of rejecting those who might appear to them to have accepted employment, on dependent principles. By the use of the time this has long been perverted to very different and unconstitutional purposes; for it is under this Bill, that members, wishing to vacate their seats, solicit the favour of the Minister.[1]

There was a good deal of support for the view that the combination of the Chiltern Hundreds and resignation was 'a strange perversion of an act of parliament'.[2] Burke supported Grenville's proposal on the grounds that it would 'obviate the present mischief of a power in the minister to give undue preferences to his friends and favourites',[3] and Fox supported it because it would deprive the Government of at least one opportunity of showing 'partiality'.[4]

But in spite of strong support Grenville's motion was defeated in the House by 173 votes to 126, and the provision of an alternative method of resignation from the House of Commons was not seriously considered again by the House for more than a century.[5] Robert Vernon Smith's suggestion, during the debates on corrupt compromises in 1842, that the solution lay in substituting a proper method of resignation for the 'barbarous fiction' of the Chiltern Hundreds, met with no support. Henry Drummond Wolff's statement, in July 1880, that early in the next session he would move for a committee to report 'whether it is desirable to provide by statute some means whereby members can relinquish their seats under the control of the House, and independently of the

---

[1] *Parl. Hist.*, xviii. 413-14 (15 March 1775).
[2] *Ibid.* 416. The phrase was Lord Folkestone's.   [3] *Ibid.* 419.
[4] *Ibid.* 418-9. North admitted that he had just refused the Chiltern Hundreds to Nathaniel Bayly, member for Westbury, because he had made a 'rule never to grant an opportunity of this nature to any person to oppose his friends'.
[5] The Middlesex petition of Dec. 1779 protested against the 'Abuse and Perversion of that Act (1707)' from which 'the Power claimed by the Minister to vacate seats in Parliament is derived'. But the bill presented by the supporters of the petition provided, not for an alternative method of resignation, but only for the transfer of members from one constituency to another in the same parliament. The motion to commit the bill was defeated, on 29 Feb. 1780, by 66 votes to 29 (*Commons' Journals*, xxxvii. 676). Grenville had gone to the House of Lords in October 1779.

Government of the day',[1] seems to have been a tactical move in the Fourth Party's game of obstructing Gladstone's Government. The promised motion was never made, perhaps because Gladstone, who was, he said, 'not at all enamoured of this power placed in my hands', declared himself 'decidedly of the opinion that some better system ... might be devised' to replace 'the only ordinary method by which a member of parliament can vacate his seat'.[2]

But in January 1893 a more promising phase seemed to open, for Sir William Harcourt, chancellor of the exchequer in Rosebery's Liberal Government, after defending himself for granting the Chiltern Hundreds to a member, Jabez Balfour, guilty of fraud, showed that, like George Grenville, he was interested in the question of resignation for its own sake and wished to divorce it from the Chiltern Hundreds.[3] His defence, based on Gladstone's statement of August 1859, was that the chancellor had no duty or right to investigate suspicious applications. He pointed out that the stewardship of the Chiltern Hundreds was no longer 'an honourable office',[4] and said that he himself would always prefer to give it to an undesirable member than to a good one. 'The whole proceeding', Harcourt added, 'is merely a constitutional fiction equivalent to resignation. It is certainly an anomalous and inconvenient fiction. A former member of this House, Sir Henry Drummond Wolff, in 1880, intimated that he would move for a Committee to alter the system. I am sorry he did not do so, because I think it would be very desirable that another form of resignation should be established in this House.'[5] In July 1894 Harcourt's grant of the Chiltern Hundreds to Bernard Coleridge, member for the Attercliffe division of Sheffield, was questioned in the House, on the

---

[1] *Hansard*, 3rd series, ccliv. 1533-4.
[2] *Ibid.* 1531.
[3] Harcourt's maiden speech, on 23 Feb. 1869, was in opposition to Lord Bury's motion to repeal s. 26 of the 1707 Act (*ibid.* cxciv. 211-219).
[4] The words 'especial trust and confidence in the care and fidelity' of the steward were taken out of the appointing warrant in 1861. They crept in again later, and were finally removed in 1877.
[5] *Hansard*, 4th series, viii. 51.

The Stewardship of the Chiltern Hundreds

grounds that his father, Baron Coleridge, had died before the application was made, and the seat was therefore already vacant. A select committee was appointed to enquire into the Coleridge case and also into 'the Law and Practice of Parliament in reference to the Vacating of Seats in the House of Commons, and whether it is desirable that any, and if so what, changes should be made therein'. In August 1894 the committee presented to the House [1] the evidence it had taken, the minutes of its proceedings and several Appendices, including a valuable memorandum submitted by Harcourt summarizing the history and then practice with regard to the grant of the Chiltern Hundreds,[2] and recommended that it be reappointed in the next session to consider its report. The committee was reappointed in February 1895, and in May reported separately on the Coleridge case — declaring that the fact of succession to the peerage disabled from membership of the Commons, though not, of course, from appointment to the Chiltern Hundreds — and reserved 'the other matters referred to them for a further Report'.[3] But as the committee did not meet again, this further report, like Wolff's promised motion, was never made.

The next step in this sorry story confirms the impression that Providence did not favour those who attempted to disturb what Balfour called 'a dodge... discovered in the middle of the 18th century'. On 19 February 1901, George Walter Erskine Loder, Conservative member for Brighton, introduced a private member's bill providing that a member wishing to resign should make written application to the Speaker, that the Speaker should lay the application before the House, and that, after fourteen days, the House should grant or reject it.[4] The proposal was very similar to George Grenville's and was no luckier. The bill was printed, as the Members of Parlia-

---

[1] *Parliamentary Papers*, 1894, xii. (278).
[2] This memorandum, printed as Appendix 5, had been prepared for Harcourt by F. S. Parry, a treasury official, in 1893. Only Parry's preface and conclusion are omitted. [3] *Parliamentary Papers*, 1895, x. (272).
[4] Among Loder's supporters were Sir Charles Dilke, a member of the 1894 and 1895 committees, and T. M. Healy, a member of the 1895 committee.

ment (Resignation of Seats) Bill, and ordered to be read a second time on 8 May, but its second reading never took place — it was postponed seven times and on 26 June the bill was withdrawn.[1]

Perhaps the advocates of a simple method of resignation, controlled by the House of Commons, in place of the accidental method supplied by application for office — 'the Chiltern Hundreds'— which had deprived the House of complete control over its own members, failed because most members of parliament were less interested in the constitutional undesirability of the 'dodge' than in its usefulness to them as individuals. If, with them, we leave the heights of constitutional theory for the plains of political fact, we see that the Chiltern Hundreds introduced an important new element to political life: a class of by-elections caused not by death, disqualification or removal to the House of Lords, but merely by members' decision to retire. It was a large class. In the century from 1747, the beginning of the parliament in which John Pitt applied for the Chiltern Hundreds, to 1847, the end of the parliament of corrupt compromises, there were 787 applications[2] for the Chiltern Hundreds and for similar offices, of which only two — the stewardships of the manor of East Hendred and of the manor of Old Shoreham — received more than a handful of applications. This is an average of 36 a parliament, or nearly 8 a year.[3] The figures for the century after 1780, when the practice was fully established, throw light on the circumstances which led members to retire before and after the Reform Act of 1832. In the thirteen parliaments of the half-century from 1780 to 1832 there were 549 applications, 10 a year, and in the twelve parliaments of the half-century from 1833 to 1885 there were 413, 8 a year. But although the number of applications was smaller in the half-

---

[1] Of the 153 private members' bills introduced in 1901, only 4 became law.

[2] This total does not include 23 applications for the office of escheator of Munster, which was used for vacation, by Irish members only, in the period 1801–26.

[3] Excluding the four parliaments before 1774, when the number of applications was still small (71), the average was 40 a parliament, or 9 a year.

The Stewardship of the Chiltern Hundreds

century after 1832, and fluctuated rather less from year to year, there was no steady decline; indeed, in this half-century, the largest number of applications (56) came in the 1841-7 parliament, and the next largest (51) in the 1880-5 parliament.[1] The Reform Act did not merely reduce the number of applications: it disfranchised the boroughs which had, before 1832, produced about three-quarters of the applications — the rotten and pocket boroughs — and so affected the reasons for which applications were made.[2] Of the 86 boroughs disfranchised or partly disfranchised in 1832, 76 had produced applications for the Chiltern Hundreds. East Looe, Bletchingley and Yarmouth headed the list with 35 applications between them, 6 or 7 applications were common, a single application was very rare. Some of these applications were, of course, made for personal reasons, including the wish to stand for another constituency, but most of them were made for political reasons arising out of the relationship between the applicant and the patron of the borough for which he sat. Members retired because their patron wished to provide a seat for a relative, because he disapproved of their conduct in the House or because they were unwilling to support there a policy he approved, or, sometimes, in face of a common danger.[3] The Reform Act, by weakening the relationship between member and patron, and reducing the number of boroughs where this relationship was of primary importance, weakened the force of the most important political reason for application for the Chiltern Hundreds.[4] But the numerical implications of this weakening were to some extent offset by

---

[1] The largest number of applications in the half-century before 1832 was 69, in the 1812-18 parliament; but the 1830 parliament, with 18, and the 1831 parliament, with 20, had the largest annual averages.

[2] Hardly any applications came from county members.

[3] For example, 90 per cent of the applications in the 1830 and 1831 parliaments came from members for condemned boroughs.

[4] By diminishing the difference in status between constituencies — especially between borough and county constituencies — the Act also virtually put an end to applications made for the purpose of moving from one constituency to another. In the period 1747-80 nearly half the applicants moved immediately to another constituency, and although the proportion declined after 1780 it rose again to half in the parliaments of 1830 and 1831.

the development, after 1832, of a new political reason for retirement, arising out of the relationship between members and their constituents. This new political reason was, potentially, stronger than the old, because it was of general effect.

Old and new political reasons for resignation are found side by side in the parliament of 1841-7, which had a larger number of applications than any other parliament of the half-century after the Reform Act. There were, during this parliament, 49 applications for the Chiltern Hundreds and 7 for three other stewardships,[1] and only 15 of these 56 applicants ever sat in the House of Commons again.[2] Moreover, a quarter of the applications for the whole parliament were made in January and February 1846,[3] the period of the struggle for the repeal of the Corn Laws in the House of Commons. With two or three exceptions, these were political applications made because of changes in the applicants' opinions about the Corn Laws: of the new members, only three (two Irish and one Scottish) voted for repeal, and their votes did not conflict with their predecessors' opinions.

Among the applications of January and February 1846 are several of the old kind, depending on relationship between member and patron. For example, at Chichester the free-trader Lord Arthur Lennox was forced to apply for the stewardship of the manor of Hempholme by his elder brother, the fifth duke of Richmond, president of the Agricultural Protection Society, and was replaced by Richmond's more amenable son, Lord Henry Lennox. In April 1845 there had been a similar family shuffle at Woodstock,[4] where John

[1] The stewardships of Poynings manor and of the manors of Hempholme and Northstead. None of these had been previously used for vacation, but Northstead, first used in 1844, has been used ever since. Of the three, only Poynings manor was an active office: it was used in 1841 and 1843 but never again.

[2] Eight in the same parliament, seven more in later parliaments.

[3] The thirteen applications of Jan. and Feb. 1846 led *Punch*, in Feb., to remark that 'The Hundreds have not been so gay for many years past. . . . There is some talk of races for the Chiltern Hundreds, if they continue their present attraction.'

[4] Woodstock was a family preserve of the duke of Marlborough but since his family was large enough to lack homogeneity the borough was not without election contests — for example, the contest between the marquess of Blandford and a younger son, Lord John Spencer Churchill, in 1838.

The Stewardship of the Chiltern Hundreds

Winston Spencer Churchill, marquess of Blandford, was ordered to apply for the Chiltern Hundreds by his father, the duke of Marlborough, because he refused to hide his free-trade opinions. He was succeeded by the protectionist J. H. Loftus, and, when Loftus went to the House of Lords in December 1845, by the duke's younger son, Lord Alfred Spencer Churchill, who held the seat only until he had voted against repeal and, at the 1847 general election, retired in favour of the marquess of Blandford.

The resignation of Thomas Francis Fremantle, member for Buckingham, though voluntary, still depended primarily on his sense of obligation to his patron, the duke of Buckingham, who had resigned from the Government in 1842 on the Corn Law question. Fremantle had, however, been re-elected in February 1845, after his appointment as chief secretary for Ireland, and had then pledged himself to his constituents to maintain the 1842 Corn Law. His double obligation led him to apply for the Chiltern Hundreds in February 1846, although he was in favour of repeal and reluctant to embarrass the Government, and he was succeeded by the marquess of Chandos. No other seat could be found for Fremantle and he therefore resigned his office of chief secretary for Ireland. In this he was succeeded by Lord Lincoln, member of parliament for the county of Nottingham, who, through the influence of his father, the duke of Newcastle, was himself defeated at the ensuing by-election because of his free-trade opinions. Lincoln returned to parliament in May 1847 as member for Linlithgow; Fremantle never returned.[1] Relationship between member and constituents, instead of member and patron, produced the resignation of Anthony Ashley Cooper, Lord Ashley, member of parliament for Dorset.[2] By Feb-

---

[1] He was appointed deputy chairman of the Board of Customs and remained a civil servant until he retired in 1873.

[2] Ashley's comment on his resignation was: 'Many will condemn me, some for doing that which they ought to do; others for appearing to sanction the principle of delegation . . . I could justify such a vote (for repeal) before God . . . but I have entered into relations with men and must observe them' (E. Hodder, *Life of Shaftesbury*, ii. 132). This was Ashley's second application

ruary 1846 Ashley was convinced that 'public necessity and public welfare both demand the repeal of the Corn Laws'. He was not pledged to his constituents to oppose repeal, but he believed that at the time of his election there had been 'between the electors and myself an "honourable understanding" that "Protection of some kind should be maintained"'.[1] He therefore applied for the Chiltern Hundreds, refused to stand for re-election and was succeeded by H. K. Seymer, a reliable protectionist.

The Government was, naturally, politically embarrassed both by the resignations of January and February 1846 and by its failure to win by-elections. 'We are in a great turmoil here over elections,' Peel wrote, 'many are convinced, who talk of resigning their seats. They feel that they cannot conscientiously vote against me, yet are inclined either to give up Parliament, or to pass through the ordeal of re-election'.[2] But Peel's personal embarrassment was provoked by constitutional rather than political considerations. He was aware that many of the resignations were a response, not to conscience, but to pressure from 'certain peers'— Marlborough, Richmond, Newcastle, Buckingham are examples — whose action threatened 'the constitutional freedom of election',[3] and he was even more concerned about the conscientious resignations, which seemed to derive from a mistaken conception of the status of a member of parliament. In the House of Commons in January he referred to the changed opinions of 'some of the most honourable men that ever sat upon these benches', and gave as examples, apart from Ashley, H. C. Sturt, the other member for Dorset, and Lord Henniker, member for East Suffolk, who both applied for the Chiltern Hundreds

---

for the Chiltern Hundreds. The first, in Sept. 1831, was made in order to vacate his seat at Dorchester and contest a by-election for the county of Dorset in the anti-Reform interest. His opponent, W. F. S. Ponsonby, had also vacated his seat, for Poole, by accepting the Chiltern Hundreds. Ashley was successful and voted against the Reform Bill (Hodder, i. 118, wrongly puts this contest at the 1831 dissolution).   [1] Hodder, *op. cit.*, iii. 127.

[2] *Private Correspondence*, iii. 337 (Peel to Hon. William Peel, 31 Jan. 1846).

[3] *Ibid.*, 338 (Peel to the queen, 14 Feb. 1846).

and were succeeded by protectionists,[1] and two members who offered to apply but were asked by their constituents not to do so, William Patten, member for North Lancashire, and William Tatton Egerton, member for North Cheshire.[2] But Peel regretted that members of parliament should feel that it was against their conscience to vote for a measure they had come to believe in, and he rejected the theory on which their feeling was based: that members were tied to the views of their constituents even if they had not given pledges to them. 'I have great doubts', he wrote to Sir Howard Douglas, member for Liverpool, who apparently considered resigning because of his reluctance to vote against the Government, 'as to the propriety on constitutional grounds of vacating a seat by a voluntary act of the holder of it. I should think, however, from all I hear from Liverpool, that your constituents would entreat you to remain, and to exercise your free judgment from a review of present circumstances, unfettered by past declarations of opinion.'[3] Members who resigned because they did not share their constituents' views were, Peel thought, subscribing to a theory of dependence more extreme and more dangerous than those who resigned because they did not share their patrons' views.

Peel was not alone in regarding resignation as a constitutional problem, nor in fearing that resignations effected because members did not share their constituents' views were

---

[1] The editors of Peel's *Private Correspondence* (iii, 337) state that Henniker was asked to stand again for East Suffolk and was 'triumphantly returned' as a free-trader. In fact, his successor, E. S. Gooch, retained the seat until his death in 1866, when Henniker succeeded him.

[2] Ten of the applications came from county members: they included also W. H. Dawnay, member for Rutland, Francis Charteris, member for East Gloucestershire, and George Darby, member for East Sussex. The three borough applicants were Lennox, Fremantle and H. B. Seymour, member for Midhurst.

[3] *Private Correspondence*, iii. 337. Douglas did not apply for the Chiltern Hundreds, but the exercise of his 'free judgment' led him to vote against repeal. He justified his vote, 'painful and reluctant in some respects', in the House on 13 Feb. 1846 (*Hansard*, 3rd series, lxxxiii. 855). The other member for Liverpool, Viscount Sandon, voted for repeal — also reluctantly — because he regarded it as inevitable and was unwilling to weaken the Government (*ibid.* 596-601 (9 Feb. 1846)).

evidence of that intrusion of the electorate into politics which the Reform Act had precipitated. Roebuck, for example, considered that resignation in obedience to the commands, implied or explicit, of constituents, endangered the independence of parliament, and asked 'what was the meaning of not being a delegate, but a representative, but that during the term of service in Parliament one must be guided by his own personal convictions?'[1] The few precedents for the conscientious resignations of 1846 seemed to be linked directly with the Reform Act. For example, in May 1833, Croker declared that 'nobody knew why'[2] John Cam Hobhouse not only gave up his office, the Irish secretaryship, but also applied for the Chiltern Hundreds, on the grounds that the Government's policy with regard to the Assessed Taxes was contrary to his constituents' opinions,[3] and Greville condemned resignations of this kind as 'one of the fruits of the Reform Bill'.[4] But, even before the Reform Act, Peel himself had known the difficulties of members faced with 'the painful alternative of disregarding the dictates of their own consciences or of acting in opposition to the opinions and disappointing the hopes of their constituents'.[5] In February 1829, after his decision to support Catholic Emancipation, he applied for the Chiltern Hundreds in order to vacate his seat for the University of Oxford.[6] He later confessed that he then acted 'upon the impulse of private feelings, rather than upon a dispassionate consideration of the constitutional relation between a representative and his constituents',[7] and came to apply to the 1846

[1] *Hansard*, 3rd series, lxxxiii. 822 (12 Feb. 1846).
[2] Croker, *Correspondence and Diaries*, ii. 210.
[3] Pledges, like shorter parliaments, were regarded as a Radical device for tying members more closely to their constituencies. But, in fact, Hobhouse, less Radical than his constituents, had refused to give the pledges they asked of him in April 1833, at the by-election following his appointment as Irish secretary.
[4] C. C. F. Greville, *A Journal of the Reigns of George IV and William IV*, ii. 369. [5] *Memoirs*, i. 312.
[6] After his defeat at the ensuing by-election a 'convenient' vacancy was created for him at Westbury by the application of the member and patron of the borough, Sir Manasseh Lopez, for the stewardship of the manor of East Hendred. [7] *Memoirs*, i. 312.

The Stewardship of the Chiltern Hundreds

resignations something like the judgment Croker had delivered on his — that it was 'a democratical and unconstitutional proceeding, and a precedent dangerous to the independence of the House of Commons'.[1] It was a precedent: there can be no doubt that the conscientious resignations of 1846, especially those not based on explicit pledges, marked an important advance in the control of the electorate over the elected. To find these resignations side by side with resignations forced by disapproving patrons only indicates that in this, as in other electoral ideas and practices, the parliament of 1841–7 was a half-way house. Dependence, whether on patron or on constituents, produced a constitutional unbalance which could only have been righted by providing members with a simple method of resignation, controlled by the House alone.

Because this was not done, the accident which in the middle of the eighteenth century tied the Chiltern Hundreds to the problem of resignation established a constitutional anomaly which grew steadily more anomalous. It may perhaps be defended to-day on the grounds that it adds to the 'variety and colour of life',[2] but it cannot be maintained either that this loophole in the Commons' control over its membership was ever desirable, or that the loophole has been harmless. Nor has it been easy to force the Chiltern Hundreds to fit into a problem which is foreign to it: much time has been spent in deciding what legally makes it possible to describe an office which is unpaid, without duties, and in the gift of the chancellor of the exchequer, as an office of profit granted by the Crown,[3] in ensuring that the Chiltern Hundreds should be

---

[1] *Diaries and Correspondence*, ii. 7.

[2] Evidence of Sir William Holdsworth before the select committee on offices or places of profit under the Crown (H.C. 1940–1, *Reports from Committees*, iii. (120) p. 588).

[3] From Spring Rice's opinion, in 1839, that the stewardship of the Chiltern Hundreds was 'an existing and active office' (*Parliamentary Papers*, 1839, xii. p. 9) to the recommendations of the 1941 select committee that the offices of steward of the Chiltern Hundreds and of the manors of East Hendred, Northstead and Hempholme should 'continue to be deemed offices of profit under the Crown, acceptance of which by a member of the House of Commons causes him to vacate his seat' (H.C. 1940–1, *Reports from Committees*, iii. (120) p. xxxvi).

exempted from legislation affecting other Crown offices,[1] in discussing technical problems such as whether application, or promise to appoint, constitutes acceptance, how long an appointed steward remains a steward, and how soon another may be appointed,[2] and, finally, in considering whether there are any circumstances which justify the House of Commons in interfering with the chancellor's undoubted right to grant the office. The only real defence of the Chiltern Hundreds is negative and equivocal: it has produced an interesting chapter of constitutional history. By making possible the growth of a large class of by-elections — in theory 'voluntary' but in practice usually a response to pressure from outside the House of Commons — and so providing a new vehicle for the expression of opinion both inside and outside the House, the stewardship of the Chiltern Hundreds has greatly enriched the electoral history of the last two hundred years. A comparable enrichment could hardly have taken place if a rational system of resignation had superseded what Balfour, who was no iconoclast, called the 'most curious of the many curious survivals in our Parliamentary constitution ... by which the immemorial Rule of Parliament, that a man could not resign, was evaded ... (by) the curious practice of taking an office of emolument under the Crown, an office which carries with it no emolument, and which is not, in any but the most technical sense, under the Crown at all'.[3]

[1] For example, see the schedules to the Re-election of Ministers Acts of 1919 and 1926 (9 Geo. V, c. 2, and c. 19) and the House of Commons Disqualification (Temporary Provisions) Act of 1941 (4 and 5 Geo. VI, c. 8).

[2] Although in 1846 Goulburn thought that the Chiltern Hundreds should not be granted to more than one person on the same day, this has occasionally been done, and is technically possible since the appointing warrant expressly revokes the grant to the last steward. It is now customary but not essential to grant the Chiltern Hundreds and Northstead alternately.

[3] *Hansard*, 4th series, ciii. 212 (17 Feb. 1902).

A. ASPINALL

THE REPORTING AND PUBLISHING OF THE HOUSE OF COMMONS' DEBATES 1771-1834

THE year 1771 witnessed the famous struggle between the House of Commons and the printers of the London newspapers : a struggle which ended with the tacit abandonment by the House of its prescriptive but anachronistic [1] right to prohibit parliamentary reporting.[2] The ultimate result of this new freedom was to change the whole character of the constitution. The gradual creation of a politically educated public opinion was destined to make parliament, even in its unreformed state, increasingly sensitive to that opinion — with results that were strikingly seen in 1807 when, after a long campaign by evangelicals and humanitarians, parliament abolished the slave trade ; again in 1829, when the agitation in Ireland, skilfully directed by O'Connell and the Catholic Association, compelled the Wellington Ministry to cede Catholic Emancipation ; and in 1832, when public opinion everywhere in the British Isles forced a reluctant legislature to reform itself.

The freedom achieved in 1771 was very far, however,

---

[1] Yet as late as 1832 a member of parliament could defend the retention of that privilege of the House as a security for the freedom of debate. Speaking the language of a seventeenth-century puritan, Lord Milton declared he could conceive of a situation in which it might be necessary for the independence of parliament that no one should betray to the Executive what took place in the House. (*Parl. Deb.*, 3rd Series, ix. 1042.)

[2] The House of Lords silently followed the example of the Commons in 1775 rather than engage in a similar conflict with Wilkes and the London newspapers.

from complete. First, there remained on the journals the resolutions of the Long Parliament (22 March 1642) — resolutions renewed in slightly different language in 1695, 1697, 1722, 1728 and 1738 — which declared it to be a breach of the privileges of the House for any person to report the debates. The breach was uniformly connived at after 1771 except in cases of scandalous misrepresentation. Throughout the nineteenth century the House of Commons held the view that this privilege could not be abandoned and the publication of the debates formally recognized unless they were officially reported; and so full, so accurate and so impartial had the reports become by the 1830s that there was little demand for such a change of practice.[1]

Second, the debates could not be adequately reported until journalists were allowed in the gallery. The Standing Order of 31 October 1705 prohibiting the entry of strangers into the House remained on the journals and was renewed sessionally [2] until 1845, when it was substantially modified.[3] Originally (1662) resorted to for the purpose of preventing interruption of the proceedings of the House, and inconvenience and discomfort to members from the want of sufficient accommodation for strangers, the Standing Order was used in the 1770s to prevent the publication of the debates; and the gallery

[1] See *Parl. Deb.*, 3rd series, ix. 1036, for Joseph Hume's tribute to the work of the parliamentary reporters (31 Jan. 1832). He reminded the House that he had often urged the propriety of having the debates officially reported. On 6 July 1832 *The Times*, referring to a suggestion to that effect made in the House, remarked, 'The nature of the system only requires to be explained, in order that the meanest comprehension may estimate it at its exact worth'. William Tooke advocated official reporting on 22 May 1834 (*Parl. Deb.*, 3rd series, xxiii. 1228).
[2] With slight verbal changes. 'Ordered, that the Serjeant-at-Arms attending this House do from time to time take into his custody any stranger or strangers that he shall see, or be informed of to be in the House or Gallery, while the House, or any Committee of the Whole House, is sitting. Ordered, that no Member of this House do presume to bring any stranger or strangers into the House or Gallery thereof, while the House is sitting.'
[3] 'That the Serjeant-at-Arms attending this House do from time to time take into his custody any stranger whom he may see or who may be reported to him to be in any part of the House or Gallery appropriated to the Members of this House. That no Member of this House do presume to bring any stranger into any part of the House or Gallery appropriated to the Members of this House while the House or a Committee of the Whole House is sitting.'

House of Commons' Debates, 1771–1834

was generally closed.[1] Opinion in the Commons during those years was overwhelmingly against the admission of the public. There was, as yet, little recognition of the importance of having the debates faithfully reported, so that the people might know what their representatives were doing, and be in a position to judge their fitness for re-election. By 1770 parliament had begun to fear the growing power of public opinion, fostered by the gradual rise of the newspaper press as a 'Fourth Estate of the Realm'; and the House of Commons had no wish to make itself accountable to the nation for its proceedings.[2] Lord North was all against opening the gallery even on Budget days,[3] and by 83 votes to 16 the House

[1] It would probably be difficult to find a precedent for the action of the House of Commons on 26 May 1778 when, although the gallery was cleared, one gentleman was allowed to stay. That was Garrick, whose presence, said Burke, did the House honour; 'a man from whom every Member in that House must hold himself indebted on the score of oratory' (*Morning Post*, 28 May 1778).

[2] Rigby discovered another argument. 'When they [strangers] are thus indulged, scarce a day passes without some of the members being put to much inconvenience, and frequently they have been pushed about and insulted.' (*Parl. Hist.*, xix. 210 [30 April 1777].) The results of the more liberal policy adopted by the Lords in 1775 were hardly calculated, in the short run at any rate, to change opinion in the Commons, for more than once, members of the Commons listening to the Lords' debates whilst standing below the Bar alongside the general public, had had their pockets picked. (*Ibid.* 1203 [27 May 1778].) Cf. *ibid.* 210 [30 April 1777]. Cf., also *ibid.*, 672; and the *Morning Chronicle*, 3 Feb. 1778: 'The House of Commons, and the avenues leading thereto, were yesterday so crowded with strangers, that it was with the utmost difficulty the Members could get to the door of the House. At last a number of persons forced themselves into the Gallery in so rude and unjustifiable a manner as to oblige Nathaniel Webb, Esq., instantly to move for the Gallery to be cleared, which was ordered by the House. A great number of ladies, who had taken their seats as soon as the Speaker came down, kept them after the male strangers were turned out, and thought themselves snug for the remainder of the evening, but their happiness took a turn in less than five minutes upon a motion from Governor Johnstone, who rose up in his place and moved that the ladies might be directed to retire. After the dismal sentence had been pronounced by the Speaker, and as the ladies were retiring, one in particular seemed much hurt, and was heard to say "that she should hate the name of Governor Johnstone to the latest hour of her life". Some of these ladies had entered the House as early as noon — particularly, a party brought by Sir George Savile; and more than a score had to wait for some hours before hackney coaches could be found to carry them home.' Ladies were never again admitted to the 'Strangers' portion of the gallery (*Parl. Hist.*, xix. 674 n. See also *Parl. Deb.*, 3rd series, xxxiii. 812; xxxv. 1074–83; Colchester, *Diary and Corresp.*, i. 421; ii. 124, 486.

[3] 'Though it was on very fair public ground that . . . [strangers] had heretofore been admitted on that day.' (*Parl. Hist.*, xix. 209.)

decided (30 April 1777) to keep the gallery shut.[1] In 1778, however, the Speaker, with the acquiescence of the House, relaxed the operation of the Standing Order, but it was occasionally enforced.[2] Until 1875[3] he was obliged to order the instant withdrawal of strangers when any member took notice of their presence.[4] Moreover, the House would sometimes not content itself with clearing the gallery: it would also threaten with its severe displeasure (in other words, with imprisonment) members themselves who, in the absence of the regular reporters, took notes of the speeches and sent them to the press.[5]

Third, even when journalists were permitted to enter the gallery, neither they nor any other strangers were allowed to take notes, until, apparently, 1783. Before that date, notebooks and pencils were used surreptitiously, and in fear of

[1] *Parl. Hist.*, xix. 209, 211 ; *H. of C.J.*, xxxvi. 458.

[2] On 8 March 1784, 3 March 1785, 28 May 1790, 7 June 1793, 24 Nov. 1795, 14 June 1798, 6 July 1803, 6 July 1807, 2, 6, 8, 9, 12, 19 and 27 Feb., and 23 March 1810 ; 4 and 5 March 1813, 26 Jan. 1832, and 29 July 1833. (These are the dates between 1781 and 1834.) See *Parl. Hist.*, xxi. 615 [18 May 1780] : copied from the *Morning Chronicle*.

[3] There was no more zealous advocate in parliament of the freedom of the press than Sheridan, but even he did not suggest the abandonment of the Standing Order. He wished it to be modified so that its exercise should depend, not upon the caprice or pleasure of a single member, but on the decision of the House. His motion, limited though it was, was defeated on 6 Feb. 1810 by 166 to 80 (*Parl. Deb.*, xv. 345), but his view prevailed in 1875.

[4] The Standing Order was very rarely enforced after Feb. 1810, when Charles Yorke, the First Lord of the Admiralty, made himself exceedingly unpopular, especially with the newspaper proprietors, by enforcing the exclusion of strangers during the debates on the conduct of the Walcheren expedition. He professed to be apprehensive lest a garbled publication of the evidence might be made by the newspapers, and he maintained that the public would not suffer, since the evidence was to be officially published with a delay of only a few days. The duke of Richmond, the lord lieutenant of Ireland, commented, in a letter to Richard Ryder, the Home Secretary (4 Feb. 1810) : 'I hope Yorke will carry his point of keeping the Gallery clear. Those who are most inclined to mischief can't speak half so well unless they think some of their rebel friends are in the Gallery' (Richmond MSS., Nat. Lib. of Ireland, 502.)

[5] *Parl. Hist.*, xxxiii. 1487 ; *Morning Chronicle*, 15 June 1798 ; Colchester, *Diary and Corresp.*, i. 156. This threat, however, was exceptional. On 31 Jan. 1832 the House refused to take action against *The Times* and the *Morning Chronicle* which, on the 27th, had published reports of the proceedings on the preceding day, when the Standing Order was enforced. Hume and Warburton avowed that they had taken notes of what had passed, and had given them to reporters. (*Parl. Deb.*, 3rd series, ix. 1035, 1043.)

House of Commons' Debates, 1771–1834

the Serjeant-at-Arms and his underlings.[1]

Fourth, every newspaper reporting a speech which someone complained of as libellous, was liable to action for damages or to prosecution, the member himself being protected by parliamentary privilege. But if a member published his own speech as a pamphlet, or revised a manuscript report of it, or sent notes to the newspaper, he too became liable for the publication. For example, Creevey in 1813 was found guilty of publishing a libel contained in a speech of which he had sent a corrected copy to a Liverpool newspaper.[2]

Finally, until 1853 the gallery was always cleared for a division,[3] and often was not reopened at all when the debate was resumed, or was reopened after a considerable delay.[4]

[1] I think 1783 is the correct date. There is no reference in the journals of the House to the removal of the prohibition, which was certainly in force in 1782 when James Stephen was a reporter. Writing in 1822, he said, rather vaguely: 'For many years past, I believe between thirty and forty, both Houses have relaxed that rule' (*Memoirs*, p. 291). His statement is obviously incorrect so far as the House of Lords was concerned. The *Morning Chronicle* declared on 3 Feb. 1810: 'We remember a time, during the Administration of Lord North, when the Gallery was once shut. The reports of the proceedings, however, went on in the newspapers the same. They were given by members themselves, till at length the good-humoured Lord in the Blue Ribband stepped across the House to Mr. Fox, and said, "Really, Mr. Fox, since we have turned reporters ourselves, the speeches are so clumsy, there is so much misrepresentation and so much nonsense that we must open the Gallery door in our own defence".'

[2] He was fined £100. He had revised his speech to correct misrepresentation in several newspapers. He said: 'Mr. Justice Bailey considered the sending of a speech made in Parliament to a newspaper as a degradation, although he must have known that it was the practice at all times, of the most distinguished persons, in both Houses to publish their own speeches'. Fox, the champion of the liberty of the press, had himself said in 1788 that 'he did not hold the opinion that because members in the House may not only with propriety, but with strict regard to their duty, hold certain language and declare certain sentiments upon any topic under their consideration, the public prints were warranted in giving those to the world at large. The freedom of speech he considered as the first and most essential privilege of Parliament . . . and he could easily imagine many cases in which it would be a gross libel and breach of privilege in a newspaper to publish such words as he would find it necessary to make use of in his place' (*Parl. Deb.*, xxvi. 898-921).

[3] *Ibid.* 3rd series, cxxix. 1112. A division took between twenty and thirty minutes. The princess of Wales was, with other strangers, compelled to retire on 23 Jan. 1810. See, too, Lord Colchester's *Diary and Corresp.*, i. 519 (15 June 1804).

[4] *E.g., Morning Chronicle*, 4 March 1785: 'After the division there was a debate which lasted till near eleven, but as the Speaker would not suffer strangers to be admitted into the Gallery after the division, we quitted the House at 10 o'clock, and know not how it ended'.

231

Essays Presented to Sir Lewis Namier

To that extent, then, the debates still went unreported.

Throughout this period, and, indeed, until 1908, when parliament tardily decided to have the debates officially reported, and reported substantially verbatim, the newspapers [1] were the principal sources drawn upon by *Hansard* and its predecessors. Under what conditions, then, did the reporters work?

There was no 'public' gallery in the House of Commons which was destroyed by fire in 1834.[2] A single gallery was divided by a bar into sections, like the 'floor' of the House beneath it.[3] The two sides were occupied by members themselves on crowded days.[4] The part 'below the Bar', accommodating about two hundred people, was reserved for the general public, who were admitted either by a member's introduction [5] or by queueing, sometimes for hours before

---

[1] The London newspapers only, during this period. The provincial papers, as a rule, merely copied from the London papers. On rare occasions, however, a provincial paper contained an elaborate report of a debate in which local interests were concerned. J. H. Tremayne, M.P. for Cornwall, wrote to his father on 6 April 1825: 'If you read the *Cornwall Gazette* you will have seen the debate on the tin and copper duties given at length, which it was not in the London papers'. (Tremayne MSS., Truro Record Office.)

[2] There was no gallery at all in the House of Lords, and, at the end of the eighteenth century, no one in boots was allowed 'below the Bar'. All strangers were compelled to stand, and the doorkeepers were under strict orders to allow no one to take notes (Hardcastle, *Life of John, Lord Campbell*, i. 108). Notetaking was prohibited as late as 1807 (Buckingham, *Court and Cabinets of George III*, iv. 150). Whilst speaking in support of the Slave Trade Abolition Bill on 5 Feb. 1807, Lord Grenville was interrupted by the earl of Morton, who complained that a person had been taking notes at the Bar. *The Times* next day had a reasonably full report of this incident, of which there is no notice at all in the *Parliamentary Debates*. Eldon remarked that it was the duty of the lord chancellor to put an end to the practice of taking notes. Holland replied that the whole House rather than any individual peer was the conservator of its privileges; and Lord Morton said that if the debate took that turn he should feel obliged to move that the House should be cleared of strangers. *The Times* reporter stated that the order against taking notes was then strictly enforced by the attendants.

[3] The portions 'within the Bar' were known as the side galleries.

[4] Royalty was allowed in the side galleries. When Alexander I of Russia visited the House of Commons on 20 June 1814, it was arranged that he should sit 'where the Duchess of York, &c. usually' sat — in the gallery on the Speaker's right hand. (P.R.O. 30/9/16. Lord Yarmouth to the Speaker, 19 June 1814.)

[5] The eldest son of a member had the privilege of admission by courtesy (P.R.O. 30/9/14, Part 1. Wm. Dacres Adams to the Speaker, 24 Nov. 1804). Wm. Allen, the Quaker, wrote on 4 Feb. 1791: 'I had a great inclination to

House of Commons' Debates, 1771–1834

four o'clock, when the House usually began public business.¹

The reporters were restricted to the back row of the gallery. According to one of them, however, it was actually the best for hearing, and in that position they had no 'neighbours behind them, to help the motion of their pencils with their knees and elbows'.² But, as William ('Memory') Woodfall once told Mr. Speaker Addington, the reporters were continually jostled by members' constituents passing and repassing their seats.³ J. P. Collier, who was on the staff of *The Times* in 1819, attributed the occasional inaccuracy of his own reports to this sort of confusion.⁴ The *Morning Post* thus referred to Sir William Meredith's speech of 11 June 1779:

Sir William spoke a great deal, but a loud *snoring* in the Gallery prevented much of what he said from reaching the ears of the strangers in the Gallery. Whether the *snoring* arose from the want of taste in the persons who slept so soundly, or from any soporiferous effluvia from the Hon. Baronet, it is not our province to decide.⁵

Peter Finnerty, of the *Morning Chronicle*, once presumed to take notes from the front row, although, having been a

hear the debate. . . . A friend whom we met with in the Lobby got a line from a Member to the doorkeeper of the Gallery, for our admittance' (*Life of Wm. Allen*, i. 12).

¹ A new Speaker received from his predecessor a list of persons allowed to sit 'below the Bar', under the gallery. From this list he was not allowed to deviate by the House. There is, apparently, no copy in the papers of Charles Abbot, but evidence exists that, at the beginning of the nineteenth century, the following enjoyed the privilege: members of the royal family; peers with hereditary seats in the House of Lords, together with their heirs apparent or heirs presumptive; the Scottish judges (and, presumably, the English judges too); and the King's Prime Serjeant-at-law, or, when there was no person holding that office, the senior King's Serjeant. In addition, our ambassadors or ministers to foreign courts, upon leave of absence, but only on such days 'for which business was fixed relating to their appointments'. Limited permission seems also to have been extended to under-secretaries of state and one or two principal treasury officials, but not to the private secretary either of the First Lord of the Treasury or of the Secretary of State: permission, that is, for the day 'for which any business was appointed relating to that particular Department' (P.R.O. 30/9/14, Part 1).

² Wm. Jerdan's *Autobiography*, i. 85.
³ Sidmouth MSS., Woodfall to Henry Addington, 25 Nov. 1790.
⁴ *Parl. Deb.*, xl. 1164 (15 June 1819).
⁵ *Morning Post*, 12 June 1779.

reporter for twenty years, he knew the rules. He declined to close his book when ordered to do so by the messenger of the House, and told him to 'go to Hell!' For that indiscretion he narrowly escaped being committed to Newgate. Two other reporters who had moved into the front row were not proceeded against, because they had promptly stopped writing.[1]

The reporters had no priority right of admission. When an important debate was expected, they had to struggle hard against the fierce competition for seats from the general public. So great was the curiosity to hear Burke's speech on economical reform on 11 February 1780, that many people failed to get into the gallery. Among them was William Woodfall, who was therefore unable next day to give more than a brief summary of the debate, based on information from friends.[2] The situation was even worse on 23 May 1803, when there was a debate on the renewal of the war with France: not a single reporter secured a seat.[3]

[1] *Parl. Deb.*, xl. 1182-8 (15 June 1819).

[2] *Morning Chronicle*, 12 Feb. 1780. Cf. Woodfall's remarks on 10 July 1782: 'Feeling it to be a day of great public curiosity and expectation, the Printer yesterday made it a point to attend the Parliament House at an hour more than usually early; but unfortunately for him, such was the eagerness of the crowd (who had obtained admission into the Lobby) to make sure of hearing what might pass, that they suddenly overpowered the door-keepers, and, pressing onward through the front door of the House, filled the Gallery in a second. The consequence was, the Printer was obliged to undergo the very irksome task of waiting about the House the whole day. What follows is a summary state of the debate, furnished by a friend.' Woodfall also failed to secure a seat on 7 May 1782.

[3] *Parl. Hist.*, xxxvi. 1386; Stanhope's *Life of Pitt*, iv. 46; Malmesbury, *Diaries and Corresp.*, iv. 256. The crowd had been waiting to get in since eight o'clock in the morning. Just before half-past three, when the doors were opened, the people outside were extremely disappointed to find the gallery 'nearly filled with the friends of Members, or persons smuggled into the Gallery through the body of the House. Of the whole number outside, many of whom had remained there for seven hours, very few, not more than four or five, gained admission.' *The Times* added: 'The public will, no doubt, have to regret the omission of a debate in which every person in the country is deeply concerned, but they will, we are confident, do us the justice to believe that every exertion was made on our part to obtain admission. We cannot contend with impossibilities, but we sincerely trust that some arrangement will be shortly made to remedy an inconvenience which equally affects the people and their representatives.'

The inconvenience was quickly remedied. Speaker Abbot wrote, in his diary, 24 May 1803: 'Settled with the Serjeant-at-Arms . . . that the Gallery door should be opened every day, if required, at twelve; and the Serjeant

House of Commons' Debates, 1771–1834

The entrance of 'strangers' was often very noisy. William Woodfall described the scene in 1790. As a veteran reporter, he was treated with great respect by his fellow-journalists, and he tried to induce them to behave more seemly:[1]

In vain have I called out from the smoking room (for that ancient name, the First Committee Room into which the Gallery empties itself, still preserves), 'Softly, Gentlemen ! Recollect you are going into the House of Commons and not into a bear-garden !' My remonstrance has ever been considered as a piece of irony, and laughed at as a ridiculous appeal to reason in the moment of madness.[2]

Sometimes the pressure in the passage leading to the gallery was so severe that people were in danger of having a leg or an arm broken.[3] Sir Thomas Lawrence, the portrait painter, once had a narrow escape from sudden death whilst struggling for a seat.[4] On 24 November 1795, the House being engaged in the business of a 'Call', the gallery was not opened until after eight o'clock. People then rushed in so noisily that some of them tried to produce silence by calling out 'Hush !' Several members, however, mistook this sound for a hiss, and

would let the housekeeper understand that the "newswriters" might be let in in their usual places (the back row of the Gallery) as being understood to have the order of particular members, like any other strangers' (Colchester, *Diary and Corresp.*, i. 421).

[1] Sidmouth MSS., Woodfall to H. Addington, 25 Nov. 1790.

[2] 'On Wednesday evening last', someone wrote to the *Gazetteer and New Daily Advertiser* (9 June 1779), 'I got into the Gallery . . . I think I never got into such company before except at a bull-bait or a cock-fight.'

[3] *The Times*, 24 May 1803.

[4] P.R.O. 30/9/16. He recalled the incident many years later, in a letter to the Speaker (20 Feb. 1816), who acceded to his request for a special card of admission for that evening. He wanted to hear Castlereagh's defence of the recent treaty settlement of Europe. Cf. the *Morning Herald*, 18 Feb. 1783 : 'By . . . half past four the House was crowded with the greatest number of members that ever met there since the beginning of the present reign. The side galleries could scarcely contain all those who could not find room in the body of the House, either to sit or stand, and the front Gallery was so full of strangers, and the footways leading into it were so completely choked up by those who could not get seats, that those who were within, and nearly overcome with heat, found it impossible to get out. One gentleman had like to have been squeezed to death.' One day in May 1802 Woodfall said that he had been 'jostled among the mob' in the House of Lords until he was 'black and blue all over', after fifteen hours on his legs (on 13 and 14 May). [To Lord Auckland, 14 [? 15] May 1802. (Add. MSS. 34455, f. 498.)]

had the gallery cleared. After more than an hour's penance the strangers were allowed to return, Sheridan meanwhile having made an eloquent plea that, in view of the critical state of the war, the public should know what was being done. But even Cobbett, the democrat, was against having the gallery open as a matter of right, and said that, had he been a member, he would have voted against Sheridan's motion to modify the Standing Order (6 February 1810):[1]

That is quite out of the question, for, such would be the noise and tumult upon all occasions of great public interest, that the Members would be unable to hear one another, and, of course, nobody in the Gallery could hear them. There must be, at once, an end to all debate-reporting, at least. A few persons might catch here and there a part of the debate with their ears; but no debate could ever go forth to the public.

Every part of the House was crowded to excess on 25 February 1813 when Grattan initiated a debate on the Catholic question. According to the *Courier*,

The greatest difficulty was experienced by the Members in passing until a body of constables were directed to clear the entrance to the Lobby. The moment the Gallery door was opened, a rush took place which threatened at one time to be attended with fatal consequences. We are, however, happy to say no serious accident happened. The noise and confusion which were occasioned by this tumultuous ingress of such a body of people into the Gallery excited the attention of the Speaker, who observed, 'That if the disturbance in the Gallery continued, he trusted some hon. Member would feel it his duty to move the Standing Order for the exclusion of strangers'. This had the effect of producing a state of comparative silence.[2]

Disorder on the 'floor' of the House, increasing with the lateness of the hour, added to the difficulties of the reporters. Anxious to get to their beds, members beeame more and more impatient for the adjournment or the division, and would-be speakers were discouraged by loud cries for the Question. When, on 20 March 1782, the Speaker angered the Opposition

---

[1] Cobbett's *Pol. Register*, 17 Feb. 1810.
[2] *Courier*, 26 Feb. 1813.

by calling on Lord North instead of Lord Surrey, as had been expected, there followed what Woodfall described as 'a scene of clamour and confusion unexampled in the annals of Parliament'. Everyone's ears were 'stunned with the noise', and one member, Mr. Baker, shouted 'till he was absolutely hoarse'.[1]

When James Stephen reported the debates for the *Morning Post* in 1781 and 1782, at a salary of two guineas a week, no one in the gallery was allowed to take notes : [2]

> To use a pen or pencil ... was deemed a high contempt, so much so that I once saw a gentleman taken into custody and turned indignantly out, merely for taking down a figure or two with his pencil when Lord North was opening his Budget.[3] We were obliged, therefore, to depend on memory alone, and had no assistance in the work, one reporter for each House being all that any paper employed.

At that time Woodfall was not only the editor and printer but also the sole reporter of the *Morning Chronicle*. Whenever an important debate required his attendance in the House of Lords, there was no report, or only a very brief report, of the proceedings in the Commons. Sometimes he sat in the gallery, without moving, for thirteen hours. Reaching home at six, seven or even eight o'clock the following morning, he then had to begin writing what he modestly described as 'A hasty sketch of the debate' — which occupied up to eight columns of the paper — and also to superintend the printing.[4]

---

[1] *Morning Chronicle*, 21 March 1782. On 26 May 1778 there were violent scenes in the House, with fifty members on their legs at one moment, shouting 'Order !', 'the Chair !'. The Speaker was so disgusted with their behaviour that he said they were not fit to be described as gentlemen. (*Morning Post*, 27 May 1778.) See, also, *H. of C.J.*, xlviii. 11 (14 Dec. 1792).

[2] *Memoirs of James Stephen* (ed. M. M. Bevington), pp. 291-4.

[3] There seems to be no corroboration of this statement in *H. of C.J.*, but its accuracy must, I think, be accepted.

[4] See Add. MSS. 34453, f. 147, for Woodfall's own account of the manner in which he composed his report of Lord Auckland's speech in the House of Lords on 6 Jan. 1795 : 'I sat down the instant I came home, and made minutes, brief indeed, but enough to rouse my recollection of the whole that passed. I have been these two days [16 and 17 Jan.] employed in drawing the arguments of the speakers from the short heads, that cost me from eight at night till four in the morning, into the length and circumstantial detail that belonged to them.'

He was always apologizing to his readers for the extreme hurry in which his 'sketch' was written, and for the lateness of the printing. The newsmen who had to deliver papers out of town (to such distant 'villages', for example, as Hampstead, Highgate or Kentish Town) must have become terribly impatient when an all-night sitting of the House prevented them from finishing their work before the afternoon. Especially during those years when note-taking was forbidden, and when no reporter had colleagues who could share the work, the labour, as Woodfall said, was obviously great, the task toilsome, and the assiduity of the journalist unremitting. At the close of the Session he took the earliest opportunity of thanking the public for submitting so uncomplainingly to the inconvenience resulting from late publication. 'During the whole parliamentary campaign the rigour of his service has been softened by the fostering hand of public protection.'[1] Close confinement for long hours, night after night, with the excessive heat reducing some people to an almost fainting condition, occasionally made Woodfall (and others, no doubt) extremely ill; he would assure his patrons that he would resume his labours as soon as he recovered his strength.[2]

On 26 November 1795 the *Oracle* newspaper had the following typical comment on one of the speakers in the debate: 'Mr. Addington ... followed ... but in such a tone of voice as enabled us to collect no more than a few detached sentences rendered perfectly inaudible at the distance we were placed, and one or two classical quotations.'[3]

The position of the gallery made it impossible for the reporters to hear members whose voices were not powerful; and even in the clearest speakers phrases were often lost or

[1] *Morning Chronicle*, 19 July 1781. Cf. *ibid.*, 12 July 1782.
[2] *Ibid.*, 9 March 1782. Cf. *ibid.*, 19 June 1782: 'The Printer felt himself so exceedingly fatigued with the heat of the House, he was too much depressed to be capable of doing anything like tolerable justice to so very important a debate'.
[3] Almost invariably from the Latin classics. On one occasion a Greek quotation was so unfavourably received by the House that the wit, Mr. Courtenay, remembering this, refrained from following that example, as he too 'wished to address himself to the country gentlemen', who, for the most part, were quite incapable of appreciating such gems (*ibid.*, 26 April 1796).

misunderstood. In the course of the debate on 4 May 1812, for example, W. H. Lyttelton referred to the recent appointment of Colonel McMahon as the Prince Regent's private secretary, and the *Morning Chronicle* reported him as having described the Colonel as a 'gamester and spendthrift'. McMahon wrote to him, complaining of these epithets, and saying that he had never gambled and had never been rich enough to be extravagant. Lyttelton, in reply, said that he had written to the editor desiring him to correct the report: he had said, not that the Colonel was a gamester and spendthrift, but that 'he [Lyttelton] would rather give hundreds of thousands to a Nelson or a Wellington than a single farthing to a Gaveston or a Despenser'.[1] He had been alluding to the favourites of Edward II.

The reporters never complained of Canning's inaudibility, but he spoke so fast, especially when excited, that they could not keep up with him. Sir William Young, too, 'spoke with such rapidity and in so indistinct a manner that it was with greatest difficulty we could understand him'.[2]

The back row of the gallery may have been the best for hearing, but it was obviously the worst for seeing, and the newspapers were full of complaints that, as the speaker could not be seen (members often spoke from *under* the gallery) he could not be named. Also, speeches were often attributed to the wrong person. The *Oracle* of 4 December 1795 informed its readers : 'In our report of yesterday ... to the observations of Mr. Sheridan was prefixed the name of Mr. Erskine, who did not speak in that debate'.

During this period, though there was some shorthand, there was no verbatim reporting.[3] Heavy taxation of newspapers before 1836 tended severely to limit both the sale and

[1] *Letters of George IV*, i. 72-3. On 10 Nov. 1795 J. T. Stanley was reported as saying that 'at every meeting ... of a public nature, the Constitution and existing establishments had more friends than Ministers' (*Parl. Register*, xliii. 121 [10, not 9 Nov., as there stated].) 'Ministers' was obviously a mistake for 'enemies'. The reporter had misheard.
[2] *Morning Chronicle*, 18 Feb. 1796.
[3] Campbell, the lord chancellor, and himself a parliamentary reporter at the beginning of the nineteenth century, considered that the non-existence of

the size; and although the public appetite for parliamentary debates was almost insatiable, the reports were much curtailed, especially before the 1820s. That was so even when the entire newspaper was given over to an important debate. Those occasions were necessarily few, because then, as always, advertisements were the lifeblood of a newspaper and could not be indefinitely withheld. Many speeches had to be omitted altogether, and even those of the 'great guns' like Fox and Pitt could not be given in full. In Pitt's time a typical London newspaper consisted of only a single sheet, about 25 by 19 inches, folded once so as to make four pages, with four columns to the page. Even if the debate filled the whole paper (and the usual space was much less than half) it ran to only about 19,000 words, or, in point of time, about $2\frac{3}{4}$ hours. When very small (and almost unreadable) type was used, the report could be expanded seventy per cent or more.[1] An important debate rarely went on for less than eight hours, and sometimes it lasted twelve, fourteen and even sixteen hours. The extent to which the newspaper reports were condensed can readily be estimated.

By 1815 a slightly larger sheet was being used: about 32 by 21 inches; and the abolition in 1825 of the statutory restrictions on the size of a sheet meant that, in the late 1820s, a newspaper like *The Times* normally consisted of a single sheet three feet by two — nearly twice as large as the one at the beginning of the century. *The Times* doubled its size on 19 January 1829 — being printed on a single sheet, four feet by three, containing 48 columns. The largest hitherto manufactured, it could be folded twice and cut so as to make eight pages of the usual size.[2] The intention was that *The Times* should appear in that form only occasionally during the parliamentary session. Sometimes as much as 18 columns,

shorthand reporting greatly improved the quality of a speech. 'If Pitt could have been taken down *verbatim*, all his sentences, however long and involved, would have been found complete and grammatical, but it would have been sometimes stiff and cumbrous and vapid.' (Hardcastle's *Campbell*, i. 106.)

[1] *E.g. True Briton*, 31 Dec. 1796.

[2] This device was adopted to circumvent the stamp duty: a supplementary sheet would have been taxed even though given away.

House of Commons' Debates, 1771–1834

representing about 54,000 words or about eight hours of the debate, were devoted to parliamentary proceedings: but those were still exceptional performances.

During the last quarter of the eighteenth century the *Morning Chronicle* usually had the fullest reports, and, until the paper changed hands in 1789, they were generally written by Woodfall.[1] How, it may be asked, in pre-1783 days when note-taking was prohibited, did he contrive to report a debate in nearly eighteen columns? For example, on Saturday, 23 February 1782, his 'very slight sketch'[2] of the preceding night's debate occupied 6½ columns. He worked all day Sunday at the concluding portion, which filled 11 columns on the Monday.[3] On occasions of this sort he must have relied

---

[1] As late as 1803 some people thought that the *Morning Chronicle* had the best reports (Add. MSS. 35724, f. 48). The *True Briton*, too, at that time had admirable reports, filling the whole, or nearly the whole paper. It declared on 6 Dec. 1798: 'We have the satisfaction of hearing from every quarter that our report of Mr. Pitt's speech on Monday night in the House of Commons was by far the most accurate and faithful of any that was given'. Occasionally the *Oracle* had a fuller report than the *Morning Chronicle* (e.g. 27 Nov. 1795) and the debate which followed the division on 30 Nov. 1795 took up more than half a column in the *Oracle*, and only a few lines in the *Chronicle*. For the debates, said Canning in 1794, 'the *Sun* is vile; the *Star*, though an Opposition paper, is better, and the *Morning Chronicle* better still' (A. Aspinall, *Politics and the Press*, p. 295). A year later, he thought that the *Oracle*'s debates were well done, but that those of the *Morning Post* were not worth reading. 'Indeed, it grows so stupid as well as mischievous that I have thoughts of leaving it off entirely.' Henry Hobhouse (the permanent under-secretary of state in the Home Department) informed Peel on 13 Jan. 1825 that Dr. Stoddart, the editor of the *New Times*, hoped by getting better reporters to rival *The Times* and *Chronicle*, 'and, of course, to merit and obtain your recommendation' (Add. MSS. 40372, f. 108). On the 31st Stoddart wrote to Peel: 'As Mr Hobhouse was kind enough to say he would mention to you the arrangements which have been made for rendering the *New Times* more effectual in the humble support which it gives to Government, I take the liberty of forwarding you a copy which shows the first result of those arrangements in the improved *external* appearance of the paper. The approaching session will, I hope, exhibit a still more important improvement in the parliamentary reports' (Add. MSS. 40372, f. 289).

[2] So dull was the debate on the navy estimates on 13 Feb. 1782 that Woodfall told his readers that he should give 'barely a few hints of the principal objections stated' — yet his 'slight sketch' ran to more than 8 columns.

[3] One can find an even more striking example. The debate of Friday, 8 March 1782, was given in 6 columns on Saturday the 9th, a further 6 columns on Monday the 11th, another 4½ on the 18th and 4½ more on the 19th. This represents between 3 and 3¼ hours of the debate, which lasted about 10 hours. Other newspapers, too, made great efforts to give full reports. For example, the *Gazetteer* of 11 Feb. 1780 published a 4½-column account of the Lords' debate

on something more than his extraordinary memory. The explanation is that he had friends on both sides of the House who supplied him with their own notes.[1] In that way he could sometimes give a 4-column report of a debate in the Commons after he himself had spent the whole night listening to the peers.[2] Thus, on 22 February 1780 he said he could 'give his readers only a word or two [actually, he gave them a column] of intelligence respecting the business of the day in the House of Commons, which he collected from the information of the Members, his friends'. The intricate Budget figures given by the newspapers the day after the chancellor's speech at times when note-taking in the gallery was still prohibited, were evidently furnished by members; and the preliminary reports were supplemented, a day or two later, from information again supplied by them. Thus, the *Morning Chronicle* stated on Wednesday, 27 February 1782, the day after its first report of the Budget speech: 'By way of supplement to our account of Monday's debate . . . a correspondent has favoured us with the following accurate state of the Budget as opened by Lord North, with each article arranged under its proper head'.[3] On 28 February 1782 Woodfall printed a 4½-column sketch of the Commons' debate the previous even-

on the 8th, with additions of 4 columns on the 12th and 6 columns on the 14th. On 25 Jan. 1782 the *Morning Herald* had a 5-column (the *Chronicle* a 6½-column) report of the debate in the Commons on the 24th. On the 26th the *Herald* copied word for word the *Chronicle*'s concluding part of that debate — a remarkable example of piracy.

[1] A. Aspinall, *Politics and the Press*, p. 444. Woodfall stated on 18 Feb. 1783 that he had 'prevailed on a friend' to report the previous day's debate in the Lords, whilst he himself attended in the Commons. He could not, of course, always rely on members for a report or for notes when he himself could not attend. Thus the *Morning Chronicle* had no report of the Commons' debate on 31 Jan. 1782, whilst the *Morning Herald* had nearly 2 columns. The *Herald*, unlike the *Chronicle*, had two reporters in 1782.

[2] E.g. *Morning Chronicle*, 13 June 1781.

[3] A double column of figures followed. On 19 Dec. 1779 Woodfall asked Charles Jenkinson, then secretary-at-war, for a correct statement of the estimates voted in the House of Commons the previous day, and explained that, 'to avoid an error', he had declined attempting to report in that day's paper what the sums actually were. He went on to express the hope that 'as Almon has promised an exact account shall be laid before the public tomorrow in his *London Courant*, Mr. Jenkinson will have no objection to the *Morning Chronicle*'s having the same advantage' (Add. MSS. 38212, f. 274).

ing, when he was in the House of Lords. 'The following', he said, 'is as good an outline of it as his casual conversations with different Members would enable him to sketch.' Again, on 7 March 1782, after being similarly absent, he stated that his 4-column report of the Commons' debate originated thus: 'He learnt the greater part... from a friend, who did him the favour to relate so much of the debate to him'.[1]

So vigorously did the newspapers protest whenever the reporters were excluded, that members apparently seemed to think that the publication of their speeches was desired more by the editors than by themselves. If that really was their impression it was erroneous. As far as the personal convenience and interests of the proprietors were concerned, there was no question of hardship: they were better able to satisfy their advertising friends and to increase their income. It was the public that was so grievously disappointed; and on one occasion when strangers were ordered to withdraw, some people in the front row of the gallery hissed, and 'behaved in the most indecent manner'.[2]

Although members might protest that they cared very little whether the press reported their speeches or not, some of them cared a good deal, and saw to it that correct copies were published.[3] For example, on Wednesday, 30 May 1781, the *Morning Chronicle* stated: 'The following is an authentic copy of the speech of Mr. Estwick, the Agent for the Island of Barbadoes, against the petition of the sugar refiners in the

[1] Woodfall was given an account of the course of the debate on 8 May 1780 after the exclusion of strangers in anticipation of a division (*Morning Chronicle*, 9 May 1780).

[2] The *Courier*, 3 Feb. 1810; the *Sun*, 3 Feb. 1810. See also the *Courier*'s remarks on the 7th. William Eden's speech of 11 June 1779, reported in the *Morning Chronicle* in 21 lines next day, was amplified in the *Morning Post* on the 14th, in nearly 2½ columns. The *Gazetteer* of the 14th declared: 'The very mutilated and imperfect accounts which have appeared in the public prints relative to the debate on Sir William Meredith's motion in the House of Commons on Friday, has induced a correspondent, who was present, to favour the *Gazetteer* with an authentic account of the important proceedings of that day, which will appear in this Paper tomorrow'. There were nearly 5 columns of it.

[3] 'It is very unlucky', wrote Burke, 'that the reputation of a speaker in the House of Commons depends far less on what he says than on the account of it in the newspapers' (*Epistolary Corresp. of Burke and French Laurence*, p. 152).

House of Commons on Monday last'.[1] On 5 June 1781 the *Morning Chronicle* gave Wraxall's speech eleven days earlier 'more in detail than it has yet appeared'.[2] Reporting John Courtenay's speech on 15 June 1781, the *Chronicle* merely said, 'Mr. Courtenay in a most able manner attacked the Marriage Act, and at first onset so hid his argument under the veil of irony as to make it a second time almost doubtful which point he intended supporting'. Evidently dissatisfied with this equivocal statement, Courtenay sent a report of his speech to Woodfall, who, on the 19th, printed 'A more copious account [in $2\frac{1}{2}$ columns] of the speech ... than we could find time to lay before our readers in Saturday's paper'. One may guess that the letter signed 'Memory', published in the *Morning Chronicle* on 28 February 1781, was written by Courtenay himself:

> Observing the speech of Mr. Courtenay relative to the reformation of the Civil List to be much misrepresented in some of the public prints, as if that gentleman had only indulged a rich vein of ridicule, without serious argument, against the virtuous Herculean struggles of Opposition to cleanse the Augean stables, I think it a justice to Mr. Courtenay, as I was present during the debate, to send you the substance of that gentleman's speech, on your printing which, it will appear he can be as argumentative as a Bishop, without his dullness.

Woodfall told his readers on 9 March 1782 that, as he had not reached home until after three o'clock in the morning, 'and being, in consequence of the very great heat of the House extremely fatigued and indisposed', he had been unable to write anything more than a 'very slight outline' [in 6 columns] of the night's debate. Yet that report, in the third

---

[1] It took up more than a column, and was in the first person.

[2] In one column. William Adam's speech of 24 April 1780 was revised in the *Morning Chronicle* as late as 8 May (in more than 3 columns, as against little more than half a column on the 25th). Fox's was similarly revised on 10 May, in 4 columns. Woodfall added the comment: 'The above is but a rude and imperfect sketch of what Mr. Fox said on the occasion. The distance is so great, and so many different debates have passed the mind of the reporter since the 24th of April, that his memory was not so much at his command as it in some cases has been.'

person, included what was obviously a full account, in the first person, of James Martin's speech.¹ Martin must have written it out whilst in the House, and handed it over to Woodfall in the early hours of the morning.²

One can hardly doubt that it was the action of members in supplying Woodfall and other printers with notes and verbal information, that, in 1783, defeated the attempt to forbid note-taking in the gallery. Long after the removal of the ban, members frequently sent corrected reports of their speeches to the newspapers.³ A curious illustration of the anxiety of members to be adequately reported is afforded by the statement of a reporter employed by the *Morning Post* in 1810: he said that he had been offered money by a member in return for a particularly good report of the speech which he was about to make: ⁴

To the note I gave no answer, and to the hon. gentleman's speech I paid precisely that attention to which . . . it appeared to me to

¹ It is reproduced in *Parl. Hist.*, xxii. 1122-5.
² The *Morning Chronicle*'s report of the Lords' debate of 4 Feb. 1782 affords a striking illustration of the communication of an individual speech to the press for immediate publication. The *Morning Herald*'s account of this debate is quite different from that of the *Chronicle*, with the significant exception of Lord Abingdon's speech, which is absolutely identical, in the first person, and with the Latin quotation. Abingdon must have written out two copies of his speech, and communicated them that same night to both papers. It is in *Parl. Hist.*, xxii. 972-4. See Add. MSS. 34420, f. 72, for an example of Woodfall's being helped by the speakers ('a firm phalanx of powerful allies') to revise for publication in a pamphlet the debate in the Irish House of Commons on Friday, 12 Aug. 1785 (he had gone over to Dublin specially to report the debates on the proposed new commercial treaty between Ireland and Great Britain). He said he should have made 'a sad hand' of the business without that assistance, on account of his want of familiarity with faces, sentiments and political connexions. 'My chief personal business', he added, 'has been to throw in the little by-blows which are material (though from the general style and tenor of their reports here they seem to have no idea of their importance) and to correct and meliorate the violence done to grammar and English by such of the members as attempt in committing their speeches to paper to change the first person to the third.'
³ The *True Briton* of 20 Feb. 1796 stated: 'We give the following as a more full and correct copy of Sir Richard Hill's speech . . . than what appeared in our Paper of yesterday'.
⁴ Cobbett's *Pol. Register*, 17 Feb. 1810. George Rose, the joint secretary of the treasury, wrote to Lord Auckland, 24 Dec. 1793: 'He [*i.e.* Woodfall] has for many years had £400 a year for giving the speeches of Mr. Fox and Mr. Sheridan much more at length and better than he did those of Mr. Pitt and Mr. Dundas; all which time, too, the politics of his paper were very trimming'

be entitled. The next day the hon. Member enclosed to me a cheque upon his banker. This I instantly returned, accompanied by a few lines in which I observed that he had entirely mistaken my character, and, I firmly believed, the character of all my coadjutors, if he imagined that we were to be influenced in the performance of . . . a public duty by any private consideration. . . . To a gentleman, the reporter of another paper, this hon. Member made a similar application, and from him he experienced a similar line of conduct.

When there was an important debate on Irish affairs the Irish secretary would send to Dublin a full report of his own speech, for the ministerial newspapers. Thus, William Wellesley-Pole wrote to the lord lieutenant, the duke of Richmond, on 4 February 1812,[1] 'Flint sent an account of our debate to Sir Charles Saxton after the House broke up this morning. I spoke so very late that no good report of me can be in today's papers. However, a very copious report will go by the express and should be inserted in our papers. On this I will write a line to Saxton'.[2] Four days later the *Dublin Journal* published a 6-column report of the debate, Wellesley-Pole's speech occupying more than half this space. Then, on the 15th, there appeared the special report of that speech, in nearly 8 columns — and this was only a portion, the rest following on the 20th in 5 more columns. The editor remarked, 'Mr. Pole's speech, of which we have given an outline, occupied two hours and a half in the delivery, and was received throughout with repeated cheers and the most marked attention'. Wellesley-Pole wrote to the lord lieutenant on 17 March 1811, with reference to an Opposition motion on the Catholic question ten days earlier: 'I hope to be able to send you some copies of my speech in a day or two. I have corrected it, and I hope its circulation will do good.'[3] The speech was doubtless

(*Journal and Corresp. of Lord Auckland*, iii. 165). For the Government subsidies paid to the *Morning Chronicle* until 1789, and later to Woodfall's newspaper, the *Diary*, see A. Aspinall, *Politics and the Press*, p. 69.

[1] Nat. Lib. of Ireland, Richmond MSS., 984. Cf. *Journal and Corresp. of Lord Auckland*, iv. 87 (plans for the accurate reporting, and circulating in Ireland, of Pitt's speech on 31 Jan. 1799).

[2] Flint and Saxton were under-secretaries in the Irish Office in London.

[3] Nat. Lib. of Ireland, Richmond MSS., 752.

House of Commons' Debates, 1771–1834

circulated in pamphlet form at the expense of the Irish Government.[1]

Members, in fact, frequently revised their speeches for publication as pamphlets.[2] Either they wished the country to know what they had really said (or would have liked to say), or else they wanted to guard against error and misrepresentation.[3] The *Morning Chronicle*, announcing on 27 March 1795 that Fox's speech of the preceding Tuesday would appear shortly, declared that the newspaper report had been 'carefully revised, enlarged and collated with the notes of several Members of the House'.

At the request of Lord Grenville and Lord Mornington, Matthew Montagu, M.P. for Tregony, took down in shorthand Pitt's Budget speech in 1792, and it was afterwards corrected for the press by Pitt himself. He, however, unlike Canning, revised only a few of his speeches.[4] Huskisson sometimes wrote out his at length, and the drafts were later used when a three-volume edition of them was being prepared.[5] J. Wright, the printer, wrote to Peel on 10 March 1826:[6]

As a correct report of your speech of last night [on the criminal law] will certainly be looked for by the public and as you may not

---

[1] On 29 June 1813 Peel replied in the House to some observations of Sir Henry Montgomery respecting the lord lieutenant, the duke of Richmond. Next day he wrote to William Gregory, the Civil under-secretary in Dublin: 'Enclosed is a more correct report of what I did say than what the papers have inserted. It is of more consequence that it should appear correct in the Irish papers than here' (Add. MSS. 40284, f. 36).

[2] Joseph Marryat's speech of 26 Jan. 1810, upon Manning's motion on the subject of marine insurance, was published by the special committee at Lloyd's, price 1s. 6d.

[3] Charles Yorke's speech on 17 Dec. 1790 is given in the *Parliamentary History* in only seven lines (xxviii. 1060). On the 18th he wrote to his uncle Lord Hardwicke, asking him to 'send a short account' of his speech 'to the Cambridge Paper, to prevent misrepresentation' (he was member for Cambridgeshire). (Add. MSS. 35392, f. 194).

[4] Colchester, *Diary and Corresp.*, i. 75; Introduction to Pitt's *Collected Speeches* (3 vols., second edition, 1808). Some of them 'were communicated by respectable members of the House of Commons from private notes in their own possession'. See also Introduction to Therry's edition of Canning's *Speeches* (6 vols., 1836). The facsimile there of some of his corrections of his speech on Portugal, 12 Dec. 1826, shows with what care Canning remodelled it.

[5] Add. MSS. 38767-8.

[6] *Ibid.* 40386, f. 1. It was Wright who edited Huskisson's speeches.

be able to spare time to write it out yourself, I beg leave to say that I will immediately prepare, if such should be your wish, as full a report as I possibly can, and submit it for your correction in the same way that I have just done the enclosed very important speech of Mr. Huskisson, and published it at a shilling, provided the Home Department would take of me a certain number of copies as has been the case with Mr. Huskisson's speech. I would engage to send you half of it on Sunday morning, and the rest on Monday.

P.S. I enclose you a few sheets of the manuscript of Mr. Huskisson's speech, by which you will see the manner in which I propose to write it out.

Members themselves sometimes reported the debates when the gallery was shut — as, for example, on 5 March 1813 when the affairs of the princess of Wales were under discussion. Creevey wrote, next day :[1]

I was determined to try how far I could proceed in reports of debates when the professional reporters were excluded ; so I took my pen, ink and paper into the Gallery, and in the face of the whole House set to work at 6 o'clock ; and when I had finished my notes of Johnstone, Castlereagh and Whitbread's speeches I retired to write them out fair, and I did not finish till one this morning, when they went to the *Chronicle*, and are there, you see, in that paper of today. I was relieved by Parnell, who finished the rest, and I have been complimented universally and most warmly today for the *Chronicle* and my part of this report.

Neither Woodfall nor, we may suspect, his fellow-journalists, would have claimed that their reports accurately represented what was said in parliament: the conditions of reporting were all against it. The same may be said of 'corrected' speeches. *The Times* had some pertinent remarks about them in 1832 :[2]

If this version [3] contain passages which the noble or honourable orator repents him of, or which may be disagreeable to his constituents, he strikes them out, of course ; and if (which after having heard the speeches of others, is not improbable) any good

[1] Creevey typescript, in the possession of Sir John Murray.
[2] *The Times*, 6 July 1832.
[3] That of the *Mirror of Parliament*, which 'is an authentic record of the speeches which noble lords or hon. members, after a day's reflection, think they *ought* to have made'.

things occur to him as things which he might have said with advantage, it is not to be expected that he will resist this temptation of inserting them, though he never thought of uttering them at the time. Now, it can hardly be necessary to suggest that no reliance is to be placed upon reports of the proceedings in Parliament which are conducted upon such a system as this.

Parliament always felt that, whether the debates were to be published by permission or by connivance, it was right and proper that they should be fairly reported, and not, as Charles Wynn put it (14 June 1819), 'converted into an engine to gratify private malice or party purposes'.[1]

From time to time members complained of wilful misrepresentation of their speeches. Fox said in 1788 that he scarcely ever looked at a newspaper report without finding examples, but he thought it beneath him to take any notice of it himself.[2] Yet how could he expect fairer treatment from politically hostile newspapers when he described them as 'the Minister's miserable prints'?[3] Editors freely admitted that, in view of the difficulties under which reporters worked, and the haste with which the reports were prepared for publication, casual misrepresentation, at any rate, was inevitable. Wilberforce was once very angry with the *Morning Chronicle* for scandalously misrepresenting his speeches, yet he abandoned his intention of publishing correct versions as pamphlets.[4] Fourteen years later (in 1812) he was making similar complaints against that newspaper.[5] Repudiating charges of this nature, the *Chronicle* on one occasion remarked that parliament possessed an adequate security against misrepresentation, in the number and rivalry of the newspapers.[6]

[1] *Parl. Deb.*, xl. 1146.
[2] *Parl. Hist.*, xxvii. 718.
[3] *Parl. Register*, xxxvii. 182 (21 Jan. 1794).
[4] *Life of Wilberforce*, by his sons, ii. 324 ; iii. 75-6.
[5] *Ibid.* iv. 6-7. It was, however, to the *Morning Chronicle* that he sent a corrected copy of his speech on the slave trade on 6 June 1814 (*ibid.* iv. 187).
[6] *Morning Chronicle*, 31 Dec. 1798. The Irish newspapers were worse offenders than the English. W. V. Fitzgerald once wrote to Peel, when Irish secretary (the letter is undated) : 'I see the *Freeman's Journal* makes free with us — puts assertions into our mouths and then gives us the *lie* without circumlocution. The *Evening Post* says that I was *inarticulate* from *rage*' (Add. MSS. 40207, f. 192).

Writing in 1822, James Stephen was very critical of his successors in the gallery. They were prone 'to gratify their political and personal predilections and antipathies' with 'a shameful partiality and injustice'. They fully reported the speeches of members whom they liked, dismissing in a few lines or ignoring altogether those of members they disliked.[1] Windham's was the most notorious example of a member being unreported who had quarrelled with the press:[2] an example which prompted Perceval, when prime minister, to talk about 'the impossibility of suffering the newspapers to go on to report debates as they now do, suppressing systematically the entire speeches of particular Members', and adding that the Government would have to interfere to put an end to tyranny.[3] Whether it ever occurred to Perceval that the solution was to have the debates officially reported, we do not know.[4]

In spite of James Stephen's strictures, one may say with confidence that, on the whole, the reporters performed a difficult task competently and impartially. Amongst their number was a considerable proportion of university-trained men, some of whom rose to great eminence in literature, law and politics. It is, of course, possible to find criticisms of their work,[5] but by 1830 there was general admiration for the

[1] *Memoirs of James Stephen*, p. 292. Cobbett wrote to his colleague, John Wright (13 March 1808): 'I have before me a letter from Lord Folkestone complaining bitterly of the curtailing of his debate by the reporters. He requests me to desire *you* to be *full* upon it. I shall advise him to write out his speech' (Add. MSS. 22906, f. 364). The reporters always dealt fully only with subjects which excited public interest, and many questions were passed over without any notice at all.

[2] In July 1833 *The Times*' reporters refused to report any more of O'Connell's speeches until he apologized for having asserted that some of their reports were designedly false (*Parl. Deb.*, 3rd series, xx. 6, 67-95). See also *ibid.* xxiii. 1243, and xv. 336, for the case of Tierney; also, *Farington Diary*, v. 21, 196; vi. 28-9.

[3] Colchester, *Diary and Corresp.*, ii. 261. For allegations of suppression as late as 1832 during the fierce controversy over the Reform Bill, see *Parl. Deb.*, 3rd series, xiii. 908.

[4] George Dawson expressed the hope (20 June 1832) that one of the first objects of the reformed parliament would be 'that the front row of the Gallery should be occupied by gentlemen under the control and superintendence of the House, and who should be responsible to it for . . . giving authentic, impartial and official reports of the debates' (*ibid.* 909).

[5] *E.g.* Lord Haddington to Mrs. Huskisson, 20 Oct. 1831 (referring to his

way in which it was done. That result could not have been achieved unless conditions in the gallery had improved since the turn of the century, and unless the increasing prosperity of the leading newspapers had made possible the employment of six or seven times as many reporters as in the days of Woodfall and Stephen.[1] By 1824 they were allowed to enter the gallery after the door had been locked against other strangers; and they had secured a private entrance from the corridor of the gallery into the gallery itself, thus enabling them to avoid the crowd. Although the gallery was still cleared for a division, they were no longer thrust downstairs, and they could reoccupy their seats before the admittance of other strangers.[2]

The various collections of *Debates*[3] were, then, compiled chiefly from newspaper reports. All the editors seem to have

recent speech on the Reform Bill as reported by the *Mirror of Parliament*): 'If you were to see the stuff sent to me by the shorthand writers you would believe me when I assure you that though I corrected that stuff as well as I could, I am not answerable for all the grammar of the enclosed. I found infinite difficulty in making anything of it, but perhaps that was as much the fault of the speaker as of the reporter' (Add. MSS. 39948, f. 138). Charles Ellis wrote to his friend Lord Granville, 10 March 1826 : 'Dudley made an admirable slavery speech in the Lords on Tuesday. But it is shockingly reported. It would seem as if the reporters had been quite mystified, and not to [have] had a notion of what he was at ! It was in his very best and most caustic manner' (P.R.O. 30/29/9. Granville MSS.). See also Buckingham, *Court of George IV*, i. 145, 289-90.

[1] According to the writer of the article on Newspapers in the *Westminster Review* (July 1824, p. 204) it was Perry, the editor and proprietor of the *Morning Chronicle*, who 'brought to its present degree of accuracy and usefulness' the reporting of the debates. Each reporter took notes in the gallery or at the bar of the House of Lords for one, or two hours, and was then relieved by his successor. He retired to write from his notes the speeches he had heard, and the reports of the early part of the debate were printed whilst it was still proceeding. In 1819 *The Times* had thirteen or fourteen parliamentary reporters (*Parl. Deb.*, xl. 1165).

[2] *Westminster Review*, July 1824, p. 206. In 1833 the number of parliamentary reporters was between forty and fifty, some of them, said Peel, 'holding commissions in the Army and Navy, several at the Bar, most of them having received an academical education, and occupying, therefore, the situation of gentlemen' (*Parl. Deb.*, 3rd series, xx. 86).

[3] There is an incomplete list in the *Bulletin of the Institute of Historical Research*, x. 171-7. The following should be added, though they are not so important as *Debrett* (and the continuation of that series by Woodfall and Stockdale), Cobbett's *Parliamentary History*, and Cobbett's *Parliamentary Debates* (continued by Hansard):

(a) *Jordan's Parliamentary Journal*, which apparently started with the debate

Essays Presented to Sir Lewis Namier

invited members to submit notes or corrected reports of their speeches.[1] For example, the preface to one volume of Woodfall's *Parliamentary Register* had this remark: 'Those noble-

on 13 Dec. 1792. The volume containing the debates from 13 Dec. 1792 to 14 Feb. 1793 consists of vi+473 pp. It is the only one in the British Museum. When the series came to an end I do not know; the volumes were still appearing in 1795.

(*b*) The *Senator; or Parliamentary Chronicle* (28 vols., 1790–1801).

(*c*) Woodfall's *New Parliamentary Register*, of which there is no copy in the British Museum. Its dates are therefore uncertain. It was in progress in 1781. On some occasions, when Woodfall had no room for a continuation of a certain debate, he would say, at the end of his report in the *Morning Chronicle*, 'To be continued in this paper, if an early opportunity serves; if not, in the *New Parliamentary Register*' (*e.g. Morning Chronicle*, 11 Dec. 1781, and 28 Jan. 1782). In an advertisement published in the *Morning Chronicle* on 14 Dec. 1781, the proprietors of the *Register* begged leave 'to return their grateful acknowledgments for the assistance with which they have been honoured in their endeavours to complete the volumes of the Debates of the preceding Session, which shall be published with all the dispatch that can accompany the determination to execute the work with care'. Woodfall had no great opinion of his rivals: 'My competitors are of the most paltry kind of publishers; they rely on the dispatch of their publishing; hence their *Senator, Jordan's Reports*, &c. are nothing more, with very few exceptions indeed, than transcripts from the newspaper reports with all their errors'. He added, 'My stronghold is the fullness, the truth and the accuracy of what I state' (to Lord Auckland, 17 Jan. 1795, Add. MSS. 34453, f. 147).

(*d*) *An Impartial Report of all the Proceedings in Parliament on the late important subject of a Regency* [Comprising the debates in both Houses from 20 Nov. 1788 to 10 March 1789]. London. Printed and sold by J. Bew, 1789. [620 pp. plus an Appendix.]

(*e*) *Cobbett's Parliamentary Register* (May-Dec. 1820). See M. L. Pearl's *Cobbett: A Bibliographical Account of his Life and Times*, p. 114.

(*f*) The *Parliamentary History and Review*; containing Reports of the Proceedings of the two Houses of Parliament during the Session of 1825, with critical remarks on the principal measures of the Session. London, 1826. There are two volumes in the British Museum: the debates for 1825 and 1826. The first volume is in 808 pp., double columns, and the commentary on the debates begins on page 603.

(*g*) The *Mirror of Parliament*, 1828–41.

(*h*) *Bell's Parliamentary Debates and Biographical Sketches of Senatorial Characters*. This was in progress in 1807. See an advertisement in the *Courier*, 9 July 1807.

[1] The *Mirror of Parliament* seems to have had greater support from members than *Hansard* had. Cobbett, projecting his own *Parliamentary Register* (the actual title was, of course, different) in Nov. 1803, when Woodfall's *Parliamentary Register* was coming to an end, told Windham that its success would largely depend on the 'correctness and amplifications which the speeches of our friends will receive *from their own* hands'. He added: 'Whatever is sent must be sent us the next day or two days after the debate takes place' (Add. MSS. 37853, f. 101). Most, in fact, of the various collections of *Debates* were published, in the first place, in weekly, fortnightly or monthly parts: hence the need for speed in compilation. See Add. MSS. 34453, f. 141, for Woodfall's

men and gentlemen who favour the reporter with a minute of their speeches, are requested to send them to Mr. Stockdale's or the Reporter's house, as early as possible after they are delivered'. No member took more trouble to be correctly reported than Windham. His connexion with Cobbett during the first six years of the nineteenth century is well known,[1] but on the subject of his speeches Windham wrote chiefly to Cobbett's co-editor, John Wright. In February 1810 Windham made a quite uncalled-for attack on the press and the reporters. Cobbett remarked:[2]

Of all the noblemen and gentlemen for whom Mr. Wright has corrected or inserted debates; of all the persons whom he has ever obliged in this way, he never obliged anyone so much as Mr. Windham; nay, I am of opinion that he has done more to oblige Mr. Windham in this way than he has ever done to oblige all the other Members put together. This seems hardly credible, but it is the fact.[3]

If Wright, said Cobbett, had been paid for all the trouble he had been put to over Windham's speeches, he would have received something like £500:[4]

request to Lord Auckland (8 Jan. 1795) for a revised report of his speech on the 6th, for publication, apparently, in Woodfall's *Impartial Report of the Debates* (33 vols., 1794–1803). 'If I receive it by Monday evening or Tuesday noon it will be in time, although, could I have stimulated the publisher's men to have worked as hard as I have done since Parliament met, I should have been able to have published my second Number by next Tuesday'. How contemptuous of the efforts of his predecessors and rivals Cobbett was, may be judged from his advertisement of the fifth volume of his own *Parliamentary Debates* (1805). He reminded his readers 'of the promise which, at the outset of the work, he made, of rescuing the proceedings of the British Parliament from the disgrace of a slovenly and unintelligible mode of publication'. The draft is in Add. MSS. 22906, f. 84. Cf. Wm. Windham to Thos. Amyot, 6 Dec. 1803: 'What you will receive . . . is taken from a new *Parliamentary Register*, which has been undertaken by Cobbett, and which will far surpass in impartiality as well as accuracy (I am persuaded) any of the *Parliamentary Registers* that have been published hitherto' (*ibid.* 37906, f. 105).

[1] Cobbett's letters to Windham are in Add. MSS. 37853.

[2] *Cobbett's Political Register*, 10 Feb. 1810. Windham's speech (6 Feb. 1810) is in *Parl. Deb.*, xv. 329-31.

[3] For some indignant protests by parliamentary reporters against Windham's attack on their characters, see Add. MSS. 37889, ff. 5, 11. One writer pointed out that, for the most part, they had no other connexion with the conduct of the newspapers than the mere exercise of the duty of reporting.

[4] *Cobbett's Political Register*, 10 Feb. 1810.

Innumerable are the times that he has sent for this bankrupt [1] to his house to consult him about the correcting and publishing of his speeches. . . . In the printer's (Mr. Hansard's) bill for the debates of the very last Session, there is the following charge against us : 'Corrections, revises, slips, &c &c, of Mr. Windham's speeches (various), £9 11 6d.' During the 14 volumes of Debates, *alterations* of the sort above-described, made with Mr. Windham's own hand, upon slips sent to him at his request, and without any possible view of gain on our part, have cost us upwards of £70. Mr. Wright has sent him *proofs*, and even *revises* . . . down into Norfolk,[2] and . . . the publication of the last volume of Debates was *delayed* for weeks in order solely to oblige him. Mr. Windham, who has such a contempt for the reporters and the Gallery, has not once or twice but many times asked this 'bankrupt' whether he was *well heard in the Gallery* ; what *impression his speech produced* ; and consulted with him how he should *modulate his voice, how* and *where* he should *stand* so as to be *best heard in the Gallery.*

T. C. Hansard never had his own reporters : he would send members the best newspaper reports of their speeches and ask for them to be corrected. A little known collection, *The Senator; or Clarendon's Parliamentary Chronicle*, was apparently the work, to some extent, of the proprietor's own reporters, for in 1795 he stated that he had engaged 'the same reporters' for that Session as in the four previous ones'.[3] We do not know whether they were employed exclusively by him,

---

[1] Windham had referred in his speech to some of the reporters and conductors of the press as 'bankrupts, lottery-office keepers, footmen and decayed tradesmen', and it was known that in mentioning bankrupts he had John Wright in mind (Wright had gone bankrupt as a bookseller in 1801).

[2] See Add. MSS. 37888, ff. 21, 47, for two newspaper reports of his speeches on the Local Militia Bill, sent to him by Wright for correction, with requests that they should be returned as soon as possible.

[3] Advertisement in the *Courier*, 7 Jan. 1795. When, in 1824, the journalist Edward Clarkson proposed to publish a new collection of *Parliamentary Debates* under the title of the *Parliamentary Record*, he told Peel, the Home Secretary, whose patronage he desired, that he wished to secure permission for a reporter to be in the House of Lords, 'as near the Woolsack as possible', and another in the Commons, at the Clerk's table — 'the great cause of inaccuracy in newspaper reports being the distance of the reporters and their consequent inability to hear all that is said'. He went on : 'The position of these privileged reporters will resemble that of the reporters in the French Chambers, who take their seat for the purpose of accurate record beneath the orator in the Tribune' (Add. MSS. 40371, f. 176).

House of Commons' Debates, 1771–1834

and it is possible that he had an arrangement with one of the newspaper proprietors, or with his reporters, to be supplied with material, for a fee. Whenever the House sat very late, the reporters' notes could hardly, for lack of space, be used at all for the last hours of the debate [1]— except when the 'hasty sketch' was completed on a subsequent day. Debrett's *Parliamentary Register*, for example, generally had a much fuller report than any newspaper, of the concluding part of a lengthy sitting. It is most unlikely that all the late speakers sent their speeches to Debrett, and therefore he might have been able to use the newspaper reporters' notes.

The *Mirror of Parliament* certainly had its own reporters.[2] Sir Edward Knatchbull, M.P. for Kent, wrote to his wife, evidently on 4 February 1830 (the letter is undated):[3]

My speech [introducing the Amendment to the Address] is badly reported. The *Mirror of Parliament* people came to me. I rather complained. The reply was, 'You speak so fluently, without any stopping or hesitating, that it is most difficult to take down your words. We hear you well, but you never give us time to pause.'[4]

---

[1] This difficulty always remained. John Wright, the printer, said, with reference to Huskisson's speeches, which he edited: 'From the lateness of the hour at which some of the speeches were delivered, a very imperfect report has been preserved. For instance, one of the best speeches ever made by Mr. Huskisson was in 1825 on the Law of Merchants Bill, but it took place at *one* in the morning, and was not therefore reported' (*ibid.* 38758, f. 267 [21 Jan. 1831]).

[2] *Parl. Deb.*, 3rd series, xx. 87 (29 July 1833). The cost must have been very heavy for a periodical with a limited circulation (a leading morning newspaper would at that time pay its reporters well over £3000 a year in the aggregate). 'Night after night', the editor, John Henry Barrow, once remarked, 'and week after week, the unremitted labours of all parties connected with this undertaking were renewed' (preface to the volume beginning with the debate on 14 June 1831). *The Times*, 6 July 1832, said that the reporters for the *Mirror of Parliament* had frequently been reporters for the morning newspapers, including *The Times* itself. Charles Dickens was one of the *Mirror*'s reporters, after having been similarly employed by the *True Sun* (Forster, *Life of Dickens*, i. 75-6).

[3] A copy of this letter was kindly shown to me by Sir Hughe Knatchbull-Hugessen.

[4] The *Mirror of Parliament*'s reports were generally rather longer than *Hansard*'s, but it gave fewer division lists. *The Times*, 6 July 1832, suggested rather patronizingly, that the *Mirror of Parliament* was 'a most useful and creditable publication, especially in giving the debates on private bills, &c., for which a morning newspaper cannot find room'.

Essays Presented to Sir Lewis Namier

Debrett is much fuller than Cobbett's *Parliamentary History*, but its continuation by Stockdale, from 1803 to 1812, is decidedly inferior to *Cobbett's Parliamentary Debates*. Both Debrett and Cobbett made good use of pamphlet speeches, but the newspaper reports used by the latter were often inferior to Debrett's. Cobbett left out many debates altogether, the best known example being those relating to the Combination Acts of 1799 and 1800. Occasionally, however, one can find a fuller report of a member's speech in *Cobbett*. His co-editor, John Wright, was in the gallery sometimes,[1] but, in general, neither Cobbett nor Debrett employed his own reporters.

Both compilations could have been more satisfactory. Newspapers giving the fullest reports were not always used: and that may also be said of Hansard, who had no serious competitor until 1828. The *Parliamentary History* is badly arranged and indexed. The debates are not always given in chronological order, and the lists of speakers are incomplete. In both *Debrett* and *Cobbett*, a debate was sometimes attributed to the wrong day,[2] and they could assign one speech to different members; and similar errors are to be found in *Hansard* and the *Mirror of Parliament*.[3] Neither *Debrett* nor *Cobbett* is in the least reliable when one wishes to find out

[1] On 21 Nov. 1803 Cobbett wrote to Windham, asking him to send a member's permit for the Gallery for use the following day, 'as Mr. Wright, who is my reporter [*i.e.* for *Cobbett's Political Register*, which then included a *Supplement* of the debates], must be there very early, or he will not get a place' (Add. MSS. 37853, f. 101).

[2] *E.g.* the debate of 14 Dec. 1796 is wrongly given in the *Parliamentary History* as on the 13th. Those of 3, 10 and 20 Nov. 1795 are wrongly given in *Debrett* as on the 2nd, 9th and 19th respectively.

[3] A speech against the Habeas Corpus Suspension Bill on 17 May 1794 was made by Mr. Miller according to *Debrett* (xxxvii. 282); by Ralph Milbanke according to *Cobbett* (xxxi. 530.) On 4 Feb. 1830 *Hansard* attributes one speech to Lord Tullamore; the *Mirror of Parliament* the same speech to Ewart. There is a similar error in the case of William Bankes (*Mirror of Parliament*, 1828, i. 33) and George Bankes (*Parl. Deb.*, N.S., xviii. 84), on 31 Jan. 1828. Inaccuracies were not always corrected by Debrett when they were put right in subsequent issues of the newspaper whose report he copied. Even the newspaper could make a mistake about the date. For example, the *Morning Chronicle* of Saturday, 14 May 1796, was wrongly printed Saturday the 13th; and the *Public Advertiser* of Wednesday, 15 May 1793, was printed 1 May. Monday, 21 March 1796, is given in *Debrett* as the 20th.

how often members spoke; and the numbers on a division are often wrongly recorded.

I have said nothing about the 'silent speeches' of members of parliament — their votes, that is. The question of the division lists merits separate treatment.

NORMAN GASH

ENGLISH REFORM AND FRENCH REVOLUTION IN THE GENERAL ELECTION OF 1830

THE view that the English general election of 1830 was strongly and sympathetically affected by the July revolution in France is one that has never been seriously challenged even though it has not always been wholeheartedly accepted. One of the most authoritative exponents of this opinion was Halévy. In his *History of the English People* [1] he stated that the news of the events in France, coming when the borough elections had just started and the county elections were about to begin, 'provoked in England an indescribable storm of popular feeling which swept the country and was most unfavourable to the government'. But Halévy was basing himself on much contemporary assertion. One of the tory contentions in the Reform Bill debates was that Grey's ministry had only come into power because of the artificial excitement caused by the French revolution. The strongly conservative *Annual Register* in its review of the year argued that as a result of the events in France 'the general election took place in a period of greater public excitation, directed towards great changes in the frame of the government, than had occurred since the period of the French Revolution', and added that in no popular election did any candidate find himself a gainer by announcing himself as an adherent of the Government.[2] Wellington himself attributed to that excitement the major responsibility for his parliamentary defeat in November 1830. 'The adminis-

---

[1] Vol. iii, 3 (1927 edn.). [2] *Annual Register*, 1830, p. 146.

tration was beaten by two events', he wrote at the end of December. 'First, the Roman Catholic question; next, the French Revolution.' But though he admitted that over Catholic Emancipation 'we estranged our own party', he thought the ministry would still have been too strong for the whigs, 'if the French Revolution had not occurred at the very moment of the dissolution of Parliament'.[1]

In war the duke had rarely had occasion to supply explanations for defeat. Politics, as he had been finding out, was a different matter. In both, however, the retrospective accounts of beaten commanders are less valuable than their utterances during the actual campaign. Wellington, before his parliamentary defeat, showed no awareness that the general election had made it impossible for his ministry to continue. At the beginning of September he told Vesey Fitzgerald that what the government lacked was not numbers in the House of Commons but talent in the cabinet. In October he wrote to the duke of Northumberland, then lord lieutenant of Ireland, that though men's minds were unsettled on a variety of political questions, he hoped the meeting of parliament would tend to tranquillize them and that the government would get through its difficulties.[2] In this mood of mild optimism he was not peculiar. To few people did the result of the general election seem at the time to clarify what was admittedly a confused political situation. If the ultra-tory *Standard* announced [3] that the result would be the formation of a strong 'country' party, the whig *Morning Chronicle* talked with confidence of the overthrow of the squirearchy at the recent elections.[4] On two points only was there general agreement: that the government had been neither influential nor popular; and that there would be a strong movement for enquiry, retrenchment and reform in the new session. Party men in government and Opposition made the conventional claims to have gained on balance from the elections.[5] But nice statistics

[1] Wellington, *Despatches*, new series, vii. 382-3. [2] *Ibid.* 240, 295.
[3] 14 Aug. 1830. [4] 18 Aug. 1830.
[5] A. Aspinall, *Three Early Nineteenth Century Diaries*, Introd. p. xxi. There

of this kind were almost irrelevant. Neither before nor after the election did the government command a majority in the House of Commons. Even when Wellington was writing to Fitzgerald, the Treasury whips were calculating that less than a half of the House could be reckoned as firm supporters.[1] This, of course, did not necessarily spell doom to the ministry. The House was not based on a rigid two-party system and the organized body of the Opposition numbered less than two hundred. In these circumstances, though the position of the government was not easy, there was at least room for manœuvre. The question posed by the 1830 election was not whether the government had lost outright control of the House of Commons, but whether the character and temper of the new House would deprive the government of its ability to manœuvre successfully any longer.

It was privately admitted by the ministerialists during the autumn that they could not hope to stay in office without a reinforcement of 'speaking talent' in the Commons. But, when it came to the point, no reinforcement was available except on condition of parliamentary reform. It was true that when the ministers abruptly resigned in November 1830, it was on another issue; but they did so to evade the question of reform and to put responsibility for that subject on their successors. Whatever Grey's personal feelings were on taking office, parliamentary reform was an inescapable legacy left to him by the outgoing government.[2] The subject on which men soon began to differ, however, was whether this irresistible demand for reform was simply the culmination of a long domestic agitation, or the fortuitous result of a coincidence during the summer of an English general election with a French revolution.

The chronological coincidence was, in fact, rather finer than is generally realized. On 28 July *The Times* reported the

is a Treasury list in the Peel Papers (Brit. Mus. Add. MSS. 40401, f. 140) of thirty-eight contested elections in England and Wales, of which tory successes are claimed in twenty-four, whig in fourteen.

[1] A. Aspinall, op. cit., pp. xxi-xxii.
[2] Cf. Wellington to Northumberland, 17 Nov. 1830 (*W.N.D.*, vii. 361).

promulgation of the Polignac ordinances. On 2 August came the news of rioting in Paris and republican successes; and on 3 August the English newspapers were able to give detailed accounts of the fighting and announce the formation of the provisional Government. By that date, most of the English elections were already over. In many constituencies electoral activity had started in early July and by the middle of the month candidates were taking the field all over the country. By 29 July the first elections had started and by 3 August *The Times* could report the results in over sixty constituencies and the return of over 120 members. The difference between the timing of the county and borough elections was not quite so uniform or distinct as Halévy suggested; but in general the elections in the uncontested English boroughs were decided in the last two days of July and the first two days of August; the counties and most of the contested boroughs in the first week or ten days of August.[1]

Yet how many elections were actually contested in 1830? Even in the twenty years after the Reform Act the average number of constituencies contested at a general election was only just over half. Before the Reform Act the proportion was undoubtedly smaller, even though exact statistics are hard to obtain. H. S. Smith, in his *Contested Elections* (1842), records only sixty-one contests in England and Wales at the general election of 1830. As he ignored the fifty-six rotten boroughs disfranchised in 1832 the real figure is slightly higher. But of those omitted constituencies only eight were contested in 1830, and only one of them (Stockbridge, Hants) made its return after 2 August. Even allowing for the omissions and possible defects in Smith's compilation, it is probable that little more than a quarter of the 269 English and Welsh constituencies were contested in 1830. It is true that uncontested elections frequently concealed a decision of some sort, and might even reflect a measure of public opinion. But it would necessarily be a decision taken some days,

---

[1] In Scotland and Ireland the majority of the elections took place in the second and third weeks of August.

perhaps weeks, earlier and not likely therefore to be influenced by sudden extraneous events at the time of the election itself. But even with the contested elections, the real consideration is whether they were decided after the news of the successful July revolution had reached the English public through their morning newspapers on 3 August. The official *Return of Members of Parliament* (1878) gives just over a hundred English and Welsh constituencies with the date of the election return in 1830 as 3 August or later. These were not all contested, though they naturally contained a higher proportion of contests than the earlier elections. Of the sixty-one contests listed by Smith, twenty-six were already decided by 2 August. His figures must, as already indicated, be scaled up slightly. But as all but one of the contested boroughs he omitted to consider concluded their elections before 3 August, the revised total is only thirty-six. Exact figures are impossible until the whole election is subjected to large-scale research. Yet the tentative conclusion must be that probably less than forty contested constituencies in England and Wales were decided after 2 August. If so, the amount of voting open to the direct impact of the July revolution was considerably restricted.

It would be wrong, of course, to take into account merely the actual votes cast after that critical date. Atmosphere and emotion are important in politics though they are not easily translatable into statistics. Even candidates certain of their seat might be infected by popular enthusiasms or impressed by strong views among their constituents at the time of their election. Of the intense interest roused by the news from France there can be no doubt. It started not merely with the Paris riots or the Polignac ordinances but with the elections to the new French Chamber early in July. At the beginning of the month there were press comments on the probable course of the elections in France and on 9 July *The Times* had a leader on the political problems facing Charles X. French internal politics continued to occupy a large share of the

Reform and French Revolution in General Election of 1830

foreign news and between 20 and 23 July *The Times* devoted its chief leading article almost daily to the French situation. Once the revolution broke out, both the national and the provincial press gave extremely full reports; and up to the end of August, *The Times* at least continued to make a feature of French news.[1] Indeed, while providing its readers with a steady flow of report and comment on affairs in France, the newspaper curiously omitted to give any general review of the results of the general election in England.

The issue, however, is not whether the British reading public took a marked interest in the revolutionary proceedings in France at this date, but whether they were prepared to draw analogies between the contemporary situation in the two countries or to derive inspiration from abroad for a forward movement at home. Some undoubtedly were; and it is perhaps symptomatic that the most important of these were drawn from the extreme wings of English politics — the ultra-radicals and the ultra-tories.

As early as the middle of July, Burdett was already using the coincidence of Liberal successes in the French elections with the start of a new and popular reign in England to urge all reformers to unite in exploiting circumstances so favourable to a reform movement.[2] With the outbreak of the revolution in Paris, the French analogy became a feature of lower-class Radical propaganda. Hume, appearing for the first time as prospective member for Middlesex in an unopposed election, told the crowd on nomination day (5 August) that if they needed an example, a glorious one might be found in a neighbouring state; and though he had too high an opinion of his country to think that the occasion would ever arrive for such proceedings as had lately taken place in France, he hoped the

---

[1] See esp. 12-14 and 30 Aug.
[2] *The Times*, 17 July. Burdett was returned unopposed for Westminster on 31 July. His speech from the hustings was devoted entirely to parliamentary reform with no reference to foreign affairs, and he expressed the conviction that the next session of parliament would be of vital importance in view of the great issues that would be brought up in it.

people of England would be as sensible of their rights as the people of France.[1] Cobbett in his *Political Register* contended that the effect of the French revolution must be to hasten reform in England, and in a series of speeches and lectures in the late summer and autumn proceeded to ram home the point with his usual vigorous and repetitive technique. On 16 August he presided at a dinner of Radical reformers at the London Tavern and delivered an address of congratulation to the people of Paris which was subsequently reprinted at that stronghold of Radicalism, Birmingham. Between 9 September and 7 October he delivered a set of eleven lectures on 'The French and Belgian Revolutions and English Boroughmongering' at the Rotunda in Blackfriars Road.[2] But two factors limited the effect of Cobbett's arguments. The acceptance of the July revolution as a direct political inspiration was a doctrine preached mainly to the proletarian Radicals. It is true that the whig *Morning Chronicle*, pursuing its own line of parliamentary reform, admitted in a leader of 7 August that there was much in Cobbett's view. But this was exceptional. The people in whose minds his arguments found readiest approval were for the most part the poorer, unenfranchised classes who at most could only have an indirect influence on the elections. In the second place, his propaganda developed its main strength after and not during the elections. This was perhaps inevitable. If the July revolution presented a lesson to the British public, it was one that required at least a few days for absorption. In fact, it was not until the elections were largely over that the Radical spokesmen began generally to elaborate the analogy of French revolution and English reform. From their point of view it would have been better had the events in Paris preceded rather than accompanied the English elections. The coincidence was a little too exact.

An illustration of this delay in Radical reaction, which was possibly not uncommon elsewhere, was furnished by the

[1] *The Times*, 6 Aug.
[2] M. L. Pearl, *Wm. Cobbett*, pp. 162, 165.

Reform and French Revolution in General Election of 1830

Radicals in Leeds. At the end of May they had held a meeting on Hunslet Moor and resolved that it was desirable to form a political union.[1] But during the actual election there is little evidence that they did more than heckle the orthodox candidates on the question of reform; and their influence on the result was negligible. It was not until 18 August, almost a fortnight after the Yorkshire election was concluded, that they held another open-air meeting at Elland, at which they founded their Union and dilated in many speeches on the impetus given to the reforming spirit in the country by the French revolution.[2] It was not until 16 October, nearly two months later, that they celebrated the triumph of the people in France with a public dinner (at 1s. 6d. a head) at which Foster, the editor of the Radical *Leeds Patriot*, declared in a characteristic passage that 'from the noble efforts made in Paris and in Belgium, from "the feast of reason" which is now spreading, the game is at last at the feet of the operative classes'.[3] Yet if the game was one of returning their own representatives to parliament, it was in August or even July rather than October that it should have been played. By the time the Leeds Radicals had founded their union and perorated on France, all they could hope to do was to influence representatives who were already elected and to whose election they had been uniformly hostile.[4]

The Government undoubtedly took these signs of revolutionary contagion seriously, but what they feared was not an alteration in the parliamentary balance of power but a direct threat to law and order, particularly in the northern industrial districts. 'The success of the Mobs', wrote Peel, the home secretary, in the middle of October, 'and either the unwillingness or inability of the soldiers to cope with them in Paris and Brussels, is producing its natural effect in the Manufacturing

---

[1] A. S. Turberville and F. Beckwith, 'Leeds and Parliamentary Reform, 1820–1832' (Thoresby Society, *Miscellany*, xli).
[2] *Leeds Mercury*, 21 Aug. 1830.
[3] *Leeds Intelligencer*, 21 Oct. 1830.
[4] The ultra-Radicals in Leeds had broken with the Liberals in 1829 and it was not until 1832 that they allied with the tories over factory reform.

districts here, calling into action the almost forgotten Radicals of 1817 and 1819, and provoking a discussion upon the probable results of insurrectionary movements in this country.'[1] There were rumours of plots to seize the arms depôt at Carlisle and a more credible account of the disturbed and ominous situation in Manchester, where the master manufacturers, like the troops in France and Belgium, seemed unwilling or unable to combine in self-defence. At the end of October there were several cabinet discussions on the dangerous state of the country, and simultaneously came reports of the serious disorders in Kent which heralded the widespread rioting among the country labourers of the south of England the following month.[2] These disturbances, however, formed an administrative rather than a political problem and came after, not during, the general election.

It was left to the ultra-tories, from their superior station in the political world, to make more timely use of the French revolution. Not only were they themselves in a state of profound discontent with their own government, but the anti-clerical character of the July revolution was in their eyes an immediate recommendation for an event which in a more normal state of mind they might have regarded very differently. Obsessed as they were by the dangers of Catholicism, they ignored the aberration of political principle involved in their support for revolution. Nevertheless their tactics were shallow and patently opportunist, and it is questionable whether they were approved by more than a minority even among the general conservative elements in the country. Their propaganda scarcely convinced themselves; it did not convince many others. In essence their campaign was a continuation of the vendetta against Wellington and Peel that had started the previous year with the Government's decision to grant Catholic Emancipation. From that date Wellington in particular had become the target for ultra-tory abuse. Indeed,

---

[1] Peel to Hardinge, 14 Oct. 1830 (B.M. Add. MSS. 40313, f. 76).

[2] Ellenborough, *Diary*, ii. 400-8. See also J. R. M. Butler, *Passing of the Great Reform Bill*, pp. 94-5.

on the eve of the general election it was remarked that if the Government was not outstandingly popular, it was not strongly opposed on matters of policy by any section in parliament except the ultra-tories.[1] The unrelenting hostility of that group was characteristically shown at the end of July when the *Standard*[2] greeted the news of the Polignac ordinances with the ironic enquiry whether things were any better in England, and whether, if the French legislature was in as bad a state as the English, there would be much loss in its dissolution. With the outbreak of the revolution in Paris, however, the *Standard* recovered from this false start, went over to the popular side, and tried instead to damage Wellington's position by identifying him with the party of reaction in France. In the worst journalistic style it first, on 2 August, hinted at Wellington's complicity with Polignac, and then, the following day, demanded that Wellington should publicly deny the charge or else resign. A few days later Sir Richard Vyvyan, one of the more unbalanced of the ultra-tory country members, took up the running. At the Cornish county election meeting at Bodmin on 6 August, he delivered a rambling and, at times, almost unintelligible speech, in the course of which he compared Peel's metropolitan police with the French gendarmerie and Wellington with James II. The purpose of his oratory, however, was clear enough. He called on all parties to join in an 'anti-Wellington party'; he argued that Catholic Emancipation was not an isolated question but part of a general struggle in Europe between Liberalism and representative government on the one side, tyranny and despotism on the other; and he spoke of the evident connexion between Wellington's actions and the ordinances of Polignac.[3] The *Standard* immediately exploited this new ally, and for the rest of August and into September continued to insinuate that the prime minister had been an accomplice of the fallen and discredited French Government.[4]

[1] *The Times*, 14 July.   [2] 28 July.
[3] See the full account in the *Standard*, 9 Aug.
[4] See *e.g. Standard*, 10, 28 Aug., 3 Sept.; *The Times*, 10 Sept.

The fact remained, however, that scarcely a person of consequence was found to believe the charge. From the outset *The Times* championed the government on this issue and dismissed the story as the invention of a stupid and malignant faction. The *Morning Chronicle*, the chief Liberal organ, also defended Wellington, though in more lukewarm fashion, against this particular calumny.[1] An excess of generosity was not to be expected from political opponents, but the whig Liberal party as a body preferred to leave the Polignac legend as the monopoly of the *Standard* and the rest of the ultratory press. Only the impressionable and heedless Brougham yielded to the temptation. But when, at a Liberal election dinner at York on 13 August, he unwisely allowed himself a reference to the friendship that had existed between the British Government and the Polignac Administration, he met with little response from his audience.[2] The speech itself was not one of Brougham's happier efforts, and though he received the doubtful honour of a favourable notice in the *Standard*, he was sharply reproved by *The Times* for this half-hearted and irresponsible repetition of the Polignac story.[3] Whatever Wellington's faults were as a politician, no sensible person could have thought him an accomplice to the reactionary policy of the French Government. The British public of all classes and opinions condemned the French king and his ministers, and approved the July revolution; they had little reason to believe that their own Government did not share those sentiments.

United as Englishmen were in welcoming the revolution, however, they were not necessarily conscious of any need to extract from the scenes enacted in France a lesson for their own political behaviour. Indeed, the comments passed in the press and in public speeches on the French revolution are more characteristic of a mature and stable political society than of a country ripe for rebellion. The analogy that pre-

[1] *E.g.* 31 July, 4 Aug. 1830.
[2] *Leeds Mercury*, 14 Aug.
[3] *Standard*, 16 Aug.; *The Times*, 17 Aug.

Reform and French Revolution in General Election of 1830

sented itself most strongly to the ordinary English mind was between 1830 and 1688. What England had achieved a century and a half ago, France was now after a long interval endeavouring to emulate. Hobhouse, the Radical, speaking from the hustings at the Middlesex election, declared that the heroic exertions of the French had rendered them worthy of obtaining what England had struggled to secure at her own revolution, a free press and a free parliament, and adjured the crowd to look upon the French as brothers.[1] Colonel Jolliffe, a tory contesting Surrey, congratulated the French people on having released themselves from the chains of popery and priesthood.[2] Western, a whig, said at the Essex election that every one must rejoice at the glorious efforts being made in France to consolidate their liberty on the basis of representative government — 'such a government as England possessed, such as he trusted it always would possess'.[3] This satisfied and insular outlook was even more remarkably expressed by Jeffrey at a meeting at Edinburgh, when he observed that the recent behaviour of the French would mean that Britons would cease to regard them with contempt.[4] The analogy between 1830 and 1688, which rapidly became a stock theme in the national press, was echoed in the counties. The *Leeds Mercury*, one of the most influential of the provincial newspapers, used the comparison to refute the agitation of the ultra-radicals. To admire the French revolution and call for a similar change in England, it observed, was to show a profundity of ignorance. 'Why, we had *our* "Glorious Revolution" a hundred and forty years ago.' France was only copying our example and imitating our institutions. Why should Englishmen play the monkey trick of 'mimicking those who are imitating us?'[5]

Englishmen of moderate views (and in 1830 they probably constituted the bulk of the electorate) were prepared to admit defects in their constitution and wished to have them

---

[1] *The Times*, 6 Aug.
[2] *Morning Chronicle*, 9 Aug.
[3] *Ibid.* 7 Aug.
[4] *The Times*, 24 Aug.
[5] 21 Aug. 1830.

reformed; but they could not see that there was any essential similarity between the political situation in France and in England. Even in the charitable efforts made to relieve the victims of the fighting in Paris, the same attitude was apparent. Meetings were held in many parts of the country for the joint purpose of congratulating the French and raising subscriptions to assist those who had suffered in the struggle. But it was a general movement and not confined to the Radicals;[1] and speeches made on such occasions struck the same note of robust, humanitarian and slightly complacent approval.[2]

It would be fallacious, moreover, to assume that the profound interest created in England by the news from France was accompanied by an equally profound interest in the result of the general election; or that the people most interested in the one were also most concerned with the other. General elections under the unreformed system, with its eccentric representation and limited franchise, were of a more specialized nature than they became later in the century. The 1830 election, in the contemporary confusion of issues and parties, was not calculated to arouse particular national excitement. For the professional politicians the case was different; but it is possible that for the public at large the elections were obscured rather than illuminated by the sensational events on the Continent. *The Times*, on 4 August, discussing the tremendous public interest in the news of the July revolution, remarked 'indeed, it far exceeds even that for the home elections, in the mass of the people, those being excepted of course from its influence who are personally engaged in the latter'. A week later the *Morning Chronicle* took the same view.

The paramount interest and importance of the triumphant progress of freedom in France has, in some measure, diverted public attention from scenes at home which otherwise could not have failed to arrest it. But we must not suffer ourselves to lose

[1] Though this is the implication in Halévy, *op. cit.*, p. 5.
[2] *E.g.* see the account of the meeting of the Marylebone ratepayers on 11 Aug. (*Morning Chronicle*, 12 Aug. 1830).

Reform and French Revolution in General Election of 1830

sight of the elating prospect which so many of the late Elections have opened to the friends of liberty in this country.[1]

Mark Philips, who two years later became the first elected member for the city, at a public dinner at Manchester to celebrate the July revolution, found it necessary to remind his audience not to forget, in their admiration for the 'glorious burst of freedom' in France, that some of their own institutions were not altogether compatible with 'the spirit of the age'.[2]

There was therefore perhaps less connexion in men's minds between the French revolution and the general election than might otherwise be supposed. In any case, however, the reform question had already been taking on a new significance before the election and, even without the continental disturbances, would probably have become a major issue in the new parliament. The reasons for this are not hard to find. For over twenty years Catholic Emancipation had overshadowed all other domestic controversies in British politics. Now that debate had ended, and at the same time the manner of its ending had deeply divided the party in politics which stood for a 'conservation' of the existing constitution. Not only was the way clear for parliamentary reform to move into the front rank of active parliamentary issues, but some of the ultra-protestant tories had been driven by their exasperation and sense of impotence to look favourably on suggestions for a change in the structure of a legislature which they had patently ceased to control. The 1830 session had seen three plans for parliamentary reform put forward from different parts of the House,[3] and though at the start of the year there had been signs of a whig alliance with the Government, the failure of Grey and Althorp to secure a postponement of the dissolution in July left the whig leaders in a hostile mood when the elections began. Even the *Annual Register* admitted that the spirit of opposition was at

---
[1] 12 Aug.   [2] *The Times*, 30 Aug. 1830.
[3] By the tory marquess of Blandford, by Lord John Russell, and by Daniel O'Connell.

work in all quarters before Polignac issued his ill-fated ordinances the other side of the Channel.¹ Reform perhaps would have been a better word than opposition. *The Times*, which was far from being anti-Governmental, suggested on 12 July a threefold test for electoral candidates: repeal of the Corn Laws, economical reform and the establishment of parliamentary representation for great and populous towns. The *Examiner* selected the same three topics — cheap bread, economy and parliamentary reform — as the issues of the day; and this diagnosis was quoted with the inference of agreement by the tory *Standard*.² A variation of the theme was provided by E. T. Bainbridge, one of the two whigs returned for Taunton, who declared on 26 July that he followed Lord John Russell in singling out religious liberty, the slave trade and parliamentary reform as the issues 'paramount in the arena of politics'.³ The Parliamentary Reform Association, dedicated to the third of these objects, prepared for the oncoming elections with a meeting on 16 July at the Freemasons' Tavern. J. B. Monck, M.P. for Reading, took the chair, and Burdett, Hobhouse and Hume were among the several hundred present. Various Radical motions were passed in favour of the ballot, universal suffrage and the formation of reform associations throughout the country; and Burdett urged the need for combining with the Birmingham Union and all other classes of reformers. A few days later he turned precept into example by going to Birmingham to attend the Union's first annual meeting. Here, on 26 July, almost the eve of the Paris riots, he delivered another speech, which consisted largely of a long retrospect of the course of the parliamentary reform movement in England.⁴

For professed parliamentary reformers to agitate for parliamentary reform was perhaps not in itself very remarkable. Of more significance was the deliberate agitation given to the question by the influential whig *Morning Chronicle*.

---

¹ *Annual Register*, 1830, p. 144.   ² On 19 July.
³ *The Times*, 29 July.
⁴ *Ibid.* 17, 29 July; *Morning Chronicle*, 17, 30 July.

Reform and French Revolution in General Election of 1830

The French elections earlier in July had already provided an occasion for a discussion in *The Times*, the *Globe* and the *Westminster Review*, among others, of the representative system in England; and the *Chronicle* in three successive numbers [1] devoted a leading article to a comparison of the British and French electoral systems and an exhaustive review of the issues raised in the general press discussion of parliamentary reform. Further leaders on the same topic appeared almost daily as the election drew nearer. Consistent encouragement was given to the reform movement in the country at large, including even guarded support for the ballot. The Reform Association's activities received its blessing; Brougham's candidature for Yorkshire was approved; and Cobbett himself received favourable mention. On 20 July, in a burst of feeling, the newspaper expressed the hope that the triumphs of Liberalism in the French elections would make the people of England 'ashamed of the beastly orgies' of their own. What was most impressive in the *Chronicle*'s prolonged campaign, however, was not an attempt to rouse a factitious excitement but its cool and realistic analysis of the actual defects and characteristics of the existing system: the decline in Government influence, the silent change in the electoral structure resulting from the greater diffusion of wealth and growing respectability of the electoral classes; venality in borough, subservience in county constituencies; the crippling expense of contested elections and its effect on the supply and character of candidates. All this, moreover, was being reiterated to its readers day after day for almost a month before the elections started.

In the end, of course, what counted was not what the newspapers said but how electors and candidates behaved. If the question is, how far the general election was influenced by the July revolution and how far that influence worked against the Government and in favour of reform, the answer must ultimately be sought in the elections themselves. And until the 1830 general election is analysed constituency by

[1] 10 July (Saturday), 12 and 13 July.

constituency, that answer cannot be complete. Yet the electoral realities of even a few constituencies will at least throw some light on the question. Three have been selected for enquiry. All were large constituencies; all were contested; and all decided their elections after 2 August. If the influence of the French revolution was an appreciable factor in 1830, it is presumably in this kind of constituency that it would show most clearly.

The first example is Southwark, the only metropolitan constituency in 1830 to be contested. It had a scot and lot franchise, the electors being reckoned at about 5000, and enjoyed a reputation for returning only 'popular' candidates. The three who came forward in 1830 included both the sitting members. Charles Calvert, who had represented the borough since 1812, was a London brewer and a landowner, with country houses at Hounslow and Dorking, and brother to Nicholas Calvert, the member for Herefordshire. The other was Sir Robert Wilson, an army officer who had been a public supporter of Queen Caroline and was dismissed from the service in 1821 for his conduct at her funeral.[1] He had sat for the borough since 1818. Both men were Liberal whigs and members of the recognized Opposition. Their challenger was John Harris, a wealthy master-hatter of Southwark Road who, at the outset at least, appeared to be the unpopular candidate. In their speeches on nomination day (30 July), Calvert emphasized economy and the need for cheaper living; Wilson, retrenchment and reform, including a moderate measure of parliamentary reform; and Harris his independence and local connexions. The only reference to foreign affairs was made by Wilson, who proclaimed that they had not in their country to fear either the double-headed monster of fanaticism and despotism threatening others, or any peril to the liberty of the press and of the constitution. The poll went to the sixth day and, as the candidates addressed the crowd from the hustings at the end of each day's polling,

---

[1] He was reinstated when the whigs came into power at the end of the year.

Reform and French Revolution in General Election of 1830

their speeches gave ample indication of the sentiments they held or thought their audience would wish them to hold. From the start Harris, the challenger, went into the lead, to the obvious surprise and discomfiture of his two Liberal opponents, who were now left jockeying for second place. Harris was at first cautious in his utterances on public themes, though he was clearly a ministerialist supporter of moderate conservative views. As his majority daily increased, however, he became more expansive. He openly proclaimed himself a friend to the government, with the safe reservation that he would oppose them if they usurped more power over the public than was necessary; he promised to support every measure of economy and retrenchment that was compatible with the dignity of the empire; and on the subject of parliamentary reform he ended by a declaration in favour of extending the franchise to such populous towns as Leeds, Manchester and Birmingham, and of any rational measure that did not infringe rights properly and legally used for the benefit of the people.

Between these impeccable if guarded statements and the declarations of the other two candidates there was in the end little to choose; and the two Liberals, against whom there was perhaps some echo of resentment for the vote they had given in favour of Catholic Emancipation the previous year, were forced back on a recital of their past services to the borough in an effort to win favour. It was significant, however, that neither of them made any attempt to exploit the news of the July revolution. Calvert, indeed, who after the first two days was at the bottom of the poll and might have been tempted to a demagogic appeal, made no recorded reference whatever to France. Wilson made an allusion but only in terms of admiration and encouragement for a generous people struggling to be free; and the Beer Bill played just as important a part in his oratory as the Continent. Harris, too, made passing reference to foreign affairs, but chiefly in order to congratulate his audience on having a patriot king and a Ministry that would never have done what they had seen attempted in a neighbouring kingdom. On this note of satisfaction the poll ended, with Harris more than two hundred votes ahead of his rivals.[1] When, a week later, the chairing of the successful candidates took place with the traditional party processions, Wilson's banners displayed such popular legends as 'Wilson and Magna Carta', 'Wilson and the poor Negro', and those for Harris equally Dickensian inscriptions such as 'Charity and Christian benevolence' and 'Harris the Poor Man's Friend'. Neither side troubled to enliven these time-honoured sentiments by exotic allusions to tyrannical Bourbons or brave Frenchmen.[2]

The second example is that of a medium-sized borough in the provinces — Reading, the county town of Berkshire, with a scot and lot franchise, an electorate of over a thousand, and a strong Liberal tradition. The sitting members, J. B. Monck and C. F. Palmer, were both whig Liberals. Monck perhaps, as a professed parliamentary reformer and a supporter of Hume, was something stronger. But he retired at the end of the session and two candidates came forward to secure the vacant place. The first was Stephen Lushington, the barrister, politician and reformer, who had first entered parliament in 1806 and since 1826 had sat for Tregony. He was strongly supported by Monck, and the two men, together with Palmer, met the Liberal electors at a public meeting in the middle of July. This was later to bring on a charge of 'coalition', though Palmer took care otherwise to act alone both in his canvass and on the hustings. The other challenger was Charles Russell, land-owner and East India proprietor, whose father's seat was at Swallowfield, a few miles from the town. Russell stood as an independent but his attitude was fundamentally conservative and he was supported by much of the business and commercial interests of the borough.[3]

[1] The final figures were : Harris, 1664 ; Wilson, 1434 ; Calvert, 995.
[2] The course of the election can be followed in *The Times* and the *Morning Chronicle*, 31 July–6 Aug. and 13 Aug. Some additional details are given in the *Key to Both Houses of Parliament* (1832).
[3] Further details of Palmer and Russell may be found in my *Politics in the Age of Peel*, pp. 283-4.

Reform and French Revolution in General Election of 1830

On public issues he was noncommittal and his party concentrated on attacking Lushington, whose support for the Anatomy Bill furnished a pretext for an inconsequential but popular charge of 'body-snatching' and the appearance of the legend 'No dead bodies' on one of Russell's election flags.

Palmer's supporters made the usual references to his Liberal principles; support for parliamentary reform and governmental economy, opposition to monopolies. The Beer Act [1] of the previous session came in for much discussion and it was alleged, no doubt with truth, that Palmer had incurred the hostility of the powerful brewing industry at Reading for his vote on that measure. Perhaps it was not accidental that a brewer, Blackall Simonds, was chairman of Russell's election committee and that it included two other members of the Simonds family. But Palmer, when he came to speak from the hustings on nomination day, struck a different note. He had sat in parliament for twelve years, he said, and though for the first six he had not supported the king's ministers, yet when he saw them adopting a system in the interest and for the welfare of the country, he had voted with them, though exceptionally opposing on specific measures. Lushington, both in the speeches of his supporters and in his own utterances, took his chief stand on parliamentary reform, with which he linked the question of economy. It was because M.P.s were not elected by the mass of the people, he argued, that an excessive burden of taxation was laid on their shoulders; it was a reproach that Birmingham, Manchester and Leeds were without representation. Russell was less precise. He stressed his independence and freedom from pledges; he denied allegations that he approved of either colonial slavery or East India monopoly; and he said he would support the Government if their measures were good, even though he did not wish to imply that the ministers were free from blemish. This cautious advocacy probably reflected a general feeling among the Reading conservatives. The *Berkshire Chronicle*,

[1] It was intended to break down the virtual monopoly of public-houses by the breweries.

the organ of the party, had expressed the hope at the outset of the election campaign that the duke of Wellington would continue as prime minister, if necessary with the admission of a few whigs into the Government. This was all the more magnanimous since the newspaper still regretted the passing of Catholic Emancipation and could not forbear at the end of the session from congratulating its readers on the dissolution of the 'anti-national parliament'. When the polling began, proceedings were confused and disorderly, largely as a result of the constant challenging of voters and the delay while cases were referred to the returning officer's legal assessor. The poll lasted the full six days, with voters brought from Brighton and sick men from their beds. When it closed, Lushington was at the foot of the poll, thirty votes below Russell. There was a further interval of suspense while the assessor decided on a number of doubtful votes, but his final judgment, while it narrowed the gap, did not reverse the placing of the last two candidates.[1]

When the result was known, Palmer made a speech to the crowd in which he again drew attention to the different spirit of the ministers compared with that when he first entered parliament. No inroads, he assured them, were being made on the constitution by the existing government; and as long as the rights of the people were observed, and careful economy in expenditure practised, he would continue his support of the king's ministers. This moderate attitude of Palmer, consistently maintained before and after his election, was in contrast with the more emotional rhetoric of the other Liberal candidate. Lushington, for example, was the only speaker who was reported as having made direct allusion to the July revolution. That was on nomination day, when he warned his hearers that the time was a pregnant one and the Govern-

[1] The final result was: Palmer, 522; Russell, 471; Lushington, 452. Lushington's party made various allegations of corrupt and illegal practices against Russell, and a petition was presented against his return at the opening of the new parliament. It was withdrawn before the case was heard, however, possibly because of the probability of an early dissolution following the accession of Grey's Ministry.

ment must be careful; he for one would never sanction interference in France. But it is doubtful whether the Reading electors were much swayed by considerations of this kind, even though that day (2 August) was the one on which the daily press first gave reports of the fighting in France. The *Reading Mercury*, which made its weekly appearance also on that day, devoted a leader to the topic and, for a provincial paper, gave ample space to French news. A week later it published another leader, praising the French and suggesting the opening of a subscription for the victims of the struggle. But it was not a party issue and the *Mercury*, though a Liberal paper, made no attempt to draw analogies with the political situation in England. The Conservative *Berkshire Chronicle* was even more discouraging and aloof. While reporting the events in France fairly fully, it made no comment other than a small note at the head of the column to the effect that, whatever the effects on Europe, it could be stated definitely that 'His Majesty's Government will not mix the country up in the struggle between arbitrary power and insolent democracy'. Nevertheless, even the triumphant Blue party paid its tribute to the July revolution. At a banquet held early in September to celebrate Russell's return, one of the official toasts was to 'Louis Philippe, King of the French'; though according to the *Mercury*, a hostile witness, this was coolly received and many of the company refused to drink it.[1] But whatever was thought privately on that issue, the electoral decision was clear. The candidate who had stated his trust in Wellington's Government had been returned at the head of the poll; the man least likely to support Liberal measures had secured the second seat; and the proclaimed parliamentary reformer, who alone had thought fit to allude to the French example, had been defeated.[2]

The last election contest for consideration is that for

---

[1] This account of the Reading election is mainly based on the files of the *Reading Mercury* and the *Berkshire Chronicle*, July–Sept. 1830.
[2] In the critical Civil List division in Nov., Palmer voted with the majority against the Government, Russell with the minority in their support.

Yorkshire — the largest constituency in the kingdom, the only county to return four members, and memorable in 1830 for electing Henry Brougham, the self-advertised champion of parliamentary reform and the first 'stranger' to represent Yorkshire since the seventeenth century. His election was, in fact, the one sensational event in an otherwise colourless general election, and many observers on both sides took it as an example and a portent. It was in the flush of his Yorkshire victory that Brougham tabled his motion for parliamentary reform at the opening of the new session, and it was to avoid a debate on his motion that the ministers resigned after their Civil List defeat. Yet any detailed examination of the Yorkshire election of 1830 shows how many local and accidental features decided the outcome, and how little influence is to be attributed to foreign events.

The dominating factor in the 1830 Yorkshire election was the prohibitive expense of a contest. The great struggle of 1807, which cost the Fitzwilliam and the Lascelles families over £100,000 each, had been the first contested election in Yorkshire since the fall of Walpole and might well have been regarded as earning Lord Milton a seat for life. Yet in 1826, the first election at which four members were returned, another contest threatened. Five candidates took the field, and though Bethell, a liberal tory, withdrew on the eve of the poll, the election expenses had by that time mounted to £150,000.[1] This was more than most candidates would care to face a second time and in 1830 three of the four sitting members announced their retirement. Only Duncombe, a tory, was left in the field at the beginning of July when electioneering began. Both the Liberal seats were left vacant. Marshall, the wealthy Leeds flax-spinner, who had been brought in when Morpeth declined nomination in 1826 and in all probability spent something like £26,000 on that occasion in merely preparing for a contest,[2] was old and ill-

---

[1] *Parliamentary Representation of Yorkshire*, ed. A. Gooder, ii. 154-5 (Yorks. Arch. Soc. *Records*, xcvi).

[2] The Fitzwilliam expenses in 1826 amounted to £26,000 (see 'Earl Fitzwilliam and the Corn Laws', by David Spring, *American Hist. Review*, lix. 301),

Reform and French Revolution in General Election of 1830

fitted for public life. Milton gave as his ostensible reason for retiring the advanced age of his father, Earl Fitzwilliam, and the consequent probability that he would be called to the upper house sometime during the next parliament. But there is private evidence that after his experience at the previous election he was unwilling to risk once more the expense of a contest.[1] There was no lack of suitable candidates to succeed them; the difficulty was lack of money. It was not, wrote George Strickland to Milton, a question of apathy as regards the election, but 'every name being coupled with a determination not to spend any money, no person knows how to act'.[2]

The situation was complicated by the emergence of a freak candidate, the eccentric Martin Stapylton of Myton Hall, who stood on the sole issue of purity of election and promised to poll every voter who would come to the hustings at his own expense. After some delay Bethell, the 1826 candidate, came forward as tory colleague to Duncombe; and Lord Morpeth was persuaded to take Milton's place on the Liberal side. There were now four candidates for the four seats. But the position was far from satisfactory to the Liberals, who were in the dilemma of either contenting themselves with one member or bringing on a contest which few were prepared for and every one feared. None of the whig gentry could afford a contest from his own resources and it became therefore a question of finding some one whom the Liberal party in Yorkshire would agree to return without expense. A preliminary meeting at Leeds on 14 July between representatives of the country gentlemen and the leaders of the West Riding Liberals made it clear, however, that the freeholders of that district, who formed the majority of the

---

and Marshall subsequently recorded in his *Memoir* (privately printed) that the joint expenses on the Liberal side totalled £53,000.

[1] See the letter from Tottie, the Liberal agent, to Lord Milton, 3 July 1830, in the correspondence of the third Earl Fitzwilliam (Wentworth Woodhouse Muniments, Sheffield Library). For permission to use this and the following extracts from the same source, I am indebted to the Earl Fitzwilliam and the Trustees of the Wentworth Woodhouse Settled Estates.

[2] *Ibid.* Strickland to Milton, 11 July 1830.

Liberal electors in the county, would not journey to York at their own cost merely to vote for a whig country squire. Even for Morpeth there was no enthusiasm. 'Under these circumstances and with the experience recently afforded of the taste for expense among Yorkshire Freeholders,' wrote Tottie, the Liberal agent, to Lord Milton from Leeds, 'it becomes a rather serious matter to invite any Independent Gentleman to come forward on Whig principles. I do not find that any one is seriously thought of here by our Friends and I cannot name an Individual in the County that they would be likely to invite with a pledge of support free of expense.'[1]

It was at this point that Baines, the influential editor of the *Leeds Mercury*, made his sudden and successful proposal to bring in Brougham. It was not a new idea of Baines. In 1812 he had suggested Whitbread or Brougham to succeed Wilberforce. But outside the Baines circle in Leeds (the 'Bainesocracy' as its enemies called it), it is unlikely that Brougham was envisaged as a possible Yorkshire candidate until the *Leeds Mercury* of 17 July, in a carefully prepared leader, came out with the proposal. The tactical opening for this bold stroke had been already furnished by the meeting on 14 July at which, in return for a grudging acceptance of Morpeth's candidature, the whig representatives agreed that the West Riding Liberals should be entitled to put forward a candidate of their own. Nevertheless, Brougham was not a candidate easily stomached by the country gentlemen and it was only after an angry meeting at York on 23 July that his candidature was approved; and then only after the whig squires had been flatly told by the Leeds delegation that Brougham would be proposed whether they accepted him or not. To this ultimatum the whigs were obliged to submit. Indeed, there was no real alternative. The York meeting had been summoned to choose two Liberal candidates to be returned free of expense. Brougham was at least a candidate for whom the men of the West Riding would go of their own

[1] Letter from Tottie to Milton, 14 July 1830.

Reform and French Revolution in General Election of 1830

accord to vote; and though the withdrawal of Stapylton on the second day of the polling turned the actual contest into a farce, there can be no doubt that Brougham would still have been triumphantly returned if the election had gone its full length. Brougham's nomination, and virtually his election, were thus assured some ten days before the Paris revolution broke out.

There is, however, another aspect to the election: the motives of Brougham's backers and his own views on the great issues of the day. Among the proximate causes for the choice of Brougham by the West Riding Liberals was the prominent part he had taken in the slavery debate of 13 July. The powerful dissenting interest in Yorkshire, in fact nearly all the old Wilberforce party except the Anglicans, were prepared to put out their strength on behalf of an anti-slavery candidate of such national eminence. Indeed, Brougham's name was already in the minds of some of them at the Leeds meeting with the whig spokesmen on 14 July. Once his candidature was assured, the dissenting churches took an active part in the campaign and dissenting ministers were prominent both in the West Riding delegation that secured his nomination at York on 23 July and later on the hustings. 'There is enthusiasm in the cause,' reported Tottie to Milton on the 24th, 'and anti-Colonial Slavery is the basis of it.'[1] In his canvass and on nomination day Brougham took care to pay full recognition to this element in his candidature.

Yet he himself could scarcely have regarded slavery as the dominant issue of the election. As the 1830 session had drawn to a close, he had become convinced of the need for pulling down a Government which showed no signs of

---

[1] *Ibid.* 24 July. The annual national conference of the Wesleyan Methodists was taking place in Leeds at the time of the election (28 July-9 Aug.), and on 30 July the conference passed a series of resolutions condemning slavery and urging all Methodists with the vote to use it on behalf of those candidates who pledged themselves to the entire abolition of slavery within the empire. Earlier, the Yorkshire Protestant Dissenters Association for the Abolition of Slavery, meeting at Leeds on 21 July, pledged itself to support Brougham and urged its members to vote for abolitionist candidates. (*Leeds Intelligencer*, 5, 12 Aug.; *Leeds Mercury*, 24 July.)

admitting the whigs to a share of office; and for that purpose a more direct attack would be required.¹ The Leeds Liberals had secured his nomination and it could not be forgotten that Leeds was one of the great unrepresented trinity which all reformers quoted as an example of the absurdity of the parliamentary system. As recently as March 1830 a public meeting in Leeds had sent up to London the largest petition known in the history of the town, praying for retrenchment and parliamentary reform. Baines himself, the chief promoter of Brougham's candidature, had been a parliamentary reformer from his early days. Even before Brougham's name was publicly mentioned, the *Leeds Mercury* had raised the issue of reform in an election leader devoted to 'this most important of all subjects' and urged all reformers to unite in continuous agitation.² When Brougham's election campaign started in earnest, it became apparent that if dissenters and Quakers were inspired by the slavery question, the merchants and manufacturers were mainly concerned with parliamentary and economical reform. Brougham from the start made parliamentary reform one of his chief topics. On 27 July, in company with Morpeth, he appropriately opened the Liberal election campaign with a visit to Leeds. In a speech to an audience reckoned at ten thousand, he dwelt at length on parliamentary reform. After defining his aims as the extension of the franchise to all inhabitant freeholders, and of representation to all great towns, he told his hearers that the parliamentary weakness of the government offered an immense opportunity to reformers, and that the 1830 election would carry the great questions of parliamentary reform, revision of the Corn Laws, and extinction of colonial slavery, just as surely as the County Clare election had carried Catholic Emancipation.³ The same theme was continued in his

---

[1] Cf. A. Aspinall, *Brougham and the Whig Party*, pp. 173-4.
[2] 12 June 1830. See also E. Baines, *Life of Edward Baines*, pp. 80, 139-50.
[3] Full reports of this speech are given with only minor verbal variations by the *Leeds Mercury* and *Leeds Patriot*, 31 July, and the *Leeds Intelligencer*, 29 July. The *Mercury* secured a scoop by also bringing out a special supplement containing Brougham's and Morpeth's speeches on 28 July.

canvass of the other industrial areas of the West Riding, and echoed, though more cautiously, by Morpeth. On nomination day, 5 August, Morpeth indeed placed the emphasis of his speech on parliamentary reform; and in an eloquent passage recalling the eighteenth-century Yorkshire movement and the tradition of Savile and Wyvill, it formed the peroration of Brougham's final address. Eight weeks later there took place at York the formal election dinner of the two Liberal members. In the interval Brougham's thoughts had ripened and he chose this occasion to unfold in public his grand plan of parliamentary reform. Formerly, he said, he had been restrained from bringing forward such a measure by the fear of being charged with having no constituents. Now he had been relieved from that imputation and 'I will leave in no man's hand, now that I am member for Yorkshire, the great cause of parliamentary reform'. He ended by announcing his intention, on the opening of parliament, to bring forward as its first great measure, one for its own reformation.[1]

In this development of Brougham's thought, there is little evidence that the influence of the French revolution played a decisive part. His adoption of reform as an electioneering platform, like his candidature, had preceded the news of the disturbances in Paris; and the tone of his supporters during the election indicated no new inspiration from abroad. In his Leeds speech of 27 July he made an approving reference to the example set by the Liberal successes in the French elections; and later, in reply to a question at Sheffield, he said it was no business of England to interfere in the affairs of France. On the hustings on 5 August he even expressed his belief that the ministers were not so 'mad and frantic' as to risk war by intervention in continental affairs.[2] Indeed it

[1] *Leeds Intelligencer*, 30 Sept.; *Leeds Mercury*, 2 Oct. See also Brougham, *Life and Times*, iii. 38-47, for his own recollections of the campaign. The letter from Strickland (p. 41) should obviously be dated 23 July, the day of the Liberal meeting at York.

[2] *Leeds Mercury*, 7 Aug. It should not be inferred, of course, that Brougham was uninterested in the French revolution. See Aspinall, *Brougham and the Whig Party*, p. 178, for his insistence on writing the article in the *Edinburgh Review* on that topic, in which he not only repeated a modified version of the

is possible that his remarks about Wellington a few days later were the result of a sudden and unhappy impulse. Though he later defended them, they were not characteristic of his election campaign as reported in the local press. When the election banquet was held at the end of September, his remarks on France were singularly moderate. He expressed the hope that the new French government might be established 'firm as well as free', and reminded his audience that 'the Schoolmaster', in the cant phrase of the time, was a friend of good order and government and his lesson was ill learnt if they did not know that resistance to tyranny was one thing, opposing anarchy another.[1] The *Leeds Mercury* maintained an equally cool and detached attitude. It welcomed the emergence of liberal institutions in France, dismissed as an 'idiotic proposition' the notion that the British government wished to interfere, and saw in the general pride and pleasure with which Englishmen of all ranks applauded the July revolution a proof of the dissemination of whig principles throughout the country.[2] But it sought to derive neither inspiration nor example from the events in France. Indeed, in a final summing-up on 14 August, it emphasized the character of Brougham's election as the careful and deliberate choice of the Yorkshire freeholders.

This is no ebullition of popular feeling arising out of *temporary* circumstances. There is no reason whatever for any degree of excitement at this period. We are in the midst of profound peace ; we are suffering under no panic ; religious dissentions have been terminated by the glorious measures of 1828 and 1829 ; we have a popular king and a not unpopular government. Whatever expression of public opinion takes place, therefore, must spring from the deliberate, deep-seated convictions of a sober and reflecting people.

Polignac story, but asserted that the battle of English liberty had really been fought and won at Paris (*Edinburgh Review*, lii. 1, 'The French Revolution of 1830'). Nevertheless, the account of the Yorkshire election given by Brougham himself, minimizing the French issue and emphasizing the movement for parliamentary reform (*Life and Times*, iii. 46-7) is upheld by the contemporary reports in the local newspapers.

[1] *Leeds Intelligencer*, 30 Sept. ; *Leeds Mercury*, 2 Oct.
[2] 21 Aug. 1830.

Reform and French Revolution in General Election of 1830

The *Mercury* was a partial witness and there was more to the Yorkshire election than this. Nevertheless the substance of its argument cannot easily be controverted; nor can its relevance be confined to one constituency.[1]

Evidence from a limited number of elections is necessarily of itself limited. But incomplete as it is, it must at least cast some doubt on much of the generalized comment on the 1830 election that has passed into print. Seen in detail, the most striking feature of these individual elections is the importance of local and personal factors, and of domestic issues, rather than any signs of external stimulus. Government was weak but it is not true that opposition to Government was the only passport to electoral favour; and there was perhaps more respect for Wellington and Peel than has been commonly thought. Traditional party divisions existed but there were no clear party policies, and candidates came to terms as best they could with the electorate. The scene is at once more complicated and more human than the artificially simplified version offered later by observers after the event. In most constituencies the elections probably followed a familiar pattern, and if the news of the revolution brought an additional excitement, it was of a vague and diffused kind. What could not be doubted was that many electors wanted reform of some sort or another — parliamentary reform, economy, abolition of slavery, cheap bread — and that irrespective of party many candidates expressed a greater or less degree of willingness to support those objects in the House of Commons. Brougham and Burdett were probably right in saying that the new parliament would inevitably see great changes; and in that case it was clear that Wellington's minority Government, if it could not direct those changes, was bound to give way to another. But in the elections themselves, even those relatively few contested after 2 August, it is difficult to discern

---

[1] This account of the Yorkshire election is partly based on a paper entitled 'Brougham and the Yorkshire Election of 1830', read to the Thoresby Society, in November 1954.

that the news of the French revolution was more than an accidental and superficial feature. Certainly there is little indication that the electors consciously thought of themselves as following in the footsteps of the Paris revolutionaries. The English public was immensely interested in the July revolution, but its attitude resembled less the deference of an admiring disciple than the more characteristic posture of John Bull giving comfortable and mildly patronizing approval to the belated efforts of a less fortunate neighbour. What coloured in retrospect the circumstances in which the general election of 1830 was fought, was the fact that it was followed by a disturbed autumn, the resignation of Wellington's government early in the new session, and its replacement by a new Ministry courageous enough to bring forward a measure of parliamentary reform that is still a landmark in British political history. But that, in the summer of 1830, was hidden in the future; and it was left to another general election to win the battle of reform.

EDWARD HUGHES

THE CHANGES IN PARLIAMENTARY PROCEDURE, 1880–1882

A NECESSARY, if formidable, corollary of the *History of Parliament* will be a series of studies tracing the development of parliamentary procedure. Professor Neale has already done this for the formative Elizabethan period; Professor Notestein has explained the importance of the standing committees of the House of Commons which emerged in the early Stuart period and continued until they were swept away by Althorp in 1833.[1] For the student of the eighteenth century there is the important 'Liverpool Tractate',[2] possibly the work of Jeremiah Dyson, besides Hatsell's famous 'Precedents'. But apart from Dr. Cyprian William's standard treatise on private bill legislation, the story of procedural developments in the nineteenth century has yet to be written. It is a difficult and complex problem; even Gladstone confessed that it was 'blind work'.[3] Members fiercely contended at the time, and it will scarcely be disputed now, that the new rules of 1882 were revolutionary in character: Mr. Newdegate, an old tory whip, declared that they were a 'direct attack upon Parliamentary government'.[4] They constitute the real watershed between the ancient parliamentary régime and modern practice. Previously, for most of the session the Government had only two 'Government nights' a week, both constantly liable to serious inroads; after 1882 it could claim, so the critics said, four nights a week and it enjoyed large new powers of

---

[1] *Hansard*, **275**, p. 356.
[2] Edited by Dr. C. Strateman.
[3] Add. MSS. 44195, f. 82 (to Speaker Brand).
[4] *Hansard*, **268**, p. 347.

closing a debate. It is impossible in a short paper to do anything like justice to the complex technical questions involved. From the material in the Gladstone papers, however, it is possible to trace how Government policy took shape and to some extent to discover who was responsible for particular aspects of it. The present paper is concerned with this strictly limited object. It will not attempt to trace the long struggle in the Commons over the new rules which extended over nine months and fills several volumes of *Hansard*.

What was the problem that confronted Gladstone in 1880? Stated in its crudest terms, it was that systematic obstruction by the Irish members had created a serious 'block' in parliamentary business, although in the course of debate the prime minister—wiser than some of his Cabinet colleagues—denied that the new rules were occasioned by or directed merely against Irish filibustering. In a notable speech introducing the resolutions, he explained that the problem was a much larger and older one.[1] 'Before the Reform Act the position of a member of this House was one of perfect ease and convenience, I may say, with regard to the physical and mental possibility of meeting the grave calls upon him.' He recalled how as a boy he had sat in the gallery of the old House and how, at that date, the House, as a matter of course, normally disposed of its business by six or seven p.m. and was permitted to adjourn; but how from that moment (1832) forward 'the position . . . was fundamentally altered'. 'At once the pressure and calls upon the House were felt to be painful and almost intolerable.' In a word, from the time of the Reform Act 'there was a sudden and vast expansion of Parliamentary duty'. The causes of this, he contended, were twofold: the many-sided demands of an enlarged empire on the one hand, and 'social' questions on the other. True, the House had not flinched from these constantly increasing labours and from time to time it had adopted important time-saving devices,

[1] *Hansard*, **266**, pp. 1124-95. Speaker Denison declared in 1871 that late sittings had 'converted honourable service into almost intolerable slavery'. *Report of the Select Committee on Procedure* (1871), p. 28.

The Changes in Parliamentary Procedure, 1880–1882

but, even so, the gap between 'increasing labours' and 'decreased power' had widened and much needed legislative reforms were being held up.[1]

Obstruction was not novel in 1880 or a monopoly of the Home Rulers. The biographer of Palmerston had noted its existence as early as 1844; but it was developed as a fine art by Parnell and certain Liberals in the late 1870s. James Bryce in an article in the New York *Nation* of March 1881 claimed that 'obstruction as a Parliamentary weapon was invented by some young Tories in the year 1872 in order to resist the passage of a bill for reforming the army: it was revived by Mr. Parnell in 1876 and practised with much tenacity and ingenuity during that and the three following years'. John Morley in an article in the *Fortnightly Review* of October 1881 described Mr. James Lowther as 'the original patentee' of the art of political obstruction 'before Parnell patented his continuous brake and brought the heavily freighted parliamentary train to a permanent standstill'.[2] After 1880 Lord Randolph Churchill and the members of the Fourth Party who became experts in this 'black art' took delight in pointing out that Hartington and Chamberlain, both notable champions and indeed the alleged authors of the new rules, had themselves practised obstruction with no small success in 1879 on the occasion of the Army Discipline Bill. Indeed Chamberlain was dubbed 'the high priest of obstruction'. The first effective move against it was made

[1] A Government paper showed how the average length of the session had increased from a total of 1000 hours in 1880 to 1400 in 1881; the hours the House sat after midnight from 100 to 238, and whereas formerly a session lasted about six months, it was now extended to nearly eight. Earlier Lord Sudeley had shown that increasing numbers of members took part in debates (*Hansard*, 250, p. 1453). It was stated that after the 1867 Reform Act members introduced 'a familiar, chatty', less formal style of debate 'unsuited to good work' and were socially inferior (*Quarterly Review*, 145, 233; *Frazer's Magazine*, xxiv, 545). Stafford Northcote pointed out that 'the House now takes a much larger share in the direct control of the Executive' (*Hansard*, 266, p. 1155).

[2] *Fortnightly Review*, xxx, 528. For Parnell's audacious question ('What is obstruction?') addressed to the 1878 committee and his subsequent flouting of the new rules, see *Quarterly Review*, 145, 243. Gladstone defined obstruction as 'a disposition either of the minority of the House or of individuals to resist the prevailing will of the House otherwise than by argument'. *Report of Select Committee on Procedure* (1878), 42, 119.

towards the end of Disraeli's administration — Stafford Northcote's standing order of 28 February 1880 which empowered the Speaker or the Chairman of Committee to suspend individual offenders.[1] This measure received general support from both sides of the House. The principle of dealing with individual offenders continued to be stock tory policy long after the effectiveness of the new standing order had been called into question. So far as obstruction was concerned the problem which faced Gladstone's second ministry was not new in kind, only new in intensity. The prime minister himself was well aware that it tended to obscure a more fundamental problem.

In the half-century since the great Reform Act not a decade had passed without a select committee on procedure — Gladstone stated that there had, in fact, been fourteen such; Hartington put the figure at twenty.[2] Giving evidence before the committee of 1854, Speaker Shaw Lefevre had declared:[3]

> My belief is that the House will some day or other be obliged to adopt a summary mode of putting an end to useless debate. . . . My fear is that the House will be obliged to resort to it (*i.e.* the closure) at last, but I think it desirable to put off the day of its adoption as long as possible.

Again, his sorely tried successor, Denison, told the Lowe committee in 1871:

> I am aware that in most public assemblies it has been found necessary to have recourse to some such expedient, but I should be disposed myself to try what could be done by other means rather than proceed at once to that extremity.

Similarly the 1878 committee, when pressed on the question, was 'not prepared to recommend whether the power of formally closing a debate and coming to a decision on the

---

[1] *Hansard*, **250**, pp. 1450 *seq*. Leonard Courtney (M.P. Liskeard) suggested that a 'Committee of Order' be appointed at the beginning of each session. *Ibid*. pp. 1474-5.

[2] *Ibid*. **267**, p. 1334. See especially the reports of 1848, 1854, 1871 and 1878.

[3] *Report of the Select Committee on Procedure* (1854), pp. 51, 56, quoted by Gladstone. *Hansard*, **266**, p. 1137.

The Changes in Parliamentary Procedure, 1880–1882

main question ... is one which, under certain restrictions, might be beneficially exercised'. Many Englishmen, of course, knew about the working of 'la clôture' in France or of the 'Previous Question' in America.[1] Gladstone declared that these select committees had never led to adequate results and 'were what I may, for practical purposes, accurately call total failures'.[2] The moral was obvious. There was, in this matter, an 'impotence', an 'insufficiency of power', in the House itself; 'the government alone could supply the necessary motive force to effect the reform that was so sorely needed'. Accordingly, he explained, the government have 'charged themselves with the duty which they would gladly have avoided or delegated to other hands'. 'The function was not primarily theirs', but in face of the total failure of the House to reform its own procedure, the government had no alternative but to accept responsibility, devise a plan and carry it through as it would any other aspect of policy. That was the essence of the government's case. We shall have occasion later to note Gladstone's earnest desire to make the issue a non-party one.

His first move was a foreign office 'circular' of 25 August 1880, instructing our diplomatic representatives to report on the methods used by foreign legislatures for restricting debate.[3] Gladstone claimed that in formulating its proposals the government had obtained 'all the aid we could on the subject from its living and recognised authorities'. Whom had he in mind? Clearly, Speaker Henry Brand — though the Premier was careful to add that there was 'no intention of bringing the Speaker, directly or indirectly, into the slightest responsibility for any of the recommendations' — and Sir Thomas Erskine May, the experienced principal clerk of the House. As long ago as 1849 Erskine May had published his

[1] Guizot and Mr. Curtis, a member of Congress, had given evidence before the 1848 committee.   [2] *Hansard*, **266**, p. 1124.
[3] *Ibid.*, p. 1304. Tory critics were not slow to point out that 'the Mother of Parliaments' had no business to follow the example of foreign legislatures whose origins were either 'revolutionary' or the creation of despots, and they disagreed with some of the examples which Gladstone cited.

293

Remarks and Suggestions with a view to facilitate the dispatch of Public Business in Parliament, followed in 1854 by a cogent article in the *Edinburgh Review* [1] in which he advocated the setting up of a number of 'Grand' or 'Standing Committees', two of which eventually materialized in 1882. Now, when Gladstone first became chancellor of the exchequer in 1852, the passage of his budget resolutions was greatly facilitated by recent changes in certain standing orders for which May was indirectly responsible, and since 1865 correspondence between the two men had ripened into friendship.[2] It was Erskine May who provided the material in the form of secret memoranda which served as the basis for the Cabinet's discussions. The most important of these is the *Memorandum on Changes of Procedure since 1832*,[3] which provides the necessary background to the problem.

Gladstone was greatly attracted by May's scheme of grand or standing committees. Some such delegation of powers, the prime minister later confessed, 'undoubtedly involves, in my opinion, by far the most important part of the entire question'.[4] We now know that his own first approach to the problem proceeded along such lines. On 23 October 1880 he drew up the following memorandum.[5]

Confidential

OBSTRUCTION AND DEVOLUTION

(1) The question of obstruction in the proceedings of the House of Commons has grown to such a magnitude that it seems to require the consideration of the Government during the present recess.

(2) We have subjects more or less in prospect, some of which may present increased inducements to this practice. On these it seems likely that obstruction may present a further aggravation of character.

---

[1] Reprinted in 1881.   [2] Add. MSS. 44154 *passim*.
[3] *Ibid.* f. 98. See May's evidence, *Report of Select Committee* (1854), pp. 23-44; *ibid.* (1871) on Closure, pp. 1-36.
[4] *Hansard*, **273**, p. 1700.
[5] Add. MSS. 44764, ff. 109-127, 152 (original draft); 44625, f. 4.

The Changes in Parliamentary Procedure, 1880–1882

(3) Even without taking obstruction into account, while legislation has fallen into great arrear, the labours of Parliament have become unduly and almost intolerably severe.

(4) It is the extreme pressure of business which is the secret of the strength of the obstructor proper and which makes it pay him so well to pursue his vocation at all costs. Were the time at the disposal of the House equal to the calls upon it, it would be, in respect of him, a fund virtually unlimited, and it would no longer be so well worth his while to draw upon it.

(5) The work of encountering him by repression is extremely difficult and, as matters now stand, of doubtful issue. In the case of the Irish obstructor, this repression might answer his purpose by supplying him with a new national grievance, and as his extremist resistance would probably be popular with his constituents, the House might find that it had more than a merely personal conflict to handle.

(6) It will also be admitted that any serious changes in the rules of the House of Commons, if repressive of the liberty of debate, would be grave public evils, even should we be able to avert, by their means, evils greater still.

(7) It is worth while to enquire whether there may not be a way, different from that of repression, but in case of need auxiliary and preparatory to it, by which we may neutralise or reduce within more moderate bounds both the scandalous evil of obstruction and the heavy inconvenience of prolonged and manifold legislative arrear.

(8) This way of proceeding I shall call devolution. By devolving upon other bodies a portion of its overwhelming tasks the House of Commons may at once economise its time, reduce its arrears, and bring down to a minimum the inducement to obstruct; for obstruction will then be only the infliction of suffering, whereas now it is the frustration of purpose, the defeat of duty.

(9) At the same time, whatever repression can do for us will still remain not less than before at our command.

(10) Of this devolution, part may be to subordinate and separate authorities. On this portion of the subject I do not now touch. But part may also be to sub-formations out of the body of the House itself on something like the same principle, though not in the same form, as that on which the French Chamber divides work among its Bureaux.[1] I shall here rudely sketch some portion at least of

[1] On these see *Traité pratique de droit parlementaire* by Jules Poudra and Eugène Pierre. This work was cited by Erskine May. The Bureaux were

what I think may hopefully be undertaken in this direction.

(11) But I must add that besides the defeat of obstruction and the improvement of our attitude for dealing with arrear, I conceive that devolution may supply the means of partially meeting and satisfying, at least so far as it is legitimate, another call. I refer to the call for what is styled (in bonam partem) 'Local Government'[1] and (in malam) 'Home Rule'.

(12) One word more must be added to these introductory sentences. During a Parliamentary recess, since Mr. Brand became Speaker, and when we were last in office, there was a small meeting at Palace Yard at which Sir T. Erskine May attended. He then gave a general opinion in favour of the devolution of a portion of the duties of the House to Grand Committees. The suggestion was generally approved. It evidently meant something beyond, and distinct from what is intended in a mere extension of the practice of referring Bills to Select Committees.[2] But the idea was not at the time pursued into much detail. It forms, I need hardly say, the groundwork of the suggestions here appended.

(13) They might be extended in scope as well as in particulars beyond the present sketch ; but this will perhaps suffice at least for raising a very important and rather many-sided question.

W. E. G.

October 23, 1880

It will have been noted that Gladstone did not as yet contemplate any form of closure : his panacea was devolution. Indeed his admission 'that any serious changes in the rules of the House of Commons, if repressive of the liberty of debate, would be grave public evils', testifies to his essential conservatism. One of his former Liberal colleagues, Robert Lowe, now Lord Sherbrooke, was more courageous. In an out-

chosen by ballot : for their working, see a confidential memorandum by J. G. Dodson, Add. MSS. 44252, f. 87 (24 Nov. 1880).

[1] The Government intended to introduce a Local Government Bill in 1882 but it got crowded out of the parliamentary time-table (Add. MSS. 44252, f. 169).

[2] There had been a great extension of the practice of referring bills to Select Committees since 1811. The tories preferred them to the proposed standing committees (*Hansard*, **18**, 1218-24 ; **19**, 106-7, 123-9, 244). For the procedural changes in 1811, occasioned in part by the Irish Union, *ibid.*, **19**, 245. Saturday sittings had ceased in 1793. According to Whitbread the Chairman of a Select Committee 'takes a prominent part in the discussions and generally produces the Report' (Add. MSS. 44476, f. 85).

The Changes in Parliamentary Procedure, 1880–1882

spoken article in the *Nineteenth Century,* October 1880, under the title 'Obstruction or Clôture', he stepped forward boldly as *avvocato di diavolo* against the dragon of 'boundless and predetermined loquacity'. Obstruction, he insisted, with a glance at certain Liberals, had thrived 'by sufferance': it was to be met 'not by patience and meekness, but by resistance', though he confessed that he had been driven to this conclusion 'with the bitterest regret and the most extreme reluctance'.[1] It was a dilemma shared by many Liberal members.

Meanwhile, Gladstone submitted his own memorandum to four of his colleagues and invited their comments. It is not possible to print them all *in extenso.* Hartington, the former Liberal leader, replied:[2]

I think the plan very well worth careful consideration. But if developed to an extent which would give the House of Commons real relief from the pressure of work it would entail so vast a change in the practice and (recent if not former) traditions of the House that it would encounter immense opposition; and I should scarcely expect to see it carried, even if approved, in less than two or three Sessions. But the importance of the reform, if it could be worked out, would equal its difficulty.

Childers, secretary of state for war, thought the suggestion of grand committees 'most valuable'.[3]

But I venture to urge that although the appointment of Grand Committees will relieve the pressure on the House [he continued], this will be far more satisfactorily effected by establishing County bodies, like the Conseils Généraux in France, and transferring to them large masses of business which Parliament has shown itself utterly unable to transact with proper care and deliberation. However we may improve parts of the machinery, the machine itself is inadequate for the task imposed on it; and I believe that a large and liberal measure of County Legislative bodies, not mere

---

[1] In their reviews of the reports of the select committees on procedure both the *Quarterly* and the *Edinburgh Review* had criticized the inadequacy of the proposed reforms (*Edinburgh Review*, 133, pp. 57-89; 134, pp. 587-99; *Quarterly Review*, 145, pp. 231 *seq.*; 146, pp. 181 *seq.*).

[2] Add. MSS. 44625, f. 4.

[3] He pointed to a danger that would have to be guarded against, viz., lest the chairmen of standing committees became permanent and more powerful than the responsible minister, as had happened in the United States.

County boards, is an absolute necessity. There is no English-speaking community where this necessity is not recognised. The United States of America could never be held together, or decently governed from Washington, without State Legislatures. We have adopted the principle for the government of four million Canadians and for the federation of the Cape Colonies and it must soon be adopted for Australia. It is the only possible answer to Home Rule.[1]

W. E. Forster, the Irish secretary, likewise welcomed the plan and hoped that the cabinet would give it 'practical consideration'. 'It holds out hope of real diminution of the work of the House and I believe it would ultimately lessen Irish obstruction by satisfying so much of the Home Rule as is a real grievance.' The reply of J. G. Dodson, president of the Local Government Board, was less encouraging. For seven years, 1865–72, Dodson had been a successful Chairman of Ways and Means and was therefore something of an authority on questions of procedure.[2] He pointed out that Erskine May, the great advocate of standing committees, in his evidence before the select committee on procedure in 1878 had abandoned an earlier scheme for dividing up the entire House into six or seven grand committees. 'The advocates of Grand Committees', Dodson stated,

> have always felt and admitted, in general terms, that great measures and measures of a party character, could not be disposed of by reference to them, and that they could only dispose of Bills of detail, or of compromise or of consolidation — in fact, very much the same sort of Bills that the House now consents to adopt from a Select Committee or a Commission.

He also pointed out the great practical difficulty of ensuring that the majority party was adequately reflected in the composition of each committee, and that there would be special difficulties in the allocation of Scottish and Irish mem-

---

[1] In Jan. 1882 Childers proposed to divide the entire House into seven 'general panels' (Add. MSS. 44130, f. 8 ; 44252, f. 155).

[2] For his account of the historical development of this post, see his letter to Gladstone (*ibid*. 44252, f. 19). On the death of Speaker Denison in 1872 Dodson was passed over in favour of Henry Brand (*ibid*. ff. 23–31).

The Changes in Parliamentary Procedure, 1880–1882

bers. His conclusion ended on a different note. 'I have for some years gradually, though reluctantly, been coming to the conclusion that the House will eventually have to determine to take power to bring a debate or a Committee to a close. The existence of such power would be a great check to obstruction, though no doubt there might be cases in which the obstructors might seek to promote its exercise and pose as victims.' 'The power of proposing it should perhaps be limited to the government, who would exercise it under such a keen sense of responsibility to the House and to the public that they would not be likely to resort to it except in a case they could plainly justify.'

Later Dodson was assigned the special task of preparing memoranda for the Cabinet on the working of the closure in certain of our self-governing colonies as well as in foreign legislatures, while on important technical matters, *e.g.* estimates and supply, he was a recognized 'authority'.[1]

Encouraged by these replies, Gladstone decided to print his memorandum and 'circulate' it to members of the Cabinet. In a covering letter, dated 11 November 1880, he added the following remarks:[2]

(1) I admit that the revival for practical purposes of Grand Committees would revive the name more than the thing and would be in the main new, though holding on to the old.

(2) It seems essential that if any plan of this kind be adopted there should be a simple method of appointment and one, so far as may be, self-working; and the body, once appointed, should not be open to easy change.

(3) It may be question[ed] whether the House has yet attained a sufficient consciousness of the existing and impending evils to be willing to face a drastic remedy, but unless it has arrived at this willingness, I believe it will have still to draw upon its stock, if any, of unexhausted patience before getting rid of obstruction or reducing arrear.

Prophetic words!

A month later news had leaked out that the Government

[1] *Ibid.* ff. 87, 151, 163, 175-86.   [2] *Ibid.* 44625, f. 4.

intended to introduce resolutions against obstruction immediately. The report called forth the following letter from Dr. Lyon Playfair, Chairman of Ways and Means.[1]

Obstruction   ATHENAEUM CLUB, PALL MALL,
                              11*th December*/80.
DEAR MR. GLADSTONE,

I see an apparently official notice in *The Times* today that Resolutions regarding Obstruction are immediately to be introduced to the House.

Allow me, as Chairman of Committees, to suggest one or two considerations. I would be very unwilling to limit the number of speeches to any member on the subject matter of a Bill or clause of a Bill. But I think it would be quite fair to limit each member to a single speech on the Motions :

(*a*) That the Speaker or Chairman } leave the Chair.

(*b*) That Progress be reported.

This alone would cut away a good deal of obstruction. I once counted Biggar's speeches on the latter motion and he spoke 8 times on a single motion.

I suggested this limitation of speech to Lord Randolph Churchill and Mr. Gorst and they told me (last session) they would support it.

(2) I further suggested to these two great obstructors that they might go a step further, but they dissented from the following proposition, viz.,

that the House deciding by $\frac{2}{3}$ majority on either of the above motions that the House should proceed with the Bill or particular clause of the Bill, it should be gone on with till the subject matter be determined, that is, no further Motions for delay should be allowed in regard to that one subject.

---

[1] Add. MSS. 44280, f. 174. Dr. Playfair later came in for some very sharp criticism from members of the Fourth Party and the Irish Party for his action in suspending Irish M.P.s *en bloc*, some of whom were not in the House at the time. The Opposition was unwilling to entrust the same powers to the Chairman as to the Speaker. Playfair was in ill-health and was succeeded in 1883 by Sir A. Otway (*ibid.* ff. 182-98). For Lord Randolph Churchill's views on closure see W. S. Churchill, *Life of Lord Randolph Churchill*, i. 156, 214-16; ii. 176.

The Changes in Parliamentary Procedure, 1880-1882

I only wish, just now, to allude to these two small parts of the subject of obstruction because I think they could be readily carried and they would remove at least two of the chief instruments of obstruction.

Yours sincerely,
Lyon Playfair

It would appear from this that Playfair was the unwitting author of what Gladstone later described as the 'detestable' suggestion of a two-thirds majority for purposes of applying the closure, and that Gorst had lately changed his mind on the main question.

Meanwhile the prime minister had begun a correspondence with the Speaker, who replied from his Sussex home:[1]

Glynde, December 18, 1880.

I have now to answer your letter of the 15th having had in the meantime the advantage of consulting Sir T. E. May.

The House under the existing crisis would be thoroughly warranted in passing a resolution, setting aside our ordinary modes of proceeding, for the purpose of passing a Bill or Bills essential to the Public Safety.

I cannot cite a precedent precisely in point, because the situation is without precedent; but as you know, there are many precedents for granting additional time to Government, founded generally on the plea of urgency — a plea which certainly prevails at the present juncture.

A Resolution might be drafted in the following terms:

'That Government Notices of Motion and Orders of the Day relating to Ireland . . . have precedence over all Notices of Motion or Orders of the Day untill the House shall otherwise order.'

I have left the blanks to be filled up by such measure or measures as you may decide; and you may think it right to include the remedial as well as the repressive measure.

With respect to the adoption of a resolution to have continuous sittings, although it has its advantages, I have doubts as to the expediency of such a course, because the resolution itself might

---

[1] Add. MSS. 44194, f. 230.

become the subject of a protracted debate ; and, as you know, the House has the power to sit continuously to pass the several stages of a Bill without any resolution, and would, no doubt, pursue that course on the occasions supposed, on the intimation of its necessity from the responsible Minister of the Crown.

Continuous sittings are, of course, a severe trial upon the House. I don't quite see why you propose to except the Committee from such a condition, for on the principle of salus populi, suprema lex, we should sit till an urgent measure had passed.

There lies behind a graver question than the above with which the House may have to deal. What is to be done if actual rebellion shews itself within the walls of the House in the form of wilful and persistent obstruction with the deliberate intention of stopping its action ? I do not expect that this state of things will actually arise, for I have faith in the moral force of the will of the House and that its will will prevail over all obstacles.

But we must be prepared for such a crisis. What else can we do but commit ?

I have no doubt that you have considered this emergency. It is constantly present to my mind and I really don't see what other course, in the face of absolute defiance, is open to the House.

This letter was circulated to members of the Cabinet. On the same day Gladstone received a note from Hartington.[1]

I apprehend, also, that the country will by that time [the re-opening of parliament in January] be and in fact now is in a state which will not admit of any further delay . . . or concession to obstruction. I do not mean to say that fair debate ought not to be permitted but I do think that obstruction will have to be sharply dealt with.

The subject was clearly under discussion in government circles during the Christmas recess, although there was apparently some delay in the circulation of official papers.[2] By the middle of January 1881, Gladstone had drafted a set of

[1] Add. MSS. 44145, ff. 163, 175. Lord E. Fitzmaurice and Mr. Thorold Rogers furnished Hartington with precedents, 'the result of a search of an hour or two', of the Speaker's powers to suppress disorder.
[2] Ibid. f. 173 (Hartington to Gladstone, 10 Jan. 1881). 'Dodson told me that he had not seen a Circulation Box which you sent round last week containing he Speaker's letter and a Memorandum by Sir E. May. . . .'

urgency rules. These were discussed by the Cabinet on the 19th and copies forwarded to the Speaker and Erskine May for their comments. The original draft of Rule I read as follows:

That whenever the House shall have voted 'That the state of public business is urgent', the powers of the House for the regulation of its business shall be [vested in] and remain with the Speaker (until Mr. Speaker shall declare the state of public business is no longer urgent).[1]

Erskine May commented: 'If such powers were entrusted to the Speaker . . . he would be brought into violent conflict with the obstructive party and the authority of the chair might be impaired'. Not all the members of the Cabinet, apparently, sufficiently appreciated this important principle; Hartington was a great advocate of the Speaker 'taking the initiative' and was 'still inclined to think that the Speaker should be urged to take the responsibility on himself' (of declaring a state of urgency).[2] Speaker Brand was fully alive to the danger.

I have no hesitation in assuming any authority which the House may for the public good impose upon me [he told Gladstone], but there is some danger that by a process of this kind, the authority of the Chair may be permanently impaired; — and although on personal grounds I am willing to make any sacrifices, resort should not be had to a proceeding which may injuriously affect the Chair and which may be regarded as high-handed until all other means have been exhausted and the necessity has actually arisen.

My belief is that a well considered resolution for closing the debate may be a means for delivering the House from the tyranny of obstruction under which it now suffers and I should advise an attempt in this direction before you adopt your Resolution of urgency making the Speaker absolute.[3]

Meanwhile, Brand had addressed the following letter to Stafford Northcote, leader of the Opposition, in an effort to

[1] *Ibid.* 44626, ff. 23, 26, 76 (with May's marginal comments); 44765, ff. 80-87.
[2] *Ibid.* 44145, ff. 175, 178. Hansard, **268**, p. 345.
[3] Add. MSS. 44195, f. 8.

get concerted action by the major political parties on the matter.[1]

Private   *January* 19, 1881.

MY DEAR SIR STAFFORD NORTHCOTE,

The tactics of Members, commonly known as the Third Party,[2] have been clearly disclosed by their proceedings since the meeting of Parliament. Their tactics may be shortly described as a determination to stifle discussion under cover of our present Rules and Orders. They exercise a monopoly of debate for themselves, and thus effectually shut out all freedom of debate for others. The House is now, through this action of this Party, paralizzed [*sic*] ; and this state of things, if allowed to continue, will bring Parliamentary Government into contempt.

This is the tenth day of the debate on the Address, and I have reason to believe that the same tactics will be repeated upon the Report of the Address ; and that throughout the Session (and I may say throughout the Parliament) every available opportunity will be seized by the same Party to paralizze the action of the House.

The question arises, What is to be done ?

I have given very anxious consideration to this matter and have come to the conclusion that the best way to meet the crisis is to take power to close a debate, subject to certain conditions for the protection of minorities.

I have embodied my ideas in the enclosed Draft Resolution, and I submit it to you for your consideration.[3]

I shewed this Draft last night to Mr. Gladstone and to Lord Hartington ; and it shall go no further until you have considered it and given me your opinion.

Both Mr. Gladstone and Ld. Hartington, without expressing

---

[1] Add. MSS. 44195, f. 2.

[2] This designation is interesting. *The Times* of 7 Sept. 1880 referred to their 'half serious nickname of the Fourth Party', quoted by W. S. Churchill, *Life of Lord Randolph Churchill*, i. 152 ; *Hansard*, **274**, pp. 1254, 1364, 1437, 1511.

[3] 'That on a Motion being made, during any Debate, in the House or in any Committee of the Whole House "That the Debate be now closed", the Speaker or the Chairman, may, if he think fit, desire any members who support such motion to rise in their places ; and if not less than 40 members so rise, he shall thereupon put the Question, no debate adjournment or amendment being allowed ; and if such Question be resolved in the Affirmative, the original Question shall be forthwith put from the Chair.'

a definite opinion, were disposed to entertain the Resolution favourably as a basis for consideration.[1]

Mr. Gladstone asked me 'What would be your opinion', adding that he was desirous upon such a matter to obtain your co-operation, and that before taking any action he would confer with you in the hope, if possible, of coming to a common understanding.

Upon this statement of Mr. Gladstone, I volunteered to submit the enclosed to you in the hope that it might at least point the way to that common understanding.

When you shall have considered the enclosed, I shall be glad to confer with you, and I forbear to lengthen this letter by entering into details, waiting to hear what you have to say upon the matter.

This was the position at the end of the month when the Irish members exceeded all bounds in their opposition to the proposed Coercion Bill. From a quarter to four o'clock on the afternoon of Monday, 31 January, the House was kept in continuous session until it was terminiated by the dramatic intervention of the Speaker, at nine-thirty on the morning of Wednesday, 2 February, a total of $41\frac{1}{2}$ hours.[2] 'The dignity, the credit and the authority of this House', the Speaker solemnly declared, 'are seriously threatened and it is necessary they should be vindicated. Under the operation of the accustomed rules and methods of procedure the legislative powers of the House are paralyzed [sic] and a new and exceptional course is imperatively demanded.' This courageous stand won general approval from both sides of the House: Mr. Speaker had become 'our deliverer', 'our guardian angel'.[3] The prime minister subsequently gave notice that on the following day he would move urgency resolutions 'enabling

---

[1] The Speaker also forwarded a copy of this letter to Sir Richard Cross but had received no reply from either when he wrote to Gladstone on the 22nd. 'The Speaker told me just now', Hartington wrote to Gladstone on the 20th, 'that he had had some further conversation with Cross and that he and Northcote are evidently alarmed that some proposal may be made to which they cannot give their approval without consulting their friends. He thinks that if you give notice tomorrow of any Resolution in definite terms, to which Northcote's assent has not been obtained, it will place him in a very difficult position . . .' (Add. MSS. 44145, f. 183).

[2] Erskine May referred to it as 'the memorable sitting' (*ibid.* 44154, f. 139). In the same letter he cites other instances of long sittings.

[3] *Hansard*, **266**, p. 1142 (Gladstone's words).

the House', so Bryce explained to his American readers, 'to entrust the Speaker with almost dictatorial powers'. 'Last week was the most remarkable one in the history of our Parliament since the great Civil War,' Bryce added, 'the changes made in the rules of the House of Commons have been both greater and more sudden than anyone had ventured to dream of two months ago.'[1] The urgency rules 'framed' by Brand were a modified version of Gladstone's earlier draft.[2]

With singular lack of tact a section of the Irishmen played straight into the Speaker's hands and twenty-seven were forthwith suspended.[3] Indeed it was generally admitted that the urgency rules were particularly stringent and the House breathed a sigh of relief when they were lifted.[4]

Even with urgency rules, the parliamentary breakdown in 1881 was wellnigh total. In a forthright article in the August issue of the *Fortnightly*, John Morley declared:[5]

> The Parliamentary breakdown has in one sense been the most signal of any on record. Parliament met in January and will probably not be prorogued till September, but a Session prolonged beyond precedent is likely to be characterised by barrenness without parallel. The Parliamentary collapse is almost painfully complete. Measures of pressing urgency affecting the vital interests of the United Kingdom are blocked. Nothing can be done. The Parliamentary machine has broken down, and the paralysis of the legislature is at last being recognised as a grave public peril. . . . If Parliamentary Government has to continue a possibility in this country, the reform of Parliamentary procedure must be taken in

---

[1] *The Nation*, xxxii. 164-5, 'The Adoption of the Clôture'.

[2] Add. MSS. 44195, ff. 20-22 ; *Hansard*, **257**, p. 435 ; **271**, p. 1396.

[3] Gladstone later commented on 'this most extraordinary error', *Hansard*, **266**, p. 144 ; **274**, pp. 1830, 1835. Cf. Bryce's contemporary account, *loc. cit.* For Bryce's speeches on the new rules, *Hansard*, **267**, pp. 1379-84 ; **274**, pp. 386 *passim*.

[4] It was found necessary, later in the month, to frame additional rules 'for bringing the labors of a Committee to a close' (Brand to Gladstone), Add. MSS. 44195, ff. 17, 24-31. *Hansard*, **268**, pp. 1070, 1343. For a criticism of the urgency rules, see Burt, *Nineteenth Century*, ix. 618.

[5] *Fortnightly Review*, xxx, 263. Morley gave strong support throughout to the new rules (*ibid.* 392, 677 *passim*). See also Frederic Harrison's 'The Deadlock in the House of Commons', *Nineteenth Century*, x. 317-40.

hand without any longer delay. Even a Government by ukase may come to be preferred to the Government of a legislature which cannot legislate.

It had always been recognized that the Speaker's urgency rules were 'exceptional' and unrepeatable: he himself had stated at the time that the House would have to address itself to a permanent reform of its procedure.[1] There could be no question, therefore, of making Brand's rules standing orders though ex-Speaker Lord Eversley told Erskine May that he was in favour of so doing. And since it was obvious that the House itself lacked a 'sufficient propelling power' to devise and carry through a new code, the unenviable task fell to the government. In the autumn of 1881 the 'authorities'— Brand, Erskine May and Dodson — were called in again and the two last submitted important memoranda which served as a basis for the deliberations of the Cabinet. It is clear from their correspondence with Gladstone how dependent he was on these men not only for the actual proposals but later, on May particularly, for 'drawing' them in parliamentary form. When parliament was prorogued in August 1881, Gladstone sent Brand a copy of his earlier paper on '*Devolution and Obstruction*' and invited him, in consultation with May, to consider the whole question of procedure '*ab initio*'.[2] Accordingly, after 'much consideration and mutual conference' they submitted, early in November, a memorandum that had been prepared by May.[3] 'We have two special objects in view,' Brand explained, '(i) To repress disorder or irregularity or the abuse of Rules; (ii) To facilitate the progress of business by the revision of our Rules and Practice'.

He did not expect the government would encounter much opposition on the first,

---

[1] Brand preferred to describe the proceedings of 31 Jan. as 'exceptional' rather than 'irregular' or 'illegal' (Add. MSS. 44195, f. 89). In reply to a question by Ashton Dilke the prime minister agreed that the urgency rules 'by no means cover the whole of the case' although the Government had then (21 Feb.) not arrived at any positive conclusion (*Hansard*, **257**, p. 2033; **268**, p. 1383).
[2] Add. MSS. 44195, f. 65, 'as if we had never received the Cabinet Paper'.
[3] *Ibid.* 44154, f. 79.

but you will meet with strenuous resistance to the second from many quarters — from Sir Stafford Northcote, from Lord R. Churchill and from the disaffected Irish because none of these wish to facilitate the progress of business *in your hands*. It will remain to be seen how far you can depend upon your own supporters. Discipline is no doubt important and in present times essential, but I attach infinitely more importance to the second branch of the above subjects. I hope that the scheme of Standing Committees, upon which both May and I have given much thought, will commend itself to you. I attach great importance to it and believe that in practice it will work well.

The unanimity of these 'great authorities' on this aspect of reform is remarkable. Nevertheless a notable difference is evident. True, the new rules eventually made provision for the setting up of two standing committees (for Law and Trade) but they were relegated almost to an appendix.[1] Devolution no longer occupied first place. At what precise date during 1881 Gladstone decided that Rule I should be 'To establish the Clôture'— it appears in those words in an undated set of 'Notes' in his hand[2]— it is impossible to say, but for him it marked a radical conversion. This much is clear from a letter to May.

Private & Confidential

HAWARDEN CASTLE, 22 *Nov.* 1881.[3]

MY DEAR SIR THOMAS MAY,

... I had the benefit of a conversation with the Speaker on the clôture. On that subject I differ a little from many, (1) in expecting immense difficulty in passing it, (2) in anticipating from it insufficient benefits. In my view, obstruction with us thrives very much more through the multiplication of questions, than through the undue prolongation of particular debates. To put an end to a debate by Clôture requires a very strong case. It is usually not difficult to save appearances as far as to avoid obviously creating such a case.

---

[1] *Hansard*, **275** (Appendix), 'The New Rules of Procedure'.
[2] Add. MSS. 44765, f. 80, endorsed 'January or February, 1881', which, however, is clearly associated with the proposed urgency rules.
[3] (Gladstone to Sir T. E. May) *ibid.* 44154, f. 92.

The Changes in Parliamentary Procedure, 1880–1882

This remedy could not be used except at intervals comparatively distant. I should anticipate much larger advantage from the previous question, in a form which would, I suppose, be new : a form, which on a Resolution, as a clause in a Bill, should render it possible at any time to move that all remaining amendments, or other motions on such Resolution or Clause should be put without discussion. I do not know whether this would be feasible. But I have a strong impression that clôture, when obtained, would not do the work we want done.

'I myself', he later confessed to the House, 'have been one of the most reluctant and slowest to be convinced of the necessity of such.'[1] (If the House sensed the prime minister's misgivings on this point it is not surprising that it took nearly nine months to carry it.)

May replied :[2]

There can be little doubt that *La Clôture*, in any form, would be strenuously opposed ; and many opponents would be found in the Liberal Party.

If the rule were adopted, I think it would only be applied in extreme cases, of which there have been some recent examples.

The putting of the remaining clauses and amendments in Committee on a Bill was provided for last session on one of the Speaker's Urgency Rules and proved very effective.

You will see from the Paper I am preparing that nearly all the changes of procedure during the last 50 years have been in the direction of reducing the number of Questions and opportunities for debate.[3]

As originally drafted, Rule I provided, under certain safeguards, for the closing of debate, but it contained also a 'very startling' proposal which provided 'that any amend-

---

[1] *Hansard*, **266**, p. 1138. Morley observes that 'the necessity for the closure was probably the most unpalatable of all the changes forced on Gladstone by change in social and political circumstance' (*Life*, ii. 363-4). He adds the surprising statement : 'his papers contain nothing of interest or novelty upon the question either of devolution or of the compulsory stoppage of debate'. Cf. Magnus, *op. cit.*, p. 298.

[2] Add. MSS. 44154, f. 94, dated 23 Jan., but clearly in error for Nov., as the beginning of the letter is in reply to Gladstone's queries concerning the working of the French Bureaux, ff. 86, 88.

[3] *Ibid.* f. 98 ('Memorandum on Changes of Procedure since 1832', 29 Nov. 1881).

ments on the Paper, as well as the main question, shall be forthwith put from the Chair'.¹ Brand took strong exception to this, as well as to a reference to obstruction in the proposed rule, and these parts were eventually dropped. For the rest, he told Gladstone, 'I quite approve of the remaining Rules... and I think that you will carry them substantially, provided you don't alarm the House with an explosion from the second barrel of No. I'.² In another letter he suggested that 'we adopt the word "close" instead of clôture which is french and of closure which is frenchified'— a change which commended itself to the prime minister.³ He also recommended the inclusion of Rules 7 and 8 of the urgency rules: 'I think that they would be accepted by the House and work well'.⁴ When told of the Cabinet's decision to try a limited, experimental scheme of two standing committees, he wrote: 'I must say... that in my opinion a large scheme, fully considered, would have a better chance of floating than a tentative experiment such as that now proposed by the Cabinet, but which I thankfully accept if the better way cannot be followed'.⁵ With his running commentary on detailed technical points, we need not here be concerned. Suffice to say that he strongly advised Gladstone not to change the order of the resolutions and put Rule I last as suggested by the Opposition. 'You run the risk of wearying the House over the less important Resolutions and it will be urged that enough has been done and that Resolution I may be thrown overboard.'⁶ He rejected the suggestion of the American 'Previous Question'.⁷ Similarly he 'hoped and believed that you will sustain the principle of

---

[1] *I.e.* anticipating the guillotine. Brand stigmatized it as 'very strong, too strong in my opinion for acceptance by the House, and not required *at present*' (my italics).

[2] Add. MSS. 44195, f. 77.   [3] *Ibid.* ff. 89, 91.

[4] 'Again, you should pass a Rule regulating Supply founded on the Resolution of 1873 (proposed, I think, by Lowe) otherwise our Supply rights will continue to be chaotic' (*ibid.* f. 77).

[5] *Ibid.* f. 85. He had written earlier, 'For my part I am strongly in favour of delegating to Standing Committees much of the work now undertaken by Committees of the Whole House. This would be a real measure of relief to the House and facilitate the progress of business in many ways' (*ibid.* f. 77).   [6] *Ibid.* ff. 84-7.   [7] *Ibid.* f. 119 (7 Oct.).

The Changes in Parliamentary Procedure, 1880–1882

a bare majority as the foundation of Rule I', though he added later, 'the arithmetical puzzle in your own Rule will ever be a trial to the Chair but it must be accepted for the protection of minorities in consequence of the adoption of the sound Parliamentary principle of Government by majority'.[1] He stigmatized the tory proposal of a two-thirds majority, or other fractional variants, as 'new-fangled'. Finally, he advised that the government should make the new rules, if adopted, standing orders 'so as not to have to fight the battle or any part of it over again'.[2]

It was the proposal to apply the closure by a 'bare' or 'simple' majority that fired the parliamentary heather.[3] A month before the resolutions were tabled May had written: 'There is a strong prejudice against a bare majority which may be appeased by requiring that there shall be more than 200 supporting the closure . . . or less than 40 [in opposition]. In reality this is a bare majority, for the motion would be carried if 199 opposed it, but the safeguard of numbers would probably satisfy doubting and reluctant minds'.[4] This is the origin of the 'arithmetical puzzle' in the rule. Actually what Gladstone was concerned to do was to ensure reasonable protection to small minorities — large ones could take care of themselves — while, at the same time, to prevent a 'tyrant' or 'dominant' handful of members from frustrating the evident sense of the House.[5] The puzzle disappears when it is realized that Gladstone was concerned, not with the question of the size of the majority, but with the number of the quorum required at different levels so as to ensure that a mere handful

---

[1] *Ibid.* f. 123 (19 Oct.). He pointed out that under Gibson's rule 'the Chair will be called upon not only to resolve that puzzle but must be satisfied also that the closure is demanded by two-thirds of the House'. See Churchill, *op. cit.*, ii. 176.

[2] Add. MSS. 44195, f. 121.

[3] See Marriott's amendment to Rule I and the protracted debates thereon (*Hansard*, **266**, p. 232).

[4] Add. MSS. 44154, f. 107 (18 Jan. 1882) Gladstone gave notice of the resolutions relating to procedure on 7 Feb. (*Hansard*, **266**, p. 97 ; **267**, pp. 1148, 1760).

[5] The adjectives were Speaker Brand's. (Add. MSS. 44195, ff. 108, 121.) On large minorities, see Bright's speech (*Hansard*, **268**, p. 319).

of members should not prevent the application of the closure. 'It is altogether a question of quorum', declared Harcourt. But it was not easy to draft in a single resolution a proposal to establish what Dodson called a 'major' and a 'minor' clôture, and certainly Erskine May recognized the apparent inconsistency. He wrote on 20 February 1882, the day on which the prime minister moved the resolutions:[1]

> Your modification of the first Resolution will, I trust, satisfy the doubting members of your own party who have expressed fears that small minorities would be unduly coerced.
> But as the principle of a simple majority is so far compromised it will now be asked why a large minority is not to have the same protection as a small one.
> To this, however, I think it will be a fair and sufficient answer that a large minority needs no such protection. Its members and debating power, its moral force and the support of public opinion insure it against coercion.
> The initiative of the Speaker will afford protection to minorities whether great or small—but more especially to the former, as with a minority approaching 200 it will scarcely be possible for the Speaker to affirm that it is the evident sense of the House [2] that the debate should be closed.

On such reasoning the government based its case.

The opinion was widely held at the time and repeatedly asserted in the course of debate that Chamberlain was the author of the new rules: that closure, like caucus, was a 'Brummagem' product.[3] The full correspondence of Gladstone with May and Brand effectively disposes of this myth. The following, hitherto unpublished, letters from Chamberlain show that he took up the subject rather late and that his main rôle was to steel the prime minister against trying to conciliate the tories.

---

[1] Add. MSS. 44154, f. 141. For J. G. Dodson's comments, *ibid.* 44252, f. 151.   [2] See Rule I.
[3] *Hansard*, **266**, pp. 1170, 1709; **274**, p. 1454. Hinde Palmer (M.P. Lincoln) stated that Chamberlain 'was the chief person who wants the clôture', although Hicks-Beach pointed out that Chamberlain 'had never favoured the House with his views as to this matter' (*ibid.* **274**, p. 1274).

The Changes in Parliamentary Procedure, 1880–1882

HIGHBURY, MOOR GREEN,
BIRMINGHAM.[1]

21 January (1882)

I attached some importance to the reference to obstruction in No. 1 as I thought it would greatly strengthen our position in the House and the Country and would be an unanswerable proof of our intention not to interfere with legitimate discussion. The arguments of the Speaker, however, seem to me very strong and I now think the balance is against the insertion of this qualification.[2] I agree also with the Speaker as to the difficulty of carrying No. 2 and should be disposed to omit it from our first proposals. It can be considered afterwards by the help of No. 1 if circumstances show it to be necessary.

(same date) [3]

I think it would be a great pity to burden our proposals with provisions for Urgency.

The House could only be reconciled to such excessively stringent rules by an emergency, and as the power of Closure would enable a majority to deal promptly with such a condition, if it should arise, I think it much better not to attempt this provision at the present time. I think the proposal to allow Bills to be taken up in the succeeding sessions of the same Parliament in the stage in which the prorogation finds them, would be popular in the House and deserves careful consideration. I do not agree with Mr. Dodson's objection,[4] for if this change were made, the earlier stages of the Bills would be seriously contested, instead of being allowed, as now, to be taken with insufficient examination in the faith of their not being able to be pushed further.

Private members would like this alteration and it would help to sweeten our other proposals to them.

[1] (Chamberlain to Gladstone) Add. MSS. 44125, f. 115.
[2] *Supra*, p. 310. The reference to obstruction was dropped. Dodson had pointed out that 'the words "For the purpose of obstruction" somewhat weaken the rule but they make it so incomparably more difficult for the Opposition to resist before the House and the country that it is safe to retain them (*loc. cit.*).
[3] Add. MSS. 44125, f. 115.
[4] *Ibid.* 44252, f. 153. 'The suspension of bills from Session to Session is most questionable', Dodson commented on 20 Jan. '. . . the change interferes with the Royal Prerogative of putting an end to all business by a Prorogation'.

Essays Presented to Sir Lewis Namier

BOARD OF TRADE, *January* 26, 1882.[1]

I was surprised to hear Lord Richard Grosvenor[2] say that Mr. Dillwyn[3] would oppose the Closure and that 30 members would follow him on the Liberal side.

If this had been correct it would have been a serious difficulty in our way but, fortunately, it is the very reverse of the fact.

On May 17, 1881, Mr. Dillwyn moved the adoption of a series of Resolutions including a closure more stringent, I think, in some respects than ours. I enclose a Copy of these Resolutions, all of which are worth consideration; and I may add that Mr. Dillwyn told a friend of mine last week that experience had only confirmed his conviction of the necessity of these changes.

I am convinced that there is no fear of serious opposition to our proposals from the advanced Radicals. The only member of that section who is doubtful is Mr. Rylands.[4]

BOARD OF TRADE, *June* 22, 1882.[5]

I see you are to be asked today a question as to the Procedure Resolutions and as to whether any compromise or concession is to be made on the Clôture.[6]

It is to be noted from the statements of Mr. Raikes[7] and others and from the articles in the *Standard* that the Tories intend in any case to oppose the scheme of devolution; and consequently the effect of a concession on the first Rule will only be to transfer their obstruction to the proposal for Grand Committees.

I am convinced that any change of front under the circumstances

[1] Add. MSS. 44252, f. 118.
[2] The Government Chief Whip.
[3] M.P. for Swansea. He had opposed the introduction of clôture in 1880. For his speech on the new rules, *Hansard*, **268**, pp. 385-93.
[4] M.P. for Burnley (*ibid.* **274**, pp. 302, 1611). Rylands and Dillwyn were described as 'the Palladins of the liberties of the House'.
[5] Add. MSS. 44125, f. 156.
[6] On 20 June Mr. John Gorst drew attention to a speech at Banff by R. W. Duff, a junior lord of the Treasury, in which he said: 'I believe the Government are determined to pass the Procedure Rules, if possible, before Parliament rises; and, if not, though of course I am not in Cabinet secrets, I believe by calling an Autumn session for the purpose'. This hint of a special session was not denied or confirmed at the time by Gladstone (*Hansard*, **270**, p. 1768).
[7] M.P. for Preston and a former Chairman of Ways and Means (*ibid.* **267**, pp. 1301-15).

The Changes in Parliamentary Procedure, 1880–1882

will be most disheartening to our friends in the country, but my chief object in writing is to say that I am informed on the best authority, that the feeling of indignation at the prolonged incapacity of the House to fulfil its duties is very strong and has only been restrained hitherto by doubts as to the necessity or expediency of public demonstrations. If, however, an autumn session is announced for dealing with the question I am assured that the recess will be utilised for an agitation which will embrace every constituency in England and will be directed to strengthening the hands of the Government and securing support for their proposals — in their integrity.

Pray do not reply to this.[1]

HIGHBURY, 18*th October* (1882) [2]

I agree with every word of Harcourt's memorandum.[3]

I fully admit the serious nature of the struggle and in fact I doubt if we can succeed at all unless we allow it to be known at once 1st, that the session will be prolonged into January, if necessary ; and 2nd that the decision will be considered as involving the fate of the Government.

But under these conditions ultimate victory is certain.

Without venturing on confident predictions, I believe that the effect of abandoning Closure would be to transfer the fight to the Resolutions concerning delegation.

I have not the slightest faith in conciliating the Tories, except by surrendering all our projects of legislation. They have worked themselves up into a real panic about revolutionary legislation and they will do nothing to facilitate the effective progress of business in the present House of Commons

But if we go on, on the present lines, it seems probable that the opposition will exhaust itself on the Closure fight and when that is once out of the way they may be unable to rally their followers

---

[1] Endorsed by Gladstone : 'Agst. change of front on Procedure'. The National Liberal Federation had issued a 'circular' on the subject. It was this which gave offence to the tories and gave rise to the mistaken view that Chamberlain was the author of closure (*ibid.* **266**, pp. 1172, 1186. See an article by George Baden Powell in the *Contemporary Review*, xlii. 544-51).

[2] Add. MSS. 44125, f. 206.

[3] Home Secretary. I have not yet succeeded in tracing this memorandum : there is a later one by him in Add. MSS. 44200, f. 186. *Hansard*, **267**, pp. 1753-1765.

for continued opposition to the remaining Rules. In fact 'Closure' may well turn out to be the Tel-el-Kebir of the campaign.[1]

I venture to differ from Mr. Gladstone as to the importance of the closing power and the probable frequency of its use. I believe that obstruction will continue under any system and that the closure will gradually come into general use as it has done in France where its operation provokes no comment and no complaint.[2]

The present position is this : it is agreed by both parties that some form of closure is necessary and the only question is by what majority it may be exerted.

The innovators are the Tories who would introduce the unconstitutional practice of a two-thirds majority.[3]

The effect would be formally to acknowledge the right of a 3rd minority to postpone indefinitely a decision on any proposal to which they object and practically to dictate the policy of the country.

Indeed the whig Hartington and the Radical Chamberlain were substantially agreed on the matter. In fact, the tory critic who called Hartington 'the author of this measure' was nearer the truth. In a famous speech to his constituents at Nelson on 17 December 1881, he hinted plainly that the country would no longer tolerate the frustrating postponement of legislation by obstructionists.[4] 'If you want any of those things done', he declared, 'I have no hesitation

---

[1] And so it proved.

[2] Cf. W. S. Churchill's prediction, 'The victory of Closure will be complete' (*Life of Lord Randolph Churchill*, i. 221).

[3] See Lord Randolph's notable speech on 1 Nov. 'I own I am a firm believer in the general infallibility of simple majorities' (*ibid.* 214-22). Cf. Gladstone's earlier enunciation of the principle : 'there is but one sound principle in this House and that is that the majority should prevail' (*Hansard*, **266**, p. 1146).

[4] Hartington had favoured the adoption of closure as early as 1878 (*Report of Select Committee on Procedure* ; *Hansard*, **267**, pp. 1309-11, 1318-34 ; **274**, p. 1281). Raikes declared that this speech let 'the biggest political cat ever seen out of the flimsiest of bags'. 'I am of opinion', declared Hartington, 'that no remedy will be found adequate which does not give to the House and to a majority of the House far greater powers than it now possesses for the purpose of disposing of its own time and of deciding what subjects it will discuss and at what length it shall discuss them.' He contended that 'time belongs to the House' and 'it is not a personal right or privilege of members : . . . except in this House, liberty of speech does not extend to providing a man with an audience' (*ibid.* **268**, p. 328 ; *Fortnightly Review* (1882), p. 402).

The Changes in Parliamentary Procedure, 1880–1882

in saying that the first thing to do is to reform the existing procedure in Parliament.' And it was Hartington who insisted that the Government treat the vote as one of confidence. *The Times* was sadly wide of the mark in appealing to him to lead a Liberal revolt on the issue. In the event Chamberlain was right in his prognostication that the Radicals would support the Government and that once the fight over Rule I was won the tories would not strenuously oppose the others. Only three English Liberals, Courtauld (Maldon), Marriott (Brighton) and Taylor (Leicester) voted with the tories on the crucial 'Closure division' of 10 November 1882 :[1] by 1 December the other Rules had been adopted.

The fight had been a long one. The resolutions which embodied the new rules had stood on the Notice Paper ever since 20 February and it had required a special autumn session to pass them.[2] The earnest desire of Gladstone and the Speaker to win tory support and to treat the question as a non-party issue failed from the start.[3] We cannot now go

[1] Add. MSS. 44628, f. 155. There were 27 other English and 'Scotch' Liberals who did not vote on the division ; 17 of these had paired. Three other Liberal members, Cowen (Newcastle-on-Tyne), Walter (Berks) and Sir E. Watkin (Hythe), who, Morley stated, 'can hardly be classed among the regular supporters of Government', had voted with the Opposition on Marriott's amendment in March (*Hansard*, **268**, p. 426). The Irish voting on the main closure resolution was as follows : 27 Parnellites and 5 other Home Rulers voted against the Government along with 21 Irish tories, while 8 others abstained ; 25 Irish M.P.s voted with the Government. Cf. the statement in *Life of Lord Randolph Churchill*, p. 150, that 'the Irish Party voted in a body' against the amendment which proposed a ⅔ majority.

[2] During the special autumn session 'procedure' had precedence. See Gladstone's statement, *Hansard*, **273**, p. 2051 : Add. MSS. 44217, f. 207.

[3] Gladstone informed Sir Stafford Northcote in advance of the proposals and got the following reply :

                                  30 St James Place, *February* 4, 1882
  Private
My dear Mr. Gladstone,
    I am much obliged by your letter and the copy of the Resolutions which I have read with care. I propose to show them to some of my late Cabinet Colleagues whom I shall meet this evening, and I will then take care to impress on them the strictly confidential character of the communication.
    My first impression is that there will be no insuperable difficulty in coming to an agreement upon the great majority of the resolutions in the spirit in which they are proposed ; but that there will be a sharp divergence between us and you upon the first of them.
    On the whole I think we shall discuss them with more advantage across

into the detailed causes of this. Suffice to say that Stafford Northcote, the tory leader, was prepared to compromise on the other rules, but was adamant on the closure, and that Cross tried to persuade the Government to postpone the proposal for standing committees.[1] Above all, the long fight admirably illustrates what Bryce described as 'the extreme conservatism of the House of Commons in all that concerns its forms'.[2]

Much of the opposition to the new rules turned on the fear that they would gravely prejudice the rights of private

> the floor of the House than in a private conference, but should I find on further consideration reason to change this opinion I will take advantage of your kind suggestion and will communicate with you either late this evening or the first thing in the morning.
> You may rely on my doing my best in any case to bring about a settlement on the very important questions which are raised and which so closely affect the House of Commons irrespective of Party. (Add. MSS. 44217, f. 191.)

On the 6th of May there was an important sequel. Gladstone privately informed Northcote that the Government was willing to accept Gibson's amendment with a view to speeding up the passage of the procedure resolutions.

> With a view to this end [he wrote] and adverting to the fact that you are now acting together as a party and also to the character and especially the length of the debates thus far on the 1st Resolution of procedure, we are prepared, without having modified our own ideas, to accept the amendment of which notice has been given by Mr. Gibson, with the intention of allowing the Resolution, thus altered, to be fairly tested by experience, provided we are assured in the House (for I do not ask from you any undertaking or any reply to this note beyond acknowledgement) that you and the heads of your party will, on that basis, use exertions to expedite the action of the House on Procedure and will enter on the consideration of the remaining Resolutions in what I may term the spirit of co-operation indicated in your note of Feb. 4 in relation to them.
> I think I need not here trouble you with any statement of the motives which have led us to adopt this course but the suggestion is tendered with a conciliatory aim. (*Ibid.* f. 203.)

Owing to the Phoenix Park murders immediately afterwards this suggestion was never acted upon. Gladstone later explained to the House that, in the changed circumstances, both sides subsequently claimed complete freedom of action (*Hansard*, **273**, p. 1696. Add. MSS. 44195, f. 98, for Brand's unavailing appeal to Northcote).

[1] *Ibid.* f. 138. Sir Richard Cross appealed to the Speaker on 18 Nov. to urge Gladstone not to press this session the resolutions *re* standing committees, 'a matter about which he and his friends were very anxious'. By that date Northcote was a sick man, and about to set out on a Mediterranean cruise (*ibid.* 44217, f. 210).

[2] Bryce, *The Nation, loc. cit.* Burke had declared that 'the forms (of the House) were the entrenchments of minorities' (*Hansard*, **19**, 106-7).

The Changes in Parliamentary Procedure, 1880–1882

members and play into the hands of the disciplined party battalions — a fear justified by subsequent developments. It was fitting, therefore, that the most respected 'Independent' in the House, Samuel Whitbread, M.P. for Bedford, should have played a most important minor rôle in the detailed suggestions relating to standing committees. For it was his *Memorandum* of 3 February 1882 on *Grand Committees*, dealing with their composition and the method of appointment of such and of their chairman, that was eventually adopted in preference to various schemes of members of the cabinet.[1] Since 1868 Whitbread had steadily refused office and he was to refuse more offers, including a privy councillorship in 1882, since he was convinced that he could be more useful as an 'independent' member.

> It seems to me [he told Gladstone] that an independent member of Parliament, especially in times of political difficulty like those through which we are passing, has less chance of being useful if he is seen to be accepting for himself marks of distinction which fall naturally and properly to those who have borne the burthen of official life. I do not presume to judge for others, but for myself I hold this view strongly.[2]

He represents perhaps the last in a long parliamentary tradition. As such he will have a special appeal to the scholar whom we seek to honour.

[1] Add. MSS. 44474, ff. 124-32 ; 44476, ff. 83-93 ; 44195, ff. 85, 111, 117; 44252, ff. 153-5, 163 (for Dodson's proposals).
[2] *Ibid.* 44417, ff. 89-91 ; 44476, f. 170 ; 44440, f. 193. He was chairman of the committee of selection and had been a member of the 1878 committee on procedure (*Hansard*, **268**, p. 336).

G. H. BOLSOVER

ASPECTS OF RUSSIAN FOREIGN POLICY, 1815–1914

IN 1815 Russia emerged from the Napoleonic wars firmly established as one of the Great Powers of Europe. By 1914 she had become a World Power as well. In Europe she made no new permanent territorial gains during these hundred years. In 1829 she forced Turkey to cede her a small but important area at the Danube mouth. But she lost it in 1856 along with part of Bessarabia which she eventually recovered in 1878. Apart from this, her western frontiers underwent no change and were the same in 1914 as in 1815. This was in complete contrast to their considerable extension westwards during the preceding century and hardly bore out the dire warnings about further Russian conquests which circulated in Europe, particularly between 1815 and 1856. The reasons for this halt in her territorial expansion into Europe were complex. But they are to be found mainly in the opposition of the other European Powers, in an intermittent feeling among those responsible for her foreign policy that she was perhaps big enough already, and in a realization that the risks involved in acquiring new territory in Europe had grown too great. Even though her territorial expansion into Europe was halted, she had considerable influence in European affairs. It was at its peak between 1815 and 1856 when it was thought in some quarters to be excessive if not preponderant. Afterwards it declined somewhat. But it was always much greater and more continuous than in the eighteenth century.

Outside Europe, Russia made considerable territorial gains between 1815 and 1914 in the Caucasus, central Asia and the Far East. It was these which provided the basis for her

Aspects of Russian Foreign Policy, 1815–1914

development from a European into a World Power. In the Caucasus, she had largely completed the process of expelling Persia and Turkey by the early years of Nicholas I's reign. But it took her more than another thirty years to stamp out insurrection among the Caucasian peoples and bring the whole region under her effective control. In 1878 she again extended her Caucasian frontier southwards by forcing Turkey to cede her Batum and the district round Kars. But this marked the limit of her advance in the area. Her conquests in central Asia were prepared during Nicholas I's reign by advances from Orenburg to the Aral Sea and from the Irtysh to Lake Balkhash; and by the early 'sixties she was in a position to carry her frontier rapidly southwards on a broad front until it reached the upper Oxus in the 'seventies, the Atrek and the Murgab in the 'eighties, and the Pamirs in the 'nineties. In 1871 she also occupied the Chinese district of Kuldja which she held until 1881 when the greater part of it was restored to China. In the Far East she induced China to cede her the Amur region in 1858 and the Ussuri region in 1860. This planted her along the northern and eastern boundaries of Manchuria and the western shore of the Sea of Japan and brought her into direct contact with the northern tip of Korea. In 1853 she also began to establish herself in the northern part of Sakhalin Island which was claimed by Japan. At first she had to be satisfied with a share in Sakhalin. But in 1875 she induced Japan to recognize her sovereignty over the whole island in exchange for the Kurile Islands which she had long claimed to be Russian. By contrast she decided to abandon the establishments which the Russo-American Company had maintained or established along the American shore of the Pacific since its foundation in 1799. This led in 1841 to the sale of the small Russian colony at Fort Ross in California to private American interests and in 1867 to the sale of Alaska to the U.S. government.[1]

---

[1] For a survey of the work of the Russo-American Company based on material in the Russian archives, see S. P. Okun, *The Russian-American Company* (R) (Moscow-Leningrad, 1939).

Essays Presented to Sir Lewis Namier

Russia's territorial expansion in Asia during the middle and later years of the nineteenth century can hardly be said to have been deliberately planned by the Russian government. It was due much more to the enterprise and energy of governors-general and soldiers in outlying areas, who often took the initiative without or even against instructions from St. Petersburg which was too far away and had too poor communications to keep them under effective control. Men like Muraviev in the Far East and Kaufman, Cherniaiev and Skobeliev in central Asia had a vision of Russia's imperial mission in Asia which impelled them to press forward with the extension of her frontiers before Britain could forestall and thwart her, as they believed she aimed to do. They showed little regard for the fears of international complications and the concern over financial cost which troubled Government officials in St. Petersburg, and whenever it came to a choice, the tsar in the end always preferred to accept rather than renounce the territories which their initiative was bringing him. As Nicholas I said when he intervened to save Captain Nevelskoy from demotion to the ranks for disobeying instructions and planting the Russian military flag and a military post at the mouth of the Amur in August 1851: 'Where the Russian flag has been run up, it must not be hauled down'.[1]

. . . . .

Throughout the whole period from 1815 to 1914 the tsar retained the right to direct and control Russia's foreign policy as autocrat. In 1837 a report on the Russian foreign ministry, drawn up for the guidance of the future Alexander II, described it as 'merely the faithful executor of the intentions' of Alexander I and Nicholas I. 'Its every action', it went on, '... was carried out under the orders and direction of the tsars themselves.'[2] Many years later Gorchakov expressed similar views about his own position as foreign minister in relation to

---

[1] See the article on G. I. Nevelskoy in the *Russian Biographical Dictionary* (R) (St. Ptbg., 1896–1916).

[2] See for this report *Collection of the Imperial Russian Historical Society* (R), vol. 31 (St. Ptbg., 1880), pp. 163-95.

Aspects of Russian Foreign Policy, 1815–1914

Alexander II. 'In Russia', he said, 'there are only two people who know the policy of the Russian cabinet: the emperor who makes it and myself who prepares and executes it.'[1] Even the constitutional changes which followed the 1905 revolution left the tsar's control of foreign policy unimpaired. 'The emperor', proclaimed article 12 of the fundamental laws of 1906, 'is the supreme director of all the external relations of the Russian state with foreign powers; he also sets the course of the international policy of the Russian state.'[2]

All five tsars who ruled between 1815 and 1914 took their responsibility for foreign policy seriously and were diligent in hearing and reading reports from their foreign ministers and in studying dispatches from their ambassadors and envoys abroad. But they varied considerably in character and ability and consequently in their grasp and control of matters of state. Alexander I had a natural talent for diplomacy and derived enough personal pleasure and satisfaction from handling foreign affairs to act in a real sense as his own foreign minister. Nicholas I was a much less perceptive and sensitive man with far narrower views. But he had as vigorous a sense of purpose and much greater determination, and though rather less of his own foreign minister than Alexander I, he developed a close personal interest in foreign affairs and was able to view and direct Russian foreign policy in an equally co-ordinated and coherent fashion. This was not so true of their successors, who had none of Alexander I's diplomatic gifts or Nicholas I's iron will. Alexander II approached them closest in interest in foreign policy and ability to see it in the round. But Alexander III was too ungifted intellectually to develop any very great liking for foreign affairs, and while not devoid of will-power, he was more inclined to harness it to his prejudices than to a coherent view of Russian foreign policy. He also preferred to live quietly in his own family circle and was averse to the meetings and conferences with

[1] See B. E. Nolde, *Bismarck's St. Petersburg Mission (1859–1862)* (R) (Prague, 1925), p. 39.
[2] See *Collection of the Laws of the Russian Empire* (R), ed. A. A. Dobrovolsky (2nd ed., St. Ptbg., 1913), Book I, p. 2.

foreign rulers and statesmen which all three of his predecessors had willingly participated in. Even when he received a foreign ambassador, it was something of an event. Nicholas II was equally fond of the quiet and seclusion of family life. But he never shirked meetings with foreign rulers and their ministers, and foreign ambassadors found him much more accessible than his father. The trouble was that in matters of state he was sadly lacking in comprehension and will-power, and in foreign affairs he merely fumbled and blundered through problems of growing complexity and importance which he mistakenly imagined that he understood and could cope with.

The tsar was always helped by a minister of foreign affairs who had charge of the foreign ministry and the Russian diplomatic and consular services. He was invariably a man with long experience of diplomacy, and once the tsar had selected and appointed him, he usually left him in office till the end of his reign. Three foreign ministers spanned between them the eighty years from 1816 to 1895. Nesselrode served as Alexander I's foreign minister from 1816 to 1825 and as Nicholas I's from 1825 to 1855. In April 1856, when he finally retired, Alexander II replaced him by Gorchakov, who served as foreign minister for the remaining twenty-five years of Alexander II's reign and the early months of Alexander III's reign. In April 1882 Alexander III appointed Giers to be foreign minister and kept him in office till the end of his reign in 1894. Giers also served Nicholas II for a few months and died in office in January 1895. These long years of service allowed to Nesselrode, Gorchakov and Giers were due in part to their expert knowledge of foreign affairs and their readiness and ability to play the subordinate rôle to which the autocracy restricted its ministers. But they also showed that the tsars themselves were capable of a high degree of loyalty and attachment to those whom they selected to serve them. The pattern changed with Nicholas II, who had six foreign ministers within the twenty years between 1894 and 1914. Giers, Lobanov-Rostovsky and Muraviev all died in office between 1895 and 1900. The others fell victim to Nicholas

Aspects of Russian Foreign Policy, 1815–1914

II's inherent mistrust of ministers in general. Lamsdorff, whom the tsar appointed in December 1900, was dropped in 1906 after he had twice been driven to the point of asking the tsar's permission to resign. Isvolsky, who followed him, was relieved of the foreign ministry in 1910 and became ambassador in Paris. Sazonov, who followed Isvolsky, survived in office until 1916.

However long the foreign minister held office, Russian foreign policy remained the tsar's foreign policy. The foreign minister helped the tsar by gathering and sifting information and advising on and recommending possible courses of action. But it was the tsar alone who had the power to make decisions; and once he had made them, it was the foreign minister's duty to put them into effect. The Saxon chargé d'affaires in St. Petersburg said of Nesselrode even as late as 1852 that in the eyes of Nicholas I he was 'nothing but . . . an official who enjoyed his confidence only so far as business required'.[1] Gorchakov, according to Bismarck, 'pour exprimer sa soumission à la volonté de l'empereur, se compare à une éponge à laquelle la pression de la main de l'empereur fait rendre le liquide dont elle est pénétrée'.[2] To the French ambassador in St. Petersburg over forty years later, Lamsdorff was 'un ministre des Affaires étrangères à la russe, c'est-à-dire qu'il n'avait pas la direction de la politique étrangère, mais seulement de la diplomatie de la Russie, avec la charge d'adapter celle-ci à celle-là'.[3]

But even if it was the tsar alone who had power to decide in foreign affairs, the foreign minister could to some extent influence his decisions as a channel through which the tsar received information and transmitted instructions and perhaps even more as an interpreter of the information and executor of the instructions. In 1895 Lobanov-Rostovsky called it a 'fiction' to say that 'the tsar himself directs his foreign

[1] Vitzthum von Eckstädt, *St. Petersburg and London 1852–1864* (London, 1887), i. 5.
[2] *Die politischen Berichte des Fürsten Bismarck aus Petersburg und Paris*, ed. L. von Rashdau (Berlin, 1920), i. 30.
[3] M. Bompard, *Mon ambassade en Russie, 1903–1908* (Paris, 1937), p. 4.

policy'. 'Without his minister', he told Lamsdorff, 'he can do nothing'.[1] Nicholas II was young and fresh on the throne at the time, and Lobanov was exaggerating. But his remarks form a necessary corrective to the more usual view which tends to minimize the foreign minister's influence. The extent of this influence and its effects on the formulation of policy cannot be measured precisely from the material at present available. It varied from one tsar and foreign minister to another and depended very much on the tsar's confidence in his minister's views and ability. But in general the influence of Nesselrode and Giers seems to have increased with the passage of time. Gorchakov's, on the other hand, was greater in the early years of Alexander II's reign than towards its close.

Even the most trusted foreign ministers had to acknowledge definite limits to their influence. None of them had the strength of character and will to impose their views if the tsar disagreed, and they could never be certain that the tsar might not take important initiatives against their advice, as in January 1853, when Nicholas I sounded the British ambassador about a possible partition of Turkey, or even without their knowledge, as in July 1905, when Nicholas II signed the treaty of Björkö with the Kaiser. The tsars also regarded their direct dealings with other monarchs as a personal matter which their foreign ministers need not necessarily know about in detail, and for many years they and the Hohenzollerns regularly used their military representatives at each other's courts as a channel for particularly intimate and confidential exchanges of views. Another limitation on the foreign minister's influence was that the tsar could always turn elsewhere for advice and help. For several years after 1816 Alexander I entrusted relations with the East and the Slavs to Capodistrias, not to Nesselrode, and gave him the same rank and the same right to report directly to himself. Nicholas I sometimes passed over Nesselrode and the foreign ministry in a different way by selecting intimates like Orlov and Menshikov for

[1] Quoted in *Istorik Marksist* (R), vol. 20 (Moscow, 1930), p. 118.

important special missions abroad. The tsar also took advice on various aspects of foreign policy from other ministers such as the ministers of war, finance, navy and the interior. Sometimes he might consult these other ministers individually, possibly without the foreign minister's knowledge. At other times he set up special committees such as the Asiatic committee and the Amur committee or ordered joint discussions at special ministerial meetings. In such cases the foreign minister took part and sometimes presided. In the Caucasus, central Asia and eastern Siberia, the tsar also invested his viceroys and governors-general with special military and diplomatic powers which became particularly important in times of territorial expansion and made their influence on relations with neighbouring states much more effective than the foreign minister's far away in St. Petersburg. In some respects the foreign minister was not always complete master even within the foreign ministry and the diplomatic service. The Asiatic department, which was created in 1819 and covered the Ottoman empire as well as Asia proper, long enjoyed a special status within the ministry, and even though the minister gradually brought it under stricter control, it continued to have a more specialized staff than the other departments and remained more nationalist and aggressive in outlook.[1] The foreign minister also suffered on occasion from ambitious ambassadors like Ignatiev, Saburov and Mohrenheim, who had policies of their own to further and who were capable of writing dispatches directed much more towards the tsar than the foreign minister to whom they were addressed.

These many faults in the machinery for administering foreign affairs came to a head over Far Eastern policy during the first half of Nicholas II's reign when the foreign minister found himself increasingly overshadowed by the ministers of finance and war and the tsar allowed the Bezobrazov-Abaza

[1] For information about the organization of the ministry of foreign affairs, see *Collection of the Imperial Russian Historical Society, loc. cit.*; and *Outline of the History of the Ministry of Foreign Affairs, 1802–1902* (R) (St. Ptbg., 1902), particularly pp. 86–98, 121–32, 160–8, 181–2, and 203–6.

clique of political adventurers to form what the war minister called a 'black cabinet'.[1] This 'black cabinet' rapidly undermined ministerial authority and eventually persuaded the tsar to appoint a viceroy in the Far East and to create in St. Petersburg a special committee on Far Eastern affairs under Bezobrazov's control. The resulting confusion helped to make war with Japan inevitable. Matters improved after the constitutional reforms of 1906, which provided for a certain degree of co-ordination among ministers through the council of ministers and its chairman. But Nicholas II remained opposed to any ideas of Cabinet responsibility or ministerial solidarity and was particularly reluctant to let the council of ministers discuss foreign affairs. Constitutionally the council was entitled to discuss them whenever the tsar commanded it or the foreign minister considered it necessary or they affected other ministries.[2] But Nicholas II still thought of them as essentially his own concern, to be treated between himself and the foreign minister with the minimum of interference from the council of ministers and its chairman.[3]

The conditions under which Russian foreign policy was decided and conducted afforded little scope for the influence of the press and public opinion. It was 1865 before the press was even partly freed from preventive censorship, and it continued to be shackled by Government restrictions until after the 1905 revolution. This did not stop the emergence of first-rate newspapers and periodicals, which took a keen and serious interest in foreign affairs from the 'sixties onwards. But their circulation remained relatively small, and even by 1900 a total of 50,000 to 60,000 subscribers was considered very good. Some of them gained considerable influence over their readers and helped to stimulate their interest in foreign policy; and by 1910 it seemed to Milyukov that the whole public was beginning to become interested in foreign affairs.

---

[1] See 'Diary of A. N. Kuropatkin' for 4 Aug. 1903 in *Krasny Arkhiv* (R), vol. 2 (Moscow, 1922), p. 48.
[2] See *Collection of the Laws of the Russian Empire* (R), Book I, p. 147.
[3] See *Out of my Past. The Memoirs of Count Kokovtsov*, ed. H. H. Fisher (London, 1935), pp. 217 and 359-60.

Aspects of Russian Foreign Policy, 1815-1914

At the same time he admitted that in the past it had shown something which was 'not quite indifference to, and not quite prejudice against, concern with foreign policy'.[1] But even when press and public interest in foreign affairs emerged, it was rare for the tsar and his ministers to let pressure from public opinion shape their policy. The most notable exception occurred during the Near Eastern crisis of 1875-8, when intense public sympathy for the Balkan Slavs, which marked the culmination of Slavophil and Panslav teaching over many years, helped to push the Russian government into a more forceful policy than it might have adopted otherwise. On occasion the views of prominent journalists like Katkov of the *Moscow Gazette* or Suvorin of the *New Times* might find favour with the tsar and his advisers. But this was because they were attractive in themselves, not because they had public backing, as seems evident from the increase in Katkov's influence on Alexander III even after his paper's circulation had started to fall. In any case, the tsar eventually rejected Katkov's sustained plea for a 'free hand' policy which the rest of the press loudly supported. Instead, he accepted the advice of Giers and concluded the reinsurance treaty with Germany; and the only immediate result of the press agitation for a 'free hand' policy was to make him keep the treaty secret in view of the public's growing antipathy towards Germany as an ally.[2] Even the Duma was allowed no effective say in foreign affairs. It became its practice to discuss them publicly once a year when the foreign ministry's estimates were before it, and on five occasions between 1906 and 1914 the tsar authorized Isvolsky and Sazonov to make a report in the Duma on foreign relations. But Nicholas II was always too jealous of his prerogatives to let the Duma do more than talk about foreign policy.[3] On the other hand, the

---

[1] P. Milyukov, *The Balkan Crisis and the Policy of A. P. Isvolsky* (R) (St. Ptbg., 1910), pp. 133-4.
[2] See I. Grüning, *Die russische öffentliche Meinung und ihre Stellung zu den Grossmächten*, 1878-1894 (Berlin, 1929).
[3] Isvolsky reported three times and Sazonov twice. Isvolsky's first report, on 27 Feb./11 March 1908, dealt with relations with Japan and the situation in

growing public interest in and discussion of foreign affairs, first in the press and later in the Duma, slowly began to exert a real if indirect influence on foreign policy. In some respects it helped to strengthen the nationalist outlook, which had been gaining ground since the mid-nineteenth century and was increasingly affecting even higher bureaucrats and ministers. This tended in its turn to make Russian foreign policy less flexible by narrowing the freedom of action of the tsar and his foreign minister, who could now expect strong public criticism and possible opposition even within the Government if they neglected what the press and public conceived to be Russia's national interests. Isvolsky discovered this to his cost in 1908 during the Bosnian crisis. Sazonov met with similar difficulties in 1913 over Serbia. But in 1913 the tsar himself stood firm, and in the last resort it was the tsar's attitude which was still decisive.[1]

. . . . .

Between 1815 and 1914 Russian foreign policy was concerned almost entirely with four geographical areas of interest: Europe; the Near East, particularly the Straits and the Balkans; the Middle East, particularly central Asia and Persia; and the Far East, particularly China and Korea. Russia was never very active in all four of these areas at the same time. During the first half of the nineteenth century, her attention was focused on Europe and the Near East, which overlapped politically as well as geographically. But after her defeat in the Crimean War she switched for a time to the Middle East. During the 'seventies and 'eighties, the

the Far East. His second report, on 4/17 April 1908, dealt with the situation in the Near East. His third report, on 12/25 Dec. 1908, was a general survey. Sazonov's first report was given on 13/26 April 1912 and his second on 10/23 May 1914. On each occasion he made a general survey of Russian foreign policy. An examination of the stenographic reports of the public sessions of the Duma shows that it devoted much less than 1 per cent. of its time to discussion of foreign affairs. How much of the budget commission's time was spent on foreign affairs it is impossible to ascertain as reports of its meetings were not published.

[1] See S. Sazonov, *Fateful Years, 1909–1916* (London, 1928), pp. 74-6 and 78-9.

Aspects of Russian Foreign Policy, 1815–1914

Near East again claimed most of her attention. But at the end of the nineteenth century she began to concentrate on the Far East, until her defeat in the Russo-Japanese War again led her to focus on the Near East. These frequent switches from one area to another should not be misinterpreted. They in no way implied that Russia had completely lost interest in the area from which she turned. They simply meant that she was meeting formidable obstacles which impelled her to halt and concentrate her energies elsewhere. But however much she reduced her activity in an area, she never suspended it entirely and was ready to increase it again when circumstances became more favourable.

Behind Russian foreign policy stood the resources of a vast, sprawling empire with a large, rapidly increasing and overwhelmingly peasant population. It had emerged from the Napoleonic wars with considerably increased territory and prestige and was thought in some quarters to be getting too powerful for the good of the rest of Europe. But it was already suffering from debilitating social ills which grew worse as the remedies were postponed or applied in half measure. Russia's system of government was also inefficient, unwieldy and excessively bureaucratic; her population was sparse east of the Volga; her communications were poor; and she was much slower than the other Great European Powers to embark on industrialization. But she always kept a bigger standing army than anybody else, and in May 1905 Plehve, the minister of the interior, reminded Lamsdorff that it was her bayonets, not her diplomats, which had made her.[1] Between 1815 and 1914 Russia was at war for much less time than in most earlier centuries. But her bayonets added considerable weight to her foreign policy even if they now flashed on the parade ground rather than on the battlefield: it was still her big standing army rather than her underlying weaknesses which impressed her neighbours in Europe and Asia; and her military reputation was maintained by her three victorious wars against Persia and Turkey and her successful colonial

[1] See *Mémoi es du Comte Witte (1849–1915)* (Paris, 1921), p. 104.

campaigns in central Asia, and was hardly more than temporarily impaired by her defeats in the Crimean War and the war against Japan. In Asia, Russian foreign policy had another useful adjunct in commercial penetration, and at the end of the nineteenth century some of her ministers tried for a time to cover her bayonets with such modern agencies of imperialism as the Russo-Chinese Bank and the Loan and Discount Bank in Persia. But before long the bayonet-point again showed through.

.   .   .   .   .

In Europe, Russia played a very active and key rôle for nearly forty years after 1815 under both Alexander I and Nicholas I. She set herself two major and interdependent aims: to maintain the 1815 territorial settlement, of which she had been one of the leading architects; and to uphold monarchical government against liberal and democratic revolutions. The 1815 settlement had not entirely satisfied Alexander I in its distribution of Polish and Saxon territory. But it had sanctioned the partition of Poland between Russia, Austria and Prussia, and assigned Alexander I the lion's share of even ethnically Polish territory. It had also made central Europe sufficiently strong under Austrian and Prussian leadership to be able to withstand France but not to exclude Russian influence. For these and other reasons, Russia stood firmly behind the settlement, and as she considered France the chief potential threat to it, she joined Britain, Austria and Prussia in the quadruple alliance of November 1815, which aimed at keeping France within her 1815 frontiers and excluding Napoleon and any of his family from the French throne. Under the Bourbons, France's policy remained relatively moderate, and Russia's attitude towards her was not unfriendly. But after the 1830 revolution, when Louis Philippe replaced Charles X, Russian fears of French aggression immediately revived, and Nicholas I reacted by trying to resurrect the quadruple alliance. He also wanted to enforce the Vienna settlement against the Belgians when they separated from Holland and repudiated King William I. The attitude of Britain, the hesitations of Austria and Prussia, and his own preoccupation with the 1830 rising in Poland, all combined to prevent him from organizing armed action against France or enabling William I to reimpose his authority on Belgium. But he at least succeeded in keeping the breach in the Vienna settlement to a minimum and to an area where Russia had no vital interests. He also remained doubtful and suspicious of the France of Louis Philippe, and from 1830 onwards his policy became essentially anti-French in orientation. What the Russian Government feared most, especially after the 1830 revolutions in France, Poland and elsewhere, was that the extreme revolutionaries would eventually gain control in Paris, that revolutions would follow in central Europe and Italy, and that France would use the revolutionary movement to try to overthrow the whole 1815 settlement. The inevitable result would be a general European war in which the Poles would fight to resurrect a Poland with the 1772 frontiers and Russia might face another and more dangerous 1812.

This fear partly explains why Russian backing for the territorial settlement of 1815 was accompanied by support for monarchical government. As a monarch himself, the tsar naturally upheld monarchical government in self-defence. But he also supported it because he regarded kings as the best curb on general European revolution, which would inevitably threaten Russia with dismemberment if the revolutionaries tried to resurrect Poland; and this, the Russian envoy in Berlin insisted in 1848, 'est et doit être le dernier but des victoires républicaines'.[1] Alexander I through the Holy Alliance and the Troppau protocol and Nicholas I through the treaty of Berlin both made support for fellow-monarchs a cardinal principle of Russian policy; and both found willing allies in the Habsburgs and the Hohenzollerns, who had partnered them in partitioning Poland and who had similar

[1] *Peter von Meyendorff, politischer und privater Briefwechsel, 1826–63*, ed. O. Hoetsch (Berlin and Leipzig, 1923), ii. 42.

vested interests in monarchical government and the 1815 settlement. This led them to join the tsar in upholding the right of rulers, when asked, to intervene and support each other against internal disorders as well as against external attack. Nicholas I, to whom revolution was very much the universal and unsleeping enemy, envisaged Austria and Prussia as Russia's 'moral barrier' against France; and he hoped to keep them sufficiently strong and stable to halt the revolutionary spirit at a distance from Russia or at least exhaust it before it reached her frontiers.[1] On the other hand, his insistence on the principle of intervention against revolution helped to lose him the backing of Britain, which moved steadily away from her partners in the quadruple alliance and supported France in asserting the principle of non-intervention. Liberals and democrats everywhere anathematized the tsar as Europe's policeman, and their detestation of him reached its climax in 1848-9 when he played this rôle as never before. In the spring of 1848 during the first great surge of revolution, when the republic was proclaimed in France and Russia's 'moral barrier' in central Europe collapsed, it looked for a short time as though Russia would find herself facing, to quote her envoy in Berlin, 'la lutte avec la Pologne, soutenue avec toute l'Europe, France, Allemagne, Hongrie, etc., etc.'[2] But this threat of a new 1812 soon passed, and the tsar was left free to devote his power and influence to re-establishing the old order, at least in central Europe and Italy where he stood solidly behind the Habsburgs from the moment they began to resist the revolution. By contrast, he was critical of the Hohenzollerns, whom he found too ready to flirt with revolution. In July 1848 he moved troops into Moldavia and Wallachia to maintain order and curb Rumanian nationalist agitation, and in the spring of 1849 he sent 100,000 men

[1] S. S. Tatischiev, *The Foreign Policy of Nicholas I* (R) (St. Ptbg., 1887), pp. 25-34, quoting from an unpublished memorandum of Baron Brunnow entitled 'On the general principles which lie at the basis of our foreign policy', which was written in 1838 and formed part of a survey of the history of Russia's foreign relations for the future Alexander II.

[2] *Meyendorff, op. cit.*, p. 42. See also L. B. Namier, *1848* : *The Revolution of the Intellectuals* (London, 1946), particularly pp. 40-65.

Aspects of Russian Foreign Policy, 1815–1914

across Galicia to help the Habsburgs against the revolutionaries in Hungary. He also opposed Prussian dynastic and German nationalist designs on Schleswig, discouraged the Prussian Government from persisting in its challenge to Austrian leadership in Germany, and helped towards the restoration of the Germanic Confederation; and at the end of 1850 Nesselrode felt entitled to report that 'depuis 1814 la position de la Russie et de son souverain n'a jamais été ni plus belle ni plus grande'.[1]

Russia's rôle in European affairs became much less active and effective after Nicholas I's death and the end of the Crimean War. The new tsar and his advisers all agreed that the country's interests now demanded 'une concentration de ... forces et ... intelligence à l'intérieur' and that 'toute activité extérieure qui y ferait obstacle devra être soigneusement exclue'.[2] Their determination to subordinate foreign affairs to domestic reforms inevitably prescribed a more limited policy than under Alexander I and Nicholas I; it persisted even during the unification of Italy under Piedmont and Germany under Prussia and was one of the important factors which helped Cavour and Bismarck to achieve these drastic changes in the Vienna settlement and the European balance of power. Russia's experiences in the Crimean War had also destroyed her former readiness to back Austria to the hilt and had revived and strengthened her old friendship for Prussia, whose helpful attitude during the Polish rising of 1863 made relations closer still. After the Crimean War she angled for friendship with France, chiefly to weaken the Anglo-French-Austrian guarantee treaty of April 1856, and prepare the ground for an eventual revision of at least the Black Sea clauses of the Peace of Paris. But she also hoped

---

[1] *Collection of the Imperial Russian Historical Society*, vol. 98 (St. Ptbg. 1896), p. 296.
[2] See Gorchakov's letter to the Grand Duchess Olga of 14 March 1862 printed in C. Friese, *Russland und Preussen vom Krimkrieg bis zum polnischen Aufstand* (Berlin, 1931), p. 352; and Nesselrode's memorandum of 11 Feb. 1856 printed in *Lettres et papiers du Comte de Nesselrode, 1760–1856*, ed. A. de Nesselrode, xi. 112–16.

that by offering Napoleon III the prospect of friendship with monarchical powers such as herself and possibly Prussia, she would be able to keep him from allying himself with revolutionary forces and furthering what Gorchakov called 'the revolutionary principle of nationalities'. In March 1859 these different currents merged and produced a secret Russo-French agreement which made Russia benevolently neutral towards France in the subsequent Franco-Austrian conflict over Italy and prompted her to move troops to the Galician frontier and warn Prussia and the German Confederation against helping Austria.[1] But this policy of co-operation with France, which was very much Gorchakov's in inspiration, naturally lost much of its attraction for the tsar when its expected advantages for Russia failed to materialize and when, instead, revolutions occurred in southern and central Italy and France continued to manifest her traditional pro-Polish sympathies. As an alternative, Russia tried to supplement her close friendship with Prussia by better relations with Austria and began to re-emphasize the 'politique monarchique et anti-polonaise' which Nesselrode claimed to the end to be in the 'véritable intérêt de la Russie et de la dynastie'.[2] During the Schleswig-Holstein crisis of 1864 the tsar gave the king of Denmark only moral support against Prussia and Austria and quietly acquiesced when the two Powers compelled the king to cede them the duchies. Russia repeatedly urged Prussia and Austria to work together in German affairs in the belief that a struggle for supremacy between them would inevitably weaken Germany, strengthen the forces of revolution, and open the door to foreign intervention which might even reach to Poland.[3] But in 1866, when Prussia won her swift and decisive victory over Austria, the tsar accepted the consequent drastic reorganization of Germany, though

[1] For the text of the agreement in a Russian version see 'The History of the Franco-Russian agreement of 1859' in *Krasny Arkhiv*, vol. 3 (88) (Moscow, 1938), pp. 183-255.   [2] Nesselrode, *op. cit.*, pp. 112-16.
[3] See in particular Gorchakov's report to the tsar of 3 Sept. 1865 printed in *Krasny Arkhiv*, vol. 2 (93) (Moscow, 1939), pp. 107-11 ; and the tsar's letter to King William I of 7/19 March 1866 published in *Die auswärtige Politik Preussens, 1858-71*, vol. vi (Oldenburg, 1939), pp. 703-4.

Aspects of Russian Foreign Policy, 1815–1914

he had serious qualms about Prussia's effacement of some of the German dynasties and complained to King William that it had dealt the 'monarchical principle' a 'severe blow'.[1] From now on he was drawn even closer to Prussia by his uneasiness over Austria's Balkan policy, and in 1870 he helped her to establish the German empire by bringing pressure on Austria to remain neutral during the Franco-Prussian War. In return Russia received Prussia's backing when she repudiated the Black Sea clauses of the Peace of Paris.

After 1870 Russia faced a Europe dominated by Germany, whose military power greatly complicated the defence of Russia's western frontier. But she could console herself that Germany had been united through the pro-Russian Prussian monarchy, not through popular revolution with its implicit threat to resurrect Poland. Her Government disliked the new republican régime in France, and in 1873 the fears aroused by the Paris Commune impelled the tsar to join the Habsburgs and Hohenzollerns in a *Dreikaiserbund* in support of monarchical government and the social order. On the other hand, Russia's attitude towards Germany and France in the 1875 'war scare' indicated her reluctance to see France further weakened to Germany's advantage. In general, after 1870 Russia tended to subordinate her policy in Europe to her policy in the Near East and areas outside Europe. Giers believed that basically it was only the Near Eastern and Polish problems which affected her interests;[2] and from 1870 onwards her chief concern was less European affairs in themselves than how to use them to further her aims elsewhere, above all, in the Near East. During and after the Near Eastern crisis of 1875–8, the Russian government attached exceptional importance to friendship with Germany both as a cover for her western frontier and in the belief that German power and influence could be used to prevent an anti-Russian coalition between Britain and Austria; and Bismarck was so anxious

---
[1] *Ibid.* viii. 42–3.
[2] *Die grosse Politik der europäischen Kabinette, 1871–1914*, ed. J. Lepsius, etc., vol. iii (Berlin, 1922), p. 328.

to keep Russia aloof from France that he willingly co-operated with her and urged Austria to do the same. In 1878 panslav influences pushed the Russian government into demands which inevitably provoked British and Austrian opposition; and when Russia found herself obliged to give way, her resentment concentrated mainly on Germany, which reacted with a secret defensive alliance with Austria in 1879. But fundamentally the Russian government still regarded Germany's friendship as the best safeguard against anti-Russian coalitions, and in 1881, after using Bismarck's help to effect a reconciliation with Vienna, Russia joined Germany and Austria in a new *Dreikaiserbund*. Under it, she agreed in effect to abandon France to Germany's devices in return for a German promise not to help Britain against Russia and to back Russia's Near Eastern policy within stipulated limits. But it proved difficult for the Russian government to continue this pledge to accept even a preventive German war against France. This was partly due to its growing reluctance to see the European balance of power weighted still more in Germany's favour. But it was also due to the value which it was beginning to attach to French naval power as a possible factor against Britain.[1] In 1884 the Russian government renewed the *Dreikaiserbund* for another three years. But by 1887 Alexander III was too irritated with Austria to renew it a second time. He was still prepared to maintain Russia's alliance with Germany in spite of press clamour for a 'free hand' policy. But he now promised Russia's benevolent neutrality in a Franco-German war only if France attacked

[1] This seems clear from the following extract from Shuvalov's summary of his fourth conversation with Bismarck, on 17 May 1887 : 'C'est alors que je transmis au Prince les instructions No. 1 qui exprimaient d'une manière plus que précise la declaration, que j'avais à faire au sujet de notre engagement de neutralité en cas de guerre entre l'Allemagne et la France, j'assurais le Prince qu'il n'y avait de notre côté aucune arrière-pensée, que l'Empereur tenait à la conservation de l'équilibre européen, que de même que Sa Majesté était prête à accorder Sa neutralité bienveillante dans un conflit de revanche, qui aurait pour but d'arracher à l'Allemagne des provinces acquises, de même Sa Majesté ne saurait voir un coup mortel porté à l'une ou l'autre des parties belligérantes. — La France nous était nécessaire comme puissance navale dans des complications d'avenir, etc. etc.' (*Krasny Arkhiv*, vol. 1 (Moscow, 1922), p. 116).

Germany, not if Germany attacked France.[1] In 1890 the Russian government wanted to prolong the Russo-German alliance for a further period and was very much disturbed when William II refused and began instead to adopt a pro-British orientation. This made it so afraid of the possibility of a hostile Anglo-Austrian-German coalition that in self-defence it swallowed its dislike of republicanism and concluded first an *entente* and later an alliance with France which lasted until 1917. Essentially, it committed Russia to oppose any further change in the European balance of power to Germany's advantage through a German attack on France, and ensured in return that she herself would not be left isolated against a hostile Anglo-Austrian-German coalition. For her, the point of the Franco-Russian alliance was really directed at Britain and Austria rather than Germany; and before long certain Russians even began to contemplate a Franco-Russian-German alliance against Britain. But soundings in Paris after the treaty of Björkö in 1905 showed that France would never enter an alliance with Germany; and by now Russia had become too dependent on French loans to jeopardize the Franco-Russian alliance by trying to insist. Instead, French counter-pressure on Russia and more particularly Germany's policy in the Near East gradually made her readier to give the alliance an anti-German twist. But the Russian government still remained unwilling to risk war simply over German dominance in Europe and to recover Alsace-Lorraine for France.

. . . . .

[1] The Russian Government insisted that this reservation should be written into the alliance only when Bismarck made it clear that in view of Germany's commitments to Austria he would have to exclude a Russian attack on Austria from the eventualities in which Germany was committed to benevolent neutrality towards Russia. But on the other hand, it had stated right at the start of the talks that it was negotiating on the assumption that Bismarck did not intend to attack France and that his object was 'se garantir d'une agression française, en comptant sur notre neutralité bienveillante dans l'éventualité d'une *guerre de revanche*'. See *ibid. loc. cit.*, p. 92. There is some new information from the Soviet archives about the Russian attitude during the negotiations for the reinsurance treaty in an article in *Istoricheskiye Zapiski* (R), vol. 18 (Moscow, 1946), pp. 200-54.

Essays Presented to Sir Lewis Namier

In the Near East, Russia faced a declining Turkish empire, which she had fought at intervals for over a century and deprived of most of the Caucasus and the whole northern Black Sea coast between the Don and the Danube. The Turks still possessed, in Constantinople, the Straits and the Balkans, territories which Russia considered of cardinal importance to her for a mixture of strategic, economic and emotional reasons; and she seemed certain to try to break Turkey's hold on them by continuing her policy of conquest and dismemberment. But the tsar and his advisers were already wondering whether a policy adopted when Turkey was strong was necessarily best now she was in decline. They had begun to realize that if Turkey's rule ended, Russia would not be left to dispose of Turkey's heritage by herself. The other Great Powers would also insist on taking part, and the resulting new order might suit Russia's interests much less than a weak Turkey. This led the tsar to decide towards the end of the Russo-Turkish war of 1828–9 that Russia must now work to maintain Turkey and keep her weak and under Russian influence. The first results of this new policy were Russian support for the sultan against Mehemet Ali of Egypt and the Russo-Turkish alliance of Unkiar Skelessi of July 1833. But the tsar tended to think of Russian influence in Turkey in terms of a Russian protectorate over the sultan's Christian subjects: an idea which neither the sultan nor the other Powers could stomach and which the sultan resisted with British and French backing to the point of war with Russia. Defeat in the Crimean War forced Russia to renounce her claim to a special and preponderant influence in Turkey and crippled for many years the Black Sea fleet which had helped to sustain it. She still followed the policy of preserving a weak Turkey and trying to make her friendly, particularly in the late nineteenth century and the years before 1914. But it never entirely superseded and tended to alternate with her older policy of working to undermine and destroy Turkey, which, as the crisis of 1875–8 showed, strongly appealed to Slavophils and Panslavs and could still influence even the

Aspects of Russian Foreign Policy, 1815–1914

Government, particularly when the sultan fell too much under the influence of the other Powers and ignored Russia's advice and when his Christian subjects rebelled and looked to Russia for aid.

However hard the Russian government might try to preserve Turkey as a weak state under Russian influence, it was never certain that the sultan's rule could be upheld; and if his rule ended, it wanted to be able to safeguard Russian interests in the ensuing international discussions by having sufficient forces available to seize vital points like the Bosphorus beforehand and also a previous understanding about the future of Turkish territory with other interested Great Powers. This led it to pay special attention to the Black Sea fleet, except when the Treaty of Paris forbade Russia to maintain one, and to try from time to time to reach agreement with Austria and Britain on what to do with Turkish territory if Turkish rule ended. But Russia's approaches to Austria and Britain never produced any permanent or far-reaching understanding and rather aroused uneasiness as a suspected move in a Russian plan to destroy Turkey. The Russian government's views on the shape of a possible new order also changed appreciably as time went on. At one stage Nicholas I was prepared to let Austria take everything between the Danube and the Adriatic, with Constantinople and a bridgehead in Asia Minor for himself. At other times he thought in terms of 'independence' for the Balkan nationalities under 'joint Russo-Austrian protection' or of independence for some parts of the Balkans and partition of the rest between Russia and Austria, with Russia taking Moldavia and Wallachia and Bulgaria as far as Constanza. Constantinople would become a free city and either the fortifications of the Straits would be razed or Russia would garrison the Bosphorus and Austria the Dardanelles. Britain might take Egypt and perhaps Cyprus and Rhodes or Crete.[1] But

---

[1] For further details, see my article on 'Nicholas I and the Partition of Turkey' in the *Slavonic and East European Review*, vol. xxvii, No. 68 (London, 1948), pp. 115-45.

with the subsequent growth of nationalism in the Balkans the Russian government moved away from a possible partition of Balkan territory between Russia and Austria towards independent statehood for the Balkan peoples. It also came to oppose a permanent British occupation of Egypt in view of the Suez Canal's importance to Russia's maritime communications with the Far East. About Constantinople, it eventually decided that if Turkish rule ended it could never allow any other Power, whether great or small, to take it. In general, it also adopted Alexander III's view that Russia's chief aim should be 'to establish ourselves at the Straits once and for all and know that they will be permanently in our hands'.[1]

Russia had important commercial and strategic interests in the Straits dictated by the economic and defence needs of her southern provinces. But the Straits had also acquired an emotional significance, symbolized in the phrase that they were 'the key to her house' and ought to be in her pocket. In many respects they were no more important to her than the Straits between the Baltic and the North Sea.[2] But while the Sound caused her relatively little anxiety, the Bosphorus and the Dardanelles exercised her constantly, largely because she thought that Turkey's hold on them was becoming insecure and that their fate might have to be settled at any moment. All Russians were agreed that when Turkish rule ended, Russia could never allow any other Power to possess the Bosphorus, and many of them felt that she ought to take both Straits for herself. But in the meantime she had to try to safeguard her commercial and strategic interests with the Straits in Turkish hands and prevent any developments which would make her own eventual possession of them impossible. Her commercial interests presented least difficulty and were satisfactorily met by Turkey's agreement to keep the Straits open to merchant shipping. But her strategic

[1] See Alexander III's letter to General Obruchev of 12/24 Sept. 1885 in *Krasny Arkhiv*, vol. 3 (46) (Moscow, 1931), pp. 180-1.
[2] See Baron Rosen, *Forty Years of Diplomacy* (London, 1922), ii. 101, 'In reality these straits of the Bosphorus and the Dardanelles can just as little be considered to represent the key to our house as the strait known as the Sound....'

Aspects of Russian Foreign Policy, 1815–1914

interests were very much harder to safeguard, if only because the aims of other Powers never coincided with her own to the same extent as over trade through the Straits. She tried two main lines of approach. The first was an alliance with Turkey which aimed to make her secure in the Black Sea by committing the sultan to close the Dardanelles to hostile warships. She tried it in 1833 in the Treaty of Unkiar Skelessi. But by 1839 determined British and French opposition and Turkish vacillation had led her to adopt a different approach aiming at an international solution. This was embodied in the Straits Conventions of 1841 and later, under which Turkey was pledged to close the Straits to foreign warships and the Powers to respect the closure.

But even this international solution had its limitations. First, Turkey was still free to open the Straits to her allies if she herself went to war, which obviously made Russia's security in the Black Sea incomplete; and in 1871 she saw even this limited security curtailed when Turkey gained the right to open the Straits to her allies in peace-time if she thought that the maintenance of the Treaty of Paris required it. Secondly, at the Congress of Berlin the British delegation claimed that the undertaking of the Powers to respect the closure of the Straits was an undertaking to the sultan alone, not to each other as well, which would greatly reduce its value to Russia if the British claim were generally accepted. Thirdly, the closure of the Straits to foreign warships, while increasing Russia's security in the Black Sea, prevented the use of her Black Sea fleet in other areas, which particularly handicapped her during the Russo-Japanese war. The Russian government tried hard to overcome these difficulties. In the 'eighties it secured Germany's and Austria's rejection of Britain's interpretation of the Straits Conventions and support for its own thesis that Turkey would commit an act of war against Russia if, when herself at peace, she opened the Straits to a Power at war with Russia. In the middle 'nineties, after strong pressure from the Russian ambassador at Constantinople, who expected British naval intervention, the tsar almost sanctioned a Russian assault on the Straits. At the same time, Salisbury's changed attitude towards Turkey seemed to the Russians to indicate a possibility of an eventual agreement with Britain which might bring them the Straits in return for support for British designs elsewhere in Turkey, particularly Egypt. But Lobanov-Rostovsky attached too much importance to the Suez Canal to pay what was expected to be Salisbury's price.[1] Later, under Isvolsky's inspiration, the Russian government tried with limited success to prepare for a new international arrangement over the Straits under which, whilst remaining in Turkish hands, they would be open to Russia and closed to other Powers. Russia's concern over the Straits increased appreciably during the Italo-Turkish and Balkan wars, particularly when her trade through the Straits suffered for a time. But it was not until 1915 that she could persuade Britain and France to agree that they should become hers.

Russia also took a keen interest in the Christians in Turkey, who were mainly Orthodox and Slavs like the Russians themselves. She tried to induce the Turkish Government to treat them less arbitrarily, which aroused the suspicion that she intended to use them to undermine Turkish rule. But neither Alexander I nor Nicholas I favoured subversive, revolutionary activities even in Turkey, and their concern over the treatment and status of the Balkan Christians stopped short of the idea of independence for them, except in the 1820's when the Greek revolt and the attitude of the other Powers forced Nicholas I's hand over Greece, and in 1853-4 when the tsar expected the advance of his troops into Turkey to start a general Christian insurrection. Later in the century, with the growth of Slavophil and Panslav ideas in Russia and nationalism in the Balkans, the Russian government's attitude changed appreciably. The panslavs believed that it was Russia's historic mission to free the Balkan Slavs from Turkish rule, and their views greatly influenced the Russian public

[1] See V. Khvostov's article on 'The Near Eastern Crisis, 1895-1897' in *Istorik Marksist*, vol. 13 (Moscow, 1929), pp. 19-54.

Aspects of Russian Foreign Policy, 1815–1914

and even the Russian government during the 1875–8 crisis, which led to war between Russia and Turkey and ended in independence for Serbia, Montenegro and Rumania. But Russia's support for the idea of independence for the Balkan peoples was always counteracted by her wish to preserve Turkey: it was not until 1908–9 and after the Italo-Turkish war that it again took practical form in her backing for Bulgarian independence and for the Bulgar-Serbian alliance of 1912; and initially she had envisaged this alliance as a protective measure against Austria rather than as a move to deprive Turkey of Macedonia and other areas.[1] The Russians and the Balkan peoples also found that close contact with each other was apt to produce disillusion and antipathy rather than greater friendliness, and, as developments in Bulgaria during the 'eighties showed, the Russian government tended to expect a subservience which the Balkan nationalists deeply resented and resisted. This made the Russian government resentful on its side, and it began to think more of how to use the Balkan peoples and less of how to help them.[2] But as Isvolsky discovered in 1908–9 and Sazonov in 1912–13, the Russian public was still too sentimental about the Balkan Slavs for the Russian government to be able to jeopardize or neglect their interests.

Russia's policy in the Near East encountered strong opposition from Britain, who suspected that she wanted to destroy Turkey and become its heir. It persisted until after the turn of the century, in spite of Russia's efforts to allay British suspicions, and pushed Britain into war with her in 1854 and to the verge of war in 1877–8. France also tended to oppose Russia in the Near East during the first half of the century and joined Britain and Turkey against her during the

---

[1] See in particular the telegram of the acting foreign minister to the Russian envoy in Sofia of 21 Sept./4 Oct. 1911 printed in *International Relations in the Epoch of Imperialism* (R), 2nd series, vol. 18, pt. ii (Moscow, 1938), pp. 71-2.

[2] In Sept. 1885 Alexander III wrote to General Obruchev: 'We have had enough of doing popular things to the detriment of Russia's true interests. The Slavs must now serve Russia and not we them. This is my view on the present political situation.' See *Krasny Arkhiv*, vol. 3 (46) (Moscow, 1931), pp. 180-1.

Crimean War. But France's opposition lacked the depth and persistence of Britain's and was later largely nullified by the Franco-Russian alliance. This British and French hostility gave added importance to Russia's relations with Austria and Prussia with which she was already allied in Europe. Prussia had no direct interests in the Near East and was concerned only with how Near Eastern problems affected Great Power alignments and the general European situation. But Austria was as much interested in the Near East as Russia herself, and Nicholas I tried hard to keep her on Russia's side by working to preserve Turkey and undertaking to satisfy Austrian interests if Turkish rule ended. He never expected armed Austrian and Prussian support for Russia in a war with Britain and France over Near Eastern affairs. What he wanted from them was benevolent neutrality, which would safeguard Russia's western frontier and restrict hostilities to the Near East. But his expectation that the Balkan Christians would revolt and irrevocably end Turkish rule if Russian troops crossed the Danube in 1854 so disturbed Austria, which wanted to maintain Turkey, that instead of becoming benevolently neutral, she successfully tried to keep hostilities away from the Balkans by forcing Russia to evacuate the Danubian Principalities and temporarily occupying them herself. After 1870, when Russia resumed an active policy in the Near East, she tried to avoid new coalitions against her by friendship with Germany and agreement with Austria on their respective interests and aims in the Near East. The agreement worked until the San Stefano treaty which alienated Austria and led her to co-operate with Britain against Russia. It was later renewed in a different form to allow for Russo-Austrian co-operation in avoiding drastic changes and sharing influence in the Balkans. But the clash between Russian and Austrian interests in the Balkans proved too strong for lasting compromise and strengthened panslav elements in Russia in their belief that Russia would eventually have to settle accounts with Austria as well as with Turkey. Towards the turn of the century, Germany also began to develop direct interests

Aspects of Russian Foreign Policy, 1815–1914

in the Near East, particularly through the Berlin-Baghdad railway project, which Russia found disturbing and which led to increased German support for Austria's Balkan policy. On the other hand, Russia was able to achieve a *rapprochement* with Britain which, together with the French alliance, assured her of British and French support for her interests in the Near East as long as she continued to pitch them within moderate limits.

.   .   .   .   .   .

In the Middle East Russia pursued an active policy of expansion which caused rivalry and complications with Britain mainly through its possible effects on Britain's position in India. At first, she concentrated on the western flank of the Middle East in Transcaucasia, where she forced Persia to concede her a frontier on the Araxes in 1828 and Turkey to abandon western Transcaucasia in 1829. Her original avowed aim was to keep her borders well insulated from British power in the Middle East by trying to turn Persia and the vast area between her south Siberian frontier and the Sutlej into a kind of neutral zone in which she and Britain would be merely commercial not political rivals.[1] But her government proved no more able to prevent the extension of Russian rule to central Asia than the British government the extension of British rule to Sind, the Punjab and beyond; and a rising tide of suspicion, fear, and national pride and prestige on both sides helped to carry the frontiers of the two empires rapidly towards each other, instead of keeping them widely apart. Russian rule was extended initially by the energy, initiative and rivalries of local commanders and officials, by the desire to expand Russian trade, and by a grow-

[1] In his instructions to the newly-appointed Russian envoy to Persia of 28 April 1858, Gorchakov wrote: 'Nous avons longtemps été avec le gouvernement britannique les seules puissances répresentées à la cour de Perse. Pendant 15 ans un accord tacite s'est établi entre nous et le cabinet de Londres afin de faire de la Perse et de l'Asie centrale comme une zone de neutralité placée entre nos possessions respectives et destinée à prévenir tout contact immédiat. . . . La guerre d'Orient y a mis un terme.' *Documents collected by the Caucasian Archeographical Commission* (R), vol. 12 (Tiflis, 1904), pp. 595-9.

ing belief that Russia had a great civilizing mission to fulfil in Asia. But later, particularly during and after the 1875–8 crisis in the Near East, certain military and political leaders also wanted a forward policy in central Asia in order to be better able to threaten British India and so counteract or buy off British opposition to Russia in the Straits.[1] Nicholas II, whose wilder dreams of conquest embraced Manchuria, Korea, Persia, the Straits and even Tibet,[2] put the same idea more bluntly when he wrote to his sister at the beginning of the Boer War:

... you know I am not proud, but I *do like knowing that it lies solely with me* in the last resort to change the course of the war in Africa. The means are very simple — telegraph an order for the whole Turkestan army to mobilise and march to the frontier. ... The strongest fleets in the world cannot prevent us from settling our scores with England precisely at her most vulnerable point.[3]

Within fifty years Russia's advance into central Asia carried her frontier over 800 miles southwards on a broad front until it reached the approaches to India in north-east Persia and Afghanistan. This inevitably alarmed the British government, particularly after successive Russian statements that it would go no further. In 1869 the British made a vaguely worded proposal to establish a neutral zone between the two empires, directed primarily towards keeping Russia north of the Oxus. But they abandoned it when the Russian government wanted to limit the zone to Afghanistan, in which Britain had taken special interest since the 'thirties. During the discussions, Russia assured Britain that Afghanistan was

---

[1] See the following extract from a memorandum of the war ministry drawn up by General Obruchev in 1877 and quoted in S. Skazkin, *The End of the Austro-Russian-German Alliance* (R), vol. i, 1879–1884 (Moscow, 1928), pp. 126-127. 'India is the main concern of Britain, and the Bosphorus is only important to her as a means of attacking our southern coasts unimpeded in case of need'; 'on the other hand ... our chief concern is in the Bosphorus; and the possibility of attacking India is important only as a means of winning concessions from Britain in the Straits question which is vital to us.'

[2] See 'Diary of A. N. Kuropatkin' for 16 Feb. 1903 in *Krasny Arkhiv*, vol. 2 (Moscow, 1922), p. 31.

[3] Quoted in B. H. Sumner, *Tsardom and Imperialism in the Far East and the Middle East, 1880–1914* (London, 1942), pp. 7-8.

entirely outside Russia's sphere of action. But she soon established contact with the amir, and in 1878 she openly challenged British influence by sending a Russian general to Kabul. This provoked Britain into a show of strength which brought war with Afghanistan and recognition by the amir of Britain's right to control his foreign relations. Russia now renewed her assurances that Afghanistan was entirely outside her sphere of action. But she continued to have serious differences with Britain over the delimitation of Afghanistan's ill-defined northern frontier, which she hoped to push as far south as possible; and it was not until 1895, after several dangerous crises, that agreement was finally reached. During the Boer War, Russia threatened Britain's exclusive influence in Afghanistan by pleading her own need for direct relations with the Afghan government on frontier and trade questions. She also improved her means of action in the area through the Orenburg-Tashkent railway, which was finished in 1906 and supplemented the new Transcaspian line with its branch to Kushk opposite Herat. But her defeat in the Russo-Japanese war temporarily weakened her and prescribed a holding not a forward policy in the Middle East; and in 1907 she signed a convention with Britain, under which she agreed that Afghanistan was outside her sphere and that on political matters she would still deal with it through Britain. In return, Britain promised not to change Afghanistan's political status and agreed to direct contacts between Russian and Afghan frontier authorities on local, non-political matters. During the next few years, Russia succeeded in greatly increasing her trade with Afghanistan, and by 1914 she was urging Britain to make northern Afghanistan more accessible to Russian influence and enterprise. But she envisaged a bigger area than Britain would accept.[1]

Persia was another area of Russo-British rivalry in the Middle East. Until 1828 Russia had been taking territory

---

[1] See the article by I. Reisner on 'The Anglo-Russian Convention of 1907 and the Partition of Afghanistan' in *Krasny Arkhiv*, vol. 3 (10) (Moscow, 1925), pp. 54-66.

from north-west Persia as she pushed across the Caucasus. But after 1828 she worked to maintain Persia and strengthen Russian influence at Teheran, partly because she had not yet digested the Caucasus and partly because she feared that further Russian encroachments in the north would make Persia turn to Britain or lead Britain to seize southern Persia. To some extent, she and Britain co-operated in trying to avoid disputed successions to the Persian throne and other internal complications likely to promote Persia's disintegration. But in the 'thirties the activities of the Russian envoy in Teheran made Britain suspect that she was encouraging Persia to expand eastwards into Afghan territory and to take Herat, which was regarded as one of the gates to India. Britain's counter-measures led to friction with both Persia and Russia. But even during the Crimean War Russia made no real attempt to use Persia against either Turkey or Britain and preferred her to remain neutral. In 1858 Gorchakov still insisted that Russia's interest was to maintain Persia's independence and integrity as 'un état neutre destiné à nous garantir d'un contact immédiat avec la puissance anglaise en Asie'. He also welcomed Persia's attempts to develop contact with other Powers and saw in them no danger for Russia and for Persia 'un point d'appui contre la pression anglaise'.[1]

Russia's subsequent expansion through central Asia, which absorbed the Turcomans among others, brought her for the first time into direct contact with north-east Persia and greatly increased her means of pressure on Teheran, particularly after she built the Transcaspian railway during the 'eighties parallel with the new Perso-Russian frontier. She now began to follow a more vigorous policy in Persia, aimed, in Alexander III's words, at gaining a 'predominating influence'[2] and combating British influence even in southern Persia and the Persian Gulf. At times Nicholas II even dreamed of eventually taking Persia. Russia steadily extended her influence throughout northern

[1] *Documents collected by the Caucasian Archeographical Commission*, loc. cit., pp. 595-9.
[2] V. N. Lamsdorff, *Diary, 1891–1892* (R) (Moscow, 1934), p. 215.

Aspects of Russian Foreign Policy, 1815–1914

Persia by such means as trade, the shah's Russian-officered Cossack brigade, road building, shipping on the Caspian, telegraphs, insurance, loans to the Persian government, and the Persian Loan and Discount Bank which she established in 1890, at first under another name, as a counterbalance to the British-controlled Imperial Bank of Persia. In contrast to Gorchakov's attitude in 1858, she now set herself to hinder the spread of other foreign influences and enterprise in Persia by trying to block railway construction; and in 1890 and again in 1900 she was able to secure a pledge from the shah that for the next ten years he would allow no railways to be built without Russian consent. She also started to extend her influence into southern Persia and the Persian Gulf by opening consulates and a subsidized shipping line between Odessa and the gulf ports. These various enterprises proved costly, and not all the Russian leaders were convinced that she was wise to strain her resources by trying to challenge British influence in the south. But she remained firmly opposed to any 'spheres of influence' policy in Persia until her defeat in the Russo-Japanese War impelled her to adopt a holding policy in the Middle East and to switch her main energies from Asia back to the Near East. This led to the Anglo-Russian Convention of 1907 under which Russia promised not to extend her own influence to or work against British influence in a defined zone in south-east Persia. In return she gained a corresponding promise from Britain about a defined zone in northern Persia, which her military leaders unsuccessfully tried to extend southwards to include the area bordering on western Afghanistan. The rest of Persia was to remain accessible to the enterprise of both Powers as before. For the time being, this partition of influence with Britain dashed Russia's hopes of eventually controlling the whole of Persia. But, as subsequent developments showed, she found it increasingly difficult to keep her policy in Persia within the framework of the 1907 agreement either in her own zone of influence or in the rest of Persia outside the British zone.

.   .   .   .

In the Far East, as in the Middle East, Russia pursued a policy of expansion from the mid-nineteenth century onwards. Under pressure from Muraviev, the governor-general of eastern Siberia, who thought to forestall suspected British designs in the north-west Pacific, she induced China to cede her the Amur region in 1858 and the Ussuri region in 1860. In 1875 she also established her claim to Sakhalin against Japan. She now looked southwards with the idea of rounding off her recent territorial gains by the acquisition of an ice-free port and naval base in Korea, which many Russians regarded as destined to be absorbed in the Russian empire. But after 1891 her policy changed radically in aim and scope when the Government decided to build the Trans-Siberian railway to link her far eastern provinces with Russia proper and help in their defence and development, and more particularly when it planned to shorten the length of the railway and avoid certain construction difficulties by carrying it across Chinese territory in Manchuria instead of wholly within Russian territory round the bend of the Amur. Some Russians wanted to run the railway merely across the northern tip of Manchuria and thought that China should be induced to cede Russia the territory affected. But Witte, the minister of finance, had other and more grandiose ideas. Witte's plan was to carry the Trans-Siberian railway through the heart of Manchuria with the consent of the Chinese government and make it the basis for Russian commercial and economic penetration into Manchuria, Korea and as much of the rest of China as possible. Unlike some of his colleagues, Witte had no interest in immediate territorial acquisitions along Russia's border. He wanted instead to keep China from disintegrating, to establish and maintain intimate relations with the Chinese government, to bring it under Russian influence by lending it money and supporting it against other Powers, and to secure from it railway, trade and economic concessions which would turn the whole of north China into an exclusive Russian preserve and still enable Russia to extend her influence in the rest of China on the same footing as other Powers. At bottom,

Aspects of Russian Foreign Policy, 1815–1914

Witte's programme was unrealistic. Russia still lacked the economic and financial resources to penetrate and exploit large areas of China, and her Far Eastern provinces remained sparsely populated and exposed to pressure from the Chinese, who were already settling in large numbers in Manchuria.[1] Other and economically stronger Powers than Russia also had important interests in China which they were certain to defend against Russian pressure. But Witte was so vigorous and powerful a minister that his views about China carried considerable weight and greatly influenced Russia's Far Eastern policy for over a decade. At the same time the tsar also listened to other ministers and unofficial advisers like Bezobrazov, who advocated different aims and methods from those of Witte. The result was that Russia's policy in the Far East lacked continuity and consistency and ended by involving her in war with Japan.

Russia first began to unfold her policy of economic imperialism in 1895 at the end of the Sino-Japanese War over Korea, when she helped China by manœuvring the Japanese out of the Liaotung peninsula and securing her a loan to meet her war indemnity to Japan. The same year Witte established the Russo-Chinese Bank with French financial support as a spear-head of Russian economic penetration in China. In 1896, on Witte's initiative, Russia made a defensive alliance with China against Japan, and Witte persuaded the Chinese government to grant a concession for a railway across Manchuria to a specially created Chinese Eastern Railway Company, which received very wide privileges in Manchuria and was controlled by the Russian finance ministry through the Russo-Chinese Bank. But in 1898 Witte's policy of economic penetration in friendship with China was seriously endangered when the Russian foreign minister used Germany's seizure of Kiaochow to persuade the tsar to occupy Port Arthur and

---

[1] Kuropatkin, the war minister, was very worried about the effects which Chinese settlement in Manchuria would have on the security of Russia's frontier. See 'Diary of A. N. Kuropatkin' for 5 Jan. 1903, in *Krasny Arkhiv*, vol. 2 (Moscow, 1922), pp. 21-2. See also *The Memoirs of General Kuropatkin on the Russo-Japanese War* (R) (Berlin, 1911), pp. 75-7.

Dalny in the Liaotung peninsula and extort a 25-year lease on them from the Chinese government. Witte at first opposed this move. But when the tsar approved it, he tried to make it serve his own policy by securing a concession for the Chinese Eastern Railway Company for a branch line to Port Arthur from the main Manchurian line. On the other hand, the Russian seizure of Port Arthur naturally alarmed the Chinese government and made it less friendly towards Russia. In 1900 the Boxer movement led to a Russian military occupation of the whole of Manchuria, and Witte hoped to use the presence of Russian troops to secure far-reaching concessions from China which would have turned Manchuria and the whole of northern China, including Mongolia, into an exclusive Russian sphere of influence.[1] By contrast, the minister of war would have been content to acquire northern Manchuria and the navy minister an ice-free port and naval base in Korea. But Russia's ambitious plans in the Far East had already caused so much uneasiness in Japan and Britain that in 1902 they came together in defence of their Far Eastern interests. Russia might still have averted Japanese hostility if she had been prepared to abandon her designs on Korea. But the tsar was now under the influence of the Bezobrazov-Abaza clique, which wanted no withdrawals in the Far East, least of all in Korea. The result was that in February 1904 Japan stopped trying to negotiate with Russia and attacked Port Arthur, and Russia's defeat in the ensuing war cost her southern Sakhalin and her hold on the Liaotung peninsula, both of which she had to surrender to Japan in the Peace of Portsmouth.

Even after the Russo-Japanese War Russia was far from adopting a passive rôle in the Far East. But she now switched from a policy of trying to extend her exclusive influence over the whole of north China through friendship with the Chinese government to a policy of entrenching it in the border areas through co-operation with Japan. In 1907 she made a secret

[1] See B. A. Romanov, *Russia in Manchuria, 1892–1906* (R) (Leningrad, 1928), chapters 5 and 6, pp. 240-465.

agreement with Japan under which Japan recognized Russia's special position in north Manchuria and Outer Mongolia and Russia Japan's special position in south Manchuria and Korea. In 1910 she and Japan signed a second secret agreement which recognized the right of each to defend its special interests in its own agreed sphere in Manchuria and also envisaged common action if these special interests were threatened. Two years later in a third secret agreement Japan recognized Russia's special interests in the western half of Inner Mongolia and Russia Japan's special interests in the eastern half.[1] Russia's changed attitude towards China naturally led the Russian government to welcome the Chinese revolution of 1911, in the belief that it would cause the disintegration or at least the weakening of the Chinese empire. Some Russian officials even urged that Russia should take advantage of the revolution to seize territory from China for herself, and their advice was not without influence on the tsar. But Sazonov, who had the situation in Europe and the Near East constantly in mind, successfully steered the Government away from a policy of immediate territorial acquisitions, which would have caused complications with Britain, France and America, and kept it to its policy of spheres of influence, for which he hoped to secure French and British approval.[2] At the same time Russia favoured the anti-Chinese movement among the Mongols of Outer Mongolia and used it to bring the area much more under her influence. But while she compelled China to agree to Outer Mongolia's autonomy and to settle its political and territorial problems jointly with herself, she was unwilling to support the Mongols in their demand for a completely independent state.[3] She also used China's difficulties

[1] For the texts of these treaties, see E. B. Brice, *The Russo-Japanese Treaties of 1907–1916 concerning Manchuria and Mongolia* (Baltimore, 1933), Appendices B, C, and D.

[2] See 'The Chinese Revolution of 1911', in *Krasny Arkhiv*, vol. 5 (18) (Moscow, 1926), particularly pp. 75-6 and 96-7. There is also a great deal of information about Russia's far eastern policy at this time in *International Relations in the Epoch of Imperialism* (R), 2nd and 3rd series.

[3] See the article by A. Popov on 'Tsarist Russia in Mongolia in 1913–14' in *Krasny Arkhiv*, vol. 6 (37) (Moscow, 1929), pp. 3-68.

to entrench her influence in other border areas. But from now on, she was increasingly handicapped in the Far East by her preoccupations elsewhere, and when she finally became involved in war with Germany and Austria in 1914 she had no option but to concentrate on the struggle against them in Europe.

E. H. CARR

'RUSSIA AND EUROPE' AS A THEME OF RUSSIAN HISTORY

THE greatest political upheaval of our times provides fresh illustration of the historical commonplace, first established by Tocqueville, that revolutions are less revolutionary than they appear at first blush, and interrupt the continuity of the nation's history less sharply and less radically than their sponsors like to pretend. The Russian revolution, like the French revolution, was followed by a struggle within the nation — no less acute for being sometimes masked in revolutionary phraseology — between the element of change and the element of continuity, with the latter asserting itself ever more powerfully as the years went on. But, though this analogy between the two great revolutions of modern times has been frequently remarked, it is less often noticed that the tension between the elements of change and continuity in the aftermath of the Russian revolution presented peculiar features of its own. In the French revolution, as in the English revolution of the seventeenth century, the forces in play on either side had worn the same national colour. Though the French revolution quickly assumed an international rôle, the initial impetus, the dominant ideas of the revolution, had come from within the nation itself. The genesis of the Bolshevik revolution was infinitely more complex. While in one aspect it could be said to stem from a native revolutionary tradition which went back to Pugachev and had been an obsessing theme in Russian politics, thought and literature throughout the nineteenth century, the irruption of Marxism into Russia, like the irruption of Christianity into the Roman empire, meant the acceptance of a creed, claiming indeed universal validity, but carrying the stigmata of an alien origin. The direct inspiration of the Bolshevik revolution and the basis of its ideology came from western Europe; its principal leaders had spent long years there; their training and outlook were predominantly western. The revolution which they made in Russia was conceived by them not primarily as a Russian revolution, but as the first step in a European or world-wide revolution; as an exclusively Russian phenomenon, it had for them no meaning, no validity and no chance of survival. Hence the re-emergence of the features of the old order after the revolutionary flood had receded took the form not merely of the restoration of an earlier ideological and institutional framework, but of a national restoration. The defeated social forces which now re-emerged to make their compromise with the new revolutionary order and insensibly to modify its course were also national forces reasserting the validity of a native tradition against the influx of foreign influences. What happened in the aftermath of the revolution, and especially after Lenin's death, had a dual character. Seen in the perspective of the revolution, it represented the familiar reaction of the principle of continuity against the onset of revolutionary change. Seen in the perspective of Russian history, it represented an attempt of the Russian national tradition to reassert itself against the encroachments of the west.

. . . . .

It is customary to trace the differences between Russia and western Europe to the schism between Rome and Byzantium. The rift did not at first seem vital or irreparable. In the Middle Ages the thought of western as well as eastern Christendom was confined to the prescribed channels of religious orthodoxy. But, in the thirteenth and fourteenth centuries, while the development of Russian civilization was arrested and threatened with extinction under the Mongol

'Russia and Europe' as a Theme of Russian History

yoke, the western world rediscovered the legacy of classical antiquity. Eastern Christendom, clinging to Old Slavonic instead of Latin as its ritual language, remained immune from the Greek discovery of the supremacy of reason and the Roman invention of the rule of law. Western Christendom incorporated the classical in the Christian tradition, reconciling secular with divine reason and human with divine law.[1] The gulf broadened when the Renaissance set in motion the process which emancipated the human reason from theological leading-strings and laid the foundations of an autonomous secular culture. The ideal of the independent and self-sufficient individual, which flowered in the Renaissance and formed a main ingredient in the western civilization of the next three centuries, found no echo in Russia, where earlier Christian conceptions of collective responsibility and collective salvation continued to prevail unimpaired. The rule of the tsars rested, at any rate down to the time of Peter the Great, on a theocratic foundation; the conception of a secular art or a secular literature was still unborn. Western belief in the potency of 'free' thought, advancing through a salutary conflict of opposite opinions towards an empirical and conditional conclusion, which was the basis of the Protestant doctrine of toleration, remained anathema to the Russian tradition of an absolute and divinely attested truth.

If, however, we are to consider Russian history from the standpoint of Russia's 'backwardness' and isolation from the characteristic developments of western Europe, the main reason for this phenomenon should be sought not so much in any initial divergence between eastern and western Christendom as in the conditions which maintained and widened that divergence and caused Russia's material progress to lag

---

[1] Ivan Kireevsky, the Slavophil philosopher, in one of his early essays, wrote that 'the invasion of the Tatars and their influence on our whole subsequent evolution was rendered possible only by one reason: *the absence of the classical world*'; later he attributed the heretical development of the west primarily to the influence of 'the classical world of ancient paganism', which represented 'the victory of formal human reason' (*Polnoe Sobranie Sochinenii I. V. Kireevskogo* (1911), i. 101, 111-12).

behind that of western Europe. The vast expanse of territory, unbroken by any well-defined geographical features or ethnographical divisions, which went to make the Russian State, and the inclement climatic conditions prevailing over the greater part of it, were the real foundation of Russia's backwardness in comparison with the material development of western Europe. The great distances over which authority had to be organized made state-building in Russia an unusually slow and cumbrous process; and, in the unpropitious environment of the Russian steppe, forms of production and the social relations arising from them lagged far behind those of the more favoured west. And this time-lag, continuing throughout Russian history, created disparities which coloured and determined all Russian relations with the west. The first contacts of the rising Russian State with western Europe, which began on an extensive scale under Ivan the Terrible in the latter part of the sixteenth century, revealed all the disadvantages of Russia's backwardness in face of the west; and these disadvantages were still more conspicuously shown up in the ensuing 'period of troubles' and of the Polish invasions. Henceforth the development of State power in Russia proceeded at a forced pace under the watchword of military necessity.[1] The outstanding place occupied by Peter the Great in Russian history is due to his success in building in Russia a power capable of confronting western European countries on comparable, if not equal, terms.

This historical pattern of the development of the Russian State had three important consequences. In the first place, it produced that chronically ambivalent attitude to western Europe which has run through all subsequent Russian thought and policy. It was indispensable to imitate and 'catch up with' the west as a means of self-defence against the west: the west was admired and envied as a model, as well as feared and

[1] The exposed frontiers of France, compared with the sheltered strategic position of Great Britain, have often been quoted as the reason for the rise of strong autocratic monarchy in France in the seventeenth and eighteenth centuries and failure to follow the British path of constitutional development: the same argument applies in a more extreme form to Russia.

'Russia and Europe' as a Theme of Russian History

hated as the potential enemy. Secondly, the pattern of development rested on the conception of 'revolution from above'.[1] Reform came not through pressure from below, from an under-privileged class or from oppressed masses, expressing itself in demands for social justice or equality, but through pressure of external crisis, resulting in a belated demand within the ruling group for an efficient authority and calling for a strong leader to exercise it.[2] Hence reform, which in the west normally led to a curbing and dispersal of State power, meant in Russia a strengthening and concentration of that power. Thirdly, the pattern imposed by these conditions was one not of orderly progress but of spasmodic advance by fits and starts — a pattern not of evolution but of intermittent revolution. The function of Peter the Great, succeeding to the unfinished work of Ivan the Terrible, was, within the space of a single lifetime, to transform a mediaeval into a modern society, and, using European models, to drive his backward and reluctant subjects by forced marches to new tasks in a new world. Progress in Russia thus acquired a spasmodic and episodic character.

[1] The phrase appears to have been first used by the French Liberal journalist Girardin, who, in *La Presse* of 6 June 1848, distinguished between two types of revolution : '*from above* (*par en haut*), which is revolution by initiative, by intelligence, by progress, by ideas ; *from below* (*par en bas*), which is revolution by insurrection, by force, by despair, by the streets'. Proudhon, quoting this passage in *Confessions d'un révolutionnaire*, attacked as 'revolutionaries from above' not only Louis XIV, Robespierre, Napoleon and Charles X, but also Saint-Simon, Fourier, Owen, Cabet and Louis Blanc, who favoured the organization of labour 'by the State, by capital or by what authority soever' (*Œuvres complètes de P.-J. Proudhon* (1876), ix. 26-7).

[2] This process, of which the first example in Russian history is the mythical appeal of the dispersed Slav tribes to the Varangian Rurik to 'come and rule over us', was commonly quoted by Russian writers, as proof of the essentially pacific and defensive character of Russian power in contrast with that of the west: 'The European states were formed through conquest. Enmity is their fundamental principle. Government came there as an armed enemy and established itself by force over conquered peoples. . . . The Russian State, on the other hand, was founded not by conquest, but by voluntary invitation of the governed. . . . Thus, in the foundation of the western State, violence, slavery and enmity ; in the foundation of the Russian State, free will, freedom and peace' (*Polnoe Sobranie Sochinenii K. S. Aksakova*, i. (1861), 8). One result of 'revolution from above' in Russian history was the phenomenon, rare in the west, of repression applied to those who resisted change, *e.g.* the Old Believers in the seventeenth century, the *boyars* under Peter the Great.

In Europe, in most civilized countries [wrote Nicholas Turgenev], institutions have developed by stages; everything that exists there has its source and root in the past; the Middle Ages still serve, more or less, as the basis for everything that constitutes the social, civic and political life of the European States. Russia has had no Middle Ages; everything that is to prosper there must be borrowed from Europe; Russia cannot graft it on her own ancient institutions.[1]

And the same point was made by a western traveller:

Russia alone, belatedly civilized, has been deprived by the impatience of her leaders of the profound fermentation and the benefit of slow natural development. . . . Adolescence, that laborious age when the spirit of man assumes entire responsibility for his independence, has been lost to her. Her princes, especially Peter the Great, counting time for nothing, made her pass violently from childhood to manhood.[2]

Nor was such progress wholly maintained. Peter's death in 1725 was followed by a period of nearly forty years in which weak successors went as far as they dared to nullify his work by transforming it on traditional Russian lines. The alternation of violent advance and no less violent reaction continued to mark the uneven course of Russian history.

The consequence of this development was to leave in simultaneous existence, within the loose and ample structure of the Russian State, social, economic, political and cultural forms which in western Europe seemed to belong to different stages of civilization and were regarded as incompatible with one another. In Russia elements of servile, feudal and capitalist society continued to exist side by side; and this anomaly could not fail to create new divisions and set up new tensions. In the eighteenth century the complex of traditions and beliefs known in the west by the vague name of 'humanism' at length reached Russia. But it came in the form of a foreign extravagance imported from the west, and scarcely penetrated beneath the surface of Russian society and Russian conscious-

---

[1] N. Turgenev, *La Russie et les Russes* (1847), iii. 5.
[2] De Custine, *La Russie en 1839* (Brussels, 1843), iv. 153-4.

'Russia and Europe' as a Theme of Russian History

ness. Its effect was to deepen and perpetuate the wide cleavage that separated rulers from ruled: Russia was now more sharply than ever divided between a 'society' which solaced itself for the backwardness of Russian life in the contemplation of western ideas and the enjoyment of the trappings of civilization, and the 'dark' mass of the Russian people plunged in the immemorial Russian tradition of poverty and ignorance. Russia became the land of extremes — of the extremes of luxury and indigence, of the most advanced thought and the most primitive superstition, of uninhibited freedom and untempered oppression. The gulf between west and east in Europe was doubled by a gulf within Russia itself, between a superficially westernized society and an authentic Russian people. The rift between east and west was no longer purely external. It had inserted itself into the composite fabric of the Russian State.

. . . . .

These complexities reached their peak in Russian nineteenth-century history — a fruitful period which revealed all the contradictions and all the potentialities of Russian development in exuberant profusion. The period opened under the stimulus of a fresh impact from the west. 'The veritable history of Russia', wrote Herzen, 'begins only in 1812.'[1] The French revolution and the wars of Napoleon had carried all over Europe the twin ideals of constitutional freedom and national self-realization, the rights of man and the rights of nations. The victorious ending of the war did not mean the eradication from Russian soil of the seeds sown there by the revolution. Nicholas Turgenev, returning to Russia from western Europe in 1816, noted the rapid dissemination of western ideas:

> The impulse given to men's minds by recent events, or rather by the agitation produced by those events, was evident. With the return of the Russian armies to their country, *liberal ideas*, as they were then called, began to spread in Russia. Independently of the regular troops, great masses of recruits had also seen foreign

[1] *Polnoe Sobranie Sochinenii i Pisem A. I. Gertsena*, ed. Lemke, vi. 209.

lands : these recruits of every rank, when they recrossed the frontier, returned to their homes, where they related what they had seen in Europe. Events spoke more loudly than any human voice. It was a veritable propaganda.[1]

This exuberance of ideas finally gave birth to two distinct and, in some ways, contrasted movements. The cause of constitutional liberty was taken up by the so-called 'westerners', whose admiration of western models was unqualified. The cause of Russian nationalism, which was complicated from the first by a certain ambivalence towards the west, was to be the theme of the Slavophils.

The fierce controversies that raged between westerners and Slavophils have left in the minds of historians a somewhat distorted and exaggerated picture of basic antagonism. It is true that the two groups can be broadly contrasted as 'westerners' and 'easterners' in their view of past Russian history and future Russian development, though both drew their original inspiration from the west. It is not true that they can be contrasted as reformers and conservatives, or as revolutionaries and reactionaries, though some of the ideas of both were at different times borrowed by conservatives and reactionaries. Both westerners and Slavophils were the offspring of the French revolution. Both belonged to the nascent Russian intelligentsia — a fluid and ill-defined group in Russian society, lacking the solid foundation which the intellectuals of the west found in a powerful manufacturing and trading class,[2] and united only in their hostility to a

---

[1] N. Turgenev, *La Russie et les Russes* (1847), i. 80-1.

[2] The weakness of the Russian bourgeoisie was a familiar theme from the early years of the nineteenth century onwards : 'The bourgeois, a respected and influential class in all other countries, are with us contemptible, poor, tax-ridden, and deprived of the means of existence. . . . In other countries they populate the cities, but our cities exist only on the map' (quoted from A. A. Bestuzhev in V. I. Semevsky, *Politicheskie i Obshchestvennye Idei Dekabristov* (1909), p. 99). Cities in Russia first obtained official recognition in a decree of Catherine II of 1785. The view that the 'rootlessness' or 'classlessness' of the Russian intelligentsia, due to the absence of a bourgeoisie, gave it a specifically anti-bourgeois character, and that this differentiated it fundamentally from its western counterparts, is the theme of the well-known work of Ivanov-Razumnik, *Istoriya Russkoi Obshchestvennoi Mysli* (3rd ed., 1911). But even this view seems

'Russia and Europe' as a Theme of Russian History

Government which stifled or distorted every form of literary and artistic activity. It was typical of the weakness of the Russian intelligentsia that westerners and Slavophils consumed their energies in mutual recriminations on a theoretical plane, and remained without direct influence on the public policies of their time. Yet they jointly marked the emergence of a new focus of social and political discontent which, in various forms, remained active down to 1917. Throughout the nineteenth century the cause of social and political emancipation and the cause of national emancipation, sometimes in alliance, sometimes in mutual antipathy, provided the ferment which inspired and fertilized all Russian thought.

The westerners were the first to take the field. The demand for political and social rights, which crystallized during the first half of the century in the two concrete demands for a constitution and for the emancipation of the serfs, led to a significant new alignment. Hitherto the reforming influences of the west had worked in Russia in a sense favourable to the autocracy, or, at any rate, not incompatible with it, and had received the official encouragement and patronage of successive tsars. Even Alexander I had toyed with constitution-making, and had emancipated the serfs in his Baltic provinces. Henceforth the westerners would be the enemies of autocratic rule, seeking, like the Liberals and Radicals of the west, to wrest constitutional rights from reluctant monarchs; and this meant in Russian terms that they became cosmopolitan revolutionaries, while the tsar, forgetting the westernizing zeal of his most famous predecessors, became the upholder of a national theocratic tradition. The new positions were staked out on both sides in the famous Decembrist rising of 1825, which was the recognized starting-

to accord to the Russian intelligentsia a greater ideological cohesion than it, in fact, possessed. The westerners spoke for the rising group of professional men and civil servants, who had a smattering of western culture and were greedy for the fruits of western thought. The Slavophils are sometimes said, not very convincingly, to have spoken for the smaller land-owners against a régime primarily based on the interests of the great nobility; but, apart from a prejudice against the employment of foreigners and the imitation of foreign methods in administration, they can hardly be said to have had a political programme.

point of the whole nineteenth-century revolutionary movement. Hitherto in Russian history 'revolution from below' had been known only in the form of a spontaneous peasant *jacquerie*. Now the seeds of an urge for 'revolution from below' had been sown among the governing classes side by side with the older urge for 'revolution from above'. The Decembrists were primarily westerners, and official resistance to their ideas therefore tended to be couched in national slogans. To the revolutionary cry of 'Liberty, Equality, Fraternity', Nicholas I's minister Uvarov opposed the patriotic motto, 'Autocracy, Orthodoxy, Nationality'.[1]

The founder of the philosophy of westernism was Chaadaev, whose diagnosis of the Russian past in his famous 'Philosophical Letter', written in 1829 and first published in 1836, remained the *locus classicus* on the subject:

> First, brutal barbarism, then crude superstition, then a savage and humiliating foreign domination of the spirit which later became the legacy of the national power — there is the sad picture of our youth. . . .
>
> While the edifice of modern civilization was rising out of the struggle between the energetic barbarism of the peoples of the north and the lofty philosophy of religion, what were we doing? Driven by a fatal destiny, we were seeking in wretched Byzantium, the object of the profound contempt of these peoples, the moral code in which we were to be reared. . . .
>
> Confined in our schism, nothing of what was happening in Europe reached us. We stood apart from the world's great venture. . . . Although we bore the name of Christians, when Christianity advanced in majesty along the path traced by its divine founder, and drew the generations after it, we stood still. While the whole world was building anew, we created nothing: we remained squatting in our hovels of log and thatch. In a word, we had no part in the new destinies of mankind. We were Christians, but the fruits of Christianity were not for us.[2]

---

[1] The motto seems to have been coined in a memorandum from Uvarov to the Tsar in 1832 (N. P. Barsukov, *Zhizn' i Trudy M. P. Pogodina*, iv (1891), 82-5); Uvarov became minister of Public Instruction in 1834.

[2] *Sochineniya i Pis'ma P. Ya. Chaadaeva*, ed. Gershenzon, i (1913), 78-9, 85-6.

'Russia and Europe' as a Theme of Russian History

Of the Slav peoples only the Poles had been westernized; and, as Herzen later said, 'with the exception of Poland, the Slavs belong to geography rather than to history'.[1] Chaadaev's diagnosis of the Russian past led inevitably to the conclusion that 'we must speak the language of Europe', and that 'the more we seek to unite with her, the better it will be for us';[2] and Chaadaev's own formula of *rapprochement* with the west was union with the Catholic Church. But, while his interest was primarily historical and religious, he afterwards confessed that 'the young generation, to which I belong, dreamed of reforms in the country, of systems of administration such as we find in European countries, an order of society based on that of those countries, in a word, of constitutions and everything pertaining to them', though he exculpated himself from ever having criminally attempted to put such ideas into practice.[3]

The publication of Chaadaev's 'philosophical letter' infuriated the authorities. Its author was officially pronounced insane and placed under medical supervision. Its impact on the young Radicals whose first political memory was the Decembrist insurrection was correspondingly great; Herzen in a well-known passage has described its effect on him when he first read it in his exile in Vyatka.[4] For the two decades which followed the Decembrist insurrection, the vast majority of the younger generation of the rising Russian intelligentsia unhesitatingly accepted the fundamental thesis of Russian isolation from Europe as the cause of Russian backwardness. Granovsky, in his famous Lectures of the 1840s in the University of Moscow, differed from Chaadaev in putting the issue on a secular basis, but continued to seek the foundations of

[1] *Sobranie Sochinenii i Pisem A. I. Gertsena*, ed. Lemke, vi. 203 : this is a paraphrase of Herder, who had written that the Slavs 'occupy more space on the earth than in history' (*Herders sämmtliche Werke*, ed. Suphan, xiv (1909), 277).
[2] *Sochineniya i Pis'ma P. Ya. Chaadaeva*, ed. Gershenzon, i (1913), 137 : these phrases occur not in the so-called 'first' letter written in 1829 and published in 1836, but in the 'third' letter written earlier in 1829 but not published in Chaadaev's lifetime. [3] *Ibid.* i. 335.
[4] *Polnoe Sobranie Sochinenii i Pisem A. I. Gertsena*, ed. Lemke, xiii. 126.

European civilization and, by implication, of Russian backwardness in the Middle Ages. Kavelin, in an article of 1847 in *Sovremennik*, praised Peter the Great for having made the emancipation of the individual personality the central theme of Russian history (hitherto the family, or earlier still the tribe, had been the unit of Russian society), and thus set Russia on the western path of development.[1] Herzen and Ogarev, Stankevich and Bakunin, Belinsky and Turgenev were merely the outstanding figures in a generation of young Radicals who, whatever the other differences dividing them, assumed, almost without argument, that in politics and in literature, in art and in manners, Russia could emerge from her isolation only by closer contacts with Europe, and overcome her backwardness only by following well-tried western models.

The movement led by the Slavophils [2] was more complex and slower to take shape than that of the westerners. It, too, owed its initial inspiration to the ferment of the French revolution which, culminating in the defeat of Napoleon's invading armies by Russian forces and the appearance of Alexander I in Paris and Vienna as the recognized peer of the other European sovereigns, gave a powerful impetus to Russian national consciousness and Russian national pride. Russia had vindicated her right to be a nation like the other great European nations, with all the prerogatives of nationhood. The demand to assert an independent national tradition made itself heard above all in literature. Karamzin created, and Pushkin perfected, the new Russian literary

---

[1] *Sobranie Sochinenii K. D. Kavelina* (n.d. [1897]), i. 5-66.

[2] The name was first applied in derision to Shishkov, the president of the Imperial Academy, who published in 1803 *Considerations on the Old and New Style in the Russian Language* and launched a campaign to defend the exclusive use of words with Russian roots against the westernizing innovations of Karamzin. In 1811 he published *Considerations on Love for One's Country*, and in the following year succeeded Speransky as secretary of state, being primarily concerned to arouse Russian patriotism in the struggle against Napoleon. He was minister of Public Instruction from 1824 to 1828, when he retired. The Slavophils never applied the name to themselves. As Khomyakov pointed out, the word had a foreign root: they would have had to call themselves *Slavyanolyubtsy* (*Polnoe Sobranie Sochinenii A. S. Khomyakova* (1900), i. 96-7).

language, and laid the foundations of a great national literature; and these achievements, while they sprang from imitation of the west, gave a strong impetus to national pride and national self-consciousness. In 1825 Küchelbecker wrote in the short-lived but significant literary magazine *Mnemosyne*:

> Russian literature should generously and freely acquire all the treasures of Europe and Asia, but acquire them in such a way as not to lose her independence and national character. It is necessary for the glory of Russia that a truly Russian poetry should at length be born, that holy Russia should become the first State in the universe, not only in the political world but also in the moral world.[1]

And in the programme for the *Moskovsky Vestnik*, founded to replace the defunct *Mnemosyne*, Venevitinov complained that Russian thought and Russian literature had been distorted by imitation of European forms and needed to recapture their native essence (*samobytnost'*).[2] The movement had a strong Germanic tinge of primitive folk-lore, and indulged in romantic extravagances like the wearing of beards and of old Russian national costume. The early Slavophils were steeped in the writings of German romantic thinkers from Herder to Schelling.[3] The romantic doctrine of national particularism was the basis of their creed: hardly anything that they wrote of the Russian *narod* had not already been written by German philosophers of the German *Volk*.

---

[1] Quoted in A. Koyré, *La Philosophie et le problème national en Russie* (1929), p. 149.

[2] D. V. Venevitinov, *Polnoe Sobranie Sochinenii* (1934), pp. 217-20.

[3] Herder was apparently the first to depict the Slavs as a gentle, industrious, submissive people held down throughout history by the energetic Germans and barbarous Tatars; though 'now sunk so low', however, they would one day be 'freed from their slave chains' and, 'refreshed by their long, idle sleep', cultivate their fair lands in peace (*Herders sämmtliche Werke*, ed. Suphan, xiv (1909), 277-80). Hegel preached the historical mission of successive nations. Schelling treated history as a struggle between the sons of Seth, the peace-loving patriarchs, and the sons of Cain, the 'heaven-storming Titans'; for Khomyakov the Slavophil it was a struggle between the 'Iranian' principle of freedom and submission to the divine will (the Slavs naturally represented this principle) and the 'Kushite' principle of necessity and enslavement. For some account of these doctrines, see N. V. Riasanovsky, *Russia and the West in the Teaching of the Slavophiles* (Harvard, 1952), pp. 215-18.

The paradox of the essential superiority of primitive Russia over advanced and cultured Europe was not entirely new. Half a century earlier an argument had been found which converted the notorious Russian backwardness into a positive asset. Fonvizin, then on a visit to France, had written in a letter of 1778:

> If here they began to live before us, at any rate we, in beginning to live, can give ourselves whatever form we please, and avoid the shortcomings and evils which are rooted here. *Nous commençons et ils finissent.* I think that he who is being born is happier than he who is dying.[1]

An article of Kireevsky which appeared in 1830, and must count as one of the earliest Slavophil pronouncements, while still admitting the low level of Russian culture and its indebtedness to Europe, drew the same encouraging conclusion from Russia's backwardness:

> European civilization served as the cradle of ours: our civilization was born at a time when the others were already completing the cycle of their intellectual evolution, and, where they have stopped, we are only beginning. As the youngest sister of a great family, Russia before entering the world is already rich with the experience of her elders.

In Europe stagnation had set in: 'political and moral progress has come to an end'. In the whole of the civilized world only two countries were exempt from this stagnation: the United States of America and Russia. But the former was too distant and too one-sided in the English character of its civilization. Russia was destined to succeed to the legacy of Europe, and 'we shall repay her a hundredfold what we owe to her'.[2] In another article written two years later, after a visit to Europe, and entitled *The Nineteenth Century*, Kireevsky reiterated that 'we must labour to acquire this western civilization, which is the synonym of civilization as such'; but he continued to believe that, once this was acquired, his compatriots were

---

[1] *Sochineniya, Pis'ma i Izbrannye Perevody D. I. Fon-Vizina*, ed. P. A. Efremov (1866), pp. 272-3.
[2] *Polnoe Sobranie Sochinenii I. V. Kireevskogo* (1911), ii. 37-9.

destined to become 'the new representatives of humanity', who would inherit the fruits of European civilization and 'extract from it the germs of a new development'.[1] Then, 'when the *common civilization of Europe* becomes identical with *our particular essence*', a new civilization will be born, 'truly Russian and big with beneficent consequences for Russia and for humanity'.[2] The conception that Russia was not merely a nation among nations, but had a unique mission to transcend nationality by becoming the archetype of universal humanity, became a central tenet of the Slavophil creed. 'The Russian nation', wrote Konstantin Aksakov in the 1850s, 'is not a nation, it is humanity; it is a nation only because it is surrounded by nations having exclusive national essences, and its humanity therefore appears as nationality.'[3] It was in this spirit that Dostoevsky was later to find in Pushkin the quintessential Russian, the prototype of the 'all-man', and to declare, through the mouth of Shatov in *The Devils*, that Russia was 'a god-bearing nation'.

The most specific practical item of Slavophil doctrine, belief in the significance of the Russian peasant commune as a form of social organization, also owed something to western inspiration. In the early 1840s a Prussian official named Haxthausen made an extended tour of Russia for the purpose of studying Russian institutions and published a detailed work on them. The most striking feature of his report was his praise of the peasant commune, which he treated as a specifically Russian institution and a sure bulwark of social stability against the threat of revolution. This belief in the peasant commune was enthusiastically embraced by Slavophil writers and provided an important reinforcement of the Slavophil creed. Individualism was denounced as the characteristic vice of the west, leading in religion to Protestantism, in politics

---

[1] *Ibid.* i. 103-4.
[2] *Ibid.* ii. 61.
[3] *Polnoe Sobranie Sochinenii K. S. Aksakova*, i (1861), 630. Similarly, Samarin maintained that, whereas Catholicism and Protestantism represented two different sides of Christianity, Orthodoxy was the one universal Christian faith (*Sochineniya Yu. F. Samarina*, v (1880), 4-8).

to the social contract theory of obligation, in economics to *laissez-faire* capitalism. The peasant commune embodied the Russian virtue of collective living, which implied the self-abnegation of the individual and a realization of personality through the community.[1] Above all, its existence seemed to afford the proof that Russia could follow her own path of social development, and was not destined, as the westerners — and indeed the early Slavophils themselves — believed, to advance through imitation of western models. The peasant commune, which for Haxthausen was the distinctively Russian bulwark against revolution, became for the Slavophils the distinctively Russian form of a future socialist order, the pledge of a specifically Russian socialism.[2]

The assertion of the peculiar prerogatives and destinies of the Russian nation, which lay at the root of the Slavophil movement, made its political position ambivalent.[3] In the hands of Nicholas I and Uvarov, Russian nationalism could be used to confound the westerners and to stifle the cause of political liberty and even of those reforms which the Slavophils themselves desired. In the hands of the Slavophils, Russian nationalism could be invoked not only against the westerners, but also against the autocracy. If the westerners stood condemned for attempting to import foreign ideas and practices, and to mould Russian national life on western models, the same taint rested on a dynasty descended from Peter the Great, the imitator of the west and perverter of the Russian tradition, who had even abandoned the Russian capital, Moscow, for a new western capital called after his name. It

---

[1] This was the theme of a famous article by Samarin in the *Moskvityanin* of 1847, written in reply to Kavelin's article already quoted (*Sochineniya Yu. F. Samarina*, i (1877), 28-105).

[2] Herzen had taken this point as early as 1851 : 'Is not socialism, which divides Europe so decisively, so profoundly, into two camps, accepted by the Slavophils as by us ? It is the bridge across which we can join hands' (*Polnoe Sobranie Sochinenii i Pisem A. I. Gertsena*, ed. Lemke, vi. 285).

[3] 'For the Slavophils', as Herzen afterwards said, 'good relations with the Government were a misfortune rather than a desired fact' (*ibid.* 278); C. Quénet, *Tchaadaev et les Lettres philosophiques* (1931), p. 408, distinguishes between the 'dynamic *narodnost*' of the Slavophils and the 'static *narodnost*' of Uvarov.

'Russia and Europe' as a Theme of Russian History

was a dynasty wholly German in blood, which used French rather than Russian as the language of its court and preferred Germans to Russians in its administrative posts.[1] It, too, stood condemned for seeking to impose a rational western routine on the mystical Orthodox harmonies of Russian society. The Slavophil attitude to the State was curiously and characteristically ambivalent. Exalting the peasant commune as the ancient and authentically Russian unit of society, the Slavophils condemned not only the Romanov State, but any State whatever. 'The State as a principle', wrote Konstantin Aksakov, 'is evil. . . . The lie resides not in this or that State, but in the State itself as an idea, a principle.' Yet, though anarchist strains can be detected in the Slavophil creed, the Slavophils were, in practice, the reverse of anarchists. Moral condemnation of the State as evil was not incompatible with political acceptance of the State as a necessary evil. Aksakov himself arrived at an unqualified justification of autocracy, an explicit contrast between 'powerless people' and the 'all-powerful Government':

> The Russian people is not a State people, that is to say, it does not strive for State power . . .
> The peculiarity of the Russian people is that it is an unpolitical people, that it seeks no share in the Government, and does not wish to limit governmental power by any kind of conditions ; in brief, it contains no political element, and therefore does not hold within itself even the germ of revolution or of a constitutional system. . . .

[1] The Russians who had protested against Anna's horde of German advisers (the 'bironovshchina') were the forerunners of the Slavophils. Herzen has a well-known passage on this 'instinctive' Slavophilism as a factor in Russian history : 'Slavism or Russianism — not as theory or doctrine, but as wounded national feeling, as dark recollection and healthy instinct, as opposition against exclusively foreign influence — has existed since the time when Peter I shaved the first beard. . . . It appears with the party of the Dolgorukovs under Peter II, as hatred of the Germans under Biron, it was embodied in Catherine under Peter III, and in Elizabeth who supported herself on the then Slavophils in order to obtain the throne. All the dissenters are Slavophils. The whole white and black priesthood are Slavophils. The soldiers who demanded the dismissal of Barclay de Tolly because of his German name were the predecessors of Khomyakov and his friends' (*Polnoe Sobranie Sochinenii i Pisem A. I. Gertsena*, ed. Lemke, xiii. 122). Herzen, like the Slavophils, attacked Nicholas I as one of those 'Germans who want to russify themselves' (*ibid.* x. 90).

The Russian people, not having in itself a political element, has separated the State from itself and does not wish to exercise State power. Not wishing to exercise State power, the people reserves for the Government unlimited State power. In exchange for this the people reserves for itself moral liberty, liberty of life and spirit. . . .

To the Government the right of action and therefore of law; to the people the right of opinion and therefore of speech.[1]

Though this position was not reached in the early stages of the Slavophil movement, a profound gulf separated the basically anti-political attitude of the Slavophils from the zeal for political reform displayed by the westerners.

Into this fanciful amalgam of romanticism, nationalism and obscurantism the Slavophils introduced one original and fruitful *motif*. The contrast between a corrupt and self-indulgent ruling class contaminated by contact with the west and the Russian people living its traditional life in undefiled Slav purity was a constant Slavophil theme. Konstantin Aksakov denounced the ruling class, society, under the title of 'the public' (he deliberately chose a foreign word): 'the public is a purely western phenomenon . . . and constitutes our perpetual link with the west'. But this contrast led the Slavophils, almost unwittingly, to the dim realization of an immense social problem.

The public speaks French, the people speaks Russian. The public follows Paris fashions, the people has its Russian customs. The public . . . eats meat, the people fasts. The public sleeps, the people has long ago risen and is at work. The public despises the people; the people forgives the public. The public is only 150 years old; you cannot count the age of the people. The public is transient; the people eternal.[2]

The formula is naïve and literary. The condition of the Russian people was still a subject for sentimental description

[1] *Rus*, 1881, No. 28, 12-13, quoted in *Sobranie Sochinenii V. S. Solov'eva* (n.d.), v. 200-3. Dmitri Khomyakov wrote that in order to have the liberty to live its interior life in peace, the people had unloaded on the monarch chosen by it the burden of the external organization of the State; in Russia the rôle of authority is 'to carry the burden of the people' (quoted in A. Gratieux, *A. S. Khomyakov*, ii. 185).

[2] K. Aksakov quoted in L. Brodsky, *Rannie Slavofily* (1910), pp. 121-2.

rather than for remedial action. But, while the early Liberals and Radicals — the so-called 'men of the 'forties' — were busy canvassing the empty prospects of constitutional democracy, the Slavophils reached down, however tentatively, to the nerve-centre of the Russian question, the destiny of the Russian peasant, and were the first representatives of that curious but important phenomenon of the latter half of the century — the 'conscience-stricken gentry'. As early as 1854 Pogodin, an official historian much influenced by the Slavophils, warned the authorities where the real danger lay. There was nothing to be feared, he wrote, from a Russian Mirabeau or a Russian Mazzini; but Stenka Razin or Emelyan Pugachev had only to call, and the people would follow.[1] Two years later, a Russian convert to Catholicism denounced Slavophilism as 'la formule russe de l'idée révolutionnaire'.[2]

.   .   .   .   .

The events of 1848 in Europe had the effect of narrowing the gap between westerners and Slavophils: and it was the former rather than the latter who gave ground. The westerners, however firmly they preached the need to follow western models, were never impervious to the idea of a peculiar Russian national mission. Already in 1837 Chaadaev in his *Apologia of a Madman*, which was the reply to his condemnation, had reached a conclusion diverging widely from that of his peccant 'letter':

If we have arrived after the others, it is in order to do better than the others, in order not to fall into their faults, their errors, their superstitions. It would, in my opinion, be a strange misunderstanding of the rôle which has fallen to our lot to reduce us to a clumsy repetition of the whole long series of follies committed by nations less favoured than we are, to a recapitulation of all the calamities undergone by them. . . . Still more: I have the intimate conviction that we are called on to resolve the greater part of the problems of the social order, to bring to fruition the greater part of the ideas which have arisen in the old societies, to pronounce

[1] Quoted in K. Stahlin, *Geschichte Russlands*, iv (1939), 43-4.
[2] I. S. Gagarin, *La Russie sera-t-elle Catholique?* (1856).

judgment on the gravest questions which preoccupy the human race. I have often said it, and I like to repeat it : we have somehow been constituted by the very nature of things as a veritable jury for many causes which are being pleaded before the great tribunals of the human spirit and human society.[1]

Belinsky, in spite of drastic changes in his attitude to philosophy and politics, retained throughout his life (he died prematurely in 1848) an unshaken faith in the west. Yet he too, like the Slavophils, eagerly asserted the claim of a Russian universal mission to mankind. 'Every nation has in it something whole, peculiar, particular, individual', he wrote in an article of 1838 on Fonvizin, and went on :

It does not become us to be Germans any more than Frenchmen, since we have our own national life, a deep, powerful, original life ; the destiny of Russia is to receive in herself all the elements of the life, not only of Europe, but of the world. . . . We must not and cannot be Englishmen, or Frenchmen or Germans, because we must be Russians. But we shall take as our own everything that forms the exclusive characteristic of the life of every European nation, and we shall take it not as an exclusive characteristic, but as an element in the fulfilment of our life, the exclusive characteristic of which must be many-sidedness, not an abstract many-sidedness, but a living concrete many-sidedness, having its own national physiognomy and national character.

And in the famous article on the battle of Borodino a year later he declared that 'the man for whom *ubi bene, ibi patria*, is an immoral and soulless creature unworthy to be called by the sacred name of man'.

Other westerners were at this time more cautious, or more absorbed in hopes of salvation from the west. But when in 1848, in Herzen's words, 'the February revolution came and shuffled all the cards in Europe', disillusionment spread rapidly : the westerners 'lost all their possessions in the promised land'.[2] Herzen was the most conspicuous of those

[1] *Sochineniya i Pis'ma P. Ya. Chaadaeva*, ed. Gershenzon, i (1913), 230-1 ; that these observations cannot be read as a mere official apology, but represent a real evolution in Chaadaev's opinions, has been shown by C. Quénet, *Tchaadaev et les Lettres philosophiques* (1931), pp. 263-83.

[2] *Polnoe Sobranie Sochinenii i Pisem A. I. Gertsena*, ed. Lemke, x. 97.

'Russia and Europe' as a Theme of Russian History

westerners who, disappointed in the west, renewed their faith in Russia in terms scarcely distinguishable from those used by the Slavophils. Herzen proclaimed the peculiar virtues of the Russian peasant commune, and, in his open *Letter to Michelet*, declared that in Russia the future belonged to the peasant just as in western Europe it belonged to the factory worker.[1] Bakunin, after experiences of 1848 in several European countries, staked all his hopes for the future on the revolutionary aptitudes of the Slav, and especially the Russian, peasant. Turgenev, almost alone, remained an unrepentant and uncompromising westerner; but, when he wrote that 'we Russians belong by language and species to the European family, *genus Europaeum*, and must therefore by the unchangeable laws of physiology travel along the same road', Herzen coolly rejoined that 'Cain and Abel were brothers, but had very different careers'.[2] Once, however, it was admitted that Russia need not travel the same road of progress already pioneered by the western nations, and had a peculiar destiny of her own, outstanding differences with the Slavophils melted away. When Konstantin Aksakov died in 1861, Herzen in *The Bell* seized the occasion for an eloquent eulogy of him and Khomyakov — 'opponents who were nearer to us than many friends'— and reflected how, 'like Janus or the two-headed eagle, we faced different ways while *our heart beat as one*'. It was the final burying of 'a family quarrel of fifteen years ago'.[3]

As had happened before in Russian history, and as was to happen again, the impact of the west had set in motion processes which, before they could fructify, had to be transformed and reabsorbed into the Russian environment and the Russian tradition.

· · · · ·

Reform came, when it came, not from the ineffectual efforts of westerners or Slavophils, but in accordance with the recurrent pattern of Russian history, from a crisis of

---

[1] *Ibid.* vi. 293-7, 434-56. [2] *Ibid.* xv. 302-3. [3] *Ibid.* xi. 11-12.

military defeat by the superior forces of western Europe. Nicholas I died while the Crimean War was being ignominiously lost. Both westerners and Slavophils welcomed the result as a salutary lesson — the first instance in Russian history of revolutionary defeatism;[1] and, with Alexander II on the throne, the cry went up once more to overcome the clogging backwardness of Russian administration, to modernize the structure of Russia, to 'catch up with' the west in order to make Russia a match for the west. For the wonderful five years which followed Alexander II's accession every one seemed in agreement. The plan to modernize Russia's economic and political organization on western lines, culminating in the emancipation of the serfs, was hailed by the autocracy as a 'revolution from above' in the grand manner of Peter the Great, though a new note in Russian history was struck by Alexander's admission that the revolution from above had been necessary to forestall a revolution from below. It was greeted by the surviving westerners as a belated but necessary step on the way to representative government and capitalism: backward Russia was advancing along the welltried western path. It was welcomed by the Slavophils, who contrived to see in it a tribute to the transcendent qualities of the Russian *mir* and a return to simpler forms of Slav society which had been submerged for two centuries beneath an alien despotism. In essence, Alexander's 'revolution from above' was Russia's first step — corresponding to the step which England had taken in 1649, France in 1789 and Ger-

[1] The argument that defeat in war was an asset to Russia because it hastened internal change, which played so conspicuous a part in Bolshevik propaganda in the first World War, seems to have been first heard at this time. 'The purpose of the war was to damage Russia,' wrote Herzen, 'but it has brought her only benefit' (*Polnoe Sobranie Sochinenii i Pisem A. I. Gertsena*, ed. Lemke, x. 3). What is more surprising is that the Slavophils took the same line. 'This is the way it should have been — it was necessary for the Russian Government to be shown up and exposed to ridicule', wrote Ivan Aksakov in an unpublished letter of 25 Jan. 1856 (quoted in A. A. Plotkin, *Pisarev i Literaturno-Obshchestvennoe Dvizhenie Shestidesyatykh Godov* (1945), p. 19); and the defeats in the Crimea 'did not distress us unduly since we felt that the defeats were more bearable and even more beneficial than the situation in which we had been' (*Zapiski A. I. Kosheleva* (Berlin 1884), p. 82).

'Russia and Europe' as a Theme of Russian History

many after 1848 — in what Marx called the bourgeois revolution, the revolution which overthrew the feudal order and was to pave the way to modern capitalism and modern democracy.

The emancipation of the serfs seemed at the outset to have achieved little, since the great land-owners were able to stultify positive efforts to improve the lot of those whom the decree emancipated. But it broke down many barriers, created new interests and new alignments, and opened a new epoch. After 1861, though the old names of westerners and Slavophils remained in use, they no longer had the same — or, indeed, any precise — meaning. Reaction followed the initial liberalizing reforms of Alexander II. But the struggle between reform and reaction in the 1860s could not, any more than the struggle under Nicholas I, be explained in terms of a conflict between western and national strains of thought. In effect both western and Slavophil camps split into conservative and radical movements. Among the westerners, the split was between the 'fathers' and the 'sons', between the 'men of the 'forties', men like Herzen and Turgenev, who remained faithful to the watchwords of political liberty and reform, and the 'men of the 'sixties', radicals or nihilists like Chernyshevsky and Pisarev, who raised the banner of socialism and revolution. Among the Slavophils, the sentiment of Russian national pride and of the civilizing mission of the Slav race found crude and vigorous expression in a campaign for Russian expansion in central Asia and in south-eastern Europe — the Russian counterpart of the growing imperialist fervour of western Europe; and the political panslavism of the 'sixties and 'seventies, a thoroughly conservative and chauvinist doctrine, ousted the mild and predominantly cultural Slavophilism of the 1840s.[1] But the same period saw the birth of the *narodnik* movement, which was, in sub-

---

[1] This second wave of Slavophilism may be said to have begun with the creation in 1856 of the journal *Russkaya Beseda*, in which Koshelev, Ivan Aksakov and Belyaev were the principal collaborators. It reached its high-water mark, after the deaths of Kireevsky (1856), Khomyakov (1860) and

stance though not in name, a Slavophil movement of the Left, borrowing from the older generation of Slavophils its idealization of the Russian peasant, its denunciation of an alien and oppressive autocracy, and its conscience-stricken awareness of the profound rift in the fabric of Russian society, so that the disputes of the 1830s and 1840s between westerners and Slavophils were reproduced in the quarrels of the 1860s and 1870s between westernizing Radicals and *narodniks*. If Russian messianism, in the hands of the panslav school, issued in crude forms of Russian chauvinism, it was always deeply penetrated by a consciousness of Russian backwardness and poverty, of the bleakness of the Russian land and the 'darkness' of the Russian people. The despised and rejected would put down the mighty from their seat; the humble and meek would inherit the world. The sense of a Russian national mission was never wholly divorced from the notion of a national purification and regeneration which would enable Russia to purify and regenerate the decaying west. Thus, Russian messianism, like the Slavophilism out of which it had sprung, could accommodate itself without much difficulty to revolutionary ambitions, and inspired Bakunin to see the salvation of mankind in the destructive, yet creative, turbulence of the Russian peasant. Even political panslavism had

Konstantin Aksakov (1861), with the Slav congress held in Moscow in 1867. But the Slav committee set up by this congress proved too moderate for the panslav chauvinism of the next decade, and it was dissolved in 1877. The panslav movement in its latest and most extreme form was represented by Danilevsky's *Russia and Europe* (1871) and Dostoevsky's *Journal of a Writer* (1876–7). Danilevsky has become best known in recent years as a precursor of Spengler; but, as R. MacMaster has shown in *Journal of Modern History*, xxvi, No. 2 (June 1954), pp. 154-61, the resemblance between them stops short at a crucial point. For Spengler, each cultural-historical type of civilization is self-contained and has its own incommunicable values : one type makes no contribution to any other, and there is no sense in which one is higher or lower than another. For Danilevsky, the different cultural-historical types have all made their contribution to a common pool of experience ; what distinguishes him from Herbert Spencer and the political Darwinists of the west is that, for him, it is the higher Slav, not the lower 'Germano-Roman' type, which is destined to sum up in itself and transcend the contributions of previous types. Slav nationalism masquerading as universalism brings Danilevsky into line with the other late panslav theorists. But he was never a popular writer, and seems to have had little influence.

'Russia and Europe' as a Theme of Russian History

its revolutionary side. For the same panslavs who proclaimed Russia's national mission to conquer and civilize also called loudly for a revolt to liberate the oppressed Slav peoples; and Bakunin found no difficulty in venting his hatred of Germany and of the Habsburg empire in a creed of revolutionary panslavism.[1] In the 1870s, when western tendencies in Russian thought were once more in eclipse, official chauvinistic panslavism and revolutionary *narodnik* terrorism, both authentic offspring, legitimate or illegitimate, of the original Slavophil movement, seemed to divide the Russian stage between them.

This time, however, the check once more administered, both from the Right and from the Left, to the encroachment of western ideas and institutions proved of short duration. Before the end of the century both panslavism and nihilism were in eclipse, and Russia was once more subject to predominant western influences. The emancipation of the serfs, by breaking the legal fetters which riveted the peasant to the land, created the raw material of an industrial proletariat and made possible the development in Russia of a 'free' labour market, the essential condition of the advent of industrial capitalism. In other words, it played the same rôle in Russian history as the enclosures had played in the early stages of the industrialization of Great Britain. The process advanced slowly in face of inertia and obstruction.[2] But at the beginning of the

---

[1] These tendencies did not escape notice in Germany. In Nov. 1875 Wilhelm I wrote to Alexander II of Russia: 'I fear the nihilist party which, in conjunction with the Slavophils, holds a hostile language towards foreign countries in order to profit by any awkward conflict for their subversive plans' (*Die grosse Politik der europäischen Kabinette, 1871–1914*, iii (1926), 127). Bismarck, in a letter of 10 Sept. 1879 to the king of Bavaria, spoke of 'the in part militarist, in part revolutionary, tendencies of panslavism' (Bismarck, *Gedanken und Erinnerungen* (1913), ii. 266).

[2] The original Slavophils had eulogized rural handicrafts as specifically Russian, but had not protested against the incipient growth of factory industry in the 1840s (M. Tugan-Baranovsky, *Russkaya Fabrika v Proshlom i Nastoyashchem* (3rd ed., 1922), pp. 219-21). The new Slavophils of the 1860s opposed industrial development in all forms: their text-book was A. K. Korsak, *O Formakh Promyshlennosti . . . v Zapadnoi Evrope i Rossii* (1861), which argued that Peter the Great had set Russia on a fatal path by introducing large-scale industry.

1890s, the pressure of a fresh military threat from the west, when Germany failed to renew her treaty with Russia and Russia turned to France for reinsurance, at length forced the pace. The Franco-Russian alliance stimulated an abundant flow of capital investment to Russia for the purpose of building up Russia's industrial and military strength. Under these impulses Russian industry, and especially heavy industry, developed in the twenty years before 1914 at an astonishingly rapid rate. And this development brought about the same division between westerners and Slavophils (though they were no longer called by these names) which had marked the great controversies of the 1840s and 1860s. On the Right, Witte, strong in the support of western finance and closely following western models, was confronted by the stubborn resistance of the land-owing interests, which eventually forced his resignation, though not in time to arrest the process of industrialization. On the Left, the same split occurred between the Marxist founders of the Russian Social Democratic Party, whose scheme of bourgeois and proletarian revolutions required Russia to tread the western path, and the Social Revolutionary heirs of the *narodniks*, who placed their faith in the Russian peasant as the begetter of a specifically and distinctively Russian revolution. Thus Lenin logically found himself in the strange situation of regarding Witte, the champion of the industrialists, and even Stolypin — who, after the downfall of Witte, made a desperate bid to modernize agriculture by developing small-scale peasant capitalism in the countryside — as progressive phenomena. The struggle between westerners and Slavophils, between acceptance of western models and influences and the assertion of a particular national tradition, continued in new forms and under new names, though it had ceased altogether to correspond to the struggle between Left and Right.

The process of industrialization in Russia at the end of the nineteenth century exhibited many of the characteristic features of Russian development in the period after Peter the Great. First of all, Russian heavy industry, almost from the moment of its birth, was geared to the production of 'war potential', including railway construction, rather than to the needs of a consumer market; in a population consisting largely of peasants, who were self-sufficient at a low subsistence level, a large-scale consumer market could not come into existence. Industry was 'planned' in the sense that it depended primarily on Government orders, not on spontaneous market demand, and was financed by loans accorded for political reasons rather than for the traditional 'capitalist' motive of earning commercial profits; in these respects it anticipated much that was to happen under the Five Year Plans thirty years later. Secondly, the tardy arrival of industrialization in Russia meant that it skipped over many of the earlier stages through which the much slower growth of industrialization had passed in western Europe — the gradual transformation from the single-handed craftsman to the small workshop, and from the first primitive factory to the giant agglomeration employing hundreds and thousands of workmen. Russian industry, the youngest in Europe and in other respects the most backward, was the most advanced in respect of the concentration of production in large-scale units.

Thus, the hot-house development of Russian industry, in its haste to catch up the time-lag by an intensive borrowing from western models, once more skipped the gradual, formative stage of adolescence, and carried it at one step from infancy to adult stature. In so doing, it created a social structure sharply differentiated from that of the older industrial communities of western Europe, so that western influence, and even conscious imitation of western models, failed to reproduce in Russia the characteristic western pattern. The rapidity and belatedness of Russian industrial development shaped the human factor on both sides of industry on distinctive lines of its own. In the west, something of the spirit of the earlier *entrepreneur*, attentive to the changing conditions of the market and in close personal contact with his workers, survived even in the manager of modern industry; in Russia, the industrial manager was from the first the administrator, the organizer, the bureaucrat. In the west, the industrial worker contrived to retain, even in the age of mass production, something of the personal skills and independent spirit of the artisan. In Russia, the vast majority of the new generation of industrial workers were still peasants in factory clothes. A 'grey mass' of peasants was transformed overnight into a 'grey mass' of factory workers. But to drive the peasant into the factories and force on him the rigours of factory routine required — before, as after, the revolution of 1917 — a harsh and relentless discipline, which shaped relations between industrial management and the industrial worker on lines of a sharply defined class hostility. Weak and backward as it was, the Russian proletariat provided a more fertile soil than the advanced proletariats of the west for the proletarian revolution. What had begun in the traditional Russian fashion as a 'revolution from above' was for the first time creating some of the conditions for a 'revolution from below'. Once again, a process set in motion under western influence and in imitation of the west had developed a peculiar national character of its own.

The political history of Russia in the latter half of the nineteenth century reflected its economic foundations. Just as the emancipation of the serfs was a belated attempt to modernize the Russian economy on western lines, so the political reforms which accompanied it were an attempt to bring an obsolete system of government up to date by borrowing and adapting western Liberal and democratic institutions. The courts were reformed, rudimentary social services established and an enlightened — though scarcely democratic — machinery of local self-government grafted on to the rigid, age-old trunk of autocratic power. But, just as the Russian economy developed in a forcing-house at a temperature maintained by pressures from without, so the political reforms grew not from the strength of their own indigenous roots, but under alien impulses from western Europe; and the product was something which, though ostensibly imitated from the west, had a national character all its own. The long-standing failure to develop an active bourgeoisie and independent urban communities could not be repaired in a moment, and had far-reaching consequences. Like German liberalism in 1848, Russian liberalism lacked the solid social basis which western liberalism found in an energetic and prosperous class of manufacturers and merchants.[1] The Russian Liberal was an isolated intellectual, the conscious imitator of a western model. Personally sincere, he was without political weight; in the time of crisis he could not play the rôle of his western counterpart. From the Russian political equation, as from the economic equation, the middle term was absent. The Russian intelligentsia was no substitute for the western middle class. Institutions and social groups, deriving directly from imitation of western models, were quickly transformed in Russian conditions into something alien to the west and distinctively national.

. . . . .

The history of the Bolshevik revolution fitted perfectly into this complicated national pattern. No previous innovator in Russian history had drawn so frankly and unreservedly as Lenin on the experience and example of the west, or had spoken in terms of such open contempt of Russia's native backwardness. The doctrine that the Russian revolution was merely the forerunner of the much more important German, European and eventually world-wide proletarian revolution, and was indeed dependent on such a revolution for its own survival, was an extreme expression of the traditional belief of Russian reformers in the backwardness of Russia and in the need to imitate, and learn from, the west. The Russian national tradition was weighed and found wanting in almost every field. The Russian past was condemned root

[1] Trotsky had written in 1901 : 'Pure liberalism with all its Manchester symbols of faith faded in our country before it blossomed : it did not find any social soil in which to grow. Manchester ideas could be imported, . . . but the social environment which produced those ideas could not be imported' (L. Trotsky, *Sochineniya*, xx. 85-6). Ten years later he wrote of the 'bourgeoisification' and 'Europeanization' of the Russian intelligentsia, meaning by this that it had lost its intellectual independence and become the tool of the ruling class (*ibid*. xx. 351-2).

and branch. The very name of Russia disappeared from the official title of the new authority, which with presumptuous universality described itself simply as a 'workers' and peasants' Government'. If the temporary headquarters of the proletarian world revolution had been set up in Russia, this was no more than an unexpected and rather disconcerting accident. Yet within a few years, innovation undertaken in time of emergency in conscious imitation of the west was reabsorbed into a national setting, and took on a specifically national colour. In this sense, 'socialism in one country' was a repetition of what had happened countless times before in Russian history.

Premonitory symptoms of this development might have been detected, even before the revolution, in the revolutionary movement itself. Marxism came to Russia, not merely as a western doctrine, but as a doctrine requiring the development of Russia on capitalist lines in direct and conscious imitation of the west;[1] only when Russia had followed the west on the path of industrialization could she fulfil her Marxist destiny. 'Let us recognize our uncultured condition, and go to school to the capitalists', was the conclusion of a famous article by Struve, the founder of 'legal Marxism'. In the 1890s Russian Marxists found themselves in the anomalous position of sharing and applauding the aims of Witte, the arch-capitalist and protagonist of the policy of industrialization. The first organized Russian Marxist group had been founded in the 1880s by Russian *émigrés* in western Europe. The Russian Social Democratic Workers' Party, which was created at the turn of the century, borrowed, in token of its creed and ambitions, the name of the German Social Democratic Workers' Party, which it did not cease to regard as its model and mentor. Nothing in Russian history seemed so unimpeachably and unreservedly western, so free of any national taint, as the Russian Marxist movement.

[1] For the not very successful efforts of some early Russian Marxists, and of Marx himself, to evade this requirement, see E. H. Carr, *The Bolshevik Revolution, 1917–1923*, ii. 388–93.

'Russia and Europe' as a Theme of Russian History

Yet contrary symptoms were not slow to develop. Lenin was early alive to the impracticability of simply reproducing western models on Russian soil.

> A movement beginning in a young country [he wrote in 1902 in *What is to be done?*] can be successful only if it transforms the experience of other countries. And for such transformation it is not enough merely to be acquainted with this experience and to copy out the latest resolutions: one must know how to adopt a critical attitude to this experience and test it independently.[1]

Scarcely had the Russian Social Democratic Workers' Party begun to organize itself when, at the congress of 1903, the split occurred between Bolsheviks and Mensheviks. The apparently trivial differences proved significant, the split deep and lasting. Henceforth Russian Marxists were divided on the issue whether their party should stick to its western model or adapt itself to specifically Russian conditions, whether it should organize itself as a broad party of opinion or equip itself for the conspiratorial activities which were the only means of action open to the Left in Russia. Unconsciously, but from the very first moment, the Mensheviks were the westerners in the party, the Bolsheviks the easterners.[2] And the issue quickly broadened out into fundamental questions of Marxist doctrine. The Bolsheviks, as practical revolutionaries, were brought face to face with the dilemma of the Russian peasant, who constituted more than 80 per cent of the population of Russia. Lenin understood that no Russian revolution could be made except in a broad-based alliance with the Russian peasantry, whose revolutionary potentialities were amply attested in Russian history; and, while he firmly

---

[1] Lenin, *Sochineniya* (2nd ed.), iv. 380.
[2] The preponderance of Jews, which was marked throughout the party, was particularly great among leading Mensheviks, almost all of whom were Jews: Stalin early remarked that the Russian element in the party was Bolshevik (*Sochineniya*, ii. 50-1). Of the Russian left-wing groups, the 'economists' were the counterpart of the German 'revisionists', the Mensheviks of the western Social Democrats; only the Bolsheviks, as the experience of Zimmerwald showed, had no western counterpart (except, with reservations, the tiny group of German Spartakists, who were a special product of the war, and, incidentally, owed their ideological programme to Polish-Lithuanian leadership).

rejected the *narodnik* hypothesis with which Marx had toyed in the 1880s, he postulated as the culminating point of the first phase of the Russian revolution a 'democratic dictatorship of workers and peasants'. Finally, in 1917, by ostentatiously borrowing the *narodnik* agrarian programme of the Social Revolutionaries and embodying it in the land decree, Lenin firmly anchored the Bolshevik revolution to the Russian national tradition of peasant land-hunger and peasant revolt. Already in 1917 Bolshevism was Marxism applied to Russian conditions and interpreted in the light of them.

The incorporation of this 'eastern' element in the amalgam of Bolshevism had not escaped the attention of critics. As early as 1904 the keen-eyed Trotsky, then in his Menshevik period, had noted that the main Bolshevik strongholds in Russia, outside the two capitals, were the factories in the Urals, and taunted the Bolsheviks with striving to 'preserve their social-democratic Asia'.[1] A Menshevik journal which appeared spasmodically in Petersburg after the 1905 revolution dubbed the Bolsheviks 'Slavophilizing Marxists'.[2] Plekhanov, as well as the Mensheviks, denounced Lenin's attitude towards the peasantry as non-Marxist and a revival of *narodnik* heresies.[3] In 1912 the Menshevik Axelrod [4] was preaching the need 'to Europeanize, *i.e.* radically to change, the character of Russian Social Democracy, . . . and to organize it on the same principles on which the party structure of European Social Democracy rests'; and Lenin angrily retorted that 'the notorious "Europeanization" about which Dan and Martov and Trotsky and Levitsky and all the liquidators talk in season and out of season' was 'one of the chief points of their opportunism'. How was the character of *any* Social Democracy, how were '*radical* changes' in it, to be determined? Clearly, argued Lenin, in terms of 'the

[1] N. Trotsky, *Nashi Politicheskie Zadachi* (1904), p. 69.
[2] *Sotsial-Demokrat* (Petersburg), No. 2, 6 Oct. 1906, p. 5.
[3] *Chetvertyi (Ob"edinitel'nyi) S"ezd RSDRP* (1934), pp. 133-4.
[4] In 1896 Plekhanov had written to Axelrod: 'You are first and foremost a European, and that is someone whom it is important to have in any Russian party' (*Perepiska G. V. Plekhanova i P. B. Aksel'roda* (1925), i. 138) — a remark equally revealing for both.

'Russia and Europe' as a Theme of Russian History

general economic and political conditions of the country in question'. Axelrod was like 'a naked savage who puts on a top-hat and imagines himself for that reason a European'.[1] Trotsky retaliated in similar style in 1916 when, in reviewing the collection of articles by Lenin and Zinoviev on *Socialism and the War*, he dubbed the authors 'narodniks from Chelyabinsk'.[2] When Lenin proclaimed the ambition of the Bolsheviks to seize power from the hands of the Provisional Government, it was a common charge that he was acting as a disciple of Bakunin, not of Marx; and no less an opponent than Milyukov compared him with the Slavophils: 'Gentleman Lenin merely repeats gentleman Kireevsky or Khomyakov when he asserts that from Russia will come the new word which will resuscitate the aged west'.[3]

Such criticisms left Lenin unmoved. He felt himself heart and soul a westerner. In his conception of the party, he could appeal to an older western tradition — the tradition of the Jacobins; he had proudly claimed the name when it was first hurled at him by Trotsky as a term of abuse.[4] In his reliance on Marxism, he appealed more often to the Marx of the period before 1848, to Marx the active propagandist of revolution, than to the later Marx, the student of the contradictions and inevitable downfall of capitalism. It was the earlier Marx who had lived and worked in conditions most nearly comparable to those now confronting Lenin; and the episode of the Paris Commune showed that, even much later, he had abated nothing of his enthusiasm for the practice of revolution. That the Marxism of the Bolsheviks was as authentic, and therefore as 'western', as the Marxism of the

---

[1] Lenin, *Sochineniya* (2nd ed.), xvi. 41-2.

[2] Quoted in G. Zinoviev, *Litsom k Derevne* (1925), p. 24 : I have not been able to trace the original. Zinoviev, as late as 1925 (*ibid.* p. 26) retorted that the party would 'not concede an inch to "European" pseudo-Marxism dressed up in a "Left" Trotskyist guise'.

[3] Quoted in Bunyan and Fisher, *The Bolshevik Revolution, 1917–1918* (Stanford, 1934), p. 42.

[4] See E. H. Carr, *The Bolshevik Revolution, 1917–1923*, i. 33, 35 ; Plekhanov also accepted the imputation of 'Jacobinism', contrasting this favourably with Axelrod's humanitarian liberalism (*Perepiska G. V. Plekhanova i P. B. Aksel'roda* (1925), i. 44, 192 ; ii. 118).

Mensheviks was a perfectly tenable view. But the discrepancies between them were patent. Of the two strands which went to make the composite fabric of Marxist teaching, the Bolsheviks represented primarily the revolutionary, voluntarist element,[1] the Mensheviks the evolutionary, determinist element. The Bolsheviks spoke of the need to act in order to change the world, the Mensheviks of the need to study the forces which were changing it and to conform their action to these forces. Finally the Bolsheviks put their faith in a conscious minority which would lead the masses and galvanize them into action; the Mensheviks more cautiously awaited the moment when the hidden forces of change would ripen and penetrate the consciousness of the masses, this last divergence being directly reflected in their views of party organization. On all these issues the views of the Mensheviks rather than those of the Bolsheviks coincided far more closely with the prevailing attitude of western Marxists; and this alone sufficed to give Bolshevism, whatever the sources of its inspiration, a certain Russian, or non-western, colour. The belief in the need for a group of highly conscious and highly organized professional revolutionaries to lead the unconscious and 'spontaneous' action of the mass of the workers was a far more accurate response to Russian than to western conditions. On a longer view, it might also be said to have equipped the Bolsheviks to cope, far more effectively than the Mensheviks, with the irrational tendencies permeating modern mass society.

.   .   .   .   .

The traditions of the Russian past created a soil in which Bolshevism could easily develop the latent anti-western elements in its composition, and merge its Marxist messianism in an older Russian messianism. 'History', said Sokolnikov a few weeks after the revolution, 'clearly shows that the salt

---

[1] Plekhanov in 1905 accused the Bolsheviks of introducing into Marxism the voluntarism of Mach and the idealists (Lenin, *Sochineniya* (2nd ed.), vii, 267, note 121).

'Russia and Europe' as a Theme of Russian History

of the earth is moving gradually eastwards. In the eighteenth century France was the salt of the earth, in the nineteenth century Germany: now it is Russia.'[1] But the shift entailed the introduction of specifically Russian elements. The time-honoured Russian pattern of spasmodic advance, hastening to catch up with the west and, in the process, skipping over intermediate stages through which western progress had passed, was repeated in the preparations for the Russian revolution. Trotsky's theory of 'permanent revolution' was devised to meet the dilemma arising from specifically Russian conditions — the absence in Russia of a powerful bourgeoisie capable of realizing the bourgeois revolution which was a necessary stage in western conceptions of Marxist development; and Lenin, while formally rejecting the theory, adopted in 1917 what was virtually the same expedient of making the Bolshevik seizure of power do simultaneous duty as the last act of the bourgeois revolution and the first of the socialist revolution. Russian history had experienced one more violent and abrupt transition from 'childhood' to 'manhood'.[2] Even the initial appeal of the 'workers' and peasants' Government' to the world for peace and brotherhood among the nations might have seemed to reflect the long-standing claim of the Russian people to fulfil a universal, and not a purely national, rôle. As the new régime found itself isolated and driven to the wall by its enemies, domestic and foreign, and exposed to

---

[1] *Protokoly Tsentral'nogo Komiteta RSDRP* (1929), p. 206. The element of Russian messianism was, of course, not unknown to other revolutionary schools of thought. Tolstoy wrote in his diary on 29 June 1905 that 'as the French were called in 1789 to renew the world, so also are the Russians in 1905' (L. N. Tolstoy: *Polnoe Sobranie Sochinenii* (1937), 151); and Mackenzie Wallace, after reading a work of the Menshevik Dan, recorded in a manuscript note of May 1907 (preserved with his papers in the Cambridge University Library) that 'the writers of this school [the S.D.s] . . . all believe that the Great Revolution of Russia, which is to surpass in its magnificent and beneficent effects the Great Revolution of France, is already thoroughly ablaze and cannot possibly be extinguished by any human efforts, for who can oppose successfully the revolution of the elemental forces'.

[2] A writer in the *émigré* symposium *Smena Vekh* published in 1921 declared that 'Russia, in the few months of the Provisional Government, had run through all those illusions of the democratic order which it had taken Europe more than a hundred years to outlive' (*Smena Vekh* (2nd ed., Prague, 1922), p. 109).

the hazards of civil war, the old pattern of revolution from above began, imperceptibly at first, to substitute itself for the revolution from below which had carried the Bolsheviks to victory in October 1917; and the dictatorship of the proletariat fell into the mould of reforming autocracy. Finally, when peasant discontent forced the 'retreat' into NEP, another jarring, but irresistible, Russian force had imposed itself on the original Marxist conception of the revolution. The question which the Bolshevik leaders had to ask themselves in 1921 was essentially the question which had divided the westerners and the Slavophils. Would the triumph of socialism in Russia be achieved by following the western path, or by following a specifically Russian line of development? If the first answer were accepted, reliance must be placed on the development of industry and of the proletariat, if necessary, at the expense of the peasant. If the second answer were accepted, reliance must be placed on conciliating the peasant and winning his support for increased agricultural production as the pre-requisite of an advance to socialism. As always in Russian history, a clear-cut choice between the two answers was impossible. Russia could neither unconditionally pursue nor totally reject the western path. In NEP Lenin found the compromise between the two answers — the 'link' between proletariat and peasantry which would for a time make it possible to travel the two roads simultaneously. But the compromise, which was also a 'retreat', had ideological implications; and these implications also carried reflexions of the Russian past. The resistance of the Russian peasant to Marxism was the resistance of the traditional Russian way of life to western innovation.

Thus, during the first years of the régime, while the revolutionary impetus continued to predominate, familiar features of the Russian landscape and the Russian outlook slowly emerged from beneath the revolutionary flood. As the Soviet Government became more and more openly the heir of Russian State power and attracted to itself traditional feelings of Russian patriotism, it proclaimed its mission in terms which conveyed to sensitive ears unmistakable echoes of the Russian past. Moscow, the third Rome and now the centre of the Third International, was once again conscious of its mission to renew, out of the fullness of its uncorrupted youth and vigour, the decrepit and decadent west, was once again courting a hostility from the west which it attributed to the envy and malice inspired by its achievements, and was once again covering its material backwardness by boastful assertions of its superior spiritual essence. The fulfilment of the eschatological promises of Marxism was delayed, like the Second Advent, far beyond the original expectations of the faithful; and, when this delay bred the inevitable current compromises with power and expediency, the process of degeneration from the pure ideal took on specifically Russian forms in a Russian context. Primitive Christianity decked itself in the trappings of imperial Rome, communism in those of the Russian national State. Though it soon transpired that the compromise was not all on one side, the transformation was incongruous, and scandalized some believers. But, as the cause of Russia and the cause of Bolshevism began to coalesce into a single undifferentiated whole, the resulting amalgam showed clear traces of both the original components out of which it had been formed; the idiom was a blend of both elements. This process, subtle and undeclared, was well advanced when Stalin first propounded the hybrid doctrine of 'socialism in one country'.

HUGH SETON-WATSON

THE INTELLECTUALS AND REVOLUTION: SOCIAL FORCES IN EASTERN EUROPE SINCE 1848

THE events of 1848 in central Europe have been well described as The Revolution of the Intellectuals. From the brilliant work of Sir Lewis Namier which bears that title,[1] and which is mainly concerned with German, Polish and Czech political trends in the year of revolutions, two points may here be selected as of special interest. These are the distrust of Liberal intellectuals for peasant masses, and the contempt of the 'historical' nations for those which lacked, or were believed to lack, a history.[2] The two attitudes were connected, for the unhistorical nations were even more overwhelmingly composed of peasants than were the historical. The Germans despised the Danubian peoples, the Poles the Ukrainians. German and Polish intellectuals alike feared and disliked the peasants of their own nation. The Czechs held a rather special position. They were 'less historical' than Germans or Poles, but 'more historical' than the lesser nations of the Danube valley. The Czech masses were still peasants, but from their ranks business men, skilled workers and intellectuals were rapidly emerging. The Czechs challenged German supremacy, and had a certain distrustful sympathy for nations more submerged, and peasant masses more primitive, than their own.

[1] L. B. Namier, *1848: The Revolution of the Intellectuals* (1946).
[2] By these are meant primarily Ukrainians, Slovaks, Rumanians, Serbs, Croats, Slovenes and Bulgarians.

Social Forces in Eastern Europe since 1848

In the Danube valley in 1848 were already present the forces that in the following decades shaped the fate of half Europe, and in the present century have spread over most of the world. The next period saw the growth of the intelligentsia as a social and political force in its own right, among both 'historical' and 'unhistorical' nations in Eastern Europe. The interconnexion of social and national revolt, and the fusion of socialist and nationalist doctrines, both imported from western Europe and both developed into messianic dogmas, first took shape in the Danube valley, the Balkans and Russia in the late nineteenth century, but have become the outstanding features of Asian and African history in our own time.

At the beginning of the nineteenth century the social and political structure of eastern Europe was fairly simple. The masses were peasants; the dominant social class was a landowning nobility; merchants and industrial workers were unimportant elements; and political power was held by a monarch ruling through a bureaucracy. The significant differences between east European states were political rather than social. They concerned the relative power of monarch and nobility.

In Russia the monarch overshadowed his subjects. The nobility was not, as it had been in western Europe in earlier periods, an active political force. In Russia the nobility can be described, with little exaggeration, as a bureaucracy enjoying land-ownership as the reward of State service. The concessions of Peter III and Catherine II did something to increase its power, prestige and class-consciousness, but the process had not gone far by the time of Nicholas I, who successfully reversed it. In Poland before the partitions the opposite was the case: the nobility had all the power, the monarch none. After the partitions Poland, of course, shared in the development of the three conquering Powers. In the Habsburg lands the balance of power between monarchy and nobility was more uncertain, but tended to incline in favour of the monarchy. This was, however, less true of Hungary than of the Austrian lands. After 1867 the Hungarian nobility, whose social status and prestige had remained great, obtained great political power too. In the Balkans, Turkish military bureaucracy was imposed directly on the peasants, and the intermediate strata were of little if any importance.[1]

To these lands the nineteenth century brought two great explosive forces — the industrial revolution and the political ideas of eighteenth-century western Europe. These forces were imported from the west, and made their impact on societies which were culturally unprepared for them, and in which the forces through which they had operated in the west were extremely weak, if not entirely absent. There are, of course, wide variations. In Russia, Hungary, Poland, the Balkans and the South Slav provinces of Austria the business element was extremely weak, and only tiny minorities had had any contact with west European culture. In the German provinces of Austria commercial capitalism was long established, a system of schools was well developed, and the influence of secular culture was not confined to a small élite, or even to those who could read and write. The Czechs and Slovenes had to some extent shared the social and cultural development of the Austrian Germans.

The impact of these new forces on eastern Europe produced three main social consequences.

Firstly, the introduction of modern factory industry created business classes and working classes. The status and problems of the working class in Hungary, Poland and Russia at the end of the nineteenth century were very similar to those of the British working class at the beginning of the century. The rôle of the business man, however, varied considerably. In Britain, and on the whole in western Europe, private initiative and the search for private profit were the driving force behind industrial development. In Russia the driving force was State policy, and private initiative its instrument. Both Russian and foreign capitalists made profits,

[1] This is less true of the Rumanians and Greeks than of the Serbs, Bulgarians or Albanians.

but the Government closely controlled the direction of industrial growth, whose main aim was the military and imperial greatness of Russia. In Hungary the rôle of private initiative (largely Jewish or German) was greater, but State policy was a very important factor. The liberated Balkan states were at first a happy hunting-ground for foreign capitalists, in search of profits, and to some extent of strategic advantages, for their own countries. It was not until the 1930s that Balkan Governments began more seriously to consider industrial growth from the point of view of State interests. The rulers of Poland did likewise at the same time.

Secondly, throughout eastern Europe, as the business of government became more complex, the numbers and power of the bureaucracy increased. It became a social category in its own right, the real ruling class. In those countries where at mid-century large landed estates had prevailed in agriculture — Russia, Hungary, Poland, Rumania — both the economic and the political power of the land-owners declined in the last decades before 1914. Between 1877 and 1914 the amount of land belonging to noble land-owners in Russia was reduced almost by half, and most of this passed into peasant hands. Sons of land-owners went into the bureaucracy. They formed a 'middle class' in the purely economic sense, but not a 'bourgeoisie' in the social or cultural sense. This large bureaucratic class,[1] of noble origin and inspired by the ethos of the nobility, controlled Russian economic as well as political life. Both the business men and the remaining large land-owners were dependent on it. In both Hungary and Poland the same process took place from the mid-nineteenth century onwards, though it had not gone so far as in Russia by 1914.[2]

[1] I am not using the word in its Marxist sense, of a category determined by its relationship to production. Land-owners and capitalists are 'classes' to Marxists, bureaucrats are not. I am concerned with social groups which have a social and political significance of their own. It seems to me both legitimate and convenient for one who does not regard Marxist definitions as *ipso facto* valid to use the word 'class' in the present context.

[2] Poles, of course, could not obtain bureaucratic posts in Russian Poland, but they could do so in other parts of the Russian empire. In Austrian Poland they could do exactly as they liked. The mass influx of Polish gentry into bureaucratic jobs, however, came after the achievement of independence in 1918.

It reached its highest point between the World Wars. Much the same could be said of independent Rumania and of Croatia.[1] In the Balkans there was some variety. In Serbia and Bulgaria, where no native nobility existed at the time the Turks left, the ruling class was from the beginning a bureaucracy recruited from children of peasants, Orthodox priests and village tradesmen. In Greece the power of the bureaucracy, recruited in the same way, was limited by a native business class which had a very long tradition of private enterprise, and soon acquired much of the west European bourgeois ethos. Albania, a society in which tribal and feudal elements combined, remained untouched by modern influences until after the first World War.

Thirdly, there arose throughout eastern Europe another social group, with a significance and a rôle of its own, the intelligentsia. This consisted essentially of persons who had received a modern secular education, but were not Government officials.[2] It corresponded approximately to the 'free professions' in the west. It performed the same functions, but its social predicament was utterly different. The graduate of a Russian university in 1880 belonged to the culture of nineteenth-century Europe. The mass of the Russian people, however, lived in the Middle Ages. The difference between the Russian intellectual and the Russian peasant was not the same as the difference between an educated and an uneducated person in a western country. Voltaire and a French agricultural labourer, Mr. Gladstone and a British docker, lived on different cultural levels, but they belonged to the same culture.

---

[1] Children of the Croatian nobility actually had better chances in the bureaucracy under Hungary before 1914 than in Yugoslavia between the wars. In the latter State the best jobs were, on the whole, reserved for Serbs, though it is going too far to say that the Serbs had a monopoly.

[2] It is not easy to distinguish Government officials from Government employees. In Russia, for example, nearly all teachers, and all provincial and county agricultural engineers, veterinaries, statisticians, etc. — the hard core of the Russian intelligentsia — were Government employees (of ministries or *zemstvos*), but were not normally regarded as bureaucrats. It was almost inconceivable that a high official of the central Government apparatus, whatever his educational qualifications, should regard himself as a member of the intelligentsia.

Social Forces in Eastern Europe since 1848

The ideas of Voltaire, the rhetoric of Gladstone, derived — even if by tortuous routes — from the reality of France or Britain. The Russian intellectual and the Russian peasant belonged to different cultures. The ideas of the Russian intellectual did not derive from Russian conditions, but were imported prefabricated from abroad. The cultural gap between intelligentsia and masses was not equal throughout eastern Europe. In Rumania, Serbia and Bulgaria it was as wide as in Russia. In Poland and Hungary it was narrower. Yet the relationship in these two countries differed from the relationship in Russia and the Balkans in degree rather than in kind.[1] In German Austria, intelligentsia and masses belonged to the same culture, while in the Czech and Slovene lands the relationship conformed rather to the German than to the Russian pattern.

The admixture of these social groups differed in each of the chief regions of eastern Europe, but three main types of pattern can be distinguished.

In the German and Czech provinces of Austria, and to some extent in Prussian Poland, the growth of the industrial classes kept pace with that of the intelligentsia. Education also began to affect rural as well as urban populations. In short, social and cultural development closely followed that of north-west Europe earlier in the century.

Further east and south, among the historical nations the intelligentsia and the bureaucratic middle class gained greatly in numbers and influence, but the industrial classes lagged behind. The two most obvious instances are Russians and Hungarians. Lesser examples are the Poles of Galicia and the Rumanians of the Old Kingdom, while Croatia, Russian Poland and Georgia approximate to this pattern. Special problems arise in regions where the dominant social group and the masses are of different nationality, but neither of them constitutes the dominant nation in the State. The most

[1] It is dangerous to generalize about Poland owing to its division into three. The relationship in Russian Poland came nearest to the 'eastern' pattern, that in Galicia was similar to the Hungarian, while that in the Prussian portion — culturally the most advanced — came nearest to the German pattern.

striking examples are the Polish-Lithuanian and Polish-Ukrainian borderlands within the Russian empire. Here the land-owners were Poles, the intelligentsia consisted mainly of Poles and partly of Jews, and the masses were White Russians or Lithuanians or Ukrainians, but the bureaucrats were almost exclusively Russians. In the Baltic provinces the dominant social group were Germans, the masses Letts and Esthonians, while posts in the bureaucracy were disputed between Germans and Russians, the later steadily gaining ground from the 1880s. In Finland, the social supremacy of the Swedish minority over the Finnish masses was challenged before the end of the century both by the formation of a strong Finnish middle class and by the pretensions of Russian nationalism to control of the Finnish civil service.

Among the unhistorical nations of eastern Europe, the first component of a middle class to emerge from the peasant masses was an intelligentsia, followed by a bureaucratic element only when an independent State had been achieved. Thus by 1914 the Serbs of the Kingdom[1] and the Bulgarians had both intelligentsia and bureaucracy; the Slovaks and Ukrainians little more than a rudimentary intelligentsia; the Serbs and Rumanians of Austria-Hungary a rather stronger intelligentsia, a few bureaucrats and a few prosperous provincial merchants. Among the Protestant Finns, Esthonians and Letts education was more widespread and of higher quality than among the Catholic or Orthodox nations of eastern Europe, and among the Finns an efficient business class soon appeared. In general, the social and cultural development of these Baltic nations, though it started later, resembled that of the Czechs and Austrian Germans: it approximated to a 'western' rather than an 'eastern' model.

There were certain nations which, though they were hardly touched by western influences until the mid-nineteenth century, possessed a long tradition of commercial enterprise,

---

[1] Of the independent Serbian state created in the nineteenth century. Nearly half the Serbian nation lived outside its boundaries — in Croatia, Dalmatia, Bosnia and in Hungarian and Turkish territory.

Social Forces in Eastern Europe since 1848

which enabled them to adjust themselves very quickly to nineteenth-century capitalism. They quickly developed not only an intelligentsia but also a business class, which operated not only in their national territories but also among their economically less gifted neighbours. The most important of these were the Greeks, whose national home was on both shores and on the islands of the Aegean, but whose business activities extended over the whole domain of the Ottoman empire and the Mediterranean and Black seas, and even farther afield. A second were the Armenians, whose home lay in the highlands of eastern Anatolia and Transcaucasia, but whose *diaspora* was nearly as wide as the Greek. A third were the Volga Tatars, most of whom lived in the former khanate of Kazan, but who carried both goods and ideas far into central Asia. These Tatars may perhaps be called the Czechs of the Moslem world. Their aristocracy had been russified, they were a nation of peasants and bourgeois, the latter including both business men and intellectuals. No other group in the whole Moslem world was so quickly or deeply affected by western economic and cultural influences as the Volga Tatars, who were the pioneers of Turkish nationalism and democracy.

The position of the Jews is, of course, unique. They had no national territory, no land-owners or peasants or bureaucrats. Their history had fostered equally their ability for intellectual and for business activity. The industrial revolution gave them opportunities both as employers and as workers, and none were better fitted than they to make use of the new schools and universities. But they were faced by the hostility of Governments and Churches, and later also of the aspirants to urban middle-class status from the nations among whom they lived, whether dominant or subject, historical or unhistorical. The Russian Government and Russian Orthodox Church distrusted them, first for their religion and then for the radical or revolutionary ideas which spread with special speed among them. They denied them civil rights, and restricted the areas in which they might reside, the schools they might attend, and the professions they might practise. Yet, though victims of Russian rule, the Jews incurred the hatred of Polish nationalists for their loyalty to the Russian State, and of Ukrainian peasants in their rôle as village shopkeepers. In Hungary the Government treated the Jews well, and this brought on them the hatred of the Slovaks and Rumanians who resisted the 'Magyarization' pursued from Budapest. At first the religious and nationalist motives prevailed in east European anti-semitism. It was not until after 1918, when both historical and unhistorical nations had acquired stronger middle classes, that economic rivalry inflamed it further.

. . . . .

Political ideas came first to the historical nations, and it was these which first split up into political parties. They had more numerous intelligentsias than the unhistorical. Knowing their national supremacy to be secure, they could afford to divide on ideological or social issues. For the unhistorical nations, national unity was essential for national survival, let alone for attainment of national independence. The small intelligentsias of the unhistorical nations could do nothing without mass support. Moreover, the gap between them and the masses, from which they had only just emerged, was much narrower than in the case of such historical nations as Poles, Hungarians or Russians, whose intelligentsias, at least at first, were recruited from a nobility with exclusive traditions.[1]

Nationalism and liberal democracy reached eastern Europe together, and both were already popular with the intellectuals of the historical nations by 1848. In the second half of the century they were followed by socialism. Nationalism was not essentially a revolutionary doctrine whereas, at least in its youth, socialism was. Nineteenth-century nationalists

[1] It has been pointed out *above* (p. 395) that the Russian nobility had not been an active force in history, in contrast to west European nobilities. But this does not mean that it did not have the contempt of a nobility for the masses. It lacked political power, but not social arrogance.

could hope to achieve their aims, which did not necessarily go so far as the establishment of independent sovereign states, by peaceful and constitutional means. Marxist socialists at least professed to believe in the necessity of a revolutionary cataclysm.

In practice, the relative importance of nationalism, liberalism and socialism in the different regions of eastern Europe was determined in about equal measure by the social differences discussed above and by the differences of political régime.

In the German and Czech provinces not only were the industrial classes strong, but constitutional government and civil liberties were assured. Various German and Czech parties, of varying degrees of liberalism or nationalism or radicalism, proclaimed their ideas in parliament, press and public meeting. Socialism became a mighty force, and, as in western Europe, declined in revolutionary ardour as it increased in numbers. Among the Czechs, perhaps more than among the Germans, nationalism cut across class divisions. It was never easy to say whether a Czech social-democratic worker felt more solidarity with a German worker or with a Czech bourgeois. But among both nations the three forces of liberalism, nationalism and socialism remained strong. It was unsafe to predict that any one of them would kill the other two.

In Hungary, liberalism and radicalism fused with nationalism among the ruling class of Magyar land-owners and bureaucrats and Jewish business men. Liberal principles and centralized government went together. Both were equally progressive, both equally derived from the French Revolution. Those who objected to a central administration, a single Magyar state language and a single Magyar patriotism were reactionaries. Magyar peasants and workers did not have the vote, but the unity of the enfranchised minority of the Magyar nation against the unhistorical nations was impressive. The socialist movement, led by a small section of the intelligentsia and supported by the working class of

Budapest, Hungary's only important industrial centre, was but a small dissident group, and even it was not wholly free from Magyar nationalism.

Among the unhistorical nations of Hungary social classes had hardly yet appeared. Nationalism derived its leaders from the small provincial intelligentsias, its mass strength from the peasants. The leaders of the Serbian and Rumanian national movements in Hungary were confirmed liberal-democrats, who refused to resort to revolutionary methods, even when the Government violated constitutional principles. The Slovaks and Croats were less devoted to democracy. The devoutly Catholic majority of Slovaks was influenced by the Church's hostility to liberal doctrine: only among the Protestant minority was liberalism strong. A similar Catholic conservatism existed in Croatia. It was opposed both by Liberal groups, whose main strength came from the *bourgeoisie* of the Dalmatian coastal cities, and by the peasant movement of the Radić brothers, the one serious force of social revolution in the kingdom of Hungary.

In the Balkan countries the united front of the whole nation, which had existed in the last years of Turkish rule, broke up when national independence had been won. Class differences were at first no wider than among the unhistorical nations of Hungary, and differences in wealth were probably smaller right up to 1918. But before long a privileged bureaucracy was formed, peasant discontent became sharper and more articulate, and the growth of an intelligentsia familiar with the latest western ideas and isolated from the peasant masses began to create a political climate favourable to revolution. Political conditions were an unstable combination of comparative freedom of speech and parliamentary institutions with fairly corrupt and brutal administration. In Rumania the land-owning nobility still had great power, and the presence of a large Jewish population gave rise to anti-semitism. In Serbia, Bulgaria and Greece class differences were much smaller, and there was no 'Jewish problem'. In all three countries nationalism was still unsatisfied. Desire for the unredeemed lands (Transylvania, Bessarabia, Bosnia, Macedonia) made for national unity. But in all three countries social discontent was also strong, and socialist ideas made their appeal to the intelligentsia. In Rumania the doctrines of the Russian populists had their intellectual champions, but restricted franchise and police pressure made a mass peasant movement impossible. Marxist socialism was negligible. In Serbia populism was influential in the 1870s, but later gave place to non-socialist radicalism, in which intellectuals and peasants combined, and which took shape in several political parties differing but little from each other. In the last years before 1914 Marxist socialism began to be important. In Bulgaria both populism and Marxism were much stronger, perhaps because government was more brutal than elsewhere in the Balkans, perhaps because the influence of the Russian revolutionary intelligentsia was greater.[1]

It was in the Russian empire that revolutionary forces were strongest, and that the intelligentsia had the greatest part to play. The cultural gap between intelligentsia and masses was not wider than in the Balkan states recently liberated from the Turks, but the political system was incomparably more oppressive. Until 1905 there were no central representative institutions, no political parties were allowed, and there was no freedom of speech on matters of internal politics. After 1905, it is true, a constitutional régime was established,[2] parties were permitted, and freedom of speech and press were fairly wide. But habits of mind formed in the preceding fifty years of bitter struggle and political persecution could not be quickly discarded.

Socialist ideas reached Russia before the social and econ-

[1] The founder of Rumanian socialism, Dobrogeanu-Gherea, born under the name Katz in Russia, had been a member of the Land and Liberty group in the 1870s. Svetozar Markovic, the first eminent Serbian socialist, had acquired his populist ideas in Russia. So had several of the Bulgarian revolutionaries of 1876, the founders of the Bulgarian state. Blagoev, founder of Bulgarian Marxism, had organized a Marxist discussion group in Russia in 1885.

[2] The third and fourth Dumas (1907 and 1912) were elected on a very restricted franchise. Nevertheless they provided a public forum for the discussion of political issues such as had never before existed in Russia.

omic conditions, from which they had been derived by their west European authors, had made their appearance. The first socialist groups in Russia, populist since the 1860s and Marxist also since the late 1880s, were composed solely of intellectuals. It was not until the 1890s that working-class support became important, and even up to 1917 it was certainly less in reality than Russian Marxists have believed, either then or now. It would be wrong to suppose that the whole Russian educated class consisted of revolutionaries. But it is probably true that its great majority was utterly alienated from the existing régime, and so disliked the revolutionaries less than the established disorder. And it was from the ranks of the educated class that the minority of professional revolutionaries was recruited. Certain weeds can grow only in certain soils. If the intelligentsia as a whole had not been disaffected, if the régime had not quite failed to enlist its loyalty, the professional revolutionary would not have become a significant figure of Russian life.

The autocracy which until 1905 prevented Russians from asking for political and social reforms, and still more from forming organizations to pursue them, also prevented the non-Russian nationalities, who formed 55 per cent of the empire's population, from asking for equal status for their languages, religions and cultures with the Russian, and still more from forming associations to work for national autonomy. Thus nationalists, no less than socialists, were driven to revolutionary methods. The non-Russian nationalist intellectuals were thus much more sympathetic to socialist ideas than were the nationalist intellectuals of central Europe. Nationalism and socialism were more closely interwoven in the Russian empire than in Hungary or the Balkans. Almost all the Ukrainian nationalists in Russia — in contrast to the Ukrainian nationalists of Austrian East Galicia — were socialists, whether populist or Marxist. The Polish Socialist Party (PPS) was the strongest single party in Russian Poland and, but for a brief interval in 1905–6, it was much more nationalist than socialist. It was even able to some extent to impose its

Social Forces in Eastern Europe since 1848

nationalist and revolutionary outlook on the socialist movements of Austrian and Prussian Poland, which had the opportunity to develop moderate labour movements within constitutional states, and would perhaps have done so if left to themselves. In Finland the socialists were the largest single party after 1905, drawing their support from a much larger section of the nation than the working class. Originally a class party, they were driven into nationalism by the russification policy of Nicholas II. The Armenian Dashnyak party was also socialist, though populist rather than Marxist. The only non-Russian region of European Russia in which the strongest political party was definitely not nationalist was Georgia. Here social democracy was the strongest force, and it followed the Menshevik faction of the RSDRP, many of whose leaders were, in fact, Georgians. But even these convinced internationalists were forced by the events of 1917–18 to choose national independence for Georgia.

. . . . . .

All these forces of social and national revolution had matured in eastern Europe in the first decade of the twentieth century. Assisted by two World Wars, they were to find catastrophic expression in Bolshevism and Nazism. It is interesting to note the common ground between the two great conquering heroes of these two secular religions. Both 'the greatest German who has ever lived' and 'the teacher of genius of all progressive humanity' came from that border zone between proletariat and petty *bourgeoisie* where class and national hatreds naturally meet. Joseph Djugashvili, the cobbler's son, expelled seminarist and part-time observatory clerk, and Adolf Hitler, the customs official's son and housepainter, had intellectual or aesthetic pretensions which they were able to satisfy only when they had attained absolute political power over their compatriots. Both belonged, not to the intelligentsia, but to an ill-defined group placed between it and the masses, swollen with contempt and fear of both alike. It is interesting also to note where they had their political apprenticeship. Hitler's ideas were formed in Vienna, the centre of a multi-national empire, the stronghold of anti-semitic fanaticism, a great city which to the young Hitler 'appeared the embodiment of racial incest'. Stalin's active political career began in Baku, an urban agglomeration rather than a city, remarkable not for its culture but for its oil, but resembling Vienna at least in the racial variety of its inhabitants, which found its most striking expression in the pogroms in which Tatars and Armenians massacred each other, with delighted encouragement from the Russian police.

The last half-century has seen the triumph of the revolutionary forces, and their transformation into totalitarianism — a 'society of a new type'. It would, however, be wrong to ignore those forces in eastern Europe after 1848 which were working in a different direction.

The constructive features of the Austro-Hungarian empire have often been pointed out, and there are signs at present that their cult is reviving. Undoubtedly the lands of the Habsburg monarchy formed a cultural, economic and political unity in central Europe, whose disappearance left a gap that has not yet been filled. The cultural unity is symbolized, for western minds, by the highest achievements of Austrian composers, by the best performances of the Viennese theatre and opera, to which may perhaps be added an impression, popularized and bowdlerized by the cinema, of the elegance of high society in Vienna and Budapest. But, of course, it was much more than this. It extended to the food and drink, the personal habits and manners of at least the urban population of the whole monarchy. It included, for example, the special form of Victorian architecture that is found in all provincial cities of the Hungarian plain and that, long after the frontiers had changed, made such towns as Novi Sad and Timişoară and Žilina and Vác look so alike. The cement of this culture which, like all great cultures, was both sublime and banal, should not be underrated. The economic unity was more marked within Hungary, with its natural frontiers and its balance between industrial Budapest and the rural

Social Forces in Eastern Europe since 1848

periphery, than in the more scattered 'lands represented in the Reichsrat', but it was certainly preferable to the network of tariff barriers that succeeded the monarchy's fall. During the last half-century great economic and social progress had taken place. The growth of industry was relatively even more impressive in Hungary than in Austria, but the integration of new classes into society was confined to the German and Czech provinces. Elsewhere social change exacerbated rather than mitigated national or class hatred. Political unity centred around the Habsburg dynasty, and this too should not be underrated as a positive factor. Franz Joseph has a greater share than any other Austrian in the responsibility for his country's ruin, even if his sins were of omission. Yet his person still commanded widespread loyalty right up to his death, from Magyars and Slavs and Latins as well as from Germans.

It is less generally realized that there is a parallel for every one of these positive features in imperial Russia. The highest cultural achievements of St. Petersburg surpassed those of Vienna. At a lower level, Russian culture in the sense of personal values and tastes and way of living held powerful attractions even for non-Russians who distrusted or hated Russia, such as Baltic Germans and Poles. The empire formed a vast economic unit. Moscow's industries were linked by waterways with the oil of Transcaucasia and the raw cotton of central Asia. Textiles made in Russian Poland were sold in the Far East, and the products of the Volga valley or the northern forests reached Europe through Riga or Rostov-on-Don. Even social development was rapidly moving in the same direction as that of western Europe. The Russian working class was not only increasing, but was becoming more skilled and more urbanized. It was ceasing to be a materially exploited and socially uprooted proletariat, like that of Britain in the 1820s, and was approaching at least the status of the working class of Germany in the age of Bismarck. A section of the peasantry benefited from Stolypin's reforms, though pressure of population on poorly exploited resources kept the majority poor and primitive. The whole peasantry enjoyed enormously better opportunities of education, and many *zemstvos* made solid contributions to rural welfare. Russian business men were beginning to emancipate themselves from the tutelage of the bureaucracy. Even the intelligentsia was somewhat less disaffected. Political progress was smaller than cultural, economic or social. Yet even here there was change. The third and fourth Dumas helped to form a sane public opinion. Even bureaucrats began to learn the facts of political life. The dogma of autocracy was a mighty obstacle to progress, to which there was no parallel in Austria-Hungary. Nicholas II as a ruler was also inferior to Franz Joseph: his faults were positive as well as negative. In 1914 he probably commanded less loyalty among his non-Russian subjects than Franz Joseph among his non-German. But the decline of the prestige of the tsar among Russians has been exaggerated by both Russian and non-Russian writers, under the influence of revolutionary mythology. The institution of monarchy held the Russian empire together, though it also strengthened the forces of disintegration. The task which some Russian statesmen had set themselves, of combining monarchy with reform, was certainly difficult but not absurd.

But war brought the triumph of the destructive forces over the positive, and shattered both empires. Yet war was not a mere external misfortune. It was the result of the diplomacy of the two imperial Governments, and in a more general sense of the social and national conflicts within all eastern Europe.

Special pleading and naïve sophistication have so combined to confuse twentieth-century minds, that it is necessary to recall the simple truths that the first World War was brought on by the Sarajevo murder; that behind the murder were the conflicts between the Habsburg monarchy and its South Slav subjects, and between Vienna and Belgrade; and that behind these were Austro-Russian rivalry for control of the Balkans and Russian fear of German designs on the Straits and Asia Minor. These factors, not the rivalry of

British and German capitalists for colonial markets, brought war. Strategic and economic factors were interwoven, with the strategic usually predominant. But it can certainly be argued that one factor in the decision to risk war was a sense of hopelessness on the part of Austrian and Russian statesmen about the internal contradictions of their empires. This feeling is not incompatible with the facts of internal progress and cohesion that were also unmistakably present. In 1914 it was in Austria rather than Russia that war was regarded as a helpful diversion from internal discontents. Russia had tried this gambit in 1904, against Japan, with discouraging results. Her leaders ten years later had less liking for it, but when Austro-German action deprived them of choice, they hoped that war would restore a sacred union.

Though it cannot be proved from the documents, one cannot but feel strongly that the explosive social and national conflicts in eastern Europe had a direct connexion with the outbreak of war between the German Powers and Russia. Yet that is far from saying that the war was the inevitable outcome of ineluctable historical processes. The men of 1914 had the power to keep the peace or make war, and they chose war. The responsibility of Berchtold or Moltke is greater than that of Prinsip, for the foreign minister or chief of General Staff of a great empire must be credited with knowing and understanding more than a twenty-year-old Balkan student. The men of 1914 cast aside the forces of progress within east European society, and gave free rein to those of destruction. It is not suggested that Austro-Russian or German-Russian tensions could have been removed, or problems 'finally solved'. But postponement of war for a decade or more was possible, and the history of the whole world could then have been radically different.[1]

. . . . .

[1] By the 1920s both Russian industry and the Russian army would have been immensely stronger, the Russian war effort would have been very different, and Lenin might well have died in exile a disgruntled doctrinaire without disciples.

After the war the same problems persisted, and the same revolutionary forces grew stronger, in Poland, the Danube valley and the Balkans, while they were largely, if not wholly, replaced by new problems in Russia.[1]

The Czech lands continued to be an exception to the general east European pattern. Their social and cultural development continued to follow that of western Europe. This was not, however, true of Slovakia. The Austrian republic was also an essentially western State, with the familiar western conflicts between capital and labour, Catholicism and secularism, complicated by the problem of pan-German aspirations which cut across both issues.

Elsewhere the social structure remained that of an 'underdeveloped' rather than an industrial society. There was a measure of industrial progress, especially in Poland and Hungary, and throughout the region urban influences made themselves felt in the countryside. But urban society was not dominant, and the industrial classes were not the most important social categories. These were the peasantry at the base of the social pyramid and the bureaucracy and the intelligentsia at the top.

After 1918 Hungary[2] was the only country of the region in which large landed estates dominated the agricultural scene, though there were parts of Poland and Albania in which they still played an important part. In Czechoslovakia and Rumania, and in the formerly Habsburg territories acquired by Yugoslavia, large estates were divided between the peasants. These land reforms were on such a scale as to merit the title of 'agrarian revolution'. They were accompanied by universal suffrage and competition for the peasants' votes, and by a great expansion of rural education. Though politics often degenerated into demagogy, village schools were seldom

[1] Russia, of course, lost Finland, the Baltic provinces and her western borderlands, but kept the Ukraine and her Asian territories and reconquered Transcaucasia.
[2] By this is, of course, meant the small state created by the 1920 Treaty of Trianon, with a population almost purely Magyar. In the first part of this essay we have used the word to denote the whole pre-war multinational kingdom of Hungary.

of high quality, and many villages still had no school, it would be absurd to deny that both the material and the moral status of the peasants improved in the first post-war years. Peasants' children had chances to make careers, such as had never before been within their reach. They were no longer passive herds for politicians to lead, they were beginning to feel themselves citizens. The land reforms did not, however, solve the economic problem. Rural population continued to grow faster than agricultural output improved, and faster than new jobs were created in industry, while overseas emigration was artificially restricted. The economic depression of the 1930s fell heavily on Danubian, Polish and Balkan peasants. In slump conditions the pressure of over-population became more severe. Thus the first hopeful decade was followed by a period of misery and unrest. This was no less true of the Balkan states where there had been no large estates since liberation from the Turks, than of the Danubian states whose land reforms had come after the war. Conditions became favourable to revolutionary movements, of 'right' or 'left', throughout the region.

Everywhere the ruling class was the bureaucracy. Its hold over the business class was perhaps less firm in the 1920s than it had been in imperial Russia, but in the 1930s it was greatly reinforced. Old industries were more closely controlled, and new industries were created in large part by State enterprise, with key positions held by men trained as bureaucrats or army officers, not as business men. In Hungary the process already noted, by which the children of the land-owning class were merged in the bureaucracy, was accelerated. In the 1930s it was an anachronism to say that Hungary was 'ruled by feudal magnates'. As in imperial Russia, so in inter-war eastern Europe, the ruling bureaucracy was the stronghold of authoritarian nationalism.

In nearly all the region, the intelligentsia suffered from frustrations similar to those of the intelligentsia of imperial Russia. There was the same gulf between themselves and the masses, the same contrast between the twentieth-century western ideas they had learned at school and university and the mediaeval reality of the villages from which they or their parents had sprung. The gulf was not everywhere the same: it was perhaps narrowest in Poland and widest in Macedonia.[1] But throughout the region intelligentsia and peasants belonged to different cultures, in a sense to which there was no parallel in contemporary north-western Europe.[2] These contrasts inevitably made revolutionary ideas attractive. Personal frustration in the eastern Europe of the 1920s was not so marked as in imperial Russia. There were many more careers open to educated young east Europeans than there had been for their predecessors under the bureaucracy of the Tsars. But the depression of the 1930s changed this. Unemployment among the intelligentsia, especially among university graduates, became a major problem. Thwarted ambition and social conscience combined to recommend some bloody short-cut to Utopia.

For a time the liberal or radical democratic groups that had existed before 1918 appeared to have gained in strength, and parliamentary systems worked. In defeated Hungary and Bulgaria they never had much chance. Pilsudski proved more than a match for the Polish National Democrats. In victorious Yugoslavia and Rumania the two strongest parties of this sort, the Serbian Radicals and the Rumanian Liberals, fell into the hands of newly rich capitalists and bureaucrats who had no interest in remedying administrative abuses. In Slovakia only a minority believed in liberal democracy. Its vigorous growth in the Czech lands is due to a social and cultural climate absent from the rest of the region. Peasant movements were another disappointed hope. The two most radical of these, the Polish and Bulgarian, both strongly influenced by Russian populism, were suppressed by force. The Rumanian peasant movement had a brief upsurge of mass

---

[1] It was still wider in Albania, but here the intelligentsia was so small that the problem hardly existed.

[2] In south-western Europe (Spain, Portugal and Italy below the Apennines) it did and still does exist. Carlo Levi's brilliant *Cristo s'è fermato a Eboli* throws much light on the abyss between cultures.

fervour, in which intellectuals of populist outlook played a part. But it soon fell into the hands of conservative lawyers and business men, and became a party of interests rather than of social change. The Croatian peasant movement kept its pre-war militancy, but this was diverted by circumstances into nationalist channels. The strongest socialist movement in eastern Europe was the Polish, which, after independence had been won, reverted to its original rôle of a working-class movement. Unfortunately it made the mistake of supporting Pilsudski's dictatorial plans, and thereafter felt his heavy hand. Hungarian socialism was reduced to a secondary rôle by the double disaster of Béla Kun's communist régime and the subsequent counter-revolution. In Serbia and Bulgaria the pre-war rôle of the socialists passed to the communists, who were effectively repressed by police terror.

National antagonisms were not reduced by the international settlement of 1919–20. The unhistorical nations, now armed with State machines of their own, did not show themselves more generous than their old masters. Even the Czechs behaved worse to the Sudeten Germans than the Vienna Government had behaved to them, though not, it is only fair to add, as badly as the chauvinist leaders of the Sudeten Germans would have treated the Czechs had they ever been in power in Habsburg Vienna. The Serbs showed little consideration for the 'brotherly' Croatian people, and still less for the Hungarian and Albanian minorities. The Rumanians rivalled them in their treatment of Hungarians and Ukrainians. The historical Poles celebrated the recovery of their own freedom by denying freedom to several million unhistorical White Russians and Ukrainians. Defeated Bulgaria and Hungary were resolved to regain their *irredentas*, — Macedonia, Thrace and the lands of St. Stephen's Crown. It is tempting to regard these nationalist policies as the work of the ruling bureaucracies and *bourgeoisies*, or of dispossessed Hungarian land-owners, but it is misleading. It is true that in the victorious Succession States the nationalist leaders came mostly from the small rising intelligentsia of the unhistorical nations. It is true that Hungarian nobles who had lost estates in Transylvania or Slovakia felt an understandable bitterness, and that thousands of Hungarian officials expelled from the lost provinces, and thousands of Macedonian and Thracian refugees in Bulgaria formed important pressure-groups. It is also true that in some 'mixed' areas peasants of different nationalities remained good friends. But nationalist demagogy undoubtedly enlisted popular support, mainly in the towns, but also in the villages, especially in the depression years. The initiative came from the intelligentsia, but the masses followed.

In the 1930s another phenomenon of imperial Russia, the professional revolutionary, made his appearance. Like his Russian counterpart, he sprang from the younger generation of the intelligentsia. Personal discontent and social protest were his driving force, peasant misery gave him his chance. He might choose the 'extreme left' or the 'extreme right'. The cultural, historical and political circumstances of different countries produced different results. In Serbia and Bulgaria in the 1930s communism attracted a large proportion of the most able and thoughtful young intellectuals, especially university students and recent graduates. Though their doctrines were Marxist, not populist, there was much in their attitude to the peasant masses, in their sense of an obligation to serve the people and raise it up out of its misery, that recalled the *narodnik* students in Russia in the 1870s. That this basic attitude should have drawn Serbian and Bulgarian students to communism, can be explained in large part by traditional sympathy for Russia, and in the case of Serbia by hostility to Germany and fear of Hitler's imperialism.[1]

In Greece too, communism made some progress among the intellectuals, as a reaction first against the sterile feud between royalists and Venizelists, and then against the

---

[1] In Bulgaria, for obvious historical reasons, anti-German feeling was much less strong than in Serbia. Nevertheless it did exist, and made some contribution to the popularity of communism.

Social Forces in Eastern Europe since 1848

Metaxas dictatorship. This was revealed in the rôle played by young intellectuals in the communist-led war-time resistance. In Albania the intelligentsia numbered at most a few hundred, but it included at least a score or two of devoted young communists.

In Rumania exactly the same mentality drove young intellectuals to the opposite extreme. Here the national enemy was Russia, and there was little hostility to Germany as such. Hitler's anti-semitism made him popular. Rumanian university graduates, in search of a job in the economic depression, found many of the jobs in business, journalism or the law filled by Jews. Traditional Rumanian anti-semitism, religious and cultural, was strongly reinforced by an economic motive. The young Rumanian intellectuals, largely of peasant stock, sincerely sympathized with the peasant in his misery, and wished to serve him and raise him up. The source of peasant poverty and of their own frustrations seemed to be the same: Jewish exploitation. Among the leaders of the Iron Guard were police spies and gangsters, but the movement contained thousands of honest young revolutionaries, who were the Rumanian equivalent of Russian *narodniki* of the 1870s.

In Hungary a similar trend was found in the various fascist or 'right radical' groups, of which the most important was the Arrow Cross Party led by Szálasi. These contained many idealistic young unemployed intellectuals, full of anti-semitic fury and social revolutionary fervour. There was also a small group, peculiar to Hungary, which was a more exact replica of Russian *narodnichestvo* than any other in eastern Europe. These were the 'village explorers', intellectuals who devoted themselves to detailed study, on the spot, of the condition of the Hungarian peasants and agricultural proletariat. They were more practical than their Russian predecessors,[1] and produced some first-class sociological

---

[1] They were more practical than the Russians who 'went to the people' in the mid-1870s. But, of course, one can hardly deny to the People's Will of 1879–81 great practical ability of another and more deadly kind.

books. They were socialists, but not Marxists. They included some of the best minds of their generation. Unfortunately the fate of Hungary in the 1930s and 1940s gave them no chance to influence policy.

The one east European country where the intelligentsia was of little importance as a revolutionary force between the wars was Poland. This was in striking contrast to the situation in Poland under Russian rule before 1914. With the establishment of Polish independence the national-revolutionary intelligentsia became the new ruling group. Pilsudski himself was its leader. His legionaries soon lost their revolutionary purity, and settled down comfortably as bureaucrats or colonels or even bank-directors. In the younger generation, which grew up under Pilsudski and his successors, and which inevitably reacted against the dictatorship, intellectuals were to be found in all political parties, but did not exercise over any a leadership such as that which can be observed in Rumania and the Balkans, or even in Hungary. The socialist movement was led primarily by workers, the peasant movement by peasants, though both had intellectuals among them. There were anti-semitic groups, with intellectual leaders and members inspired by both ideological and economic motives. But Polish anti-semitism never attracted such mass support, or had such a social revolutionary character, as Rumanian or Hungarian. In fact, though outward appearances might not suggest this, Poland was a more modern society, with stronger organized democratic forces, than any other in eastern Europe except Czechoslovakia. Though her eastern provinces in 1939 might still look like the Russia of Gogol, most of the country, and most of its people, were being very rapidly westernized. But they still had a long way to go.

Thus in eastern Europe between the wars, as in Austria-Hungary and Imperial Russia before 1914, there were both positive and destructive forces, but the balance was still more favourable to the destructive than it had been in the old empires. Industry and education developed fast, and the peasants probably gained more than they lost. But nationalism was more virulent, and politicians more irresponsible, than before 1914. There was a larger number of ruling groups, and few of them had any experience or traditions of government. The depression of the 1930s was the worst economic blizzard that had ever struck eastern Europe since the advent of capitalism. Their west European patrons could not or would not help them withstand it. The implacable hostility of Bolshevism, and the rise of Hitler, over neither of which the east Europeans had any control, sealed their doom.

In these conditions it is not surprising that the intellectuals turned to revolutionary gospels, or that these won mass support. But, like the Russian revolutionaries before them, the east European revolutionaries were too weak to seize power by their own efforts. Only war gave them their chance.

. . . . .

In Soviet Russia during the NEP period (1921–8) the social structure was not so very different from that which existed in the east European states.

In the towns, it is true, the differences were substantial. The industrial classes had suffered heavily. The old business class had been destroyed as such, by deliberate policy. Its place was not nearly filled by the so-called Nepmen, to whom Lenin gave a free hand in small-scale industry and trade, and some of whom made quite large fortunes. The working class was greatly weakened, not by deliberate policy but as a result of the civil war. The ablest workers became party leaders, State officials or army officials, while a large part of the unskilled dispersed in search of food to the countryside from which they had only recently come to the towns. The advance in skill which the Russian working class had made between 1890 and 1914 had been lost: the workers of the 1920s were once more a primitive proletariat. Nationalization of large-scale industry, banking and transport enormously increased the power of the bureaucracy, which, as has been noted above, even before 1917 had a strong grip on the national economy. Urban society in Soviet Russia thus consisted essentially of two classes, bureaucrats and unskilled workers.

But in rural Russia the similarity with eastern Europe was unmistakable. Once they had emerged from the horrors of civil war and the extravagances of 'war communism', the peasants could congratulate themselves on one solid gain, the same gain that the peasants of Rumania and Yugoslavia and Czechoslovakia had made. The landlords' estates had been distributed among them. Russian agriculture, like that of the Balkan states, was based on small peasant properties.[1] But the Russian land reform, like the east European measures, did not solve the economic problems. On the one hand, pressure of population on inadequate arable land of low crop output continued. On the other hand, the peasants ate more of what they produced. They had little incentive to produce more, as they were not offered a fair exchange for it, in manufactured goods. Thus the Government's food supply problem became intolerable.

The radical transformation of Russian society came with Stalin's revolution in the 1930s. The main purpose of collectivization of agriculture was to create a new centralized coercive machine, by which sufficient foodstuffs could be extracted from the villages at absurdly cheap prices, and peasant boys and girls could be drafted into the new industrial centres and public works. This purpose was achieved, at the cost of several million human lives and of about half the livestock population of the country. What was not achieved was a substantial increase in crop output per acre, or a substantial improvement in the skill or education of the peasants who remained in the villages.

Urban society was altered beyond recognition. Millions

---

[1] It is, of course, an error, though a very widespread error, to imagine that before 1917 most of the agricultural land in Russia belonged to large estates. Large estates accounted for about a fifth of the arable land, peasant holdings for nearly four-fifths. Still, landlords' estates were large and numerous enough to excite peasant envy. They also played a more important part in the agricultural economy as a whole than their mere extent would suggest.

of unskilled workers poured in from the countryside, and were dragooned into some sort of a labour-force. State-initiated industrialization was carried through on a scale as yet unknown in history. After twenty years the Soviet working class had advanced in skill and education well beyond the level of 1914, while its numbers were at least ten times as large. At the top of the social pyramid emerged a great industrial bureaucracy, which performed all the functions of nineteenth-century British capitalists except that it did not own the factories and did not pursue private profits. It is not enough to call it a 'managerial class'. It possessed many of the characteristics which, until Stalin's revolution, were generally regarded as specific to a capitalist *bourgeoisie*. The Soviet manager could only survive by adopting most of the practices of the most rugged individualists of the American 'open frontier' era. Illegal barter deals, bribery of workers, hoarding of surplus stocks, submission of false returns, and every sort of lobbying at the central ministries flourished as never before. Moreover, the new dominant social group strangely acquired many of the ethical and aesthetic values of the nineteenth-century capitalist. It had the same taste for pompous palaces, anodyne literature and nice catchy tunes, the same hatred of originality in the arts, the same dreary respectability in private life, or at least the same outward conformity to respectability. If 'bourgeois philistinism' has anything to do with a *bourgeoisie*, then the Soviet ruling group was a *bourgeoisie* — not a private capitalist *bourgeoisie* but a State *bourgeoisie*.

Thus by 1941 the urban sector of Soviet society had moved nearer to that of nineteenth-century western Europe than had urban society in eastern Europe, while the rural sector remained 'under-developed', a curious combination of a level of efficiency and culture no higher than that of the Balkans with a highly centralized political hierarchy which enforced a form of neo-serfdom.[1]

---

[1] Under serfdom, abolished in Russia in 1861, the peasant had to divide his working time between cultivating his own plot of land and that of his master;

The Soviet political system, however, was something new. Not only did the Bolshevik party monopolize power, but the content of power was expanded. A network of communications and an apparatus of propaganda as 'modern' as any in the world enabled the party to exercise not only negative but positive control over its subjects. Traditional dictatorships forbade people to do or say certain things. Stalin's government told them what they must do and say and think. Its claims were not limited to the public lives of its citizens: they reached into their private lives as well. Most important of all, it recognized no moral inhibitions. Even the most tyrannical of despots of the past had been held back by some moral or religious taboos. Under Stalinism everything was relative except the power of the boss. This was totalitarianism, a new form of government.

National conflicts were not so visible in the Soviet Union as in eastern Europe. This was partly because the nationalism of the 45 per cent non-Russian population of the Soviet Union[1] had not developed so far before 1917 as that of the Poles or of the nations of the Habsburg monarchy and the Balkans. But the main reason was the effectiveness of totalitarian government in repressing discontent. Nevertheless the changes in Soviet 'nationality policy' bore witness to the survival of nationalism, and to the continued interconnexion of national and social conflicts. The greatest sufferings during collectivization of agriculture fell on Ukrainians and Kazakhs. The purge of 1937–8 was especially severe in the Ukraine, Caucasus and parts of central Asia. A special problem was the newly created intelligentsia of the Moslem peoples of the Soviet Union. Denied a modern education under the tsars,[2] they could now send their young men and

---

under the *kolkhoz* system, as stabilized after 1935, the peasant's time was similarly divided between work on the communal lands and on the private plot which, by a reluctant compromise, the State allowed to each family. The communal lands were communal only in name, for the first claim on their output belonged to Government agencies, which bought it at derisory prices.

[1] The loss of the western borderlands in 1918 had reduced the proportion of non-Russians approximately from 55 per cent to 45 per cent.

[2] With the important exception, noted above, p. 401, of the Volga Tatars.

Social Forces in Eastern Europe since 1848

women to universities, whence they emerged as qualified engineers and doctors and bureaucrats. It does not follow that they were grateful for these new opportunities. In the heyday of 'Magyarization', young Slovak or Rumanian subjects of the kingdom of Hungary who learned Magyar and studied in Budapest could make careers. But they used the knowledge and positions they acquired, not to expound to their fellow-nationals the virtues of Magyar culture, but to lead them in the struggle for national independence against Budapest. *Mutatis mutandis*, the same was true of the intelligentsia of British India or French Indo-China. Totalitarian government prevents the expression of such aspirations: it does not necessarily prevent their existence.

Stalin's industrial revolution 'modernized' Russian society. The rise of the Soviet State *bourgeoisie* and skilled working class were factors that made for 'normalization', for the removal of the strains of perpetual revolution. Against these normalizing forces was the force of the totalitarian régime, strengthened firstly by the foreign danger (imaginary in the 1920s, but real enough after 1933), and secondly by the catastrophic upheaval associated with the name of Yezhov. It is too ingenious to argue, as some do,[1] that Stalin organized the Great Purge with the deliberate aim of keeping society liquid, of preventing the crystallization of new classes. The Purge started for different reasons, and gathered speed by its own mechanism. But it did to some extent have this effect. Yet in a sense it also helped on the 'normalizing' process. For the victims, though by no means all 'Old Bolsheviks', did include almost the whole revolutionary vanguard of 1917–20. The younger men who succeeded them in the key posts in State and economy, were much more thoroughly impregnated with the ethos of the new State *bourgeoisie*.

Russia had not fully recovered from the *Yezhovshchina* when Hitler struck.

. . . . .

[1] For example, the extremely interesting *Russian Purge*, by F. Beck and W. Godin (1951).

Eastern Europe was the immediate occasion for the outbreak of both phases of the second World War — in 1939 and in 1941.[1] In a deeper sense it was also one of the causes of the war. German imperialism was, in 1939 as in 1914, a factor external to eastern Europe. But eastern Europe, in 1939 still more than in 1914, was a field of unrest which invited aggression. Social conflicts and national hatreds divided the east European states still more bitterly than they had divided the two great empires in 1914. The east European governments could not even draw on the dwindling capital of tradition which had been available to the Habsburgs and Romanovs, and which they had blindly squandered.

The main difference in the international balance of power in and around eastern Europe, between the inter-war period and the last decades before 1914, was the absence of Russia. This was a result of the implacable hostility of the Soviet leaders towards 'the capitalist world', and to a lesser but considerable extent to the hostility of the British and French rulers towards Bolshevism. The natural interest of Russia in the balance of power in Europe was forgotten on both sides. It was forgotten that the battle of the Marne had been partly won in East Prussia, and that Russia had been saved, at least for three years, on the fields of Flanders. Both sides paid dearly for forgetting these lessons, France in 1940 and the Ukraine in 1941. But dogmatic hostility was a fact. Despite the Franco-Russian alliance of 1935, there were three camps in Europe in the 1930s — the West, the Axis and the U.S.S.R.— each equally hostile to the other two. Hitler was the gainer. He too paid the price, but he had a long run for his money.

If disruptive forces within Austria-Hungary and Russia had impelled both Powers to war in the years before 1914, they were also present in eastern Europe in the 1930s. But it is also true that the east European governments were

[1] British people are inclined to forget that for half of Europe the war began in 1941. Published documents show that disagreements with Russia about Bulgaria and the Straits, and to a lesser extent Rumania and Finland, were decisive in causing Hitler to attack in June 1941.

Social Forces in Eastern Europe since 1848

anything but bellicose. Beneš yielded at Munich rather than be accused of having started a European war. Colonel Beck and General Metaxas fought when there was no other way out. Admiral Horthy was tricked into war by one prime minister, after another had committed suicide, and he kept his contributions to the Axis war effort to a minimum. King Boris of Bulgaria was more fortunate in his geographical position, and did even less. The only two States which can be said to have chosen war — on opposite sides, though they had been allies — were Rumania and Yugoslavia. But both had been submitted to intolerable provocation — the seizure of Bessarabia by Russia and the imposition of the hated Tripartite Pact on Yugoslavia.

Except on the special Stalinist argument that to declare war on the Soviet Union is to commit a crime against humanity,[1] it would be difficult to make a case for war-mongering against the east European rulers of 1939 to 1941. They were, for the most part, victims of forces beyond their control. In so far as they had a choice, their fault was appeasement, not bellicosity. More profoundly, by their failure to deal with social problems, and by their exasperation of nationalism, they had given Hitler his chance.

. . . . .

The Stalinization of most of eastern Europe which followed the war was a result not of revolutionary action from within but of Soviet military conquest from without. Revolutionary forces were there, and revolutions were badly needed. But it was precisely those who wished to make real revolutions, by and on behalf of their nations, who suffered most from the communist leaders imposed by Soviet might. Such men were Nikola Petkov in Bulgaria, Béla Kovács in

---

[1] For this crime Premiers Bárdossy of Hungary, Antonescu of Rumania and Filov of Bulgaria, and President Tiso of Slovakia were executed after the war. Many other prominent persons were executed in eastern Europe for various war crimes, but in the case of the four above mentioned, it was made clear at their trials that their most grievous offence was to have declared war on the U.S.S.R.

Hungary and the socialist and peasant leaders in Poland, not to mention the Czech democrats.

The one country in which a real revolution took place was Yugoslavia. The inspiration was Stalinist and foreign, but Marshal Tito's armies were raised on Yugoslav soil and his civil administrators were men and women who proved their powers of leadership in a hard school. The autochthonous nature of the Yugoslav dictatorship was the basic reason for Moscow's decision to destroy it, and when it withstood the shock, it evolved even further from its original model. This is not to say that the Tito régime represented the 'will of the people', or was the best that Yugoslavia could ever have had, for in this context these are meaningless phrases.

Elsewhere was imposed a régime which combined some features of Lenin's Russia with many more features of Stalin's. Totalitarian institutions and rapid industrialization started immediately the communists had seized power, not, as in Russia, a decade later. The State *bourgeoisie* in the People's Democracies was not, as in the Soviet Union, an unintended product of the industrial revolution, but was created ready made. Its members included a fair proportion of former private capitalist bourgeois, and all were persons who had been intellectually formed under a pre-Stalinist régime.

The Stalinist State *bourgeoisie* has its own frustrations and discontents, but they are not the same as those which afflicted the pre-1917 intelligentsia of Russia, or the pre-1945 intelligentsia of the Balkans. Its predicament is perhaps more comparable with that of the French *bourgeoisie* of the eighteenth century. It has much of the substance of power, and good material conditions of life, but it lacks social recognition and security. This applies both to the intelligentsia in the strict sense [1] and to the whole upper layer of society —

---

[1] In the sense defined above, pp. 398, that is, in the sense accepted in imperial Russia. Understanding of Soviet society is made more difficult by the practice of the Soviet authorities of using the term 'toiling intelligentsia' to cover all who do not work with their hands. This heterogeneous group is described not as a 'class' but as a 'class stratum'. The State *bourgeoisie*, of

the managers, bureaucrats and experts who form the State *bourgeoisie*. The special predicament of the intelligentsia of imperial times — of living in a different century and a different culture from the masses — is much less characteristic of Soviet Russia, where urbanization and mass education have greatly narrowed the gap. Nevertheless, the differences between town and country are still very big, especially in the Moslem regions.

In eastern Europe the problem inevitably takes a nationalist form. Nationalism is rooted in both the past and the present, in memories of past national independence and of freedom at least greater than any permitted under Stalinism, and in the conflicts of interest inevitably generated by industrial development. Industrialization generates a State *bourgeoisie*, and the State *bourgeoisie* generates nationalism. The greater the pride of the Polish or Hungarian State bourgeois in the industrial machine which he feels that he has himself created, the more intolerable it seems to him that it should be exploited by a foreign Power.

Perhaps the most interesting problems for the next period of the history of Russia and eastern Europe are whether the social group created by the State-initiated industrial revolution, having acquired many of the ethical and aesthetic values of the nineteenth-century private capitalist *bourgeoisie*, will put forward the most essential of all the nineteenth century bourgeois's demands — political freedom; and whether, if it does so, it will find any means of obtaining it.

. . . . .

In the last hundred years eastern Europe has been impelled far along the path of industrialization and secularization of the western type. The real achievements of the Soviet régime, which are impressive, are essentially those of Victorian capitalism, both in the output of goods and in the formation

---

course, consists only of the upper layer of this 'toiling intelligentsia', while the intelligentsia in the strict sense consists only of those engaged in more strictly intellectual professions.

of social classes. It is not in the economic and social results, but in the political means and the cost in human lives, that the experience of eastern Europe differs utterly from that of the lands of classical capitalism. The victims include not only the dead of two world wars, but millions of Jews destroyed in the gas chambers, of Serbs and Poles slaughtered by Hitler's orders, of Ukrainian peasants starved to death in their own fields, and of Russians and others worked to death in the Arctic north.

Was the achievement worth the price? Omniscient Marxists, whether Stalinist or neo-Leninist, will blandly murmur about 'historical functions'. All this was necessary to create a new and just society. The trouble is that the society is not very new, and even less just. Nostalgic conservatives will point out how much better was life under Habsburg or Romanov. One can agree with them. This only increases the historical responsibility of those who brought their empires to ruin. In this many had a hand, but in the last resort none more than Nicholas and Franz Joseph.

It is not more helpful to scold the east Europeans for not approaching their tasks in the spirit of Mr. Gladstone. Liberal ideas, like the institutions and manners which expressed them, had grown up in the west during several centuries. Eastern Europe could not spare centuries to develop. It could not escape western economic and cultural influences, nor the military threat first from France and then from Germany. It had to adjust itself to these new forces. This is not to say that all that happened was inevitable, still less that it was morally justifiable. But eastern Europe (including Russia) was the first part of the world in which western ideas, imported ready made, were used to remould societies neither economically nor culturally prepared for them.[1]

[1] Before the nineteenth century European rule over Asiatic or African territories had had very little effect on their societies. Japan embarked on westernization considerably later than Russia or the Balkans. In North America the European colonists built a new European society, and the native population and native traditions played no part. Possibly the history of Spanish and Portuguese America can show some exceptions to my statement.

Social Forces in Eastern Europe since 1848

The recent history of Asia, Africa and Latin America has shown that many phenomena previously considered to be specifically Russian or specifically east European were not so at all, but were merely characteristic of the impact of western influences on non-western societies.

The Russian nineteenth-century intelligentsia had specific features which cannot be found elsewhere, but the essential predicament of the Russian intelligentsia was in no way unique. It has appeared in the twentieth century in China, India, Egypt and West Africa, to give only the most obvious examples.

The nationalism of the small nations of eastern Europe also has its specific features. But the emergence among subject nations, large and small, historical and unhistorical, of rabid nationalist movements, in which slogans of national and social revolution are fused by techniques of mass demagogy, has not been confined to the Danube valley. Its ravages can be clearly seen in south-east Asia, the Middle East and other lands.

The history of eastern Europe since 1848 also shows that private capitalist enterprise is not the only possible driving force for an industrial revolution, but that it is characteristic only of north-west Europe and North America. The belief that all societies must pass through capitalism, shared by Leninists and prophets of free enterprise, derives from a common Victorian insularity. Examples of a different process were visible already before 1914 in imperial Russia and imperial Japan. The Soviet Union, of course, furnished the most striking example of all. It is being followed in the 'Popular Democracies'. A different type seems to be evolving in Yugoslavia. Other types again are likely to appear in Turkey, Mexico, Egypt and other lands.

These developments place the history of eastern Europe since 1848 in a different perspective, which observers in 1914 could hardly have foreseen. Eastern Europe should be of interest to a wider circle of historians than those engaged in what are misleadingly called 'Slavonic studies'. The wider interest of eastern Europe's history lies in those aspects of social and cultural development in which it resembles or differs from the history of western Europe on the one side and of the non-European 'under-developed' countries on the other. But to see these resemblances and differences it is necessary to see eastern Europe as a whole. It is also necessary to see the real social forces, without preconceived notions of the universal validity of Victorian categories. Of all these social forces, that which perhaps most deserves attention is the intelligentsia. In this, as in so many fields of historical enquiry, Sir Lewis Namier has been a pathfinder.

STANLEY MORISON

PERSONALITY AND DIPLOMACY IN ANGLO-AMERICAN RELATIONS, 1917

A PRINCIPAL point of interest for the historian of the recent past must continue to be A.D. 1917. Of all the events of that year the resort to unrestricted submarine warfare was the most tremendous in its possibilities and consequences. Germany proclaimed the use of this weapon from 31 January. The United States entered the war on 6 April. It is proposed here to notice the methods employed by personalities engaged in the making of policy, as it affected Anglo-American relations, the immediate issues of war and the preparation for peace, during this year.

Documents concerning America's neutrality, the acceleration of her war effort, and its co-ordination with that of Britain, the various American peace initiatives and the drafting of the Fourteen Points, are presented in Professor Charles Seymour's several publications, in Mr. Ray Baker's *Life of President Wilson* and in the memoirs of Lansing and McAdoo ; more recently Lord Elibank,[1] Sir Campbell Stuart,[2] Sir Arthur Willert[3] and others[4] have added to the literature of the subject.

Throughout the period under review peace, no less than war, was a constant topic of discussion among neutrals.

---

[1] Arthur C. Murray (now Lord Elibank), *Master and Brother* (London, 1945) ; *At Close Quarters* (London, 1946).
[2] Campbell Stuart, *Opportunity Knocks Once* (London, 1952).
[3] Arthur Willert, *The Road to Safety* (London, 1952).
[4] Samuel R. Spencer, jr., *Decision for War* (Rindge, N.H., 1953).

Also, schemes to end the war were ventilated among restricted circles in the belligerent countries in spite of the fact that the enemy's manner of conducting the war, combined with the dominating political authority of the German generals and admirals, and the superiority of their military position, left the Allies with no alternative but to outfight them. There were no possibilities for Allied diplomacy, though there was an opportunity for propaganda. The American ideal of Peace without Victory was voiced by Wilson in a famous speech delivered ten days before Germany proclaimed the unlimited use of the submarine weapon.

As is well known, Colonel House was then the most powerful personality, apart from Wilson, in American foreign policy. A source of his strength was that in spite of his personal views he had loyally espoused the president's policy of neutrality. He never compromised himself as pro-British, and was careful to remain on the best terms with Bernstorff, even in the early part of 1917. In fact, House's attitude towards Germany was so 'correct' that Bernstorff left a cordial message for him: 'Give him my love and tell him he is the best friend I have in America. He has saved me many times and but for him it would have been impossible for me to have remained as long as I have.' House was not embarrassed. Anything he had done for Bernstorff had been consonant with neutrality. Simultaneously House had maintained contact to an even closer degree with a member of the British embassy, fresh from the front at Ypres, Sir William George Eden Wiseman, Bt., then thirty-two years of age. House had met him for the first time on 17 December 1916, and found in him a man who, independently, came to conclusions about Germany which were similar to his own. They became close friends and when Wiseman, shortly after, became responsible for the British Intelligence Service in America, the two men saw each other with increasing frequency. By the spring of 1917 they were intimate and lived in the same apartment house in Fifty-third

Street. The young diplomat became House's closest British confidant.[1]

House's consistent maintenance of neutrality and his desire to hold the confidence of German and British alike is characteristic. He had, in truth, long since concluded that America must actively intervene on the side of the Allies, and believed that now the time had come when he should so inform the president. The events of February and March were decisive for him as well as for Lansing. But Lansing was known to be pro-British, and the president kept his thoughts to himself. The secretary of state knew nothing of the president's mind. On 19 March, in desperation at the lack of direction of policy, Lansing invoked the influence of House. A week passed, and there was no sign that House had intervened. All that was known in the State Department was that Wilson was not well.

With his perfect sense of the *tempus loquendi*, 'the president's intimate friend' arrived at the White House on 27 March. Wilson's mind had developed farther than Lansing had led House to expect. The question he put to House was whether he thought Wilson should ask Congress to declare war, or whether he should say that a state of war existed and ask for the necessary means to carry it on. House advised the latter. 'I am afraid', he writes, 'of an acrimonious debate if he puts it up to Congress to declare war'.[2] Yet the president stayed irresolute. He did not believe 'he was fitted for the Presidency under such conditions'. House then began to speak in a way that made him feel, 'as Mrs. Wilson told me later, that he was not up against so difficult a proposi-

---

[1] I am grateful to Sir William Wiseman for permission to refer to the papers relating to the period 1916–19 which he presented to Yale to be kept with the House collection.

[2] Charles Seymour, *The Intimate Papers of Colonel House* (Boston, 1926–8, 4 vols.), ii. 464. House began to keep his diary on 25 Sept. 1912. I am obliged to President Emeritus Seymour for his permission to examine the full script of the diary, House's correspondence and other relevant material, for this article ; also, for permission to quote extracts from *Intimate Papers* and from the unpublished portions of the diary. The particulars given are of the American edition, referred to as 'Seymour'.

tion as he had imagined; ... everything that he had to meet in this emergency had been thought out time and time again in other countries, and all we had to do was to take experience as our guide and not worry over the manner of doing it'. House ended by saying that Wilson 'had taken a gamble that there would be no war, and had lost; and the country would hold it to his discredit unless he prosecuted the war successfully'.[1] Next day, 28 March, Wilson discussed with House the substance of the message he was to give to Congress. Its substance, as given on 2 April, was that a state of war existed. Germany was making 'warfare against mankind', and America recognized the situation.

Made when it was, the nation's decision owed much, apart from the president, to Secretary Lansing, and more to Colonel House. The message had taken a course consistent with the tradition of American foreign policy. She had assumed belligerency on a maritime issue, in defence of neutral rights against Germany. It was, moreover, a decision consistent with past protest against the British blockade. The message was evidence that America was still in earnest about her principle of rights at sea, as affirmed against Britain on many occasions. American protests against British maritime action had been continuous from 1914.

Immediately after Wilson's message of 2 April 1917 advising Congress to recognize that the country was in a state of war, the British Government considered the dispatch to Washington of a special mission which should place at the disposal of the American Government the experience gained by Britain in the course of three years of struggle. The suggestion was put to House.[2] On 9 April Congress responded to the message and on the same day Wilson decided to welcome an Allied Mission. The first British Mission, led by the foreign secretary, Mr. Balfour, included Lord Cunliffe of the Bank of England, Rear-Admiral Sir

---

[1] Seymour, *op. cit.*, ii. 465.
[2] By Sir Eric Drummond on 5 April.

Personality and Diplomacy in Anglo-American Relations, 1917

Dudley de Chair, Major-General G. T. M. Bridges and Mr. (now Lord) Layton. On arrival they were met by House, with whom Balfour discussed the best means of ensuring the fullest co-operation between the two Governments. Among the subjects mentioned were the documents now known as 'The Secret Treaties'. Discussions between Britain and America of the terms of peace could no longer be evaded. Wilson decided not to speak directly to Balfour on the subject but to appoint House to talk to him about it. The president was now more, rather than less, determined to emerge in due time as the grand architect of peace, with the assistance of his 'second personality', of whom he said that 'his thoughts and mine are one'.

But both Wilson and House were faced by the fact that it was necessary to abandon the old position of 'Peace without Victory'. The situation, in fact, was more serious than they knew. As the Germans had calculated, the three months that had elapsed between the German declaration of unrestricted submarine warfare and the American declaration of war, had rendered Britain desperate. The period coincided with the staggering blow dealt by the collapse of Russia. German divisions were coming west. France was virtually out of action. Italy was in sore straits. German submarines were sinking British ships faster than they could be built. There was also the question of where the money was to be found for food and shipping. These were the circumstances in which 'Peace through Victory' had to be organized. Meanwhile time was on the side of the German General Staff. Balfour thought Washington lacked the knowledge and experience that would enable it to measure the situation, and that a special envoy to remain in Washington was desirable. His importance would be such that Grey, whose personality was known to be highly agreeable to House, should be asked to undertake the direction of a new Mission. The former foreign secretary could not be induced to accept, especially as Balfour's original simple idea of an *ad hoc* personal liaison was extended by the War Cabinet into an organization to regularize, co-ordinate and supervise the many British agencies engaged in the purchase of foodstuffs and munitions, and in the conduct of the mass of business connected with shipping. The Cabinet were minded to create a new mechanism embracing more than anything that had been expected by House, Drummond, Wiseman, Balfour or Spring-Rice. The new Mission would not be designed on conventional lines.

On 31 May the foreign secretary, on the way home, received a memorandum from the War Cabinet. Taking its text from Balfour's report, it considered the waste of time, power and money resulting from mutual competition while current purchasing agencies were left undirected, by a 'single energetic and influential man of good business capacity and wide knowledge'. The War Cabinet recognized that 'Mr. Balfour's Mission had done excellent work', but decided that 'much remains to be done', especially 'with a view to bringing home to the United States Government the realities of the present war situation, and the necessity of immediate and strenuous co-operation in the war, with the least delay possible'.

Foreseeing the objection that the appointment would be resented as an encroachment upon the regular diplomatic representation, the War Cabinet concluded by saying that the office was extra-diplomatic. It was a position that by no means corresponded with the anticipations of embassy circles. They thought it quite insufficient to say that the newly appointed British 'representative in the United States' would have no diplomatic duties, and that these would remain 'in the same hands as heretofore'.[1] 'The same hands as heretofore' took the strongest exception to the War Cabinet's new scheme. It was quite different from what the foreign secretary wanted. The ambassador hated it.

But the embassy repugnance to the scheme, as such, was insignificant compared with their opposition to the personage

[1] The text of the War Cabinet's memorandum, as given to House by Wiseman on 31 May 1917, is in Seymour, *op. cit.*, iii. 84-5.

the War Cabinet had designated to work it. The memorandum concluded by saying that 'In the opinion of the War Cabinet Lord Northcliffe is suited for such an appointment, and they propose making the appointment at once with the duties above enumerated'.[1] The bare idea of Northcliffe's coming to America in any official capacity whatsoever infuriated the ambassador. It was outrageous that such a man should be head of a Mission which could not now fail to appear to have at least as much public importance as the embassy itself. With Balfour's authorization, Spring-Rice immediately went to see House, showed him the message and Balfour's reply which expressed the belief that so grandiose a scheme at so early a date in the association of the Powers would be premature. Moreover, added the ambassador, 'if it was intended to send Northcliffe or anyone else', then the consent of the president 'should first be obtained'; for, he reminded House, 'The President and the President alone was the Government of the United States'.[2]

House may well have remembered his first meeting with Northcliffe, in 1915, when he talked like an extremist. On 5 May, House and L. J. Maxse lunched with Northcliffe, who then insisted that British statesmen did not appreciate the 'magnitude of the task before them, that they were not meeting the situation with anything like the determination and ability the occasion required'.[3] When they met next on 13 January 1916, 'Northcliffe talked rather foolishly about the length of the war, the blockade, the Dardanelles, the Kaiser's health, and gave us much misinformation'.[2]

This, probably with other recollections, was remembered when Spring-Rice visited House. At that time, neither Balfour, Spring-Rice nor Wiseman understood that the calculations of the German General and Naval Staffs left the Allies with no justification for diplomacy 'as usual'. Even

[1] Seymour, *op. cit.*, iii. 85. [2] *Ibid.* i. 421.
[3] *Ibid.* ii. 125.

Balfour did not realize the pass to which Britain had come as the principal financier of the war, in terms of cash and credit. Neither House nor the others saw that America needed to understand 'the magnitude of the task', and to face the situation 'with the determination and ability the occasion required'. America did not know at the beginning of June how close the Allies were to ruin and defeat. At that moment it seemed perfectly reasonable for House to think that America could look upon herself as an arsenal of resources rather than as a reservoir of men. Accordingly, he would be bound to regard Northcliffe as an extremist. Wiseman's attitude was no different. Northcliffe's belief that the end of the war was far off was linked with the belief that the German menace to Britain was to be nullified only by decisive defeat. House, on the other hand, was convinced in 1916 that to crush the Germans would be dangerous, and that war should not be waged beyond the point at which they would make concessions; in effect, that peace must, sooner or later, be negotiated.

Foremost among those in 1917 who were still resolute for victory, knew what the word implied, had an idea of the effort required, and had faith in Allied power to achieve it, was Northcliffe. During 1916 he had never ceased to condemn weak men and weak measures. The slightest public mention of peace by negotiation earned his vehement condemnation. His most widely circulated newspapers daily trounced ministers for 'half-heartedness', 'flabbiness', and 'lack of decision'. Asquith was always 'feeble'; one day Balfour was 'too old for his job' (then the Admiralty); next day he was denounced as an 'idle septuagenarian'; Grey was a 'semi-invalid'. The demand for action, vigour and decision was incessant. 'When will the war end? When we have a Government that is in earnest, knows the value of time, and has a backbone.' The nation was urged to get rid of the 'limpets'; Haldane, Grey, Balfour, McKenna and others. Two days before the new Government came into office, Northcliffe's journals, selling by the million, were heavily attacking Balfour. When the composition of Lloyd George's Government was known, Balfour's translation from the Admiralty to the Foreign Office was headed, 'How to lose the War'. It is not surprising that Balfour should object to Northcliffe as head of any Mission that could overshadow the accredited representative of H.M. Government, appointed by his own Foreign Office in the usual manner.

But in Northcliffe's mind, before and after 8 December, nothing should be 'as usual'. He had in view the conscription of the whole man and woman-power of the country, the rationing of all primary foods and other measures that (common form as they became in the second World War) seemed revolutionary in the first and yet were, in his mind, the only way to victory. Any Government that stood in the way of such a programme must give way to another, more resolute and efficient. A. G. Gardiner's statement in the Asquithian *Daily News* of 9 December exaggerates Northcliffe's power in the spring of 1917: 'Having destroyed one Government, Lord Northcliffe is going to exercise the powers of a dictator over its successor'. He had not yet the power but he possessed the ambition. The situation in London was similarly presented to American Liberals in the *Atlantic Monthly* of March 1917 by 'A British Observer' (possibly also 'A. G. G.'): 'Mr. Asquith has been dethroned and Mr. George reigns in his stead by virtue of the will of Lord Northcliffe'. House and 'Our Friend' (as 'A. G. G.' is referred to in House's correspondence with Wilson) had an hour-and-a-half together on 11 January 1916; and it is not to be imagined that 'A. G. G.' should have left House unwarned as to the manner of man he thought Northcliffe to be.

Northcliffe was then, indeed, at the height of his popularity among the public. Equally, he was at the lowest point of detestation among the politicians. Both sides of both coalitions agreed that only a Johnsonian definition fitted Northcliffe's 'patriotism'. If the Lloyd George ministers were highly apprehensive of his next move, the Asquithians were, of course, more outspoken against him and all his ways. The plaster 'Northoleon' was lampooned in Fleet Street, vilified as a false patriot and stigmatized as a blackguard assassin of politicians. Few public men in the spring of 1917 could be found to say a good word for Northcliffe, or any of the causes he championed. Many who believed in the necessity for a more vigorous prosecution of the war held that the cause was embarrassed by Northcliffe's 'mud slinging' campaign for victory. One or two believed that he could be ignored. After all, he had never occupied a place in Government; he possessed nothing but his newspapers: but this was to ignore the degree to which Northcliffe's newspapers were supported by a great mass of soldiers and civilians. Whether he was in the Government or out of it, so long as he controlled more than half of the total newspapers read in London and affected, by example, many provincial journals, Northcliffe would cease to be a power only if his health should fail. That his attitude to the war would change was unimaginable. As for his health, in April 1917 he had never been better in his life, or so much enjoyed his sense of power; or felt so much confidence in his estimate of the situation, or so happily revelled in the execration that his name evoked among all 'limpet' politicians and their following. The apostle of victory's recent visit to the front had been an intense inspiration. His meetings with the soldiers had taught him more than he could expect to learn from his connexions with Lloyd George, Curzon, Bonar Law, Milner or Arthur Henderson, who daily met as the War Cabinet from 9 December 1916. These were the five men responsible for appointing Northcliffe head of the British War Mission to America in succession to Balfour.

Before it was decided in April 1917 to send Balfour to confer with the United States Government, House's private opinion had been sought and Wilson's consent secured that the visit would be useful and the visitor agreeable. House then recommended that the Mission be announced as 'diplomatic'; and advised that any military and naval members of the Mission be of minor rank. It was, therefore, firmly in House's mind at the end of May that the successor to Balfour should also be of diplomatic rank; and, if Grey could not be secured, another comparable name should have been suggested; not, of course, that of one who lacked the recommendation of the foreign secretary. For one that had even earned his anathema House, inevitably, had nothing to say. Finally, it is certain that House had not forgotten what 'Our friend A. G. Gardiner' thought of him; also that the President, whom he knew to have a particular regard for 'A. G. G.'s' judgment of men and integrity of disposition,[1] would expect the worst of Northcliffe and those he would bring with him. House also knew that the president would not look favourably upon any Mission that could be made to look like another British attempt to storm the White House.

For all these reasons, House had no difficulty in agreeing with Balfour, Wiseman and the ambassador. Somehow the proposal of the War Cabinet must be rejected, evaded or circumvented. Whatever happened, Northcliffe must not set foot in America as a British envoy: that was certain. When House decided to recommend to the president that it would be better if Britain were 'not to send anyone at present', he felt he was on firm ground. The president's telegraphed reply was everything that the foreign secretary, the ambassador, Wiseman and House could have desired: 'Action mentioned in your letter of yesterday would be most unwise and still more unwise the choice of person named'.[2] That Wilson was, at this time, extremely antipathetic towards Northcliffe is not open to doubt. Two or three days after this telegram was sent to House, Wilson is found instructing the secretary of the Navy, Daniels, 'to avoid a man recently

[1] The entry in House's diary under 12 Jan. 1915 notes that 'after dinner the President read from A. G. Gardiner's sketches of prominent men until half-past eight'. Cf. House to Wilson, 11 Jan. 1916 (Seymour, *op. cit.*, i. 350), 'Our friend A. G. Gardiner was with me for an hour and a half yesterday. I gave him more time than to others because I wanted to increase, if possible, his already high opinion of you.' (*Ibid.* ii. 119.)

[2] Wilson to House, in Ray Stannard Baker, *Life of Woodrow Wilson*, vii. 96; viii. 100.

sent over here by Lord Northcliffe, and I want to have as little to do with him as possible, because I don't believe in Lord Northcliffe any more than I do in Mr. Hearst'. Thus it had been satisfactorily settled that Northcliffe should not come. It remained for the State Department to arrange the matter through the diplomatic channels.

The War Cabinet's decision to send Northcliffe was, of course, not publicly known, and had Washington telegraphed promptly to London the nomination would assuredly have been reviewed. But either Lansing was not informed with the necessary speed, or he deemed the matter not to be urgent; for, as it turned out, the next action was public. On 7 June the New York newspapers announced, 'Lord Northcliffe's acceptance, at the request of the War Cabinet, of the position of head of the British War Mission in the United States, in succession to Mr. Balfour'. The source of this paragraph was unknown. It forced Lansing immediately to telegraph Page: 'Department is informed on authority that British Government is contemplating sending Lord Northcliffe on special Mission to this country. Department feels that nothing can be gained by sending another commission or a commissioner. Impression made by Mr. Balfour was so favourable it would seem better to let matters stand as they are rather than send anyone at this time.'[1] So much for Lansing. As for House, he was constrained by the announcement to write to Wilson to say he was 'sorry Northcliffe is coming. I thought Balfour's cable had headed him off.' In the meantime, Wiseman learnt also that Page had approved his coming and had thought he would be acceptable to the president. Page's report was in characteristically cordial, exaggerated, terms. He liked both the Mission and the appointment, and said so in a telegram which emphasized the nature of Northcliffe's purely 'commercial and not diplomatic errand; nor do his duties have any reference to what Mr. Balfour did'. And, Page added, 'He knows the U.S. better than any Englishman except Bryce'.[2] He said

[1] Baker, *op. cit.*, vii. 102.   [2] Ibid. 104.

more, doubtless because he was necessarily ignorant of the feeling created against Northcliffe in Washington and New York. Page won his point so far as to stay the immediate action against Northcliffe. While this correspondence was proceeding, Northcliffe was on the ocean, unaware that he was to confront the situation created by Spring-Rice's intervention with House. The difficulties were increased by Northcliffe's failure to take advantage of Balfour's arrival in London before he left. Of this fact varying interpretations were current. The truth was that the interval between Lloyd George's expression of his wish, and Northcliffe's boarding ship in obedience to it, was thirty-three hours. It was he, probably, who informed the New York press on the 6–7 June. In such haste he had accepted the work, which was to prove the greatest effort of his life. He left in a second-class American steamer with his valet as his only companion. What was America to do with him when he arrived? The situation is indicated in House's note:

> Sir William Wiseman talked with me for nearly an hour on Thursday. We discussed Northcliffe's proposed visit. The much feared action was taken before Balfour's return; Northcliffe will arrive on the St. Paul tomorrow. Wiseman and I decided to make the best of it, and try to guide Northcliffe so as to make his visit a success rather than a failure, which it bids fair to be. He is to be surrounded with people who will keep him straight. When we discussed Northcliffe's coming with the Ambassador it was our intention to let him run amok, but after enjoying the thought of this, Wiseman and I decided the matter was too serious and that we should help when we could.[1]

On 10 June Northcliffe arrived in New York. As he stepped off the ship, in his blue serge suit, soft grey hat and red-checked tie, and carrying a malacca cane, he radiated health and confidence. He had prepared a written statement and refused to add to it, except to say that he would have no time

[1] House, 9 June 1917. This extract is from the unpublished portion of House's diary. Other unpublished portions hereafter referred to are indicated as 'House'. The published portions here used are referred to as 'Seymour'. See above, p. 433, note 2.

for social engagements. He declined comment on censorship, the state of the war or any related subject, and would say nothing even about his own immediate business. He had known since he first came into publishing that he was no organizer, no administrator; he was a creator and visualizer. He believed he admired America more, and understood Americans better, than any other man upon whose services Britain could call. His acceptance of the task did not mean that he, with Lloyd George at the head of the Government, had any less dislike of official trammels or, that he had overlooked the prime minister's mixture of motives in making him, of all people, the offer; only that he absolutely agreed with Lloyd George's principal official motive: the time had passed for 'Diplomacy as Usual'.

The new British envoy was met on arrival at New York by one of his own staff, Mr. (now Sir) Arthur Willert, the correspondent in Washington of *The Times*. The ambassador was not represented.[1] Willert conducted his chief to Wiseman's office. House's letter of 12 June is brief but descriptive:

> Northcliffe was not received by any of the staff of the British Embassy, and he was angry beyond words.[2] He told Wiseman that he had been offered the Ambassadorship but had declined it. His Government requested him to get in touch with Sir William Wiseman. The British Government have given him the widest possible powers and it would therefore seem necessary to give him proper consideration. . . . While Sir William was with Northcliffe yesterday Hearst sent a request to him to the hotel. Northcliffe refused to see the Representative, and sent word to Hearst to come if he desires. In the event he comes, Northcliffe would tell him some home truths that would be good for his soul.[3]

By this time, House had so thoroughly accepted the situation that, simultaneously, he wrote to Northcliffe a welcoming letter: 'I hope that you will call on me at anytime that you

---

[1] Sir Arthur Willert relates his abortive attempt to persuade the ambassador to move, and his decision that it would be improper to advertise Northcliffe's arrival. Cf. Willert, *The Road to Safety* (London, 1952), p. 99.

[2] The scene is described by Willert. 'There ensued one of the most formidable explosions of temper that I have ever witnessed' (*ibid.* p. 100).

[3] House to Wilson, 12 June 1917.

think I can be of assistance', and expressed his delight at his safe arrival.[1]

On the 27 June Page's delayed personal report to the president was received at the White House. The ambassador now wrote in the style that Wilson most disliked: 'He [Northcliffe] is perhaps the most powerful man now living in Great Britain — how much by reason of and how much in spite of his methods it would be hard to say'. Ignoring all disputes over contraband, and Northcliffe's forthright championship of the strict interpretation of the Declaration of London, Page proceeded, in the enthusiastic Anglophil manner that so infuriated Wilson, to say that 'For the twenty years I have known him he has done our country steady and useful service in his vast influence on British opinion'.[2] But now Northcliffe had to be accepted, for he had already arrived, with authority, which, after an initial explosion in the embassy, he was determined to exercise. This being so, it was now imperative to reverse the anti-Northcliffe drive. House reported to the president that the ambassador had now seen his *bête-noire*.

His first meeting with Northcliffe was at the Embassy where he had invited him to dinner. Strangely enough, he chose this place and occasion to insult him. He had asked Northcliffe to come a few minutes in advance of the guests in order that he might express his opinion of him. Northcliffe started to leave before the dinner, and if it had not been for the opportune arrival of the French Ambassador, who was also one of the guests, he would have done so.[3]

[1] House to Northcliffe, 12 June 1917.
[2] Page to Wilson, 22 June 1917. (Hendrick, *W. H. Page*, ii. 385.)
[3] House to Wilson, 27 June 1917. Cf. the account of Willert who was present: 'When he [Northcliffe] entered the study the Ambassador was sitting at his desk and did not move for some seconds. Then he leapt up, took a few steps towards his guest and stopped with his hands behind his back and said he had never expected to have to receive him in his home. Northcliffe stood still and said nothing. "Yes," the Ambassador went on, "you are my enemy." He then accused Northcliffe of having inserted in a newspaper a letter hostile towards him. . . . Northcliffe replied that he had had no responsibility for the letter and said, "But if you feel as you say you do towards me, I had better leave your house at once", and turned towards the door. At this Spring-Rice came quickly forward and offered his hand, saying, "The war makes strange

There was little doubt that, the British embassy apart, Northcliffe had been 'received'. It appeared that he had business that was more urgent than House had anticipated. His diary records a telephone conversation with Wiseman on the night of 28 June when House was in Massachusetts. Northcliffe, it appeared, had received such an urgent message from the prime minister to 'see me immediately' that House concluded there was nothing to be done but for him to go to New York. However, Wiseman and he talked over the matter on the telephone on the 29th, and they decided that in view of other cables of a more imperative nature, it was better for Northcliffe to go at once to Washington. The whole business, House now found, was 'freighted' with too much importance 'to waste time upon conventionalities'. The matter was nothing else than British credit and the way to save it. The means could not be as 'usual'. House thus addressed the president:

29th June 1917.

DEAR GOVERNOR,

Things began to break yesterday afternoon in British quarters. Spring-Rice is at Woods Hole and McAdoo at Buena Vista and the machinery became clogged. As usual, Sir William took hold and is trying today to see what can be done.

Northcliffe received a message from Lloyd George to come here and advise with me before moving further. He was ready to take the ten o'clock train this morning when I received, through Sir William, the June 28 cable from Balfour which I sent you by Lansing. I therefore advised Northcliffe to go to Washington immediately rather than come here which he has done.

By putting together what I gather from Washington and Sir William, the trouble that has come about concerning finances is largely a matter of misunderstanding with some fault on both sides.

Sir Richard Crawford tries to work through Administration channels. Sir Hardman Lever works partly through Morgan & Company, and it is not certain that the Morgans have not lent a helping hand to this crisis.

The British understood that we would take care of certain

bed-fellows and we must work together whatever our personal feelings." North cliffe took his hand' (A. Willert, *op. cit.*, p. 104).

Russian obligations they have been carrying. They claim if they had not been under this impression they would have arranged to take care of the matter in a different way. What they need is $35,000,000 on Monday, $100,000,000 on Thursday and $185,000,000 a month for two months beginning ten days from next Thursday.

This is a staggering amount and indicates the load Great Britain has been carrying for her allies. It seems to me that we should have some definite understanding with England as to what money she will need in the future and how far she can count upon us.

It seems absurd to be giving her comparatively small amounts the frequent publication of which make a bad impression on our people. Would they not stand one large amount better than these lesser amounts constantly brought to their attention?

Affectionately yours,
E. M. HOUSE.

Northcliffe arrived at the White House on 30 June, two days after House and Wiseman had conferred over the telephone. He was handicapped with a career that was supremely objectionable to the president, a Mission that had hardly been comprehended and a status that was still in controversy. All that the new British envoy had to commend him was his information and his personality. He had come to give the president privately an item of news as sensational as any that he had ever had to 'break': Britain was all but bankrupt. The interview was satisfactory, and as the immediate matter was one of finance, Northcliffe was presently conducted to the secretary of the treasury, William McAdoo.[1] The kind of impression Northcliffe made upon him is described by the secretary himself:

In the course of our conversation I discussed with him the proposed Inter-Allied Committee in Europe, and told him frankly that I felt somewhat impatient with what appeared to me procrastination on the part of the allied governments in dealing with a matter of such outstanding importance. I have met few men who had such quick comprehension as Lord Northcliffe. It was never

[1] 'Sir William has just telephoned that Northcliffe was satisfied with his interview with the President' (House, 30 June 1917).

necessary to explain anything to him twice. He reminded me more of the highest type of American business executive than any foreigner I have ever known. He was dynamic, his phrases were vivid, his ideas crisp and clear, and he had a way of getting down at once to the vital thought in any question under discussion. Northcliffe's strong point was determining how to do things.[1]

Northcliffe's success was so immediate, and so unexpected in the foreign office and the embassy, that Balfour and Spring-Rice found it necessary to assure House that he could, with complete diplomatic propriety, give Northcliffe his confidence. On 13 July Spring-Rice reported to Balfour that he had pointed out to House in New York that

as Lord Northcliffe had not received any diplomatic commission, it was not, strictly speaking, necessary to ask for the President's consent to his Mission. The Mission had regard to the organization of the various British agencies in the United States. This was a matter for the British War Council. Had the matter been less urgent I had no doubt that the President's opinion would have been taken etc.

He proceeded to commend Northcliffe for the extremely favourable impression he had made.

A few weeks sufficed to give Northcliffe a sure estimate of the general situation and the extent of House's influence. He wrote home that 'the President is the whole Government. He is the absolute head of the Army, Navy, and Civil Service, and next to him in importance is Colonel House, who lives not in Washington, but twelve hours' journey away.' Describing the simple style in which House chose to live, 'at the rate of about, in English money, fifteen hundred a year', he said that 'One of the reasons of his power with the President is that he wants nothing for himself. He could have any office he chose.' The man himself was 'gentle, quiet and unassuming. . . . He is now at the head of the United States politics, and before the end of the war will be one of the heads of the World's politics'.[2]

[1] W. G. McAdoo, *Crowded Years* (London, 1932), p. 400.
[2] Northcliffe's confidential letter to selected members of his newspaper staffs, 12 Aug. 1917.

Personality and Diplomacy in Anglo-American Relations, 1917

House, for his part, was fast becoming attached to Northcliffe. An entry in the diary regrets the ambiguous position in which he found himself:

> I would prefer to be as frank as he is, but the exigencies of the occasion forbid. ... However, I talk to Northcliffe as frankly as I can upon all subjects. The difference here again, is that, he in turn, has too many confidants. Northcliffe is a dominating man with boundless energy. I like him the more I see him.[1]

If the diplomatic difficulties had been largely overcome, and Northcliffe found he could afford to ignore the ambassador, it remained to get on with the job. The atmosphere in Washington was still unwarlike, Northcliffe thought. He took a poor view of the U.S. Cabinet of 'sentimental Radicals'. The war was not popular and much needed to be done to rouse the great nation. 'Only the gigantic and obtuse blundering of the Germans could have got these people into the War. Now they are in, I think it will very difficult to get them out.' Yet, the nation as such was all apathy. 'It is the President who is the War'.[2]

In the heat of July and August the situation was depressing but there was no time to lose. Northcliffe worked like a titan, touring as he had never done before; speaking, as nobody had yet spoken, on the text: 'The war has only just started'. He wore out himself and his staff in these months by incessant efforts to educate the American people. Northcliffe's grandest effort was not supererogatory. Americans even in Washington had little conception of the extent of British expenditure in life, shipping and money. Accustomed as they were to figures they thought of as huge, the losses in manpower and shipping, the figures of finance and expenditure had risen to dimensions wholly strange to them. The imperative needs compelled Northcliffe to urge new ideas notably upon the responsible leaders but also upon the people. He put all his strength of heart and body into the task of convincing America of the war's overmastering urgency, of the vital

[1] House, 13 Aug. 1917.
[2] The quotations are from the letter of 12 Aug. 1917.

necessity for speed and of the absolute requirement of efficiency.

If any proof is required that Northcliffe's mind was genuinely dedicated to what he had regarded ever since August 1914 as the supreme task facing Britain, it may be found in the speeches, lectures and interviews he delivered in all parts of the United States after his arrival in June. In that abnormally hot summer he was tireless, meeting and speaking personally to hundreds of individual Americans as well as to vast audiences. Northcliffe spared himself nothing. His energy was superabundant, his popularity unlimited, his success spectacular, his conduct irreproachable, his modesty, as House and others admitted, 'surprising'. To the astonishment of all, Northcliffe, the supposed egoist and demagogue, behaved throughout as a statesman — not indeed, as a highly trained official, or conventional envoy. His attack on the problem was individual and unusual. Even those who would have preferred another man and another method respected his energy. This was the summit of Northcliffe's career, and he may have known it. He certainly could not fail to realize that the problems he had been set, in the conditions that obtained at the end of May, were bound to develop to a point beyond his terms of reference and his personal capacity. The point was reached within four months of his arrival.

It has been seen that when he arrived, the absolutely immediate need was not, as the War Cabinet had originally thought, that of creating a system of 'co-ordinating' the British agencies; nor of 'bringing home to the United States Government the realities of the present war situation' nor even the necessity of arousing their 'immediate active and strenuous co-operation in the war'. At the moment of Northcliffe's arrival the vital need had shifted. The urgency was for funds wherewith to pay for what had been and what was being bought for Britain. It has been seen how Northcliffe had succeeded with the American secretary of the treasury, McAdoo, in averting temporarily the catastrophe that immediately threatened the credit of Britain. He had done this with the help of a picked staff, principal among whom were Sir Charles Gordon, the Canadian and virtual administrator of the Mission; his deputy, the Hon. R. H. (now Lord) Brand; Sir Thomas Royden; Sir Hardman Lever; and Sir Richard Crawford.

But although the urgency was alleviated for the time being, a radical solution in the way of a big loan was needed if Britain was to have the money with which to continue the war. Between 1 April 1914 and 14 July 1917 she had spent the then fabulous sum of £5,161,471,000,[1] gold. As Northcliffe cabled home in the late summer, the American Government staggered under the weight of such figures. Nevertheless, she was mistress of the situation . . . 'as regards ourselves, Canada, France, Italy and Russia. Loan to us strongly opposed by powerful section of Congress. If loan stops, war stops.'[2] The necessary first step was, according to McAdoo, the creation of an inter-allied economic council.

To accomplish this was a task beyond the instructions of Northcliffe. All he could do from Washington was to recommend that cause, and determine to back it up by his own presence in London. He urged the appointment of a British representative with the authority to arrange vitally important loans, while he would remain, for the time being, in charge of commercial affairs and propaganda. On the advice of House, Northcliffe put forward the name of Reading, then Lord Chief Justice. It was not until 31 August that Reading was able to assure Northcliffe that he could leave London for Washington. The announcement was made during renewed talk of peace. On 17 July the Reichstag had passed a motion for peace on the basis of 'No Annexations: No Indemnities'. This resolution evoked responses in England which were made firmer by the sacrifices demanded by the policy of victory, and the knowledge that the Allies could not count upon divisions from across the Atlantic until the

[1] Bonar Law to Northcliffe, 20 July 1917, *apud* Isaacs, *The Life of Lord Reading*, p. 59. [2] H. Wickham Steed, *Through Thirty Years*, ii. 143.

lapse of months. On the third anniversary of the outbreak Lloyd George found it necessary to warn London not to be more concerned to end the war than to win it. The way to win it, serious people in Washington thought, lay through an Allied staff having the necessary organizing capacity and overriding authority. It was recognized that nationality and particularist feelings on both sides had long obstructed Allied unity, and it was believed that Lloyd George, aware as he was of the position, would need to be pressed before he would consent to an agreement that might appear to subordinate Britain to France. On 15 August Northcliffe informed the prime minister that 'Colonel House who rarely raises his voice said with some emphasis "McAdoo will insist on the Inter-Allied Council"'.[1]

Northcliffe was in his best form at this time. While impressing the Americans with his energy and promptitude in decisions and action he was tactful toward everybody, and conciliatory even to the embassy. He knew he was doing well, and sent a disarming message to Balfour: 'I am every day convinced that had your visit been prolonged, you personally, by reason of your influence with Americans, could at that time have made agreements that would have solved our present difficulties'.[2] So modestly did Northcliffe bear himself in August, though war was his text he did not attack peace.

That month Pope Benedict XV had circulated a 'Peace Note' to the powers, an answer to which was not easily found. The Allies were not united on their 'Peace Points' and they left it to the president to reply to the pope. When published on 29 August it was received with no enthusiasm by the Allies. What the pope had really done was to illustrate to the world how different the war aims of the president were from those of the Allies; there was a difference in principle. This being made so clear, the president decided on 2 September to ask House to get together a group to collate documents on

[1] House, 15 Aug. 1917.
[2] Northcliffe to the foreign secretary, House, 26 April 1917.

war aims and prepare a memorandum for his guidance. Wilson directed House on 19 September, adding that Lansing 'volunteers the opinion that you were the only one to do it'.[1] Thus House began what was later known as 'The Inquiry' which resulted in the drafting of the Fourteen Points.

While this study of peace terms was being mooted the prime minister wrote to House urging that it was essential that a representative of the United States should be appointed to London 'as soon as possible'. This dovetailed with the scheme to place Reading in Washington in charge of finance, and both fitted into the American idea of a grand inter-allied General Staff, towards which Lloyd George was suspected of being as cautious as the Americans were known to be eager. Northcliffe set himself to put forth every exertion to accomplish the American plan. Meanwhile, Reading was on the way across the Atlantic. He arrived on 12 September and, with all Northcliffe's support, immediately took a firm grasp of the financial emergency. Reading was no more enthusiastic over Northcliffe than House, Wiseman and the others had been. Northcliffe himself, however, at this time was another man. A long official message of his alludes to the effort Reading was 'making indefatigably amidst great difficulties'. He had already achieved a degree of success that could not have been 'brought about by anyone not possessed by his ability, charm, and tact'.[2]

House, gifted as he too was with charm and tact, had in the months that had intervened since Northcliffe's arrival become captivated by him, as an entry in the diary for August had shown.[3] Three months later his feeling was akin to a mystified admiration. In due time Reading came to see House. The Lord Chief Justice indulged in some relatively mild denigration of Northcliffe which moved House to write that 'I wish to say, however, that I like Northcliffe the more I see him. He does what he promises, and he rings

---

[1] Seymour, *op. cit.*, iii. 170, 174.
[2] Northcliffe to the prime minister, Balfour, Bonar Law and Churchill (House, 30 Sept. 1917). [3] See above (p. 449) for the entry, 13 Aug. 1917.

true. I am constantly wondering how well we analyse him. There must be more to him than his critics see, for how could he have made the success he has? I confess he is a puzzle to me.'[1] This was House's judgment on Northcliffe in the middle of October.

Preparations were now being made for the dispatch of the American Mission to London. When the British War Cabinet, at Wiseman's instigation, urged their preference for House, he expressed his disinclination to abandon other tasks, the most interesting of which, to him, was 'The Inquiry'. His reluctance was the stronger for his conviction that, as his connexion with 'The Inquiry' was known, his arrival in London then would be interpreted in some quarters as connected with possible peace moves, for which he was not yet ready. House did, however, consent to take charge of the Mission. The principal business was to effect the closest co-operation between the Allies and America and to represent America in a general council of the Allies. Meanwhile, the British Mission made ready to leave. Northcliffe and Reading took the same ship and would, according to the official announcement, remain in Europe during the period of the 'Conference of the Allied Governments'. The American War Mission left Halifax, N.S., on 29 October, and arrived at Plymouth on 7 November. Next day it became known that the second Russian revolution had broken out and that the Bolsheviks, with Lenin at their head, had seized power in Petrograd. The conference of the Allied Governments was more than ever justified and, it was appreciated, more than ever urgent. The American Mission was rapidly installed at Chesterfield House. Apart from agitating in favour of an inter-allied General Staff, Northcliffe's private intention, now that Reading had been secured for Washington and House for London, was to concentrate upon war propaganda, and that not only in America. He had been led by House to understand that the right kind of propaganda in enemy countries could drive a wedge between the enemy Govern-

[1] House, 18 Oct. 1917.

ments and their populations.¹ What he did not then understand was that such propaganda presupposed an agreed Allied peace programme.

There is no sign that Northcliffe was more than vaguely aware that, for propaganda purposes, it was, or would be, necessary to assume that the war had already been won; an assumption intensely repugnant to him. But hesitant as he was about talking peace before victory, he was certain that no meeting of the Council of the Allies would be complete without his presence. He knew the value of what he had done in America, and his return to England was timed to permit of his attendance in Paris on 22 November. This, of course, was the conference at which House was due to attend, in accordance with the instructions of the president 'to represent me in the general conference presently to be held by the Governments associated in war with the Central Powers'. It is possible that Northcliffe's intimacy with House, and the opportunity he had to observe the extent of his influence, had led Northcliffe to consider how far his present position might carry with it the possibility of increasing his own power. What is certain is that House had now come to entertain an almost superstitious respect for the force of Northcliffe's personality and for his ability to dominate the War Cabinet. Equally, House cherished an unlimited belief in his own capacity, aided by Wiseman, to guide Northcliffe, as he had guided Wilson, in the right direction. Just as Northcliffe had an ascendancy over Lloyd George and the War Cabinet, House and Wiseman would inspire Northcliffe. They had successfully 'guided' him in New York and Washington, and were disposed to 'guide' him in London, and by his help and that of Reading, to influence Lloyd George.

The prime minister had not yet returned from his visit with the French premier to the Italian front, which had

¹ Northcliffe to the prime minister: 'House had referred again and again to propaganda. . . . The war was being fought without imagination; propaganda should be spread in Germany by airplanes and other means' (House, 15 Aug. 1917).

collapsed at Caporetto. Lloyd George was in Paris, striving against the British military chiefs, to set up the Supreme War Council. He was destined, on his return, to be the object of unrestrained criticism from the partisans of the army. Lloyd George was due to reply in the House of Commons on the 19th. With this debate on his mind, and at this critical point of the war — Russia totally lost and Italy virtually out of the war — it was necessary for the prime minister, incidentally, to ponder the disposal of Northcliffe. His nuisance value, at this point of the nation's future, was obviously undeniable and might become nearly infinite. Could he or could he not be made to return to America alongside Reading? In any event, it would be necessary to control him, either by renewing his American appointment or by finding him something new. He had been got rid of — once; he had done wonders; he had 'behaved'. Therefore he could 'behave' again. It was a fact, too, that his newspapers had virtually suspended attacks on the Government. In these circumstances, if they would only last, there was nothing the prime minister would not do for Northcliffe.

Meanwhile, House was losing no time in seeing the principal personalities and in gathering impressions of the trend of events, military and political; the tendency of thoughts, war aims and peace aims. On 9 November Milner is recorded in House's diary as 'able enough and judicious enough to see where this war is leading Europe, and he has a keen desire to bring it to an end in some way that will not make the sacrifices futile'.[1] On 11 November, Wiseman presented the head of the American Mission at Buckingham Palace. The king invited House and Mrs. House for lunch next day. Nothing could have gone more smoothly for the personalities that enter this narrative. Yet it was not certain that Northcliffe would continue to 'behave'. House notes that he had that day met with a journalist who prophesied that:

Lloyd George and Northcliffe will have a row, and as he expressed it, 'many wigs will fall upon the green'. He said he was

[1] Seymour, *op. cit.*, iii. 227, 232.

Personality and Diplomacy in Anglo-American Relations, 1917

present when George asked Northcliffe to go to the U.S. and was surprised when Northcliffe consented. Later he said he was with George when a third friend asked why Northcliffe was sent to America, and whether it was not because he was becoming troublesome. George admitted that this was his reason.

When everyone asks me, from the King down, about Northcliffe's career in the U.S. I tell them he has been surprisingly modest; that he has taken advice and altogether done well.

Loulie and I lunched with the King and Queen at Buckingham Palace.[1]

There is no reason to doubt that one of Lloyd George's reasons for offering Northcliffe the Washington appointment was that he was 'getting troublesome' at home, or that Northcliffe was unaware that this was the fact. That Northcliffe's motive for accepting was purely patriotic is also not to be doubted. Whether his patience at home now would be equal, or that he would not again be getting 'troublesome' was very much to be doubted; the more so since the war situation was so gravely unfavourable to the Allies. On 13 November, House had a talk with Northcliffe, who had just concluded his reading of a mass of data supplied to him by his several newspapers and other private agencies and personal information services. He found him pessimistic over England and optimistic over America. They talked vaguely over the opportunities that presented themselves now that the prime minister had returned, and whom House had not visited. Northcliffe said he would effect a meeting.

A date had been set for the inter-allied meeting to which the Americans had so long attached primary importance. But it was known the prime minister, with so much other business on his hands, had voiced the fear that he might be prevented from attending. This became known to House on the 14th. The information depressed him so much that he talked to Wiseman about it. They met on the 15th. House's diary for that day furnishes an example of his method:

Wiseman and I decided this morning to read the riot act to Mr. Lloyd George. He told someone yesterday that he did not

[1] House, 12 Nov. 1917.

believe he would go to the Paris Conference. Wiseman and I believe he will. I asked Wiseman to ring up Lord Northcliffe and tell him if Lloyd George did not go to the Conference, I would not go myself, and I would advise the French Government to call it off. I asked him to say to Northcliffe that if this were done it would have a disastrous effect throughout the Allied countries and would exhilarate Germany.[1]

House's position was that the conference needed full authority 'not indeed for what it may do in its deliberations, but for its moral effect'. When Wiseman spoke to Northcliffe, 'he thoroughly agreed with my position', and agreed to intervene with the prime minister. House was so satisfied that he believed 'that Northcliffe can be used to club Lloyd George into any plan we think wise.' Wiseman had even greater confidence. He told House that 'Northcliffe is willing to be guided by the President and me [House], having suddenly conceived a great respect for our opinion'. House and Wiseman were delighted with the prospect of effecting American policy with the willing assistance of their 'club'.[2] The 'club' had, in the due course, met the prime minister and asked him when he proposed to see House. He replied 'tomorrow'. Whereupon Northcliffe said to him, 'Sit down and write Colonel House the most cordial invitation you know how, to dine with you tonight'.

The reader will prefer to trace the next stages in an extract, albeit a long one, from House's diary, and will himself, perhaps, draw the obvious inferences (for the recital of which the space here available is insufficient):

Later in the day, Wiseman telephoned from the Prime Minister's residence asking if it would be convenient to have Lloyd George come to Chesterfield House at once. Of course, I answered yes. He said when the Prime Minister decided to call on me instead of asking me to come to him, his secretaries were struck dumb. It is the first time, so he says, that the Prime Minister has made such a call.

[1] House, 15 Nov. 1917.
[2] The term 'club' occurs in House's letter to the president. 'Northcliffe has been splendid. He holds a club over the P.M. and threatens to use it unless he does as desired' (House to Wilson, 16 Nov. 1917). The quotations made above occur in House for the dates cited.

Personality and Diplomacy in Anglo-American Relations, 1917

Before Lloyd George arrived, the Lord Chief Justice came apropos of nothing. It was evident to me, though, that Lloyd George had asked him to come. We talked a few minutes before the Prime Minister was announced. I told Reading that it was absolutely essential that the Paris Conference be held and why, and I thought George had made a mistake in announcing his plea for a Supreme War Council before the Conference was held. It should have been announced then, and if it had been, there would not have been the slightest criticism from any source, because everyone would have thought it had been decided upon by common agreement, and that the United States was largely responsible for it.

Reading agreed to this but excused George on account of the urgency of the situation in Italy, an excuse I did not accept because the Italian morale was stiffened not by that decision but by the announcement that Great Britain and France had decided to send troops to Italy to help hold that front.

I called Reading's attention to the importance of Lloyd George working cordially with me. If he did, I thought his Government could not be overthrown. In saying this I intended a covert threat which I think Reading caught. At this stage, the Prime Minister and Wiseman came in. George greeted Reading with enthusiasm, saying how delighted he was that he should have happened to be here at this time. He was just the man he wished to be present, for he had something very disagreeable to ask me. I marvelled that a man of George's ability should undertake to act so patent a farce.

He made a long speech urging me to consent to a postponement of the Interallied Conference. I listened quietly, for Reading had told me in advance of his coming what he would say, and I had told Reading that I would consent to postpone the Conference for a week but no longer. Reading and I had talked it out so all the arguments George gave were mere repetitions. Because of the Italian situation; because of the lack of a French Ministry, it would be futile to have a conference before these two situations composed themselves.

George wished to postpone it until a more distant date but I insisted upon naming the 29th of November, and this was finally agreed upon. He is to send for Balfour and have him communicate with the French Government and explain the reasons it will not be possible to hold the Conference on the 22nd. France is to be told that the situation in Italy is the cause of the postponement, and Italy will be told that it is because of conditions in France.

Thus it was agreed that the conference should be postponed a week. The American eagerness to ensure that the conference not only met, but enjoyed the fullest measure of authority, arose from the position that Wilson had taken towards the papal Peace Note, the reply to which the Allies had left to him. House was bound to bear in mind American ideas on peace, as well as on war, and behind all the urgency for men and munitions there lay the pressure for terms and conditions of peace or war.

One of House's principal visitors at this time was Lansdowne. In conversation with House he 'condemned . . . the folly and madness of some of the British leaders. . . . He believes that definite war aims should be set out — aims that are moderate and that will appeal to moderate minds in all countries. . . . [He advocated] a more liberal sea policy, bordering on the plan for the freedom of the seas, which indeed he was good enough to say that he had obtained from me during my last visit here'.[1] House gave Lansdowne encouragement, though there is no proof that he recommended the publication of any manifesto. It is more probable that House at this moment saw himself as the standing inspirer of the president, acting in the near future as the prime co-ordinator of some sort of triumvirate responsible for the drafting of the Allied peace programme. Tyrrell told House on the 14th that he had been instructed to prepare a memorandum on the subject and it was understood between them that House should explore Lloyd George's mind at an early opportunity.

Although House was regularly communicating with Northcliffe, the entries in his diary show that he abstained from all conversation with him on peace aims. They had talked about propaganda as a weapon of war, and found themselves in agreement on a fundamental principle: the German Government and the German people were distinct; therefore they could be divided. But in House's just mind, Northcliffe was not a constructive peace-maker but a master

[1] Seymour, *op. cit.*, iii. 233 (14 Nov. 1917).

war-maker, one of the few in England able to divine the thing to be done to win the war, and direct the way of doing it quickly — that is to say, at this time they saw eye to eye on such matters. For instance, the entries in House's diary prove that Northcliffe and House knew enough to forecast a substantial change in the British Air Arm. Also House assumed Northcliffe's presence at the forthcoming meeting of the inter-allied War Council, to the creation of which both of them had contributed. Equally, House, in conversation with the prime minister, took advantage of the opportunity to praise Northcliffe's work in America, and also Reading's. Already, however, Lloyd George had put forward Reading's name and also that of Northcliffe for an elevation in rank, while appreciating the fact that the latter's name would not be received by the king with any enthusiasm.

But there was about to occur an incident that reversed the prime minister's own feelings towards Northcliffe. On November 15 Lloyd George invited Northcliffe to lunch at Downing Street. The prime minister, on this occasion, plied the British Commissioner in the United States, and chairman of the War Mission, as Northcliffe's official position still was, with attention. In the course of the lunch Lloyd George threw out the suggestion that his guest might take over the Air Ministry which, as he proposed in the near future, might be created out of the old Air Board, secretary of which was Lord Cowdray. Another appointment would need to be found if the proposed change were accepted by the War Cabinet. Cowdray, of course, was, at this time, unaware of any project to make a change in his Board or in his personal position. It would appear that Lloyd George understood from Northcliffe's demeanour that he might be willing to consider the appointment. He persuaded Bonar Law to approve accordingly.[1] He waited, however, for a sign from Northcliffe that he would accept the appointment if offered to him.

So far so good. Lloyd George had begun the process

[1] Frank Owen, *Tempestuous Journey* (London, 1954), p. 421.

of tying Northcliffe down; he would not now be 'troublesome'; and his position would be conspicuous, even if it carried with it no seat in the War Cabinet. That body consisted of Bonar Law, Carson, Curzon, Milner, Barnes and Smuts, besides himself, and Northcliffe would be called in as required. This was a perfectly satisfactory arrangement in Lloyd George's mind, and he hoped that afternoon that Northcliffe would say 'Yes' if the Air Ministry should be offered to him.

On that evening Northcliffe made one of his rare appearances at the House of Commons. He was present at an official dinner, given in honour of the American War Mission by the foreign secretary. No doubt the Government was encouraged by Northcliffe's acceptance of this invitation which presented a notable departure from habit. During the dinner Northcliffe apparently said nothing about the sounding which Lloyd George had made earlier in the day in connexion with the proposed new Air Ministry.

But between lunch and dinner Northcliffe had composed a letter addressed to the prime minister which criticized disunity in war control, weakness in eradicating anti-war propaganda, failure to mobilize the whole man-power of the country and refusal to introduce compulsory food rationing. As for office, he flatly refused to entertain the idea. 'I can do better work if I maintain my independence and am not gagged by a loyalty that I do not feel to the whole of your Administration.' The old Northcliffe had returned, in full venom. His final sentence must have seemed to be hard to believe: 'I have none but the most friendly feelings towards yourself'. It can only have been felt by the prime minister as an utter and complete departure from all the usages of public life, and as a deliberate and advertised personal affront, for Northcliffe had communicated his letter of rejection to the news agencies before dinner, and before the prime minister could possibly have received it. Lloyd George first heard of it on the telephone from Lord Beaverbrook, who had been informed by his newspaper. The prime

Personality and Diplomacy in Anglo-American Relations, 1917

minister is reported to have been enraged beyond words.[1] He knew he had only sounded Northcliffe as to his possible willingness to entertain the offer; he had not made the offer. He was, therefore, justified in deciding that it was unforgivable for Northcliffe to subject the head of the Government to such treatment, above all at a time when he and Allied ministers were facing the worst reverses and the gravest decisions of the war.

What, then, was Northcliffe's position? What part did he think he could play on the stage as it was being set in November 1917?

The answer to these questions is not obvious. It was impossible for him to have accepted the Air Ministry, or any other, even if it entailed a seat in the War Cabinet, enlarged to six to include him. He had too often demanded a smaller War Cabinet than five, but the real reason was that Northcliffe knew better than ever before that he could not succeed as head of any department. He must leave the stage free for the players while he assumed some measure of responsibility for the superior direction. It was the war as a whole that engrossed his mind. That was his earlier attitude, and even had he felt tempted to head a department, he would have envied House's possession of freedom and power, though he could have no use for the secrecy which was House's natural medium. As for Northcliffe's main policy, he regarded Britain as, henceforth, having to play second fiddle to the United States: his conviction that the war could only be won from America carried with it the proviso that America must be fully represented in all Allied councils. He knew this from experience; from the president, from McAdoo and from House. As to himself, he knew that Reading's presence in Washington as financial expert created the conditions in which he would, perhaps, return to America. Americans needed to be put in a position to see for themselves what was wanted and that the Allies were in agreement upon it. This was the basic idea of the inter-allied conference for

[1] Frank Owen, *op. cit.*, p. 421.

which House, Northcliffe and Wiseman were pressing. Northcliffe hoped the conference would comprise the strongest team that the Allies could assemble.[1] This was the state of mind Northcliffe was in before he went to lunch with Lloyd George.

But this is not all that is to be said of Northcliffe's 'state of mind'. Of the principal persons then influential in Anglo-American relations, House was the senior. He was 59, Reading was 57, Northcliffe was only 52. But, youngest as he was of these three, Northcliffe bore a heavier burden. Back in England, he began the process of meeting the cost of the arduous summer he had spent in the United States. He had expended nearly all his physical capacity upon that effort, and was quickly to discover that he had no reserve upon which to draw for the later war work that he wished to do. Northcliffe was certainly active after the autumn of 1917 but he never again rose to the heights he had attained in the summer. By November his intuitions had become unreliable, his opinions inconsistent, his physical capacities overstrained. These deficiencies were manifest to few at that time. Certainly House was unaware of the change in Northcliffe's health. But the truth is inescapable: his effort in behalf of Anglo-American relations and the policy of peace by victory had permanently exhausted him. It was his greatest success and fated to be his last. This, therefore, was the Northcliffe who lunched with Lloyd George on 15 November, the climax of his career, when the prime minister was willing to do almost anything for him — this was the Northcliffe who, in the evening, destroyed nearly all his influence in a vain effort to ascend to a new pinnacle of power over policy, over the country, over the Government and over Lloyd George, over everybody.

To this megalomaniac state of mind House had, directly and through Wiseman, contributed. The coincidence of

[1] The *New York American*'s correspondent on Friday 16 Nov. said that Lord Northcliffe's last statement before leaving, 'As quoted here officially' was that 'We must have a Supreme War Council and I am going back to fight for it'. He meant, of course, the inter-allied Council.

Personality and Diplomacy in Anglo-American Relations, 1917

events did the rest. It was in the morning of the 15th that House and Wiseman decided to use Northcliffe as 'a club' to force Lloyd George to act on any 'plan' they thought 'right'. Within an hour or two Northcliffe was with Lloyd George at lunch and in the afternoon he had written his letter 'clubbing' the prime minister into subservience to him. It was a position that no prime minister could tolerate, and however 'splendid' House thought Northcliffe was, his prior publication of the rejection letter was indefensible. It marked the end of Northcliffe, though not immediately. For the moment the prime minister contented himself with avoiding any risk of similar treatment from him. He was more than ever wishful to get rid of him and may have perceived that he was not in robust health. In the meantime, on the night of the 15th, he had to face the immediate entailments of Northcliffe's letter, including the furious anger of the secretary of the Air Board, Cowdray — not one to whom he would wish to present a genuine grievance.

Northcliffe's rejection letter appeared in all the newspapers next morning — the 16th, when the hierarchy of the American War Mission was due to be received at Buckingham Palace. Naturally House was present as its head, and the prime minister and the foreign secretary in attendance. At lunch, House writes:

> I sat between the Queen and the Prime Minister, but my conversation was mostly with the Queen and was all of a more or less intimate character. She recalled with some amusement my prediction that Northcliffe would begin an attack on the Ministry, and cited his letter to the morning press declining to accept a Cabinet position as evidence. . . .

The entry continues:

> After lunch, Lloyd George, the King, Queen and Royal Family had each of the Mission brought up to talk to them separately. This took from half to three-quarters of an hour. Meanwhile Lloyd George and I stood apart telling jokes and laughing at his predicament with Northcliffe. I told him something of Northcliffe's visit and of how perturbed we were when we heard he was

coming. He said of course you know why I sent him.

I gave him an account of the way we took him in hand and of how we had tried to steer him straight. George thought it a remarkable achievement, but he said towards the end, 'I notice before he left, Northcliffe was doing much more talking, and I expected every day to have to recall him'.

I asked if Northcliffe was to return to the United States. He replied, 'I hope you will ask for him because I should like to send him. I would even be willing to take Roosevelt for a while in exchange, although' he added quickly, 'not permanently.' He spoke of Roosevelt having 'lectured' the British Government when he was here, telling them among other things, how to govern Egypt.

We had a good time and I am afraid the King and Queen, who I know dislike George, wondered how I could be on such friendly terms with him.[1]

It might appear from this entry that House had been rendered less enthusiastic about Northcliffe, but it was not so in fact, though he may well have found it prudent on this occasion to talk in a detached fashion about him. House still believed that Northcliffe would be more useful outside Whitehall. His report to the president dated the 16th is explicit. House was enthusiastic over Northcliffe's 'open' letter. 'Northcliffe has been splendid. ... With this combination of Wiseman, Reading and Northcliffe, things are being accomplished with more rapidity than I have ever experienced here.'[2] In the afternoon of the same day (*i.e.* of the publication of Northcliffe's rejection letter and the visit to Buckingham Palace) House was due to keep an appointment. It was with Northcliffe:

I returned to Chesterfield House in order to see Northcliffe. Later, while I was talking with him, Sir Charles Gordon and Geoffrey Dawson, Editor of *The Times*, joined us. My talk with Northcliffe was along general lines. He spoke of the Government's lack of efficiency. He thought there were only two men in it of any value, George and Milner, but Dawson included Geddes and Carson, and so it goes. No two opinions alike.

[1] House, 16 Nov. 1917.
[2] House to Wilson, 16 Nov. 1917; Seymour, *op. cit.*, iii. 240.

Northcliffe criticized Balfour's and Bonar Law's inefficiency and said they should be gotten rid of forthwith. He included Jellicoe in this group. He referred to Jellicoe as 'the man who ran away from a fight'.[1]

That evening House dined with Lord and Lady Reading, when Lloyd George and Wiseman were also present. After dinner, House pressed the prime minister on his ideas of peace terms, and found himself compelled to abandon the effort for the time being as 'useless'. The French and British could not agree. 'Great Britain cannot meet the new Russian terms of "no indemnities and no aggression" [*sic*] and neither can France. Great Britain would at once come in sharp conflict with her Colonies and they might cease fighting, and France would have to relinquish her dream of Alsace and Lorraine.' So, House concluded to wait until he returned to Washington when he would 'advise the President to do it. We are not embarrassed by any desire for territory and commercial gain, therefore we are in a better position to outline peace terms than any of the belligerents'.[2]

Next day, the 17th, Northcliffe was received in audience by the king, and a week later the *London Gazette* announced that he had been raised to the rank of viscount, a distinction now first given to a newspaper proprietor. With the highest public recognition, Northcliffe made ready to attend the Paris conference. As he was still chairman of the British War Mission, he could insist upon a place in the British delegation, and later, if his hosts were willing, he could return to America. All that was against him in the United States was that he had embarrassed some of the American 'Moderates' by taking 'The war has only begun' as his text. But whether he would or would not return to America was still undecided. Northcliffe's future, intensely gossiped about as it was, did not reach typographical expression until the 19th. On that afternoon the *Globe* published an interview in which Northcliffe said that —

[1] House, 16 Nov. 1917.
[2] House, 16 Nov. 1917; Seymour, *op. cit.*, iii. 233.

My direct and indirect connexion with the Government convinces me that it needs wholesale revision ; some of its members are tired and some are unsuitable. At the termination of the Allied Conferences in London and Paris, I propose accepting an invitation to visit various fronts, to take a week's holiday.

He then added, by way of confusing the issue, that he would then 'return to my desk as head of the British War Ministry to New York and Washington'. That he had other ideas is made clear elsewhere. House's awareness of Northcliffe's ambition to enjoy equality with, and even superiority over, statesmen, is disclosed in an entry made towards the end of the month.

Lord Northcliffe came in the afternoon to discuss the Censorship which he declares to be stupid and useless. He says he pays no attention to it himself, and that the British Government dare not interfere. He certainly is an unruly member. Lloyd George wants him back in America because he wishes to get rid of him here. Northcliffe also insists upon going to the Inter-Allied Conference at Paris, and he handles himself just as if he were Dictator of England, and, in a way, he is, for the Government are afraid of him.[1]

After noting other calls on the 20th, House proceeds : 'The King asked me to come to the Palace between five and eight o'clock. I went at seven, the only available hour I had.' They talked for half an hour or more.

The King was full of Northcliffe and his dictatorial assumptions. He asked me to find out quietly, without using his name, whether the Prime Minister intended to let Northcliffe go back to the United States. He also wanted to know whether the Prime Minister would take General Sir William Roberston, Chief of Staff, to Paris for the Inter-Allied Conference. I told him I was sure he would, and I was also certain Northcliffe would return to America whether the Prime Minister desired it or not.

I promised to send the King word about these matters by Sir William Wiseman, whom I declared to be one of the most efficient men of his age I had ever met.[2]

The disposal of Northcliffe was not yet settled and the

---

[1] House, 20 Nov. 1917. [2] House, 20 Nov. 1917.

Personality and Diplomacy in Anglo-American Relations, 1917

continuation of this day's (20 November) entry illustrates the growing disparity between American and Allied peace aims. The ancient and important differences relating to American maritime doctrine continued to offend Britain. American idealism had yet to be reconciled with continental realism, Dominion ambition, French revanchism, Italian irredentism and Russian aspiration. The 1915 agreements were still held valid by France and Italy. The possibilities for House's peace programme were not happy. The entry of the same day reports another instalment of the discussion that House had begun with Lloyd George four days earlier. The activities of Lenin and Trotsky had made peace a highly embarrassing topic throughout Allied official circles.

> The Prime Minister and Lord Chief Justice took dinner with us. We had a long and intimate talk afterwards. George and I did practically all the talking, Reading, as usual, being the listener.
> I pinned George down to British war aims. What Great Britain desires are the African Colonies, both East and West, an independent Arabia, under the suzerainty of Great Britain. Palestine to be given to the Zionists under British or, if desired by us, to be under American control. An independent Armenia and the internationalization of the Straits.
> I made no comments since he, Balfour and I are to have a conference tomorrow upon the same subject. We discussed at length the possible military problems which would come before the Supreme War Council. I find he is willing to take Robertson, Chief of Staff, to France for consultation. This will allay some of the ill-feeling in army circles. We discussed the Russian situation at considerable length. I urged on them a suggestion regarding Roumania which is that she should be made the rallying point for Polish and Cossack troops that are willing to continue fighting. He looked upon this with approval. . . . I got Lloyd George to promise to remain in Paris until after the Inter-Allied Conference adjourned and until the Supreme War Council had formulated definite military plans for the coming year.[1]

In an interval during the same evening the conversation turned to other affairs and personalities. 'We talked of

[1] House, 20 Nov. 1917; for a portion of this passage, see Seymour, *op. cit.*, iii. 235-6.

Northcliffe. He [Lloyd George] evidently is afraid of him and, unfortunately, Northcliffe knows it.' Within a few days the prime minister was to show markedly less fear of the would-be dictator, and House could write that 'George is constantly ridiculing Northcliffe. . . . I replied that I had learnt to like him and that he could send him to America and we would welcome him'.[1] A week later, House advised a hesitant Northcliffe, in answer to his question, not to accept any definition of his position as chairman of the British Commission that would tie him more or less permanently to Washington or New York, but to travel 'back and forth' at intervals between both America and Britain. He would thus keep in touch with conditions in both countries. Northcliffe replied that this had been his conclusion.

> He spoke of someone being near Lloyd George. He thought that while George had courage, at times he neglected to do necessary things. . . .
> Northcliffe believes (he has expressed this to me frequently) that George's incurable timidity at certain times, is due to his humble origin and the fear of criticizing the Aristocracy; he says he has a brother who is a carpenter and quite without education.[2]

But Northcliffe continued to have his uncertainties. His doubts increased. They were destined to be of long standing. His relations with the prime minister worsened gradually and became so negligible that they cease to be mentioned in House's diary or in his correspondence.

A contributory reason for House's silence about Northcliffe was his preoccupation with the subject he continued to avoid in his talks with him: peace. On the 21st, House told Balfour that he thought it 'necessary and pertinent' to make an announcement of general war aims and of the formation of an international association for the prevention of future wars. When the American Mission crossed the Channel they forthwith became involved in discussion with the military side of the Allied Council. They had also to consider

---

[1] House, 1 Dec. 1917. [2] House, 6 Dec. 1917.

a rumoured proposal from Austria for a separate peace and the more serious risk, even virtual certainty, of a separate peace between Russia and Germany. Meanwhile, Allied strength and American unpreparedness, compared with Germany's military might on land and submarine successes at sea, afforded little basis for optimism in Paris. Moreover, the throwing of the whole subject of war aims into the arena of public argument by the reproduction, which began in *Pravda* on 7 November (o.s.), of the London agreements of 1915, amounted to a major diplomatic triumph for Germany. The existence of these agreements had been acknowledged in Washington by Balfour, but no step had been taken, despite House's efforts, towards proposals which, by substance and sanction, could be accepted by America as the associated Power. The Bolshevik revelations strengthened House's determination to bring peace before the Paris War Conference due, after the week's postponement to which House had agreed, to assemble on 29 November. The statement made to the press in the evening of the 22nd, when the American Mission arrived in Paris, contained the striking sentence that 'We have in view no material gain, but what we want is an assurance of permanent peace'. A later *communiqué* included among the objects of the conference, 'the comparison and, in broad outline, a coordination of war aims' with the 'inauguration of the new Allied War Council'. But House quickly found himself unable to place before the conference any resolution dealing with peace and decided to reserve it until he should see Wilson. Nor was he assisted by the publication of a peace letter from an English source.

House maintained his reserve on the subject even after 29 November. This was the day of publication of Lord Lansdowne's letter of which, it has been seen, he had been told — as certain circles in London were aware.[1] Riddell (whom House failed, no doubt deliberately, to contact or utilize, though he was one of the prime minister's closest friends) recorded in his diary on the 4th December, that Lansdowne

[1] For Lansdowne's visit to House on 14 Nov. 1917, see above (p. 460).

had discussed his letter with F. W. Hirst (former editor of the *Economist*) and Lords Loreburn, Morley and Curzon, as well as House.[1] Curzon is said to have disagreed with certain paragraphs, but to have agreed to publication. When Riddell told the prime minister and said that he had reason to think that Colonel House was cognizant of, and approved of, the letter Riddell added that 'it is a serious matter. I am told he [House] suggested the passage as to the freedom of the seas.' Lloyd George answered, ' I think you may be right. Of course the time will come when it will be necessary to re-open the question of peace, but the moment is unfavourable. . . . At the moment we could not secure fair and able terms'.[2]

In Paris, necessary steps were taken to see that its effects were small. The conference gave no consideration to the letter and held consistently to its agenda : war and war only. Experts made their several reports on the desirable course of action as to supplies, shipping and transport, etc. The heads of the American and British War Missions appear to have taken no personal part in the open discussions, so that there was nothing spectacular about them, apart from the fact that House made one of his rare speeches — and this made no mention of peace. The net diplomatic result procured in Paris by Lansdowne's letter and its publication on the day of the opening of the conference was to increase all official aversion from the subject. Lansdowne had succeeded only in blocking peace and blocking House.

Two days after the conference had concluded, the names of House and Northcliffe occur in the news. 'Mr. House' it was then announced —

accompanied by General Bliss, Chief of Staff, Admiral Benson, Chief of Naval Operations, and the members of the American Mission, and Lord Northcliffe left Paris yesterday morning at 7 o'clock for the G.H.Q. of the American Expeditionary Force.

---

[1] These were all friends of House. It may be as well to record that in addition to A. G. Gardiner, House was in touch, from time to time, with Brailsford and Lansbury.   [2] *Lord Riddell's War Diary*, p. 298.

Personality and Diplomacy in Anglo-American Relations, 1917

The Party returned to Paris 4 December. Mr. House and Lord Northcliffe were both particularly pleased with General Pershing's staff organisation.

Next day, in complete secrecy, House with his party left Paris and embarked at Brest.

On 18 December House reported to Wilson and acknowledged his failure to persuade the Allies to prepare a plan or statement of their war aims. The president having listened, agreed to undertake forthwith the task of laying down the conditions upon which America would make peace. The way was thus opened for the drafting of the Fourteen Points, the initial steps towards which House had taken, with presidential sanction, in the work of 'The Inquiry'.[1] It was to be House's later task, in behalf of the president, to obtain the concurrence of the *Entente* to these 'Points'—an enterprise fully as difficult as any he had shouldered. In the course of it, he was to find it necessary to get Northcliffe to make a special visit to Paris in order to help persuade Lloyd George to accept House's interpretation of Point Two, which dealt with the 'absolute Freedom of navigation upon the Seas' etc. The story of the failure of this proceeding and Northcliffe's ambiguous attitude toward Point Two lies outside the scope of an account limited, as the present is, to the events of 1917.

For contrasting reasons, the power of Northcliffe and House waned with the victory for which both had striven. By the end of 1918 both men were in partial eclipse. In the case of Northcliffe, the explanation lies in the state of his health which, even in the middle of 1916, entailed a combination of megalomania and aberration of the kind displayed in the manner of his rejection of the Air Ministry. In House's case, illness was only temporary, and it was Wilson's presence in Paris that affected his position. The year 1917, therefore, was the finest year for both. Four years were to elapse before Northcliffe again visited America. The occasion came in 1922 when his doctors urged that a world cruise might restore his health. In the intervening years Northcliffe had not lost

[1] For 'The Inquiry', see above (pp. 453-4).

touch with House, nor did time efface the impression Northcliffe had made. After controversy had long abated, and Northcliffe had been dead five years, House wrote to his biographer to say that 'Northcliffe had never received the credit due to him in the winning of the War'. His own nation, if represented by the distinguished diplomat who was permanent head of the Foreign Office in 1917, saw him in a different light: 'Northcliffe went over [to the United States] making no secret that he hoped to effect some big coup for his own glorification. . . . He was a complete failure and returned to Europe in a few weeks' time.'[1] Some may believe that the barbs of Lord Hardinge are as wide of the mark as those loosed by the jealous Washington bureaucracy at Colonel House. The 'grand inquisitor and eloquent listener from Texas' was accused of assisting the British by shelving discussion of Point Two of the Fourteen Points, which dealt with the 'Freedom of the Seas'.[2] Thus the accumulated resentment of the petty professional avenged itself for the intrusion of personality into diplomacy.

[1] Viscount Hardinge, *The Old Diplomacy* (London, 1937), p. 213.
[2] See the article in the *New York World*, 9 Dec. 1919. House, according to the inspired writer, had been blandished by Wiseman, and deceived the president.

A. J. P. TAYLOR

THE WAR AIMS OF THE ALLIES IN THE FIRST WORLD WAR

NONE of the Great Powers entered the war of 1914 with defined war aims. Each took up arms for an ostensibly defensive reason; and the programme of each was limited at first to victory in the field. All anticipated short decisive battles and expected the war to be over by Christmas. These expectations were not fulfilled; and the belligerents found themselves, unwillingly enough, with time on their hands to define what they were fighting for as well as what they were fighting against. The Germans had the easier task. They had won the first campaigns, though not the war itself; and their war-programme boiled down to keeping all or part of what they had gained — control over Belgium and northeastern France, domination of the Balkans or, in more general terms, a consolidated *Mitteleuropa*. The Germans made only tactical variations in these aims until October 1918. The Entente Powers found it harder to be precise. In one way, they were less pressed for terms. While the Germans wanted to end a war which they had already won, the Allies would not be called on for their terms until they had reversed the effect of the first German victories. Until the end the practical war aim of the French was to expel the Germans from 'the national territory'; of the British to liberate Belgium; of the Russians to survive as a great military Power.

The Allies could not maintain this negative position. A purely defensive war lacked inspiration. The peoples demanded the prospect of a better world; and the need for this was reinforced when the Allies, Great Britain in particular, appealed to public opinion in the United States. Further, the Allies needed to define their war aims towards each other. In 1815 Gentz cynically described the task of the Congress of Vienna as 'dividing among the victors the spoils of the vanquished'; and, though this was an exaggeration in regard to the settlement of Vienna, or even in regard to that of 1919, relations among victors certainly change fundamentally when the vanquished fall out of the balance. The Russians were well aware that Great Britain and France had sought their friendship mainly, if not solely, from fear of Germany; the French appreciated that their disputes with Great Britain in the Near East were likely to be renewed once German power disappeared. Moreover, the French and the Russians — both heavily engaged against Germany — feared that Great Britain might steal a march on them elsewhere in the world; and though the British could not help doing this, they wished to give their allies an assurance against it all the same.

War aims were, in fact, weapons of war. The public programmes were designed to maintain morale and to win American approval; the secret treaties to give the Allies confidence in each other. Like most treaties, they were a promise that their relations would remain the same when the circumstances which caused these relations altered. Later on, when the secret treaties became known and when the peace settlement aroused perhaps unreasonable disappointment, it was widely held that the secret treaties expressed the real war aims of the Allied rulers and that the public programmes were a fraud on the Allied peoples, on the Americans, and even on the Germans. This was not so. The secret treaties did not contain Allied war aims in the strict sense. They attempted rather to secure the relations of the Allies between themselves; they defined solutions for the problems which would follow the defeat of Germany, not the objects for which Germany should be defeated. It is not surprising, in the circumstances, that the secret treaties were made. What is surprising is that these treaties clashed so little with the public statements. And most surprising of all that the Allies managed to reach a general, even an idealistic, programme when their only practical aim remained, to the end, the defeat of Germany.

The British were the first to begin the process of definition. In Russia the imperial Government did not trouble much about public opinion and used only the old slogans of Holy Russia and a Life for the Tsar. In France parliamentary government was suspended until the end of 1914, and everything subordinated to national defence. Parliamentary life went on in England, and with it a free press. There was also the peculiar circumstance that a Liberal Government was in power; and until the very last minute the principal newspapers supporting the Government had been the most opposed to war. Now these same newspapers had to show why they were the most strenuous in supporting the war. It is a great mistake to suppose that the two wings of the Liberal party welcomed estrangement from each other. Perhaps Lloyd George had sometimes thought of splitting the party and putting himself at the head of a Radical-Labour coalition; but he had not done it. And on the other side, if Asquith or Grey had really felt themselves nearer to the Conservatives than to the Radicals, they would have gone over to the Conservatives; they did not do so. All Liberals rejoiced that the war had reunited them; and the basis of this reunion had to be an idealistic programme. The great Liberal editors, such as Scott of the *Manchester Guardian* and A. G. Gardiner of the *Daily News*, recognized indeed that war was a defeat for Liberalism and a victory for the evil forces which they personified in Lord Northcliffe; but they believed that this defeat could be transformed into a victory if war was made to serve some nobler cause.

Scott had a hard core of realism. He concentrated on winning the war once he had failed to avert it — hence his support two years later for the Lloyd George–Bonar Law coalition even against Asquith and the bulk of the Liberal party. When the *Manchester Guardian* looked towards the future early in 1915, Scott called on the moderate L. T. Hobhouse; and that wise man spoke out against any early reconciliation with Germany. 'The peacemakers will err seriously if they set to work after the war as though the revelation of the mind of German statesmanship were to count for nothing'. Hobhouse wanted the Triple Entente to become a permanent federation, holding all the power in Europe. He was not afraid to hold out the example of the Holy Alliance and warned that this failed only when its idealism became too dogmatically international. The Supreme Council of the Allies, he thought later, should control Europe. In time the neutrals could be added with a subordinate voice, and last of all the defeated Powers.

Gardiner was not so cautious. On 8 August he repudiated any quarrel with the German people and announced 'we are fighting for the emancipation of Germany'. He had already hit on a simple explanation of the conflict: 'this is not a war of peoples but of despots and diplomatists'. H. G. Wells added his voice. 'The defeat of Germany will open the door to disarmament and peace throughout the earth'. On 7 August he called the war the *Sword of Peace*. On 14 August he did even better. He invented the phrase which was to echo round the world, at first as an inspiration, later in bitter mockery. He discovered *The War to End War*. There would be 'a Peace League that will control the globe'. A little later Eden Phillpotts held out the same prospect to the Germans in more high-flown terms:

> And our revenge shall be to bid you hear
> Ineffable music from the olden time.

Yet there was no cleavage between the idealists and the practical statesmen except in their mode of expression. The outlook of Lowes Dickinson, who invented the phrase 'the League of Nations' and who (as his so-called historical works show) did not blame one nation more than another for the war, shaded imperceptibly into that of Gilbert Murray or H. G. Wells, who were convinced that the war had been caused by German militarism; and their outlook in turn shaded into that of Grey and Asquith. No British statesman would be content with the liberation or restoration of Belgium, though this had given the occasion for the war. Grey, for instance, said in November 1914 that there could be no peace that would permit 'continuance or recurrence of an armed brute power in central Europe'; the future peace must provide for 'an end of militarism for ever and for reparation to ruined Belgium'.

Certain practical conditions were already foreshadowed. Since final victory was assumed, the disappearance of the German fleet was assumed also; and it seemed unnecessary to stipulate this in the peace terms. The acquisition of the German colonies was assumed in the same casual way. But what should happen on the continent of Europe? Gladstone provided the ultimate inspiration for Liberal foreign policy. He had not only believed in the national principle; he had sympathized with Russian aims and had protested against the German annexation of Alsace and Lorraine. All the Liberal writers insisted that Alsace and Lorraine should return to France, though the most Radical (such as Brailsford) wanted this to be preceded by a plebiscite. Most of them supported 'a Greater Servia' and Rumanian claims to Transylvania, though Rumania was neutral. The only other concrete grievance they discovered was that of the 'Bulgarians' under Serbia in Macedonia — certainly even-handed justice against an ally. H. G. Wells held that 'an unchallenged Russia will be a wholesome check and no great danger for the new Greater Servia and the new Greater Roumania.' Only Brailsford dissented: 'Within a year from the breaking of Germany's power . . . , our Imperialists will be calling out for a strong Germany to balance a threatening Russia'. The statesmen agreed with the writers. Asquith regarded the ethnographical principle as 'the only one which was serious and lasting'— a phrase which Tsar Nicholas II underlined with satisfaction. Grey approved the French claim to Alsace and Lorraine, though there was, of course, no British commitment to France on this point. He, too, sought concessions to Bulgaria and to Rumania — perhaps more to win them as allies than to satisfy abstract justice.

The French began to define their war aims only towards the end of the year when the first shock of battle was over. They too wanted a settled peace for the future, but in their case it was precise security against Germany, not a general system of world order. Delcassé spoke of 'the destruction of the German Reich and the weakening of Prussia'; Viviani described the war as 'defence against the German desire to control Europe'. On 22 December Deschanel, president of the Chamber, first formally laid claim to Alsace and Lorraine. He brought in also the liberation of Belgium, but the emphasis was not so strong as it was in British policy. The British regarded Belgium as a special case which came before all else. The French lumped together Belgium and north-eastern France (in which they included Alsace and Lorraine); and they unconsciously extended to their own territory the 'massive reparation' which the British projected for Belgium alone. Farther east the French were a good deal less enthusiastic than the British about 'the national principle'. They dreamt of some miracle by which the defeat of Germany would not involve the defeat of Austria-Hungary also; they cared less for Serbia than for Poland — a subject remote from British speculation; and they fondly supposed that Russia's ambitions would be met by 'the freedom of the Straits'.

The Russians had certainly not formulated a clear picture of their aims even at the Straits when they entered the war. But, with their incurable taste for future precision to offset their present confusions, they were the first to sketch a programme of territorial changes. Early in September Sazonov, the foreign minister, defined his guiding principles as 'destruction of German power and the principle of nationality'. Russia would take eastern Galicia and advance to the line of the Niemen. Poland, conveniently under Russian suzerainty, would take eastern Posen, Silesia and west

The War Aims of the Allies in the First World War

Galicia. France, of course, would recover Alsace and Lorraine. Belgium would acquire some German territory; Schleswig and Holstein would return to Denmark; and the kingdom of Hanover would be restored — as much to please the British royal house as to weaken Prussia. The Habsburg monarchy would be dismembered into three Succession States — Austria, Bohemia, Hungary. Rumania would receive 'part of Transylvania', but not Bessarabia on any account ('not an inch of Russian land' was Nicholas II's phrase). Serbia would receive Bosnia and Hercegovina, Dalmatia and northern Albania; Greece, southern Albania; and Bulgaria part of Macedonia. In short, the full national programme of small independent states — except for Poland — but no word of the Straits. Later in the autumn the Russian experts tried to formulate a solution for the Straits question, but arrived only at the conclusion that all plans were equally bad. Even 'the active solution' of a Russian occupation of Constantinople would so absorb Russia's resources as to leave her without strength elsewhere. Better to be content with the vague aims of 'destroying German and Austrian attempts to challenge Russia's prestige as a Great Power' and 'freeing Europe from militarism'.

These speculations were far removed from a policy. There was no serious exchange of ideas between the Entente Powers on war aims during the first winter of the war. Since they also failed to exchange ideas even on the conduct of the war, this is not surprising. The only tie between them was the treaty signed on 5 September 1914, by which the three Powers promised not to make a separate peace nor to pose peace terms to the enemy without previous agreement. This was, in fact, the only real commitment ever made by the Entente Powers. It was not necessary to act on it until some prospect of peace negotiations appeared, and by then Russia was out of the war. But Russia was pushed into making practical demands early in 1915, though more against her allies than against the enemy. The British project for forcing the Dardanelles — though originally provoked by the Russian generals — alarmed the diplomats; they feared that Constantinople might fall from the feeble hands of the Turks into those of the western Powers. On 4 March, without preliminary warning, Sazonov informed the French and British ambassadors in writing that 'any solution would be unsatisfactory and precarious' which did not give Constantinople and the shores of the Bosphorus to Russia. 'The Imperial government hopes that these considerations will be treated sympathetically by the allied Powers.'

The Russians expected resistance from the British. They were mistaken. The British had long written off their old interest in the Straits. They were now impatient to launch the Dardanelles campaign; and, lacking trained soldiers themselves, were anxious to keep Russia active on the eastern Front. A Russian attempt to reach Constantinople first (in fact, regarded by the Russian General Staff as impractical) would have much disturbed British policy. On 12 March Grey, with the approval of the Opposition leaders, Lansdowne, Bonar Law and Balfour, declared British approval of Russia's claims 'subject to the war being carried on and brought to a successful conclusion and to the desiderata of Great Britain and France in the Ottoman empire and elsewhere being realized'. He followed this up the same day with some immediate conditions: Constantinople should become a free port; the Mohammedan Holy Places and Arabia should remain under independent Mohammedan dominion; and the neutral zone of Persia, as defined in the agreement of 1907, should become a British sphere. On 20 March Sazonov agreed to these conditions, with some slight adjustments in Persia and a free hand for Russia in her own zone.

The French turned out much more difficult. Delcassé persistently deluded himself that the Russians would be satisfied with internationalization of the Straits. Faced with Sazonov's demand, he offered only 'a friendly attitude' and a reminder that the Straits, along with all other questions, must be settled by common discussion according to the agreement of 5 September 1914. When this met with a cool reception, he fell back on the excuse that England would never agree to the Russian claims. Disappointed here also, he tried delay. On 5 April 'he struck his forehead and said that he had forgotten to send instructions to St. Petersburg'. There was no averting the inevitable. On 10 April the French Government also declared their agreement to Russia's claims on similar conditions to those that the British had made on 12 March. But, in the gloom of giving way, the French failed to define these conditions. The Russians had been generous during the period of delay. Nicholas II had said: 'take the left bank of the Rhine; take Mainz; go further if you like'. He had agreed to support French claims to Syria, Cilicia and Palestine — with some reserve over the Holy Places. Delcassé failed to take up these offers. The French were so angry at having to give way over Constantinople and the Straits that they did it finally without claiming a reward. If they had struck a bargain in April 1915 they would have had Russian backing when they came to negotiate over the Near East with Great Britain. As it was, the Russians were free to join with the British in forcing further compromises on the French.

The agreement over Constantinople and the Straits, though later the most maligned of the secret treaties, was not strictly a war aim at all. It did not lay down terms which the Entente would impose on the enemy; it only defined what they would settle between themselves if they won the war. The Treaty of London with Italy which followed shortly after had a different character. It laid down what Italy 'will receive', and this certainly implied an obligation on the Entente Powers to continue fighting until Italy's aims were achieved. Russia was already at war; she had only to be persuaded to remain there. Italy was a neutral; she had to be brought in, and the French, at any rate, considered that she would be a decisive gain. The Italians claimed Tyrol, Trieste with Istria, and Dalmatia. The British and French made no objection. These were all traditional objects of Italian nationalism; and support for them no more implied approval for the dismemberment of Austria-Hungary than had support for the unification of Italy fifty or sixty years before. Sazonov, fearing a new rival at the Straits, did not want Italy in the war. He was overruled by his western allies and by his own General Staff. He held firm only over southern Dalmatia which he insisted should go to Serbia. This was a fine display of Slav solidarity; more immediately, southern Dalmatia was the price with which Sazonov hoped to persuade Serbia into surrendering Macedonia to Bulgaria. The Allies were certainly tied to Italy's war aims by the Treaty of London. It was a more important consideration that Italy was tied to them also. Once having staked her claims she could not recede from them. She was the most opposed of the Entente Powers to the dismemberment of Austria-Hungary; yet she had to pursue her claims even at the price of this dismemberment, and became finally the most intransigent Entente Power so far as Austria-Hungary was concerned.

The Russians tried to stave off Italian intervention in the Ottoman empire before the Treaty of London was signed. They proposed to stipulate that Italy should endorse the agreement of the Triple Entente over the Straits without seeing it. This was too much. Indeed the Treaty of London promised 'an equitable share' of Asia Minor to Italy; but Great Britain and France formally reaffirmed to Russia their pledge over the Straits when Italy entered the war. The pledge was thus directed now against Italy as well as against themselves. The French had a more pressing anxiety. They wished to define the plans concerning the Ottoman empire which they had made Russia endorse. But this demanded negotiations with the British, and they had plans of their own in the Near East. They had already promised the Sherif of Mecca that Arabia should be an independent State in order to bring him into war; and they interpreted 'Arabia' generously, so long as it did not extend to the valley of the Euphrates. Grey evaded negotiation with the French at the time of the Straits agreement. They renewed their insistence in the autumn, when Georges Picot came to London to negotiate with Sir Mark Sykes. The French assumed that the British would be content with Mesopotamia; and they intended to claim for themselves Syria, Cilicia and Palestine.

This did not meet with British approval. They demanded Haifa for themselves, as outlet for a railway from Baghdad; Beirut for the 'independent' Arab State; and, most serious of all, Palestine as an international State. In the agreement with Russia Grey had stipulated only for the independence of the Mohammedan Holy Places; it now turned out that he had felt as strongly about the Christian Holy Places and, when Picot protested, Sykes answered that Russia would never agree to their passing under French control. This was a curious revival of the great issue in the Crimean War, but with Russia and Great Britain this time in alliance against France. The French would be left with a thin strip of Mediterranean coastline, deprived of its best ports. Sykes finally gave up Beirut; and, as Picot was still dissatisfied, he added a platonic approval to any extension of claims in Armenia that the French cared to make. This would put a wedge of French influence between the British sphere in Mesopotamia and the Russian sphere in northern Persia; and Kitchener laid down the proposition that it was undesirable for the British 'to be in immediate contact with a great military monarchy'. In this way the French, without knowing it, received title (temporary as it turned out) to the oilfields of Mosul.

The Sykes-Picot Agreement, signed on 3 January 1916, postulated the approval of Russia. Sazonov offered to sign it blindfold on 19 February. The western Powers did not take him at his word, principally because each wished to play Russia off against the other. Sykes and Picot came to Petrograd armed with invitations for Russian backing. Sykes gave Sazonov a map marked with objections that he might usefully make; Picot persuaded Sazonov to promise to oppose the British plans for Palestine — a promise which he did not fulfil. For, when the Russians looked at the agreements, they were horrified to see the French claims in Armenia, which extended even to the frontier of the Russian zone in Persia. Henceforth Sazonov was busy opposing the French claims and had no time to worry about Palestine. Sykes joined Sazonov; and the two forced concession on Picot. The French line was withdrawn in Armenia; in exchange it extended somewhat farther north in Cilicia, into purely Turkish territory. More striking still, Sykes and Picot, in their anxiety for Russia's approval, acquiesced in her claiming the whole of Armenia — rather to the annoyance of the Russian General Staff, who regarded it as too big a morsel and who were, in any case, incapable of conquering it. In this way Russia was paid twice over for agreeing to the Anglo-French partition of the Near East: beforehand with Constantinople and the Straits, afterwards with Armenia. Yet at bottom the Russians did not want either price; they wanted 'a Turkey as large and independent as possible' as a buffer between themselves and any western Powers.

The three allies reached general agreement in April 1916 on these questions; points of drafting, such as the future of the Capitulations and the open door for trade, dragged on until September, and even then some details remained unsettled. This agreement over Asiatic Turkey was also not strictly a war aim. It too merely laid down what each would allow the others to do when the Ottoman empire collapsed. There was no promise of mutual support, though, of course, an implied condition that one ally could not claim his full share if the others were disappointed. Though the agreements were secret, the two western Powers would have liked to make them public — the French to show their own people that they were not being cheated in the Near East, and both Governments to encourage Russia to remain in the war. Asquith hinted at the agreements when a Russian parliamentary delegation visited England in May; and the agreement over the Straits was described in the Duma in December — without any effect on Russian war-weariness. All this talk alarmed the Italians. They saw themselves being left out of the

The War Aims of the Allies in the First World War

partition of the Near East, and claimed the fulfilment of the promise made to them in the Treaty of London. The Allies insisted that Italy must first declare war on Germany, which she did in August 1916. Now it was the turn of the original Allies to hesitate. They feared rightly an Italian explosion when it was revealed that the Ottoman empire was already partitioned. Grey finally persuaded his two partners that the agreements should be regarded as binding only when Italy declared herself satisfied. No doubt he would not have lamented if the condition were never fulfilled.

The Italians were told of the Asiatic agreements on 5 October. They were indignant and answered by demanding for themselves a zone of Asia Minor which, on the one side, would take Adana and Mersina from the French zone and, on the other, would, at Smyrna, approach dangerously near the Russian territory at the Straits. The British made no objection. The French and Russians, however, were united in opposition; and a conference at London met with complete deadlock early in 1917. Meanwhile the discussion of genuine war aims had begun in earnest. This sprang from the increasing desire of the western Powers to draw in the United States. Quite apart from the practical need for American assistance, the Allies — Great Britain in particular — looked to America for help in providing some stabler basis of peace than mere victory. The Allies still thought that they could win the war; but then the United States should, in Grey's words, 'come into some general guaranty for world-wide peace'. Grey returned to this idea again and again. He wrote on 22 September 1915: 'would the President propose a League of Nations binding themselves to side against any Power which broke a treaty?'

This was not far from Wilson's own outlook. Though determined to preserve American neutrality in the present war, he hoped also to act as the guarantor of a future peace, provided this was enlightened enough. His ideas for such a peace corresponded closely with those of the English Liberals, for he too was a Gladstonian. He too regarded the German annexation of Alsace and Lorraine as a crime. He declared: 'Russia's ambitions are legitimate', and said: 'I cannot help sympathizing with Russia's aims to secure natural outlets for its trade with the world'. He did not share the fears of his adviser House about Russia and wrote in December 1914: 'Austria-Hungary will go to pieces altogether — ought to go to pieces for the welfare of Europe'. He was constantly hinting that the Allies should announce enlightened war arms so that he could then prepare to guarantee them. Early in 1916 the British tried to oblige him. Asquith, Grey, Lloyd George and Balfour met House at Lord Reading's and sketched terms which House thought the president would approve: 'the restoration of Belgium, the transfer of Alsace and Lorraine to France, and the acquisition by Russia of an outlet to the sea'. There was, however, an equivocation. Wilson only meant to guarantee these terms after the Allies had won the war — and then only if they behaved generously in other ways. The British ministers hoped to lure Wilson into imposing these terms on Germany; and House encouraged their delusion.

In August 1916 Grey told the American ambassador that there could be no discussion of peace terms until France agreed, and added a new condition: 'an impartial enquiry who began the war and who is responsible for it?' This academic point was not pursued. Meanwhile the British went on speculating what they should propose either to the French or for themselves. Robertson, chief of the General Staff, produced a memorandum on 31 August, saying that Alsace and Lorraine must 'presumably' go to France. But Austria-Hungary should be kept in being: 'this limits the power of Russia and the Slav states, and prevents the Mediterranean becoming a French and Italian lake'. In general, 'it is in the interests of the British empire to leave Germany reasonably strong on land, but to weaken her at sea'— a curious outlook for one who held that all British effort should be concentrated on the western Front. Balfour followed on 4 October with a very different policy. He wanted to reduce

The War Aims of the Allies in the First World War

the Central Powers and to apply everywhere 'the principle of nationality'— in Alsace and Lorraine, and for the benefit of Italy, Serbia and Rumania. 'I should greatly like to see it applied in Bohemia also.' But he would *not* like to see the old kingdom of Poland restored. 'If Germany is relieved of all fear of pressure from Russia, France and Britain might be the sufferers and Russia might be diverted to the Far East.' He waved aside all fear of Russia: 'The more Russia is made a European rather than an Asiatic power the better for everybody. . . . Whatever trouble Russia may give us in Mesopotamia, Persia and Afghanistan, I do not think she will attempt the domination of Europe, still less succeed in securing it.'

The two continental allies were also revolving these problems. The Russians had by now little interest in general principles. Their greatest anxiety during the course of 1916 was to ward off any suggestion of Polish independence by their western allies. Sazonov said to Paléologue, the French ambassador, in March: 'Beware of Poland. It is dangerous ground for an ambassador of France.' Sazonov hit on the idea of buying off French interest in Poland by the offer of a free hand for France on the western frontier of Germany — an idea which he did little to develop before his fall from power in July. The French became alarmed that Russia was moving towards a separate peace; and they, in turn, contemplated offering Russia a free hand on Germany's eastern frontier. Briand, the French prime minister, soon thought better of this. He was becoming the protagonist of national independence — the first French statesman to make the liberation of Serbia a war aim (3 November 1915), and the first Allied statesman to receive Beneš, representative of the future Czechoslovakia (February 1916). It ill became him to renounce French interest in Poland; or, if he did so, it must be cloaked by some striking French gain — in other words, the left bank of the Rhine. Both Grey and Briand were thus moving towards a formulation of war aims — Grey principally to interest the Americans, Briand more to console the Russians.

In September 1916 Briand offered to undertake the task. He had not completed it when the Entente was caught unawares by President Wilson's Note of 18 December, which invited both sides to state their peace terms. The British at first wanted to reject the suggestion. Lloyd George called it 'a sort of insult' to put both sides on the same level. Briand, however, pulled out his unfinished draft, adding to it a protest 'against the assimilation established in the American note between the two groups of belligerents'. Briand's Note declared that it was impossible to discuss peace terms until there was 'a satisfactory settlement of the present conflict'; and he confined himself to the general principles of 'reparation, restitution and guarantees'. The British now took up the running. At the inter-allied conference in London on 27–28 December they objected that the Allies would be suspected of shady designs if they did not state some concrete aims. Ribot, who represented France, was a more practical man than Briand and agreed with them. A new paragraph of concrete aims was therefore tacked on, though Briand's assertion of the impossibility of defining such aims still remained to contradict it. This paragraph had then to be settled with the Russians and the Italians. Balfour had proposed to refer to 'a free autonomous Poland'. The Russians objected; and the issue was dodged. The Italians objected to including 'the South Slavs' in the list of nationalities to be liberated. The more harmless word 'Slav' was substituted; but to make the list look more practical the 'Czecho-Slovaks' were added, though without any realization that this implied the destruction of the Habsburg monarchy.

This Note was handed to the Americans on 10 January 1917. It demanded 'the restoration of Belgium, of Serbia and of Montenegro and the indemnities which are due them; the evacuation of the invaded territories ...; the reorganization of Europe, guaranteed by a stable régime and founded as much upon respect of nationalities ... as upon territorial conventions and international agreements'. Then came the practical aims: 'the restitution of provinces

The War Aims of the Allies in the First World War

or territories wrested in the past from the Allies by force . . . , the liberation of Italians, of Slavs, of Roumanians and of Czecho-Slovaks from foreign domination; the enfranchisement of populations subject to the bloody tyranny of the Turks; the expulsion from Europe of the Ottoman Empire'. Finally, 'the intentions of His Majesty the Emperor of Russia regarding Poland have been clearly indicated in the proclamation which he has just addressed to his armies'. This list had some curiosities. Alsace and Lorraine were mentioned only by implication — though what other provinces or territories had been wrested from the Allies by force? Belgium was put on a level with Serbia and Montenegro despite her protests. The partition of the Ottoman empire appeared in an idealistic Gladstonian dress. And the future of Poland remained at Russia's discretion.

Neither the British nor the French government was happy about this Note. Both wished to underline some of its implications. On 13 January Balfour, who had recently become foreign secretary, followed it up by a supplementary Note to Washington, justifying at length 'the expulsion of the Turks from Europe' and the dismemberment of the Ottoman empire. He also laid down three conditions for a durable peace (apart from 'the success of the Allied cause' as a preliminary): 'existing causes of international unrest should be, as far as possible, removed or weakened'; 'the aggressive aims and the unscrupulous methods of the Central Powers should fall into disrepute among their own people'; 'behind international law and all treaty arrangements . . . some form of international sanction should be devised which would give pause to the hardiest aggressor'. The Americans were being offered an effective League of Nations such as Wilson had often proposed, and were given to understand that the partition of the Ottoman empire was Great Britain's only concrete war aim. Lloyd George supplied a further gloss in February. Asked by Lansing, the American secretary of state, for assurances against the 'virtual dismemberment of Austria-Hungary', he answered that 'the peoples of the

Entente Governments such as Slavs, Roumanians, Serbs and Italians, as well as Bosnia and Herzegovina, must by the principle of nationality be freed from Austrian control'; but Bohemia and Hungary would remain intact — not only a contradiction of his previous sentence, but a repudiation of the declaration made on 10 January in favour of the Czecho-Slovaks. Lloyd George added the curious remark that he wanted to see the United States at the peace conference in order to check the colonial demands of South Africa and Australia, and even of the British people.

Briand defined his aims in a letter to Paul Cambon at London on 12 January. Alsace and Lorraine should go to France not as a conquest but as a 'disannexation', and this should include the valley of the Saar. The German territory on the left bank of the Rhine should form a neutral buffer State. For the rest, Belgium should be restored; Denmark should receive Schleswig; Poland should become autonomous; Rumania and Serbia should make 'legitimate acquisitions'. Evidently Briand did not regard Italian ambitions as a French war aim; and he remained discreetly silent about Constantinople. He had also different views about the League of Nations. Where the British wanted a general system of security, Briand projected a league of victors. The Entente 'should be united more closely by treaties of alliance, in order to compose permanently an association of strength which would make itself respected'. This was much the policy which Hobhouse had advocated against the weight of Liberal opinion. Briand's statement was met in London with disapproving silence.

With Russia Briand did rather better — or so he thought. An inter-allied conference met at Petrograd in February 1917. Its main purpose was to co-ordinate Allied military plans and to keep Russia in the war. But the French had also policy in view. For one thing, they wanted Russia to join them in resisting Italian claims in Asia Minor: if the Russians would keep the Italians out of Mersina and Adana, the French would keep them out of Smyrna. For another thing, the

The War Aims of the Allies in the First World War

French wanted Russian backing for their scheme to make a buffer state on the left bank of the Rhine. Doumergue, the French delegate, had as instructions only Briand's letter to Paul Cambon of 12 January. He got nothing from the Russians concerning Asia Minor except an exclamation of disapproval about Smyrna; but he did exceptionally well over the left bank of the Rhine. No sooner did he raise the subject than the tsar endorsed every French demand: Alsace and Lorraine and the Saar in full sovereignty; the left bank 'an autonomous and neutral state' occupied by French troops until the enemy states had completely fulfilled all conditions and guarantees laid down in the peace treaties. The Russian ministers were taken aback by their master's precipitancy: he had promised to support the French demands without claiming anything for Russia in return. However, they soon put matters right. They stated their claims in Paris; and Briand, out of touch with Doumergue and unwilling to wreck his negotiations, agreed to them. He tried to postulate something about the future of Poland, was overruled, and on 12 March gave Russia 'full freedom to determine her western frontiers'.

The Russian Revolution soon deprived this agreement of any meaning. The revolution had more serious effects. The new Russian leaders were soon talking of a peace with 'no annexations and no indemnities'; and this phrase forced western statesmen into idealistic competition. On a more practical level, Russia was obviously tumbling out of the war, and this made Italy more important to the western Allies. As a further complication, the new Austrian emperor Charles made a secret offer of peace to the French in March. The Austrians recognized that the Entente had certain claims against Germany — Alsace-Lorraine and the restoration of Belgium; some claims against Austria-Hungary in favour of the Serbs, Rumanians and Italians; and, finally, the Straits to Russia. Charles proposed to endorse the claims against Germany on conditions that the Entente dropped those against Austria-Hungary; and he would even support the western Powers against Russia. Lloyd George and Ribot were tempted by these proposals. They made some slight reservation in regard to Serbia, but none in regard to Rumania — despite the formal pledge to support her claims which France had made the previous year when Rumania entered the war. Neither had qualms about the Straits, the French indeed much pleasure at thwarting Russia; and both statesmen welcomed the prospect of making a purely European peace without either Russia or the United States — neither of whom was informed of the negotiations.

Italy, however, had to be won over. For she was, after all, the only Power actually fighting Austria-Hungary. On the other hand, Lloyd George and Ribot were pledged not to reveal to Italy that they were negotiating with Emperor Charles. They therefore invited Sonnino, the Italian prime minister, to meet them at St.-Jean-de-Maurienne on 19 April, ostensibly to resolve the deadlock in the negotiations over Asia Minor. Sonnino refused to depart in the slightest from the Italian claims which had been recognized in the Treaty of London; this made it pointless even to hint at the possibility of a separate peace with Austria. But the British were anxious to get Italian agreement over Asia Minor. They were caught by their ingenious argument of the previous autumn that the agreements should become effective only when Italy acquiesced; for now, with Russia almost out of the war, they needed Italian support against France. Earlier the British had worked with Russia in order to diminish France's share and especially to keep her out of Palestine. Now Russia was useless, and the British were indifferent to her claims. When Sonnino continued obstinate, Lloyd George withdrew from the room and returned with a British Staff map on which Smyrna (hitherto a Russian interest) was allotted to Italy. Sonnino pulled out another copy of the same map, which the British had put forward at the London Conference of the previous January, and on which the gain to Italy was Konia, adjacent to the French sphere. He then agreed to take both, while Ribot and

The War Aims of the Allies in the First World War

Lloyd George sat by in bewildered admiration.

No formal agreement was reached at St.-Jean-de-Maurienne, though the letters exchanged later in August conventionally bear its name. The Italians continued to demand precision throughout the summer. When the French delayed, the British suggested a direct Anglo-Italian agreement, which would, of course, have been pointed against the French. This spurred the French to action, and letters defining the spheres of interest of the three countries were exchanged on 18 August. The French belatedly insisted on Russian approval — to wreck the agreements rather than to please their failing ally. The agreement therefore began with the words, 'under reserve of Russian assent'. No reply came from Russia before the Bolshevik Revolution of November put an end to allied relations. The agreements over the Ottoman empire remained in considerable confusion. The French and the British held that the so-called Agreement of St.-Jean-de-Maurienne had lapsed from lack of Russian approval; and they never acknowledged Italy's claim again. But was it the only agreement that lapsed when Russia fell out of the war? The original Sykes-Picot Agreement of January 1916 was a consequence of the Straits Agreement made in March 1915 and postulated Russian approval also. This was obtained in May 1916 when the Sykes-Picot Agreement was superseded by a three-sided exchange of letters. Did not Russia's renunciation of the Straits cast some doubt on the other agreements? In particular, could the Sykes-Picot Agreement be resurrected as though later negotiations had never been?

These questions were to cause much trouble at the end of the war. Meanwhile the British put increasing emphasis on their promises of national independence to the Arabs — promises which they intended should operate against the French, but not against themselves. They also took new precautions in regard to Palestine, which was dangerously near the Suez Canal. The Holy Places had been effective in keeping France out of Palestine so long as Russia was both

Orthodox and an active belligerent. When Russia became first a secular republic and then fell out of the war, the British needed some other instrument. They found it in Zionism. On 8 November, one day after the Bolshevik Revolution, Balfour announced that 'His Majesty's Government view with favour the establishment in Palestine of a national home for the Jewish people'; and the British were soon talking of Palestine as a national State without reserve — which indeed it became when enough Jews were persuaded to settle there. Abraham and David succeeded where the saints of the Orthodox church had failed. Palestine became a British, not a French care.

The partition of the Ottoman empire was a side-issue, however fascinating to the respective foreign offices. The great purpose of war aims became increasingly to satisfy public opinion in the Allied countries and in the United States. On 6 April the United States entered the war, though as an associate, not an ally. Balfour went over to Washington. While there, he discussed war aims with House and, more vaguely, with Wilson. On 28 April he showed House a map with the projected partition of Turkey-in-Asia and ran over the usual points — Alsace-Lorraine; restitution and reparation of all occupied territory; Bosnia and Herce-govina for Serbia; Macedonia for Bulgaria. House and Balfour differed over Poland. House wanted it as a strong barrier against Russia, and asked Balfour 'not to look upon Germany as a permanent enemy'. Balfour, however, 'was more impressed with the German menace than he was by the possible danger from Russia'. House also told Balfour that the proposals for Turkey-in-Asia were 'all bad'. Balfour was unrepentant, but did not scruple to jettison British commitments elsewhere. He 'regretted the Treaty of London', and agreed with House that Constantinople should be 'internationalized'. Evidently he regarded the secret treaties as a statement of aims by the ally concerned, with no obligation by Great Britain to support them, nor even perhaps not to oppose them.

The War Aims of the Allies in the First World War

On 30 April Balfour and President Wilson also surveyed the future, agreeing only on 'the internationalization of Constantinople'. Balfour thought that Wilson ought to know about the secret treaties, which characteristically he had failed to bring with him. A packet was hastily sent from London, which Balfour passed on to the President on 18 May. Wilson later denied all knowledge of the treaties; and Balfour could not remember what was in the parcel. It contained, in fact, the text of a statement by Balfour to the Imperial War Conference, emphasizing that 'the practical destruction of the Turkish Empire was one of the objects desired by the British government'; two copies of the Treaty of London; the so-called Sykes-Picot Agreement regarding Asia Minor and ascribed to May 1916 (in other words, the agreement as modified by Russian participation); the exchange of letters with Russia in March-April 1915 concerning Constantinople and the Straits; and the Treaty of Bucharest with Rumania. Wilson never acknowledged receipt of this curious collection. In January 1918 Balfour wrote to Wilson about the secret treaties, adding cheerfully: 'it is not probable Italy will prolong the war in order to obtain her Adriatic claims'. Wilson ignored all these communications. His only war aim was the defeat of Germany; and he intended that the Allies should make peace on their own terms, which he would then endorse if they were sufficiently enlightened. Apart from the 'internationalization' of Constantinople, his only indication was to express to the French his approval of a 'scientific' peace, which would not reproduce 'the enormity committed by the Germans when they took Alsace-Lorraine from France'. This might be an endorsement of France's principal war aim; equally it might be a warning against it.

During the summer of 1917 the British and French Governments were pushed farther towards definition by the idealistic wind blowing from Russia. On 5 June the French Chamber of Deputies passed a 'peace resolution', demanding the return of Alsace-Lorraine, 'together with liberation of invaded territories and just reparation for damage'. Further, there must be 'durable guarantees for peace and independence for peoples great and small, in a league of nations such as has already been foreshadowed'. The Senate passed a similar resolution, but omitted the reference to a League of Nations. The French Socialists wished to postulate a plebiscite even for Alsace-Lorraine. When this was refused, they withdrew from the Government in September.

On 29 June Lloyd George had a shot at war aims in a speech at Glasgow. He dwelt at length on reparation for Belgium; gave one sentence to Serbia, three paragraphs to Mesopotamia, and one paragraph to the German colonies. The peroration of his speech demanded 'the democratization of the German government'. There was nothing about the League of Nations nor about the dismemberment of Austria-Hungary — not even a mention of Alsace-Lorraine. A month later, on 30 July, Balfour, the foreign secretary, was a little more precise in the House of Commons. Though he would not discuss 'how you are going to deal with such a great and ancient monarchy as Austria', he said: 'what we desire, of course, is that the nationalities composing that heterogeneous State should be allowed to develop on their own lines'. He also expressed, his 'own opinion, which is that, while France fights for Alsace and Lorraine, we should support her'. It was Kühlmann, the German secretary of state, not Balfour, who finally provoked Lloyd George into formally endorsing France's claim. Kühlmann implied in the Reichstag that the British would make peace without thought of Alsace and Lorraine, if Germany restored Belgium. On 11 October Lloyd George replied: 'However long the war may last, this country intends to stand by her gallant ally, France, until she redeems her oppressed children from the degradation of a foreign yoke'. It had taken more than three years of war to turn Alsace-Lorraine into a British war aim.

The shape of the war changed fundamentally in its last year. Russia had ceased to fight and soon made a separate peace. Italy was exhausted, France hardly less so. The British had to increase their contribution in ideas as well as in men if they were to hold their own with the United States. The collapse of Russia was not an unmixed disaster. The agreement over Constantinople could be forgotten; the sacred principle of internationalizing the Straits could be proclaimed — with American approval. Moreover, Poland could be resurrected, after being jettisoned by France the previous March. On 27 December Pichon, foreign minister under Clemenceau, said of Poland: 'We do not separate her cause from ours . . . we want her one, independent, indivisible'. The British did not share this enthusiasm for Poland. Indeed, in December 1917, Smuts, negotiating in Switzerland with an Austrian representative, suggested that Poland, together with Rumania and Serbia, should unite in a federation under the Habsburg emperor.

This, of course, was not official British policy. Balfour clearly disapproved of it. Once the chief opponent of the national principle in Ireland, he now backed it elsewhere and no doubt enjoyed overbidding the former Radicalism of his prime minister. Speaking in the House of Commons on 6 November, he emphasized the recovery of Alsace-Lorraine and the liberation of Armenia and Poland as idealistic war aims — Armenia a particularly shrewd stroke at the Gladstonian tradition. These were casual hints. Lloyd George devised a more elaborate programme. He was in competition both with the Bolsheviks and with Wilson: Lansdowne's 'peace letter' of 29 November 1917, urging a *status quo* peace in return for the liberation of Belgium, was a further challenge to him. He secured the approval of Asquith and Grey, the principal leaders of the Liberal Opposition, and on 5 January 1918 gave at the Trade Union Congress the most precise definition of British war aims. There were two clear negatives. 'The break-up of Austria-Hungary is no part of our war aims. . . . Nor are we fighting to deprive Turkey of its capital or of the rich and renowned lands of Asia Minor and Thrace, which are predominantly Turkish in race.' The secret treaty of March 1915 was safely forgotten, the agreement with Italy hardly less so.

Essays Presented to Sir Lewis Namier

On the positive side, 'the first requirement' was the complete restoration of Belgian independence and reparation for her devastation. In this the British Government had not wavered since the beginning of the war. Lloyd George added, less justifiably, that this was also the first requirement of the Allies. Next came the restoration of Serbia, Montenegro and the occupied part of France, Italy and Rumania; and 'we mean to stand by the French Democracy to the death in the demand they make for reconsideration of the great wrong of 1871'. Lloyd George then dwelt at length on the dangers of a separate peace between Russia and Germany. He added as an afterthought the single sentence: 'We believe that an independent Poland, comprising all those genuinely Polish elements who desire to form part of it is an urgent necessity for the stability of Western Europe'. He endorsed two other national claims: 'the satisfaction of the legitimate claims of the Italians for union with those of their own race and tongue'; and 'that justice be done to men of Roumanian blood and speech in their legitimate aspirations'. Neither the Czechoslovaks nor the Yugoslavs were mentioned. Outside Europe the Straits were to be 'internationalized and neutralized', and 'Arabia, Armenia, Mesopotamia, Syria and Palestine are in our judgement entitled to a recognition of their separate national condition'. The secret treaties were tactfully repudiated: 'new circumstances have changed the conditions under which those arrangements were made'.

Lloyd George turned with obvious relief from these topics to the German colonies, which 'by the general principle of national self-determination' were never to return to Germany. He ended by a reference to the economic and other difficulties that would follow the war; but all he had to contribute to solving these problems was the single sentence: 'a great attempt must be made to establish by some international organization an alternative to war as a means of settling international disputes'. This would 'limit the burden of armaments and diminish the probability of war'. There was no reference to the German navy — a curious omission. Clearly

The War Aims of the Allies in the First World War

Lloyd George felt committed to Belgium and to the French demand for Alsace-Lorraine. He honoured the Sykes-Picot Agreement, but disregarded the Treaty of London (or regarded it as synonymous with Italy's national claims — which it was not) and gave no thought to the Agreement of St.-Jean-de-Maurienne. Indeed 'the maintenance of the Turkish empire in the home lands of the Turkish race' was a direct repudiation of it. Italy had suffered the disaster of Caporetto since the agreement was made, and no doubt Lloyd George thought that she was lucky to remain in the war at all.

Lloyd George's programme was endorsed by Clemenceau in a single sentence on 6 January. The other allies did not express an opinion. This programme just managed to anticipate President Wilson's. He had earlier sought an agreed statement by the Allies; and House, his confidential adviser, spent the autumn of 1917 in Europe for this purpose. He failed, and Wilson therefore decided to act on his own. The final spur was the prospect of a separate peace between Germany and Russia, which Wilson hoped to prevent by an idealistic statement. On 8 January he announced the Fourteen Points to Congress. These partly — but only partly — coincided with Lloyd George's programme, though they had been drafted independently. There were four general propositions: 'open covenants of peace, openly arrived at'; 'absolute freedom of navigation upon the seas'; 'the removal, so far as possible, of all economic barriers'; and 'adequate guarantees given and taken that national armaments will be reduced'. There was to be 'a free, open-minded, and absolutely impartial adjustment of all colonial claims'. All Russian territory must be evacuated.

Then came the practical terms. 'Belgium must be evacuated and restored.' 'All French territory should be freed and the invaded portions restored, and the wrong done to France by Prussia in 1871 in the matter of Alsace-Lorraine . . . should be righted.' The clause concerning Italy was carefully designed to supersede the Treaty of London: 'a readjustment of the frontiers of Italy should be effected along clearly recognizable lines of nationality'. The claims of the Czechoslovaks were also repudiated: 'the peoples of Austria-Hungary . . . should be accorded the freest opportunity of autonomous development'. Though Rumania, Serbia and Montenegro were to be evacuated and restored, there was no hint that any of them should receive any acquisition of territory. Nor was it clear that the Ottoman empire was to be be dismembered. The non-Turkish nationalities were merely offered 'an undoubted security of life and an absolutely unmolested opportunity of autonomous development'. The Dardanelles were to be permanently opened under international guarantees — the Bosphorus was apparently forgotten. The pledge to Poland was a good deal more specific than any given by a British or French statesman: 'an independent Polish state . . . which should include the territories inhabited by indisputably Polish populations, which should be assured a free and secure access to the sea, and whose political and economic independence and territorial integrity should be guaranteed by international covenant'. The final point defined the future League of Nations: 'a general association . . . for the purpose of affording mutual guarantees of political independence and territorial integrity to great and small States alike'. There was one most striking omission. No word of the Fourteen Points referred to the democratization of the German Government.

The Fourteen Points contained nothing that Wilson had not said before. But previously he had expressed academic approval of aims which the Entente were to realize; now he made them his own. 'The program of the world's peace is our program; and that program, the only possible program, as we see it, is this.' Lloyd George virtually endorsed the Fourteen Points on 18 January: 'President Wilson and myself laid down what was substantially the same programme of demands for the termination of the war', though he expressed some doubt about the freedom of the seas. None of the other Allies made any public statement. The Italian Government contemplated a protest, but thought better of it.

The War Aims of the Allies in the First World War

The Serb minister at Washington said privately that ignoring his country was 'the absolute bankruptcy of Allied policy'.

Wilson laid down further general propositions in later speeches. None of them added to his practical programme except the principle stated on 4 July: 'the destruction of every arbitrary power anywhere that can separately, secretly, and of its single choice disturb the peace of the world'. It was on the basis of this clause that Wilson demanded assurance that Germany had become a democratic country, when the Germans sought an armistice in October. There was a more important change of policy in the last months of the war: the Allies jettisoned Austria-Hungary. The attempts at a separate peace with her had broken down. What is more, the Italians, in their desperate condition, grasped at any assistance and in April 1918 organized a Congress of Oppressed Nationalities at Rome, where they sat side by side with Yugoslavs, whom they hoped shortly to oppress. The real gainers were the Czechoslovaks, whose claims the Italians could back unreservedly without risk to themselves. The Allies had, too, the example of Russian Bolshevism before their eyes. They feared similar developments in central Europe when the Habsburg monarchy broke up; and nothing did more to endear the principle of national self-determination to them than the anti-Bolshevik achievements of the Czech legion in Siberia.

At the end of May an Entente conference met at Versailles intending to launch a grandiose programme of national liberation, but it broke against Italian reluctance to recognize Yugoslavia even now. On 3 June it declared in favour of 'a united and independent Poland with free access to the sea' and expressed 'lively sympathy for the Czechoslovak and Jugoslav people'. Beneš, who was conducting Czechoslovak affairs in Europe, decided that he could not be held back any longer by the Yugoslavs. He went ahead and obtained recognition on his own. On 28 June France recognized the Czechoslovak National Council as 'supreme organ of the nation, and the first basis of a future Czechoslovak government'. On 9 August Great Britain accepted the Czechoslovaks 'as an Allied nation' and recognized the National Council 'as the present trustee of the future Czechoslovak Government'. On 2 September the United States outbid the Allies and recognized the National Council 'as a *de facto* belligerent government'. Czechoslovakia was thus legally in existence before the end of the war. Poland got a mere grudging acknowledgment in October, Yugoslavia none.

In October the Central Powers were defeated and sought peace negotiations on the basis of the Fourteen Points and Wilson's 'subsequent pronouncements'. Wilson made it clear that the programme of national autonomy had been made out of date by later events. In any case the armistices with Bulgaria, Austria-Hungary and Turkey were concluded on a purely military basis without reference to the Fourteen Points or any other political programme. The Germans were, however, informed on 5 November that the Allied governments were willing to make peace on the terms of the Fourteen Points and the principles enunciated in Wilson's subsequent addresses. They made two reservations: one — directed more against the United States than against Germany — concerning the freedom of the seas; the other that 'compensation will be made by Germany for all damage done to the civilian population of the Allies and their property by the aggression of Germany by land, by sea and from the air'.

One final gloss was added to Allied war aims before the Peace Conference met at Paris. Clemenceau and Foch came to London on a triumphal visit from 30 November to 3 December. They wished to secure British backing for their claim to the Saar and their plan for a separate Rhineland, which had been endorsed by Russia in the far-off happy days of February 1917. They did not succeed. Lloyd George refused to create 'a new Alsace-Lorraine in Europe'. Nevertheless Clemenceau held out a tempting bait. He would agree that Palestine should become a British, instead of an international, mandate; and he would transfer Mosul

The War Aims of the Allies in the First World War

— with its oilfields — from the French to the British sphere. Lloyd George accepted this 'verbal agreement'. What did he give 'verbally' in return? According to his own account, nothing. Not only did he reject Foch's scheme for the Rhineland: he asserted at the Supreme Council on 20 March 1919 that even the Sykes-Picot Agreement had been superseded by an Anglo-French statement of 7 November 1918, which promised 'to encourage and help the establishment of native governments and administrations in Syria and Mesopotamia'. On the other hand, Tardieu, one of Clemenceau's associates, said in the French Chamber that Clemenceau had yielded over Mosul and Palestine 'because he needed both general agreement with Great Britain and her local support in Syria'; and he described Clemenceau's price as 'total support given by England to the French plans in case of American objections'. Clemenceau certainly kept his bargain. Perhaps Lloyd George did also. Not only did Syria become a French mandate after some British objections: France got the Saar for fifteen years and an occupation of the Rhineland which Clemenceau intended should be permanent.

For the rest, Alsace-Lorraine returned to France. Belgium was liberated. Poland and Czechoslovakia became independent national states. The Rumanians got more than they deserved, though less than they demanded; the Yugoslavs less than they deserved, but more than they hoped for. Russian ambitions were swamped in the storm of the Bolshevik Revolution. Italy did not make the gains which she had been promised in the Treaty of London. She had been the most calculating and the most grasping of the Allies; and was consequently the more disappointed in a peace settlement where ideal principles counted for much more than 'the secret treaties'.

J. W. WHEELER-BENNETT

MEN OF TRAGIC DESTINY: LUDENDORFF AND GROENER

I

GERMANY is perhaps the only country in which in modern times the military caste has exercised a predominant influence in the political sphere and in which eminent soldiers have played a leading rôle in the formulation of both foreign and internal politics. In the main this has been to her ultimate detriment and the story of this military participation in politics is fraught with irony and tragedy. As in every story there are good and bad elements, heights of victory were reached and moments of nobility attained, but there were also depths of malfeasance and astounding instances of broken faith.

In no way is this story better exemplified than in the curiously interwoven lives of Erich Ludendorff and Wilhelm Groener, both men of tragic destiny, who were fated to sway the fortunes of Germany, and in some degree of the world as a whole, on certain momentous occasions. Of the two, Ludendorff achieved the greater eminence and yet was doomed in all things to fall just short of victory. Perhaps the ablest military strategist to be produced by the first World War, and certainly one of the greatest military organizers that the world has ever seen, Ludendorff, at the height of his power — and for the last two years of Wilhelm II's reign he dominated Germany as had none other since Bismarck — was his own worst enemy, nullifying as politician what he had achieved as a soldier; a political Jekyll for ever warring against a military Hyde. Groener, on the other hand, was the more tragic figure of the two, for he was fated to play a leading rôle in the obsequies of both the Second Reich and the Weimar system, and to be the victim of base betrayals on both occasions. It was laid upon him to perform duties in his country's service which caused him to be vilified and traduced by his fellow-soldiers. Few men have given more selfless service to their country, both as soldier and statesman, and few have been treated with greater lack of gratitude.

II

Wilhelm Groener was born in Ludwigsburg on 22 November 1867, the son of a non-commissioned officer in the Württemberg army. From earliest childhood he was destined for a military career, but, because his parents were poor, he was unable to receive anything more elaborate than the excellent education of the normal German schools, and here he distinguished himself by his unusual command of language and an outstanding gift for expression. At last the military goal was reached; on his eighteenth birthday (1885) Groener entered the 121st Infantry Regiment as an ensign, and for the next twenty years his life was that of an ordinary army officer, filled with the minute and strict detail of regimental service and staff routine.

This period was one of the most crucial in the history and development of German military strategy. The great Moltke had essayed to safeguard the new German empire, which he and Bismarck and William I had created, by preparing to meet the possibility of a simultaneous war with France and Russia. His plan of campaign, designed in 1880, envisaged an attack in full force in the east and defensive tactics in the west, where he was even prepared to retire before the French armies to a position behind the Rhine. In time, however, the military and political conditions which had influenced Moltke's decision changed, and his successor, Count von Waldersee, so far modified the plan as to provide for two alternative strategies, according to the season of the year. If war broke out in summer, the main attack would be in the east against Russia; if in the winter, in the west against France. It was the second of Moltke's successors, the great military genius, Count Alfred von Schlieffen, who, with the dawn of the century, finally abandoned the Moltke plan and adopted one based on precisely opposite principles. France had by this time become the more dangerous adversary for Germany; hence the rules of strategy demanded that, regardless of the season of the year, the main attack should be in the west. This would be delivered by the strengthened right wing of the German army through northern France and Belgium against Paris, whilst there would be a strategic retreat before the French armies on the left in Alsace-Lorraine. In the meantime, the eastern Front must look after itself until the decisive battle in the west freed sufficient forces for an offensive against Russia.

As a young and rising officer, Groener became a deep admirer of Schlieffen's genius and a strong devotee of his policies, in so far as they were made known to junior officers. His intense study of the potential Western Front and his application of these studies to the immediate problems of strategy commended him to his superiors who were perhaps agreeably surprised to find such aptitude in a young Swabian whose family was not of the military caste.

On his appointment, with the rank of major, as instructor at the *Kriegsakademie* his courses were eagerly followed by the young officers who came under his influence. Among this group of disciples were a number who later achieved fame and notoriety: Freiherr von Willisen, the mystery man and 'good genius' of the Imperial German Army, whose activities during the first World War have become a military classic, as yet remaining unchronicled, and whose liaison between the Government and the army in the early days of the Republic was of such vital importance; Kurt von Hammerstein-Equord, later to succeed Seeckt and Heye as commander of the *Reichswehr*; and Kurt von Schleicher,

Men of Tragic Destiny: Ludendorff and Groener

who was to become the *feldgraue Eminenz* of Weimar Germany and the viper which Groener had taken to his bosom. To these young men Groener seemed inspired, and much of the ability which they later displayed was attributed to his early training. His quality of human understanding, his gift for brilliant exposition, the clarity of his mind and the coolness of his judgment revealed him to them not only as an instructor above the average, but as a soldier whose genius, given the opportunity, must carry him very high in military command.

Yet Groener, throughout his army career, felt himself to be a lonely man, a Swabian unable to fit in completely with the rigidity of the Prussian military machine. The machine, however, was neither unmindful nor unappreciative of his high qualities, and the interest of that inner group of officers who were continually on the look-out for outstanding talent, ensured him an appointment on the Great General Staff, where there began his rivalry with a contemporary — Erich Ludendorff — with whom his life was to be linked so strangely.

When in 1906 the unfortunate younger Moltke — whom Groener was later to dub *der Feldherr wider Willen* — was appointed, at the whim of Wilhelm II, to succeed Schlieffen, he found that among the younger officers who must necessarily on their records receive high appointments were two outstanding candidates, Wilhelm Groener and Erich Ludendorff. They formed a strange contrast, for though neither belonged by birth either to the nobility or the military caste, Ludendorff, the Prussian, approximated more closely to tradition than did Groener, the Swabian, with his Württemberger background of poverty.

III

Born at Kruszewnia in Posen and two years older than Groener, Erich Ludendorff was the eldest son — his younger brother became the eminent astronomer of Potsdam — of a minor official in the Prussian State Railways administration. He received his early training at the Cadet School at Ploen and the Lichterfelde Military Academy, and was gazetted a lieutenant in the Marine-Infantry in 1882, at the age of eighteen. Throughout his school-years his more aristocratic contemporaries never allowed him to forget that he lacked the 'von' of nobility before his name, and this *snobbismus* spurred Ludendorff, like the young Bonaparte at Brienne, to a fierce application to his studies in order to excel the efforts of his fellows and thereby command their deference.

This passion for work and attention to detail won the recognition of Ludendorff's superiors. He rose rapidly through the regimental ranks, was promoted captain in 1893 and the same year received his first taste of work on the General Staff, later being attached to the Fourth Corps at Magdeburg. But he was still unknown, and his appointment as a major on the Great General Staff in 1906 came as a surprise to all in the military world, save to that inner circle of officers who continually sought outstanding talent.

But this passionate addiction to work took toll of Ludendorff in other ways. His spirit became impervious to the finer humanities. He was blessed with neither Groener's appreciation for natural beauty nor his intellectual attainment, and he lacked the Swabian's jovial sense of humour. With his mind enmeshed in a net of military detail no streak of aestheticism coloured Ludendorff's nature. 'He was a man blind in spirit,' his medical director once confessed. 'He had never seen a flower bloom, never heard a bird sing, never watched the sun set. I used to treat him for his soul.'

Neck-and-neck Ludendorff and Groener easily outdistanced other competitors for the 'plum' position on the General Staff, the head of the Operations Section. The merits of both were carefully weighed and both seemed to be admirably suited. The selectors turned to minutiae to influence their choice. After lengthy consideration, Groener was passed over on the grounds that, as his father had been a paymaster, he was not of the military caste. Ludendorff was not an officer's son either, but there had been officers in his family for generations, and this turned the scale in his favour. He became Chief of Operations, and to Groener fell the parallel post of Chief of Transport.

The unhappy Moltke took it upon himself in 1908–9 to sanction certain fundamental changes in the Schlieffen Plan with regard to mobilization and operations. These changes originated largely from proposals of Ludendorff which envisaged a sudden attack on Liège, the abandonment of the strategic retreat in Alsace-Lorraine and the weakening of the right wing to make possible a 'break-through' in the south between Toul and Épinal, there being a *sine qua non* in Ludendorff's mind that at least three new corps should be added to the army.

To these proposals Groener made the liveliest opposition. He strongly deprecated the abandoning of Schlieffen's fundamental principle that the right wing must be kept strong at all costs and feared that too much faith would be placed in the 42-cm. mortars which Ludendorff proposed to use against Liège. There was a danger, he warned, that over-estimation of technical inventions would tend to destroy the creative imagination of Staff officers, rendering them too prone to mental rigidity in warfare.

The alternative plan which Groener urged upon Moltke was one which, had it been adopted, might well have altered the course of the early weeks of the war. Groener was satisfied, after studying the reports of his former pupil Willisen, that the line of the Vosges could be held with a comparatively small number of troops. Two army corps could, therefore, be withdrawn from Alsace and concentrated on the lower Rhine, thereby strengthening the German right even beyond the conception of Schlieffen. Groener hoped, by thus additionally strengthening the German right, to force the French into violating Belgian neutrality in order to forestall a German attack from that quarter and thus, by shifting the stigma of this action to France, to fight the early battles of the war under favourable political and military conditions.

Between the proposals of Groener and Ludendorff, Moltke characteristically hesitated; finally he attempted a fatal compromise. He adopted Ludendorff's plan without pressing for the formation of the three additional corps upon which it had been based, and at the same time attempted to weave into it some part of Groener's scheme. This resulted in August 1914 in two divisions being immobilized in trains on the lower Rhine without any one seeming to know just why they were there.

Though he doubted the wisdom of the new Moltke plan, Groener at once began to work out the necessary details in rail and road organization which its adoption entailed and, as a result, there belongs to him the undying credit for the amazing perfection with which the transport of German troops and guns and *matériel* functioned during the first two years of the first World War.

But, like many another in Germany during those fatal July days of 1914, Groener did not believe that either politically or strategically the assassination of the Archduke Franz Ferdinand should create for Germany a *casus foederis* with Austria. To him it was impossible that a general war should result from this issue and, confident in this belief, he departed for his annual cure at Kissingen, taking with him the key of the safe in the war ministry wherein reposed the plans for the carrying out of mobilization. From the calm of this retreat he counselled caution and discretion to his colleagues on the General Staff. Twice he refused to obey an imperative summons to return to Berlin. 'If you will keep your heads and remain calm as I am doing, this thing will pass as it has passed before', he replied, and only the issue of the order for mobilization on 31 July brought him back to the capital, for it could not proceed without him.

The outbreak of the war brought Groener his promotion to colonel and his appointment as Chief of Field-Railway Transport in the west. From the Imperial Headquarters at Coblenz, and later at Charleville, he watched the famous Plan into which Schlieffen had infused his genius, wrecked and destroyed under the *main malheureuse* of Moltke. Thanks to the modifications which the Schlieffen Plan had undergone, neither wing was strong enough to carry out its offensive mission. The break-through in the south failed to materialize, and in the north, though at one moment Willisen, as chief of staff of the cavalry corps, was sitting on the eighth milestone from Calais, the attack was checked and recalled by the now famous and fatal orders which Moltke sent verbally to the commanders by Colonel Hentsch of his staff, to whose personal discretion, strangely enough, the final decision was left. It was always Groener's subsequent contention that, had Kluck and Bülow disregarded these strangely irregular instructions and pressed forward on their own initiative, the fall of Paris could have been accomplished.

Even after the disaster of the Marne, Groener urged first on Moltke and then on his successor, Falkenhayn, a return to Schlieffen's bold policy of strengthening the right wing by utilizing the excellently organized system of the German strategic railways and resuming the drive on Paris through northern France, but his advice was disregarded and German strategy developed into the great drive for Antwerp and the Channel Ports.

IV

Ludendorff's star, meanwhile, was in the ascendant. The general mobilization of July 1914 had found him Deputy Chief of Staff of the Second Army, to which was assigned the carrying out of the assault on the fortress of Liège. By a sudden and daring decision to take command of a regiment that had been brought to a standstill, and by launching a surprise attack, he was able to achieve the spectacular capture of the citadel almost single-handed, though the forts still held out for two days longer. For this gallant feat, the only occasion during the war in which he actually commanded troops, Ludendorff was decorated by the Kaiser with the coveted Pour le Mérite cross.

When the defeat and collapse of the Eighth Army in East Prussia sent a thrill of apprehension through the Imperial General Headquarters at Coblenz, Moltke inevitably turned to Colonel Ludendorff to redress the balance of disaster. 'I know of no other person whom I trust so implicitly as yourself', he wrote. 'Perhaps you may succeed in saving the position in the East . . . your energy is such that you may still succeed in averting the worst.' And General von Stein added his appeal. 'Your place is on the Eastern Front . . . the safety of the country demands it.'

Such was the mission with which Ludendorff was entrusted on his appointment as Chief of Staff of the Eighth Army, with Colonel-General Paul von Benckendorff und von Hindenburg as the 'dear old Excellency' who should be his nominal commander, the foil for his brilliance and the shield for the flame of his genius. This 'marriage of minds', which was effected at the railway station of Hanover in the early hours of 23 August 1914, is without exact parallel in history. Personally unknown to one another, and utterly dissimilar in character, each provided the necessary complement of the other. Ludendorff was the dominant husband of the union, Hindenburg the placid wife; Ludendorff was the motive force in the partnership, Hindenburg the balancing factor. The calmer nature of the older man served as a corrective for the younger's eager temperament, at once more brilliant and less stable. Ludendorff could stand the strain of responsibility when things went well but in moments of crisis he was liable to nervous distraction; Hindenburg preserved a stoic impassivity in the face of both triumph and disaster. Together they formed one of the most amazing military combinations in history.

Their joint fame became world-wide a week later, after the great victory of Tannenberg, though no impartial student of that campaign can escape the conclusion that the strategic laurels for the Russian defeat belong to their senior staff officer, Colonel Hoffmann; while the point-blank refusal of that vigorous tactician, General von François, to carry out

Men of Tragic Destiny: Ludendorff and Groener

Ludendorff's orders contributed largely to the cutting off of the enemy's retreat. Popular opinion, however, is but little affected by historical accuracy, and the names of Hindenburg and Ludendorff became inseparably linked with the destruction of Samsonov's army at Tannenberg, and with the subsequent rout of Rennenkampf at the battle of the Masurian Lakes. The winter campaign in Poland, which, after many vicissitudes, ended in the capture of the fortress of Łodz and the general retirement of the Russian armies, added greatly to their already glowing prestige and gave, both to themselves and to the general public at large, a disproportionate idea of their achievements. For the numerical superiority of the defeated Russian armies blinded many to their great weakness in guns and munitions and the poverty of their leadership.

Throughout the year 1915 and the first half of 1916, Hindenburg, Ludendorff and Hoffmann, now welded into the single symbol HLH, were in bitter conflict with the new Chief of the General Staff, von Falkenhayn, who had succeeded Moltke after the disaster of the Marne. They had forced the Russians back as far as Vilna, but the enemy had always escaped from their enveloping movements. A Cannae victory had eluded HLH, and they demanded additional troops for a drive to the north against Minsk, which should sever the Russian rail communications. This was rejected by Falkenhayn, who rightly judged that the war must be fought to a finish in the west, believing that, even were Russia forced to make a separate peace, Great Britain and France would continue the struggle. He elected to make a gigantic effort to take Verdun, and his withdrawal of troops and guns from the east rendered it impossible for HLH to make any farther advance. They were driven on to the defensive by the Russian attacks of March and April 1916, and though they were able to hold their own, they were unable to prevent the Austrian defeats at the hands of the Russians between the Pripet and the Carpathians.

The opposition of Falkenhayn to the 'Easterners' resulted

in an extraordinary exhibition of military intrigue and barratry. Ludendorff and Hoffmann lost no opportunity in egging on Hindenburg to flout and thwart the orders of the Chief of the General Staff, while Falkenhayn in his turn responded with pinpricking pettiness and obstinacy. The conduct of both sides was mean and picayune and redounded to the credit of neither party, for neither appeared to recall that the duty of a soldier is to fight the enemy and not his comrades.

But the tide was running strongly against Falkenhayn, and when the failure of the Verdun offensive was followed by the entry of Rumania into the war on the side of the Allies a full two months before he had expected it, the Kaiser yielded to the voice of popular demand, and on 29 August 1916 summoned Hindenburg and Ludendorff to the Supreme Command of the German armies in the field.

v

A definite period closed for Ludendorff on 29 August. Hitherto his undoubted genius had been exercised only in a limited sphere, for the High Command in the east, though semi-autonomous, was concerned merely with the problems of its own strategy. The consideration of national politics and the organization of the national resources had played no part in the world of HLH, whose political activities had been confined to their intrigues against Falkenhayn. They had been soldiers pure and simple; their great and deserved reputation had been built up on their military attainments alone. Now all this was changed. A stroll in the gardens of the Castle of Pless on an afternoon in high summer had altered the destinies not only of Hindenburg and Ludendorff, but of Germany and Europe. Had he but known it, Wilhelm II in that brief conversation had sealed the fate of his country, his throne and his house. For from the moment of his appointment Ludendorff conceived himself as the chief power in the Reich. It had been the original intention to appoint the Marshal and Ludendorff as Chief and Second

Men of Tragic Destiny: Ludendorff and Groener

Chief of the General Staff, but to this Ludendorff objected. For him the word 'second' no longer existed with regard to rank, and he insisted on the title of First Quartermaster-General. But before he accepted the position at all, he made it clear to the Kaiser that he must have 'joint responsibility in all decisions and measures that might be taken', and the Kaiser had given him assurance on this point.

Here was the direct corollary of the 'marriage of minds' between Hindenburg and Ludendorff. After two years of close co-operation the personality of the Marshal had become so dependent upon, and merged into, that of his lieutenant that he accepted almost unquestioned the views of Ludendorff. The combination from a military aspect proved vastly effective, but politically it was utterly unfortunate; for while in the direction of operations these two worked in complementary accord, in political affairs Hindenburg, knowing and caring nothing of State affairs, was glad to leave their conduct exclusively to Ludendorff — and Ludendorff had very definite ideas regarding the place of the Supreme Command in the government of the country. 'Not only had I to probe deeply into the wider workings of the war-direction, and get a grasp of both the great and small matters that affected the home life of the people,' he wrote, 'but I had to familiarize myself with great world questions which raised all sorts of problems'. The result of this enquiry and familiarization was the conclusion that, for the winning of the war, the entire resources and government of the country must be placed unreservedly and without stint at the disposal of the Supreme Command, who assumed responsibility for all actions taken but whose decisions must not be criticized or questioned. The military condominium of Hindenburg and Ludendorff, under the instigation of the latter, became an *imperium in imperio*, with the First Quartermaster-General negotiating independently with the Emperor, the Chancellor, the Foreign Office, the party leaders in the Reichstag, industrial magnates and trade union officials, in fact with everyone who had to be subordinated to the will of G.H.Q.

Gradually a complete dictatorship was built up on the interpretation which Ludendorff placed upon the word 'responsibility'. For example, when the Imperial Chancellor pursued some policy of which the Supreme Command disapproved, or which they considered injurious to the conduct of the war, they declared they could not assume 'responsibility' for such action and asked leave to resign. But it was the Chancellor who resigned. By exercise of this method of 'persuasion' Ludendorff forced everyone from the Emperor down to give way to him. On some occasions he obtained Hindenburg's approval for his actions; frequently he made use of his name in negotiation; always his final argument was, 'The Field Marshal and I will resign'.

In claiming these supreme powers Ludendorff was not actuated by personal ambition. Ruthless and arrogant he was, but not personally ambitious. His was the dynamic will of the fanatic, which drives straight to its goal without a thought for those who stand in its path. Himself steeped in the disciplinary obedience of the military tradition, he regarded Germany as a vast machine respondent to his will rather than as a highly sensitive and complex industrial organism, and he demanded from it that same willingness to achieve complete victory which he regarded as inherent in the German army. His handling of the 'home front' was characterized by a lack of understanding which led at last to failure and breakdown, and is in marked contrast with the successful degree of co-operation which the more sympathetic personality of Groener was able to establish between capital and labour.

In his consideration of the wider questions of national policy which affected other countries Ludendorff's limitations became still more definite. There was a marked inability to see the part in relation to the whole, a tendency to pursue a policy for its short-term advantages, regardless of what its ultimate repercussions might bring, and, above all, an assumption of omniscience which would brook no correction or opposition. It was this obstinate conviction which deprived

Men of Tragic Destiny: Ludendorff and Groener

Germany of the services of her two most enlightened wartime statesmen, Bethmann Hollweg and Kühlmann, both of whom were sacrificed by Wilhelm II at the command of Ludendorff.

The results of such a situation could not but be disastrous, for while the strategic genius of the Supreme Command was achieving military successes, their political ineptitude prevented these successes from being exploited diplomatically; and, since Germany was virtually in the state of a beleaguered fortress, the advantages gained were really only in the nature of sorties which, though they forced the enemy to retire, could not raise the siege. Thus, though the armies of the Central Powers crushed Rumania, held Russia, created the supposedly impregnable *Siegfried Stellung,* repulsed with bloody loss the Nivelle offensive, and inflicted a heavy defeat on the Italians at Caporetto, their efforts and sacrifices were nullified by the political policies dictated by the Supreme Command.

The movement towards a separate peace with tsarist Russia, fostered with such care on both sides, was brought to a sudden end in November 1916 by the insistence of the Supreme Command on the proclamation of the kingdom of Poland in the hope of raising a Polish army to fight for Germany. In effect nothing of the sort occurred; the Poles regarded this recognition of their independence as but their natural due and showed a definite disinclination to shed their blood for Germany. Grasping at a shadow, Ludendorff had missed the substance, for the advantages of a separate peace with Russia, unattended by the dangers of Bolshevism, were obvious.

Four months later, in February 1917, a further blunder of major importance attended the efforts of the Supreme Command to control policy. In face of the expressed objection of the Chancellor, Bethmann Hollweg, and regardless of the vast potentialities involved, Ludendorff and Hindenburg forced the reluctant Kaiser to declare for unlimited U-boat warfare against neutrals and belligerents alike, in a desperate attempt to break the stranglehold of the Allied blockade. The effect of this action on non-belligerent powers had been considered, and it was agreed that there were sufficient troops available to repulse any attempt of Danish and Dutch divisions to invade Germany by way of retaliation. As for the United States, it was not even considered worth-while to regard them from a military point of view, for even if American troops should succeed in crossing the Atlantic — on the impossibility of which the Chief of the Naval Staff staked his reputation — the value to the Allies of these raw untrained forces would be negligible. In any case it was hoped to bring England to her knees before any such eventuality could possibly take place. In both these expectations the Supreme Command were disappointed. England, though hard pressed, was not driven to surrender, and the United States declared war on 6 April. Three months later the first American troops landed in France, and by November they were in the firing line. In addition, the Allied blockade, now strengthened by the co-operation of the American navy, became more complete than ever.

In the summer of 1917 a not unpromising offer of mediation on the part of the Pope was rejected by Michaelis, the puppet Chancellor whose appointment Ludendorff and Hindenburg had contrived as a successor to Bethmann Hollweg, simply because the Supreme Command refused to consider the restoration of Belgian independence.

But the most outstanding example of the defeat of the soldier by the politician was in the case of the peace of Brest-Litovsk. With the object of assisting the collapse of Russia, the Supreme Command facilitated the return of Lenin to Petrograd, little thinking the virus of Bolshevism which they were injecting into the body politic of an enemy State would infect the army and civilian population of Germany. So quickly did the poison spread that by December 1917 Russia was suing for a separate peace. Germany's Secretary of State, von Kühlmann, realized what the soldiers would not admit, that a victory in the field was no longer possible for Germany, and sought therefore to prepare the way for a general peace of negotiation, but Ludendorff insisted on the imposition of peace terms so starkly brutal and annexationist in character that the world stood aghast at their rapacity.

In every sense the effect was disastrous. The Allied governments were made aware of the kind of peace they might expect from a Germany dominated by the Supreme Command, and were confirmed in their belief that the war must be fought to the bitter end to accomplish the defeat of Germany. Moreover, the publication of the Brest peace terms decided President Wilson to devote all the vast resources of America, in men, money and munitions, to the Allied cause. A degree of co-operation was established between America and the nations of the Entente which all previous negotiation between them had failed to achieve, and the artificer of this unity of purpose was Ludendorff.

Furthermore, the direct results to Germany of the treaty were entirely negative. The hope of securing large supplies of food from the Ukraine for the hungry population of the Central Powers was doomed to disappointment, and in addition it was discovered that a victor's peace must be enforced. Germany had separated from Russia the provinces of Courland, Lithuania, Esthonia and Livonia with a view to incorporating them within the empire, and a garrison had to be kept in these territories. She had recognized the independence of the Ukraine and of Georgia, and was therefore obliged to uphold with bayonets their shadow governments, which would otherwise be overthrown by the Bolsheviks. An army of occupation was maintained in Rumania, and German expeditions were sent to Finland, Baku and the Donetz Basin. The original object of concluding a separate peace with Russia had been to enable the German army in the east to be transferred to the western Front to take part in the final offensive against the Allies which Ludendorff planned for the spring of 1918, and on which he was prepared to stake all in a final gamble for victory. Yet when the great attack was launched on 21 March, a million men were still immobilized in the east, and half that number on the western Front in the early stages of the *Kaiserschlacht* might easily have turned the scale in favour of Germany. It was not until late summer, when the German losses had reached stupendous figures, that Ludendorff made his final withdrawals from the east, but then they only came a few at a time and too late.

Despite the failure of the offensive in the spring and summer, it was not until 28 September that Ludendorff would admit the necessity of an armistice, though he knew after 8 August — 'the black day of the German Army in the war'— that his 'gambler's throw' had failed and the initiative had passed into the hands of the Allies. Again his political sense failed him. Realizing that a democratization of the German political structure was a necessary preliminary for peace, he commanded a 'Revolution from Above' and a proposal for an armistice on the basis of Mr. Wilson's Fourteen Points, still ignorant of the fact that, since the Peace of Brest-Litovsk, this programme no longer represented 'a full recitation of the conditions of peace'.

In vain Prince Max of Baden pleaded for a preliminary period of negotiation, pointing out that so sudden a conversion to peace and democracy on the part of Germany indicated too openly a death-bed repentance. Ludendorff, in the last act of his supremacy, and haunted by the spectre of a complete breakdown of the army in the field, bore down all opposition and insisted upon the dispatch of the fatal telegram of 4 October. Too late he became aware of the powers which he had conjured up against Germany. When the conditions of the pre-armistice agreement arrived from Washington, making it clear that in accepting them Germany would render herself unable to reopen hostilities, Ludendorff, aghast, repudiated his part in urging the opening of negotiations and declared for a war *à outrance*.

He fell, at last, a victim to the 'Revolution from Above' which he himself had ordered. The responsibility for the conduct of the war had passed by the reforms of October 1918 from the Supreme Command to the Cabinet, and on 26 October the Chancellor confronted the Kaiser with the choice which Ludendorff had so often put before him during the past two years. Either the Cabinet or the First Quartermaster-General must resign, and in this case Wilhelm II had no choice in making his decision. Ludendorff's own weapon of an ultimatum had been turned against him. Two days later his request for permission to resign was granted, and he passed from active service, to be succeeded by his old rival, Wilhelm Groener. When the revolution of November broke out in Germany he fled to Sweden wearing civilian clothes and disguised with blue glasses.

VI

Groener's career, meantime, had been less spectacular but by no means less constructive in its contribution to Germany's war effort. For the first two years of the war he devoted himself to the perfect functioning of military transport, one of the most vital factors in modern warfare. Constant streams of reserves, food, guns, munitions and stores passed up to the Front; constant convoys of wounded and exhausted troops streamed back to hospitals and depôts. Divisions moved from one part of the line to another. Upon Groener rested the responsibility for the smooth running of this gigantic transport system, and he discharged this task with cool precision and unqualified success.

With the appearance of Hindenburg and Ludendorff at the Supreme Command in August 1916 the war took on a new aspect. The General Staff was reorganized and for the first time it was appreciated that the industrial life of Germany must be controlled and mobilized to meet the gigantic demands of the army. There developed the so-called 'Hindenburg Programme' for the economic intensification of production, a programme which depended for its success upon the complete co-operation of employers and employed.

To Groener, now a major-general, was assigned this task, his official position being head of the *Kriegsamt* of the Ministry of War, and here his flair for organization and his capacity for human understanding were his chief assets. The officials of the trade unions and Social Democratic Party had declared their refusal to work with any representative of the Supreme Command, but in an astonishingly short space of time Groener had won their co-operation, at first unwillingly and in spite of themselves, but soon in genuine admiration of his great qualities and fair-mindedness. Ebert, Scheidemann and Legien trusted Groener for his intrinsic honesty and with them he made friendships which were later to prove of high importance to Germany.

As a result of these felicitous relations, Groener was enabled to exercise a benevolent dictatorship over the German 'home front' and the Hindenburg Programme gained a high degree of achievement, the credit for which went to the Field Marshal. But Groener's success was to his own detriment. Ludendorff, jealous as ever of the one man in the army who was his possible rival, gave ear to the resentful suspicions of the great industrialists who complained that Groener's relations with the workmen were too friendly, citing his measures for the improvement of wages and the regulation of contractors' profits.

With the characteristic insidiousness of the military condominium then ruling Germany, a statement appeared in the semi-official *Lokalanzeiger* foreshadowing Groener's imminent retirement. Correctly interpreting the writing on the wall, Groener did not give the Supreme Command the satisfaction of relegating him to obscurity. He immediately placed his resignation in the hands of the Minister of War and requested an active command. His departure from the 'home front' marked the beginning of a steady deterioration in the relations between capital and labour which culminated in the revolutionary strike movement of January 1918.

For the remainder of 1917 Groener saw service on the western Front, first as a divisional and later as a corps commander, but with the conclusion of peace with Russia in the east, a new field of service was opened to him — the task of garnering the harvest of victory which Ludendorff had hoped to reap from the treaties of Brest-Litovsk of February and March 1918. By these treaties, Germany and Austria-Hungary had recognized the independence of the Ukraine from Soviet Russia and had entered into separate negotiations with her for supplies of grain and foodstuffs in which the Central Powers were so gravely lacking as a result of the Allied blockade. The task of collecting these supplies was entrusted to the army of occupation commanded by Marshal von Eichhorn, to whom Groener, now a lieutenant-general, was attached as Chief of Staff. He was considered particularly qualified for this thankless mission by reason of the very success on the 'home front' which had brought about his resignation, and if conciliatory tactics could have achieved success, he would certainly have produced results. Tribute was paid by all parties in the Ukraine to the sincerity of his efforts and to the highly efficient plan which he developed to solve the difficulties of the problem through the German-Ukrainian Trading Organization; a plan, however, which depended for its success on some measure of co-operation from the peasantry.

But not even Groener's persuasive qualities could break down the sullen opposition of the Ukrainian peasant farmer, and the organization, brilliant in conception, had depressingly meagre results. Only 42,000 truck-loads of grain in all were exported from the Ukraine during the whole period of German and Austrian occupation (March–December 1918).

Groener's efforts were still further hampered by the arbitrary tactics of Marshal von Eichhorn who, enraged at the dilatoriness and non-co-operative policies of the Ukrainian *Rada*, determined to replace it with a form of military dictatorship which would be more subservient to the wishes of the German High Command. Upon Groener devolved the duties of negotiating with the new Ukrainian ruler, General Pavlo Skoropadsky, with whom he signed an agreement on behalf of Germany on 24 April 1918 whereby that country acquired an even tighter grip on the economic life of the Ukraine. Yet the repressive measures which Eichhorn and Skoropadsky now introduced were of no greater avail than Groener's efforts had been in persuading the Ukrainian peasant to part with his crops, and throughout the summer and early autumn a series of defeats were encountered.

VII

It was while he was thus profitlessly engaged that there came to Groener, in the grey cold of Kiev, his fateful summons to Spa as First Quartermaster-General and virtual field commander of the defeated German armies in the west. The race between himself and Ludendorff was ended and his rival was crossing the Swedish frontier disguised in blue spectacles and civilian clothes. But there was no rejoicing in Groener's heart as he crossed an exhausted, war-weary Germany on his journey to Spa. He knew already the hopelessness of the task he had to face, a task which demanded of him a ruthless energy, utter self-denial and the renunciation of all glory and all gratitude. With quiet courage he assumed his new responsibilities and showed nobly that he possessed in full measure the qualities required.

On his arrival on 30 October Groener found Hindenburg saddened and bemused by the tragic train of events, which had removed the man who had been his twin soul for four long years, and which had turned possible victory into certain defeat. It was impossible for Ludendorff's successor to establish the same relationship of intimacy with the Marshal, and it was perhaps inevitable that Hindenburg should resent the change and readjustment which Groener's arrival entailed. He was not very cordial in his reception. Scarcely, however, had he and Groener exchanged greetings when they were joined by the Kaiser, who had virtually fled from Berlin where already he had been urged to abdicate, a course of action which he resolutely refused even to consider.

Men of Tragic Destiny: Ludendorff and Groener

At this period Groener was firmly opposed to any thought of the Kaiser's abdication, and so berated Dr. Drews, the Prussian Minister of Interior whom Prince Max of Baden had sent as an envoy to persuade Wilhelm II of its necessity, that the Kaiser had actually to come to the rescue of his Minister, and soothe his ruffled feathers.

'How splendid to see the solemn Groener so carried away', he remarked later to his aide-de-camp. 'I was delighted to see a South German so ready to defend the King of Prussia. *Der biedere Schwabe.*'

But 'the brave Swabian' was facing fearful realities. His first visit to the Front convinced him of the utter hopelessness of continuing hostilities. On 5 November he bluntly informed the Chancellor and the Cabinet: 'We shall have to cross the lines with a white flag. Even a week is too long to wait. It must be Saturday 9 November at latest.' Prince Max pointed out that it had been revealed in the course of the negotiations with President Wilson that the chief obstacle to favourable terms was the refusal of the Kaiser to abdicate. Would not Groener, he urged, himself dissipate the imperial illusions and force the Emperor to realize the truth? Groener refused adamantly. 'Perhaps the Field-Marshal . . .' a cabinet member began, but Groener turned on him shouting, 'The Marshal would consider himself the lowest kind of scoundrel if he abandoned the Kaiser, and so, gentlemen, would I and every honourable soldier.'

That same day Groener met Ebert and Scheidemann, and other Social Democrat and trade union leaders, men who had collaborated with him on friendly terms in 1916 and 1917. All trusted him, and Ebert begged him to urge abdication on the Emperor. If the monarchical régime was to survive, and they were not opposed to it as such, it must be based upon the trade unions and controlled by a parliamentary system, but this was impossible under the present Kaiser or the crown prince. The last chance of saving the monarchy was to entrust the government to a regent for one of the younger imperial princes.

Groener was shaken by these arguments. The honest reasoning of Ebert affected him more deeply than the distracted pleadings of Prince Max. He was now persuaded that the abdication of the Kaiser could not be long postponed, but he could not bring himself to have any part in it. Rather would he have seen Wilhelm II seek death in action. 'He should go to the front line,' he had said to Hindenburg after their set-to with Drews, 'not to review troops or to confer decorations but to look for death. He should go to some trench which was under the full blast of war. If he were killed, it would be the finest death possible. If he were wounded, the feelings of the German people would completely change towards him.' Despite Hindenburg's horror at such a suggestion, Groener still believed this to be the way of honour for his War Lord.

Throughout those fateful November days Groener used every means at his command, short of personal insistence, to convince the Kaiser of the hopeless gravity of the situation both at the Front and in the interior, in the hope that Wilhelm II would himself make the gesture of renunciation in order to save his dynasty and his people. But it soon became evident that, until he was convinced of the fact that he no longer held the loyalty of his army, the Kaiser could take no such decision, and though Groener was himself certain that the troops would fight no longer either against the enemy in their front or the revolution in their rear, he considered that it was Hindenburg's duty, as Chief of Staff, rather than his, to make this clear to the Kaiser. But this the Marshal would not do, and in the meantime revolution was running through the country like a prairie fire.

At length, however, later on the evening of 8 November, Hindenburg and Groener reached a decision. The Kaiser must abdicate in favour of one of his younger sons, or of the eldest son of the crown prince, but there must be no question of his leaving the country. Such an action would discredit the monarchy for ever. He must retire to one of his estates. It was agreed that the two heads of the Supreme Command should acquaint Wilhelm II with this decision on the following morning, and Groener retired with a heavy heart but a clear conscience.

But he awoke to find that in the night-watches other influences had convinced Hindenburg that the flight of the emperor to neutral soil was an imperative corollary to abdication, and there was no time before their audience to make him change his mind again. In silence the two leaders drove to meet their War Lord, and at the final moment of ordeal Hindenburg broke down. With tears running down his face he begged his Kaiser's leave to resign. He could not as a Prussian officer say to his War Lord what must be said to him. He had, therefore, ordered General Groener to give to His Majesty the considered opinion of the High Command.

So it was Groener, the *biedere Schwabe*, who was made the scapegoat. As a Württemberger he could use language which could not sully the lips of a member of the Prussian military caste. Upon the shoulders of this lonely South German was laid the task of disillusioning the king of Prussia.

Very simply and quietly Groener explained the situation. The army would no longer fight either the revolution or the enemy. It demanded peace, it wanted to go home. Very well, said the Kaiser, he would spare the Fatherland the horrors of a civil war; he would remain at Spa until the conclusion of an armistice and then return home quietly at the head of his troops.

So far Groener had purposely avoided the blunt statement that the army was no longer *kaisertreu*, but now he could evade the issue no longer. The myopic obstinacy of the Kaiser demanded brutal measures, and Groener used the words for which the imperial forgiveness was long delayed.

'Sire,' he said, 'you no longer have an army. The army will march home in peace and order under its leaders and commanding generals, but not under the command of Your Majesty, for it no longer stands behind Your Majesty.'

In the fierce debate which followed, Groener stood alone against the bitter reproaches of the Prussian generals, led by the crown prince's Chief of Staff, Count von der Schulenburg. Outnumbered, he stood his ground, and as the day wore on the inexorable record of events which flooded into Spa by telephone from all over Germany and from the Front proved him a truthful Cassandra.

With the final decision of the Kaiser to cross the Dutch frontier he had no part. The responsibility for that rested on Hindenburg alone. Groener had consistently opposed the policy of flight, and considered that Wilhelm II in so doing had been grievously mistaken. Like the remainder of the officer corps, he found himself released from his oaths of fealty to his War Lord and conceived his only loyalty to be to his Fatherland in this dire hour of misfortune. His attitude was commendable in the highest degree and gave a shining example to all others who were wavering and uncertain as to where their duty lay.

Groener, once the final ordeal was over, and Wilhelm II had disappeared from the scene, gave himself up to the task of bringing the field army home to revolutionary Germany with the maximum amount of efficiency and the minimum of disorder. Hindenburg, bewildered by the tragedy of 9 November, followed the lead of his lieutenant but took no initiative. It was Groener who gave the assurance to Ebert and the new Government that the General Staff and the corps of officers would support the Social Democratic régime in its fight for life against Communism. It was Groener who ordered the homeward march on 12 November, and to his genius for organization was the credit that the armies of the west returned quickly and without mishap. It was Groener's tact in handling the new 'spokesmen', which each unit was permitted to elect, which was responsible for the fact that, with the exception of some regrettable incidents in the Rhinelands, military discipline was strictly maintained.

There followed a year of bitterness and humiliation during which Hindenburg and Groener, with headquarters first at Cassel and later at Kolberg, were engaged in the gigantic task of disbanding the field armies in accordance with the Armistice

Agreement — a difficult period of adjustment and transformation. It was in these days of trial that the old friendship between Groener and Ebert gave to Germany a factor of stability without which the new-born republic might well have perished. A private telephone connected Ebert's room at the Chancellery with Groener's at General Headquarters, and along it travelled advice, admonition, recriminations and, occasionally, threats, for there were many moments when the square peg of the military machine refused to be fitted into the round hole of republican democracy. But there can be no doubt that the support given by Groener to Ebert in these critical months was of the greatest possible help in dealing with those enthusiasts on both the Right and the Left who, regardless of national patriotism, persistently gave themselves up to rocking the boat.

VIII

In Germany itself the issue between Socialism and Communism was finally settled in the bloody and abortive Spartacist risings which were suppressed with the greatest severity by the Ebert Government. Slowly and painfully the life of the country began to take on a more normal form and, as the spring deepened into summer, all eyes were turned to Paris where the Germans had been summoned to receive the Allied terms of peace. Their publication sent a shudder of incredulous horror through Germany, to be followed by an outcry of furious resentment. The country to a man was in favour of rejection and clamoured for such action by the Government and the National Assembly in session at Weimar. Ebert and his colleagues shared to the full the outraged feelings of their countrymen, but upon them rested the responsibility for the consequences which rejection of the peace terms would entail. For weeks the Cabinet and Assembly were divided; finally, 22 June, there came an ultimatum from Foch. The terms must be accepted within forty-eight hours or hostilities would reopen.

As a last resort, Ebert appealed to the army leaders. He would only agree to signing the treaty if the High Command had come to the final conclusion that there remained no chance left of armed resistance. If they believed in the smallest possibility of success, Ebert declared, he would throw the whole weight of his influence in favour of rejection.

The appeal was addressed to Hindenburg, as nominal commander-in-chief, and once again, as in the matter of the Kaiser's abdication, the Marshal buckled beneath the burden of responsibility. He knew that armed resistance was impossible, so that he dared not advise the resumption of hostilities, yet equally he could not take the responsibility for accepting the treaty. In the greater issues he lacked moral courage; he essayed once more to avoid the personal issue. He delegated to Groener the task of giving the reply to Ebert, and hence there appears in the records of the Weimar National Assembly the following passage: 'What finally decided the matter [of accepting the peace terms] was a trunk call from General Groener to President Ebert, in which the former stated that, if fighting were resumed, the prospects of a successful issue were hopeless, adding his firm conviction that in the end even the army would approve acceptance of the conditions.'

Hindenburg's name does not appear.

For the second time Groener had become the victim of Hindenburg's lack of courage, and, in the eyes of the army, the 'treachery of Weimar' was added to the 'treason of Spa'. Though he defended himself against the charge of disloyalty to the Kaiser, brought by Schulenburg and Count von Waldersee, and in 1922 extracted from a Court of Honour the verdict that he had 'acted according to his conscience, holding that thus he could best secure the interests of his country', in the matter of Weimar, Groener remained silent in the face of the attacks and calumnies which were repeatedly levelled against him over fourteen years. In all that time Hindenburg said no word in his defence nor even denied that the whole responsibility of the decision rested with Groener.

Men of Tragic Destiny: Ludendorff and Groener

'Why did you make no effort to protect your name and reputation?' a group of friends once asked Groener, and he answered us in these words: 'Because I believed that in the interests of the New Army the myth of Hindenburg should be preserved. It was necessary that one great German figure should emerge from the war free from all the blame that was attached to the General Staff. That figure had to be Hindenburg.'

IX

The work of disbanding and demobilizing the great German war-machine was completed at last. Hindenburg retired in June 1919 and signalized his farewell to the army in a moving order of the day which Groener had drafted. Three months later Groener followed his chief into retirement, hoping to enjoy with his wife and daughter in the quiet seclusion of his modest Potsdam home some modicum of rest after the demands which the strain of the past five years had made upon him.

But the period of inaction was of short duration. The infant German republic continued to be threatened alike by the extremists of the Left and Right. Communism was still a latent danger, but the immediate crisis arose from the Nationalist conservative and military leaders, who under Dr. Kapp and General von Lüttwitz attempted to seize the government in March 1920. As before in moments of crisis, Ebert turned to Groener. Much would depend on the attitude which the general officers of the former High Command adopted towards the rebellion. Hindenburg remained silent; Seeckt, as commander of the *Reichswehr*, essayed neutrality; Ludendorff, his hatred of the Weimar system burning in his blood, supported Kapp and Lüttwitz. Many former army officers looked for guidance to Groener and to that group of brilliant younger staff officers who had once been his pupils, among them Willisen, Schleicher and Hammerstein. All declared their loyalty to the Ebert government — to Hammerstein fell the duty of arresting Lüttwitz, his own father-in-law — and by their unhesitating opposition to the rebels did much to keep the army true to the government.

In the reorganization of the Cabinet which followed the Kapp *Putsch*, Groener became Minister for Transport and so continued under the chancellorships of Fehrenbach, Wirth and Cuno. For three years he devoted his organizing genius to redeeming the German railways from the chaotic condition in which the war had left them and welding them into one of the most efficient and modern transport systems in the world. He supported Cuno's policy of passive resistance to the French invasion of the Ruhr, and, when this gave way in August 1923 to Stresemann's policy of fulfilment, Groener resigned with the rest of the Cabinet and once more passed into retirement.

X

The post-war careers of Groener and Ludendorff typified in themselves the deep cleavage which existed in the military circles of Germany between those who recognized — albeit regretfully — the world of 'things as they are', and those who clung fanatically and viciously to the irretrievable traditions of the past, expending their energies in attempting to put the clock back to 1914. Groener, carrying Hindenburg with him, had recognized the new democratic order in Germany as the only instrument with which to bring about the rehabilitation of his country. He had saved it — and was to save it again — with loyal and self-sacrificing devotion, his eyes ever upon the great and ultimate goal of a Germany restored to her place among the nations.

But whereas the Swabian looked forward, the Prussian spent the remainder of his life looking over his shoulder. Ludendorff's record after the war did little to add to his reputation as a soldier, a statesman or a politician. Under the general amnesty granted by the Republic he returned to Germany in February 1919, full of hatred and contempt for the régime which had permitted him to do so. He allied himself with the ultra-nationalist elements of the Right,

Men of Tragic Destiny: Ludendorff and Groener

refusing to be reconciled in any way with the Weimar Republic, and for some time at least he was able to re-establish his old ascendancy over Hindenburg, now released from the controlling influence of Groener.

He never missed an opportunity of adding a new weapon to his armoury of hatred. One evening in the autumn of 1919, when dining with the head of the British Military Mission, Major-General Sir Neill Malcolm, and his officers, Ludendorff was expatiating with his usual vitriolic eloquence, on the way in which the Supreme Command had been 'betrayed' by the revolution on the 'home front'. His style of speech was turgid and verbose, and in an effort to crystallize the meaning in a single sentence, General Malcolm asked him: 'Do you mean, General, that you were stabbed in the back?' Ludendorff's eyes lit up and he leapt upon the phrase like a dog on a bone. 'Stabbed in the back?' he repeated. 'Yes, that is it exactly, we were stabbed in the back.' And thus was born a legend which later, in the evil hands of Adolf Hitler, was to spell death and torture and the horrors of the concentration camp for many Germans.

Ludendorff was involved in the Kapp *Putsch* of 1920, and played a more courageous rôle than Hitler in the abortive rising at Munich in November 1923, an event which brought him much personal popularity among the reactionaries. A year later he was elected to the Reichstag as leader of 'the National Socialist Party of Liberty', and remained a deputy for four years. His popularity as a political leader, which at the start had been immense, soon waned, and when at the close of 1924 Adolf Hitler was released from prison and began laboriously to build up his political machine, his followers turned with relief from the strict militarism of Ludendorff to the easier discipline of the Führer.

The final political folly came in 1925 when Ludendorff was ignominiously defeated in the first presidential ballot on the death of Ebert, and though he remained in the Reichstag until the general election of 1928, he played but a minor rôle in national and party politics, emerging only to campaign vigorously against the Young Plan. He never forgave Hindenburg for accepting this reparation agreement, and the bitter estrangement continued until the Marshal's death in 1934.

Four years of unprecedented strain and responsibility during the war had left their mark on Ludendorff. Though he withdrew to his tents in Munich, he lived a life of tempestuous isolation. His public utterances grew wilder and less comprehensible, and his attacks upon his former colleagues, Hindenburg and Hitler, became more and more savage in invective. There were those who said that he had actually suffered a stroke at Spa on the night of 28 September 1918; others attributed his morbid brooding and fierce outbursts to the effect of an automobile accident shortly before his resignation, in which he had been rendered unconscious. His later eccentricities took the form of a violent onslaught on Christianity and the belief that the downfall of European civilization was being encompassed by an unholy alliance of the Catholic Church, World Jewry and the Grand Orient.

The attacks on Christianity lost nothing in robust virility or vivid imagination, but they came to be taken less and less seriously. Ludendorff's own sincerity in proclaiming himself 'a heathen — and proud of it' is, however, undoubted, and to the end his energies were unflagging. For him the anti-Christian and anti-Jewish activities of the Nazis proceeded all too slowly, and his criticism of their lack of thoroughness led more than once, after the revolution of 1933, to the suppression of his newspaper. Unabashed, he never surrendered his liberty of thought and expression, and almost alone in the Third Reich spoke his mind without incurring personal interference. He refused in all cases to be patronized by the new rulers of Germany, and when, on his seventieth birthday, Hitler sought to make him a Field Marshal, he refused the honour, creating for himself the unique title, *Feldherr des Weltkrieges*.

His death, when it came on 20 December 1937, was not without irony, for Erich Ludendorff, foremost neo-pagan of

Men of Tragic Destiny: Ludendorff and Groener

Germany, died on the eve of the winter solstice, in a Catholic hospital in Munich, attended by praying sisters of mercy.

XI

As a soldier, Ludendorff will always be assured of a high reputation, for more than any other of the military commanders of the World War he left his mark upon modern warfare. Almost alone among his contemporaries he recognized that, even under the conditions of trench warfare, the element of surprise was still a possibility, and in his search for the achievement of surprise he developed a new offensive technique.

Had Ludendorff added to his undoubted gifts the power of devolution he would unquestionably have been a great commander. He had collected round him one of the most brilliant staffs assembled during the war at any headquarters. Men such as Bauer, Bruchmüller, Geyer and Wetzell were acknowledged experts in their own fields, and yet, as Prince Rupprecht of Bavaria has shown in his memoirs, Ludendorff was perpetually interfering in details which could and should have been left to staff officers and army commanders. It was this inability to decentralize which imposed so crushing a burden of responsibility upon him throughout the war. The normal duties of a high commander are sufficiently onerous without adding to them those of subordinates, and when to these is added the assumption of responsibility for the conduct of internal policy and national affairs, the load becomes more than any human being can carry and preserve full sanity.

For it was this passion for supreme control which led Ludendorff into the uncharted seas of political vagary and intrigue, and he provides a striking example of the dangers of an expert, brilliant in his own calling, translated to an unaccustomed sphere. He demanded unquestioning support from the 'home front' without trying in return to understand its problems. He bullied where he should have cajoled and alienated where he should have found allies. His unbounded confidence in himself and in his judgment was matched only by his complete contempt for the abilities and morale of his opponents, whether military or political, and the wisdom of a great soldier was rendered sterile by the unwisdom of a poor politician.

XII

Groener's retirement in 1923 gave him a respite from office of five years. He employed it in making a searching review of the strategy of the early months of the war on the western Front, demonstrating the disastrous effects of the 'Little Moltke's' modification of the Schlieffen Plan. The two books which resulted from his researches — *Das Testament des Grafen Schlieffen* and *Der Feldherr wider Willen* — are remarkable not only as classical military studies but also for their beauty of language and style.

It was in January 1928 that the call to duty sounded again, and that it did so was largely due to his former pupil, Kurt von Schleicher. On his arrival at Spa from Kiev ten years before, Groener had been delighted to find Schleicher as a young major on the General Staff. He had plucked him from his billet in the Press Department and had made him his personal adjutant. Thus Schleicher had accompanied Groener through the ordeals of Spa and Kolberg. Together they had weathered the trials and depressions of the revolution, and on one occasion the two of them, alone and on foot, forced their way to Ebert's rescue through a howling mob in the Wilhelmstrasse which had virtually imprisoned him in the Chancellery.

But when Groener retired in 1919, Schleicher, by means best known to himself, had set out to become a power in the land, and had begun that career of treachery and intrigue which was to carry him to the chancellor's palace and to end with the murderer's bullet. In ten years he had achieved a position sufficiently influential to dispose first of Seeckt, as commander of the *Reichswehr*, and secondly of Gessler, as Minister of Defence, and to replace them with his own nominees.

Men of Tragic Destiny: Ludendorff and Groener

Between Groener and Schleicher there existed almost parental and filial relations. Groener would often refer to the younger man as 'my son', and indeed there was every prospect of Schleicher's becoming his son-in-law. Trusting his former disciple implicitly, he had no conception that Schleicher's professed affection for him was merely part of a great scheme for self-aggrandizement.

Thus, when the Ministry of Defence became vacant in January 1928, Schleicher set about securing Groener's appointment. There were two other candidates, Willisen, his former pupil, and Schulenburg, who had been Groener's arch-antagonist at Spa and later with Waldersee his principal traducer at the Court of Honour in 1922. Now, partly due to Schleicher's blandishments and partly to his own clearer understanding of the past, Schulenburg agreed to stand aside with Willisen, and even to add his influence with Hindenburg, president of the Reich since 1925, in favour of his rival. 'We must have Groener at all costs,' he telegraphed. 'We have all been mistaken about him.'

As might have been expected, the chief opposition came from Hindenburg; for Groener, alone of living mortals, knew the truth of what had happened at Spa and Kolberg, and would, in the frequent contact which must be maintained between Commander-in-Chief and Minister of Defence, prove a constant and irritating reminder of those not very noble episodes in the marshal's career. His attempts to avoid responsibility in the light of history had not been wholly successful. 'You all blame me; but you should blame Groener', he had told his Nationalist friends reproachfully, but they remained unconvinced. Both the Kaiser at Doorn and the military caste in Germany now knew the truth.

But Hindenburg's objections were overcome and Groener re-entered government service, to be joined two years later, again as a result of Schleicher's machinations, by another of his former pupils, General von Hammerstein-Equord, as commander of the *Reichswehr*. Together they pursued the policies which their predecessors, Gessler and Seeckt, had laid down before them; an internal policy of keeping the army out of politics, and an external policy of maintaining the close liaison with the Red Army, in order to render certain German officers expertly proficient in the use of those categories of armament which had been forbidden to Germany under the treaties of peace.

Neither Groener nor Hammerstein-Equord lent themselves willingly or knowingly to any of Schleicher's subsequent intrigues, but it was largely because they both trusted and believed in him that his influence became so powerful. It so happened that, for long periods in the years 1929 and 1930, three and sometimes four Cabinet ministers were at the Hague Conferences which marked the adoption of the Young Plan, and, in addition, the ill-health of Chancellor Hermann Müller necessitated his long and frequent absences from Berlin. Groener, as acting chancellor, presided over a rump Cabinet, which became the butt of many a joke at café tables and cabaret performances. Unused and, in many ways, unsuited to the position, he leaned more and more for support upon his brilliant young assistant, with the result that Schleicher assumed the duties and powers of a Secretary of State, preparing Groener's Cabinet statements, attending to his routine business, having access to all secrets of state, and acting as the official go-between of the Government in negotiation with party leaders.

When, in March 1930, the parlous condition of German political and economic life made it evident that a new Chancellor must be found and above all one who commanded the confidence of the army, the choice of Groener, Hammerstein, Willisen and Schleicher coincided in the person of Heinrich Brüning, whom they persuaded Hindenburg to accept. Between the Minister of Defence and the former machine-gun officer there developed a relationship of mutual affection and esteem, and with Treviranus and Dietrich, Groener formed one of that inner Cabinet upon which Brüning depended so much in his heroic efforts to withstand the rising tide of National Socialism on the one hand, and, on the other, to bring the statesmen of Europe to a realization of the perils of the situation not only to Germany and to Europe but to the peace of the whole world.

The struggle was a losing one, and when, after a Cabinet reorganization, Brüning assumed the portfolio of foreign affairs and gave the additional office of Minister of Interior to Groener, the General became responsible for much of the burden of the internal phase of the battle. It was now that both Chancellor and Minister found themselves enmeshed and hampered at every turn by the intrigues of Schleicher. Using his influence with the old Marshal, scheming with the army commanders, intriguing with foreign embassies, Schleicher conceived of himself as a potential saviour of the nation, and sacrificed all loyalties to his dreams and ambitions. Convinced that his last chances for success lay in co-operation with, and possible control of, the Nazi party, he aided them clandestinely in their attacks on the Brüning government.

His final betrayal of Groener came in the early summer of 1932. Because of their subversive activities, Groener had, with the consent of the Cabinet, suppressed the Storm Troops, the Brown Army of the Nazi Party. Schleicher, with his own devilish cunning, whispered in the ears of the *Reichswehr* generals, that Groener was no longer in control of the situation and that an alliance between the army and the Nazis was necessary. He even succeeded in seducing Hammerstein-Equord from his loyalty to their mutual friend. In a session of the Reichstag on 9 May Groener was bitterly attacked by the Right. He was a sick man, his voice was failing, yet in a speech full of courage and determination he defended his policy.

The sequel was swift and dramatic. As the exhausted Groener concluded his speech and left the Chamber, Schleicher and Hammerstein informed him with cold brutality that he no longer enjoyed the confidence of the army and must resign immediately. Groener was thunderstruck. He had cherished Schleicher like a son and had purposed resigning the Ministry of Defence to him in the near future. Overwhelmed by such desertion and treachery, he appealed to Hindenburg, but, as he might have known, the Marshal 'could do nothing for him'. It was the inevitable sequel to Spa and Kolberg, and to Groener had come the fate of others who trusted in Hindenburg.

Lonely and betrayed, Groener retired to his home in Potsdam, and there received a crumb of consolation. By devious means there was conveyed to him a remark which the Kaiser, with his own memories of Hindenburg's desertion, had made to a member of his suite at Doorn: 'Tell Groener he has my full sympathy; I always expected that this would happen'.

When the Revolution of 1933 swept the National Socialists into power, fears were entertained for Groener's safety from Hitler's revenge. His colleagues Brüning, Treviranus and Dietrich were forced to fly the country, but the broad shield of the army protected him from molestation or arrest, and, by a bitter irony, it was Schleicher who fell a victim of assassination on the bloody thirtieth of June.

For seven years — until 5 May 1939 — Groener lived the life of a recluse. Apparently unresentful, he never complained of his fate and it was even difficult to get him to speak of the great events in which he had played a part. He was a soldier and a statesman of whom Germany should have been justly proud, but his actions seemed foredoomed to misunderstanding and himself to malignant calumny. History will judge him more kindly, but for the moment he stands a man of tragic destiny whose fate it had been to defend the failing causes of both monarchy and democracy in Germany; a monument to the frailty of human troth.

THE END

LIBRARY OF DAVIDSON COLLEGE

Books on regular loan may be checked out for **two weeks.** Books must be presented at the Circulation Desk in order to be renewed.

A fine is charged after date due.

Special books are subject to special regulations at the discretion of library staff.

MAY 1 8 '81			